Outline Contents

Detailed Contents

List of Abbreviations

Terms

AGA	Authorised Guarantee Agreement
CRAR	Commercial Rent Arrears Recovery

Legislation

AJA	Administration of Justice Act
CCA	Consumer Credit Act
CLRA	Commonhold and Leasehold Reform Act
ECHR	European Convention for the Protection of Human Rights and Fundamental Freedoms
FLA	Family Law Act
FSMA	Financial Services and Markets Act
LA	Limitation Act
LCA	Land Charges Act
LPA	Law of Property Act
LP(MP)A	Law of Property (Miscellaneous Provisions) Act
LRA	Land Registration Act
LRR	Land Registration Rules
LT(C)A	Landlord and Tenants (Covenants) Act
SLA	Settled Land Act
TOLATA	Trusts of Land and Appointment of Trustees Act

Journals

CLJ	Cambridge Law Journal
Conv	The Conveyancer and Property Lawyer
CLP	Current Legal Problems
LQR	Law Quarterly Review
LS	Legal Studies
MLR	Modern Law Review
SLR	Student Law Review
SLRYB	Student Law Review Yearbook

Preface

Approaching land law for the first time can seem a daunting prospect. A major aim of this text is to dispel fears, and to explain land law in an understandable and logical way. No attempt has been made to minimise the complexities of the subject simply to make it attractive or readable, for that benefits no one. However, the text is designed to explode the myths and mysteries of land law, and substitute instead a picture that is both detailed and comprehensible. There is no denying that land law is different from other subjects, not least because its language is at first unfamiliar. But different does not mean difficult. Similarly, there is a common belief that land law is boring, not as sexy or apparently relevant as other legal disciplines. This too is misplaced, for land law remains at the heart of the legal system and is the vehicle for so much that concerns our everyday lives, both at home and work. Seen in context, the issues raised in land law are as challenging and as topical as any that other law courses have to offer.

Land law is also a subject steeped in history. Many of the concepts and much of the language have their origin in centuries-old legal tradition. However, the historical dimension of land law – which in its own right is a fascinating topic for those with a passion for social and legal history – should not blind us to the reality that we live in the twenty-first century and that the everyday principles of land law have moved on. The great reforms of 1922–25 that gave birth to the reforming property law legislation of 1925 no longer seem radical and unfamiliar, and the entry into force of the Land Registration Act 2002 on 13 October 2003 heralded a new era. Of course, what we have now owes much to what we once had, but land law is a modern subject and our system is likely to be the first in the world that moves away from paper transactions in favour of electronic dealings. That said, I have resisted the temptation, which was never very great, to present land law as some kind of trendy, modernist social construct. The need for modern teaching of a modern subject does not mean the abandonment of a method of analysis that has stood the test of time. This is a book about law, based on our traditional understanding of the foundations of property law, albeit that concepts, principles and rules that are of purely historical interest have been omitted.

Land law is like a jigsaw, and this book aims to explain the rules and principles and how they fit together to form a coherent whole. The arrangement of the chapters is intended to facilitate the growth of a steady understanding of each topic and its place within the jigsaw. Many pieces are needed before the jigsaw shows a picture, so the text aims at an accumulation of understanding, rather than dropping the reader in at the deep end. There has been important case law since the previous edition, and the Land Registration Act 2002 has continued to be interpreted in the courts. The House of Lords has been reinvented as the Supreme Court, and electronic land registration has moved closer. The impact of human rights on land law continues to be explored – if not resolved – and the impact of the credit crunch has been felt in the law of mortgages. Several sections of the text have been rewritten and of necessity there has been some expansion. My aim has remained, however, to help the reader swim with the subject, rather than watch them drown in the detail.

I remain grateful to many current and former students who continue to raise questions about land law that require thought and reflection. They have done much to sharpen my thoughts and to save me (I hope) from serious error. My wife and children have moved from active disinterest in land law to quiet submission, and now simply switch on the Wii when I began to babble on about the latest developments in the Chancery Division. I remain convinced that land law is an elegant and sophisticated subject, and continue to believe that everyone I meet can be convinced of this. People now cross the street to avoid me. Many readers have commented on the absence of Cornflake from the last edition, but I am pleased to say that the dedication has been restored. Cornflake's absence did not reflect a change in substance, but merely my inattention when checking the proofs of the previous edition. The discovery of this was not a happy moment.

Martin Dixon
Queens' College, Cambridge
Candlemas, February 2010

Table of Cases

Table of Statutes

Table of Statutory Instruments

Table of European Legislation

Chapter 1
An Introduction to Modern Land Law

Chapter Contents

Introduction

Land law is a subject steeped in history. It has its origins in the feudal reforms imposed on England by William the Conqueror after 1066, and many of the most fundamental concepts and principles of land law spring from the economic and social changes that began then. However, while these concepts and the feudal origins of land law should not, and cannot, be ignored, we must remember that we are about to examine a system of law that is alive and well in the twenty-first century. It would be easy to embark on an historical survey of land law, but not necessarily entirely profitable. Of course, the concepts and principles that were codified and refined in the years leading up to 1 January 1926 – the effective date of the first wave of great legislative reforms[1] – were themselves the products of decades of development, and every student of the subject must come to grips with the unfamiliar terminology and substance of the common law. Yet the purpose of this book is to present land law as it is today without obscuring the concepts and principles on which it is built. Indeed, as we move speedily forward in our electronic age, there is no doubt that the system of land law that came into effect on 1 January 1926 is itself creaking with the strain of absorbing all that has happened to society since then. It too has had to grow and develop in response to these changes. Consequently, although the substance of modern land law remains governed by the structure established by the Law of Property Act 1925, some 85 years of social and economic changes, far-reaching judicial pronouncements and further legislation have all played a part in moulding the substantive law to the needs of the modern age. In this respect, the most significant legislative development in recent times was the enactment of the Land Registration Act 2002 (hereafter, LRA 2002). This came into force on 13 October 2003[2] and replaced entirely the Land Registration Act 1925. It heralded a new era for the law of real property, and its full effect has not yet been felt.

The LRA 2002 was the product of years of consideration and consultation by the Law Commission in conjunction with HM Land Registry. The reforms – the development of which is chronicled in detail in Law Commission Report No. 271, *Land Registration for the Twenty-first Century: A Conveyancing Revolution* – are designed to provide an updated and genuinely modern mechanism for the regulation of land of registered title. Many of the changes made by the 2002 Act are controversial – at least for some commentators – not least the prospective introduction of a system of electronic conveyancing.[3] This system – paperless, swift and, hopefully, efficient – will do much more than revolutionise the way in which land is sold or transferred. It marks the end of much ancient law (and lore) and is the clean

---

1 In particular, the Law of Property Act 1925, the LRA 1925 (now the LRA 2002), the Trustee Act 1925, the Administration of Estates Act 1925 and the Land Charges Act 1925 (now the Land Charges Act 1972).

2 An unusual date for such momentous legislation. It was chosen so as to give enough time for the reforms to take effect before another piece of amending legislation – the Commonhold and Leasehold Reform Act 2002 – was brought into force. In the event, the entry into force of the Commonhold and Leasehold Reform Act was delayed.

3 Although the LRA 2002 itself is in force, the provisions concerning electronic conveyancing, particularly section 93, are not yet operative. At the time of writing, no firm date has been set for the introduction of full e-conveyancing, although various pilot projects have been completed and others are continuing. Some aspects of e-conveyancing are in operation, particularly in relation to the discharge of mortgages. HM Land Registry hopes to introduce a form of electronic transfer of title by the end of 2010, but this remains tentative.

break with the feudal past that has been too long coming. Indeed, it is not too grand to say that the consequences of the reforms of the system of land registration already achieved by the LRA 2002, together with the gradual introduction of electronic conveyancing, have already altered fundamentally the nature of land law in England and Wales. As e-conveyancing takes hold, there will be little left untouched and land lawyers in the early years of the twenty-first century will witness as radical a change to the way we use and enjoy this precious resource called 'land' as did those lawyers who first grappled with the 1925 legislation. For a property lawyer, these are interesting times.

1.1 The Nature and Scope of the Law of Real Property

The 'law of real property' (or land law) is, obviously, concerned with land, rights in or over land, and the processes whereby those rights and interests are created and transferred. One starting point might be to consider the meaning of 'land' itself or, more properly, the legal definition of 'land' as found in the Law of Property Act (LPA) 1925. According to section 205(1)(ix) of the LPA 1925:

> Land includes land of any tenure, and mines and minerals . . . buildings or parts of buildings and other corporeal hereditaments; also a manor, an advowson, and a rent and other incorporeal hereditaments, and an easement, right, privilege, or benefit in, over, or derived from land.

Clearly, this is complicated and the statutory definition assumes that the reader already has a working knowledge of the basic concepts of land law, such as 'incorporeal heredita-ments' or 'easements'. In essence, what this statutory definition seeks to convey and what is at the heart of land law is the idea that 'land' includes not only tangible, physical property such as fields, factories, houses, shops and soil, but also intangible rights in the land, such as the right to walk across a neighbour's driveway (an example of an 'ease-ment'), the creation of a charge on land to secure a debt (a 'mortgage'), the right to control the use to which a neighbour may put his land (a 'restrictive covenant') or the right to take something from another's land, such as fish (being a 'profit' and an example of an 'incorporeal hereditament'). As a matter of legal definition, 'land' is both the physi-cal asset and the rights that the owner or others may enjoy in or over it. Consequently, 'land law' is the study of the creation, transfer, operation and termination of these rights and the manner in which they affect the use and enjoyment of the physical asset.

It is also important to appreciate why land law is fundamentally different from other legal disciplines, such as the law of contract or the law of tort. As we shall see, very many transactions concerning land or intangible rights in land take place through the medium of a contract. Thus, land is sold through a contract and a mortgage is also a contract of debt between lender and landowner. Similarly, the right to enjoy the exclusive possession of another's land for a defined period of time (a 'lease') may be given by a contract between the owner of the land (technically, the owner of an 'estate' in the land and in this context the 'landlord') and the person who is to enjoy the right (in this context the 'tenant'). Obviously, the conclusion of such a contract would bind the parties to it as a matter of simple contract law and, pending the introduction of electronic, paperless conveyancing, the contract might require one of the parties to 'complete' the transaction by executing a deed that formally 'grants' the right to the other.[4] In such cases, the contract is said to 'merge with the grant', and the contract ceases to have any separate existence as a legal concept. Indeed, in everyday conveyancing practice, the parties to such a transaction may choose to proceed directly by grant (i.e. by deed) without first formally concluding a separate contract. Clearly, however, whether the parties are bound by a 'mere' contract, or by the more formal 'deed of grant', they may enforce the contract or deed against each other: in the former case, by an action for damages or specific performance; in the latter, by relying on the covenants (i.e. promises) contained in the deed. In fact, when it becomes possible – or even compulsory – to create property rights electronically without a paper deed or a written contract, it will remain true that the parties to the 'electronic bargain' will be bound to each other. Yet the thing that is so special about 'real property rights', whether created by contract, by grant, by e-conveyancing or by some other method,[5] is that they are *capable* of affecting other people, not simply the parties that originally created the right. To put it another way, 'land law rights' are capable of *attaching* to the land itself so that any person who comes into ownership or possession of the land may be entitled to enjoy the benefits that now come with the land (such as the right to possess the land exclusively, or the right to fix a television aerial to a neighbour's property), or may be subject to the burdens imposed on the land (such as the obligation to permit the exclusive possession of another person, or the fixing of the television aerial). This is the 'proprietary' nature of land law rights and it is very different from the merely 'personal' obligations that an ordinary contractual relationship establishes. In fact, another way of describing what land law is about is to say that it is the study of the creation and operation of proprietary rights, being rights that become part of the land and are not personal to the parties that created them. This is represented diagrammatically in Figures 1.1 and 1.2.

The intrinsic ability of a proprietary right to affect a person – in his capacity as an owner or occupier of land – in addition to the person who originally created the right, means that the proper identification of what amounts to a 'proprietary right' is of particular importance. The categories of proprietary right must be defined with some care, and

Figure 1.1

Where A and B have entered into a contract for the creation of a proprietary right in favour of B, over A's land, the contract is enforceable between A and B like any other contract:

A – land owner: the grantor of the right

B – a person to whom A has granted a lease, easement or some other proprietary right in A's land: the grantee of the right

---

4   A deed is a formal written document, executed, signed and delivered as such, by the grantor of the right and witnessed as such by a third person – see section 1 of the Law of Property (Miscellaneous Provisions) Act 1989. It is no longer necessary to fix a red seal to a deed.

5   For example, by long use (prescription) or through proprietary estoppel (see Chapter 9).

Figure 1.2

Where A sells his land to X (or, more accurately, sells his right of ownership or estate in the land), the proprietary nature of B's right means that it is *capable* of 'binding' X. The proprietary right is enforceable beyond the original parties to the contract (A and B) and so B's right is potentially enforceable against X, even though X had no part in the creation of the right:

B – the person with a lease, easement or some other proprietary right in A's land, and who may be able to enforce that right against X, the transferee or purchaser of A's land, even though X had no part in the creation of the right

their creation must be established with a degree of certainty, because not every right that has something to do with land can be proprietary. If that were the case, then the practical use and enjoyment of land by the owner would become extremely difficult, if not impossible, and the value of his land would fall. For example, in Chapter 9, we examine whether a licence over land (being a permission given by the owner to another person allowing use of the land for a specific purpose, such as permission to hold a party) is proprietary or merely personal. This is especially important given that licences may arise in a huge variety of circumstances and sometimes they are given voluntarily (e.g. to a friend who is visiting) and sometimes in return for a payment (e.g. on the purchase of a cinema ticket). If licences as a category are proprietary, then the owner of the land affected might find that his land is so overburdened by other peoples' rights that it becomes difficult to use it for his own purposes. Consequently, it becomes less valuable on sale because a purchaser might also be bound to permit the licence-holders to use the land. Necessarily then, it is not all rights merely connected with land that are 'proprietary', and a proper understanding of land law must encompass an understanding of how we might be able to distinguish between proprietary rights in land and merely personal rights to use land.

The traditional starting point in a search for the 'proprietary' character of rights is the *a priori* definition of 'an interest in land' put forward by the House of Lords in *National Provincial Bank v. Ainsworth* (1965). In that case, the essential point was whether a wife's right to live in the former matrimonial home could be regarded as a proprietary right given that she did not actually own a share of the property. If it could, the right might bind a third party such as the National Provincial Bank, which had a mortgage over the land and which claim to possession might be defeated if a proprietary right existed. If, however, the right was purely personal – that is, enforceable by the wife only against the husband personally – it could never bind the land and the bank's mortgage would necessarily take priority. In deciding that the wife's right could only ever be personal (assuming she had no actual share of ownership), Lord Wilberforce stated that '[b]efore a right or an interest can be admitted into the category of property, or of a right affecting property, it must be definable, identifiable by third parties, capable in its nature of assumption by third parties, and have some degree of permanence or stability'.

So it is, then, that rights to use land must, apparently, satisfy this four-fold test before they can be regarded as 'proprietary'. As a general indication of proprietary status, this 'definition' has merit, but it is susceptible to criticism. For example, not only are 'definability', 'identifiability' and 'stability' inherently open-ended (how definable, identifiable and stable must a right be?), the definition is clearly circular, for only if a right is *already* proprietary is it *capable* of assumption by third parties. After all, the search for an answer to the question – does it bind third parties? – is often the very reason why we need to establish the proprietary or personal nature of the right in the first place. Nevertheless, perhaps we should not seek to pick over Lord Wilberforce's words as if they were enshrined in legislation or were intended to be writ in stone. What he is trying to identify are those attributes that mark out candidates for proprietary status from those rights to use land that are clearly personal, 'however broad or penumbral the separating band between these two kinds of rights may be' (*per* Lord Wilberforce). After all, proprietary rights should – indeed *must* – be definable, identifiable and stable precisely because they can affect the land for considerable periods of time irrespective of who now might own or occupy it. The definition tells us, in other words, that proprietary rights have a certain quality other than merely being connected with the use or enjoyment of land and it is this quality that makes them fit to endure beyond changes in the ownership or occupation of the land. Necessarily, this leaves room for argument and perhaps the only really certain way of identifying all proprietary rights is to make a list – to have a so-called *numerus clausus* [6] – but English law has not trodden this path and so we are left with useful, but not definitive, judicial dicta and a wealth of case law that has examined the proprietary status of rights on a case-by-case basis.[7]

1.2   Types of Proprietary Right

Generally, and with some necessary simplification for the purposes of exposition, 'proprietary rights' fall into two categories: estates in land and interests in land.

1.2.1   Estates in land

The 'doctrine of estates' forms one of the cornerstones of the law of real property, and this is as true today as it was in feudal times, even with the introduction of near universal registration of title. Theoretically, all land in England and Wales is actually owned by the Crown[8] – and all other persons may own 'merely' an 'estate in the land', rather than the land itself.[9] In this sense, an estate confers a right to use and control land, being tantamount to ownership, but with the important difference that the type of estate that is owned will define the time for which the use and control of the land is to last. In this sense, an estate in land is equivalent to ownership of the land for a 'slice of time'.

---

6   See, e.g., Rudden, B. (1987) 'Economic theory versus property law: The *numerus clausus* problem', in Eekelaar and Bell (eds) *Oxford Essays in Jurisprudence*, 3rd series, Oxford; Clarendon Press.

7   It is not only case law that can settle the matter. Sections 115 and 116 of the LRA 2002 confirm the proprietary status of previously disputed rights. Thus, rights of pre-emption, proprietary estoppel and mere equities are confirmed as proprietary.

8   The 'Crown' is neither the government, nor the reigning king or queen in a personal capacity, but a legal entity in its own right, which can be regarded as the repository of the sovereignty of the nation as expressed through a constitutional monarchy.

9   Under section 79 of the LRA 2002, the Crown may now grant itself a freehold estate in order to register its land.

1.2.1.1 The fee simple or freehold estate

When people say that they own their land, usually they mean that they own this estate in the land: 'the fee simple absolute in possession'. A fee simple comprises the right to use and enjoy the land for the duration of the life of the grantee and that of his heirs and successors. Furthermore, the fee simple estate is freely transferable ('alienable') during the life of the estate owner (i.e. by gift or sale), or on his death (i.e. by will or under the rules of intestate succession when there is no will), and each new estate owner is then entitled to enjoy the land for the duration of his life and that of his heirs and successors. Consequently, although the fee simple is, at its legal root, a description of ownership for a limited duration – as are all estates – the way in which the duration of the estate is defined and its free alienability means that, in most respects, the fee simple is equivalent to permanent ownership of the land by the person who is currently the estate owner. In practice, the paramount ownership of the Crown is irrelevant. Each fee simple owner has it within his own power to transfer the estate to another (even on death), and because the full duration of the estate may be enjoyed by a new estate owner and he may then transfer it (and so on), the estate can, and usually does, survive through generations. However, in one situation, the true nature of the fee simple estate is revealed and the land will revert to the Crown as ultimate absolute owner. If the current owner of the fee simple estate has not transferred the land during his life and then dies leaving no will and no next of kin to inherit under the rules of intestate succession, the estate has run its course and the land reverts to the Crown. This is uncommon for natural persons (but more common where an estate is held by a company that dissolves with no successors), but it does illustrate the inherent nature of the fee simple as 'ownership for a slice of time'. As we shall see, a fee simple may be either 'legal' or 'equitable',[10] although the former is much more common and the latter will arise only in special circumstances (e.g. see Chapter 4 on co-ownership).

1.2.1.2 The leasehold estate

The leasehold estate comprises a right to use and enjoy the land exclusively as owner for a stated period of time. This may be one day, one year, one month, 99 years or any defined period at all. Somewhat misleadingly, the leasehold estate (however long it is stated to last) is frequently referred to as a 'term of years' even if the 'term' is shorter than a year. The owner of a leasehold estate may be referred to as a 'leaseholder', 'lessee' or 'tenant' (sometimes 'underlessee' or 'subtenant') and the leasehold estate is carved out of any other estate (including itself), provided that its 'term' is fixed at less than the estate out of which it is carved.[11] For example, a leasehold of any duration (say, 999 years) may be carved out of a fee simple, the latter being of greater duration because of the principles discussed earlier. However, in the very unlikely event that the fee simple should actually terminate before the end of the leasehold period that is carved out of it, then the lease also

---

10 Technically, because of section 1(3) of the LPA 1925, an equitable fee simple is not an estate, but an 'interest', but nothing turns on this.

11 In the case of *Bruton v. London and Quadrant Housing Trust* (2000), the House of Lords suggested that a lease need not always be carved out of an estate in the land, but might, in some circumstances, be regarded as 'non-proprietary'. This interesting and controversial analysis is discussed more fully in Chapter 6.

terminates. Again, a leasehold can be carved out of a leasehold of longer duration. For example, X, who holds a lease of seven years from the fee simple owner, may grant a lease of three years to Y, in which case X can be regarded as the tenant of the freeholder but the landlord of Y, and Y is the subtenant in actual possession of the land. In fact, as will be discussed in Chapter 6, the fact that a lease can be carved out of any estate of longer duration means that a plot of land may have several different 'owners', each enjoying specific rights in relation to the land: for example, there may be a fee simple owner, a lessee, a sublessee, a sub-sublessee and so on. As with freeholds, a leasehold may be 'legal' or 'equitable',[12] although equitable leases tend to occur more usually in a residential rather than a commercial context.[13]

1.2.1.3   *The fee tail*

Although originally an estate in land, the fee tail is more properly regarded, since 1 January 1926, as an 'interest' in another person's land.[14] However, it is considered here because of its feudal origins as a true estate. The fee tail is an interest permitting its 'owner' the use of land for the duration of his life and that of his *lineal* descendants (not *all* heirs). A lineal descendant is a person who can show a parental, grandparental, great-grandparental (and so on) link to the person who was originally granted the fee tail. As with the fee simple, a fee tail (or 'entail') may turn out to be of very long duration indeed, save that an 'entail' may be curtailed in practice by restricting the qualifying successors to either male or female lineal descendants. For example, the fee may be 'entailed' from father to son and so on to the exclusion of daughters.[15]

At the death of the last lineal descendant (e.g. the current interest-holder who has no sons or daughters), the land will revert either to the person entitled to the estate in fee simple[16] or to the Crown if there is none. More importantly, although existing entails are unaffected, from 1 January 1997 it has become impossible to create any new interest in fee tail (see Schedule 1 to the Trusts of Land and Appointment of Trustees Act 1996). This legislative prohibition of the creation of new fee tails, coupled with the fact that it has been, and still is, possible to turn an existing entail into a fee simple (by a process known as 'barring the entail'), means that the interest in fee tail rarely survives as a feature of modern land law. Where it does exist, it may do so only as an 'equitable' interest (section 1 of the LPA 1925).

---

12 See section 1.3.1 below.

13 Primarily because parties in a commercial relationship tend to use property professionals to organise their affairs and usually this leads to a lease that complies with the formalities necessary to create a legal estate.

14 Section 1(3) of the LPA 1925 provides that the only current estates are the legal fee simple or legal leasehold because all other estates and interests 'take effect as equitable interests'.

15 Such a fee tail is at the heart of Jane Austen's *Pride and Prejudice* – the estate owner (Mr Bennet) has no son and, on his death, the surviving women must leave the land because the estate in tail will terminate.

16 Mr Collins in *Pride and Prejudice*.

1.2.1.4 *The life interest*

As with the fee tail, the life interest was once an estate proper (i.e. prior to 1 January 1926 and the entry into force of section 1 of the LPA 1925), and it is considered here because of that history. A life interest (or 'life estate') gives the holder the right to use and enjoy the land for the duration of his life. On death, the life interest comes to an end and the land reverts to the superior estate owner, who is usually a long leaseholder or fee simple owner. Somewhat confusingly, the owner of a life interest is frequently referred to as a 'life tenant', although this has nothing to do with the leasehold estate. Again, like the estate in fee tail, the life interest today may exist only as an 'equitable' interest (section 1 of the LPA 1925).

All of this may seem complicated, but the important point to remember is that an estate effectively means ownership of the land: either of virtually permanent duration (freehold), or limited by agreement to a defined period (leasehold). The other two interests represent ownership for different slices of time, but are relatively rare in practice. They will be discussed in the text where appropriate. Of course, all four estates are 'proprietary' in that they are capable of being sold or transferred during the time period for which they exist. Thus, in common parlance, the freehold or the leasehold may be sold or transferred by the current owner at any time, provided that the estate has not terminated. So, A may sell his freehold to B and C may sell ('assign') his 999-year lease to D, provided that there is still time to run.[17]

1.2.2 Interests in land

The above section considered those rights in land that give the holder the equivalent of a right of ownership for a defined period of time. By way of contrast, 'interests in land' may be used to denote those proprietary rights that one person enjoys in the land (technically, in the 'estate') of another. Good examples are the right of way over someone else's land (an easement), a debt secured on the debtor's land (a mortgage), the right to prevent an owner carrying on some specific activity on his own land (a restrictive covenant) or the right to buy another's land within a fixed time frame (an option). These are all proprietary interests in the land (in the estate) of another person and this is not an exhaustive list. As proprietary rights, they may be transferred or sold to another person (usually, but not always, as an incident of the land benefited by the right)[18] and may be binding against a new owner of the 'estate' over which they operate, as illustrated by Figure 1.2 (above).

1.3 The Legal or Equitable Quality of Proprietary Rights

In the discussion of estates in land in the previous section, reference was made to whether the estate could be 'legal', or 'equitable'. In fact, it is important to determine of all

---

17 If X is a life tenant, thus holding an estate for life, it may be sold to Y, but Y's estate will last only for so long as X is alive. Y's interest is then said to be *pur autre vie* – for the life of another.

18 For example, the benefit of an easement – such as the right to walk on a neighbour's land – will be sold as part of the benefited land, but the right to an option to buy may be sold independently of any land.

proprietary rights (i.e. of both estates and interests) whether they *may* exist as a legal or equitable right, and whether they do *in fact* exist as a legal or equitable right in any given case. To discuss whether a proprietary right is legal or equitable is to consider its *quality* as opposed to its content: the question is *not*, 'What does the right entitle a person to do on the land?' (content), but 'What is the nature of the right?' (i.e. is it legal or equitable?). Moreover, although the distinction between 'legal' and 'equitable' proprietary rights became less important as a result of the changes made by the 1925 property legislation, and will become even less important under the electronic conveyancing provisions of the LRA 2002, it is impossible to come to grips with modern land law without an understanding of (a) how the distinction between legal and equitable proprietary rights is to be made, and (b) the significance of the distinction.

1.3.1 The origins of the distinction between legal and equitable rights

Historically, the distinction between legal and equitable rights was based on the type of court in which a claimant might obtain a remedy against a defendant for the unlawful denial of the claimant's right over the defendant's land. Thus, the King's Court (or court of common law) would grant a remedy to a claimant who could establish a case 'at law', usually on proof of certain formalities and on pleading a specified 'form of action'. The court of common law was, however, fairly inflexible in its approach to legal problems and would often deny a remedy to a deserving claimant simply because the proper formalities had not been observed. Consequently, the Chancellor's Court (or Court of Chancery) began to mitigate the harshness of the common law by giving an 'equitable' remedy to a deserving claimant, even in the absence of the proper formalities required for a remedy 'at law'. This led to many clashes of jurisdiction where a claimant would be denied a remedy 'at law' in one court, but be able to secure a remedy 'in equity' in a different court, although eventually it was the Court of Chancery, administering the rules of equity, which was to prevail. In other words, what started out as a different procedure for the administration of justice eventually developed into two different sets of substantive legal principles: the common law courts dealing with 'legal rules' and the court of equity dealing with 'rules of equity'. Since the Judicature Act 1875, all courts have been empowered to apply rules of 'law' and rules of 'equity', and clashes of jurisdiction no longer occur. However, for the present, this historical diversity still echoes in the modern law. In modern land law, the distinction between legal and equitable *proprietary* rights no longer rests on which type of court hears a case, but it still has a flavour of the old distinction between the formality of the common law and the fairness of equity.

1.3.2 Making the distinction between legal and equitable rights today

In order to determine today (i.e. prior to the full introduction of electronic conveyancing) whether any given proprietary right is 'legal' or 'equitable', two issues need to be addressed. First, is the right *capable* of existing as either a legal or equitable right? Second, has the right come into existence in the manner recognised as creating either a legal or equitable right? It follows from this that there are certain rights that may be *only* equitable (there are none that may be *only* legal), and some that may be either legal or equitable, depending on how they have been created.

1.3.3   Section 1 of the Law of Property Act 1925: Is the right capable of being either legal or equitable?

The starting point must be section 1 of the Law of Property Act 1925. This defines conclusively those rights that *may* be legal. Necessarily, therefore, any rights not within this statutory definition can only ever be equitable. According to section 1:

(1)   The only estates in land which are capable of subsisting or of being conveyed or created at law are –

    (a)   an estate in fee simple absolute in possession;
    (b)   a term of years absolute.

(2)   The only interests or charges in or over land which are capable of subsisting or of being conveyed or created at law are –

    (a)   an easement, right or privilege in or over land [held as an adjunct to a fee simple or leasehold absolute in possession];
    (b)   a rentcharge;
    (c)   a charge by way of legal mortgage;
    (d)   [not relevant for present purposes];
    (e)   rights of entry [annexed to a legal lease or legal rentcharge].

(3)   All other estates, interests and charges in or over land take effect as equitable interests.

In simple terms, this means that, in the language of the distinction between *estates* and *interests*, the only *estates* that may be legal are the fee simple (the 'freehold'), provided that it gives an immediate right to possession of the land ('absolute in possession') and the leasehold (whether giving possession immediately or on the termination of a prior right, i.e. in 'possession' or 'reversion'), and the only *interests* that are capable of being legal are easements (and associated rights to enter another's land and take something from it, such as fish being *profits à prendre*), mortgages, rights of entry contained in a legal lease and the (now relatively rare) rentcharge. Given, therefore, that in the words of section 1(3), 'all other estates [and] interests . . . take effect as equitable interests', such rights as the life interest and fee tail and such other interests as the restrictive covenant, the option and the right of pre-emption will always be equitable. However, let us be clear about what this section says: it does not say that such estates and interests as are listed in section 1 *must* be legal; only that they *may* be legal. In addition, therefore, much turns on how these potential legal estates and interests come into existence.

1.3.4   The manner of creation of the right

As noted above, section 1 of the LPA 1925 tells us only what rights *may* be legal; it does not say that they *always will* be legal. In other words, even the estates and interests specified in section 1 may be equitable in certain circumstances. If a proprietary right may, in principle, be either legal or equitable, then its final quality depends on the manner by which it has come into existence and, in particular, whether the formality requirements for its creation (which are established by statute) have been observed. Generally, full formality is required for the creation of legal estates and interests, and more informality is permitted for the creation of equitable rights. Here, then, lies the heart of the (pre-electronic) legal/equitable distinction, and it has echoes of the historical division between law and equity that originated in a dispute between two sets of courts, one of which was prepared to enforce rights only if they were accompanied with the proper formality, the other of which was prepared to enforce rights when it was equitable to do so, notwithstanding the lack of proper formality.

1.3.4.1   When is a proprietary right legal in practice?

Assuming it falls within section 1 of the LPA 1925, a proprietary right will be 'legal' if it is created with proper formality. At present this has two aspects.

1   Subject to only minor exceptions, the proprietary right must have been created by deed. A 'deed' is a written document of a special kind and it goes beyond a mere written contract.[19] According to section 1 of the Law of Property (Miscellaneous Provisions) Act 1989, an instrument is not a deed unless it is expressed to be a deed on its face or by the person signing it, it is executed as a deed and is witnessed by some person other than the persons who are parties to it. Usually, a document intended to be a deed will declare itself to be a deed (it will say 'this is a deed' or similar) and will state that it is 'executed as a deed by X and Y' and will be witnessed as such by another.[20] As indicated, however, in special circumstances, certain proprietary rights can be legal without the need for a deed. For our purposes, these are in the case of certain leases for three years or less (the 'short lease exception' – see sections 52(2)(d) and 54(2) of the LPA 1925, and see Chapter 6[21]) or where an easement arises by 'prescription' (long use – see Chapter 7). These special cases will be considered where appropriate.

2   In addition to the use of a deed, *certain* potential legal estates and interests must also be registered in the manner required by the Land Registration Act 2002. Failure to so register will render the relevant estate or interest equitable even if created or transferred by a deed – sections 7 and 27(1) of the LRA 2002. These registration requirements are considered in detail in Chapter 2, but (briefly) they require: the substantive registration as registered titles of all potential legal freeholds and all potential legal leaseholds of over seven years' duration;[22] the registration of a potentially legal mortgage against the title of the burdened land; and the entry on the register of the burdened land of legal easements expressly created after 13 October 2003.[23]

To sum up then: proprietary rights will be legal where they fall within section 1 of the LPA 1925, provided that they originate in a deed (with minor exceptions) and so long as they

---

19 *Eagle Star Insurance Company v. Green* (2001).

20 Land Registry transfer forms (e.g. for the sale or gift of registered land) are deliberately cast as deeds for this purpose.

21 Leases for three years or less, giving an immediate right to possession for the best rent reasonably obtainable, provided that no lump sum is payable at the start of the lease as a condition of it being granted.

22 For exceptional cases, legal leases for a term of less than seven years may require registration, but these are of an individual and special character – see sections 4(1) and 27(2)(b) of the LRA 2002, and also Chapter 2.

23 Impliedly created easements are not caught by section 27(2), neither are those special easements that fall under the Commons Registration Act 1965 even if expressly created.

are registered, where such registration is required. This means that even a potentially legal estate or interest may fail to be legal because either no deed has been used where required, or a deed has been used but registration has not occurred where required.

1.3.4.2 *When is a proprietary right equitable in practice?*

A proprietary right has the potential to be 'equitable' for *any one* of three reasons. First, it may be excluded *ab initio* from the definition of a legal estate or interest found in section 1 of the LPA 1925. Such rights can only ever be equitable because they cannot be legal, as with a life estate, a restrictive covenant, a claim in proprietary estoppel, an option to purchase, a right of pre-emption and so on. Second, despite being within section 1, no deed may have been used where such is required. Third, despite being within section 1 and the use of a deed, registration may not have occurred, where required.

However, even if a proprietary right is potentially equitable, that is not enough. Even equitable proprietary rights are required to be created in an appropriate manner before they may exist as such. After all, let us not forget that all proprietary rights – be they legal or equitable – have the capacity to affect land for many years irrespective of who owns that land and so we must be reasonably certain that alleged proprietary rights do in fact exist. In the majority of cases, the relevant formality for the creation of an equitable property right is the use of a written instrument, either a comprehensive written contract signed by, or on behalf of, the parties to the contract, as required by section 2 of the Law of Property (Miscellaneous Provisions) Act 1989, or by a written instrument signed by the person creating the equitable right, as required by section 53 of the LPA 1925.[24] Failing the use of a written instrument, the intended right does not exist at all as a right in property: it is 'void' as a proprietary right.[25] Of course, it may still permit the person to whom the right is given to exercise the right against the person who gave it – but *only* that person – but the right is then merely personal. It would then be a 'licence'.

Of course, the requirement of a written contract or instrument for the creation of equitable proprietary rights is relatively formal, but there is a clear distinction between these instruments and a deed, not least that the latter must be witnessed. It does mean, of course, that, in the normal case, merely verbal agreements or promises cannot create property rights or obligations. Note, however, that, in *exceptional* circumstances, equity will recognise the existence of an equitable proprietary right arising from an oral contract, agreement or promise, provided that the conditions for proprietary estoppel or implied trusts (resulting or constructive) have been fulfilled.[26] As will be seen in Chapters 4 and 9 respectively, the creation of equitable rights by purely verbal dealings between the parties

---

24 The written contract will be used where the creator of the right receives a benefit in return for burdening his land; a written instrument under section 53 of the LPA 1925 is more appropriate for a voluntary grant of an equitable right, often using a trust.

25 It may be possible to save part of a written instrument by separating a valid clause from an invalid one and giving proprietary effect to the valid part: *Murray v. Guinness* (1998).

26 By section 53(2) of the LPA 1925 and section 2(5)(c) of the LPA 1989, implied trusts are a statutory exception to the formality requirements found in section 53 of the LPA 1925 and section 2 of the LPA 1989 respectively. Proprietary estoppel is an invention of equity and is justified on a policy basis in order to prevent unconscionability – see *Taylor Fashions v. Liverpool Victoria Trustees* (1982).

is not particularly uncommon, because it serves the needs of fairness – or equity – between the parties. It is an anathema to the law that a person should be able to deny that they have granted a proprietary right to another by pleading non-compliance with statutory formalities if this is their own fault. Nevertheless, the creation of equitable rights by proprietary estoppel or implied trust (i.e. verbally) are in the nature of exceptions to the rule that equitable rights usually should be created in writing, and, consequently, the relevant principles must not be so widely interpreted so as to destroy the basic formality rule itself.[27] Finally, for completeness, it should also be noted that property rights arising before the entry into force of the 1989 Law of Property Act[28] can be equitable if created by an oral contract without the need to plead proprietary estoppel or implied trust, provided that the oral contract was supported by some 'act of part performance' in pursuit of the right, as in *Thatcher* v. *Douglas* (1996), applying the now repealed section 40 of the LPA 1925.[29] This is now of largely historical interest, save that it is possible for professional conveyancers still to encounter a valid equitable right created under the old regime of oral contract plus 'part-performance'.

1.3.5 The proposed system of electronic conveyancing and the distinction between legal and equitable property rights

It may well be that the anticipated introduction of electronic, paperless conveyancing will make the distinction between legal and equitable property rights largely redundant, or certainly less significant. By virtue of section 93 of the LRA 2002, the creation or grant of certain specified property rights may be required to be carried out *exclusively* by means of an electronic entry against the registered title of the estate affected. It will not be the case that such electronic entry is optional, but that, without such entry, the alleged property right will not exist at all, even if a paper deed or written contract exists. When this system comes into operation, for those rights specified under section 93, there will be no scope for the distinction between 'legal' and 'equitable' versions of the rights specified because deeds and written instruments will be irrelevant. In such cases, the property right will either exist by reason of an electronic entry on the register, or it will not.

This full implementation of e-conveyancing and the activation of section 93 is still some way off, although a pilot scheme has been road-tested and some electronic entries connected with mortgages may now be made.[30] However, many things remain uncertain, not least whether the technology exists to make the system a reality. In addition, it is not yet clear whether all property transactions will fall within the realm of e-conveyancing (i.e. be specified under section 93 of the LRA 2002), or only the most fundamental, such as the transfer of freeholds and leaseholds and the grant of mortgages and easements. Neither can we yet know whether the courts will invent a 'default' status for rights not created electronically when they should have been, even in the face of an explicit section 93 of the LRA 2002. After all, this is exactly the function of proprietary estoppel in the face

---

27 Auction contracts are also excepted (section 2(5)(b) of the LPA 1989), as are short leases (section 2(5)(a) of the LPA 1989).

28 That is, before 27 September 1989.

29 Repealed prospectively by section 2(8) of the LPA 1989.

30 HM Land Registry has tentative plans to introduce e-transfers of certain titles towards the end of 2010.

of the clear requirements of section 53 of the LPA 1925 and section 2 of the LPA 1989. What we can conclude, however, is that initially some proprietary rights still will be capable of creation by deed or in writing, possibly even with the added choice of electronic registration, while we all get used to the brave new world of e-commerce. Presumably, in such an eventuality, the old legal/equitable distinction will have some relevance until e-conveyancing becomes mandatory.

1.3.6   The division of ownership and the 'trust'

Although the distinction between legal and equitable property rights turns, primarily, on the definition in section 1 of the LPA 1925 and the manner in which the right is created, there is a third way by which the distinction can arise. This is where enjoyment of the land is regulated by use of the 'trust'. In English law and systems derived from it, it is perfectly possible for a single piece of property (*any* property) to be owned by two or more people at the same time. This is not simply that two people may share ownership; it is, rather, that two or more people may have a different quality of ownership over the same property at the same time. In other words, one person may have the legal title to the property, and another may have the equitable title. Of course, in the normal course of events, when a person owns an estate in land (or any other property), this legal and equitable title is not separated, and the person is regarded simply as 'the owner'. However, it is the ability to split ownership that is so unique to the English legal system and other common law systems. So, for land, it is possible to have a legal owner and an equitable owner: one with legal rights of ownership; the other with equitable rights. Necessarily, these two owners must stand in a relationship to each other and this relationship is known as a 'trust'. This is what is meant when it is said that A holds land on trust for B: A is the legal owner (and trustee), and B is the equitable owner (and beneficiary).

The trust that exists between A and B can take many forms, and different rights and duties can be imposed on A (the trustee) for the benefit of B (the beneficiary), depending on how the trust was established and any relevant statutory provisions (e.g. the Trust of Land and Appointment of Trustees Act 1996 – see Chapter 4). In some circumstances, a trust will be imposed on a landowner without a deliberate act of trust creation, thus creating by force of law a distinction between the legal and equitable titles.[31] Finally, it is also important to appreciate that the creation of legal and equitable proprietary rights through the use of a trust requires compliance with a different but complementary set of formality rules to those discussed above: that is, rules similar to (but not identical with) those required for the simple creation of proprietary rights. Unless there is a 'constructive

Figure 1.3

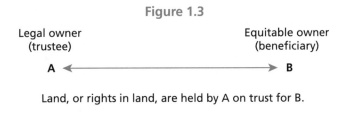

Land, or rights in land, are held by A on trust for B.

---

31 As with implied, resulting and constructive trusts.

trust', 'resulting trust',[32] or a successful claim of proprietary estoppel, a trust concerning land or any right therein must be 'manifested and proved by some writing', as required by section 53(1)(b) of the LPA 1925. This means that the existence of the legal and equitable interests under a trust concerning land depends on the trust being created in the proper manner, although the requirement here is that the trust of land must be *evidenced* by some written document, rather than actually be in writing itself.

1.4   The Consequences of the Distinction between Legal and Equitable Property Rights

It is apparent from the above that whether a proprietary right is legal or equitable may tell us many things: for example, how the right was created and whether there is any possibility of the existence of a trust. However, in times past, one of the most important consequences of the distinction, albeit much modified by statute, was the different way in which legal or equitable rights could affect the new owners or occupiers of the land over which such rights existed. As noted at the outset of this chapter, the peculiar quality of proprietary rights is that they attach to the land, and thus the right to enforce them and the obligation to honour them is *capable* of passing to new owners of the benefited or burdened land. This is the situation represented by Figure 1.2. So, for everyday conveyancing, the precise effect of a proprietary right on a third party (in the sense of their obligation to honour it) once depended crucially on whether the proprietary right was 'legal' or 'equitable'. However, while this is not yet a matter of history, it must be appreciated that, in modern land law, the effect of a proprietary right on a new owner of land depends much more on the effect and interpretation of statute than it does on the nature of the proprietary right. The impact of the now repealed LRA 1925 was considerable in this regard, and this has now been extended and consolidated by the current LRA 2002. Even in respect of the relatively small number of titles that remain unregistered, the relevance of the legal or equitable quality of proprietary rights is much reduced by the Land Charges Act 1972. That is not to say, of course, that we must not spend time understanding the distinction, not least because even now it is impossible to understand modern land law without an appreciation of the historical importance and limited present impact of it. Yet we must view the issue in perspective.

1.4.1   Legal property rights before the 1925 legislation

Prior to 1 January 1926, if a proprietary right was *legal*, it would always bind every person who came to own or occupy the land over which the right existed. As was commonly said, 'Legal rights bind the whole world', and the person entitled to enforce the legal proprietary right could exercise it against any purchaser of the land, squatter, donee of a gift and all others. So, for example, the person entitled to a legal right of way (an easement) would have been able to enjoy that right no matter who came to own or occupy the land over which it existed.

---

32 Both are exempt from formality by section 53(2) of the LPA 1925 and section 2(5)(c) of the LPA 1989.

1.4.2　Equitable property rights before the 1925 legislation

Prior to 1 January 1926, if an existing property right over land was *equitable*, it would bind every transferee of that land *except* a bona fide purchaser for value of a legal estate in the land who had no notice of the equitable right. This appears to be a complicated rule, but it can be broken down into its constituent parts. Thus, an existing equitable right over land *would* be binding on a transferee of that land in all the following cases:

1　where the transferee was not a purchaser for value, as where he received the land by will, or as a gift, or under the rules of adverse possession (squatting);
2　where the transferee did not purchase a legal estate in the land, as where he occupied the land under an equitable lease;
3　where the transferee was not bona fide, as where he acted in bad faith; and
4　where the transferee had notice of the equitable right, as where he either knew of its existence (actual notice) or knew of circumstances from which a reasonable person would have been aware of its existence (constructive notice) (*Hunt v. Luck* (1902), *Kingsnorth v. Tizard* (1986)), or the transferee's agent (e.g. his solicitor) had actual or constructive notice (so-called imputed notice).

In all these cases, the equitable right would have been binding on a transferee of the land. However, it is important to realise that, in the great majority of cases, the transferee of the land would easily fulfil the first three requirements of the 'bona fide purchaser' rule, and so could hope to escape being bound by the equitable right by disputing whether or not he had 'notice' of the right. In practice, this was usually the only real question. Consequently, the rule about equitable interests became known as the 'doctrine of notice', because it was usually the transferee's 'notice' of the equitable interest (bound by it) or lack of notice (not bound by it) that was the real issue. Unfortunately, such were (and are) the vagaries of the doctrine of notice that neither the transferee of the land nor the owner of the equitable right that was alleged to bind the land could ever be sure whether his land or his right (as the case may have been) was secure. In many cases, the 'owner' of an equitable right over land could do little to ensure its survival, should the burdened land be sold, and, conversely, a purchaser might find that the land they had just purchased was encumbered by an equitable right of which they were deemed to have constructive notice. In short, the operation of the doctrine of notice was so uncertain that the 1925 property legislation modified the rule in a radical way and thereby substantially reduced the importance of the legal/equitable distinction.

1.5　The 1925 Property Legislation and the Land Registration Act 2002

All that we have considered so far forms the basis of the modern law of real property. However, the start of the twentieth century brought with it fundamental social and economic changes, and when these were allied to the defects, mysteries, vagaries and plain injustices of the law before 1 January 1926, it was clear that wholesale reform was necessary. The detail of the legislative changes that came into effect on 1 January 1926 is considered later in the appropriate chapters, especially Chapters 2, 3 and 4, but for now it is important to realise that both substantive and structural changes were made in 1925, particularly regarding the question of ownership of land and the way in which proprietary rights could affect 'third parties' – being persons who came to the land after the proprietary right had been created. The main legislative enactments of 1925 are considered briefly below; it should be noted at this early stage that the LRA 2002 has remodelled parts of the original 1925 scheme substantially.

1.5.1   The Law of Property Act 1925

The LPA 1925 made substantive changes to the law of real property, including, as we have seen, a redefinition of what rights could be legal or equitable. It also has much to say about joint ownership of land, the creation of proprietary rights, the nature of the fee simple and leasehold estates, and much more. Although amended in parts, it remains the governing statute for modern land law.

1.5.2   The Settled Land Act 1925

The Settled Land Act 1925 is a complicated statute, designed to regulate the creation and operation of successive interests in land, as where a house is given to A for his life, and then to B for her life and then to C absolutely. It is considered in Chapter 5. Its importance is much diminished by the abolition of 'settlements' for dispositions taking effect on or after 1 January 1997 – see section 2 of the Trusts of Land and Appointment of Trustees Act 1996. It would be unusual to come across a settlement governed by the Settled Land Act today.

1.5.3   The Land Registration Act 1925 and the Land Registration Act 2002

The machinery originally established by the repealed LRA 1925 and now found in the LRA 2002 is examined in detail in Chapter 2. This new and comprehensive statute is fundamental to the modern law of real property. It creates a system whereby title to land (being the estates of legal fee simple or legal leasehold) and many other rights in that land are recorded by HM Land Registry in a register held by district offices. In essence, each title is assigned a 'title number' linked to a plot of land, under which the ownership of the estate and many other rights affecting the land are recorded. The purpose behind these provisions was – and is – to replace the haphazard system of conveyancing that existed before 1 January 1926 and, especially, to bring certainty and stability to the question of how proprietary rights affect third parties. As such, the LRA 2002 applies to what is loosely called 'registered land'.

As indicated briefly, the system introduced by the LRA 1925 was ripe for reform, and that reform has been made a reality by the LRA 2002. Although most of the central principles of land registration have remained the same under the LRA 2002 as they were under the LRA 1925 (albeit 'tidied up' to reflect modern circumstances), there is much that is different. The 2002 Act came into force on 13 October 2003 and the LRA 1925 is no more. Not all of the provisions of the new legislation will take effect immediately (e.g. section 93 and electronic conveyancing), but the LRA 2002 has already affected the way in which modern land law operates.[33]

---

33 For example, with the introduction of electronic discharge of mortgages.

1.5.4   The Land Charges Act 1972

The Land Charges Act 1972 (the LCA, originally, the Land Charges Act 1925) is also examined in detail later – see Chapter 3. Once again, it establishes a system to regulate the transfer of land and is also designed to bring certainty to dealings with land affected by the proprietary rights of other people, particularly if those rights are equitable. Importantly, land that is covered by the LCA 1972 is *not* 'registered land', and it falls outside the scope of the LRA 2002. Thus, the LCA 1972 governs what is called 'unregistered land', this being land to which the title is not entered on a register but is proved by the title deeds to the property and any related bundle of documents.

1.6   The Distinction between Registered and Unregistered Land

The fundamental distinction that every student and practitioner of property law must draw since 1 January 1926 is between registered and unregistered land. Registered land – more accurately, land of registered title – is governed by the LPA 1925, the common law and the LRA 2002. Unregistered land is governed by the LPA 1925, the common law and the LCA 1972. Most importantly of all, the registered land system and the unregistered land system are mutually exclusive. Land either falls into one system or the other, but never both at the same time. As explained in Chapter 2, the great majority of titles are already registered (over 85 per cent) and in due course virtually all land will become registered – a process that has been speeded up by the entry into force of the LRA 2002. However, at present, two systems of land conveyancing are in operation in England and Wales, side by side. What follows is an outline of the two systems, and the detail is provided later in Chapters 2 and 3. Particular attention should be paid to the way in which both systems deal with the question of the effect of proprietary interests on third parties: that is, the issue that was once governed, principally, by the distinction between legal and equitable rights and the doctrine of notice. That said, it is also important to appreciate that 'registered land' is the system intended to govern land law into the twenty-first century and beyond, and that it is already by far the predominant system. Unregistered land is of diminishing importance.

1.6.1   Registered land

1   Registered land is land to which the title is registered in a register. Every title is given a title number and the details of the current owners are registered against it. Once a person is registered as estate owner, that ownership is guaranteed by the State,[34] and prospective purchasers may buy the land in the certainty that the title has been thoroughly investigated and approved before it was first registered (e.g. as in *Habenec v. Harris* (1998)). A title that is registered under the LRA 2002 is a strong, marketable title.

---

34 Section 58 of the LRA 2002 provides that registration as proprietor of an estate is conclusive.

2   A second category of right in registered land is the *registered charge*. These are essentially legal mortgages, used to raise money for the estate owner by offering the land as security for a loan. Legal mortgages are registered against the estate over which they take effect.

3   There is another group of proprietary rights in registered land, central to the operation of the LRA 2002, called *unregistered interests that override*. These property rights, still conveniently called 'overriding interests',[35] are *automatically* binding on any transferee or occupier of the land, without the need for any kind of registration. They have priority over the rights of such transferees, whether the transferee be a purchaser or not.[36] Importantly, unregistered interests that override are not only comprised of legal rights, but include a number of equitable rights. This is because they are defined in the LRA 2002 – in Schedules 1 and 3 to the Act – and these definitions are conclusive. In fact, it is a right's status as an 'interest that overrides' that is important, not its legal or equitable quality, and thus it is the statutory status within the LRA 2002 that makes such rights binding on a third party.

4   A fourth category of right in registered land is the *protectable registrable interest*. These rights include all other proprietary rights not included in the above categories, be they legal or equitable. The fundamental point about these interests is that they will only bind a purchaser of the land if they are registered against the title that they affect. Registration is by means of a notice.[37] If they are not so registered, they have no priority against a purchaser of the affected land, meaning that they cannot be enforced against him.[38]

To conclude, three points about registered land bear repetition. First, in registered land, the effect of a proprietary right on a transferee of the land is determined by its status under the LRA 2002, especially whether it is an interest that overrides or a protectable registrable interest. Its legal or equitable quality is relevant, but not crucial. Second, under the system of the LRA 2002, the 'doctrine of notice' is entirely irrelevant, although certain provisions do make reference to the 'knowledge' of transferees of land. Third, the concept of overreaching (see Chapters 2 and 4) may allow a purchaser of registered land to defeat *certain* equitable rights, even if they appear to be technically overriding or their registration has been attempted. So, a purchaser who pays the purchase price of land to the co-owners of a legal estate will 'overreach' any equitable owners, meaning that the rights of equitable ownership *cannot* bind that purchaser, whether or not the rights fall within the definition of overriding interests or are registered protected interests.[39] The equitable owner's rights are, in fact, transferred to the purchase money that has been paid. Overreaching is a limited, but powerful, 'trump card' and is explained in greater detail in Chapters 3 and 4.

---

35 As they were known under the LRA 1925.

36 Sections 11, 12, 29 and 30 of the LRA 2002.

37 The notice is the name given to the register entry. It is *not* the doctrine of notice.

38 Note, however, as explained in Chapter 2, that even an unregistered right may be enforceable against a transferee of the land who is *not* a purchaser – such as a person receiving the land under a will or by gift: see section 28 of the LRA 2002.

39 In fact, these overreachable equitable shares of ownership cannot be registered by means of a notice under the LRA 2002 precisely because it is intended that they should be overreached: section 33 of the LRA 2002.

1.6.2   Unregistered land

Unregistered land is land to which *the title is not registered*. The title is located in the old-fashioned title deeds, and a prospective purchaser must investigate 'root of title' through examination of the title deeds in order to be confident of obtaining an unimpeachable right to the land. Further, in unregistered land, it remains true that 'legal rights bind the whole world'. This aspect of the pre-1926 common law remains important and an understanding of how 'legal' rights come into existence is therefore crucial to understanding unregistered land. However, equitable rights in unregistered land fall into three distinct and separate categories.

1   Most equitable rights are 'land charges' within the LCA 1972. As such, they must be registered against the *owner* of the land over which they take effect (not the land itself) in order to bind a purchaser of it. If they are not registered, they are not binding (they are void) and the doctrine of notice is irrelevant. It should be understood that this is an *entirely separate* system of registration from that which exists in registered land. The two different systems of registration are mutually exclusive, and operate under different statutes. The equitable rights that are land charges for the purposes of registration under the LCA 1972 are defined in the LCA 1972 itself. They are generally rights of a commercial nature (e.g. an equitable mortgage).

2   There are a number of equitable rights that do not fall within the statutory definition of land charges. Consequently, they are *not* registrable under the LCA 1972 and are not 'land charges'. Their effectiveness against a purchaser is decided by the application of the old doctrine of notice. This is a very limited class of right and provides the only example in which the doctrine of notice retains any relevance in modern land law.

3   There are certain special equitable rights that are neither land charges nor always subject to the doctrine of notice. These are the rights that are overreachable. They are equitable rights of a special character, being rights capable of easy quantification in money (e.g. equitable ownership of a proportion of a house). They may be 'overreached' so as not to be binding on a new purchaser of the land, meaning that the equitable owner may be required to take the monetary value of the right rather than enjoy the right over the land itself. This is explained more fully in Chapter 4, but its relevance here is to signpost the existence of equitable rights in unregistered land that are neither land charges under the LCA 1972, nor subject to the old doctrine of notice.

So, to reiterate with respect to unregistered land. First, in unregistered land, the distinction between legal and equitable rights is still of fundamental importance. Second, in unregistered land, the doctrine of notice is largely irrelevant, but may still play a part for those equitable rights that fall outside of the LCA 1972 and which are not overreached. Third, the concept of overreaching (see Chapters 3 and 4) also applies to unregistered land, and may allow a purchaser of unregistered land to defeat *certain* equitable rights. Fourth, over 85 per cent of all titles are registered and unregistered land is slowly, but surely, disappearing from the map. As we shall see, land that is currently unregistered becomes registered on the occasion of certain dealings with it. These 'triggers' for compulsory registration are discussed in Chapter 2. There are also procedures by which an estate owner may apply for voluntary first registration of title and the entry into force of the LRA 2002 has encouraged much greater voluntary registration. However, the point is simply that unregistered land is a fading system and soon will barely trouble practitioners and students alike. Figure 1.4 gives a diagrammatic representation of the 1925 property legislation.

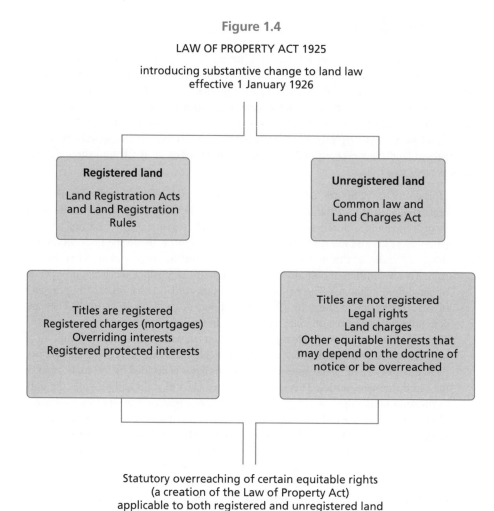

Figure 1.4

LAW OF PROPERTY ACT 1925

introducing substantive change to land law
effective 1 January 1926

Registered land

Land Registration Acts
and Land Registration
Rules

Unregistered land

Common law and
Land Charges Act

Titles are registered
Registered charges (mortgages)
Overriding interests
Registered protected interests

Titles are not registered
Legal rights
Land charges
Other equitable interests that
may depend on the doctrine of
notice or be overreached

Statutory overreaching of certain equitable rights
(a creation of the Law of Property Act)
applicable to both registered and unregistered land

1.7 Chapter Summary

The law of real property (or land law) is concerned with land, rights in or over land, and the processes whereby those rights and interests are created and transferred. Rights in or over land are different from 'mere' contractual rights, in that 'land law rights' are capable of affecting persons other than the parties who created the rights. This is the 'proprietary' nature of land law rights and it is completely different from the merely 'personal' obligations that an ordinary contractual relationship establishes. Proprietary rights can 'run' with the land and can confer benefits and burdens on whomsoever comes to own the land.

1.7.1 Types of proprietary right

Proprietary rights are either 'estates' or 'interests'. An 'estate' is a right to use and control land, being tantamount to ownership, but with the important difference that the 'estate' will define the time for which their 'ownership' lasts. An 'estate' is equivalent to owner-ship of the land for a slice of time. The two estates proper are:

1   the fee simple (or freehold); and
2   the leasehold (or term of years or tenancy).

An 'interest' is generally a right that one person enjoys over land belonging to someone else; technically, an interest is a right in the estate of another person. These include two former estates (the fee tail and life interest), but also more limited rights such as the easement (e.g. a right of way), mortgage (a debt secured on land) and restrictive covenant (a right to control a neighbour's use of land).

1.7.2   The legal or equitable quality of proprietary rights

Section 1 of the LPA 1925 defines which proprietary rights may be legal. These include the fee simple absolute in possession, the term of years absolute (both 'estates'), the easement, mortgage and right of re-entry (all 'interests'). An estate or interest not falling within this section must necessarily be equitable. For estates and interests that *do* fall within the section, their legal or equitable status will be determined by the manner of their creation.

Assuming the estate or interest falls within section 1 of the LPA 1925, the following will apply.

1   A right will be 'legal' if it is created with proper formality, which usually means by deed. Note that, in special circumstances, certain proprietary rights may be legal without the execution of a deed, such as where there is a lease for three years or less, or an easement is generated by prescription. The need for a deed is supplemented in respect of some legal rights by the need for registration under the LRA 2002.
2   A right will be 'equitable' if it is created by a written contract or instrument within section 2 of the Law of Property (Miscellaneous Provisions) Act 1989 or section 53 of the Law of Property Act 1925. In exceptional circumstances, equity will recognise the existence of a right arising from an oral contract, promise or agreement, pro-vided that the conditions for proprietary estoppel or implied trusts have been fulfilled.
3   Under the LRA 2002, it will be possible, and later mandatory, to create proprietary rights electronically.
4   A right falling outside of section 1 of the LPA 1925 may only ever be equitable, but must also fulfil the formality requirements necessary to establish an equitable propri-etary right (as 2 above).
5   The distinction between legal and equitable proprietary rights also can arise through the use of the 'trust'. One person may have the 'legal' title to property and another may have the 'equitable' title. This is common in co-ownership situations.

1.7.3   The original significance of the legal/equitable distinction prior to 1926

As well as indicating how a proprietary right came into existence and whether any trust is involved, a significant reason for distinguishing between legal and equitable proprietary rights *before* the 1925 property legislation was that this could determine their effect on third parties.

1   If the right were legal, it would always bind every transferee of the land over which it existed.

2   If the right were equitable, it would bind every transferee of the land except a bona fide purchaser for value of a legal estate in the land who had no notice of the equitable right.

These principles have been replaced to a very considerable extent by requirements of registration.

1.7.4   The 1925 and 2002 property legislation

The LPA 1925 made substantive changes in the law of real property, including a redefinition of what rights may be 'legal' or 'equitable'. It applies in equal measure to registered and unregistered land.

The LRA 2002 governs a system whereby title to land is recorded in a register administered by HM Land Registry. Provision is made for the registration of other rights affecting the land. 'Registered land' now accounts for over 85 per cent of all titles. The land registration system has been thoroughly overhauled by the entry into force of the LRA 2002.

The LCA 1972 (replacing the LCA 1925) establishes a system of registration of equitable interests in unregistered land, being land for which title is not entered on a register. Land covered by the LCA falls outside of 'registered land'. Unregistered land is now much less important, given that most titles are registered under the LRA 2002. Unregistered conveyancing will largely disappear as more titles become registered.

The Settled Land Act 1925 controls dealings with 'successive' interests in land, but only in respect of settlements in existence before 1 January 1997. Thereafter, any new successive interests are controlled by the Trusts of Land and Appointment of Trustees Act 1996.

The distinction between 'registered land' and 'unregistered land' is as follows. Registered land is land to which the title is registered: for example, the legal freehold or the legal lease of over seven years' duration. Other categories of right in registered land are: registered charges (e.g. mortgages); unregistered interests that override (being rights that are automatically in priority to those of a transferee of the land without the need for any kind of registration or notice); and protected registrable interests (being rights requiring registration to bind a purchaser of the land).

Unregistered land is land to which the title is not registered. The title is located in the title deeds and a prospective purchaser must investigate 'root of title'. In unregistered land, it remains true that 'legal rights bind the whole world', although the validity of equitable rights against a purchaser depends on their status as either land charges (requiring registration under the LCA 1972), overreachable rights or rights dependent on the doctrine of notice.

Further Reading

Battersby, G, 'Informally created interests in land', in Bright, S and Dewar, J (eds) *Land Law: Themes and Perspectives*, Oxford: OUP, 1998

Dixon, M, 'Proprietary and non-proprietary rights in modern land law', in Tee, L (ed.) *Essays in Land Law*, Devon: Willan, 2002

Jackson, P and **Wilde**, D (eds) *The Reform of Property Law*, Aldershot: Dartmouth, 1997

Chapter 2
Registered Land

Introduction

The system of registered land was perhaps the greatest of the reforms that came out of the wholesale restructuring of English property law in 1925.[1] While the original system of land registration inaugurated by the 1925 Land Registration Act (LRA 1925) had many flaws, it served well for nearly 80 years and was able to cope with the fundamental economic and social changes that took place over that time. It was not perfect,[2] but judicial management through sensible interpretation in case law ensured that it worked on an everyday basis. Today, the majority of land in England and Wales is 'registered land'[3] and is now governed by the Land Registration Act 2002 (LRA 2002). The LRA 2002 entered into force on 13 October 2003 and significantly amended the original scheme. This legislation, which is still relatively untested in the courts, replaced the 1925 Act in its entirety, and while some aspects of the old law remain operative through transitional provisions,[4] it is to the 2002 Act and the Land Registration Rules (LRR) that we must turn for the detail of the system. Consequently, this chapter will concentrate on the law of land registration as it exists today – that is, under the LRA 2002. Reference will of course be made to the 'old' law of land registration under the 1925 Act, especially where its provisions have been given longer life through the transitional provisions of the LRA 2002. However, the LRA 2002 is the guiding statute.

The 2002 Act was the product of years of consultation and evaluation and it was a joint project between the Land Registry[5] and the Law Commission.[6] The draft Bill was virtually unamended during its passage through Parliament and it is a work of clarity and principle. As well as ensuring that the substantive principles of land registration were brought up to date and expressed in clear language, the 2002 Act is also designed – in fact primarily designed – to facilitate e-conveyancing: that is, the holding and transfer of estates and interests in land electronically. This goal of a virtually paper-free conveyancing system has not yet been achieved because the e-conveyancing provisions of the LRA 2002 have not yet been triggered,[7] but the structure of registered land under the 2002 Act is designed to ensure that e-conveyancing will work when the remaining technological and legal issues have been resolved. In this sense, the 2002 Act is 'transaction-driven' – its primary aim is to ensure the quick, efficient and inexpensive transfer of estates and

---

1 It is a common misconception that land registration in England and Wales is a relatively modern phenomenon. In fact, the first legislation occurred in 1862, with further statutes in 1875 and 1897, although admittedly it was not until the entry into force of the LRA 1925 on 1 January 1926 that giant steps were taken towards a nationwide system of title registration.

2 See Law Commission Report No. 271, below note 6.

3 See below for a more accurate description of what it means to say that land is 'registered'.

4 That is, the 2002 Act necessarily has to preserve the pre-existing situation in some instances and does this by incorporating some of that law through transitional provisions.

5 The government agency responsible for administering and operating registered land.

6 In July 1998, the Law Commission published its Report No. 271 entitled *Land Registration for the Twenty-first Century: A Conveyancing Revolution*, on which the 2002 Act is based.

7 A pilot scheme was completed in 2007 and e-transfers (i.e. certain electronic dispositions) are planned for introduction in late 2010 or early 2011.

interests in land while ensuring that third-party interests in land (the proprietary rights of others in the registered estate) are properly protected. To further this in a practical way, the 2002 Act seeks to implement a number of policies through changes to the substantive law. First, it seeks to ensure that as many estates in land as is possible become registered. Second, it seeks to ensure that as many third-party rights as possible are recorded on the register of title of the estate that is affected by those rights. The necessary corollary is, of course, that failure to protect rights by registration when required may well mean that the interest ceases to affect the estate when it is sold. Third, it seeks to minimise the number and effect of those third-party proprietary rights that can be effective against the new owner of land even without being registered ('unregistered interests that override'). In turn, this will do much to ensure that the register provides a very clear picture of the legal state of the land. Fourth, eventually under e-conveyancing, it seeks to provide that the effective transfer and creation of most proprietary rights in land cannot occur unless this is achieved by an electronic entry on the e-register.

At this early stage in the analysis of the law of land registration, these policy goals may appear difficult to understand, but the point of importance is to appreciate that the LRA 2002 is designed to alter radically, through e-conveyancing, the way in which land is sold and the ways in which third-party rights in that land are held and protected. We are not there yet, but many of the provisions of the LRA 2002 make sense only if this fundamental point is appreciated. That said, it would have been foolish for the framers of the 2002 Act to ignore what had gone before. So it is that the 2002 Act builds on the principles of the 1925 Act and there is much in the new law that is taken from the old. Indeed, we can go further and say that the basics of the system operating under the 2002 Act are the same as those under the 1925 Act. There is still a register of titles, there is still a Chief Land Registrar and district registrars, and under the 2002 Act there are concepts, ideas and distinctions that are to be found in the 1925 Act. The difference is in the detail, not the basic structure, at least prior to the introduction of e-conveyancing when perhaps even our understanding of what 'proprietary rights' are might have to change. For now, however, the 2002 Act represents evolution not revolution.[8]

2.1   The Basic Concept of Title Registration

Simply put, to describe land as 'registered' means that the title to it (the estate, a right of ownership) is recorded in a register maintained by HM Land Registry and accessed through a number of district land registries around the country or increasingly online. Each title is referenced by a unique title number. In addition to information about the title itself (e.g. quality of title, general description of land and identity of estate owner), other rights and interests affecting the title may be entered on the register against the title number. Thus, while it is convenient to talk of registration of 'land', in fact the system is built on registration of title and it is not a 'cadastral system' in which it is the land itself that is recorded.[9] The fact that our system depends on registration of title, not of land, also

---

8   The Law Commission Report is entitled *A Conveyancing Revolution*, but I am grateful to Professor Edward Burn for this
      pithy turn of phrase when commenting on the 2002 Act.

9   Of course, under the LRA 2002, the physical land to which each title relates is described in the register.

means that it is perfectly possible for one plot of land to have more than one type of title registered in respect of it. Where this occurs, it is clearly identified on the register and a suitable cross-reference made. For example, a parcel of land might be identified as having a registered fee simple (a freehold owner) and a registered long lease (his tenant), and these will be cross-referenced to each other so that a purchaser of the freehold will be able to identify all registrable estates (titles) over the land that he is purchasing.

As things currently stand under the LRA 2002, not quite every 'estate' in land is a 'registrable title' because some estates are excluded for practical or legal reasons (e.g. they may be of too short duration to require the protection of registration). Currently, a registrable estate – being an estate that must be registered on its transfer or creation[10] – is either a *legal freehold* (being the fee simple absolute in possession) or a *legal leasehold* of over seven years' duration (or with over seven years left to run if it is sold by one tenant to another[11]). All other estates cannot be registered in their own right but, as discussed in the previous chapter, these two 'qualifying' titles are for all intents and purposes the most important indicia of land ownership in modern land law.[12] The Land Register is thus intended to provide a comprehensive picture of title ownership in England and Wales, and 'registration of title' has replaced 'deeds of title' as the proof of that ownership. So while the mechanics of the system are complicated, the central idea is simple enough. There should exist an accurate and reasonably comprehensive record of title to land and of third-party interests in that land in order that dealings with the land can be accomplished safely and quickly. In pursuit of this, on 1 December 1990, all land in England and Wales became subject to compulsory first registration of title, although, at that time, there were already some 13 million registered titles. Today, HM Land Registry estimates that over 85 per cent of titles are registered.

The consequence of the introduction of nationwide compulsory first registration of title on 1 December 1990 – a principle now enshrined in the LRA 2002 – is that certain transactions concerning what is currently unregistered land will trigger the requirement that the new owner seeks registration of title by application to the relevant district land registry. On such application, HM Land Registry will investigate the title, will register it and will assign a unique title number. In fact, the LRA 2002 lists numerous transactions that will trigger a compulsory first registration of a qualifying title. These 'triggers' for compulsory first registration of a previously unregistered title are:[13]

1   the transfer ('conveyance') of an unregistered freehold estate to another person,

---

10 Sections 4 and 27 of the LRA 2002.

11 The limitation to legal leases of over seven years is a practical one to ensure that HM Land Registry does not get swamped with applications to register. In due course, the trigger for registration will fall to legal leases of over three years, thus matching the trigger for the use of a deed to create a legal lease. Under the LRA 1925, the trigger for registration was legal leases of over 21 years, and so the LRA 2002 already has brought more leasehold titles onto the register.

12 Under the LRA 2002, it is also possible to register rights of ownership of other types of real property, not being estates. These 'franchises', 'rentcharges' and '*profits à prendre* in gross' give their owners specialist and limited rights over the land they are registered against. A 'manor' – an old feudal property ownership right – may no longer be registered, but can continue to be registered if it was registered under the LRA 1925.

13 See generally section 4 of the LRA 2002.

whether for valuable consideration (e.g. a sale), by gift, on death, by way of trust or under order of the court;

2   the transfer of an existing lease in the land to another person, with more than seven years left to run at the date of the transfer, whether for valuable consideration (e.g. a sale of the lease), by gift, on death or under order of the court;[14]

3   the grant of a legal lease of more than seven years' duration, either out of an unregistered freehold or out of an unregistered leasehold of more than seven years' duration (in this case, the lease will be registered, even if the estate out of which it is granted is not);[15]

4   the creation of a first legal mortgage over an unregistered freehold or unregistered leasehold with more than seven years left to run, which will trigger registration of both the mortgage and the title.[16]

There is no doubt that the great majority of transactions concerning unregistered land will be caught by these triggers with the consequence that, as HM Land Registry estimates, the vast majority of all titles to land should be registered in the near future.[17] In addition, the 2002 Act also provides for voluntary registration of titles[18] and for registration by the Crown of its land.[19] So, for example, an existing owner of an unregistered freehold can apply for voluntary first registration and thus 'convert' his land from 'unregistered' to 'registered'. Indeed, the LRA 2002 provides powerful incentives to do this. Not only are there reduced fees for registration and significant protection for persons buying a registered title, but registered land is also protected to a very great degree from claims of adverse possession.[20] A large landowner, perhaps a farmer or local authority, who is unable to keep track of all of their holdings, might well apply for voluntary first registration of title in order to obtain the security offered by the LRA 2002.[21] Some land will, however, remain of unregistered title under these provisions, but these are likely to be unusual land holdings that are rarely, if ever, transferred and so their unregistered status will be not be important.[22]

---

14 Certain shorter leases also require registration, but these are of a specialist kind. Perhaps the most important is the lease of whatever duration that gives a right to possession more than three months in the future: for example, a lease of six years' duration granted on 1 July 2010 to take effect in possession on 1 December 2010. This is registrable as a title irrespective of its duration because it cannot necessarily be discovered by inspection of the land because the possession might not have started at the time of the inspection.

15 Note the grant of a lease of more than seven years out of an existing registered estate of freehold or leasehold also must be registered. This is technically a 'disposition' of a registered estate, so is dealt with by section 27 of the Act.

16 Note the grant of a mortgage over an existing registered estate of freehold or leasehold also must be registered. This is technically a 'disposition' of a registered estate, so is dealt with by section 27 of the Act.

17 The happy consequence is that unregistered land conveyancing will be a very rare event: see Chapter 3.

18 Section 3 of the LRA 2002.

19 Section 79 of the LRA 2002.

20 See Chapter 11.

21 In fact, a number of local authorities have negotiated a block fee with HM Land Registry for the voluntary first registration of all of their holdings.

22 For example, land held by the ancient universities or by the Church of England whose retention of land is essential in order to achieve their purposes.

2.2 The Nature and Purpose of the System of Registered Land

The LRA 2002, and the Land Registration Rules 2003[23] made thereunder, contain the details of the current system of registered land. Together, they provide a statutory code that seeks to regulate the transfer, use and enjoyment of registered land, and it is imperative to appreciate that an understanding of 'registered land' is indispensable before embarking on an analysis of the substance of modern land law. The 2002 Act (and the 1925 Act before it) represent an attempt to impose a self-contained structure on a vitally important area of social, economic, family and commercial activity – the sale and use of land – and in this it is largely successful. Of course, the system of registered land is not perfect, even though the 2002 Act has resolved many points of former difficulty,[24] but that should not blind us to the importance of a thorough understanding of the 2002 Act and the principles that underlie it.

Land is one of the most important economic assets of any nation, but it is also used for a variety of social and domestic purposes that many would argue are at the foundation of a modern society. Land law has to reflect the needs of commerce, families, financial institutions, neighbours, purchasers and occupiers. It is in this context that the system of registered land must operate, for it is these masters that land law has to serve. Consequently, it is difficult to draw up a complete list of the aims and purposes of the land registration system of England and Wales, not least because the LRA 2002 is just one component of a complex system regulating land use and ownership. In this respect, it must also be remembered that many of the structural changes in the mechanics of land law originally brought about by the 1925 Act and now developed by the 2002 Act would not have been possible without the complimentary changes in the substantive law of estates and interests that were brought about by the Law of Property Act 1925. These were discussed in Chapter 1 and are an important step in the achievement of the objectives outlined below. With that in mind, we may note that our modern system of registered land is dedicated to a number of practical goals.[25]

1   To reduce the expense and effort of purchasing land by eliminating the lengthy and formalistic process of investigating 'root of title'.[26] If title is registered, the owners of land should be easily discoverable by a simple search of the register of title and the possibility of fraud should be reduced. Thus land becomes much more saleable and alienable.

---

23 As amended in November 2008.

24 As noted, although the 2002 Act replaces the 1925 LRA in its entirety, it nevertheless builds on its conceptual foundations. It has thus inherited much of its basic philosophy. In one respect, however, the 2002 deliberately departs from its predecessor in that it pays no regard to principles of *unregistered* conveyancing. The Law Commission Report is explicit that old principles of unregistered land (and those of the 1925 Act based on unregistered conveyancing) should not hinder the development of the modern law of land registration.

25 The 2002 Act is very much designed to be a practical tool to be used for the everyday business of land transfer and land exploitation.

26 Used in unregistered conveyancing: see Chapter 3.

2   To reduce the dangers facing a purchaser who is buying land from a person whose title is unsafe, unclear or difficult to establish. The purchaser can rely on the register of title to the extent that the title has been registered after investigation by the Land Registrar. In fact, under the LRA 2002, the aim is to ensure that ownership of land in England and Wales takes the form of 'title by registration' instead of 'registration of title'. Thus, title is ensured by *the fact of registration itself*, not by the documents that are sent off for registration – as made clear in section 58 of the Act. As the Law Commission commented in Report No. 271, the 'fundamental objective' of the 2002 Act is that 'the register should be a complete and accurate reflection of the state of the title of the land at any given time, so that it is possible to investigate title to land on line, with the absolute minimum of additional enquiries and inspections'.[27]

3   To ensure that a purchaser of land knows about the rights and interests of other persons over that land, thereby ensuring that the price paid reflects its true economic and social value. This can be done by ensuring that as many rights as possible must be entered on the register and by limiting those that need not be. If the purchaser is able to discover these hostile interests – either by inspecting the register or by inspecting the land itself – the purchase can be abandoned or the offer price reduced if he is unable to use the land for the purpose originally intended.

4   To enable the purchaser to buy land completely free of certain types of interest over that land, those interests then taking effect in the money paid to the seller (known as 'overreaching').

5   To provide a mechanism whereby *certain* third-party rights in land can be protected and so survive a sale of that land to a new owner. For this reason, the old unregistered land 'doctrine of notice' plays no part in the system of registered land, having been superseded by the operation of the register, in particular by the categorisation of third-party proprietary rights into three groups: those that are overreached;[28] those that are 'unregistered interests that override';[29] and those interests that must be protected by registration.[30]

6   Eventually to introduce e-conveyancing whereby the transfer of land, its mortgage and the creation of many third-party rights will be required to be achieved by electronic entry directly on to the register of title. In many instances, paper transactions with land will cease to be valid.[31] The transfer, creation and protection of many proprietary rights will be a 'one-stage' process, all to be achieved by electronic entry on the register by the parties directly.[32]

As well as these major aims, which – as we shall see – have been implemented with varying degrees of success by the 2002 Act, widespread registration of title has brought other

---

27   Law Commission Report No. 271, paragraph 1.5.

28   As noted above, overreaching 'protects' the interest by converting it into its monetary equivalent.

29   These were called 'overriding interests' under the LRA 1925.

30   These were known as 'minor interests' under the LRA 1925, a description deliberately not repeated in the LRA 2002.

31   See section 91 of the LRA 2002. It is too early to identify those transactions with land that will *not* be subject to e-conveyancing, but they are likely to be few in number.

32   In reality, of course, by their lawyers who will have had to have concluded a 'Network Access Agreement' with HM Land Registry in order to act as conveyancers under e-conveyancing.

benefits. For example, more accurate plans are provided, standardised and simple forms and procedures have replaced bulky title deeds, disputes can usually be resolved more easily, transaction costs have been reduced and confidence has been brought to the conveyancing process.

2.3   The Three Fundamental Operating Principles of Registered Land

It is sometimes said that there are three principles underlying the system of registered land against which we should judge the reality of the LRA 2002 (and the LRA 1925 before it). To some extent, however, these are no more than a restatement of what we have already noted: that land registration is about the easy, safe and efficient transfer of land and the appropriate protection of rights in land. That said, the three principles are the *mirror principle*, the *curtain principle* and the *insurance principle*, and they are discussed briefly below.

2.3.1   The mirror principle

The *mirror principle* encapsulates the idea that the register should reflect the totality of the rights and interests concerning a title of registered land. Thus, inspection of the register should reveal the identity of the owner, the nature of his ownership, any limitations on his ownership and any rights enjoyed by other persons over the land that are adverse to the owner. The point is simply that if the register reflects the full character of the land, any purchaser and any third party can rest assured that they are fully protected: the purchaser knows what he is buying and the person with an interest in the land knows that it will be protected. Yet, as we shall see, the mirror principle does not operate fully in the system of registered land in England and Wales, even under the LRA 2002. This is mainly due to the existence of a category of rights that affect the land and which bind any transferee of it (including a purchaser) without ever being entered on any register. These are the 'unregistered interests that override' – found in Schedule 1 and Schedule 3 to the LRA 2002[33] – which although much reduced in scope by the 2002 Act (when compared with the 1925 Act) nevertheless compromise the integrity of the register as a 'mirror' of the legal status of the land.

However, before we are too critical, it is important to remember that 'unregistered interests that override' (still 'overriding interests' for short), are not a mistake. Although the 2002 Act in particular desires to make the register as complete a mirror as possible, it is recognised that it is simply impractical or undesirable to make absolutely everything subject to express registration. Indeed, registration of title is not intended to replace physical inspection of the land by the purchaser as a way of discovering whether there are any adverse rights over that land. Thus, the imperatives of the LRA 2002 are to ensure that as much as possible about the land is registered *and*, for those rights that are not registrable under the Act, to ensure that they are *capable* of discovery by a normal inspection of the

---

33 Schedule 1 concerns first registration of title; Schedule 3 concerns dealings with titles already registered. However, the list of interests that override under the schedules is broadly similar.

land. Thus, the purchaser should inspect the register and the land and should thereby be able to discover all that he needs to know.[34] In this aim, the LRA 2002 largely succeeds.[35] Consequently, although the image reflected by the register under the LRA 2002 remains imperfect, the imperfection will not necessarily cause loss to a diligent purchaser.[36] Title registration exists to ease the purchaser's path, not to exclude his participation in the conveyancing process.

In fact, the register will never be a truly perfect mirror, as not everything can be expected to be entered on a register. For example, informally created rights where no property professional has been involved are unlikely ever to be registered by the parties and short-term rights (e.g. a one-year lease) or rights fundamental to the good use of land (e.g. rights benefiting the public) are either too transient or too important to be subject to a registration requirement. However, it is undoubtedly true that the changes made by the LRA 2002 to the original 1925 scheme do much to improve the reflection of the mirror. As noted already, many more interests will be brought onto the register through the operation of electronic conveyancing (as where the right will not exist at all unless it is electronically registered – see section 93 of the LRA 2002). Similarly, under the LRA 2002, fewer categories of rights can override at all, irrespective of the circumstances in which they arise,[37] and the definition of those overriding interests that remain has been altered to give the purchaser a very real chance of discovering their existence before the sale is completed.[38] Indeed, there is now a general duty to disclose unregistered rights that override to the registrar so that they may be brought onto the register when a title changes hands.[39]

2.3.2   The curtain principle

The *curtain principle* encapsulates the idea that certain *equitable* interests in land should be hidden behind the 'curtain' of a special type of trust. Thus, if a person wishes to buy registered land that is subject to a trust of land, the purchaser need be concerned only with the legal title to the land, which is held by the trustees and reflected on the title register. He need not look behind the 'curtain' of the trust or worry about any equitable rights of ownership that might exist. The reason is that any such equitable rights will be 'overreached' if the proper formalities of the purchase are observed – see sections 2 and 27 of the LPA 1925. Consequently, these equitable rights will not affect the purchaser in his enjoyment of the land. Moreover, although the interests of the equitable owners cannot affect the purchaser because of overreaching, they are not completely destroyed because the process of overreaching operates to transfer the rights of the equitable owner from the land itself to the money that the purchaser has just paid for it. Thereafter, the trustees

---

34 Thus, for those rights not capable of registration, if they are *discoverable*, a purchaser who fails to inspect the land at all, or inspects badly, cannot claim unfairness if he is bound by rights not on the register.

35 See below for a discussion of the LRA 2002's strategies in this regard.

36 As we shall see, however, if a right is registrable, then failure to register it (assuming it does not override) causes the right to be lost, even if the purchaser discovered it. This must be so, else there would be no incentive to register.

37 For example, equitable easements may not override at all.

38 For example, where there is 'actual occupation'.

39 Section 71 of the LRA 2002.

(the legal owners) hold the purchase money in trust for the equitable owners. This doctrine of overreaching (which also operates in unregistered land) is discussed more fully in
Chapter 4 on co-ownership, but for now the important point is that, once again, the aim
is to facilitate the alienability of land by freeing the purchaser from the effort and worry of
dealing with equitable owners. As we shall see, the 'curtain' principle operates effectively
in the majority of cases, but when it fails (usually because the preconditions for statutory
overreaching cannot be met), the purchaser is faced with considerable difficulties. It may
then become necessary for the purchaser to look behind the curtain as in the classic case of
Williams and Glyn's Bank v. Boland (1981).[40]

The LRA 2002 does not alter the fundamentals of overreaching and so does not resolve
most of the problems that arise when overreaching does not occur (i.e. when the purchaser
has to look behind the curtain), save to the extent that the 2002 Act redefines what
qualifies as an overriding interest.[41] The 2002 Act does, however, confirm that legal owners
of land (the trustees) have all the powers of an absolute owner, subject only to restrictions
on their powers placed on the register of title itself (see section 23 of the LRA 2002) and
this will support the overreaching mechanism when there are the required minimum of
two legal owners.[42] Similarly, the widespread use of the restriction against a title of land
when there is only one legal owner (but others owning in equity) is likely to encourage
overreaching by ensuring that a purchaser is alerted to the existence of equitable interests
and so alerted to the need to overreach (or to gain the equitable owner's consent) before
he buys.[43]

2.3.3   The insurance principle

The *insurance principle* was one of the most ambitious of the motives underlying the LRA
1925 and it continues to underpin the operation of the 2002 Act. It encapsulates the idea
that if a title is duly registered, it is guaranteed by the State. This guarantee is supported
by a system of statutory indemnity (i.e. monetary compensation) for any purchaser who
suffers loss by reason of the conclusive nature of the register. The State insures against
inaccuracies or other mistakes in the register.

The original scheme of indemnity provided by the LRA 1925 was quite narrow, but
the (relatively) wider indemnity provisions of the 2002 Act are considered later in this
chapter. The point to be grasped here is that any registration system that guarantees title
effectively will need to provide a system of compensation for those persons who suffer
loss by reason of the application of the system. A register of land titles, especially one that is
designed to be absolutely conclusive for most purposes, will always generate cases in

---

40 See Chapter 4. The bank's failure to look behind the curtain meant that its mortgage lost priority to the rights of the
    borrower's wife.

41 This is done by redefining overriding interests in such a way as to exclude most interests that are undiscoverable. See
    below.

42 Except in those cases in which the two legal owners attempt to commit a fraud by employing the overreaching
    machinery: *HSBC v. Dyche* (2009); see Chapter 4.

43 A standard Form A restriction. Entry of this restriction necessarily alerts the purchaser to the existence of an
    equitable owner because it requires purchase money to be paid to two trustees, an event that would be unnecessary if
    there were not another equitable owner.

which loss is caused to innocent parties simply because of the way the system works. If A is the 'true' freehold owner of land, but B is registered with the title by innocent mistake, and then C buys the land from B on the basis of his registered title as guaranteed by the LRA 2002, it is obvious that either A or C will suffer loss by reason of the application of the registration system. The 'insurance' principle stipulates that a registration system must provide compensation in such cases.

It is difficult to overestimate the importance of the insurance principle. It is not so much that persons who suffer loss are compensated – in reality, there are relatively few payments of indemnity because of the relatively few serious instances of loss caused by the registration system – but rather that the very existence of an indemnity provision gives confidence to those using the registration system and encourages reliance on it. By way of contrast with the system in England and Wales, the system of title registration introduced into Hong Kong has an 'indemnity cap' that limits the amount of compensation payable in the event of a loss caused by an error in the register. It is clear already that the absence of a provision providing for full compensation has eroded confidence in the system in Hong Kong and has put at risk the widespread adoption of land registration. After all, if the State is not confident enough to back its registration system by underwriting it, why should landowners?

2.4   An Overview of the Registered Land System under the Land Registration Act 2002

As noted already, land is 'registered land' when title to it is recorded in the title register, provided that the title is either the legal fee simple absolute in possession (freehold) or the legal leasehold of over seven years' duration (or with over seven years left to run on assignment[44]). These are the two important titles in current land law that, when registered, are known as 'registered estates' and the owner is the 'registered proprietor'. Title is registered usually following some dealing with the land (e.g. a sale or mortgage) and after HM Land Registry has checked the validity of the title from the documents supplied by the person asking to be entered as the registered proprietor. Access to the register is through district land registries throughout England and Wales, or online, and the register itself is an open public document, searchable on payment of the appropriate fee.[45] Each registered title is given a unique title number and its entry is divided into three parts: the *property register* describes the land itself, usually by reference to a plan, and notes the type of title (i.e. the estate) that the registered proprietor has; the *proprietorship register* gives the name of the proprietor and describes the *grade* of their title and any benefits attaching to the title (the grade of the title varies according to the extent to which HM Land Registry is satisfied that the title has been established); and the *charges register* gives details of all third-party rights over the land (except unregistered interests that override) that detract from the registered proprietor's full use and enjoyment of the land. An illustration is given below. Although this illustration appears complex, it gives a flavour of the three-fold nature of the register and the degree of detail that may be found. Titles conveyed more recently than the

---

44 Note also the need to register certain specialist shorter-term leases.

45 A simple online search currently costs £4.

one is this example may include a note of the purchase price and the identity of any lender (but not the amount lent).

Register extract

```
*******************************************************************
*Title Number: CB5341
*
*Address of Property: 16 Gunning Way, Cambridge
*
*Price Stated: Not Available
*
*Registered Owner(s): RONALD JOHN BUCKLEY of 16 Gunning Way,
Cambridge
*
*Lender(s): None
*******************************************************************
```

TITLE NUMBER: CB5341

A: Property register

This register describes the land and estate comprised in the title.
COUNTY: CAMBRIDGESHIRE DISTRICT:
CAMBRIDGE

1. (18 June 1955) The Freehold land shown edged with red on the plan of the above Title filed at the Registry and being 16 Gunning Way, Cambridge.
2. The land has the benefit of the rights of drainage under adjoining land with ancillary rights of access.
3. A Transfer dated 3 September 1956 made between (1) Albert Brian Clarke, Lawrence Martin Noakes, Quentin Pine and Gilder Pine and (2) Ronald John Buckley contains the following provision:

IT IS HEREBY AGREED AND DECLARED by the parties hereto that the Transferee and the persons deriving title under him shall not be entitled to any right of access of light or air to buildings to be erected on the land hereby transferred which would restrict or interfere with the free user of any of the land now or formerly comprised in this title number.

B: Proprietorship register – Absolute freehold

This register specifies the class of title and identifies the owner. It contains any entries that affect the right of disposal.

1. (18 September 1970) Proprietor: RONALD JOHN BUCKLEY of 16 Gunning Way, Cambridge.
2. A Transfer dated 11 April 1956 made between (1) The Mayor Aldermen and Citizens of the City of Cambridge and (2) Albert Brian Clarke Lawrence Martin Noakes, Quentin Pine and Gilder Pine contains Vendors personal covenant(s) details of which are set out in the schedule of personal covenants hereto.

Schedule of covenants

1. The following are details of the personal covenants contained in the Transfer dated 11 April 1956 referred to in the Proprietorship Register:

THE Vendors hereby covenant with the Purchasers and their successors in title that if and when the local authority shall take over the highways upon which the red land abuts and intended to be known as Hurrell Road, Persey Way, Gunning Way and Harding Way or shall require any private street works (whether permanent or temporary) to be executed there the Vendors will pay the expenses thereof apportioned to the red land and will at all times save harmless and keep indemnified the Purchasers and their estate and effects from and against all proceedings costs claims expenses and liabilities whatsoever in respect thereof.

IT is hereby agreed and declared that the dropping of the kerbs to provide accesses for vehicles over the footpaths in front of the red land shall be carried out by the Vendors at the expense of the Purchasers.

C: Charges register

This register contains any charges and other matters that affect the land.

1. The land is subject to rights of drainage and ancillary rights of access.

2. A Transfer dated 11 April 1956 made between (1) The Mayor Alderman and Citizens of the City of Cambridge (Vendors) and (2) Albert Brian Clarke, Lawrence Martin Noakes, Quentin Pine and Gilder Pine contains covenants details of which are set out in the schedule of restrictive covenants hereto.

Schedule of restrictive covenants

1. The following are details of the covenants contained in the Transfer dated 11 April 1956 referred to in the Charges Register:

FOR the benefit of the owners occupiers and tenants for the time being of all or any of the Vendors adjoining land comprised in a Conveyance dated the fourth day of July One thousand nine hundred and forty seven and made between The Master Fellows and Scholars of the College of Saint John the Evangelist in the University of Cambridge of the one part and the Vendors of the other part the Purchasers hereby jointly and severally covenant with the Vendors that the Purchasers and the persons deriving title under them will at all times hereafter duly perform and observe all and singular the said conditions Restrictions and stipulations mentioned in the Second Schedule hereto.

THE SECOND SCHEDULE above referred to CONDITIONS and STIPULATIONS

1. NO building erected on the red land shall except with the consent of the Vendors be used for any other purpose than as a separate or semi-detached dwelling house.

2. NO portion of the red land shall be used for any trade or business noisy noisome dangerous or offensive pursuit or occupation or for any purpose which shall or may be or grow to be in any way a nuisance cause of grievance or annoyance to the Vendors or to the owners or tenants of any of the neighbouring property.

3. NO outbuildings other than a garage shall be erected on the red land without the written consent of the Vendors.

4. NO drains from any house erected or to be erected upon the red land shall be laid except in conformity with plans previously submitted to and approved in writing on behalf of the Vendors and such drains shall be connected to the main sewer at the Purchasers expense.

END OF REGISTER

2.4.1   Rejection of the doctrine of notice

At this early stage in our analysis of registered land, it is also critical to appreciate that the practical operation of the system means that the old distinction between legal and equitable interests as a method of regulating dealings with land is largely discarded. Indeed, with the introduction of e-conveyancing, this distinction will cease to have great significance even in terms of how property rights come into existence. The LRA 2002 (as did its predecessor) also abandons the 'doctrine of notice'[46] as a method of assessing whether any third-party rights affecting land will bind a purchaser of it.[47] In fact, the LRA 2002 effectively establishes four categories of proprietary right[48] and the crucial issue in any given case is to identify the category into which a person's right falls and not to ask whether that right is legal or equitable, or whether the 'doctrine of notice' applies. Not surprisingly, the 2002 Act and the Land Registration Rules occasionally utilise the legal/ equitable distinction as a method of assigning specific rights to one of these different categories, but it is not the nature of the right that is ultimately important, rather it is the category identified under the Act into which it falls.

2.4.2   Registrable estates under the LRA 2002

Registrable estates are those that are capable of existing at law (i.e. as legal rights[49]) and which may be registered in their own right with a unique title number. Under the LRA 2002, there are two such estates (commonly called 'titles'), although we should note that the Act also makes provision for the substantive registration of three other types of legal registrable interest.[50] For present purposes, however, we are concerned with the two legal

---

46 For a brief description of this doctrine, see Chapter 3 on unregistered land. Even there, however, the doctrine has limited relevance.

47 Save possibly in one instance in respect of first registration of title (see sections 11 and 12 of the LRA 2002). Moreover, as we shall see, the LRA 2002 does refer in some cases to the 'knowledge' of a purchaser, or the discoverability of a proprietary right, but the Law Commission has made it clear that this does not import old doctrines of 'notice' in to registered land. The 2002 Act is to be interpreted afresh given its aims and purposes.

48 The Act itself does not specifically refer to four categories of property right, but this is the effect of its provisions.

49 Section 1 of the LPA 1925.

50 Being 'rentcharges' (an interest whereby land is charged with the payment of money by the owner to another person) 'profits à prendre in gross' (a right to take some commodity from another's land, such as fish or wood) and 'franchises' (a right granted by the Crown to hold a fair or market, etc.). These registrable interests may be registered with their own title number as befits their special character. 'Manors' may remain registered in this way under the LRA 2002 if they have been so registered under the LRA 1925, but no new applications for registration may be made.

estates that most accurately reflect 'ownership' of the land. These are legal freeholds and, with some minor exceptions, legal leaseholds granted for more than seven years.[51]

Currently, these titles are registered 'at first registration' on a transfer (or other trigger) of the previously unregistered estate or by a 'registered disposition' transferring an already registered title from transferor to transferee (as on sale). The mechanics follow a well-worn pattern whereby the transfer is effected by deed and then the deed is sent to HM Land Registry for 'registration'. Failure to register such a transfer when required means that the transferee obtains only an equitable title to the land.[52] However, it is important to appreciate that these legal titles will be the type of right most affected by the advent of electronic conveyancing. There are two points here. First, as a temporary and transitional measure, it may be possible in the future to execute a deed electronically (section 91 of the LRA 2002). If – and it is not certain – this measure is introduced, a legal title-holder may have the choice of either executing a paper deed (as now) or executing an electronic version, either of which may then be registered in the current manner. The electronic version will not actually be a deed, but it 'is to be regarded for the purposes of any enactment as a deed' (section 91(5) of the LRA 2002). Second, and much more importantly, full e-conveyancing will mean that no creation or transfer of a registrable title will be effective *at all* unless it is entered on the register and such entry will be required to be done electronically (section 93 of the LRA 2002). Consequently, when full e-conveyancing arrives, it will not be the case that a creation or transfer by deed (electronic or paper) can be executed followed by registration of that deed (as now). Instead, electronic registration will comprise the very act of creation or transfer of the legal estate and will be obligatory. Any attempt to create or transfer a legal estate that is specified in the rules as required to be done electronically by any other means will be void both at law and in equity. This is highly significant. It means that, come full e-conveyancing, it will be obligatory to transfer and register titles electronically and that paper transactions will carry no effect at all.

2.4.3   Registered charges

Registered charges derive from the power of the registered proprietor to mortgage the land in order to release its capital value. These are legal mortgages of registered land. Under the LRA 2002, the only way to execute a mortgage of registered land (leasehold or freehold) is by 'a charge by deed expressed to be by way of legal mortgage'.[53] Mortgages are considered in depth in Chapter 10. For now, it is enough to note that a legal mortgage

---

51 Sections 2, 3, 4 and 27 of the LRA 2002. The Act gives power to the Lord Chancellor to change the leasehold trigger for registration (section 5). It is anticipated that eventually legal leases of over three years will be registrable with their own title as these are the leases currently required to be made by deed. In addition some shorter-term leases are currently registrable as separate titles, but these concern special or unusual situations: sections 4 and 27 of the LRA 2002. Probably the most common is the legal lease of whatever duration that gives a right to possession more than three months in the future: sections 4(1)(d) and 27(2)(b)(ii) of the LRA 2002. Such a lease must be registered with its own title, otherwise a purchaser of the land out of which the lease is granted may not know of its existence, as the tenant may not yet be in possession.

52 Section 7 of the LRA 2002.

53 Section 23 of the LRA. For present purposes, 'charging the land by deed with the payment of money' is equivalent to a charge by deed by way of legal mortgage.

must be registered as a registered charge against the relevant title if it is to retain its character as a legal interest with the priority that this entails.[54] We should also note on a practical level that the 'charge certificate', which under the LRA 1925 was the mortgagee's evidence of title, has been abolished by the LRA 2002. Under the 2002 Act, charge certificates are not necessary because the register itself is open to inspection. Similarly, the creation of registered charges over a registered estate is likely to be an early subject for electronic conveyancing. In fact, it may well be that e-conveyancing is first employed in respect of the creation of legal mortgages because most institutional lenders are geared up for paperless mortgage transactions and already operate an electronic system with HM Land Registry for the discharge of mortgages (i.e. removal from the register) after they are paid off.

2.4.4   Unregistered interests that override ('overriding interests')

Unregistered interests that override are those rights in another person's land (in their registered 'estate') that have priority to the registered title of the registered proprietor – that is, they are binding on the land without being entered on the register of title of the land they affect. They are, quite literally, *unregistered* interests that *override* the registered title and which thus permit the right-holder (the person who claims the overriding interest) to exercise the right against the land irrespective of who is the registered proprietor and even though it is not on the register.[55]

Under the LRA 2002, overriding interests may take effect against a first registered proprietor (after compulsory or voluntary first registration of title) or against a person who becomes the registered proprietor on the transfer of a title that is already registered. Interests that override at first registration are defined in Schedule 1 to the 2002 Act and interests that override following a transfer (e.g. a sale) of land that is already registered[56] are defined in Schedule 3. The scope of these two schedules is broadly similar, but there are some important differences. In essence, Schedule 1 is wider in scope than Schedule 3 so that more rights may override under Schedule 1 against a first registration than may override under Schedule 3 against a registered disposition.

When compared with the LRA 1925, the LRA 2002 markedly reduces the scope and range of overriding interests in respect of both Schedules 1 and 3. The aim is to ensure that a potential purchaser of the land is bound only by those unregistered interests that, for policy or practical reasons, should take effect against a purchaser without being entered on a register and then only in circumstances in which the purchaser had a realistic opportunity of discovering the existence of the interest by a physical inspection of the land or by making normal enquiries of the transferor. Moreover, in pursuit of this policy of protecting the purchaser, the 2002 Act encourages a person applying to be registered with a title (e.g. a purchaser) to disclose to the registrar any known overriding interests so that they may

---

54 Sections 12 and 30 of the LRA 2002. See *Barclays Bank v. Zaroovabli* (1997), decided under the LRA 1925 but still illustrative, for an example of the consequences of failing to register a legal mortgage.

55 Sections 11, 12, 29, 30 of the LRA 2002.

56 This is known as a 'registered disposition' as it is a disposition – a transfer – of a registered title and is completed by registration of the new owner as proprietor.

then be recorded on the register.[57] Be that as it may, it remains true that overriding interests account for a substantial number of rights affecting registered land and their importance stems from the fact that they have priority without being entered on the register. Their very existence was a cause of concern to the Law Commission and HM Land Registry when devising the LRA 2002, but their social and economic importance is such that, as a class, they cannot be dispensed with. What the LRA 2002 can do is to reduce their impact, to redefine their scope, to reduce their number and to encourage their entry on the register. The extent to which this is achieved may well determine the future of e-conveyancing. The existence of a large, or powerful, group of rights that can bind a purchaser of land even though they are not on the register necessarily makes electronic, paperless conveyancing less reliable. When the register is not a perfect mirror, inspection of the land and any associated documents will still be necessary and 'pure' e-conveyancing is not possible.

2.4.5   Interests protected by registration

The LRA 1925 specified a category of property rights in another person's land that had to be registered against the burdened title if they were to be binding. Failure to ensure such registration meant that the interests generally were void against a purchaser unless they could be (fortuitously) saved by falling within the category of overriding interests. These registrable interests were known as 'minor interests'. Under the LRA 2002, there is no specific category known as 'minor interests' and generally that terminology should be avoided.[58] However, the LRA 2002 does employ the same logic as that found in the LRA 1925 and so there is a general insistence that third-party property interests should be entered on the register against the estate they burden. Failure to make such an entry may mean that the property right loses its priority against the registered proprietor, unless the right falls fortuitously within Schedules 1 or 3 (as they case may be) and so qualifies as an overriding interest.[59]

The broad and important principle of the LRA 2002 is, then, that unless the property right amounts to a registrable estate (in which case it should be registered as a title), or a registrable charge (in which case it should be registered as a mortgage), or an overriding interest (in which case it has priority without registration), it must be entered on the register of title of the burdened land by means of a notice in order to preserve its effectiveness against a purchaser.[60] Rights falling within this category may be known as 'interests protectable by registration' and they comprise the bulk of third-party rights, including the important categories of covenants, options to purchase and many easements. Indeed, these interests protectable by registration will, in time, become the major group of third-party interests in land. This is ensured under the LRA 2002 not only because the

---

57 Section 71 of the LRA 2002 places a duty on an applicant to disclose such interests, although it is a 'duty' without a sanction. Once an overriding interest is registered, it ceases to be overriding and is protected by its registration. It cannot thereafter revert to overriding status, even if it is removed from the register.

58 These interests are not 'minor' in the sense of being trivial or unimportant and a major aim of the LRA 2002 is to ensure that as many rights as possible are entered on the registered. There is, then, nothing 'minor' or secondary about these rights.

59 Sections 11, 12, 29, 30. It is considerably less likely than was the case under the LRA 1925 that a right will override under the 2002 Act if it really should have been registered.

60 As we shall see, an unregistered interest remains valid against a non-purchaser of the land under section 28 of the LRA 2002.

statute requires more rights to be registered than was previously the case under the LRA 1925,[61] but also because section 71 of the LRA 2002 provides for a general duty of disclosure whereby an applicant for registration of a title must disclose a range of overriding interests that affect his land so that they may be protected by registration. In consequence, the group of interests that override under the LRA 2002 will shrink as more and more of these rights become protected by an entry on the register of title.[62]

It is also important to remember that the mechanics by which these third-party interests may be protected through registration has changed under the LRA 2002 when compared with the LRA 1925. Under the old statute, there were a number of different methods by which a third-party interest could be protected.[63] Under the LRA 2002, substantive protection of an interest is achieved by the entry of a notice – which may be 'unilateral' or 'agreed' – and the registered proprietor may be controlled in his ability to deal with the land by means of a restriction. A restriction indirectly protects an interest because it prevents a transfer of the land unless the terms of the restriction are complied with.[64] These methods are discussed more fully below, but the point here is that the process of third-party interest protection has been simplified by the 2002 Act. Finally, we should note again that, in due course, many of these third-party rights will be capable of creation only by electronic means. In such cases, the existence of the interest, and its protection through registration, will occur by an electronic entry on the register of title of the burdened land. This will be the effect of section 93 of the LRA 2002 when e-conveyancing comes into operation.

This classification of proprietary rights into four different statutory classes – estates, registered charges, interests that override and interests protectable by registration – is fundamental to the land registration system under the LRA 2002. It enables owners, purchasers and third parties to know in advance how to protect their rights and what will happen to those rights if the land over which they exist should be sold, mortgaged or transferred. Clearly, this is a radical shift away from the old legal/equitable distinction and it represents the abandonment of the doctrine of notice in registered land. It also brings certainty and stability for persons who have rights in land that is owned by someone else. It is a process that began with the LRA 1925 and has been enhanced by the LRA 2002 and the intended introduction of electronic conveyancing will reduce even further the old legal/equitable distinction. It will still be important to know whether certain rights would have been legal or equitable (e.g. only legal estates can be registered as titles), but of more importance will be the status of a right as an entry on the electronic register or as an interest that overrides a registered proprietor.

2.5   The Operation of Registered Land: Titles

The registration of titles is the heart of registered land and this is what distinguishes it from unregistered land where title is found in the title deeds. Under section 58 of the LRA 2002,

---

61 With a corresponding shrinkage in the reach of overriding interests.

62 Of course, e-conveyancing depends on the register being as up to date as possible and the duty of disclosure is one method by which the register does become more mirror-like.

63 These were the notice, the caution, the inhibition and the restriction.

64 A restriction can be used for many more purposes than simply indirectly protecting an interest.

the registered proprietor 'shall be deemed' to have been vested with the legal estate (i.e. the freehold or qualifying leasehold) as it is noted on the register. This is irrespective of whether there has actually been any conveyance to him. Thus, a person registered as proprietor as the result of fraud or mistake has a valid title[65] and is able to rely on the provisions of the LRA 2002 as to the conclusiveness of his interest, albeit that they may be subject to a claim to have the register rectified against them.[66]

Indeed, the *raison d'être* of the registration system is that title to land depends on a person being registered as the estate owner and on no other proof of ownership and, as stated by the Law Commission, the full system of e-conveyancing envisaged by the LRA 2002 will signal a change from registration of title, to title by registration. It will be the act of registration itself that confers title and permits the registered proprietor to exercise all of the powers of an absolute owner, subject only to entries on the register.[67] As a counterpart, if the purchaser fails to apply for registration within the applicable time limit (currently two months from completion of the transaction[68]), the purchase becomes void as regards the transfer or creation of the legal estate. This means that, in the case of an outright transfer to the new owner, the legal title actually remains in the transferor until registration, who will hold on trust for the new owner,[69] and in the unlikely event of no proper registration of the estate taking place, the new 'owner' will have to rely on the other mechanisms of the LRA 2002 to protect his interest, such as relying on the category of overriding interests or interests protectable by registration.[70]

As indicated above, when a title is presented for first registration, HM Land Registry will investigate the 'root of title' and check the validity of the application to register. Obviously, this is vital given that registration has such a conclusive effect. There are, however, four possible grades of title with which a person may be registered and these reflect the fact that in some cases it may be difficult to establish a conclusive title due to the absence of relevant documents or other factual difficulties.

---

65 See *Argyle Building Society v. Hammond* (1984) applying the equivalent provision (section 69(1)) under the LRA 1925.

66 A suggestion to the contrary in respect of the 1925 Act was made in *Malory Enterprises Ltd v. Cheshire Homes and Chief Land Registrar* (2002), in which Arden LJ implied both that a registration following fraud is not conclusive as to the proprietor's title and, if title is innocently acquired from a fraudster, is not a 'disposition' within the 1925 Act. The case was settled before its scheduled appeal to the House of Lords but its ratio must be viewed with suspicion. Acceptance of the *Malory* approach would be to import principles of unregistered conveyancing into registered land and this would wholly contradict the system of registration of title and the move to e-conveyancing that the LRA 2002 is designed to facilitate. Note, however, *Derbyshire County Council v. Fallon* (2007), in which there are echoes of this unfortunate approach in reference to the LRA 2002.

67 Sections 23 and 26 of the LRA 2002.

68 And remembering that this will occur simultaneously with the purchase under e-conveyancing.

69 See *Pinkerry Ltd v. Needs (Kenneth) (Contractors) Ltd* (1992) and *Leeman v. Mohammed* (2001) illustrating the position under the equivalent provisions of the LRA 1925.

70 An example under the old law is provided by *Brown and Root Technology Ltd v. Sun Alliance and London Assurance Co Ltd* (1998), in which the transfer of a long lease was not registered by the new tenant and the Court of Appeal held that the assignee had not acquired legal title. This had the consequence that the assignee had no power to give notice to end the lease and that power remained with the assignor (the original tenant) who still held legal title.

2.5.1   Absolute title

Absolute title is the highest grade of title possible and amounts to full recognition of the rights of the proprietor. It is available for freeholds and leaseholds, although only rarely for the latter because the registrar is not usually in a position to validate the lessor's title to grant the lease (as required by section 10(2) of the LRA 2002) as well as that of the leaseholder who actually applies for registration.

Registration with absolute title to a freehold on a first registration has the effect ascribed by section 11 of the LRA 2002. This invests the proprietor with the full fee simple together with all of the benefits subsisting for the estate, but subject only to overriding interests within Schedule 1 of the Act, registered protected interests, rights of adverse possessors of which the first proprietor has notice and interests under trusts of which the proprietor has notice. These last two categories exist only to ensure that subsisting equitable ownership interests and the accrued claims of adverse possessors are not destroyed by the simple expedient of the landowner applying for first registration of title. After this event, 'notice' of these rights ceases to be important and a later transfer of the (now) registered title is governed by sections 28 and 29 of the LRA 2002.[71] A person first registered with absolute leasehold title is in the same position, save only that they are also bound by all express and implied covenants,[72] obligations and liabilities that are incidental to the leasehold estate (section 12(1) of the LRA 2002).

2.5.2   Good leasehold title

As noted above, it is not so common for a leasehold owner to be registered with absolute title on first registration simply because this requires the landlord's title to have been verified (section 10(2) of the LRA 2002). Thus, many proprietors of long leaseholds will be registered with good leasehold title. This invests the proprietor with the same quality of title as absolute title except that it is subject to any interests affecting the landlord's freehold or other superior title (section 12(6) of the LRA 2002). In other words, the proprietor with good leasehold title has a strong title, every bit as marketable as an absolute title, save only that the validity of the freehold (or superior leasehold) out of which it is carved is not admitted. Should that freehold or superior title become registered with absolute title or should the registrar become convinced of the quality of the freehold or superior title, the good leasehold owner may apply for upgrading to absolute title under section 62(2) of the LRA 2002.

2.5.3   Possessory title

If an owner cannot produce sufficient evidence of title (freehold or leasehold) on an application for first registration, he may be registered with possessory title. This is available where the applicant is in actual possession of the land and there is no other title with

---

71 Section 28 provides that the transferee who is not a purchaser is bound by *all* pre-existing property rights; section 29 provides that a purchaser is bound only by those entered on the register and those overriding within Schedule 3 to the Act.

72 Being promises to do, or not to do, certain things in relation to the land.

which he can be registered.[73] This is effectively the position of someone who relies on adverse possession as the basis of his title or a person who is unable to prove their title formally at first registration because of some disaster with the title deeds. The possessory title is, however, subject to *all* adverse interests that exist at the date of registration, not merely those that are overriding or registered protected interests – see section 11(7) of the LRA 2002 for freeholds and section 12(8) of the LRA 2002 for leaseholds. This appears, then, to be a rather unattractive title with which to be registered because the proprietor may find the land burdened by undisclosed interests, even perhaps a superior title. However, the registrar may upgrade the possessory title under section 62 of the LRA 2002 if satisfied as to the validity of the proprietor's title[74] or if an adverse possessor is able to establish title under the provisions of the LRA 2002.[75] Note also that a person registered with possessory title because of some mishap with the title deeds usually takes out title insurance whereby the title is privately guaranteed. This should suffice for a purchaser interested in buying the land from a person registered with possessory title.

2.5.4   Qualified title

Persons whose title is subject to fundamental defects that cannot be disregarded may be invested with a qualified title. However, qualified title is subject to the same interests as an absolute title *plus* any further interests that appear from the register to be excepted from the effects of registration (sections 11(6) and 12(7) of the LRA 2002).[76] It is, therefore, of limited comfort to an estate owner and only rarely does HM Land Registry agree to a request for such registration. It will do so where there is some prospect of the qualified title being converted into an absolute or good leasehold title under section 62 of the LRA 2002.

Of course, once a person is registered as proprietor with one of the grades of title noted above, any subsequent dealings with that land will then be subject to the provisions of sections 28, 29 and 30 of the LRA 2002 regarding the effect of registered dispositions – that is, transfer of land already registered. So, on a sale, mortgage or transfer of the now registered land, two issues arise: first, what is the position of the transferee (e.g. the new owner, purchaser or mortgagee); second, what is the position of a person with a 'third-party' interest in that land?

2.5.5   The new owner, purchaser or mortgagee under a registered disposition

According to sections 25, 26 and 27 of the LRA 2002, a transfer of a registered freehold or leasehold of a legal estate is not complete until the new owner is entered on the register as registered proprietor. For convenience, this is taken to be when an application to register title is made. However, the penalty for failure to register (an unlikely event due to the

---

73 Sections 9(5) on freeholds, and 10(6) on leaseholds.

74 For example, missing documents are found after registration.

75 On which, see Chapter 11.

76 This is a 'just in case' category that ensures that a qualified title is subject to those rights etc. that caused the registrar to have doubts about the title in the first place.

involvement of property professionals) is that the legal estate remains in the transferor and the new owner receives an equitable estate only, even if all of the other formalities necessary for a transfer of land have been observed.[77] This means that the new owner who fails to register his ownership is theoretically vulnerable to a subsequent sale of the land by the person from whom he took the transfer.[78] In practice, however, the transferee may well find their equitable interest protected as an interest that overrides under Schedule 3, paragraph 2 of the LRA 2002 if they are in discoverable actual occupation of the property. As we can see then, this is a good example of how the LRA 2002 has superseded traditional property law concepts because, under its system, the validity or otherwise of legal title depends crucially on the existence of registration, not on the method or manner in which that title was conveyed.

Once successfully registered, the registration is conclusive as to the title of the new owner under section 58 of the LRA 2002 and entitles him to exercise full powers to deal with the land under section 23 of the LRA 2002. Moreover, the LRA 2002 establishes exactly what types of proprietary interest affect the transferee when he becomes registered as owner. If the transferee is not a purchaser – perhaps he inherited the land under a will or received a gift – section 28 of the LRA 2002 provides that the new registered proprietor takes the land subject to all prior property rights, irrespective of whether those propriety rights were entered on the register or should have been entered on the register. This is known as the 'basic priority rule' and simply says that a transferee, who has not paid for the land, should take it as it comes. If, on the other hand, the transferee has given valuable consideration, section 29 provides that, when registered, he takes the land subject only to registered charges, overriding interests within Schedule 3 of the Act and protected registered interests. All other interests lose their priority. This is known as the 'special priority rule', and in fact it will apply in most cases because most transfers of land are for value. It means simply that a purchaser should be bound only by those property rights actually entered on the register – and therefore discoverable by inspection of the register – and unregistered interests that override that, in turn, are largely discoverable by a physical inspection of the land itself. Note, however, that whether a transfer is for value is a question of substance, not form. So in *Halifax v. Popeck* (2008), the transfer was found to be not for value (and so within section 28) even though it was portrayed by the parties and the conveyancing documents as a sale.

2.5.6   The third party with interests in the transferred land

It is inherent in what we have been considering so far that a major purpose of the land registration system is to ensure that land may be sold freely. Necessarily, this means that other peoples' rights over that land must be readily identifiable and their effect on the land must be known in advance in order to protect a prospective purchaser. As we have seen, when a registered title is transferred for value and a new proprietor is registered as owner,[79] that proprietor obtains the title subject only to unregistered interests

---

77 As illustrated by *Mascall v. Mascall* (1984) under the 1925 Act.

78 Of course, if the transfer were a sale, it would amount to a breach of contract.

79 This will include a mortgage, and registration of the mortgage. If there is no sale, the basic priority rule applies and all property rights are binding.

that override within Schedule 3 and interests entered on the register as charges (mortgages) or protected registered interests – sections 29 and 30 of the LRA 2002. All other property rights either lose their priority against the new registered proprietor or are subject to statutory overreaching. Importantly, the 'doctrine of notice' in its old, equitable sense plays no part in determining whether any third-party rights bind the purchaser and the matter is dealt with according to the statutory scheme established by the LRA 2002.[80]

2.6   The Operation of Registered Land: Unregistered Interests that Override

Much of the criticism of the operation of the system of registered land under the LRA 1925 was directed at the existence of 'overriding interests' as a category of right that bound the purchaser without a register entry. The basic principle was that a purchaser took the land subject to any existing overriding interests and these bound 'automatically' whether or not a purchaser knew about them. In fact, most of the interests that fell within the definition of overriding interests under the 1925 Act *should* have been obvious to a purchaser of land on inspection of the property, or were in the nature of public rights that did not seriously affect the registered proprietor's use of the land. Nevertheless, there were concerns about the potential for a purchaser to be bound by undiscoverable overriding interests[81] and also, of course, the very existence of the category distorted the 'mirror principle'. This in turn meant that there could not be an entirely 'register-only' system of e-conveyancing because not everything was on the register. Initially, the Law Commission considered abolishing the category of overriding interests altogether, but it soon became apparent that this was neither feasible nor desirable. Consequently, the LRA 2002 reforms the operation and scope of overriding interests in order to minimise their impact on land and, where they must be accepted, to ensure that as far as possible a potential transferee is aware of their existence before he completes the transfer.

2.6.1   Strategies of the LRA 2002

In seeking to minimise and clarify the impact of unregistered but binding rights, the 2002 Act employs a number of strategies. First, overriding interests operate in different ways depending on whether the occasion is a first registration of a title or a disposition of an existing registered title. At first registration, overriding interests are listed in Schedule 1 to the Act and take effect against the first registered proprietor whether or not that first registered proprietor gives value (sections 11 and 12 of the LRA 2002). This is because the act of first registration does not involve a transfer of land – the applicant *already* owns it – and so whether they gave value is immaterial. Likewise, the list of overriding interests in Schedule 1 is more extensive than that operating in respect of a disposition (Schedule 3)

---

80 The LRA 2002 does makes reference to the knowledge of the transferee when defining the scope of overriding interests within Schedule 3, but this is not meant to be a reincarnation of the doctrine of notice.

81 Not *undiscovered*.

precisely because the first registered proprietor should not be permitted to escape rights that bound him by applying for first registration. If it were otherwise, a person bound by a right could apply for first registration simply in order to escape an adverse right. However, the transfer of an already registered estate is the occasion for a new owner to be registered and this person may well have given value and *should* be given an opportunity to discover which rights might affect him. Consequently, the list of overriding interests in Schedule 3 is less extensive than those listed in Schedule 1.

Second, the number of potential overriding interests has been reduced in respect of both first registration and subsequent dispositions of a registered estate and there has been some redefinition of those that do remain in order to reduce their impact.[82] Indeed, while we cannot say that the list of overriding interests has been *drastically* reduced when compared with those existing under the 1925 Act, it is certain that now there will be fewer occasions on which a claimant can establish an overriding interest, particularly in relation to dispositions of land already registered.[83]

Third, an applicant for registration – either for first registration or after a disposition of a registered estate – is required by section 71 of the LRA 2002 to disclose those overriding interests of which he is aware so that they may be brought on to the register.[84] These interests will already bind the applicant – being overriding – and so their entry on the register simply confirms a priority that the right already enjoys. Obviously, the purpose here is to encourage the disclosure and registration of as many overriding interests as possible so that the register can become a truer mirror of the land. If so registered, the interest necessarily ceases to be overriding and cannot recover that status if it is subsequently removed from the register.[85] Importantly, however, failure to disclose the existence of an overriding interest does not destroy the overriding status of the right.[86]

2.6.2 Unregistered interests that override a first registration under Schedule 1 of the LRA 2002

The unregistered interests listed in Schedule 1 to the Act will override the estate of a first registered proprietor – section 11 of the LRA 2002 (freeholds) and section 12 of the LRA 2002 (leaseholds). If these interests subsequently become registered, they cease to be overriding, but of course would bind because they would then be on the register. The categories of right listed in Schedule 1 are similar to those found in Schedule 3, save only that those found in Schedule 1 are generally of wider scope.

---

82 This is particularly marked in relation to Schedule 3. There is some redefinition in Schedule 1, but it is not as far reaching.

83 Because Schedule 3 is even narrower than Schedule 1.

84 There is a special form – Form DI – that accompanies an application to register a title either on first registration or after a transfer.

85 Section 29(3) of the LRA 2002.

86 It is, after all, the applicant's land that is burdened and it would be strange if, by non-disclosure, he could destroy the priority of somebody else's right!

2.6.2.1   *Short-term leases – paragraph 1, Schedule 1: Legal leases for seven years or less*

With only limited special exceptions, legal leases originally granted for seven years or less will override a first registration.[87] Importantly, however, all leases that qualified as overriding interests under the old section 70(1)(k) of the LRA 1925 *before* the entry into force of the LRA 2002 will continue to override and no additional action needs to be taken to protect them while the current tenant remains the estate owner.[88] In other words, the new provision operates in respect of leases granted on or after 13 October 2003. Thus, while a tenant under a seven-year lease (or less) may choose to register his lease against the burdened land by means of a notice, the lease will be fully protected as an overriding interest without such registration.

The three exceptions to the overriding status of 'short leases' are of a special kind and as such are required to be registered as titles in their own right, irrespective of the length of the lease.[89] They are the grant of a lease out of unregistered land in pursuance of Part 5 of the Housing Act 1985 under the right to buy provisions,[90] the grant of a lease out of unregistered land of a dwelling house to a private-sector landlord where the tenant's right to buy is preserved[91] and the grant of a lease out of unregistered land that is to take effect in possession more than three months from the date of the grant.[92] The first two are special statutory creations and no more need be said of them. The third illustrates well the policy of the 2002 Act. A tenant under a short-term lease (i.e. seven years or less) is likely to be in possession and so his lease will be easily discoverable by an intending purchaser of the land and hence perfectly acceptable as an overriding interest – the purchaser will know of the lease. However, a lease where possession is 'delayed' may not be discoverable and hence is not suitable for inclusion as an overriding interest. It should be registered with its own title.

These provisions on short leases and their overriding effect implement one of the main goals of the 2002 Act – the creation of a land register that is more comprehensive than its predecessor wherein any potential transferee can rely on the register of title as much as possible to reveal adverse interests.[93] Moreover, it is clear that the legislation contemplates a further reduction in the threshold for leases registrable with their own titles (to leases over

---

87 Legal leases *over* seven years are registrable titles. A lease granted originally for more than seven years that is transferred with less than seven years left is *not* an overriding interest and the transfer must be registered.

88 Schedule 12, paragraph 12 of the LRA 2002. These are legal leases of 21 years or less under the previous version of this provision.

89 Section 4 of the LRA 2002.

90 Schedule 1, paragraph 1, referring to section 4(1)(e) of the 2002 Act.

91 Schedule 1, paragraph 1, referring to section 4(1)(f) of the 2002 Act and a lease within the ambit of section 171A of the Housing Act 1985.

92 Schedule 1, paragraph 1, referring to section 4(1)(d) of the 2002 Act. Clearly, leases taking effect in possession *three months or less* from the date of the grant, if they also be of seven years or less, will be overriding interests.

93 Consequently, although it is not possible to apply for voluntary title registration of a lease granted for seven years or less, unless the lease is discontinuous (section 3(4) of the LRA 2002), it is possible to enter a notice of such lease on the register of the superior title if the superior title is registered, at least if the lease was granted for over three years originally (section 33(b)(i) of the LRA 2002) and has more than one year left to run (Rule 57(2) of the LRR 2003).

three years), with a corresponding reduction in the length of leases that would qualify as overriding interests. Finally, we need to be clear that this category of overriding interest is concerned with legal leases that are *granted*. It should not be forgotten that equitable leases – whether they be the result of an enforceable contract to grant a lease or the result of a failure to register the title to a registrable lease – do not fall within this paragraph but nevertheless might take effect as an overriding interest because the tenant is in actual occupation of the land at the relevant time.[94]

2.6.2.2   *The interests of persons in actual occupation – paragraph 2, Schedule 1*

This is perhaps the most important of the overriding interests listed in schedule 1. It echoes a concept found in the old law in section 70(1)(g) of the LRA 1925, but the provision is not identical and so we cannot be certain that the old case law on the meaning of 'actual occupation' will necessarily carry through to the new Act. In particular, three points should be noted: first, there is no protection for the interests of persons in receipt of rent and profits of the land *per se* (i.e. if they are out of actual occupation) as there was under the old law; second, the enforceability of the interest protected is now to be limited to the land actually occupied by the interest-holder;[95] and third, there is no qualification relating to disclosure of the interest, as there is in relation to Schedule 3 and as there was under the old law.

Under the new Act, paragraph 2, Schedule 1 defines this overriding interest as an 'interest belonging to a person in actual occupation, so far as relating to land of which he is in actual occupation, except for an interest under a settlement under the Settled Land Act 1925'. In general terms, this means that a person claiming an overriding interest under this paragraph must prove that he holds a property interest in the land that is about to be first registered and that he is in actual occupation of that land at the relevant time. Moreover, although occasionally the interests falling within this paragraph are mistakenly called 'occupiers rights', it is clear that any proprietary interest (unless specifically excluded) may gain overriding status through this provision provided that the interest-holder is in actual occupation of the burdened land.[96] In order to understand how the paragraph works, we can break it down into smaller components.

First, the interest to be protected must be enforceable against the land immediately before first registration of title: that is, the interest must subsist in reference to land at the time of first registration. Consequently, if for whatever reason the applicant for first registration can establish that the claimed right was not enforceable against him immediately prior to his application for first registration, then the interest cannot be revived by the

---

94 The equitable lease must exist at the moment of first registration for this to be a possibility and most equitable leases should have been protected as a Class C (iv) land charge under the Land Charges Act 1972 to survive a transfer of the unregistered title to a purchaser. If they were not so registered, they would not exist at first registration.

95 Thus reversing *Ferrishurst v. Wallcite* (1999).

96 Often occupation will follow from the right itself, as with beneficial interests under trusts of land, but it need not. For example, an option to purchase given to a licensee of the land and who is in actual occupation would be overriding under this provision. Note, however, that it is the option that overrides; a licence *per se* cannot override under this section for it is not proprietary.

provisions of the 2002 Act. Actual occupation cannot protect that which does not exist. This is particularly important as it reminds us that if a third-party interest did not survive a pre-registration transfer or grant of title under the rules of unregistered conveyancing, then that interest has ceased to exist by the time of first registration and so cannot be revived as an overriding interest.[97]

Second, given that first registration involves no transfer of title – the applicant already owns the land – there is no 'registration gap' between a transfer and its registration and the owner of the unregistered interest that is alleged to override the first registration must be in actual occupation at the time the application to register is received at HM Land Registry.[98]

Third, any proprietary right, provided that it is not specifically excluded, may qualify for overriding status by virtue of the interest-holder being in actual occupation of the affected portion of the burdened land. In many cases, the interest alleged to be overriding will also be the reason the occupier is entitled to be present on the burdened land (e.g. an equitable lease or a beneficiary's interest under a trust of land[99]), but there is no necessary reason why this should be so and there are a number of examples in which it was not.[100] In this regard, although there is no compelling definition of what amounts to a property right, most instances will involve the familiar categories of leases and equitable shares of ownership, options and the like. Personal rights, such as contractual licences and bare licences, do not qualify, although rights of pre-emption (if created on or after 13 October 2003), proprietary estoppels and mere equities are now confirmed as proprietary rights and so are capable of taking effect as overriding interests.[101] Many other examples exist of rights that qualified under the previous law and there is nothing in the 2002 Act to suggest that in this respect the law has changed. Thus, in addition to the familiar categories, the right to seek equitable rectification of a document,[102] the right to seek alteration (formerly 'rectification') of the register[103] and the right to have a transaction set aside for undue influence[104] all qualify if supported by the necessary actual occupation.[105]

Fourth, in general terms, the meaning of 'actual occupation' under the 2002 Act is no different from that of its predecessor in section 70(1)(g) of the LRA 1925. It remains true that it is the fact of actual occupation that elevates the property interest into an overriding

---

97 For example, an option to purchase should have been registered as a land charge in unregistered land. If the land is sold and the option was not registered, it ceased to bind the applicant for first registration *before* he applied for that registration and so it cannot override.

98 See Rule 15, LRR 2003.

99 *Williams and Glyn's Bank v. Boland* (1981), now confirmed by section 3 of the Trusts of Land and Appointment of Trustees Act (TOLATA) 1996.

100 For example, *London & Cheshire Insurance Co Ltd v. Laplagrene Property Ltd* (1971) in reference to a vendor's lien where the occupation was due to a leaseback.

101 Sections 115 and 116 of the LRA 2002.

102 *Blacklocks v. J.B. Developments (Godalming) Ltd* (1982).

103 *Malory Enterprises Ltd v. Cheshire Homes (UK)* (2002).

104 *Thompson v. Foy* (2009), in respect of Schedule 3 to the 2002 Act, but the issue is the same.

105 Other examples include a right to rectify a lease (*Nurdin and Peacock v. Ramsden* (1998)), an 'estate contract', being a contract to purchase a legal estate (*Webb v. Pollmount* (1966)) and an 'unpaid vendor's lien', being the seller of land's right to charge any unpaid purchase price against the land itself (*Nationwide Building Society v. Ahmed* (1995)).

interest and any notions of the old equitable doctrine of notice have no part to play in determining whether such occupation exists.[106] However, Schedule 1, paragraph 1, does restrict the ambit of claims of 'actual occupation' so that the interest will override only in so far as it relates to the land actually occupied by the claimant. In other words, the legal reach of the adverse interest is limited to the factual reach of the occupation or, to use the words of Schedule 1, the interest overrides only 'so far as relating to the land of which he is in actual occupation'. This is an explicit reversal of the Court of Appeal's decision in *Ferrishurst Ltd v. Wallcite Ltd* (1999), in which Ferrishurst had been in occupation of part of the land as an underleasee but held an option to purchase the entire land comprised in the superior leasehold estate and, by virtue of that actual occupation, the right to purchase the entire land was held to override. Under Schedule 1, Ferrishurst's overriding interest would be limited to that part of the land that it did actually occupy.[107] With this qualification in mind, it remains true that 'actual occupation' is a question of fact to be determined by reference to the circumstances of each case. In many (probably most) instances, it will be a rather straightforward analysis of the facts. According to Lord Wilberforce in *Williams & Glyn's Bank v. Boland* (1981),[108] interpreting the previous provision in section 70(1)(g) of the LRA 1925, these words, 'are ordinary words of plain English and should, in my opinion, be interpreted as such . . . Given occupation, that is presence on the land, I do not think that the word "actual" was intended to introduce any additional qualification, certainly not to suggest that possession must be "adverse": it merely emphasises that what is required is physical presence not entitlement in law'.

The meaning of actual occupation under the 2002 Act was considered at some length in *Thompson v. Foy* (2009), with the analysis followed by the Court of Appeal in *Link Lending Ltd v. Bustard* (2010). Although both of these cases concerned Schedule 3 to the 2002 Act, which does have an additional requirement of 'discoverability', there is no reason to think that the meaning of 'actual occupation' itself is any different under the schedules. Indeed, it would be strange if were given the shared origin of the provisions. In *Thompson v. Foy*, Lewison J summed up the position in the following way:

(i) The words 'actual occupation' are ordinary words of plain English and should be interpreted as such. The word 'actual' emphasises that physical presence is required: *Williams & Glyn's Bank v. Boland* (1981).[109]

(ii) It does not necessarily involve the personal presence of the person claiming to occupy. A caretaker or the representative of a company can occupy on behalf of his employer: *Abbey National BS v. Cann* (1991).[110] Likewise, in *Bustard*, the claimant was in actual occupation despite being involuntarily detained in a psychiatric unit. However, we should note that this does cut both ways. So, in *Lloyd v. Dugdale* (2001), Dugdale was unable to claim an overriding interest by virtue of actual occupation because even though he personally held a proprietary right in the land (in fact an

---

106 Note, however, a different position in relation to interests that override registered dispositions under Schedule 3 of the 2002 Act.

107 The same restriction, plus others, applies in relation to unregistered interests that override a registered disposition under Schedule 3 to the Act.

108 At pp. 504, 505.

109 Per Lord Wilberforce.

110 Per Lord Oliver.

estoppel lease), and even though he was physically present, his presence was deemed to be that of an agent for his company and so he did not have an overriding interest. Similarly, in *Hypo-Mortgage Services Ltd* v. *Robinson* (1997),[111] it was held that children living with their parents – the estate owners – could not be said to be in actual occupation in their own right because their presence was wholly explained by that of their parents. Although this was an attractive solution on the facts of that case, and one that may well be followed, the decision must be approached with some care. It has long been accepted that wives do not occupy premises as a mere shadow of their husbands,[112] and while the *reason* for the occupation of children must be that they are with their parents, that does not explain why, factually, they too cannot be regarded as being in actual occupation. The issue is not, after all, by what right are they *entitled* to be in actual occupation, but whether they *are* in actual occupation on their own behalf, rather than as agent for another.

(iii)   However, actual occupation by a licensee (who is not a representative occupier) does not count as actual occupation by the licensor: *Strand Securities Ltd* v. *Caswell* (1965).[113] Of course, however, a licensee can be in actual occupation on his own behalf, but would not gain an overriding interest unless he held a proprietary right in the land, such as option to purchase.

(iv)   The mere presence of some of the claimant's furniture will not usually count as actual occupation: *Strand Securities Ltd* v. *Caswell*.[114] Note, however, Lewison J's reference to 'mere' presence and 'usually', because it is clear that the presence of furniture and the like can amount to actual occupation: especially if it reveals a sufficient degree of continuity and permanence of occupation: *Bustard* (2010). In addition, it seems clear that the nature and extent of the physical presence required to constitute actual occupation can vary according to the type of property under consideration. In *Malory* v. *Cheshire Homes* (2002), the land was derelict and unusable, but the claimant established 'actual occupation' through acts of minimal use, particularly the erection of a fence around the plot to keep out intruders.

(v)   If the person said to be in actual occupation at any particular time is not physically present on the land at that time, it will usually be necessary to show that his occupation was manifested and accompanied by a continuing intention to occupy. What this seems to mean is that what is required is a physical presence on the land, not of a temporary or transient nature, but the absence of the claimant from the property for a period or periods of time does not of itself take the claimant out of occupation, nor does it imply abandonment of occupation once achieved. A person does not cease to be in actual occupation because they are away on business or on holiday or indeed in semi-permanent hospital care. It seems, however, that if someone is absent, they must have a continuing intention to return and this was one reason why, in *Thompson* v. *Foy*, the claimant would not have been in actual occupation. While one can see the attractiveness of this view (especially for a purchaser or mortgagee), it is not clear that previous case law supported it – see for example the discussion of actual

---

111   [1997] 2 FLR 71.

112   *Williams & Glyn's Bank v. Boland* [1981] AC 487.

113   Per Lord Denning MR.

114   Per Russell LJ.

occupation in the Court of Appeal in *Lloyds Bank* v. *Rosset* (1991). We should also remember that the rationale of the land registration system is to ensure that questions concerning the state of mind of both purchasers and those claiming adverse interests is meant to be largely irrelevant. It is a functional system, based on facts, rather than a system based around the intentions of the parties. Likewise, how is a purchaser to know whether the person in actual occupation intends to return? The issues concerning actual occupation were *obiter* in *Foy*,[115] but they were material in *Link Lending Ltd* v. *Bustard* (2010), in which the claimant was absent from the land (her home) for lengthy periods while she was being looked after in a psychiatric unit. However, the land was effectively her permanent home, with all of her belongings and furniture there, and she visited from time to time and continued to pay the bills. She had a clear intention to return and thus was found to be in actual occupation, the Court of Appeal emphasising the degree of continuity and permanence of her occupation.

(vi) Finally, we might add to the analysis in *Foy* that, for the purposes of Schedule 1, where the test of 'actual occupation' is not further qualified,[116] and assuming we can rely on cases decided under the old law, it seems that the occupation need not be apparent in order to generate an overriding interest against an applicant for first registration. By way of contrast, however, it seems reasonably clear that mere enjoyment of a limited proprietary interest over the burdened land cannot amount to actual occupation. So, for example, the exercise of a right of way or other easement over the servient land does not amount to actual occupation of the servient tenement so as to make the easement an overriding interest.[117] It is also clear that more than one person may be in actual occupation for the purpose of establishing an overriding interest. This is seen most commonly in trust of land cases in which both the trustee (the legal owner) and the claimant (the equitable owner) are in actual occupation. In this sense, 'occupation' is not to be equated with 'exclusive possession'.

Fifth, there are a number of interests that cannot override under this provision. We have seen already that the overriding status of the rights of persons in receipt of the rents and profits of the land has been removed by the LRA 2002, but also excluded are interests under a settlement governed by the Settled Land Act 1925,[118] the right of a tenant arising from the service of a notice seeking enfranchisement or the grant of a new or extended lease,[119] a spouse's statutory right of occupation of the matrimonial home,[120] the rights

---

115   The judge held that the claimant had no relevant property interest.

116   Compare Schedule 3, paragraph 2, and the question of 'actual occupation' in respect of registered dispositions.

117   But see *K Sultana Saeed* v. *Plustrade* (2001), in which the Court of Appeal appeared to accept that the right to park under an easement amounted to actual occupation of the burdened land. It is respectfully submitted that this is in error.

118   The appropriate form of protection is a restriction controlling dealings. A notice may not be used (section 33(a)(ii) of the LRA 2002).

119   Leasehold Reform Act 1967, section 5(5) as amended by paragraph 8, Schedule 11 of the LRA 2002; Leasehold Reform, Housing and Urban Development Act 1993, section 97(1) as amended by paragraph 30, Schedule 11 of the LRA 2002. A notice may be used to protect the right and a restriction to alert the interest-holder to any proposed dealing with the land.

120   Family Law Act 1996, section 31(10)(b) as amended by paragraph 34(2), Schedule 11 of the LRA 2002. A notice may be used.

conferred on a person by or under an access order made under the Access to Neighbouring Land Act 1992,[121] a right arising from a request for an overriding lease under the Landlord and Tenant (Covenants) Act 1995,[122] and a pending land action, a writ or order affecting land issued or made by a court.[123] These are, of course, particular rights of a unique character and they cannot override because their protection is provided for in the special statutory regimes that created them.

2.6.2.3   *Legal easements and* profits à prendre *– paragraph 3, Schedule 1*

This category of overriding interest replaces the difficult section 70(1)(a) of the LRA 1925 and is simplicity itself.[124] Thus 'a legal easement or *profit à prendre*' may override. Indeed, prior to first registration, these rights would have bound the estate as 'legal rights binding the whole world' and so the fact that they override at first registration merely continues a priority they already enjoyed. Importantly, however, and representing a change in the law, equitable easements will *not* override a first registration of title, once again because of the interplay between first registration and the rules of unregistered conveyancing. Quite simply, prior to first registration, an equitable easement should have been registered as a land charge under the Land Charges Act 1972.[125] On sale of the unregistered title, if registered as a land charge, it would have been valid and been apparent to HM Land Registry and would have been entered as a notice against the new registered title at first registration. If not registered as a land charge, it would have been void and so should not be revived at first registration through the mechanism of overriding interests.[126]

The overriding status of all legal easements and profits at first registration is not controversial. Indeed, in many instances, these legal interests will in fact be entered against the title at first registration and will then cease to be overriding. The burden will be noted against the servient title and an entry will be made on the title of the dominant land indicating that the right is a benefit to be enjoyed with the estate. This is because, at first registration, the registrar will examine the title documents in the normal way and will make appropriate entries in the register. Similarly, any other legal easement or profit not apparent from the documents of title may be disclosed at the time of application for first registration and so be protected by way of notice.[127] Finally, it is important to compare the protection of legal easements and profits at first registration with the provisions applicable to registered dealings in which it will be seen that the situation is more complex.

---

121 Access to Neighbouring Land Act 1992, section 5(5) as amended by paragraph 26(4), Schedule 11 of the LRA 2002. A notice may be used: paragraph 26(3), Schedule 11 of the LRA 2002.

122 Landlord and Tenant (Covenants) Act 1995, section 20(6) as amended by paragraph 33(4), Schedule 11 of the LRA 2002. A notice may be used.

123 Section 87(3) of the LRA 2002.

124 In relation to registered dispositions, Schedule 3, paragraph 3 (the equivalent provision) is narrower in scope.

125 Except equitable estoppel easements who thus would appear to lose priority under this provision.

126 Note, however, that anything that overrode under the old law prior to the entry into force of the LRA 2002 will continue to do so. This could well include equitable easements (*Celsteel v. Alton* (1985)) the overriding status of which existed before the entry into force of the LRA 2002.

127 Using Form DI.

2.6.2.4   *Other permanent overriding interests – paragraphs 4–9, Schedule 1*

The above three categories represent by far the most important overriding interests, with the 'actual occupation' provisions being the widest in scope simply because it is possible that *any* proprietary right can attain overriding status if coupled with actual occupation. Nevertheless, there are other examples of overriding interest listed in the schedule.

'Customary rights' are expressly preserved in paragraph 4, Schedule 1, and encompasses rights that are enjoyed by all or some inhabitants of a particular area. 'Public rights' also remain a category of overriding interest under the new Act in paragraph 5, Schedule 1, and means these rights are exercisable by anyone, including non-landowners, simply by reason of the general law, such as public rights of way and rights of passage in navigable waters.[128] This grouping also includes 'local land charges' as specified in paragraph 6, Schedule 1. These are not to be confused with land charges under the Land Charges Act 1972 but are instead rights within the Local Land Charges Act 1975 and relate to such matters as planning, highways and other local authority matters. So rights in relation to mines and minerals may also override under paragraphs 7, 8 and 9 of Schedule 1 in similar fashion to the old section 70(1)(l) and (m) of the 1925 Act. They include rights to coal and older mineral rights. Finally in this brief survey we should note the overriding statues of public–private partnership leases (PPP leases). These are contracts involving the provision, construction, renewal or improvement of a railway or a proposed railway where one of the parties is London Regional Transport, Transport for London or a subsidiary of either.[129] A PPP lease is not found explicitly in Schedule 1 to the LRA 2002, but it is made an overriding interest against first registration by reason of section 90(5) of the Act. This status is driven wholly by the special nature of these leases and is an exception to the general policy of the Act that as few interests as possible should be excepted from substantive registration.

2.6.2.5   *Miscellaneous, time-limited, overriding interests*

Paragraphs 10–14 and paragraph 16 of Schedule 1[130] contain a miscellany of rights and interests that may also override a first registration of title. Although as a group they share some common attributes, what unites them now is that, by virtue of section 117 of the Act, the interests listed in these paragraphs will override a first registration of title *only for ten years* from the entry into force of the schedule. In other words, the interests will override a first registration for ten years from 13 October 2003 and thereafter, if they are to maintain their priority, they must be protected either by a caution against first registration in respect of land of unregistered title or by means of a notice against a registered title, for which no fee will be charged if registration is sought before the end of the ten-year period.[131] This unusual provision is justified by reference to the individual character of the rights concerned, their relative rarity and the encouragement to protection by registration through the absence of any fee in the ten-year period. As might be imagined, this is part of the goal

---

128 See *Overseas Investment Services Ltd v. Simcobuild Construction Ltd* (1995).

129 See generally section 210 of the Greater London Authority Act 1999 and the other conditions specified therein.

130 Paragraph 16 has been added by the LRA 2002 (Transitional Provisions) (No. 2) Order 2003. Paragraph 15 is inserted under the transitional provisions, Schedule 12, paragraph 7.

131 Section 117(2).

of reducing as far as possible the categories of unregistered interests that override. The provision has particular importance in relation to a first registration because, prior to the application for first registration, these interests will bind the estate as legal interests but, assuming ten years have elapsed, the applicant for first registration will find the estate free of the rights merely by virtue of his own application for first registration.[132] In such circumstances, the interest-holder will have to apply for rectification of the register in order to correct a mistake,[133] although such a claim may be denied if the first registered proprietor is in possession and objects within paragraphs 3(2) or 6(2) of Schedule 4 to the Act. Without such rectification, the interest-holder will continue to be denied their right against the first registered proprietor and any subsequent transferee under a registered disposition.

Examples of rights within this category include franchises, manorial rights, Crown rents, certain rights in respect of embankments and sea or river walls, tithes and liability to repair the chancel of a church.[134] This last was added to the list of time-limited overriding interests following the House of Lords decision in PCC of Aston Cantlow v. Wallbank (2003) that the enforcement of such liabilities did not infringe the European Convention on Human Rights.

2.6.2.6   *Transitional and special provisions concerning the rights of adverse possessors*

Schedule 1 of the 2002 Act contains no specific saving for the rights of adverse possessors to override at first registration. There is no equivalent to the old section 70(1)(f) of the LRA 1925. However, three provisions of the 2002 Act will have an impact on the rights of adverse possessors. First, for a transitional period of three years from 13 October 2003 (now of course expired), title already acquired under the Limitation Act 1980 before the coming into force of Schedule 1 had overriding status against a first registration.[135] In effect, this meant that an adverse possessor who had completed the 12-year period of limitation under the old law of adverse possession enjoyed protection for that right as an overriding interest for three years from the entry into force of the 2002 Act.[136] Second, the interest of the adverse possessor will have priority as an overriding interest if supported by the adverse possessor's actual occupation of the land at the time of first registration, irrespective of when that registration takes place. This is likely to be the case in most situations. Third, the interest will have priority if the first registered proprietor has notice

---

132 Assuming that the applicant has not in some way estopped himself from denying it. This is an exception to the general principle that first registration does not alter priorities of interests affecting the land.

133 Schedule 4, paragraphs 2(1)(a) and 5(a) of the LRA 2002.

134 Added to Schedule 1 by the LRA 2002 (Transitional Provisions) (No. 2) Order 2003.

135 Paragraph 7 of Schedule 12 of the LRA 2002, inserting a new paragraph 15 into Schedule 1.

136 An adverse possessor who has completed 12 years' adverse possession prior to the entry into force of the 2002 Act, and for whom in consequence the land would have been held on trust under section 75(1) of the LRA 1925 before the 2002 Act entered into force, 'is entitled to be registered as the proprietor of the estate' (paragraph 18 of Schedule 12 of the LRA 2002). Consequently, an adverse possessor who has completed the period of limitation should have applied within the three years' grace afforded by the transitional provision. Failure to do so now means that, on first registration, interest could be lost if the adverse possessor is not in actual occupation or the applicant for first registration does not have notice of the possessor.

of the rights of the adverse possessor at the time of first registration, irrespective of when that registration takes place.[137] In other words, only rarely and in very unusual circumstances will an adverse possessor be denied priority for their possessory title against a first registered proprietor by reason of the exclusion of a dedicated category from the 2002 Act's list of overriding interests. Note, however, that should this first registered proprietor sell the land, the purchaser under a registered disposition may well escape the claims of the adverse possessor if the squatter is not in discoverable actual occupation under Schedule 3, paragraph 2 of the LRA 2002.

2.6.2.7   *Interests removed from the category of interests that override a first registration of title: A summary*

Clearly, Schedule 1 to the Act seeks to rationalise the types of interest that can override a first registration. There are some changes in definition, but also some exclusions when compared with the previous law. First, the rights of adverse possessors *per se* no longer qualify, but protection is available if the adverse possessor is in actual occupation, or if the first registered proprietor has notice of the claim – as discussed immediately above. Second, a person in receipt of rent and profits may not claim overriding status for their interest, although once again such landlords have other means of protection. Third, equitable easements will not override a first registration, although often this will simply reflect the priority already gained by the applicant for first registration. Fourth, in respect of possessory, qualified or good leasehold title, those matters 'excepted from the effects of registration' under the old section 70(1)(h) of the 1925 Act no longer override at first registration, which should be no surprise given that the land is unregistered immediately prior to the first registration.

2.6.3   Unregistered interests that override a registered disposition under Schedule 3 of the LRA 2002

As noted above, the range of unregistered interests that override a registered disposition of the land[138] are more restricted than those that may override a first registration. Even though they are broadly similar in scope, and many of the considerations discussed above in relation to Schedule 1 are relevant here also, it remains true that Schedule 3 is narrower than Schedule 1. The principal reason for this difference is that Schedule 3 operates, by definition, when there is a transfer of land to a new owner and a primary aim of the LRA 2002 is to ensure that a transferee of a registered title is fully aware of as many adverse interests as possible before he takes the transfer. In consequence, the Act seeks to ensure that as much information as possible is entered on the register of title of the burdened land and thereby to limit overriding interests to those that could be discovered by a reasonably diligent transferee making an inspection of the land before the transfer. The aim is to eliminate the 'undiscoverable' overriding interest. We might also remind ourselves that, by virtue of section 28 of the LRA, a transferee not for value takes the land subject to all prior

---

137 Sections 11(4)(c) and 12(4)(d) of the LRA 2002.

138 That is, a transfer of the legal title, including sale, mortgage and the grant of leases, including leases for seven years or less even though they do not generally require registration (sections 27 and 29(4) of the LRA 2002).

proprietary rights[139] but, under sections 29 and 30, a transferee for value of an estate or a mortgage takes the land subject only to interests on the register and overriding interests within Schedule 3. Consequently, the scope of overriding interests under Schedule 3 matters when – as is normal – the transferee is a purchaser or mortgagee.

2.6.3.1   Short-term leases – paragraph 1, Schedule 3: Legal leases for seven years or less

This provision is almost identical with the provision found in Schedule 1. Thus, with only minor exceptions, a legal lease originally granted for seven years or less will override a registered disposition.[140] It will bind the transferee automatically.[141] Legal leases for a duration longer than this are registrable as individual titles. Likewise, equitable leases of any duration are excluded from this category of overriding interests and they must be protected by the entry of a notice on the register or take effect as an overriding interest through the discoverable actual occupation of the tenant. It is also the case, as with Schedule 1, that certain specialist leases of any duration cannot qualify as overriding interests under paragraph 1 of Schedule 3 and must be registered as individual titles whatever their duration. These are: the grants of a lease out of a registered estate in pursuance of Part 5 of the Housing Act 1985 under the right to buy provisions;[142] the grant of a lease out of a registered estate of a dwelling house to a private-sector landlord where the tenant's right to buy is preserved;[143] the grant of a lease of any length out of registered land that is to take effect in possession more than three months from the date of the grant; the grant of a lease where possession is discontinuous;[144] and finally, the grant of a lease out of registered land of a franchise or manor.[145] We might also note that the time will come when the trigger for leasehold title registration will fall below the current seven-year threshold and this will cause a similar reduction in the length of leases that may qualify as overriding interests under this provision.[146]

---

139   For example, *Halifax v. Popeck* (2008) in which the transferee was held not to have given value even though the transaction appeared to be a sale.

140   As previously, a lease that qualified as an overriding interest immediately before the entry into force of the 2002 Act under the old section 70(1)(k) of the LRA 1925 – being a legal lease granted for 21 years or less – continues to override while the original tenant remains in possession. The 2002 Act is not retrospective.

141   Section 29 of the LRA 2002.

142   Schedule 3, paragraph 1(a) referring to section 4(1)(e) of the 2002 Act.

143   Schedule 3, paragraph 1(a) referring to section 4(1)(f) of the 2002 Act and a lease within the ambit of section 171A of the Housing Act 1985.

144   Schedule 3, paragraph 1(b) of the 2002 Act referring to section 27(2)(b)(iii). These are typically 'timeshare' leases where the estate owner is given the right to possess for a fixed period of time but only one week each year.

145   Schedule 3, paragraph 1(b) of the 2002 Act referring to section 27(2)(c). These are ancient estates of a specialist kind.

146   Section 118 of the LRA 2002.

2.6.3.2   *The interests of persons in actual occupation, as restricted by Schedule 3, paragraph 2 of the 2002 Act*

As with its counterpart in Schedule 1, this is probably the most important category of interest that can override under Schedule 3. However, two important general points must be noted at the outset. First, the actual occupation provisions of Schedule 3, paragraph 2, do not mirror the sister provision in Schedule 1 and depart even more from the old section 70(1)(g) of the LRA 1925. In other words, Schedule 3 restricts, even more than Schedule 1, the circumstances in which a person may claim an overriding interest by virtue of their actual occupation. The reason is to ensure, as far as is possible, that a transferee for valuable consideration is not bound by an undiscoverable interest. Thus, while it may be true that the existing case law will be relevant in interpreting some of the provisions concerning actual occupation, there is no doubt that the 2002 Act will follow its own path. In particular, under Schedule 3, we should be aware that: there is no protection for the interests of persons in receipt of rent and profits *per se* (i.e. if they are out of actual occupation), subject to transitional arrangements; the enforceability of the interest protected is now limited to the land actually occupied by the interest-holder; the provision in respect of inquiry and disclosure has been reshaped; the actual occupation must be discoverable or the interest must be within the actual knowledge of the transferee in order to qualify as an overriding interest; and there is no protection for tenants in occupation under a three-month reversionary lease.[147] The second general point is that actual occupation is likely to be most influential in elevating property interests into overriding interests against a registered disposition when those interests have arisen *informally*. This is not only because the 2002 Act expressly recognises the proprietary status of three types of interest the status of which was previously uncertain,[148] but also because the future operation of e-conveyancing will ensure that most *expressly* created property rights will be electronically registered against the title. In consequence, when e-conveyancing becomes mandatory, the role of actual occupation really will be to rescue the interest-holder who has had no real chance to protect their interest by making an entry in the register. These will be informally created property interests and in respect of them the Act's policy is that a purchaser should not find his title compromised by an overriding interest arising by virtue of actual occupation unless the 'actual occupation' was discoverable before he purchased the land.

2.6.3.2.1   *General considerations*

The general principle under paragraph 2, Schedule 3 is that a person claiming an overriding interest must establish both that he holds a property interest in the burdened land and be in actual occupation of the land to which the interest extends within the meaning of the schedule. The potential difficulty arising because of the time lag between the execution of a registrable disposition and its later registration (the 'registration gap') has been resolved judicially by *Abbey National Building Society v. Cann* (1991). Consequently, actual occupation at

---

147   This exclusion is in addition to those types of interest that are specifically excluded from overriding status, either by Schedule 3 itself or under other legislation.

148   Sections 115 and 116 of the Act in relation to rights of pre-emption, mere equities and proprietary estoppels.

the date of *execution* of the transfer is critical.[149] Note here that *Thompson* v. *Foy* suggests that actual occupation must also exist when the disposition is registered, not only when the transaction is executed – i.e. at both moments. The judge based this on a forensic reading of the LRA 2002, but such a requirement seems to make no sense, in that a purchaser will inspect prior to execution of the transfer and not again before the transfer is registered. Why then require actual occupation at that later date? Of course, this 'problem' will disappear under e-conveyancing, and Lewison J in *Foy* does recognise that his (*obiter*) conclusion is out of step with all major commentaries. Finally, for clarity, as with Schedule 1, it is clear that *any proprietary* interest (unless specifically excluded) may gain overriding status through this provision provided that the interest-holder is in actual occupation of the burdened land at the relevant time.

2.6.3.2.2   *Conditions shared with the similar provision in Schedule 1*

Many of the considerations relevant to the position under Schedule 1 are relevant here also and are noted below. Reference should be made to the discussion above for a fuller account. First, the interest to be protected must be enforceable against the land immediately before the disposition takes place, bearing in mind that actual occupation must have been present at the time of completion of the transfer or grant.[150] Actual occupation cannot protect that which does not exist.[151] Second, as noted above, the relevant time for the interest-holder to be in actual occupation is at the moment the transfer or grant is executed under the general law and not (despite the contrary view expressed in *Foy*) the later date of registration. Third, any *proprietary* right, provided that it is not specifically excluded, may qualify for overriding status by virtue of the interest-holder being in actual occupation of the affected portion of the burdened land. Personal rights, such as licences, can never override simply because they are personal. Fourth, those interests that are excluded from qualifying as overriding interests under Schedule 1 are also excluded from qualifying as overriding interests through actual occupation under Schedule 3. Fifth, the meaning of 'actual occupation' as a state of affairs will be the same as that applicable to Schedule 1, including the fact that Schedule 3 also limits the effect of the overriding interest to the extent of the land actually occupied. However, of crucial importance is the *additional* requirements placed on 'actual occupation' before it can qualify under Schedule 3.

2.6.3.2.3   *Additional conditions for actual occupation under Schedule 3*

It is in respect of Schedule 3 that the Law Commission's policy of ensuring that 'actual occupation' operates as a warning to a prospective purchaser really comes to the fore. After

---

149   Of course, also as explained above, the 'problem' will disappear come e-conveyancing because of the simultaneous execution and registration of dispositions.

150   In *Thompson* v. *Foy*, Lewison J holds that the date of the disposition is also the date of its execution, rather than the later date of its registration.

151   Such a right may be unenforceable for many reasons: perhaps it was overreached by the registered disposition; perhaps the right-holder has waived his priority or would be estopped from enforcing it by his conduct. However, the critical point is that the claimant must have an interest that has *potential* priority to the registered disposition before any question of an overriding interest arises.

all, registered dispositions involve a transfer of title and if the transferee cannot discover binding adverse interests from the register – especially in an e-conveyancing climate – then it must be made as easy as possible to discover them by other means. Consequently, as well as the issues discussed above about what *factually* amounts to actual occupation, and which are also relevant here, Schedule 3 introduces additional conditions that further restrict the circumstances that an interest-holder can claim to be in actual occupation so as to override a registered disposition.

The first additional condition is that the actual occupation must be capable of being 'obvious on a reasonably careful inspection of the land at the time of the disposition' or the interest alleged to be protected must be within the 'actual knowledge' of the transferee at that time.[152] This is one of the critical provisions of Schedule 3 and it is not found in either the old law of section 70(1)(g) of the LRA 1925 or in Schedule 1 of the LRA 2002. It is a wholly new provision designed to ensure that a person – usually a purchaser – taking under a registered disposition cannot be subject to the priority of a third-party interest that is protected by an actual occupation that is not discoverable or a right that is not known about. In essence, the overriding effect of 'actual occupation' is disapplied (no overriding interest) when *both* limbs of the proviso are established. The first limb of the exclusion prevents actual occupation triggering an overriding interest if the 'occupation would not have been obvious on a reasonably careful inspection of the land at the time of the disposition'. Clearly, this provision will be subject to judicial interpretation because a transferee – especially a mortgagee – is likely to reach for the 'undiscoverability argument' as soon as it appears that he is going to lose priority to an overriding interest through actual occupation. However, the provision does have some interesting features. Clearly, it is the *occupation*, not the right, that must be discoverable and so the purchaser should be concerned with signs of presence not entitlement, although of course the former should alert the potential purchaser to the possibility of the latter. Likewise, the Law Commission's view is that 'apparent' occupation is to be determined by reference to the law on latent and patent defects of title and not by reference to the principles of constructive knowledge or notice that so bedevilled the law of unregistered conveyancing.[153] Whether this real, but fine, distinction is fully implemented come judicial interpretation of the provision remains to be seen. Importantly, however, the relevant test does have an element of objectivity. It is not whether the transferee actually did or did not discover the occupation, but whether the transferee *would have done so*, had he made a reasonably careful inspection of the property. In this sense, it is not necessary for the purchaser to make any additional enquires and inspections other than those that he normally would have undertaken. In fact, the purchaser does not have to inspect at all to gain the benefit of this provision and he will be released from the priority of the adverse interest if the actual occupation was not discoverable on a reasonable inspection whether he inspected or not. This illustrates well that the provision is designed to protect and not to catch out a purchaser. Finally, and obviously, the provision does not protect a purchaser just because he fails to discover occupation, even after inspecting, if the occupation was discoverable within the meaning of the schedule. This is not protection for the indolent or incompetent and in particular the schedule

---

152 Schedule 3, paragraph 2(c)(i) and (ii).

153 Law Commission Report No. 271, *Land Registration for the Twenty-first Century*, paragraph 8.62.

cannot be pleaded by a mortgagee or purchaser who fails to take routine precautions before advancing money under a registered disposition.[154]

The second limb of the exclusion is a necessary counterpart to the introduction of the discoverability condition. Thus, even if the occupation is undiscoverable, the third-party interest will still take effect through actual occupation as an overriding interest if the transferee had 'actual knowledge' of the right. Again, there are some important points here. First, the issue of 'actual knowledge' is irrelevant if the interest-holder is in discoverable actual occupation of the land. This qualification only kicks in if the occupation is not apparent – and this is likely to be rare in practice because most occupation will be apparent. Second, it follows that the interest-holder must still be in actual occupation of the land within the normal meaning of that term before the transferee's actual knowledge becomes an issue. So, if the interest-holder is not in actual occupation, then the fact that the transferee knows of the right is irrelevant. It is crucial to grasp this if the law of registered conveyancing is not to be undone by a secret reintroduction of the law of notice. Third, it is the right itself – not the occupation – that must be within the actual knowledge of the transferee. Fourth, the provision requires 'actual knowledge' on the part of the transferee and it is not intended that he could lose his priority to a third-party interest merely because he ought to have known of the existence of the adverse right.[155]

Clearly, this new provision will generate some uncertainty and is likely in the short term to lead to litigation while its boundaries are established. It replaces the old certainty of 'actual occupation' under the 1925 Act with a fairer, but necessarily more fluid, concept. It may, in the result, have little practical impact, for it is uncertain whether there will be many cases of actual occupation that are truly undiscoverable, rather than simply undiscovered. Note also that this provision in the schedule assumes that there is no 'registration gap' to worry about. As the schedule makes clear, the relevant time for assessing the 'discoverability' of the occupation and the 'actual knowledge' of the transferee is the time of the disposition. Presumably, pending the happy day when the transfer and registration occur simultaneously under e-conveyancing, the 'time of the disposition' will be taken to mean the time of the transfer, as this is the time at which actual occupation must be established.[156]

The second additional condition – additional to that required for 'actual occupation' under Schedule 1 – did in fact feature in a different form in the old section 70(1)(g) of the LRA 1925. This is the additional qualification that an interest will not override if inquiry was made of the right-holder and he failed to disclose the interest 'when he could

---

154 Thus, it would not have helped the lender in Boland, for Mrs Boland was undiscovered, not undiscoverable. In fact, it is debatable whether there were many cases under the 1925 legislation in which the actual occupation was truly undiscoverable, as opposed to undiscovered. See M. Dixon, 'The reform of property law and the Land Registration Act 2002: A risk assessment' (2003) 67 Conv 136. The 'discoverability' of the actual occupation appears to have been conceded in Bustard (2010) as there is little discussion.

155 The question arises whether imputed actual knowledge will suffice, as where the disponee's solicitor actually knew of the adverse right (assuming undiscoverable actual occupation) but failed to tell his client. Issues of professional ethics and good practice aside, it appears that such knowledge cannot be imputed because Schedule 3, paragraph 2(c)(ii) talks of the actual knowledge of 'the person to whom the disposition is made'.

156 In Thompson v. Foy, Lewison J held that the time of execution was the time of disposition under paragraph 2 of Schedule 3.

reasonably have been expected to do so'.[157] The Law Commission takes the view that this provision is simply a reformulation of the provision in the old section 70(1)(g) of the 1925 Act and that it operates by way of estoppel.[158] Thus, the inquiry must be directed towards the right-holder and it is his non-disclosure that is the key.[159] However, the provision is not identically worded to that in the 1925 Act, for the proviso is added that non-disclosure will only result in a denial of overriding status where disclosure could 'reasonably have been expected' to be made. This obviously accepts that there will be some circumstances in which it is reasonable not to disclose and in which such non-disclosure does not destroy the efficacy of the overriding interest gained through actual occupation.

What these circumstances might be is unclear. Of course, it may not be reasonable to expect certain classes of occupier to disclose their rights on inquiry – for example, those under legal or mental disability – but how far does this extend? Does the proviso anticipate that a person cannot 'reasonably be expected' to disclose if such disclosure would lead to the loss of their home?[160] One suspects that the proviso is not meant to change the law in order to protect occupiers in this way, but it is open to that interpretation. Consequently, when an inquiry is made, and until there is judicial clarification of the proviso, an intending transferee might well reflect on how far he can rely on the answers he receives.

2.6.3.3   Certain legal easements and profits – paragraph 3, Schedule 3

Paragraph 3 of Schedule 3 replaces, in relation to registered dispositions, section 70 (1)(a) of the LRA 1925. However, unlike its sister provision in Schedule 1 of the Act, the provision in Schedule 3 concerning the overriding effect of easements and profits against a registered disposition is not straightforward and requires care in its application. The matter is not helped by the elliptical language used to express what is in effect a good practical solution. In essence, because of the qualifications found in Schedule 3, fewer easements and profits will override a registered disposition than will at first registration, but this simple statement barely does justice to the complex nature of the provision.

The first point to note is that any easement that qualified as an overriding interest prior to the entry into force of the LRA 2002 continues to override irrespective of the provisions of the LRA 2002.[161] The 2002 Act looks forward to easements created after in entered into force. That said, as a general principle, paragraph 3 of Schedule 3 provides, first, that no equitable easement or profit will override, and second, that only *certain* legal easements and profits may override. All other easements and profits outside of this regime require deliberate protection by an entry on the register if their priority against a registered

---

157 Schedule 3, paragraph 2(b).

158 Under the 1925 Act, the enquiry had to both as to the occupation and the existence of the occupier's rights (if any) – see *Bank of Scotland v. Qutb* (2009). This is clearly the position under the LRA 2002, Schedule 3.

159 Thus, a lie given by the legal owner of land, does not prevent the interest of an equitable owner from being overriding.

160 For example, in the context of co-owned land, by encouraging the transferee to overreach or by the intended transferee requiring the current registered proprietor to take action to eject the occupier before the transfer takes place.

161 Schedule 12, paragraph 9 of the LRA 2002. This will include all legal easements and some equitable easements in existence at that date.

disposition is to be assured. The key to understanding this is to appreciate that legal easements and profits *expressly* granted or reserved on or after 13 October 2003 out of a *registered title* are excluded from the category of overriding interest because their creation amounts to a registrable disposition under section 27(2)(d) of the 2002 Act.[162] As such, they are 'required to be completed by registration' in order to operate as legal interests.[163] This means, in effect, that every expressly granted or reserved legal easement or profit out of a registered estate can be created only by the entry of a notice in the register of the burdened title, which of course means that the interest has no need of being overriding. If they are not so completed, they are equitable and equitable easements and profits are excluded by clear words from this paragraph.

In its turn, this means that the only new legal easements and profits capable of being overriding are either those expressly granted out of an estate that is not itself registered (e.g. a lease of seven years or less) or, more commonly, those that are impliedly granted.[164] In the former case, there is no title against which to register the interest and in the latter there is no express grant to register. Hence, the easement or profit must be capable of being overriding. Even then, however, it is clear that (save for a three-year period of grace commencing 13 October 2003 and now ended), not even all of this limited class may override. In addition to being either expressly created out of an unregistered estate or being impliedly created, the legal easement will override if, but only if, any *one* of the following additional conditions are satisfied. These additional conditions are either:

- the easement is registered under the Commons Registration Act 1965;[165] or
- the impliedly granted legal interest is within the 'actual knowledge' of the person to whom the disposition is made; or
- the legal interest would have been 'obvious on a reasonably careful inspection' of the burdened land, which, as with the similar provision on 'actual occupation', is an objective test, not necessarily requiring additional inspections and enquiries to be made, but designed to ensure that only 'discoverable' burdens override a registered disposition; or
- the person entitled to the benefit of the impliedly granted legal interest 'proves that it has been exercised in the period of one year ending with the day of the disposition' over which it is said to take effect as an overriding interest. In reality, this is a safety net for those impliedly granted interests that, while not being known of nor 'obvious' on a reasonably careful inspection, are nevertheless used for the benefit of the interest-holder.

It is apparent that paragraph 3 of Schedule 3 is not the most accessible provision of the LRA 2002. Its purpose is, however, clear enough. Apart from the transitional provisions (especially the three-year grace period from 13 October 2003 during which *all* new legal easements or profits expressly granted out of an unregistered estate or impliedly granted

---

162 But excluding interests capable of registration under the Commons Registration Act 1965: see section 27(2)(d) of the 2002 Act.

163 Section 27(1) of the LRA 2002.

164 This means easements created by prescription, necessity, common intention, the rule in *Wheeldon v. Burrows* or by application of section 62 of the LPA 1925. These methods of implied creation are discussed further in Chapter 7.

165 This applies to specialist easements.

out of any estate were overriding), its effect is to ensure that all newly expressly created legal easements or profits are entered on the register. Then, for easements within Schedule 3, the Act attempts to reach a compromise between ensuring their protection in the face of a registered disposition and the need for the purchaser to be aware of such interests before he completes his purchase. This is the reason for the qualified overriding status of such interests because the qualifications are designed to ensure that only those rights either known about (including those known about via Commons registration), obvious or useful take effect as overriding interests. In truth, it is likely that, in practice, Schedule 3 will capture virtually all qualifying legal easements, for there will be few that fall outside of its provisions.[166]

2.6.3.4   Public–Private Partnership (PPP) leases

This provision mirrors the identical provision in relation to Schedule 1. A PPP lease is not found explicitly in Schedule 3 to the LRA 2002 but is made an overriding interest against a registered disposition by reason of section 90(5) of the Act. This status is driven wholly by the special nature of these leases and is an exception to the Act's paramount aim of ensuring that as few interests as possible are excepted from substantive registration.

2.6.3.5   Other permanent overriding interests – paragraphs 4–9, Schedule 3

This block of overriding interest mirrors those taking effect under Schedule 1. Thus they include customary rights (paragraph 4), public rights (paragraph 5), local land charges (paragraph 6), and mines and minerals (paragraphs 7–9).

2.6.3.6   Miscellaneous, time-limited, overriding interests

In a similar vein to Schedule 1, paragraphs 1–14 and paragraph 16 of Schedule 3[167] contain the same miscellany of rights and interests that may override without their substantive registration. Once again, section 117 of the Act provides that the interests listed in these paragraphs will override a registered disposition *only for ten years* from the entry into force of the schedule. Thereafter, if they are to maintain their priority, they must be protected by a notice against the registered title they burden, for which no fee will be charged if registration is sought before the end of the ten-year period.[168]

2.6.3.7   Interests no longer enjoying overriding status under Schedule 3: A summary

As is evident from the above analysis, Schedule 3 to the 2002 Act both rationalises and restricts those unregistered interests which may override a registered disposition, going

---

166 For example, given the nature of easements, very few will not have been exercised within one year of the disposition. We might wonder, then, whether any practical purpose is served in excluding interests under this elaborate provision.

167 Paragraph 16 in respect of the liability to repair the chancel of a church having been added by LRA 2002 (Transitional Provisions) (No. 2) Order 2003.

168 Section 117(2)(b).

even further in this respect than Schedule 1. In consequence, there are a number of matters that now do not qualify as overriding interests. First, the rights of adverse possessors *per se* no longer qualify, but an adverse possessor who has completed adverse possession prior to 12 October 2003 has an entitlement to be registered as proprietor and this entitlement can override through discoverable actual occupation. Second, a person in receipt of rent and profits may not claim overriding status for their interest, although there are transitional provisions for those holding overriding interests by virtue of such receipt prior to the entry into force of the Act. Third, equitable easements created after the Act enters force will not override, although those that existed as overriding interests under the old law on 12 October 2003 will continue to do so. Fourth, not all legal easements and profits granted after the Act entered into force will override.[169] Expressly granted interests out of a registered estate must be completed by registration and so have no need to override. Failing such completion, they will subsist as equitable interests. Impliedly granted legal easements and profits (and those granted out of an unregistered estate such as a lease for seven years or less) can qualify if (subject to transitional provisions) they meet any one of the qualifying criteria. Legal easements that overrode under the old law on 12 October 2003 will continue to do so. Fifth, in respect of possessory, qualified or good leasehold title, those matters 'excepted from the effects of registration' under the old section 70(1)(h) of the 1925 Act no longer override a registered disposition.

2.6.3.8   *Transitional provisions*

For the sake of clarity, it is worth reminding ourselves that the 2002 Act is not retrospective. Thus, although the definition and scope of overriding interests has changed under the LRA 2002, there is no intention to deprive overriding status to those rights that were in existence and which qualified as overriding interests under the old law on 13 October 2003 when the 2002 Act entered into force. Consequently, if the right qualified under the old law on this date, then its overriding status is preserved in the following cases: the rights of persons in actual occupation and in receipt of rents and profits under section 70(1)(g) of the LRA 1925; legal and equitable easements within section 70(1)(a) of the LRA 1925;[170] and legal leases of 21 years or less within section 70(1)(k).

However, the transitional provisions regarding adverse possessors are a little more complex. It has been indicated previously that Schedule 3 of the 2002 Act contains no specific provision for the rights of adverse possessors to override a registered disposition.[171] There is no equivalent of section 70(1)(f) of the LRA 1925, although of course many such possessors will be able to rely on their discoverable actual occupation within paragraph 2 of Schedule 3. However, there is an important transitional provision concerning adverse possessors operating under Schedule 3. By virtue of Schedule 12, paragraph 18, of the LRA 2002, a person who, prior to the entry into force of the 2002 Act, had land held on trust for him under section 75(1) of the LRA 1925 – that is, a person who had completed 12 years' adverse possession by that date – 'is entitled to be registered as proprietor of the estate'. In effect, this means that a possessor who has completed the 12-year period of limitation

---

169   Those that overrode before the Act will continue to do so.

170   See *Celsteel v. Alton House Holdings* (1985).

171   The same is true under Schedule 1.

under the old law of adverse possession before the entry into force of the 2002 Act does not have to submit to the new scheme of the LRA 2002 but may achieve registration through a simple application to HM Land Registry. This is perfectly acceptable. However, if the paper owner sells the land before the adverse possessor's entitlement is realised, the adverse possessor is at risk of losing his right to be registered as proprietor of the estate. In essence, the adverse possessor must seek registration as the new owner before any sale or must rely on being in discoverable actual occupation so as to claim an overriding interest.[172] Failing this, the adverse possessor will lose priority to the new registered proprietor.[173]

2.6.4   The duty to disclose: Entering overriding interests on the register

Overriding interests are, by their nature, unregistered. If the interest becomes registered, it ceases to be overriding and takes priority instead from its entry on the register. This is likely to occur by reason of the duty of disclosure found in section 71 of the LRA 2002 under which an applicant for registration must disclose overriding interests of which he is aware so that they may be entered on the register by means of a notice. However, failure to disclose does not destroy the overriding status of the right.[174]

Importantly, however, the registrar will not enter a notice in respect of all matters that are disclosed because some interests are incapable of being protected by a notice and others do not amount to disclosable overriding interests. The first group are found in sections 33 and 90(4) of the Act and comprise: interests under a trust of land or a settlement under the Settled Land Act 1925;[175] leasehold estates granted for three years or less of the kind that are not required to be registered with their own title; restrictive covenants made between a lessor and lessee so far as they relate to the demised premises;[176] interests capable of being registered under the Commons Registration Act 1965; interests in any coal or coal mine within sections 38, 49 or 51 of the Coal Industry Act 1994; and PPP leases.[177] These interests are all protected by other means and their entry on the register would serve no additional purpose – except perhaps to clog the register. The second group are non-disclosable under Rule 57 of the Land Registration Rules and hence do not fall within the registrar's power to enter a notice. They comprise a public right, a local land charge, and a leasehold estate within Schedule 3, paragraph 1, but with

---

172   If the period of adverse possession would finish after the entry into force of the 2002 Act, then the scheme of the 2002 Act applies in full – see Chapter 11. There is no saving for partly completed adverse possession.

173   It is not clear whether the adverse possessor can apply for rectification of the register against the new owner in these circumstances.

174   The provision is intended to encourage registration, not to penalise the right-holder if the owner of the burdened land does not disclose it.

175   The former, but not the latter, may be an overriding interest through actual occupation but both may be protected to some degree by the entry of a restriction against dealings.

176   Note this represents a change in the law for a leasehold covenant relating to land outside the demise may now be registered by means of a notice.

177   This last is found in section 90(4) of the Act.

one year or less to run.[178] They are excluded from the duty to disclose because they also are otherwise protected and would clog the title.

2.6.5 The 'bindingness' of overriding interests under the LRA 2002

The existence of overriding interests remains a vital element in the system of land registration under the 2002 Act. As the above sections illustrate, their definition is reasonably clear but certainly open to interpretation in some areas, particularly the 'actual occupation' and 'easement' provisions of Schedule 3. However, we now come to another important issue concerning overriding interests. If we are satisfied that a right falls within Schedule 3 and qualifies in principle as an overriding interest, when *precisely* will it be binding against a purchaser? To put it another way, it cannot be true that a new registered proprietor will be bound by *everything* that could be an overriding interest whenever that interest came into existence or whatever the circumstances. It would be harsh indeed if, say, a new owner were bound by overriding interests that came into existence *after* he had purchased the land, or if the new owner were bound even if the right-holder had promised expressly to waive the bindingness of his overriding interest. Consequently, the following principles determine the time at which the overriding interest must exist in order to bind a purchaser automatically and the circumstances in which agreement between the parties can remove their effect.

For all categories of overriding interest, the crucial date for determining whether the purchaser is bound by an overriding interest is the date on which the purchaser makes an application to register his title at the correct district land registry, being the date of registration (sections 29 and 30 of the LRA 2002). This necessarily raises the possibility of a 'registration gap'[179] if the overriding interest arose after the purchaser had completed the contract of purchase, but before he was actually registered with title. This is particularly acute in relation to the 'actual occupation' provisions – given that a person with an interest might go in to occupation after a purchase but before registration of the title. Consequently, it is now settled that while an overriding interest established under the actual occupation provision of Schedule 3 crystallises at the date of registration, a person cannot claim the benefit of the schedule unless he has a proprietary right and is in actual occupation of the land at the time of the sale to the new owner was or when he granted the mortgage (*Abbey National Building Society v. Cann* (1991)).[180] This pragmatic decision effectively eliminates the 'registration gap' for 'actual occupation' overriding interests. It means, in practice, that a purchaser will not find the value or use of his land diminished by the emergence of a powerful adverse right in the interval between his purchase and the application for registration as the new proprietor. The proprietary right, and the actual occupation that invests it with the status of an overriding interest, must exist prior to completion of the purchaser's transaction so increasing the chances that it will be discovered in time for the

---

178 For example, a five-year lease that has already run for over four years.

179 See *Barclays Bank v. Zaroovabli* (1997) under the LRA 1925.

180 Although decided by reference to the 1925 Act, the principles of this House of Lords decision apply with equal force to the equivalent provisions of the LRA 2002. Note also the view in *Thompson v. Foy*, criticised above, that actual occupation also had to exist at the date of registration.

purchaser to react accordingly. Of course, this convenient solution will not be required come e-conveyancing, when completion of the purchase and its registration will take place simultaneously and electronically and there will then be no registration gap.

Second, the 'owner' of an overriding interest that would otherwise bind a new registered proprietor is able to waive voluntarily the priority given to their right by expressly consenting to the sale or mortgage of the land over which the right exists.[181] Indeed, in some cases, this consent will be implied because of the conduct of the holder of the overriding interest (*Paddington Building Society v. Mendelson* (1985)). In fact, a right-holder who has consented to a particular purchaser having priority over his otherwise binding right (e.g. a mortgagee 'X'), may be taken to have consented to the priority of a different purchaser who steps into his shoes (e.g. a re-mortgagee 'Y', whose monies pay off the first mortgage), at least to the extent of the monies provided by the original mortgagee even if in reality the right-holder did not know of the substitution (*Equity and Law Home Loans v. Prestidge* (1992)).

Although the precise circumstances in which a right-holder will be deemed to have consented to the sale or mortgage of the land over which the overriding interest takes effect are unclear, mere knowledge that a transaction concerning the land is proposed would not seem to be enough. Consequently, the person with the overriding interest need not volunteer information concerning their position and will not be taken to have consented simply because the transaction proceeds around them and they remain silent – having not been asked. The requirement is one of consent to the sale or mortgage, not simple knowledge of it (*Skipton Building Society v. Clayton* (1993)). However, active participation in organising the mortgage or encouraging a purchaser will be deemed to be consent. For example, an equitable owner in actual occupation who sits by while her husband arranges a mortgage will not thereby lose the priority that her overriding interest has over the mortgagee, but an equitable owner who participates by, say, explaining to the bank that the money is needed for an extension, will. This uncertainty as to the boundary between implied consent and 'mere' knowledge has led many purchasers (especially banks lending by way of mortgage) to now require all occupiers to sign express consent forms waiving such rights they might have in favour of the mortgage. This would seem to be perfectly adequate to protect the priority of the mortgage.[182]

Finally, for the sake of clarity, it is trite law that a proprietary right may qualify as an overriding interest only if it actually *exists*. This is not startling news, but it does mean, for example, that if it turns out that the alleged overriding interest is, for example, not a lease at all, but a licence, this licence can never be an overriding interest because licences are not capable of binding any third party, being merely personal rights. Likewise, even if the alleged overriding interest does exist as a proprietary right, it may be ineffective against a particular purchaser because of circumstances wholly unrelated to the operation of overriding interests *per se*. One such case has been considered above as where the purchaser gains the consent of the potential holder of the overriding interest so ensuring that that particular purchaser can never be bound. Also, therefore, if the alleged overriding interest

---

181 Note the connection with 'undue influence' cases in the law of mortgages.

182 *Birmingham Midshires Building Society v. Saberhawal* (2000). The contrary view expressed in *Woolwich Building Society v. Dickman* (1996) is based on a misunderstanding of the old section 70(1) of the LRA 1925 and certainly cannot be taken to apply to the LRA 2002.

is given by a landowner who had no power to give it, in such cases the right cannot bind the purchaser because, vis-à-vis the purchaser, it does not exist. An example is *Leeds Permanent Building Society v. Famini* (1998), in which the alleged overriding interest (a tenancy) was created by a landowner who had no power to create it, having promised the purchaser (the bank, his mortgagee) that he would not do so. The bank could not be bound by the alleged overriding interest.

2.7   The Operation of Registered Land: Protected Registered Interests under the Land Registration Act 2002

A major aim of the 2002 Act is to ensure that as many proprietary rights as possible that affect a registered title should be entered on the register. The category of protected registered interests – formerly known as 'minor interests' under the LRA 1925 – implements this policy. As such, these rights are not registrable titles, nor registrable mortgages (charges) and, by definition, are not unregistered interests that override. In practice, then, this group of interests usually comprises the rights of persons other than the owner, being typical third-party rights such as easements, restrictive covenants or options to purchase, and they may be legal or equitable. This is important because it emphasises that the role of this category of right is *not* – as it was primarily under the LRA 1925 – to protect equitable interests in land, but rather to provide a means whereby most third-party rights can be registered, both for the benefit of the right-holder and for any prospective purchaser of the land. Consequently, this category comprises rights that *must* be registered in order to ensure their priority against a purchaser,[183] being rights that *cannot* amount to unregistered interests that override,[184] and rights that *may* be registered and so enjoy protection, but which if not registered would nevertheless amount to overriding interests.[185] The latter group includes those rights that are either entered on the register by the registrar of his own volition after examining the conveyancing documents or those that are disclosed under the duty of disclosure when a transferee applies to be registered as the new owner.[186]

2.7.1   The mechanics of registration of interests: Notices

Unlike the position under the LRA 1925, registration of third-party interests under the LRA 2002 is relatively simple. There is only one type of entry that can substantively protect an interest, albeit that there are two variants.[187] This is the notice. In technical terms, a notice is 'an entry in the register of the burden of an interest affecting a registered

---

183   Section 29 of the LRA 2002.

184   For example, freehold covenants.

185   For example, a six-year legal lease.

186   As discussed below, not all third-party rights need be disclosed and so there are some rights that may not be protected by the entry of a notice.

187   One might argue that the registrar's notice – considered below – is a third variant. The use of the restriction is considered below.

estate'[188] and will be entered in the 'charges' section of the registered title affected by it.[189] Notices may be of two types: an 'agreed notice' or a 'unilateral notice', and if the former, the entry in the register must give details of the interest protected.[190] Importantly, both types of notice confer priority on the interest to which they relate (section 29 of the LRA 2002). In other words, a transferee takes the title subject to the priority of the interest protected by the notice, whether the notice be unilateral or agreed. This means that the choice of which type of notice to use depends ultimately on the circumstances in which the interest arose and the needs of the right-holder. In particular, unilateral notices should not be seen as a weaker form of protection for a third-party right.

In fact, the 2002 Act does not offer an exhaustive list of matters that may be protected by the entry of a notice, but rather it specifies what may not be so protected.[191] However, it remains true that most examples of classic third-party interests in land may be protected by the entry of a notice against the registered title. This includes, for example, a contract for sale prior to completion, an option to buy or right of first refusal (right of pre-emption), a restrictive covenant, including a covenant in a lease not relating to the demised premises,[192] a deed supplemental to a lease, a charging order charging the legal estate,[193] and an equitable charge of the legal estate, easements, claims in proprietary estoppel and some leases granted for seven years or less. Nevertheless, as indicated, there are a number of interests that may not be protected by the entry of a notice at all. Generally, these are interests more appropriately protected by the entry of a restriction or qualify as overriding interests not subject to the duty of disclosure. They are a beneficial interest under a trust of land,[194] a settlement governed by the Settled Land Act 1925,[195] a leasehold for three years or less unless it is one of the special class of such short leases that are registrable with their own titles,[196] restrictive covenants made between lessor and lessee relating only to the demised premises,[197] an interest capable of being registered under the Commons Registration Act 1965,[198] certain interests in coal and coal mines,[199] and PPP

---

188 Section 32(1) of the LRA 2002.

189 Rule 84, LRR 2003, except that a bankruptcy notice will be entered in the proprietorship register (section 86(2) of the LRA 2002).

190 Rule 84(3), LRR 2003. If the notice is unilateral, the entry may give such details as the registrar considers appropriate (Rule 84(5), LRR 2003).

191 Section 33 of the LRA 2002.

192 For example, in relation to other premises owned by the landlord such as other shop units in a commercial development.

193 A charging order charging a beneficial interest in the registered estate cannot be protected by a notice as it is not a burden affecting a registered estate per se. A restriction may be used.

194 For example, a share of the matrimonial home: section 33 (a)(i) of the LRA 2002. A restriction should be used.

195 Section 33(a)(ii) of the LRA 2002. The provisions of the Settled Land Act 1925 operate.

196 Section 33(b) of the LRA 2002. Likely to override either as a legal lease for a term of seven years or less or by reason of actual occupation.

197 Section 33(c) of the LRA 2002. Enforceable at common law or under the Landlord and Tenant (Covenants) Act 1995.

198 Section 33(d) of the LRA 2002. It should be so registered and may then qualify as an overriding interest.

199 Section 33(e) of the LRA 2002, referring generally to an interest in coal or a coal mine and specifically to sections 38, 49, and 51 of the Coal Industry Act 1994. These may override.

leases.[200] In respect of these interests, the registrar is not permitted to enter a notice of any kind and the right-holder must rely on other means of protection – either that found in Schedules 1 and 3 concerning unregistered interests that override, by use of a restriction or under the special statutory regime applicable to such rights.[201]

2.7.2   Agreed notices

Subject to the exclusions identified above, a person may apply for the entry of an agreed notice affecting a registered estate under section 34 of the LRA 2002. The registrar may only enter such a notice following an application in three circumstances: first, where the applicant himself is the registered proprietor or a person entitled to be registered as the proprietor; second, where the registered proprietor or person entitled consents to the entry of the notice; or third, where the registrar is satisfied as to the validity of the applicant's claim. Consequently, although an agreed notice will often be the result of the action of the registered proprietor or be with his consent, it may be entered even if the underlying right is contested. Of course, the applicant must furnish evidence to satisfy the registrar that such a notice should be entered and this will usually be proof of the registered proprietor's consent, or of the instrument that created the right, or a court order giving rise to the interest protected. It can, however, be any other 'evidence to satisfy the Registrar as to the validity of the applicant's claim'.[202] Consequently, if an agreed notice is entered in circumstances in which the proprietor has not actually consented, he may dispute the entry by applying for its cancellation only after it has been entered. However, while the entry of an agreed notice preserves the priority of a valid right against a transferee,[203] it does not guarantee the validity of an interest if it emerges that the interest is void as being contrary to the general law.[204] For example, the priority of a legal easement will be protected by the entry of a notice, but if it should appear that the alleged 'easement' was void under the general law, its entry on the register cannot clothe it with validity. One cannot protect what does not exist.

Finally, we should also note that certain third-party rights are protectable only by means of an agreed notice. This group is a mixed bag of third-party interests not truly proprietary in character – at least in a classical sense – but clearly requiring protection for the right-holder. They are found in Rule 80 of the LRR 2003 and comprise matrimonial home rights under the Family Law Act 1996, an Revenue charge in respect of inheritance tax liability, a customary right, a public right, a variation of a lease effected by section 38 of the Landlord and Tenant Act 1987[205] and an interest arising pursuant to an order made under the Access to Neighbouring Land Act 1992. These are clearly rights of a more limited and surgical effect and are 'agreed' in the sense of being indisputable by the registered proprietor whether he actually consents or not.

---

200 Section 90(4) of the LRA 2002. These will override.

201 For example, with leasehold covenants under the Landlord and Tenant (Covenants) Act 1995.

202 Land Registration Rule 81(1)(c)(ii).

203 Sections 28, 29 and 30 of the LRA 2002.

204 Section 32(3) of the LRA 2002.

205 Including amendments made under section 39(4) of that Act.

2.7.3   Unilateral notices

An application for the entry of a unilateral notice by a person claiming to be entitled to the benefit of an interest affecting the registered estate or charge may be made under section 34(2)(b) of the LRA 2002. In essence, it is an application for the entry of a notice without consent, although the applicant must furnish HM Land Registry with some evidence that the right exists. Assuming the registrar agrees to enter such a notice (but not otherwise), the registrar must give notice to the proprietor of the land affected, thus affording him the opportunity of challenging the notice and putting the applicant to proof of the existence of the alleged right, although the cancellation procedure operates only after an entry has actually been made. Again, as with agreed notices, although the entry of a unilateral notice confers priority protection on the interest claimed, it does not guarantee the validity of that interest under the general law.[206] Should the interest be found subsequently to have been invalid, its registration will preserve its priority against a transferee. The entry of a unilateral notice will identify the land or part thereof affected by the interest and (unlike agreed notices) it will also identify the person entitled to the right under the notice.[207]

2.7.4   Registrar's notices

Although an application by an interest-holder is likely to be the most common method by which a notice is entered on the register, the 2002 Act also stipulates a number of circumstances in which the registrar may, or must, make an entry. These notices are neither agreed nor unilateral notices *per se*, although the circumstances in which such an entry is possible make them equivalent to agreed notices in the sense that there is usually no doubt about the existence of the underlying right they protect. They might be thought of as 'registrar's notices' although that term is not used by the Act. They may be entered in a number of varied circumstances. First, certain transactions must satisfy specified registration requirements if they are to take effect as registrable dispositions under the Act and these entries are made by the registrar.[208] Second, under section 37 of the Act, if it appears to the registrar that a registered estate is subject to an unregistered interest that overrides at first registration, he may enter a notice in respect of that interest provided that the interest is capable of protection by means of a notice. Third, at first registration of a registrable estate, the registrar will note against the title any interest that burdens the land provided that it is capable of protection by a notice.[209] Fourth, the registrar may enter a notice in respect of overriding interests within Schedule 1 or Schedule 3 (assuming they are protectable by notice) that are disclosed at first registration or on a registered dis-position (as the case may be) under the applicant's duty of disclosure within section 71 of the Act. Fifth, it seems that the registrar may enter a notice in pursuance of his general power to alter the register within Schedule 4, paragraph 5, of the Act in order to correct a

---

206   Section 32(3) of the LRA 2002.

207   Presumably, this means the person entitled to enforce the interest.

208   Section 27 of the LRA 2002.

209   For example, protectable former land charges.

mistake, update the register, or give effect to a right or interest otherwise excepted from the effect of registration.[210]

2.7.5 Which type of notice? Agreed or unilateral?

As indicated above, certain special kinds of interest must be protected by means of an agreed notice and thus the right-holder has no choice but to adopt this route to protection. Yet in many cases there will be a choice, and the applicant has to consider which form of notice – agreed or unilateral – is the most appropriate. Once again, however, we can remind ourselves that there is no difference in the level of protection offered by an agreed or unilateral notice. Both confer substantive priority protection on the interest to the extent that the interest is valid under the general law. Thus, unilateral notices are not like cautions under the 1925 LRA, which gave only procedural protection. In deciding which version of the notice to use, a number of factors may be important. First, is the applicant in possession of the consent of the registered proprietor or of sufficient evidence to prove the existence of the claimed interest so as to secure an agreed notice? Second, does the applicant wish to establish the existence of his interest at the time of application to HM Land Registry (agreed notice), or is he content to wait to see whether the registered proprietor decides to accept or challenge the claimed interest, if ever (unilateral notice)? Third, does the applicant wish the identity of the interest-holder to be revealed in the register – as is required for a unilateral notice but not for an agreed notice? Fourth, and perhaps of significant practical importance, an application for an agreed notice will usually be accompanied by documents proving the interest: for example, the deed of grant or contract. These documents will form part of the public record and will be open to inspection by any person.[211] They may, however, contain sensitive information of a commercial or other kind and while it is possible to apply for documents to be given exempt status (an 'exempt information document'), a unilateral notice avoids this problem as documents do not need to be lodged and thus cannot form part of the publicly available register.

2.7.6 Removing and cancelling an agreed notice or a 'registrar's notice'

By its nature, a right protected by an agreed notice or a notice entered by the registrar under his various powers is not likely to be contested by the registered proprietor, even if it originally was made without his consent on the basis of submitted evidence or was the result of a court order. Consequently, the Act does not provide a specific mechanism for challenging such entries – any doubt should have been resolved at the time the making of the entry was considered. Nevertheless, it is apparent that there will be cases in which the removal of an agreed notice or registrar's notice is justified: for example, if the right was time limited or has been waived. Consequently, the Land Registration Rules provide a procedure for the cancellation of such a notice and the application must be accompanied by evidence to satisfy the registrar that the interest has come to an end. This is effectively an

---

210 Superfluous entries may also be removed.

211 Section 66(1) of the LRA 2002.

administrative procedure permitting the cancellation of entries by reason of the determination of the underlying right. It is not a procedure to challenge the validity of a third-party right or to challenge whether the original entry was properly made. No such provision exists under the LRA 2002 and this does much to explain the true nature of agreed and registrar's notices.

2.7.7 Cancelling and challenging unilateral notices

By its very nature, the entry of a unilateral notice is more likely to be contentious because the underlying right is not necessarily admitted. Even so, the entry will secure priority for the right (if it is valid) and potential purchasers of the land may well be discomfited by the registration of burdens that appear to affect the utility of the land they are just about to acquire. Consequently, there are two principal means by which a unilateral notice may be deleted from the register. First, the unilateral notice may be *removed* under section 35(3) of the Act; second, the unilateral notice may be *cancelled* under section 36 of the Act.

Removal of a unilateral notice under section 35 is effectively a non-contentious process for its withdrawal from the register. Application may be made only by the person registered as the beneficiary of the notice (or the personal representative or trustee in bankruptcy of such person) and the registrar must remove the notice if he is satisfied that the application is in order. On the other hand, cancellation of a unilateral notice under section 36 of the Act describes the process whereby the validity of the underlying right is challenged and the registered proprietor seeks the elimination of the notice from the register. It is, in essence, a 'prove it or lose it' process, but only the registered proprietor or the person entitled to be so registered may make the application.[212] In general terms, the application to cancel will cause the registrar to notify the person identified as the beneficiary of the notice and that person will have a period of time to object to the cancellation of the notice. Failure to object within the required period means that the registrar *must* cancel the unilateral notice. Clearly, however, the person entitled to the underlying right protected by the unilateral notice may well object to its cancellation, in which case the registrar will seek to resolve the matter between the parties and this may result in either the cancellation of the notice or its retention as an agreed notice. Where the parties cannot agree, the matter will be referred to the Adjudicator to HM Land Registry.

2.7.8 Enforcing registered protected interests

The aims of the system of registration for third-party interests are two-fold: to protect the interest in the event of a transfer of the land and to alert a prospective purchaser before he buys. Consequently, if an interest is protected in the proper way by entry on the register, it takes priority over the interest of any subsequent transferee *and* purchaser of the registered land: sections 28, 29 and 30 of the LRA 2002. For this reason, an intending purchaser will usually request a search of the register in order to discover whether there are any registered adverse interests. Following this search, the prospective purchaser will enjoy a 'priority period' in which to apply for registration of his title. If an application to register title is made within this priority period, any newly registered interest (i.e. registered after the

---

212 Section 36(1) of the LRA 2002. A person entitled must adduce evidence of his entitlement: Rule 86(2), LRR.

search was made) will not have priority to the purchaser. Any interests properly registered at the date the new owner applies for registration and not excluded by the priority period will be binding. It must be remembered, however, that, unlike unregistered land, it is the register itself that is conclusive. Thus, any registered interest that is not revealed because of an inaccurate search of the register remains binding on the purchaser because it is still entered on the register.

In such circumstances, a purchaser prejudiced by an inaccurate search may be entitled to an indemnity or may sue the registry in negligence. As a counterpart to this, any third-party interest that is not registered in the appropriate manner loses its priority over the interest of a subsequent purchaser of the land who registers their title, unless it is saved for some other reason. It is vital to appreciate that this is the case whether or not the purchaser knew or should have known of the existence of that interest. In other words, the doctrine of notice is irrelevant because loss of priority is the penalty for lack of registration.[213] Of course, in the great majority of cases, the new owner of land will be a purchaser (as opposed to a donee of a gift or devisee under a will) and he will seek security in a search of the register for registered interests. However, this is not quite the whole story and some exceptions to the loss of priority rule do exist, these being cases in which an *unregistered* interest does in fact enjoy priority over the interest of a new owner of the land. As explained below, these situations occur for specific rather than general reasons and, consequently, whenever it is alleged that an unregistered interest binds a new registered proprietor, the facts of the case are likely to be crucial.

First, an unregistered interest may nevertheless qualify as an overriding interest within Schedule 3 to the Act, typically under the actual occupation provision but not exclusively so. In such a case, it may well take priority over the interest of the new owner but *only* because it is an overriding interest. A typical example is an equitable lease, which could be registered by means of a notice, but which will usually take effect against a purchaser as an overriding interest because the tenant will be a person in discoverable actual occupation of the land.

Second, an unregistered interest (not qualifying as an overriding interest) remains valid against a person who is *not* a purchaser for value of the land: for example, the recipient (donee) of a gift, the recipient (devisee) under a will or a squatter (adverse possessor). This is the effect of the basic priority rule found in section 28 of the LRA 2002 – see *Halifax v. Popeck* (2008). In essence, such donees, devisees and squatters acquire no greater right than their predecessor and if he was bound, so are they, irrespective of registration.

Third, an unregistered interest (not qualifying as an overriding interest) remains valid against a purchaser for value who does not register their title. In such cases, the new owner has not completed a registered disposition within sections 25 and 27 of the LRA 2002. As such, he obtains an equitable title only and the unregistered interest takes priority under the basic priority rule of section 28 – the first in time prevails. For example, imagine that an equitable mortgagee fails to protect his mortgage by means of a notice, but the land over which the mortgage exists is sold to X. If X fails to register her estate, she has only an equitable title created after the equitable mortgage and thus ranking behind it. Of course, should X seek registration of her new estate, the equitable mortgage will cease to be

---

effective against the land, unless it has by that time been registered or otherwise qualifies as an overriding interest.

Fourth, an unregistered interest (not qualifying as an overriding interest) remains valid against a purchaser for value who has expressly promised to give effect to that interest and thereby gains some advantage: for example, a lower price. In such cases, if it would be unconscionable for the purchaser to deny the validity of the unregistered interest; that interest will be held binding on the purchaser by means of a personal constructive trust (*Lyus v. Prowsa Developments* (1982), approved in *Lloyd v. Dugdale* (2001)). It should be noted that this is an exceptional way in which an unregistered interest will be held to have priority and it depends entirely on the conduct of the particular purchaser against whom a remedy is sought. If, for example, that first purchaser were to sell the land on, the interest would then need to be registered in order to take effect against the second purchaser. In other words, this is a personal remedy against a particularly unconscionable purchaser. What amounts to 'unconscionable' conduct, so as to deny a purchaser the benefit of the priority rule necessarily, will vary from case to case. As mentioned previously, a purchaser who promises the vendor that he will honour an unregistered interest and thereby obtains a lower price, will be held to his agreement (*Lloyd v. Dugdale* (2001)). Again, however, it is important to emphasise that we are looking for 'unconscionability' on the part of the purchaser, not that he has old-style 'notice' of the interest, as explained in *Miles v. Bull (No. 2)* (1969). So, a purchaser who knows of an adverse interest that is not registered and is keen to complete the purchase before it is registered, thereby securing a bargain, is not acting unconscionably simply because they have been able to take advantage of the provisions of the LRA 2002.

Fifth, an unregistered interest (not qualifying as an overriding interest) remains valid against a purchaser for value where the purchaser has knowledge of the interest *and* is relying on the statute in order to perpetrate a fraud. This is similar to the situation outlined above and is an example of the old equitable rule that 'equity will not permit a statute to be used as an instrument of fraud' – *De Lusignan v. Johnson* (1973) – meaning that a person cannot plead the rule in sections 29 and 30 of the LRA 2002 as justification for their own fraudulent use of the land.[214] Again, the emphasis is not on the purchaser's knowledge or notice of the existence of the unregistered interest, but that the purchaser is attempting to use the statute to further a fraudulent design. Knowledge or notice of the unregistered interest *per se* does not make a purchaser fraudulent. In short, 'fraud' means more than acting on one's rights under the LRA 2002. It appears to include schemes deliberately designed to defeat unregistered interests, as in *Jones v. Lipman* (1962), in which the new registered proprietor who claimed to be free from the unregistered interest was in fact a company controlled by the former proprietor who had been bound by that interest. Likewise, a promise given to the right-holder to respect the right and therefore to discourage deliberately its protection by registration will amount to fraud.

2.8 Restrictions

Restrictions were in use under the LRA 1925 and they have been given an enhanced role in the LRA 2002. Although not chiefly designed to protect third-party interests directly, the

---

214 See also *HSBC v. Dyche* (2009), in which the purchaser was relying on section 2 of the LPA 1925 to commit a fraud in the context of overreaching,

entry of a restriction may well have this effect by controlling the registered proprietor's ability to sell the land or otherwise transfer it – see section 23 of the LRA 2002. In such cases, the third-party right is protected because there can be no dealing with the land. However, restrictions are not chiefly about third-party right protection – that is what notices are for – and are more directly concerned with preventing all manner of dealings with the estate by the registered proprietor by preventing entries on the register that do not comply with the terms of the restriction. In essence then, the restriction is a form of entry that places limitations on the registered proprietor's powers over the land. These limitations may be for specific events or specific periods, and may place the limiting power in the hands of others – as where another person's consent is required to a dealing with a registered title. On the other hand, the restriction can be of a general or universal nature.[215] Generally, the restriction is entered in the proprietorship section of the register and will ensure that no dealings with the registered title can occur until the conditions specified in the restriction are complied with.

Section 42 of the LRA 2002 sets out the registrar's general power to enter restrictions[216] and section 43 establishes who may make an application for an entry. Given that restrictions may be used in a wide range of circumstances, Schedule 4 to the Land Registration Rules lists 'standard-form' restrictions that are intended to cover the most common situations in which a restriction might be required. HM Land Registry encourages use of standard-form restrictions by making the application process smoother and cheaper than if a non-standard restriction is applied for. Typical examples of when a restriction might be required are where an equitable owner wishes to ensure that a sale of co-owned land is made by two trustees, thereby triggering overreaching,[217] or where a person with an option to buy the land wishes to control the registered proprietor's ability to sell the land to someone else. Restrictions are also vital in cases of bankruptcy to prevent dealings with the land that might defeat the interests of creditors. Importantly, a restriction may be entered even though the substantive right is protected by a notice. For example, a person with an option to buy the land might well protect that option by means of a notice and, in addition, seek a restriction to prevent the proprietor actually breaking the contract by selling to another.

2.9   The Operation of Registered Land: Overreaching

Throughout the above analysis, especially when considering whether and how a third-party right might be protected on a transfer of registered land, repeated reference has been made to the concept of overreaching. The following section will analyse the concept of

---

215 Section 40 of the LRA 2002.

216 In some situations, the registrar must enter a restriction.

217 See below. Consequently the application for a restriction – standard Form A in fact – can be used as a method of establishing an equitable interest in another person's land because such a restriction cannot be entered unless such an interest exists. Likewise, it prevents a sole legal owner from disposing of the land to the potential detriment of the equitable owner.

overreaching and explain how it fits into the registration system. As will be seen, it is a process whereby rights that would otherwise be binding against a purchaser according to the rules of registered land will not be so binding because of this 'statutory magic'. As a preliminary, it is also important to realise that 'overreaching' is not actually a creation of the LRA 1925 or LRA 2002; it also operates in unregistered land and in a similar fashion. It will continue to operate in much the same way under the LRA 2002 as it did under the LRA 1925. This is explained in the following sections.

Overreaching is a process whereby certain *equitable* rights in land that might otherwise have enjoyed protection in the system of registration on the occasion of a sale of that land to a purchaser for value are 'swept off' the land and transferred to the purchase money that has just been paid. When this occurs, the equitable rights are said to be 'overreached' and no longer bind the purchaser, even though they might have fitted exactly into the category of overriding interests.[218] Overreaching is, in effect, a method of promoting the alienability of land by removing certain equitable rights from the land and recasting them as a monetary equivalent. Note, however, that not all equitable rights can be 'swept off' the land by overreaching. In fact, the rights that are capable of being overreached are those equitable rights that exist behind a trust of land, being those equitable ownership rights that exist when the land is co-owned (see Chapters 4 and 5) and which have a readily identifiable monetary value. The crucial point is, then, that if overreaching occurs, a right that would have been protected against a purchaser ceases to be so protected, irrespective of whether it would have been an overriding interest under the LRA 2002 (or its predecessor). Overreaching is the purchaser's trump card. It follows that two essential conditions must be met before overreaching can occur.

2.9.1 The right must be capable of being overreached

The first condition is that the equitable right must be of the kind that is *capable* of being overreached. Not all equitable rights are 'overreachable' and so the trump card can be played only in defined circumstances. Overreachable equitable rights are defined in section 2 of the LPA 1925 and, in essence, are equitable co-ownership rights existing behind a trust of land – as in *City of London Building Society v. Flegg* (1998)[219] – or equitable interests existing behind a strict settlement.[220] Consequently, equitable interests such as the equitable easement and equitable lease can never be overreached and will bind a purchaser of the registered land (or not) according to the rules of registered land just discussed.

2.9.2 The statutory conditions for overreaching must be fulfilled

The second condition is that the statutory conditions for overreaching must be fulfilled. This means that the sale must be made by those persons and in those circumstances that together constitute an overreaching transaction (section 2(1) of the LPA 1925). These are four in number, although the first is the one most frequently encountered.

---

218 These rights cannot be protected by the entry of a notice; see above.

219 See Chapter 4.

220 See Chapter 5.

The first circumstance is that the transaction is made by at least two trustees (or a trust corporation being a limited company of £250,000 capital) exercising valid powers under a trust of land, usually in a co-ownership situation.[221] The trustees will be the legal owners of the land. The need for two trustees (legal owners) is a statutory requirement and has no relevance other than that this is the minimum number required. As we shall see in Chapter 4, the maximum number of trustees of land are four, so that if there are four trustees, all four must concur in the transaction (and likewise if there are three, etc.). The most common transaction effected by the trustees that will overreach any equitable co-owners is either the simple sale to a purchaser or the execution of a mortgage in return for funds. If there is a sale, the new registered proprietor will have overreached the equitable owners and may evict them; if there is a mortgage, the mortgagee's interest will have priority over that of the equitable owners and so, in the event that the land is sold, the mortgagee will be paid first.

As noted, the sale/mortgage in a co-ownership situation is the most common type of overreaching transaction and it will be discussed at length in Chapter 4. At this stage, it is noteworthy that section 2 of the LPA 1925 appears to assume that overreaching occurs when the sale proceeds (either from sale proper or monies advanced by mortgage) are *actually* paid to the two (three or four) trustees. This is quite natural as the rationale for overreaching and its ability to release a purchaser from otherwise binding rights is that the equitable owners take a share of the money in 'compensation' for the loss of their right to the land. However, as became clear in *State Bank of India v. Sood* (1997), many trustees will take out a mortgage of registered land (i.e. sell an interest to a purchaser) not in order to receive immediate monies, but to guarantee future borrowings from the bank, perhaps to finance a business venture. In these cases, no money is actually paid over even though there is an overreaching transaction by two or more trustees. Consequently, the question that arose in *Sood*, apparently for the first time, was whether this type of transaction is an overreaching transaction so as to give the bank priority over any equitable rights? The answer is that it is. The Court of Appeal decided that, under section 2(1)(ii) of the LPA 1925, if capital monies were to be paid as a result of a conveyance by the trustees, those monies would actually have to be paid to two trustees to overreach. However, if capital monies did not arise on a transaction (as in the case of a mortgage to secure *future* borrowings), a conveyance by two trustees would overreach the equitable owners by mere execution of the conveyance. The Court reached this conclusion through a generous inter-pretation of section 2(1)(ii) of the LPA 1925 – the overreaching section. Effectively, the Court decided that if money is *payable* on the transaction, it must be paid to two trustees; if money is not payable, overreaching occurs so long as the mortgage is properly executed. This interpretation was bolstered by two policy considerations: first, that the aim of the overreaching machinery is to encourage the free alienability of co-owned land and this should be protected; second, that although the point in this case had not been decided before, many lenders had agreed to these types of mortgage and to have held in this case that they did not overreach because no capital monies changed hands would be most

---

221 Thus, overreaching will not occur, despite a transaction by two trustees, if this is to perpetrate a fraud – HSBC v. *Dyche* (2009), in which the 'sale' by A and B to A alone was in pursuit of a fraudulent design that if permitted would have destroyed the priority of C's equitable interest.

unfortunate. These are compelling reasons because although the argument that existing commercial practice assumed the law to be as stated in *Sood* is not an attractive one, it is realistic. On the other hand, apart from the absence of any authority for this decision, there are two real difficulties: first, that the words of section 2(1) of the LPA 1925 really do seem to contemplate the actual payment of money as a precondition for overreaching (even if they did not mean to); second, and more importantly, that overreaching can be justified as a matter of principle because the equitable owners' interests take effect in the money paid to the trustees. That is why the equitable interests can so easily be swept off the land. If overreaching can occur without the payment of such monies – because two trustees have charged the land for future debts – what protection/benefit is there for the equitable owners? Where do they get their *quid pro quo* for suffering overreaching? There is no capital money for them to take a share of, or if it was represented as credit at the bank, it is likely to have been spent by the time the case comes to trial. In other words, *Sood* is almost certainly correct, but for reasons of practice not principle.

The second alternative situation in which overreaching can occur is where the transaction is made under the provisions of the Settled Land Act 1925 relating to the operation of strict settlements (Chapter 5). As we shall see, a strict settlement is, in simple terms, a device for ensuring that land is given to X for life, thence to Y. There are 'trustees of the settlement' who will not be X or Y, but X (the life tenant) or the trustees may have power to deal with the land (e.g. sell it) and this transaction can be an overreaching transaction, sweeping the interests of Y into the proceeds of sale. Settlements will become increasingly rare due to the inability to create new strict settlements after 31 December 1996.[222]

The third circumstance is that overreaching is possible if the transaction is made by a mortgagee (e.g. a bank or building society) or personal representative in exercise of their paramount powers to deal with the land, provided of course that the powers are indeed paramount to the interests of any co-owners.[223]

The fourth is that overreaching may occur if the transaction is made under order of the court: for example, under section 14 of the Trusts of Land and Appointment of Trustees Act 1996. The court has wide powers to deal with land, particularly land subject to a trust. Any order of the court transferring the land to a third party, or directing that it should be sold, necessarily effects an overreaching transaction for the benefit of the transferee or purchaser.

2.9.3 The consequences of failing to overreach

It is only if both of the above conditions are satisfied that an overreaching transaction occurs. The existence of an overreachable right is simply a question of fact and rarely gives rise to problems. However, what is more common is failure to ensure that a proper overreaching transaction has occurred, thereby denying the purchaser the trump card and preventing the overreachable equitable interests from being swept off the title into the

---

222 Section 2 of the Trusts of Land and Appointment of Trustees Act 1996.

223 In this situation, the mortgagee must prove that its mortgage ranks first in priority, which means that it must either have the consent of the owners or have *already* overreached the equitable interests by being paid to two legal owners. If it does, then it may sell. This example of overreaching refers to a different situation – the sale by a mortgagee who already has the ability to sell and it overreaches both the legal and equitable interests of the borrowers.

purchase money. Usually, this is a result of a failure to pay the purchase money to two trustees as required by the most common type of overreaching transaction, as in *Boland*. Should there be a failure to overreach, there are two possibilities to consider.

First, if the equitable interest constitutes an overriding interest,[224] the purchaser will be bound by the interest and his use of land restricted accordingly (sections 29 and 30 of the LRA 2002). Thus a mortgagee may not recover all of the money it has lent on the security of the land. In fact, as in *Boland*, on most occasions there will be an overriding interest because the equitable owner will be in discoverable actual occupation within paragraph 2, Schedule 3 of the LRA 2002 (and previously under section 70(1)(g) of the LRA 1925). After all, the land is likely to be their home.

Second, if the equitable interest is not protected as an overriding interest, the purchaser who registers his title takes the land free of that interest (sections 29 and 30 of the LRA), although a person who is not a purchaser remains bound by the interest (section 28 LRA 2002). This is not surprising, being simply an example of the priority rules referred to above. Note again, however, that it is possible for an equitable owner to enter a restriction against the title – a standard Form A restriction – preventing a sale by only one legal owner.[225]

It sometimes causes surprise that even a purchaser who fails to overreach may still take the title free from the priority of the relevant equitable interest. This can be understood more clearly if it is remembered that overreaching is an exceptional process – like a trump card – that frees the purchaser from the normal rules of registered (or indeed unregistered) conveyancing by providing an automatic priority over certain equitable interests. If the trump card fails, the normal rules of registered conveyancing come back into play. Hence, the equitable interest may still be unenforceable against the purchaser if it is not protected as an overriding interest. To sum up, then, overreaching is a special procedure and it can nullify the proprietary status of certain equitable interests in certain specified circumstances. When it works, these equitable interests are transferred to the purchase price of the land and cannot affect a purchaser. When it fails, the rules of registered land take effect in the normal way.

2.10   Alteration of the Register

It is a central tenet of the land registration system that the register should be as accurate as possible so that it can be relied on by all persons intending to deal with the land. Thus, the registration of persons as registered proprietors and the due entry of registered charges, protected registered interests and restrictions should be free from error. Of course, this is the ideal, but in practice faults in the registration process and registrations based on

---

224   Remember, under the LRA 2002, a notice cannot be entered in respect of such an interest.

225   It seems unlikely that an equitable owner can enter a restriction preventing a sale by two legal owners because, if it were possible, it would provide a means of preventing overreaching. The author's view is that such a restriction – a non-standard restriction – is possible if ordered by the court under section 14 of the Trusts of Land and Appointment of Trustees Act. However *Coleman v. Bryant* (2007) suggests that such a restriction would never be ordered.

incomplete or inaccurate evidence do occur. Indeed, registrations based on fraudulent or negligent transaction are also a possibility.[226]

Consequently, the LRA 2002 establishes a statutory scheme to deal with changes to the register and the correction of mistakes. In broad terms, section 65 of the LRA 2002, operating through Schedule 4 of the LRA 2002, establishes the circumstances in which it is possible to make an 'alteration' the register and this is complemented by a power to give an indemnity (compensation) under Schedule 8 of the LRA 2002 when a person suffers loss by reason of a mistake in the register, whether or not that mistake is corrected.[227] This new scheme, which is a substantial improvement on that established by the LRA 1925 (even after its amendment),[228] allows alterations by either the court or the registrar (as the case may be) while at the same time seeking to ensure that the integrity of the register is not compromised by allowing widespread and wide-ranging alterations to be made. In this vein, it is important to appreciate that genuine errors by HM Land Registry in the input or understanding of information are rare, and that most claims for alteration arise from apparently proper applications based on false information offered by the applicant himself, either accidentally or deliberately.

2.10.1   General conditions for altering the register

Schedule 4 of the LRA 2002 establishes the circumstances in which the register may be altered either by the court or by the registrar. These are effectively four in number: first, in order to correct a mistake; second, to bring the register up to date; third, to give effect to any estate, legal right or interest that is excepted from the effect of registration;[229] and fourth (being a power exercisable only by the registrar) to remove superfluous entries.[230] The last three of these situations cover what might loosely be regarded as administrative alterations arising from the normal operation of the register. For example, the register might be brought up to date to reflect a change in the corporate name of the proprietor, an entry relating to a good leasehold title might be added or time-expired entries might be removed as superfluous. Consequently, the substantive ground of alteration is really the correction of a mistake.[231]

---

226 See *Pinto v. Lim* (2005), in which a person got themselves registered as sole proprietor by fraud – a forged signature – and then sold the land to an innocent third party.

227 See below section 2.11.

228 Under the LRA 1925, all cases of alteration were known as 'rectification'. Under the LRA 2002, 'rectification' means a special kind of alteration, being one that corrects a mistake and which prejudicially affects the title of a proprietor and so could give rise to an indemnity.

229 That is when the grade of title was good leasehold, possessory or qualified and so certain matters (according to which grade) were unaffected by the registration of the proprietor with this title.

230 Paragraphs 2 and 5, Schedule 4 of the LRA 2002.

231 It seems that the 'mistake' to be corrected does not have to be in the register or a consequence of the operation of the land registration system. Thus, in *Cygnet Healthcare v. Greenswan* (2009), the court ordered rectification where the 'mistake' was a failure in the parties' conveyancing transaction. HM Land Registry registered what it was given, but the parties had failed to ensure that an intended covenant was ever created. It is not clear if the power in Schedule 3 is available to deal with mistakes by the parties, as opposed to mistakes within the system. However, the statute itself is silent as to this.

The LRA 2002 effectively operates a double category of alterations in order to correct a mistake. First, there are those alterations that correct a mistake and that do not prejudicially affect the title of a registered proprietor. Applications for these 'harmless' corrections of a mistake are unlikely to be common and the power to alter in their respect might well arise under the 'administrative' alteration provisions of Schedule 4. Be that as it may, the court 'must' make an order altering the register in such cases following an application unless the circumstances are exceptional,[232] whereas the registrar 'may' do so under paragraph 5, Schedule 4.[233] In contrast, the correction of a mistake that does or could prejudicially affect the title of a registered proprietor are much more serious. These are known as 'rectifications' and are subject to special rules. Both the registrar and the court may order a rectification and, where the power exists, both must do so unless there are exceptional circumstances justifying a refusal.[234]

2.10.2   Rectification

Rectification is thus a special class of alteration of the register and its importance lies in the fact that it is the principal ground on which an indemnity may be claimed. Rectification is possible when there is (1) the correction of a mistake and (2) this would prejudicially affect the title of a registered proprietor.[235] Importantly, both limbs of the definition must be established before a rectification is possible, but it is likely that the meaning of 'mistake' and 'prejudicial' will be given a sufficiently generous interpretation to ensure that most applications to alter the register will be regarded as 'rectifications'.[236] For example, it is clear that a 'mistake' does not imply fault on any person's part, nor on the part of HM Land Registry. It is used in a descriptive not a judgmental sense. So, when an innocent person is registered as a proprietor consequent to a purchase from a vendor who in turn fraudulently acquired title from X, there has been a 'mistake' in the register because X should have been the proprietor and this 'mistake' existed not only when the fraudster acquired title through wrongful registration, but also when the innocent purchaser was registered.[237] The mistake is the error in the register that omits X as proprietor – how it was caused or by whom do not stop it being a mistake. Similarly, any proposed correction of a mistake that affects the value of the land or removes land from a title or results in the removal or addition of a registered proprietor is prejudicial within

---

232   Rule 126, LRR 2003.

233   Even though these are non-prejudicial corrections, a person may well wish to see the register altered and, presumably, if the registrar refuses to alter (but it is difficult to envisage why he would), an application can be made to the court.

234   Paragraphs 3 (court) and 6 (registrar), Schedule 4 of the LRA 2002.

235   Paragraph 1, Schedule 4.

236   But see *Derbyshire CC v. Fallon* (2007), in which the court (possibly incorrectly) decided that a proposed change to the register did not prejudicially affect the Fallons' title (and so was only an alteration) on the ground that if the land was not theirs on a 'true' appreciation of their title, any change to remove the land from their registered title merely reflected pre-registration reality and so did not affect them prejudicially. Of course, this ignores the fact that the register is the true title (section 58 of the LRA 2002) and that it is not permissible to introduce unregistered land concepts of title into decisions concerning registered title.

237   *Pinto v. Lim* (2005).

the meaning of the schedule.[238] Note, however, that an alteration made to give effect to an existing overriding interest can never be a 'rectification' because it does not prejudicially affect the title of the registered proprietor, because it (the overriding interest) was already binding on that proprietor and the alteration merely openly recognises that fact.[239]

However, even if these preliminary matters are resolved in the applicant's favour, the register may only be rectified against a registered proprietor in possession in certain circumstances.[240] This is a vital provision, for it demonstrates the fundamental policy of the LRA 2002 that, save in special circumstances, the register is conclusive and should protect the title of registered proprietors, particularly those in possession of the land. In this sense, possession means physical possession of the land,[241] although such possession may exist through the agency of others such as where the registered proprietor's possession exists through the physical presence of his tenant, mortgagee, licensee or beneficiary.[242] The special circumstances in which a proprietor in possession can find themselves subject to a rectification are three-fold: first, if the registered proprietor consents; second, if the registered proprietor has caused or substantially contributed to the mistake because he has either been fraudulent or not exercised sufficient care; or third, if it would be unjust not to correct the mistake. Importantly, these are now the only circumstances in which rectification may be ordered against a proprietor in possession and the tautologous provision in the old law that such rectification was possible under an order of the court has been abandoned.[243] It is obvious that rectification may be ordered 'against' a proprietor in possession if he consents, and so too where he is responsible for the mistake on which the claim for rectification is based, although it seems that the ground is still available even if the applicant for rectification was also partly responsible for the mistake.[244] The third condition must, however, be approached with some care. Under the LRA 1925, a similar provision was held not to imply a general power to rectify merely because it was thought just and equitable to do so.[245] In one sense, it will always be 'unjust' not to correct a mistake in the register – after all, it is a mistake and this appears to be the view taken in *Baxter v. Mannion* (2010) – but it is to be hoped that the courts do not regard this as an at-large power to disturb the title of a registered proprietor in possession by applying a loose 'fairness' criterion. Rather, like the position under the LRA 1925, this can be regarded as a failsafe where, despite being in possession and not consenting and not contributing to the mistake, the registered proprietor's title is still rectified. These cases

---

238   See *Cygnet Healthcare v. Greenswan* (2009).

239   This confirms the position under the LRA 1925: *Re Chowood's Registered Land* (1933).

240   The majority of rectifications will be against such a person. Where rectification is against another, these additional conditions do not apply.

241   Section 131 of the LRA 2002.

242   Ibid. But not through an adverse possessor.

243   Taken literally, this provision meant that when a court decided that old law rectification was needed, on whatever ground, this was an 'order of the court' justifying rectification against a proprietor in possession – see *Kingsalton v. Thames Water* (2001) and *Pinto v. Lim* (2005). This interpretation (albeit highly suspect) made the protection of a proprietor in possession a mere fig leaf and it is rightly abandoned under the LRA 2002.

244   This appears to have been the reason in *Cygnet Healhcare v. Greenswan* (2009).

245   *Norwich & Peterborough Building Society v. Steed* (1992).

will be rare, for the balance in such cases surely lies with the innocent possessory proprietor.[246]

Having thus established that there is a case for rectification, and that either the rectification is not against a registered proprietor in possession or that one of the three exceptions applies, both the court and the registrar must order rectification, unless there are exceptional circumstances that justify not making the alteration.[247] This is intended to ensure that once the claimant has goes through all of the hoops of establishing a claim for rectification, that rectification should normally take place. What 'exceptional circumstances' might be is as yet unclear, but the key word is 'exceptional' rather than 'unusual' or 'equitable' or 'fair'. It is a high hurdle and it is to be anticipated that most applications for rectification that progress to this point will be ordered.[248]

2.11   Indemnity under the Land Registration Act 2002

The authoritative status of the register means that there will always be cases in which a person suffers loss because of the workings of the registered land system. The power to alter and rectify the register is one response to this. The power of the court to order an indemnity (i.e. compensation) for a person who suffers loss is another response. As originally conceived in the LRA 1925, the entitlement to an indemnity was tied to the power to order rectification and still they remain mutually supportive aspects of the system. However, under the 2002 Act, the payment of an indemnity is more clearly identified as a standalone remedy, albeit most (but not all) cases will 'piggyback' on a claim for rectification.[249] The indemnity provisions are found in Schedule 8 to the Act and triggered by section 103. Interestingly, all claims for indemnity not settled by 13 October 2003, whether relating to facts occurring before or after the entry into force of the LRA 2002 and whether rectification is ordered because of the application of the old law or the new, are governed by this schedule.[250]

2.11.1   Indemnity as the consequence of a mistake

A right to claim an indemnity arises – and usually will be made – in consequence of a mistake that would have, or does, result in a rectification. In other words, for the right to an

---

246 So, in *Pinto v. Lim* (2005), just decided under the old law, the court refused to rectify against a proprietor in possession despite having the power to do so precisely because of his innocence and the fact that the land had been his undisturbed home for the previous four years. Indeed, this was despite the fact that the applicant for rectification might have had a difficult task in securing an indemnity, whereas the proprietor in possession would not have. Note *Ajibade v. Bank of Scotland* (2006). See *Baxter v. Mannion* (2010) where rectification was ordered against a proprietor in possession because otherwise it would have been unjust – given that the land 'really' did belong to the claimant.

247 Paragraphs 3 (the court), and 6 (the registrar) of Schedule 4 of the LRA 2002.

248 If a property has been converted to take account of the special needs of the registered proprietor, it might be 'exceptional' to refuse to rectify the title against such a person even though the claimant had established his case. If refused rectification, the claimant would turn to a claim for an indemnity.

249 Paragraph 1, Schedule 8.

250 Paragraph 19(1), Schedule 12 of the LRA 2002.

indemnity to arise, there must be both a mistake on the register and the correction of that mistake must prejudicially affect the title of the registered proprietor of the land or a charge over that land, or have already done so. However, that is merely the threshold for claiming an indemnity. In addition, the claimant must also establish any one of three further grounds. First, an indemnity may be payable if the correction of the mistake has caused loss. This implies that a correction has actually been made, and that the correction (not the initial mistake) has caused the loss. An example would be where an innocent person was removed as registered proprietor in order to correct a mistake and thereby loses title to land or who claims title under a disposition that turns out, without their knowledge, to be forged and thereby suffers rectification. This is likely[251] to be the favourite claim (along with the second, which is very similar) because the amount of compensation will be assessed according to the value of the land immediately before the rectification is ordered.[252] After all, the compensation is because of the correction, not the mistake. Second, an indemnity may arise where again the register has been corrected because of a mistake in a way that causes loss to the claimant, but the loss was caused by the mistake before the rectification. Third, where there has been a mistake that would justify rectification, but the mistake is not corrected, anyone who suffers loss may claim an indemnity, but the amount of the indemnity necessarily will be assessed according to the loss when the mistake was made, rather than when the register was rectified.[253] This is because the indemnity reflects loss caused by the mistake itself, not the correction (which, after all, was denied).

However, even after establishing that there was a rectification-type mistake, plus any one of the three factual grounds identified above, the claimant may still not receive an indemnity. This is because there are limits on indemnity claims. First, the claimant loses the right to an indemnity if any part of his loss has been caused by his own fraud – paragraph 5(1)(a), Schedule 8 of the LRA 2002.[254] Second, the claimant loses the right to an indemnity if his own lack of proper care caused his loss – paragraph 5(1)(b), Schedule 8 of the LRA 2002.[255] Third, an indemnity may be reduced if the claimant has partly contributed to his loss by lack of proper care – paragraph 5(2), Schedule 8 of the LRA 2002. Fourth, the right to apply to a court for an indemnity – which will be relevant only in those relatively rare cases in which the indemnity issue cannot be settled by negotiation with HM Land Registry – lapses six years after the claimant became aware (or should have become aware) that he had a claim – paragraph 8, Schedule 8 of the LRA 2002.[256] Finally, in respect of the special cases of mines and minerals, it is only possible to claim an indemnity if there is an entry on the register confirming that mines and minerals were included in the title – paragraph 2, Schedule 8 of the LRA 2002.

---

251 Paragraphs 1(a) and 2, Schedule 8 of the LRA 2002.

252 So, rising land prices mean increasing compensation: see *Pinto v. Lim* (2005).

253 Paragraphs 1(b) and 3, Schedule 8 of the LRA 2002 and *Pinto v. Lim* (2005). Hence, the level of compensation may reflect historic land values, when the mistake was made, not current land values, when the register is rectified.

254 This may include, in appropriate circumstances, fraud by the claimant's predecessors in title unless the claimant took under a disposition for value.

255 This may also include lack of proper care by a predecessor in title unless the claimant took under a disposition for value.

256 But the right to ask HM Land Registry and to accept its offer remains.

2.11.2   Indemnity for other reasons

A person may claim an indemnity for losses caused by a range of other circumstances described in paragraph 1, Schedule 8 of the LRA 2002. These are where the loss arises from a mistake in an official search, a mistake in an official copy, a mistake in a document kept by the registrar that is not an original and is referred to in the register, the loss or destruction of a document lodged at the registry for inspection or safe custody, a mistake in the cautions register,[257] or failure by the registrar to perform his duty under section 50.[258]

2.12   An Overview of the Land Registration Act 2002

It will be apparent from the detailed analysis above that the 2002 Act represents a fundamental shift in the way we think about registered land. It has been said many times, but the aim is to move to title by registration instead of registration of title. The introduction of electronic conveyancing is the driving force behind this and is the motivation for many of the reforms of the Act. The 2002 Act is packed with significant features, but some of the most notable are highlighted below.

- Legal leases of over seven years' duration must be substantively registered with their own title number. This trigger is likely to fall further to encompass legal leases of over three years.
- Mortgages of registered land may be created only by the 'charge by deed by way of legal mortgage' (section 23 of the LRA 2002).
- Unregistered interests that override are reclassified into those overriding a first registration (Schedule 1) and those rights that override a subsequent registered disposition (Schedule 3). The former schedule is more extensive than the latter. The role of actual occupation and the impact of easements are restricted for Schedule 3 rights. The aim is to eliminate undiscoverable overriding interests in respect of a disposition falling under section 29 of the LRA 2002.
- The way in which other third-party interests (once called 'minor interests') can be protected has been rationalised and simplified. All entries by way of notice confer priority on the right, but the entry may be by way of an agreed or unilateral notice. Restrictions control dealings by the registered proprietor rather than protect rights, but if a registered proprietor cannot deal with the land, he cannot defeat a third-party right.
- Rights arising by proprietary estoppel and 'mere equities' are proprietary (section 116 of the LRA 2002) and so may be protected by the entry of a notice or a restriction or may amount to an overriding interest as circumstances require.
- The circumstances in which the register may be altered have been clarified and the indemnity provisions have been recast.
- The Crown will be able to register its land for the first time by granting itself a title.

---

257 Concerning cautions against first registration where the land is unregistered.

258 Concerning specialist interests called 'overriding statutory charges'.

A new system of adverse possession applies to registered land in all cases in which the old 12-year period of adverse possession was not completed by 13 October 2003 – the date of the entry into force of the 2002 Act. Under the 2002 Act, rarely will a registered proprietor lose title through adverse possession if he is prepared to take action to evict the adverse possessor. There will be no 'limitation period' *per se* for registered land.

Many provisions of the 2002 Act are designed to facilitate electronic conveyancing. Thus, while for a time it *may* be possible to create and transfer property rights by electronic 'written contracts' and 'deeds' (section 91 of the LRA 2002), more importantly, in due course, the creation or transfer of most property rights in or over registered land will be ineffective unless completed by electronic registration. Rights not electronically registered will not exist (section 93 of the LRA 2002). The creation of the right will occur at the time of registration, the registration gap will disappear and the register will be a truer mirror. In time, and subject only to the limited overriding rights in Schedules 1 and 3, rights not entered on the register will not exist at all.

2.13 Chapter Summary

2.13.1 The nature and purpose of registered land

*   To ensure the *free alienability of land* by easing the conveyancing process through the establishment of certainty; by eliminating the vagaries of the old doctrine of notice and thereby protecting the purchaser; by enhancing the role of overreaching and thereby removing some obstacles to the sale of land that is subject to a trust of land.
*   To bring certainty to *land ownership* by establishing a register of titles, held at local district offices and online, that is conclusive as to ownership and which is backed by a legislative and financial guarantee; by establishing a defined list of rights that can take priority over the land automatically but which should be discoverable on physical inspection of the land (overriding interests); by establishing a register of rights adverse to the land so that an intending purchaser (including a mortgagee) will be aware of what they are about to buy (registered protected interests).

2.13.2 The three principles of registered land

The mirror principle encapsulates the idea that the register should reflect the totality of rights in and over the land, so as to ease and speed alienability. The mirror is not perfect, due to the existence of overriding interests, but over time it will become considerably more accurate as more rights are registered.

The curtain principle encompasses the idea that equitable interests existing behind trusts of land should be kept off the register and dealt with through the mechanism of overreaching. This has been largely achieved, although the cases in which overreaching is not possible has meant that sometimes the purchaser must lift the curtain.

The insurance principle encapsulates the idea that the State will guarantee the efficacy of the system by providing statutory compensation (an indemnity) to persons suffering loss by reason of the operation of the system.

2.13.3 An overview of registered land and the various classes of estates and interests

Under the LRA 2002, proprietary rights fall into four broad classes, not necessarily coterminous with their quality as legal or equitable interests.

*   *Registrable titles* are the legal freehold absolute in possession and the legal leasehold of over seven years' duration. The grade of title with which the registered proprietor is registered may be absolute, good leasehold, possessory or qualified. The grade of title helps to determine the extent to which the proprietor is bound by pre-existing adverse rights. Registration as registered proprietor confers the relevant estate at law, subject to the rights specified in sections 11 and 12 of the LRA 2002 (first registration) and sections 28, 29 and 30 of the LRA 2002 in respect of dispositions of registered land.
*   *Registrable charges*, being legal mortgages.
*   *Unregistered interests that override*, being interests that take priority automatically, without registration. They are found in Schedule 1 (first registration) and Schedule 3 (registered dispositions) of the LRA 2002. The most important types are short legal leases, the rights of persons in actual occupation of the land and legal easements. There are differences between Schedule 1 and Schedule 3 to reflect their different field of operation.
*   *Protected registrable interests*, comprising most third-party rights, are protected by entering either an agreed or unilateral notice. Unregistered interests generally lose priority in the face of a disposition for value (sections 29 and 30). The one considerable exception is if the registrable interest qualifies in some way as an overriding interest.

2.13.4 Overreaching

This is a process whereby certain equitable interests are removed from the land and transferred to the cash proceeds of a sale of that land. Overreaching will occur when the equitable right is overreachable *and* a proper overreaching transaction occurs. If these conditions are satisfied, the equitable interest cannot be protected as an overriding interest.

2.13.5 Alteration and indemnity

The register may be altered and a person may claim an indemnity under Schedules 4 and 8 of the LRA 2002. An alteration that amounts to a rectification will generate a potential indemnity claim.

 Further Reading

Cooke, E, 'The Land Registration Bill' [2002] Conv 11

Dixon, M, 'The reform of property law and the Land Registration Act 2002: A risk assessment' [2003] 67 Conv 136

'Forgery and land registration: The decision in *Malory Investments v Cheshire Homes*' [2009] Conv 127

Harpum, C and **Bignall**, J, *Land Registration*, Bristol: Jordans, 2004

Law Commission, *Land Registration for the Twenty-first Century: A Conveyancing Revolution*, Report No. 271, London: HMSO, 2001

'Priorities under the Land Registration Act 2002' [2009] LQR 401

'The feudal system and the Land Registration Acts' [2008] LQR 586

Chapter 3
Unregistered Land

3.1   Unregistered Land: An Introduction to the System of Unregistered Conveyancing

As we have seen in Chapters 1 and 2, land law and the conveyancing system in England and Wales underwent radical reform with effect from 1 January 1926. However, it was as obvious then as it is now that the task of transforming a basically feudal system of law into one that could adequately serve the twentieth century and beyond could not be accomplished overnight. Thus, from the very first, it was intended that registration of title and the accompanying provisions of what was then the Land Registration Act (LRA) 1925 would be phased in, rather like e-conveyancing is being phased in today under the LRA 2002. At first, registered conveyancing was restricted geographically to the main urban areas and it was not until 1 December 1990 that all of England and Wales became subject to compulsory first registration of title. This meant that much land remained within the old system of conveyancing, sometimes known as the system of 'private unregistered conveyancing', in order to distinguish it from the State-guaranteed system established by the Land Registration Acts. Although the amount of land that remains unregistered today is relatively small and getting smaller,[1] there is a residual need to understand the basic structure of unregistered land even though it is of diminishing importance.[2]

However, even accepting the unavoidable residual role for unregistered land, it was clear a long time before 1925 that the system of 'private unregistered conveyancing' in its original form was unwieldy, complicated and inefficient.[3] The pre-1926 law that might

---

1   Very roughly, in England and Wales, 30 per cent of land by area and 15 per cent by number of titles remains unregistered. This will be either land held by private individuals where there has been no dealing with the land for a considerable time or, much more likely, land held by institutions such as universities, churches, local authorities and the Crown as these bodies tend to exist indefinitely and only infrequently deal with their land holdings. It includes large areas of foreshore, waterways and uninhabited countryside held by the Crown that are unlikely to change ownership. Under the LRA 2002, the Crown may now grant itself a fee simple estate that it can register (section 79) and many local authorities are voluntarily registering their titles under special fee arrangements with HM Land Registry. Aside from many other benefits, one great advantage for local authorities who have to keep track of large property portfolios is that land registered under the LRA 2002 is protected to a very considerable extent from a claim of adverse possession (squatting) – see Chapter 11.

2   At one time, it could have been argued that the registered land system and the unregistered land system were simply different methods of conveying land and that they shared the same substantive content. Consequently, when this view was taken, cases arising in unregistered land could be applied with equal force to similar issues arising in registered land – see, for example, *Midland Bank v. Green* (1981). However, as time marched away from 1926, it became clear that the principles applicable in the unregistered land system and those applicable to registered land were diverging. It is now a basic premise of the LRA 2002 that land of registered title should not be seen as a mere shadow or version of land of unregistered title and that different substantive principles may well apply to each. Thus, the better view now is that land of registered title is of a fundamentally different character than that of unregistered title. For example, section 58 of the LRA 2002 ensures the conclusiveness of the register of title irrespective of defects that would mar a title in unregistered land. Similarly, the law of adverse possession now operates differently in each system.

3   It was, however, popular with lawyers, but possibly only because it was familiar. Anecdotally it is said that nearly 40 per cent of solicitors engaged in conveyancing retired before or soon after 1 January 1926 rather than face, or learn, the 'new' system of registered title.

still operate pending the arrival of comprehensive registration of title offered neither certainty to a purchaser nor adequate protection for a person who enjoyed rights over that land. For example, the doctrine of notice, and especially the development of constructive notice, could mean that a purchaser was bound by a third-party equitable interest even if that interest seriously devalued the use and enjoyment of his (the purchaser's) land, and in circumstances in which the purchaser 'knew' of the right only in the most vague or technical sense. Conversely, a person seeking to enforce an equitable right over someone else's estate (e.g. an equitable easement) might find their interest void against a purchaser through no fault of their own, and in circumstances in which they could have done little to protect it. Furthermore, the lengths to which a purchaser had to go to investigate the title of a proposed seller, and the potential number of persons with whom he had to agree a sale in cases of joint ownership, made unregistered conveyancing a burdensome and expensive task.

To meet these problems, and bearing in mind that an immediate move to wholesale adoption of registered title was not feasible, a great part of the 1925 legislative reforms was directed at establishing an intermediate but temporary system of conveyancing built around familiar concepts of unregistered title.[4] This makeshift system was to apply to dealings with land that was not registered at the time of the dealing and was meant to last only 30 years pending widespread registration of title across England and Wales. As we now know, this timescale was wildly optimistic and real progress towards widespread title registration was not made until the mid-1950s. Of course, the fact that compulsory first registration of title has been required in England and Wales for 20 years (from 1 December 1990), and that registered titles now comprise the vast majority of all titles, does mean that the system of unregistered conveyancing will diminish in practical importance. Yet the time has not yet come when it can be abandoned completely. That happy day will not be with us for a while, although the entry into force of the LRA 2002 has done much to propel us speedily towards that goal.[5]

3.1.1　What is unregistered land?

To describe a parcel of land as 'unregistered' means one thing only: that the title to the land (the freehold or leasehold estate) is established from old-fashioned title deeds and is not to be found in the register of titles governed by the LRA 2002. Unregistered land is land for which the title must be proved from the conveyancing history of the land as evidenced by the documents of title (i.e. the deeds and related documents such as those creating easements) and not by inspecting a register. It does not mean that there is no provision or opportunity for the registration of other rights and interests affecting the land, for, as we shall see, 'unregistered land' has its own system of independent partial registration. It is important that this is appreciated fully. Indeed, it is essential from the outset to remember that the system of unregistered land (with its partial system of registration) operates completely separately from the system of registered land. Of course, they both deal with the

---

4　The LPA 1925 applies equally to unregistered land and was supplemented by the Land Charges Act 1925. The latter has been replaced by the Land Charges Act 1972.

5　For example, by encouraging voluntary first registration of unregistered titles through reduced fees and emphasising the relative immunity of registered land from claims of adverse possession.

same type of property rights (freeholds, leaseholds, easements, covenants, etc.), and they share the concept of overreaching, but they do so in different and mutually exclusive ways. So, if title to land is not registered under the LRA 2002, it is 'unregistered land' and is to be dealt with according to the principles considered in this chapter. It does not borrow from the system of registered land, or vice versa.

3.2   An Overview of Unregistered Land

Given that it was intended to be a temporary modification of pre-1926 practice, it should come as no surprise that the system of unregistered land relies heavily on many of the old doctrines that characterised dealings with land before the great legislative reforms. Thus, unlike registered land, the distinction between legal and equitable rights is still of crucial importance when considering dealings with unregistered land, although the doctrine of notice has been replaced in all but a few instances by the partial system of registration referred to above. In essence, unregistered land can be viewed in the following way.

3.2.1   Estates in unregistered land

Title to land is not recorded in a register, nor is it guaranteed by the State through any indemnity legislation. However, the same types of estate may exist at law and in equity in unregistered land as exist in registered land. As noted in Chapter 1, the substantive law of estates is governed by the Law of Property Act (LPA) 1925 and the 'freehold' and 'leasehold' have the same essential character when found in either registered or unregistered land, albeit that they are proved and transferred in different ways. Thus, any purchaser of an unregistered estate in land must seek out the 'root of title' in order to ensure that the seller has a good and safe title to pass on. Title is proven by an examination of the title deeds and documents relating to previous dealings with the land. In addition, a prudent purchaser will make a thorough physical inspection of the land in order to ascertain whether there are any obvious defects of title and whether there are any obvious third-party rights (e.g. frequently used easements) that might prejudice his use of the land.[6]

As title is not registered, the quality of a selling estate owner's interest is determined according to the old common law rules as modified by the LPA 1925.[7] Thus, a legal title, whether freehold or leasehold, encapsulates the essence of ownership for the duration of the estate granted and a legal estate owner of unregistered title has no fear that a proper title will be compromised by any extraneous issues affecting the land, other than those interests binding as proprietary rights according to the rules of unregistered conveyancing. With an equitable estate (e.g. an equitable lease[8]), the estate owner also enjoys full rights over the land subject to the difficulties affecting all equitable interests: that is, they rank second to any previously created equitable right and are vulnerable in the face of a sale of the land to a purchaser of a legal estate for valuable consideration.

---

6   For example, is anyone else in possession of some of the land or are there any boundary issues?

7   Contrast this with registered land, where the title is guaranteed by the entry on the register and is conclusive (section 58 of the LRA 2002).

8   Where, for example, the proper formalities for the creation of a legal lease have not been observed.

3.2.2 Interests in unregistered land: Rights over another person's estate

'Interests' in unregistered land are of the same type as interests in registered land. There are easements, mortgages, covenants, profits, co-ownership rights, options and estoppels, as these are creatures of the substantive law.[9] They are the proprietary rights over someone else's land (more accurately, over their estate in it). Once again, however, it is the machinery of unregistered land – the way in which these interests affect another person's land particularly on sale or mortgage – that is different from registered title. For the purposes of exposition, and bearing in mind that the picture produced below is necessarily simplified, we may split these proprietary interests into four different groups: legal rights; equitable rights that are registrable under the Land Charges Act (LCA) 1972;[10] equitable rights that are not registrable under the LCA 1972 because they are subject to over-reaching; and equitable rights that are neither overreachable nor registrable under the LCA 1972.

3.2.3 Legal interests

Legal interests in another person's unregistered land, such as legal easements, legal mortgages and legal leaseholds are, in the main, automatically effective against the land over which they exist, even if not granted by the current landowner.[11] Consequently, they will bind automatically any person coming into ownership or occupation of the land, be they a purchaser, donee of a gift, devisee under a will or an adverse possessor. This is the old pre-1926 rule that 'legal rights bind the whole world' and is a principle of utmost importance in unregistered conveyancing and necessarily requires a clear distinction to be made between legal and equitable estates and interests. As we have seen (Chapter 1), this distinction turns primarily on the scope of section 1 of the LPA 1925, the way in which the estate or interest has been created and the possible existence of a trust. However, once a legal right has been established over the burdened land, there is no need to make further enquiries in order to assess whether the legal right is binding. The transferee's 'state of mind', the nature of his title or indeed any other matter is not relevant: legal rights bind the whole world. We must not think, however, that this unbending rule causes hardship to purchasers. The manner of creation of legal rights means that generally they are obvious to a transferee either from an inspection of the title documents (i.e. the deed required to create them is likely to be available or referred to in other documents) or from an inspection of the land itself (e.g. a tenant for three years or less will have no deed, but is very likely to be on the land). Consequently, even though a transferee is bound by these legal rights whether or not he is aware of them, the reality is that in most cases the transferee has in fact discovered the existence of these rights before completion of the transfer.

The singular exception to the rule that legal rights bind the whole world in unregistered conveyancing is provided by the 'puisne' mortgage. A puisne mortgage is a legal mortgage

---

9 This list is illustrative, not exhaustive.

10 Previously the Land Charges Act 1925.

11 If the current landowner is the grantor of the interest, he is, of course, bound by his grant, irrespective of the proprietary effect of the interests.

over land for which the documents of title of the mortgaged land have not been deposited with the mortgagee (the lender), usually because an earlier legal mortgage already exists and this earlier mortgagee has the documents. As the *puisne* mortgagee does not have the documents of title, he does not have the ability to prevent dealings with the land (for which the documents of title are necessary), and so the *puisne* mortgagee is not protected adequately against further dealings with the burdened land. Consequently, a *puisne* mortgage is registrable in unregistered land under the special system of land charges as a Class C(i) land charge, and such registration ensures that any subsequent dealings with the land are subject to the mortgage.[12] For example, if A is the unregistered freeholder of a house and granted a legal mortgage to X bank, X bank will retain the title documents to the house and is fully protected because it has the documents and can prevent A from selling the house without paying off the mortgage. If A then grants a second legal mortgage to Y bank, Y bank cannot prevent A from dealing with the land by controlling the documents (because X bank has them) and so Y must register its *puisne* mortgage as a land charge in order to safeguard it.

3.2.4 Equitable interests that are registrable under the Land Charges Act 1972

The second category of interests in unregistered land comprises those equitable rights[13] requiring registration as land charges under the LCA 1972 (replacing the LCA 1925). 'land charges' are defined in the LCA 1972, and the majority of equitable rights over unregistered land fall into this category, including equitable easements, restrictive covenants, equitable mortgages, equitable leases and estate contracts. This is crucial, because in order to bind a purchaser of unregistered land, a land charge *must* be registered in the appropriate way.[14] Failure to register as a land charge when required renders the interest void against a purchaser.[15] Importantly, this structure leaves no room at all for the doctrine of notice in respect of interests that qualify as 'land charges', for that doctrine is replaced by the system of land charge registration. Given that very many equitable interests in unregistered land are 'land charges', this means that the doctrine of notice is very nearly redundant as a feature of modern land law.[16] Note also that the registration of land charges has *absolutely nothing* to do with registered land. It refers to an independent, name-based register that operates purely in the field of unregistered conveyancing.

---

12 For an example, see *Barclays Bank v. Buhr* (2001).

13 Plus the legal *puisne* mortgage.

14 Remembering, of course, that 'registration' does not mean registration under the LRA 2002. This is not registered land.

15 But the interest would remain valid against a non-purchaser of the land, even if unregistered, such as the recipient of a gift, or beneficiary under a will or an adverse possessor.

16 Of course, it plays no part at all in registered land.

3.2.5   Equitable interests that are not registrable under the Land Charges Act 1972 because they are subject to overreaching

Certain equitable interests in another person's land are not registrable under the LCA 1972 because they are subject to overreaching. These equitable interests are overreachable in the same way as their counterparts in registered land. They comprise equitable co-ownership interests existing behind a trust of land and equitable interests operating behind a settlement established under the Settled Land Act 1925.[17] These interests are capable of expression in monetary terms (e.g. 50 per cent ownership of a property) and can be quantified as a share of the money received by the seller when the land is sold. Thus, being overreachable, they do not clog the title of a purchaser, and have no need to be entered in the land charges register.

3.2.6   Equitable interests that are neither registrable under the Land Charges Act 1972 nor overreachable

Equitable interests that are neither registrable under the LCA 1972[18] nor overreachable comprise a miscellaneous category of equitable rights that were either deliberately or accidentally left out of the land charges system, or have developed since that system came into operation. As they are neither overreachable nor registrable, the only way in which it is possible to determine whether these rights bind the unregistered title (i.e. are effective against a person purchasing the land) is to utilise the old doctrine of notice. This is the only time that the doctrine of notice remains applicable in modern land law after 31 December 1925. As we shall see, the number of equitable rights that fall into this category is small, and all but one or two arise in very untypical situations. Nevertheless, this category represents a 'hole' in the system of unregistered conveyancing and is one of the main reasons why a brief acquaintance with pre-1926 law and the doctrine of notice is still necessary.

3.3   Titles in Unregistered Land

The reforms of the LPA 1925 apply in equal measure to estates of unregistered title as they do to estates of registered title. After all, in very broad terms, the substance of the law is the same and it is the machinery for dealing with the two systems of conveyancing that is different.[19] Thus, the number of possible legal estates (titles) is limited to two, being the freehold (fee simple absolute in possession) and the leasehold (term of years absolute) (section 1 of the LPA 1925). As is self-evident, 'the title' in unregistered land is not

---

17 As we shall see, Settled Land Act settlements are not common, and since 1 January 1997 no new settlements can be created. Thus, the majority of overreachable rights arise under the 'trust of land' governed by the Trusts of Land and Appointment of Trustees Act 1996 (TOLATA).

18 Because they fall outside the scope of its definitions.

19 Note, however, that because of the effect of the LRA 2002, particularly in the area of e-conveyancing, the substantive principles of registered land and unregistered land are likely to diverge.

recorded on a register but remains provable from the title deeds and associated documents held by the estate owner.[20] In effect, when a purchaser wishes to buy an estate of unregistered land, there has to be an investigation of the 'root of title' in order to determine whether the seller owns the land and in order to determine the quality of that ownership.[21] This will still be relevant on the occasion of a sale of unregistered land today, save that, after this last sale, the new owner must apply for first registration of title under section 4 of the LRA 2002. This is what is meant by the spread of compulsory title registration to all of England and Wales, because a sale of an unregistered estate is one of the 'triggers' for compulsory registration of title.[22]

Obviously, then, the search for a root of title for unregistered land will become less frequent as more land becomes subject to title registration, but it was once a complicated and expensive task. Today, the task is easier because the search for a 'good' root of title has been reduced to an examination of only the last 15 years of dealings with the land, not the 30 years prior to 1970.[23] What this means is that when the purchaser of unregistered land is searching the title deeds for an unbroken chain of ownership to the present seller (in order to prove title), the purchaser need only find a proper conveyance to begin the chain that is at least 15 years prior to the date of sale. So, if a purchaser wishes to buy unregistered land in 2010, he must seek out a good root of title going back to the first proper conveyance that was executed before 1995, and a purchaser is entitled to rely on this proof of ownership even if there is some undisclosed defect in the title beyond the 15-year period. In practice, this search for a root of title rarely causes hardship to prospective purchasers, especially since most title deeds are kept together or even deposited with a bank that has advanced money by way of mortgage. As we shall see, however, the shortened period for establishing good root of title has caused difficulties in other areas of the system of unregistered conveyancing, especially in relation to the operation of the land charges system.

The mechanics of a typical sale and purchase of an estate in unregistered land is essentially a matter of conveyancing procedures, and largely falls outside the scope of this text. Briefly, the seller and purchaser will enter into a contract for the sale and purchase of the property ('exchange of contracts') after settling a number of pre-contractual matters, such as price, general area of land to be sold, existence of planning law obligations, and (usually) the existence of any local authority obligations affecting the land.[24] This contract commits each party to the bargain and may be specifically enforced if one party later tries to withdraw. The actual transfer is perfected by 'completion', this being the effective conveyance of the property by deed to the purchaser. In the interval between exchange of contracts and completion, the seller must produce an 'abstract of title' from which the purchaser should be able to deduce a good root of title beyond the 15-year period. Failure by the seller to produce a good title permits the purchaser to rescind the

---

20 Or held by the lender if there is a mortgage.

21 The same is true if a long lease is granted out of unregistered title or an existing lease is assigned.

22 Others include the transfer of a legal lease with more than seven years left to run, the new grant of a legal lease of more than seven years and a mortgage of the title (section 4 of the LRA 2002).

23 Section 23 of the LPA 1969. See also the reforms to the law of co-ownership wherein the maximum number of legal co-owners is limited to four who must be joint tenants (see Chapter 4).

24 Known as 'local land charges', and not to be confused with land charges under the LCA 1972.

contract. Also in the period between exchange and completion, the purchaser will search the land charges register to discover whether any land charges registered under the LCA 1972 are binding on the land. The obvious problem with this is that purchaser is already committed to buying the property *before* he searches the land charges register.[25] This is discussed below.

3.4   Third-party Rights in Unregistered Land

It is inherent in what has been said already about the 1925 reforms, that one important aim was to bring certainty and stability to the status of third-party rights in land. There are two reasons for this, the fundamental importance of which bears repetition.

1   A purchaser of land needs to know with as much certainty as possible whether any other person has enforceable rights over the land, and the extent and nature of those rights.
2   The owner of those rights needs to be sure that his rights are protected when the land over which they operate is sold or otherwise disposed of.

It is, then, in everybody's interest to have a workable conveyancing system wherein there is a balance between potential purchaser and third-party right-holder, and which is so uniform in its operation as to allow accurate predictions of what will happen to third-party rights in the majority of real-life situations. Unfortunately, the system of unregistered conveyancing does not achieve these goals to the extent necessary to pronounce it a success. Of course, it does work – or, rather, it is made to work – but there is no doubt that the system of unregistered conveyancing adopted with effect from 1 January 1926 has not stood the test of time. There are few who will be sorry to see it disappear.

Before examining in detail how third-party rights are regulated in unregistered land, three preliminary points of crucial importance should be noted. First, we are about to consider whether a person who obtains title to unregistered land, over which an adverse third-party interest *already* exists, is bound by that interest (e.g. a right of way): in other words, does the third-party interest survive a transfer of the land? This may depend on both the nature of the third-party interest and/or the status of the new owner. Second, in *all* cases, it is vital to know whether the third-party right is 'legal' or 'equitable'. This will, in turn, depend both on the definition of legal interests contained in section 1 of the LPA 1925 and the way in which the interest originally came into existence. Hence, an easement may be legal or equitable (section 1 of the LPA 1925) and everything will depend on how it came into being. Conversely, the burden of a restrictive covenant can only ever be equitable, irrespective of how it is created (section 1 of the LPA 1925). A knowledge of the distinction between legal and equitable rights is vital if the system of unregistered conveyancing is to be understood properly. Third, if it should prove the case that a third-party right is not binding on a new owner of the unregistered land, the right may still be enforceable between the parties that created the right. For example, in *Barclays Bank v. Buhr*

---

25 It is only after exchange of contracts that the purchaser receives the abstract of title and only then that the names of previous estate owners against which to search are revealed.

(2001), the Buhrs had granted a mortgage over their land. As we shall see, this proprietary right should have been registered as a Class C(i) land charge in order to remain enforceable should the land come into the hands of a purchaser.[26] It was not so registered and hence was not enforceable by the bank against the new owner of the property – it was in this sense 'void'. Nevertheless, as between the bank and the Buhrs, the mortgage remained enforceable, as these were the parties that had created the right by a contract between them. Thus, the bank was able to recover some of its money from the proceeds of sale by suing them on this contract when the Buhrs sold the house.

3.5 The Purchaser of Unregistered Land and the Protection of Legal Rights

With the one exception noted above (the *puisne* mortgage), a fundamental principle of unregistered conveyancing is that 'legal rights bind the whole world'. So, if a person buys, is given, or comes to possess, a piece of unregistered land, he will take that land subject to virtually every legal interest over it. Such legal interests may be, for example, a legal lease granted by the previous owner or a legal easement conferring a right of way over the land. Short of obtaining a waiver or release of the right from the person entitled to the benefit of it, there is little a transferee can do to avoid being bound. However, lest this be thought to be a harsh and unfair rule, we must always remember that only specified estates and interests may be 'legal', and even then they must come into being in the proper fashion. Indeed, the most important reason why it is *not* unfair that legal rights should bind the land automatically is that they are usually perfectly apparent to a purchaser who investigates his purchase properly. This is because, first, most legal interests come into being formally, by use of a deed, which is then kept with the title documents; second, the rights are obvious to a prudent purchaser making a physical inspection of the land, as is the case where a tenant occupies the land, or the existence of an easement is indicated by a driveway. In other words, a potential purchaser will nearly always know of the existence of these rights and can act accordingly, either by offering a lower price or walking away. However, the correct view is *not* that these rights are obvious and that this is why they bind the land; rather, it is that it is necessary to have some rights that are capable of automatically surviving changes of ownership in land, and one way of avoiding any undue hardship is to ensure so far as possible that only those rights that are apparent or obvious have this effect. To recap then, the rule is that legal rights bind a transferee *whether or not* he knew about them, and *whether or not* they were, in fact, obvious from an inspection of the title deeds or land. In most cases, however, the purchaser will be so aware.

---

26 It was a *puisne* mortgage (see section 3.6.1 below), this being the one legal interest that requires registration under the LCA 1972.

3.6   The Purchaser of Unregistered Land and the Protection of Equitable Interests: The Land Charges Act 1972

A major part of the unregistered land system is devoted to the protection of equitable third-party interests in land. The most important method by which this is attempted is through a system of registration introduced by the LCA 1925 and now codified in the LCA 1972. To reiterate, this has nothing to do with any of the registration facilities available in registered land under the LRA 2002.

In order to understand the system of registration of land charges, it is important to appreciate that there are three stages in assessing whether an equitable right binds the land when the land passes to a new estate owner.

1   The first issue is whether the equitable interest is *registrable* under the LCA 1972. In other words, does the particular equitable interest fall within any one of the classes of right that are required to be registered as a land charge in order to bind a purchaser of the land? This depends on the statutory definition of 'land charges' in the LCA 1972. If it does *not* qualify, and so is *not* registrable, then the equitable interest is either overreachable (see section 3.7 below) or within the exceptional class discussed below in section 3.8.

2   The second question is, assuming that the equitable interest is registrable, has it in fact been registered and what is the effect of the registration?

3   Third, if the right is registrable, but has not been registered, what is the effect (if any) on a transferee of the unregistered land?

These three issues will be addressed below, but first the *machinery* of land charge registration needs to be examined. This is of a unique character. Unlike registered land, land charges are not entered against the title to the land – after all, this title is not entered on any register but is provable from the title documents. Consequently, land charges are registered against 'the name of the estate owner whose estate is intended to be affected' as required by section 3(1) of the LCA 1972. For example, if a registrable equitable interest is alleged to bind the land owned by Mr X, having been created during Mr X's ownership, it must be entered on the land charges register against the name of Mr X. Indeed, even if the land is then sold to Mrs Y and then to Miss Z, the land charge will remain entered against the name of Mr X. This is known as the 'named-based' system of registration, and it has given rise to a number of practical difficulties for purchasers, as we shall see below in section 3.9.

As briefly discussed above, when a person wishes to purchase unregistered land, he will make a search of the land charges register to determine the existence of any registered land charges. The name-based system means that the purchaser must make an official search *against the names* of all previous estate owners revealed in the root of title in order to discover whether any charges are registered. These names are usually readily discoverable from the documents of title provided by the seller, although the search is usually undertaken *after* the seller and purchaser have entered into an enforceable contract to sell the property, because it is only then that the purchaser has access to the title deeds and so may discover the relevant names. Of course, this means that a purchaser might discover a registered land charge that would seriously diminish the value of the land they propose to buy, yet he is bound by contract to go through with the sale. To meet the obvious injustice that this situation can create,[27] section 24(1) of the Law of Property Act 1969 provides that a purchaser shall be entitled to escape from the contract if he did not have real notice of the registered land charge at the time he entered the contract. This is a necessary modification to the normal rule that contracts for the sale of land can be specifically enforced and is justifiable because the purchaser's difficulties are generated entirely by the name-based system of registration of land charges, and not because of some act of the parties themselves.

Bearing this in mind, two important consequences flow from the making of an official search of the land charges register. First, if a search is made in the proper manner – against the correct name and in respect of the land described in the title deeds – an official search certificate is issued to the purchaser and this is conclusive according to its terms, even if the register itself says something different (section 10(4) of the LCA 1972). Thus, if a registered charge is not revealed through error, the purchaser still takes the land free of that charge (the certificate is conclusive), and the right as a right enforceable against the land is lost.[28] On the other hand, a defective search cannot be relied on, as in *Horrill v. Cooper* (2000), in which the requested search did not adequately follow the description of the land as given in the title deeds and so a 'clear' certificate in the name of the estate owner did not absolve the purchaser from being bound by the correctly registered land charge (a restrictive covenant). Second, the purchaser has a 15-day 'priority period' from the date of the official search in which to complete his purchase, safe in the knowledge that only those charges revealed by the official search will be binding against him. Charges registered in the interim (i.e. within the purchaser's priority period) will not be binding on the purchaser if completion of the purchase occurs within that period (section 11(5) of the LCA 1972). However, this presupposes that the purchaser has searched the names correctly, and that all of the relevant names have been searched. In this connection, it must always be remembered that the certificate is conclusive as to the search *requested*, and not as to the search that the purchaser should have made. This has caused some difficulties where defective searches or defective registrations take place (see section 3.9 below).

3.6.1   The classes of registrable land charge under the Land Charges Act 1972

Broadly speaking, the interests that are capable of registration as land charges are those rights that have an adverse affect on the value of the land or the enjoyment of it, and which are not suitable for overreaching, being interests that are not easily translated into a monetary equivalent. With the exception of the *puisne* (legal) mortgage, they can be referred to as 'commercial' equitable interests in order to distinguish them from the overreachable 'family' equitable interests. Although there are some other matters that can be registered under the LCA 1972 so as to bind transferees (e.g. pending land actions, writs

---

27 Because the land charge remains binding on the purchaser should he proceed to buy (section 198(1) of the LPA 1925) even though it could not have been discovered until after the contract was made.

28 It may be that the owner of the registered charge can seek damages from the registrar by suing in negligence, as occurred in respect of the register of local land charges in *Ministry of Housing and Local Government v. Sharp* (1970). However, this is not clear because section 10(6) of the LCA 1972 could be interpreted as preventing such an action.

– see section 3.6.5), we are concerned primarily with the six classes of land charge defined in section 2 of the Act. If an equitable interest falls outside of these classes, it is not registrable as a land charge.

A   Class A relates to certain statutory charges that are created on the application of an interested person under an Act of Parliament (section 2(2) of the LCA 1972). These statutory charges usually relate to some work undertaken by a public body in relation to the land (not being a local land charge), the cost of which is chargeable to the owner, or where an Act of Parliament charges land with the payment of money for very specific purposes. In either case, the 'cost' is secured by means of the Class A land charge. Although not rare, rarely do they generate problems, being extinguished by payment of the sum charged.

B   Class B relates to certain statutory charges that arise automatically (section 2(3) of the LCA 1972). These are very similar to Class A land charges, save only that the charge is not created by some person petitioning the land charges registrar but arises automatically by the effect of relevant legislation. A charge for the costs (or part thereof) of recovering property with the assistance of legal aid falls within Class B.

C   Class C is one of the most important classes of land charge. It comprises interests that can have a profound effect on the land over which they exist. Many are genuinely 'adverse' to the estate owner, being rights that control his use and enjoyment of the land, or detract from its capitalised value on sale. Class C is divided into four subclasses.

C(i)   Being a legal mortgage that is not protected by the deposit of the title deeds of the property with the lender. This is the *puisne* mortgage referred to above, and is an exceptional example of a legal interest being registrable as a land charge (section 2(4)(i) of the LCA 1972). As with all land charges, failure to register a puisne mortgage means that it will be void against a purchaser – see *Barclays Bank v. Buhr* (2001). As previously noted, this exceptional need to register a legal right is motivated by a desire to offer protection to the *puisne* mortgagee, given that it will not have control of the documents of title. It is interesting, then, that if the mortgagee fails to make use of the registration machinery that exists for the mortgagee's protection, that mortgagee will suffer the voidness of its charge if the land is transferred to a purchaser. Another solution could have been to allow the *puisne* mortgage to be binding automatically as with other legal interests, but with the option that registration as a land charge would be available if the mortgagee wished to prevent the estate owner from granting further mortgages without the mortgagee's consent. The opposing argument is that if this were the scheme, then the purchaser could not rely on an inspection of the relevant land charges register to determine the existence of a *puisne* mortgage (although, of course, this is true already of all other legal interests).

C(ii)   Being 'a limited owner's charge': that is, a charge or mortgage that a person such as a life tenant under the Settled Land Act 1925 (a 'limited owner') may be entitled to levy against the land because of obligations discharged by him – for example, because of the payment of inheritance tax on death of a previous estate owner (section 2(4)(ii) of the LCA 1972). These special charges are relatively uncommon, but it is important to appreciate that it is the charge or mortgage that is registrable, not the life interest itself.

C(iii) Being 'a general equitable charge' which amounts to a residual category that catches specific charges or mortgages not mentioned elsewhere (section 2(4)(iii) of the LCA 1972). However, this is not a completely open-ended category, for section 2 makes it clear that it does not include an equitable co-ownership interest behind a trust of land or a successive equitable interest under a strict settlement (because both may be overreached) and it does not include any charge that is a charge over the proceeds of sale of land rather than the land itself.[29] Moreover, it appears that it does not include equitable interests arising by virtue of proprietary estoppel because, according to Ives v. High (1967), these interests could not have been in contemplation of the LCA 1925 (as was) given that the doctrine of estoppel had not been developed fully at that time.[30]

C(iv) 'Estate contracts', being enforceable agreements to convey a legal estate (section 2(4)(iv) of the LCA 1972). This class is important as, among other things, it effectively includes all manner of equitable interests provided that they are 'equitable' because of a failure to observe the proper formalities that would have constituted them as legal interests.[31] Thus, equitable leases are registrable as Class C(iv) land charges, as they result from an enforceable contract to grant a legal lease (Walsh v. Lonsdale (1882), and see Chapter 6), as are equitable mortgages of a legal estate. Also included are true contracts to purchase a legal estate, such as options to purchase land (Armstrong v. Holmes (1993)) and certain rights of first refusal to buy land (rights of pre-emption). However, it is clear that only those contracts that are for the grant of a proprietary interest in land fall within this head. Class C(iv) cannot confer any protection for contracts for personal interests in land (Thomas v. Rose (1968)). Third, certain special types of claim, not truly contracts, are included in this class by reason of statute because it is desirable that they should be made registrable in order to alert potential purchasers. A good example is a previous tenant's request for an 'overriding lease' made under the Landlord and Tenant (Covenants) Act 1995.[32] In practice, then, the 'estate contract' in all of its guises is one of the most frequently registered classes of land charge, both because it can arise in a wide variety of situations and because of the effect an estate contract can have on the value of the land it affects when the time comes to sell it. For example, if A, the freehold owner, has granted B an option to purchase the land, this is an estate contract. If B then registers it against A's name, A's ability to deal subsequently with the land is much reduced; any purchaser from A takes the land subject to B's prior right to buy it. Note, however, that in order to be registrable as an estate contract under Class C(iv), the 'contract' must itself be validly created. As discussed in Chapter 1, the majority of contracts for the disposition of an interest in land currently must be made in writing, incorporating all of the terms and signed by both parties within the meaning

---

29 See, for example, Re Rayleigh Weir Stadium (1954).

30 Consequently, the equitable estoppel easement in that case was not a registrable land charge under either Class C(iii) or D(iii).

31 Thus, the class cannot include those interests that could never be legal under section 1 of the LPA 1925.

32 Section 20(6) of the Landlord and Tenants (Covenants) Act 1995.

of section 2 of the Law of Property (Miscellaneous Provisions) Act 1989. A contract that does not fulfil these conditions is not registrable as a Class C(iv) land charge because it is no valid contract at all. Likewise, those proprietary rights that may be created informally (e.g. by proprietary estoppel) are not registrable under this class, as they do not spring from a contract.

D   Class D is divided into three subclasses.

D(i)   Being an Inland Revenue charge on land in respect of taxes payable on death under the Inheritance Tax Acts (section 2(5)(i) of the LCA 1972).

D(ii)   Being restrictive covenants created after 1925, provided that they are not covenants between a lessor and lessee (section 2(5)(ii) of the LCA 1972). For example, where one landowner (A) promises his neighbour (B) that he will not carry on any trade or business on his (A's) own land, the neighbour may register the 'restrictive covenant' against A's name. However, if the covenant is made between lessor and lessee and affects the leasehold land (as where a tenant promises not to keep pets on the leasehold premises), special rules apply and these are discussed in detail in the chapter on leases.[33] These special rules – themselves a mix of common law and statute – provide an adequate system for the enforcement of leasehold covenants outside the registration scheme of the LCA 1972 (and indeed that of the LRA 2002 for registered land).

D(iii) Equitable easements, rights or privileges over land created after 1925, being easements and similar rights that are equitable because they are created informally or for an estate that is not itself legal[34] (section 2(5)(iii) of the LCA 1972). Importantly, this category does not include all equitable easements created over land after 1925, for according to *Ives v. High* (1967), it excludes equitable easements that arise by proprietary estoppel. In other words, Class D(iii) includes only those rights that could have been 'legal' if properly created, not those rights that are creations of equity alone.[35]

E   Class E relates to annuities created before 1926 (section 2(6) of the LCA 1972), being yearly sums payable to a specific person. Annuities created after 1925, provided that they comply with certain conditions, are registrable as Class C(iii) land charges.

F   Class F relates to a spouse's 'matrimonial home right' arising under section 30 of the Family Law Act (FLA) 1996 and registrable as a land charge by virtue of section 31 of that Act.[36] These rights are essentially personal rights that spouses or civil partners enjoy against their partners to occupy the matrimonial home. However, despite being personal in nature and for social and policy reasons, Parliament has determined that these rights should be treated as being equivalent to proprietary rights for certain purposes and this is put into effect by making them registrable as land

---

33 Chapter 6. See *Dartstone v. Cleveland Petroleum* (1969) for problems when such covenants affect land other than the land that is subject to the lease. Being contained in a lease, they are not registrable under the LCA 1972 but neither do they fall within the special regime applicable to leasehold covenants.

34 For example, an easement attached to an equitable lease.

35 The reasoning was followed in *Shiloh Spinners v. Harding* (1973) in respect of an equitable right of re-entry in a lease.

36 This replaces the former regime of the Matrimonial Homes Act 1983 and in most respects is identical.

charges. Consequently, if registered against a spouse or civil partner, that spouse or civil partner[37] and any subsequent purchaser, may be bound by the registered right of occupation. Such registration is relatively uncommon because essentially it is a hostile act against the owning spouse or civil partner, but it can be used as a precautionary step by one of the partners when the relationship starts to deteriorate. However, given that the spouse or civil partner against whom the charge is registered is taken to promise any purchaser that he will give vacant possession (Schedule 4, section 3(1) of the FLA 1996), the effect of registering a Class F land charge is that the partners will have to settle their differences before the house is sold. Should the partners fail to resolve matters before a sale, the consequences can be serious, as in Wroth v. Tyler (1975), in which the husband's inability to complete the contract with the innocent purchaser following the registration of a Class F land charge led to legal action and bankruptcy.

3.6.2   The effect of registering a land charge

It has been noted already that the machinery of the LCA 1972 requires a registrable charge to be entered on the register against the name of the estate owner who owns the land affected at the time the charge is created. This has three important consequences. First, in order to be sure that a registrable interest will be enforceable against a subsequent purchaser of the land, the land charge must be entered against the correct name of the estate owner that first created the right. Normally, it would be registered by the person who was first given the benefit of the right.[38] For these purposes, the correct name is the full name of the current estate owner as it appears on the title deeds of the land to be affected.[39] If an entry is made against the wrong name (or more likely an incorrect version of the right name), as in Diligent Finance v. Alleyne (1972), then an official search against the correct name will confer protection on the purchaser for the duration of the priority period, because the charge will not be revealed by the certificate, and the certificate is conclusive. The purchaser will take the land free of the incorrectly registered charge. For example, if the estate owner's name is William Smith, but the land charge is registered against Bill Smith, a purchaser who searches against 'William Smith' will take the land free of the charge, provided also that the search of name was linked to the relevant land or a reasonable description of it (Horrill v. Cooper (2000)). However, as illustrated by Oak Co-operative Society v. Blackburn (1968), if the purchaser also searches against the wrong name, then the registration of the land charge against a version of the correct name (albeit actually incorrect) will protect the land charge.[40] In other words, if both registration and search are defective as to the correct name, the registration of the charge will be effective to protect the interest, provided that the name against which it was actually registered is a reasonable version of the correct name. For example, assuming that the estate owner's

---

37 Assuming they own a legal estate in the land (section 31(13) of the Family Law Act 1996).

38 In practice, this would be the solicitor or licensed conveyancer that acted in the transaction that generated the registrable right.

39 Standard Property Investment plc v. British Plastics Federation (1987).

40 In Oak, the correct name was Francis David Blackburn, but the search was made against Francis Davis Blackburn and the purchaser was not protected by the search certificate. This reasoning was approved in Horrill v. Cooper (2000).

name is William Smith, and the land charge is registered against Bill Smith, if the purchaser searches against Walter Smith, the land charge binds the purchaser. Of course, a defective search will always lose priority to a correctly registered charge. Thus, if the estate owner's name is William Smith and the land charge is registered against William Smith, a purchaser will be bound by the land charge if he searches against the wrong name (e.g. Bill Smith) and the charge is not revealed. Also, in cases in which the search was made against the correct name but the affected land is misdescribed (as where a wrong postcode or town is requested in the search), the properly registered charge will prevail because the search certificate is only conclusive as to the actual search made, as in *Horrill v. Cooper*.

Second, the charge must be entered against the name of the person who is the estate owner of the land intended to be bound *at the time the charge is created*. So, for example, if A contracts to sell land to B, B must register this estate contract (a Class C(iv) land charge) against the name of A. This is perfectly straightforward. If B then enters into a subcontract to sell the land to C *before* B actually acquires the unregistered title, C must also register their estate contract against A, because A is the estate owner of the land that is to be bound at the time the charge is created.[41] C can only safely register against B if B has acquired title before making the contract with C and failure to register appropriately will mean that the contract is unprotected. There are then some pitfalls for purchasers involved in a series of subsales if they do not know the name of the initial estate owner (first vendor) or, as is more likely, that they do not realise they are involved in a subsale at all!

Third, having taken account of the two points above, a correct registration of a land charge has a powerful effect on the land over which it operates. According to section 198(1) of the LPA 1925, registration of a land charge is 'deemed to constitute actual notice of the fact of such registration, to all persons and for all purposes connected with the land'. Although it is expressed rather elliptically, this means that if the charge is registered, it will bind all future purchasers and transferees of the land. This 'bindingness' is expressed in terms of notice because from 1 January 1926, this system of registration was to replace the old 'doctrine of notice'. However, it is vital to remember that for a registrable land charge, registration alone means that it is binding. It does not matter whether the purchaser either actually knew or did not actually know of the existence of the charge. Registration is not just one form of alerting the purchaser to the existence of the charge; it is the only method of alerting the purchaser and therefore making them bound. As discussed below, a potential purchaser who has knowledge of such an adverse right by other means, but where there is no registration of it, will not be bound by the unregistered land charge when they come to purchase, a point well illustrated by *Midland Bank v. Green* (1981), in which the House of Lords confirmed that an unregistered option to purchase the land[42] was not binding on a purchaser even though the purchaser had known of the option (knowing that it was unregistered) and even though the sole purpose of the sale was to destroy the option.[43]

The powerful effect of properly registering a land charge against the name of the correct estate owner – in that it becomes binding on all future purchasers and other transferees of the land – is further illustrated by the fact that a registered land charge

---

41 *Barrett v. Hilton Developments* (1975).

42 It was an estate contract and should have been registered as a Class C(iv) land charge.

43 The seller was the father, the purchaser was the mother and the unregistered option belonged to the son and daughter-in-law.

remains binding on a purchaser even if he could not possibly have discovered the names of the estate owners against whom to make a search. So, a purchaser of a leasehold estate will be bound by charges registered against the name of the former owner of the leasehold estate *and* by charges registered against the names of the owners of the freehold estate out of which the lease is carved. This is so even though a leaseholder has no right to investigate their landlord's title,[44] and hence has no way of discovering the names of the freeholders against which to search. According to *White v. Bijou Mansions* (1938), this is the clear effect of section 198(1) of the LPA 1925, even though section 44(5) of the LPA 1925 would seem to say that a tenant in such circumstances is not fixed with notice of the relevant charge! Likewise, a purchaser of unregistered land has no right to view title documents that exist behind the root of title. Yet, root of title is only 15 years, so a purchaser may well be bound by charges registered against names that appear in a conveyance made more than 15 years before the date of the transaction under consideration. These names are potentially undiscoverable – the purchaser having no right of access to them – but the registered land charge is binding (section 198 of the LPA 1925). To meet this unjust situation (which was exacerbated when root of title was reduced to 15 years instead of 30, in 1970), section 25(1) of the Law of Property Act 1969 provides that a purchaser may obtain compensation for being bound by a registered land charge hidden behind the root of title if:

1   the transaction causing loss takes place after 1 January 1970;[45] and
2   the purchaser had no actual (i.e. real) knowledge of the hidden charge; and
3   the charge is registered against the name of an estate owner that is not revealed in any of the documents of title.

Clearly, this provision for statutory compensation is essential, given the prospect that a purchaser might be bound by a land charge hidden behind the root of title. It is, of necessity, a compromise and demonstrates clearly the inadequacies of the land charge system of registration.[46]

3.6.3   The consequences of failing to register a registrable land charge in general

As the paramount policy of the LCA 1972 is to protect both the purchaser of land and the owners of any third-party rights in that land (by bringing a measure of certainty to dealings with unregistered land), it is not surprising that there is a heavy penalty for failure to register a *registrable* interest. The fundamental point is that while failure to register a land charge does not affect its validity as between the parties that created it,[47] nevertheless such failure destroys its validity against any future purchasers of the land. In simple terms, if a person purchases land over which there exists a registrable, but unregistered, land charge, that purchaser and all subsequent transferees are not bound by the charge. Lack of registration equals voidness *even if the purchaser actually knew of the charge* – see section 199 of the LPA

---

44 *Patman v. Harland* (1881).

45 When a good root of title was reduced to 15 years.

46 That said, claims to compensation are very rare.

47 See above, *Barclays Bank v. Buhr* (2001).

1925, as illustrated by *Midland Bank v. Green* (1981) in the clearest terms. In that case, the sale and purchase was between husband (the original estate owner) and wife (the purchaser) for a sum considerably less than the true market value and was carried out precisely to defeat an unregistered land charge granted to their son. In a judgment that upholds the integrity of the land charge registration system to the utmost degree, the House of Lords confirmed that it was not a fraud to take deliberate advantage of the system by selling to defeat an unregistered right (there was no obligation of good faith), and that provided that the consideration paid was 'money or money's worth', it did not matter that it was less than the true value of the land.

However, this simple statement of principle hides much detail and in fact, the precise circumstances in which an unregistered land charge is void depends on the particular class of land charge and the status of the person who takes a transfer of the land burdened by the charge. After all, we should not forget that a central aim of the land charge system is to protect 'purchasers' and so we must consider also whether the 'voidness' rule applies in equal measure to persons who come into possession of the land without being purchasers. Finally, and by way of exception, we should also note there are some special circumstances in which an unregistered land charge may be upheld against a purchaser or other transferee for reasons not connected to the principles of land charge registration. The rules are not complicated, and are discussed in detail below.

3.6.4   The voidness rule

In order to determine precisely the consequences of a failure to register a registrable land charge, we must consider the precise type of land charge in issue and the nature of the transferee of the burdened land who is seeking to avoid enforcement of the land charge. This is sometimes known as the 'voidness rule', and may be expressed as follows.

1   A purchaser or transferee's knowledge of the existence of a registrable, but unregistered, land charge is generally irrelevant in determining whether it binds them when they become the new owner of the burdened land – see section 199 of the LPA 1925 as illustrated by *Midland Bank v. Green* (1981).

2   Class A, B, C(i), C(ii), C(iii) and F land charges, if not registered, *are void against a purchaser of any interest in the land* (i.e. a legal or equitable estate) *who gives valuable consideration* (sections 4 and 17 of the LCA 1972). In other words, a person who buys an equitable or legal freehold or leasehold, or who takes an equitable or legal mortgage, will obtain the land free of these unregistered land charges if they gave 'valuable consideration'. Actual knowledge of the charge is irrelevant. Moreover, as illustrated by *Midland Bank v. Green*, the consideration need only be valuable; it need not be adequate.

3   Class C(iv) and D land charges, if not registered, *are void against a purchaser of a legal estate in the land who gives 'money or money's worth'* – section 4 of the LCA 1972 – as illustrated by *Lloyds Bank v. Carrick* (1996), in which the defendant's estate contract[48] was held void against the purchaser[49] due to lack of registration. That the voidness rule for Class

---

48 It was a contract to purchase the remainder of a long lease.

49 Who was a mortgagee of the premises who had 'purchased' the estate by lending money.

C(iv) and D land charges operates only in favour of a purchaser of a *legal* estate means that its effect is more limited than that applying to the other classes. So, a purchaser of an equitable lease, or a bank lending money by means of an equitable mortgage, remains bound by an *unregistered* Class C(iv) and D land charge.[50] There is also a difference between 'valuable consideration' and 'money or money's worth', the latter being slightly narrower than the former. So, for example, a transfer of a legal estate in land to a newly married couple 'in consideration of marriage' is valuable consideration, but it is not 'money or money's worth' and the purchasers (the newly married couple) would still be bound by unregistered Class C(iv) or D land charges, but not by those of other classes.[51]

4 All land charges, *even if unregistered, are valid against a transferee of the land who is not a purchaser.* This will include a donee of the land by way of gift, a devisee under a will (i.e. the beneficiary of a gift of land) and an adverse possessor whether in the process of completing, or having completed, the requisite period of adverse possession. In all of these cases, the new estate owner will be bound by all pre-existing property rights, whether registered or not, precisely because they are not purchasers.

5 All land charges, *even if unregistered, will be valid against a purchaser who has indulged in fraud.* This is another example of the well-established maxim that 'equity will not permit a statute to be an instrument of fraud (i.e. the voidness rule of the LCA 1972)'. However, the real difficult problem is to identify what constitutes 'fraud' for this purpose. Certainly, the purchaser's mere knowledge or notice of the unregistered charge does not constitute 'fraud' on his part,[52] but neither does such knowledge even if coupled with a deliberate sale to a purchaser at an absurdly low price for the express purpose of defeating the unregistered interest as in *Midland Bank v. Green* (1981). As already noted, in *Green*, a father granted his son an option to purchase a farm. This was an estate contract and should have been registered as a Class C(iv) land charge. It was not registered. Subsequently, the father sold the farm to the mother for £500[53] deliberately to defeat the unregistered option. Nevertheless, as was made clear by the House of Lords, it is not a fraud to take advantage of one's legitimate rights, even if it seems that there has been some element of 'bad faith'. Consequently, given that the mother was a purchaser of a legal estate for money or money's worth, the unregistered option was not enforceable against the land. In sum then, the courts have taken a strict line with the enforceability of land charges and have not been prepared to permit the 'fraud exception' to make large inroads into the voidness rule. Undoubtedly, this has much to do with the powerful decision of the House of Lords in *Midland Bank v. Green* (1981), in which there is a clear preference for the certainty of the register over the apparent 'justice' of individual cases. Indeed, although in *Green* the owner of the option had recourse to other remedies (e.g. suing the solicitor who

---

50 In fact, although it is quite possible to come across persons who only purchase an equitable interest in property, it should be noted that in the great majority of cases concerning the enforceability of Class C(iv) and D land charges, the intending purchaser is a purchaser of a legal interest for money or money's worth.

51 As previously, however, the purchaser need not pay adequate 'money or money's worth' to escape unregistered Class C(iv) and D charges: *Midland Bank v. Green* (1981).

52 *Hollington Bros v. Rhodes* (1951).

53 It being worth nearer £40,000 at the then current values.

negligently failed to register the option), the case illustrates that more is needed to trigger the fraud exception than simply that the person who granted the land charge has attempted to defeat it. Perhaps the result would have been different if, say, the father had assured his son that the option did not require registration and then had sold the land to his wife. This might have generated an 'estoppel' capable of affecting the mother.

6   All land charges, *even if unregistered, will be valid against a purchaser who is estopped from denying their validity through proprietary estoppel.* Although it is likely to be rare in practice, if a purchaser of an unregistered estate either has promised or agreed to give effect to an unregistered land charge, and that promise or agreement is relied upon by the person entitled to the benefit of the land charge to their detriment, the purchaser will not then be able to plead statutory voidness against that person. He will be held to the promise or agreement, although subsequent purchasers from him may not. In such cases, the purchaser making the assurance is 'estopped' from denying the enforceability of the land charge against them[54] and the estoppel appears to impose a personal bar on the particular purchaser because of his conduct.[55] For example, in the *Green* case, if the mother (the purchaser) had promised that she would give effect to the unregistered option, she may have been bound by an estoppel[56] to give effect to it even though it was unregistered. Once again, however, this must be a very narrow exception to the voidness rule, and one that will be rare in practice.

3.6.5   Other registers under the Land Charges Act 1972

In addition to the land charges register itself, there are four other registers of matters affecting unregistered land regulated by the LCA 1972. These are the register of annuities, the register of deeds of arrangement, the register of writs and orders affecting land, and the register of pending actions. These four additional registers contain information relating to rights, remedies and related interests affecting land that are not the typical third-party interests registrable under the LCA 1972. The register of pending actions is used for the registration of disputes pending in court relating to title to land or to the existence of a proprietary interest. For example, a dispute concerning the existence of easement or whether an estate contract was made validly may be registered here. Registration ensures that any subsequent purchaser of the land is given notice of the dispute affecting his land. Similarly, the register of writs and orders affecting land contains details of any order or writ issued by a court affecting land, such as a charging order securing a debt on the debtor's land, and if registered, are binding on all persons. The register of annuities contains details of certain pre-1926 annuities that do not fall within Class E land charges, and the register of deeds of arrangements records deeds executed by a bankrupt in settlement with creditors. Again, registration ensures their validity against future purchasers of the land.

---

54 It is not clear how, if at all, this differs from the 'fraud exception' discussed above.

55 *Taylor Fashions Ltd v. Liverpool Victoria Trustees* (1982) and see *Lyus v. Prowsa Developments* (1982) for a similar result in registered land. Note also that 'estoppel' is proprietary in nature and only rarely will it operate as a personal bar – see Chapter 7.

56 Or its close relative, the constructive trust.

The land charges register and the four other registers operating under the LCA 1972 are administered centrally by the Land Charges Department of HM Land Registry, although this should not be confused with title registration proper. In addition, there are registers of land held by district councils and other local authorities that record 'local land charges'. These have nothing to do with land charges under the LCA 1972. In fact, 'local land charges' are registered against the land itself and concern charges on land or matters affecting land that may have been recorded by a local authority in pursuit of its statutory responsibilities, such as planning matters. They are discussed here, because some categories of land charge proper are defined to exclude 'local land charges'. In fact, local land charges operate in unregistered and registered land in exactly the same way: a prospective purchaser of land will make a search of the local land charges register held by the relevant local authority where the land is situated prior to concluding the contract of sale. This will inform him of any matters that may affect adversely the use to which he proposes to put the land and may reveal obligations or risks (e.g. of a nearby building development or planned road) affecting the land. As may be imagined, local land charges are very important in practice, and their discovery has ruined many a prospective sale.

3.7 Overreachable Rights

The second category of equitable rights operating in unregistered land are those that are subject to the process of overreaching. These are those equitable rights that are excluded from the category of land charges (i.e. they *cannot* be registered) because a properly conducted overreaching transaction will sweep the interests off the land and cause them to take effect in the monies paid by a purchaser for that land. Overreaching occurs in unregistered land in precisely the same circumstances as in registered land. To recap briefly, overreaching will occur when:

1   the equitable right is capable of being overreached and these are equitable co-ownership rights existing behind a trust of land[57] or behind a strict settlement (section 2 of the LPA 1925);

2   the sale is made by those persons and in those circumstances that are capable of effecting an overreaching transaction (section 2(1) of the LPA 1925). These circumstances are four in number, although the first is the one most frequently encountered:

   (i)   the transaction is made by at least two trustees of land (or a trust corporation) under a trust of land;[58] or

   (ii)   the transaction is made under the provisions of the Settled Land Act 1925 relating to the operation of strict settlements; or

   (iii) the transaction is made by a mortgagee or personal representative in exercise of their paramount powers; or

---

57 For example, as in *City of London Building Society v. Flegg* (1988), in which parents of one of the married couple held an equitable interest in the property but the legal title was held by the married couple jointly.

58 As in *City of London Building Society v. Flegg*.

(iv) the transaction is made under order of the court: for example, section 14 of the Trusts of Land and Appointment of Trustees Act (TOLATA) 1996.

As with registered land, it is only if both of these requirements are met that overreaching can occur and the equitable right can then be given effect to in the purchase money paid for the land. However, what is important to understand for present purposes is that these overreachable equitable rights are *not* capable of registration under the LCA 1972 (section 2(4)(iii) of the LCA 1972) and so the 'owner' of such an interest cannot obtain protection through the system of land charge registration just described. The reason for this is clear enough. The protection for these equitable proprietary rights is meant to be found in the fact that, on overreaching, they will take effect in the purchase money paid by the purchaser. In theory, they are not lost, but transformed into cash in a sum equivalent to the share that the equitable owner held in the property.[59]

Given then that these equitable rights are not capable of registration as land charges, is it true to say that they are nevertheless 'guaranteed' or vindicated by the overreaching machinery? It would seem not. First, and obviously, it may well be that the equitable owners do not want a cash equivalent for their interest in the land but would prefer to remain in possession. Overreaching deliberately prevents this. Second, as we have seen in relation to registered land, *State Bank of India v. Sood* (1997) decides that in some circumstances no purchase money need actually be paid to the trustees (i.e. the legal owners) to overreach the equitable interests. Thus, in *Sood*, overreaching still occurred even though the legal owners mortgaged the property to secure future borrowings and did not receive an immediate payment of a lump sum. Obviously, while this decision may well be convenient for purchasers – because overreaching still operates to protect them – it offers no comfort or protection to the equitable owner because no lump sum of money is in fact paid in which his or her interest could have taken effect. Third, as we have seen, before overreaching can occur, certain conditions must be established: for example, the paramount requirement that there must be a sale by at least two trustees/legal owners. If these formalities are not observed – because there may, in fact, be only one trustee[60] – the equitable rights are not overreached and the purchaser does not take the land *automatically* free of them. In such cases, we must still determine whether the purchaser might otherwise take free of the interest, but we cannot employ the LCA 1972 because such rights are not registrable as land charges. Consequently, we are thrown back on the old doctrine of notice and a purchaser who fails to overreach will be bound by these equitable interests if he has 'notice' of them.[61] This is unsatisfactory for both purchaser and equitable right-holder and is discussed fully in Chapter 4. For now, the two important points are: first, that certain equitable rights – those existing behind trusts of land – cannot be registered as land charges because they are susceptible to overreaching and overreaching will occur whenever the statutory formalities are complied with, even if no purchase money is actually paid; and second, if these equitable rights are not overreached, their effect on a purchaser is determined by the old doctrine of notice.

---

59 For example, a 40 per cent share of ownership equals a 40 per cent share of net proceeds of sale.

60 See Chapter 4 and *Williams & Glyn's Bank v. Boland* (1981).

61 See section 3.8 below.

3.8 A Residual Class of Equitable Interests in Unregistered Conveyancing

So far we have considered three different types of third-party right over unregistered land: legal rights; rights capable of registration as land charges under the LCA 1972; and rights capable of being overreached. In essence, this tripartite scheme was intended to encapsulate the totality of third-party rights in unregistered conveyancing, with only minor exceptions. However, in the same way that land law in this country had developed up to 1926, it has continued to develop since the 1925 legislation, and it is now clear that there is a fourth category of third-party equitable rights that do not fit into this neat scheme. Some of the rights within this category were excluded deliberately from the tripartite pattern just described, being minor exceptions made for policy reasons. Others are new rights, developed since 1 January 1926. However, whatever the reason for their exclusion from the tripartite system, the fundamental rule governing their effect on unregistered land is clear. When a purchaser buys land over which there is alleged to be an equitable right that is neither registrable as a land charge, nor overreachable, that equitable right is binding on the purchaser if he has actual, constructive or imputed notice of it. In other words, the ability of these rights (being equitable) to bind a purchaser of unregistered land depends on the historical doctrine of notice, and this is the one significant situation in which the doctrine is still relevant in modern land law. The following are the equitable rights that fall into this residual category.

1   Equitable co-ownership interests behind a trust of land and equitable successive interests under a Settled Land Act settlement – section 2(4)(iii) of the LCA 1972 – but only when there is no overreaching.[62] As noted in section 3.7 above, these equitable rights were deliberately omitted from the land charges system because it was believed most would actually be overreached. However, as we now know, it is not always true that they are. When they are not overreached, their effect on a purchaser is to be judged by the doctrine of notice.

2   Pre-1926 restrictive covenants and easements are also deliberately excluded from the LCA (section 2(5)(ii) and (iii) of the LCA 1972). These interests are excluded for the entirely practical reason that it would be very difficult to ensure their registration given that they were created before the entry into force of the land charges legislation.

3   Equitable mortgages protected by deposit of title deeds are excluded because absence of the title deeds will always be notice to an intending purchaser of the land of the existence of such a powerful adverse right. Hence, they do not need protection by reason of registration. Note, however, it is now clear that deposit of title deeds alone cannot actually create an equitable mortgage because such a mortgage does not spring from a *written* contract as required by section 2 of the Law of Property (Miscellaneous Provisions) Act 1989.[63] Consequently, no new equitable mortgages of this type can come into existence.

---

62 *Kingsnorth v. Tizard* (1986).

63 *United Bank of Kuwait v. Sahib* (1995).

4　Pre-1926 Class B and C land charges (because they pre-date the legislation), until they are conveyed into different ownership when they must be registered (because their conveyance is an opportune time to register) (section 4(7) of the LCA 1972).

5　Restrictive covenants between a lessor and lessee relating to the land held under the lease (section 2(5)(ii) of the LCA 1972). Such covenants have no need to be registered because there is a web of independent rules determining the effect of leasehold covenants on persons who were not the original landlord and tenant. These rules are discussed fully in Chapter 6.

6　Restrictive covenants between a lessor and lessee relating to land that is not part of the land leased: that is, where the covenant is found in a lease but relates to other land, such as land held by the landlord in the vicinity. These covenants are also outside the land charge registration system (because they are between lessor and lessee – section 2(5)(ii) of the LCA 1972, as above) but, because they do not relate to the land that is the subject matter of the lease, they cannot be enforced under the leasehold covenant rules. Thus, they bind purchasers of the relevant land through the doctrine of notice.[64]

7　A landlord's 'right of re-entry' in an equitable lease, as explained in *Shiloh Spinners* v. *Harding* (1973). This right, which permits a landlord to re-enter the land and terminate (forfeit) the lease when a covenant is broken, will be equitable when it is expressly or impliedly included as a term in an equitable lease. It falls outside all of the classes of land charge because of the plain words of section 2 of the LCA 1972. Consequently, it is enforceable against subsequent purchasers of the equitable lease, or an interest in it (e.g. a subtenancy) through the doctrine of notice.

8　A tenant's right to enter the property and remove 'tenant's fixtures' at the end of an equitable lease, as explained in *Poster* v. *Slough Lane Estates* (1969). Once again, this interest falls outside the strict definition of the LCA 1972 and so its validity against purchasers of the burdened land must depend on the doctrine of notice. It is a right that permits a tenant of an equitable lease to re-enter the leasehold land after the lease has ended in order to remove certain items ('tenant's fixtures') from the land.

9　Interests acquired through proprietary estoppel, as illustrated by *Ives* v. *High* (1967). These powerful and increasingly common interests are generated through the operation of the doctrine of proprietary estoppel and so arise informally by reason of interaction between the landowner and the person claiming the right. They appear to be non-registrable as land charges even if (as in *Ives* itself) the interest created is similar to a class of land charge, such as an equitable easement. The point is, however, that these rights derive from pure equity and their mode of creation is such that their owner may not be aware that they actually have an interest until the land over which they exist is sold to a purchaser. This would, of course, be too late to register and so the *Ives* decision is policy-driven. It is likely that all interests generated by proprietary estoppel are non-registrable as land charges, at least on the occasion of a sale of the land over which they exist to the first purchaser after they have been

---

64　*Dartstone Ltd* v. *Cleveland Petroleum Ltd* (1969). The position is not affected by the Landlord and Tenant (Covenants) Act 1995 because that Act annexes covenants to 'the premises demised by the tenancy and of the reversion in them', not to land outside the lease (section 3(1)(a) of the Landlord and Tenant (Covenants) Act 1995)), a view confirmed by *Oceanic Village* v. *United Attractions* (1999).

generated. Subsequent to that, the existence of the interest will be known and the owner might be required to register it if it is to be preserved should a further sale take place. However, this has not been settled – and now may never be, given the diminishing frequency of unregistered conveyancing.

10   A 'charging order'[65] made under the Charging Orders Act 1979 over the interest of an equitable owner of property is apparently not registrable in the register of writs and orders affecting land, because such an equitable interest (over which the charge is made) is regarded not an interest in land, but merely an interest in the proceeds of sale of land, as explained in *Perry v. Phoenix Assurance* (1988). Such an order would, apparently, only bind a subsequent purchaser of a legal estate by reason of the doctrine of notice. This is a consequence of an application (some would say misapplication) of the doctrine of conversion, rather than an inherent problem with the system of land charges. However, the abolition of the doctrine of conversion by TOLATA 1996 appears not to reverse *Perry* because the LCA 1972 is amended by TOLATA to provide that no writ or order 'affecting an interest under a trust of land' may be registered under its provisions (Schedule 3, section 12(3) of TOLATA 1996).

3.9   Inherent Problems in the System of Unregistered Land

Throughout the analysis presented above, reference has been made to both the nature of the system of unregistered land and the machinery for the registration of land charges. Some of the problems and difficulties that surround the operation of unregistered land are inherent in the system itself, and some have emerged because of legal, social and economic developments in the years after 1925. Some of the more important points are reiterated below.

First, the system of the registration of land charges is incomplete, in that some equitable rights are non-registrable. This means that the old doctrine of notice still has a part to play, albeit of rapidly diminishing importance since the introduction of compulsory first registration of title. Nevertheless, it is a serious criticism that a system that was intended to bring certainty to dealings with land was unable to do away with the vagaries of the doctrine of notice.

Second, the land charges register is a name-based register, and this brings several problems, of varying importance.

1   The use of wrong names or incorrect versions of names, both in the registration of a land charge and in a search of the register, causes obvious problems, as charges are not properly protected and a purchaser may obtain a search certificate on which he cannot rely safely.

2   Long-lived land charges may be registered against names which the purchaser cannot discover and cannot, therefore, search against, as where a purchaser of a lease cannot discover the names of previous freeholders and, more importantly, where names are hidden behind the root of title.

3   Land charges must be registered against the name of the estate owner of the land that

---

65   That is, a charge over a debtor's property enforcing a debt arising from a judgment of a court.

is intended to be bound; thus, subpurchasers in a chain of uncompleted transactions may register against the wrong person.

Third, the official search certificate is conclusive. Consequently, in the event that the registry fails to carry out an accurate search, a properly registered land charge may be lost. The remedy for the person prejudiced by this error may lie in the law of tort, but this remains uncertain.

Fourth, some would question whether the absolute voidness of an unregistered land charge is justifiable, especially where the purchaser has full knowledge of the unregistered charge and acts deliberately to defeat it, as in *Midland Bank v. Green* (1981). Thus, the LCA 1972 is morally neutral and is premised on the paramount need for certainty, even at the expense of those who might be thought to have a deserving case. Although the steady demise of unregistered conveyancing makes the matter less pressing, there has been much debate about whether the LCA 1972 should be applied as vigorously as it was in *Green*, or whether the purchaser's 'actual' state of mind should be as important as the registration requirement.

Fifth, the LCA 1972 does not protect the rights of persons in actual occupation of the land; rather, the position is that if a person has a proprietary right over another person's land, that right will be binding if it is either legal or registered as a land charge, or occasionally protected through the doctrine of notice. If, however, a right is registrable, but not registered, then the right is lost and the owner cannot rely on the fact that they are occupying the property. For example, in *Hollington Bros v. Rhodes* (1951), equitable tenants had not registered their equitable lease as a Class C(iv) land charge and so it was void against a purchaser, irrespective of their occupation of the land. Again, in *Lloyds Bank v. Carrick* (1996), the occupier also was held to have rights under a Class C(iv) land charge that were void through lack of registration. Yet, in both cases, if this had been land of registered title under the LRA 2002, the interests would have been protected as 'unregistered interests that override' within paragraph 2 of Schedule 1 or 3 through the right-holders 'actual occupation' of the burdened land.[66] This is a serious defect in the system of unregistered conveyancing and means that the continuing validity of a person's rights might actually turn on the chance of whether the land is of registered title or not. Such a disparity in the systems is not justifiable and there is evidence to suggest that it was not intentional, caused possibly by accidental omission of a provision protecting occupiers of unregistered land when the land charges legislation was consolidated in the original LCA 1925.

3.10 A Comparison with Registered Land

The regimes operated by the LCA 1972 and the LRA 2002 are intended to achieve some of the same objectives, albeit that the latter is far more wide-ranging than the former. In essence, both of these systems are intended to bring stability to the system of conveyancing in England and Wales by protecting purchasers of land and owners of rights over that land. The following points highlight the different methods used to achieve these goals.

---

66 The same result would have been reached under the old LRA 1925, section 70(1)(g), which paragraphs 2 of Schedules 1 and 3 replaced.

1   In registered land, nearly all titles to land are recorded on a register with a searchable, unique title number. In unregistered land, a purchaser must rely on the title deeds, and has to investigate the title in order to secure a proper root of title.

2   In registered land, third-party rights are protected through registration against the title by means of a notice or under the provisions relating to interests that override (Schedules 1 and 3 of the LRA 2002). Of especial importance is the protection given to the rights of persons in (discoverable) actual occupation within paragraph 2 of the schedules. In unregistered land, 'legal rights bind the whole world' and equitable third-party rights are protected through a flawed 'name-based' system of land charge registration, or, even worse, by reliance on the old doctrine of notice. In both systems, overreaching is available, but not always possible.

3   In registered land, an owner of an equitable right need not always register his right by means of a notice (although the LRA 2002 very much encourages such registration) but can sometimes fall back on the protection provided by interests that override, especially through the 'actual occupation' provisions. Although this compromises the integrity of the register, and poses problems for purchasers, it serves an important social purpose. In unregistered land, there is no protection for the rights of people in actual occupation.

4   In registered land, the methods of protecting an interest on the register under the LRA 2002 are now relatively straightforward and uncomplicated. Such registration is also very effective in guaranteeing the validity of the right against the burdened land. In unregistered land, the name-based system can cause considerable problems with defective searches and registrations and such registration is not effective if a clear search certificate is issued, even if issued in error.

5   In registered land, an interest that is not protected through registration (not being an overriding interest) loses its priority in favour of a purchaser of the registered title (sections 29 and 30 of the LRA 2002). The meaning of this is uncertain, but it may render the unprotected interest void henceforth. The voidness rule in unregistered land is spelt out clearly and has been applied with considerable vigour by the courts.

6   In registered land, it is the register that is conclusive, not any search thereof. In unregistered land, it is the other way around.

7   In registered land governed by the LRA 2002, it will be very rare for an adverse possessor to gain title to the land possessed, although it is still possible if the adverse possessor completed 12 years' adverse possession before the entry into force of the LRA 2002. In unregistered land, it remains possible for the estate owner to lose their estate though a successful claim to adverse possession.

3.11   Chapter Summary

3.11.1   Unregistered land and unregistered conveyancing

'Unregistered land' is land to which title is not recorded in an official register. 'Title' is found in the title deeds and related documents held by the estate owner (or his mortgagee). The purchaser will identify a good 'root of title' by examining the deeds and the land before completing the purchase.

3.11.2   The basic rules of unregistered conveyancing

A purchaser of unregistered land can become subject to another person's proprietary rights over the land, such as another person's lease or a neighbour's easement. In order to determine the precise effect of another person's proprietary rights against a purchaser's land, the following principles apply.

1   Legal rights bind the whole world, so ensuring that any legal estates or interests affecting the purchaser's land are binding on him. These legal rights may well have been obvious from inspection of the title deeds or the land itself. The exception is the *puisne* mortgage, a legal interest that is a land charge (see below).

2   Equitable rights fall into three categories.

    (i)   Land charges (being defined in six classes in the LCA 1972) must be registered against the name of the estate owner of the land that is to be bound at the time of the right's creation. If registered, they are binding on a prospective purchaser of the land, even if 'hidden' from that purchaser. If they are not registered, they are void against a purchaser of either a legal estate, or a purchaser of any interest, depending on the category of land charge. This rule of voidness is strictly applied. The land charges system suffers from many defects, not least that it is name-based. It also fails to protect the rights of those in occupation of the land, even though this protection may be available in registered land.

    (ii)   Overreachable rights, being 'family' equitable interests (such as co-ownership rights) that are capable of being accurately quantified in money. They are not registrable as land charges because it was believed they would be swept off the title by overreaching. The same conditions for overreaching apply in unregistered land as in registered land and the same difficulties exist.

    (iii)   Equitable interests protected by the doctrine of notice, being a residual category of rights that were either deliberately or accidentally excluded from the land charges system. The most important are the equitable right of co-ownership when overreaching is not possible and rights generated by proprietary estoppel. Whether a purchaser is bound by any of these rights depends on the doctrine of notice with all its vagaries.

3.11.3   Inherent problems in the system of unregistered land

Some of the problems and difficulties that surround the operation of unregistered land are inherent in the system itself and some have emerged because of legal, social and economic developments in the years since 1925.

- The system of the registration of land charges is incomplete, in that some equitable rights are non-registrable. This means that the old doctrine of notice still has a part to play.
- The land charges register is a name-based register and this brings several problems of varying importance, for example: the use of wrong names or incorrect versions of names both in the registration of a land charge and in a search of the register; land charges may be registered against names that the purchaser cannot discover and cannot search against; and subpurchasers in a chain of uncompleted transactions may register against the wrong person.

- The official search certificate is conclusive; thus, in the event that the registry fails to carry out an accurate search, a properly registered charge may be lost.
- Some would question whether the absolute voidness of an unregistered charge is justifiable, especially where the purchaser has full knowledge of the charge and acts deliberately to defeat it (*Green*).
- The LCA 1972 does not protect the rights of persons in actual occupation of the land.

3.11.4 A comparison with registered land

- In registered land, title to land is officially recorded and guaranteed whereas, in unregistered land, a purchaser must make his own investigation based on the title deeds.
- In registered land, third-party rights are protected through registration or under the provisions relating to overriding interests. In unregistered land, legal rights are safe, but equitable third-party rights are protected through a flawed 'name-based' system of land charge registration or, even worse, by reliance on the old doctrine of notice. In both systems, overreaching is available.
- In registered land, an owner of an equitable right may be able to fall back on the protection provided by overriding interests, especially through (discoverable) 'actual occupation' of the relevant land. In unregistered land, there is no protection for the rights of people in actual occupation.
- In registered land, it is not yet certain whether there is a clear 'voidness' rule because the LRA 2002 expresses the effect of non-registration in terms of loss of priority. In unregistered land, the voidness rule is applied strictly.
- In registered land, it is the register that is conclusive, not the search certificate. In unregistered land, it is the other way around.
- In registered land, adverse possession will be rare. In unregistered land, it remains a viable way of obtaining a title.

 Further Reading

Harpum, C, '*Midland Bank Trust Co Ltd v Green*' [1981] CLJ 213

Wade, HWR, 'Land charge registration revisited' [1956] CLJ 216

Chapter 4
Co-ownership

Chapter Contents

Introduction

The law relating to co-ownership of land[1] forms a major part of most land law syllabuses. More important than that, however, is the fact that this is one area of land law that can have a powerful impact on the lives of everyone in England and Wales. In simple terms, the law of co-ownership operates whenever two or more people enjoy the rights of ownership of land at the same time, whether that be freehold or leasehold land. The co-owners may be husband and wife,[2] civil partners, unmarried partners,[3] family members,[4] friends, neighbours, business partners,[5] or stand in any other relationship to each other that we can think of. In other words, 'the law of co-ownership' is a set of rules that governs dealings with property that is owned simultaneously by more than one person. It is not concerned specifically with the property law problems of married or unmarried couples. It is not a species of family law. Of course, many of the problems that exist with co-owned property arise precisely because an emotional relationship has broken down, or friends have fallen out, or a mortgage cannot be paid. However, these are the causes of the problem and the law of co-ownership is not designed specifically for these domestic eventualities. It is important to remember the fundamental 'property law' nature of co-ownership when considering the issues discussed below.

The law of co-ownership is a product of statute and the common law. The Law of Property Act (LPA) 1925 and the Trusts of Land and Appointment of Trustees Act 1996 (TOLATA) are particularly important, with the latter amending significantly the original 1925 legislative scheme. Moreover, social and economic changes also have had a great impact on the frequency with which co-ownership arises and the consequences it brings. It is no longer true that co-ownership is limited to large, country estates or to land held for investment purposes. Neither is it true that co-ownership can arise only on a deliberate conveyance of land to two or more people. The implied creation of co-ownership of land – or rather the acquisition of ownership rights by means other than a formal conveyance – is a relatively common phenomenon and an even more common claim. As we shall see, much of the law of co-ownership today concerns the rights and responsibilities of the co-owners of the family home and the way in which they interact with banks, building societies and other purchasers. This change in the role of co-ownership – or, rather, this broadening of the reach of the law on co-ownership away from purely commercial or investment land – has generated significant changes to the scheme of co-ownership as it was intended to operate originally under the 1925 property legislation. These changes have been achieved both by statute (TOLATA 1996) and by judicial development of the common law.

The law of co-ownership can be broken down into its various component parts, at least for the purposes of exposition. There is, first, the nature of co-ownership, and the types of co-ownership of land that may exist since 1 January 1926. Second, there is the statutory

---

1 Sometimes called the law of concurrent co-ownership in order to distinguish it from the law of successive co-ownership considered in Chapter 5.

2 *Abbott v. Abbott* (2007) on appeal to the Privy Council from Antigua and Barbuda.

3 *Curley v. Parkes* (2004); *Stack v. Dowden* (2007) relationship breakdown of unmarried couples.

4 *McKenzie v. McKenzie* (2003), a father and son; *Hapeshi v. Allnatt* (2010), a mother and her children.

5 *Rodway v. Landy* (2001), in which the co-owned property was a doctors' surgery.

machinery that regulates the use and enjoyment of co-owned land, and the all-important questions of why the 1925 legislation made the radical changes that it did, and why it was felt necessary to amend these further in 1996. Third, there are those statutory and common law rules governing the creation of co-ownership (the acquisition of property rights), both when this is deliberate and where it arises informally from the potential co-owners' dealings with the property and each other. Fourth, there is the impact of co-ownership on third parties, such as banks and building societies (which may have lent money to finance the purchase of the property), and on purchasers and other occupiers. Fifth, there are matters relating to the termination of co-ownership, and the methods by which one form of co-ownership may replace another.

4.1 The Nature and Types of Concurrent Co-ownership

Concurrent co-ownership of property describes the simultaneous enjoyment of land by two or more persons. It is important to remember that we are concerned here with the *simultaneous* enjoyment of property: that is, enjoyment of the rights of ownership by two or more persons at the same time. Successive interests in land, whereby two or more people are entitled to the enjoyment of land in succession to each other, are dealt with in Chapter 5. Before 1 January 1926, concurrent co-ownership of property could take a variety of forms, but for all practical purposes co-ownership since 1 January 1926 will either be by way of a *joint tenancy* or a *tenancy in common*. At the outset, it is best to note that 'tenancy' here does not mean a lease or a leasehold interest; rather, it is the description given to the *type* of co-ownership enjoyed by the co-owners, whether they own freehold or leasehold land.

4.2 Joint Tenancy

When land is owned by two or more people on the basis of a joint tenancy, each co-owner is treated as being entitled to the whole of that land. There are no distinct 'shares', and no single co-owner can claim any greater right over any part of the land than another. As far as the rest of the world is concerned, the land is treated as if it is owned by one person only and all of the 'joint tenants' share in that one ownership. In practical terms, this means that when land is subject to a joint tenancy, there is only one formal title to it and that title is owned jointly by all of the joint tenants. So, if four students co-own legal title to a house under a joint tenancy, it is not possible to say that they own one quarter each; they each own the whole. Moreover, if the land is registered, there will be but one title registered at HM Land Registry under one title number, with each co-owner registered as proprietor of that title in the proprietorship section of the register. If the land is unregistered, there will be but one set of title deeds, specifying the four owners. In essence, each joint tenant owns the total interest in the land. This really is 'co-ownership', because there are no shares, no partition of the land, but a right of ownership of the whole of the land enjoyed simultaneously with all of the other owners. The nature of the joint tenancy as a single title owned by more than one person is reflected in its legal attributes. These attributes – discussed immediately below – are regarded as the touchstone of a joint tenancy and the absence of any one is fatal to the existence of this form of co-ownership.

4.2.1 The right of survivorship (the *ius accrescendi*)

By virtue of this principle, if one joint tenant dies during the existence of the joint tenancy,[6] his interest in the joint tenancy (being his right to enjoy the whole of the land and its cash value on sale) *automatically accrues* to the remaining joint tenants. In fact, all that is happening is that the dead joint tenant drops out of the joint tenancy and the remainder continue to enjoy their rights over the whole land. The important practical point is, then, that when a joint tenant dies, no formal conveyance or written document is needed to reflect the new status quo. There is nothing to convey or transfer, so no conveyance or transfer is needed.[7] Indeed, the right of survivorship takes precedence over any attempted transfer on death: a person by his will cannot pass an interest under a joint tenancy because that interest does not belong to the deceased. The interest of the dead joint tenant accrues to the other joint tenants at the moment of death, so there is nothing to be left to a beneficiary of the will, even if an attempt has been made in the will explicitly to leave the deceased's 'share' in the land to someone else.[8] This means that a joint tenancy can either be very useful, as where it avoids the need for formal documentation when a co-owner dies,[9] or very unfair, as where a co-owner dies and is unable to leave an interest in the property to his family because it has accrued to the remaining joint tenants.

4.2.2 The four unities

Before a joint tenancy can exist, the 'four unities' must be present,[10] and it is the presence (or absence) of these unities that enables us to distinguish a joint tenancy from a tenancy in common.

1   The *unity of possession* means that each joint tenant is entitled to physical possession of the whole of the land. Unity of possession means that there can be no physical division of the land and no restriction on any joint tenant's use of each and every part of it. This includes the right to participate fully in the fruits of possession, such as receipt of rents and profits derived from the land. As we shall see, although unity of possession must exist before a joint tenancy can exist, the practical effects of it have been modified by statute so that, in some circumstances, one joint tenant may be excluded from the land on terms and conditions (sections 12 and 13 of TOLATA

---

6 As we shall see, a joint tenancy may be 'severed' to become a 'tenancy in common' or it may expire naturally on the death of the last-but-one joint tenant, leaving a sole owner.

7 For registered land, the deceased joint-tenant's name can be removed from the proprietorship register on application to the register, but sometimes this is not done until the surviving joint tenants wish to deal with the land in some way.

8 *Gould v. Kemp* (1834). Therefore, in order to pass property on death, the joint tenancy must have been brought to an end *before* death – usually by being severed and turned into a tenancy in common.

9 For example, on death of one of the husband and wife who were co-owners of the matrimonial home.

10 *AG Securities v. Vaughan* (1988), in which the House of Lords held that a flat-sharing arrangement whereby each sharer signed their own agreement did not amount to a single joint tenancy of the whole premises because of the obviously distinct rights that each had.

1996).[11] As a matter of principle, this does not destroy the unity of possession *per se*; rather, the court's powers under sections 12 and 13 of TOLATA can be used to modify each co-owner's entitlements. A similar power exists in relation to family disputes under Part IV of the Family Law Act 1996 where the court is given the power to exclude certain persons from the family home.

2   The *unity of interest* means that each joint tenant's interest in the property must be of the same extent, nature and duration. Thus, all must be joint tenants of the freehold, or of the leasehold, and in remainder or possession (as the case may be). Different qualities of right are inconsistent with the nature of a joint tenancy as a single title, jointly owned.

3   The *unity of title* means that each joint tenant must derive their title (i.e. ownership) from the same conveyancing documents. Note, however, that in certain circumstances, estate owners may still have a joint tenancy even though as a matter of formality they have each signed different documents. A good example is where leaseholders may be treated as joint tenants because this reflects the true nature of the agreement between all of the parties despite signing separate agreements with their landlord. In *Antoniades v. Villiers* (1990), an unmarried couple took a lease of a one-bedroom flat and signed separate documents. In the circumstances, which included the fact that the landlord had provided a double bed and there was only one bedroom, the court took the view that it was absurd to regard these two people as having separate and independent rights to the land. The House of Lords decided that *as a matter of law*, the two joint tenants derived their title from the same document, even though there was more than one piece of paper. Any other conclusion would have been to recognise a pretence. The matter must be one of substance, not of form. Of course, in the normal course of events, the title will have been conveyed to the joint tenants by the same document – as where man and woman buy a new house as the family home – but the simple fact that different documents may have been signed by the potential co-owners does not automatically mean that there is no unity of title and hence no joint tenancy.

4   The *unity of time* means that the interest of each joint tenant must arise at the same time, as befitting their ownership of a single title. For example, if a woman purchases a house in 2006 and in 2010, on the occasion of her marriage, grants an equal share in the house to her husband, they cannot be joint tenants: the interests of the co-owners arose at different times.[12] The same is true if, say, the interest of the husband arises informally through some act of the parties after the title has been conveyed to his wife.

4.3   Tenancy in Common

When two or more people own land under a tenancy in common, it is often said that they have 'undivided shares in land'. In other words, a tenant in common can point to a precise

---

11 See *Chun v. Ho* (2001).

12 A joint tenancy would arise, however, if the wife were to reconvey the entire house into the joint names of herself and her husband, rather than simply give him a share in it.

share of ownership of the land (e.g. one half, one fifth, one quarter, etc.), even though the land at present is undivided and treated as a single unit. The distinguishing feature of a tenancy in common is, then, that each co-owner has a distinct and quantifiable share in the land. That does not mean, however, that a particular tenant can physically demarcate a portion of the land and claim it as his own. The land is still 'undivided', and the tenant in common owns a quantifiable share in it, which can be realised if and when the property is sold. To put it another way, there is 'unity of possession' with a tenancy in common despite the fact that such a tenant can legitimately say that they own, say, one fifth of the land. So, following through the example, if four students co-own the house in which they live under a tenancy in common, it will be possible to say that they each own a defined share. This may be one quarter each, but it is perfectly possible that A owns one third, B owns one third and C and D own one sixth each. In fact, any combination of proportions of shared ownership is possible with a tenancy in common. Were the house to be sold, then the actual shares would take effect in the money paid by the purchaser, with each tenant in common receiving a sum proportionate to their share in the land. Pending that, however, the land is 'undivided', with each enjoying possession of the whole irrespective of the size of their share.

Importantly, although none of the other unities, apart from possession, must be present for a tenancy in common to exist, it may well be that they are. For example, it is likely that unity of time will exist if the co-ownership came into existence from the moment the property was acquired. Importantly, the right of survivorship does not apply to a tenancy in common, so that a co-owner under a tenancy in common may leave his share on death or may otherwise deal with it during his life. It is for this reason that a tenancy in common is often preferred where the co-owners are not closely related by family ties – the absence of survivorship means that there is no risk of a person's property assets accruing in error to his business partner instead of his family. Thus, to summarise, with a tenancy in common:

1   there is an undivided share in land;
2   there is unity of possession;
3   no other unity must be present, although others may be;
4   there is no right of survivorship and so the share may be passed on in the normal way on death or in writing during the co-owner's life.

Finally, we should note that a tenancy in common may come about through the 'severance' of a joint tenancy. This is discussed in more detail below, but it means that the parties to a joint tenancy may choose to terminate that form of co-ownership during their lives and be governed instead by the regime of a tenancy in common. This is more often than not driven by the desire to avoid the right of survivorship, especially after relationship breakdown.

4.4   The Effect of the Law of Property Act 1925 and the Trusts of Land and Appointment of Trustees Act 1996

It goes without saying that it is vital to distinguish between the existence of a joint tenancy and a tenancy in common, not least because of the right of survivorship. However, before we can examine in detail how that may be done, it is necessary to consider the regime of co-ownership established by the LPA 1925 and the further changes made by TOLATA

1996. The 'modern' law of co-ownership begins with the 1925 property legislation and those reforms help us to understand why the current law operates as it does and how that law has evolved. As will be seen, TOLATA 1996 did not change the basic principles of the LPA 1925 regarding co-owned land (and so the LPA 1925 must still be regarded as the source statute), but it does make significant changes to the detail with effect from 1 January 1997 when it entered into force.[13] To recap then, the changes made by the LPA 1925 were both changes in substance and procedure and were part of the wider plan to simplify all dealings with land to meet the economic and social challenges of the twentieth century. TOLATA 1996 took this further. The reasons for the 1925 reform are considered below, but essentially they stem from a paramount policy of ensuring the free market-ability of co-owned land combined with the advantages of the joint tenancy as a form of co-ownership, involving as it does a single title to land in which many may share. This contrasts with the tenancy in common, which presupposes several individual titles.

4.4.1   Before 1 January 1926

Before 1 January 1926, it was possible for a joint tenancy and a tenancy in common to exist in both the legal and equitable estate in the land. So, if land was conveyed 'to A and B as tenants in common', they would be tenants in common of the legal title. Likewise for a joint tenancy. Again, if land were conveyed 'to X and Y on trust for A and B as tenants in common', A and B would be tenants in common of the equitable title (in equity), with the legal title held by X and Y (as either joint tenants or tenants in common). So, if a purchaser wishes to buy the legal title of land that was co-owned, he will either have to investigate one title (joint tenancy) or all of the individual titles of the various co-owners (tenancy in common). While this causes no great hardship for a purchaser investigating the one title held by joint tenant legal owners, if the land is co-owned under a tenancy in common, the complexity of the transaction increases as the number of tenants in common increases. To purchase from A and B as tenants in common is only two titles to investigate, but to purchase from A, B, C and D is four, and so on.

4.4.2   From 1 January 1926

We have noted above that one change made by the LPA 1925 was to limit the types of co-ownership to two: the joint tenancy and tenancy in common. However, the Act also placed restrictions on the manner in which these forms of co-ownership could come into existence – see sections 34 and 36 LPA 1925, as amended by TOLATA 1996. The first and most significant point is that it has been impossible, since 1 January 1926, to create a tenancy in common at law: a tenancy in common *of the legal title* to land *cannot* exist (section 1(6) of the LPA 1925). In consequence, only joint tenancies of the legal title are possible and this is true irrespective of the words used when the land is transferred to the co-owners and irrespective of their intentions. For example, no longer is it possible to convey the legal title to land to A, B, C and D as tenants in common because this must operate as a conveyance of the legal title to A, B, C and D as joint tenants, even though the words are plain and the intentions clear. Note also, that this must mean that a joint tenancy

---

13 Reference will be made to the 1996 Act where appropriate, as this came into force on 1 January 1997.

of a legal title is 'unseverable' – section 36(2) LPA 1925 – because it is impossible to turn it into a legal tenancy in common.

Second, however, this joint tenancy of the legal title is of a special kind. The persons to whom the legal title to the land is conveyed – the intended co-owners of the legal estate – are *trustees* of the legal title under a statutorily imposed trust of land (sections 34 and 36 of the LPA 1925). Thus, in *every* case of express co-ownership of the legal title of land,[14] that legal title is held by joint tenant trustees on a 'trust of land'.[15] This statutory trust is defined in the LPA 1925 and TOLATA 1996, but essentially imposes on the trustees (the co-owners of the legal estate) a duty to hold the land for the persons beneficially interested in the land (i.e. the equitable owners) and for the purposes for which it was purchased, to which end they are given various powers of management, including the power of sale. So, given that, in the example above, the conveyance to A, B, C, and D operated as a conveyance to them as joint tenants of the legal title (irrespective of the words used), A, B, C and D will hold this land as trustees on the statutorily imposed trust of land for the 'real' owners. In this case, the 'real owners' are, in fact, A, B, C and D themselves, also known as the 'equitable owners'. In other words, they are trustees for themselves! The reasons for this apparently complicated machinery are discussed below.

Third, although the legal title to co-owned land must be held under a joint tenancy, the equitable title (the real and valuable interest) may be held either as a joint tenancy or a tenancy in common. Which form of equitable co-ownership exists will depend on the words used to create the co-ownership, the intentions of the parties and the surrounding circumstances. Again, in our case, although A, B, C and D must be joint tenant trustees of the legal title, in equity, they may be either equitable joint tenants or equitable tenants in common. In fact, in this example, they will be equitable tenants in common because it is clear from the words used in the conveyance at the time the land was acquired that this was the intended form of co-ownership.

To sum up then, all expressly created co-ownership operates behind a mechanism whereby the formal legal title is held by joint tenant trustees[16] on the statutorily imposed trust of land. The real equitable interest takes effect behind this trust and may be either a joint tenancy or a tenancy in common. Furthermore, in many cases, the 'trustees' will be the same people as those who share in the equitable co-ownership. So, if land is conveyed to husband (H) and wife (W), this will operate as a conveyance to them as joint tenant trustees of the legal title, holding on trust for *themselves* as either joint tenants or tenants in common in equity, depending on the circumstances in which the property was purchased. This is so even if the conveyance says 'to H and W as tenants in common': they will still be joint tenants of the legal title, albeit tenants in common of the equitable interest. The same mechanism operates irrespective of the number of intended co-owners, save that, by statute, the number of legal joint tenant trustees is limited to four (section 34(2) of the LPA 1925). The number of co-owners in equity is not limited, be they joint tenants or

---

14 In cases of implied co-ownership, there may be only one owner of the legal title, although the equitable title may be co-owned: see below.

15 As stipulated by sections 4 and 5 of TOLATA 1996, amending the LPA 1925.

16 As discussed below, in those cases in which there is only one owner of the legal title, but more than one owner of the equitable title, the legal owner will still be a trustee on the statutory trust of land for these equitable owners, but necessarily as a single trustee.

tenants in common. Consequently, if the land is purported to be conveyed to more than four people, it is the first four named in the conveyance who become the joint tenant trustees of the land, with all five or six, and so on, owning in equity as either joint tenants or tenants in common as the case may be.[17] The use of the trust is, therefore, a device to ensure that all legal title to co-owned land is held under a joint tenancy, while also ensuring that in equity, where the real interest lies, the co-owners can be either joint tenants or tenants in common. Indeed, in those cases – which will be many – in which the trustees are the same people as the beneficiaries, there is no real impact because of the use of the trust device. When, however, the legal owners are different from the equitable owners, the mandatory use of the trust can have important consequences for all parties.

4.5   The Distinction between Joint Tenancy and Tenancy in Common in Practice: The Equitable Interest

It follows from the fact that legal title to co-owned land must be held under trusteeship, that the important issue is to determine the nature of the co-ownership in equity for herein we find the valuable interest. Generally, the principles here are much the same as they were before 1926, although as ever, there are no immutable rules and each case must be decided on its own facts. The following are offered as guidelines only and their influence will vary from case to case. Remember at all times that we are now talking of the equitable interest only. A co-owned legal estate must be held as joint tenancy.

1   If the unities of interest, title or time are absent, a joint tenancy in equity cannot exist. In such a case, there must be a tenancy in common. For example, if the interest of one co-owner arises later than the other – as where a husband makes a successful claim by way of constructive or resulting trust to a share in his wife's property – the equitable interest will be held by way of a tenancy in common. The interests arose at different times. This is a very common way for an equitable tenancy in common to come into existence and it is the inevitable outcome of widespread use of the principles of constructive and resulting trusts.[18]

2   If the original conveyance to the co-owners stipulates that they are 'joint tenants' or 'tenants in common' *of the beneficial or equitable interest*, this is normally conclusive as to the nature of their co-ownership in equity. So, if land is conveyed to 'Rosie and Jim as tenants in common beneficially', they will be tenants in common in equity as the conveyance is conclusive as to the nature of the equitable ownership, irrespective of later events.[19] In *Roy v. Roy* (1996), a conveyance to P and D jointly was held conclusive between them as to the existence of a joint tenancy, despite the fact that D had contributed significantly more to the purchase and upkeep of the property over the

---

17   The chances of there being more than four intended owners of the land are not great, at least in connection with residential property.

18   See section 4.10.2 below.

19   *Goodman v. Gallant* (1986); *Hembury v. Peachey* (1996).

years, and that P had lived in the property for only a few months just after it was purchased. We should be clear, however, to understand the true scope of this rule. First, a written declaration[20] of the nature of the equitable interest is conclusive only for the parties to that declaration. So, in the *Roy* case, if an imaginary third party (X) had made a claim to an interest in the property, she would not have been bound by the conveyance to accept a joint tenancy unless she had also been a party to the written declaration. Second, the written declaration is conclusive only if valid under the general law: that is, it can be attacked on the basis that it was procured by fraud, misrepresentation, undue influence or any other vitiating factor. Third, it is clear from cases such as *Carlton v. Goodman* (2002), *McKenzie v. McKenzie* (2003) and *Stack v. Dowden* (2007) that the parties are bound only when a declaration refers clearly to the *equitable* interest. In these cases, there were two legal owners who necessarily were joint-tenant trustees but there was no express declaration as to the equitable ownership. Thus, in *Carlton* and *McKenzie*, when one of the legal co-owners claimed to be entitled to the entirety of the equitable interest because they had substantially paid for the property, the other joint tenant of the legal title resisted, claiming an equitable share flowing from their legal ownership. The result, again in both cases, was that the equitable ownership resided solely in one party – the main provider of the purchase price – thus demonstrating that being a legal owner under an expressly declared conveyance does not guarantee a share of the equitable title. Likewise in *Stack*, although Ms Dowden and Mr Stack were joint tenants of the legal title, Ms Dowden successfully claimed a larger share of the equitable interest because the conveyance to them had only declared the nature of the equitable title, not the size or type of each owner's share.[21]

3   If 'words of severance' are used, then a tenancy in common will exist in equity. Thus, a description of the share of each owner, or the creation of unequal interests in different co-owners, will mean that a tenancy in common must exist. A conveyance to 'A and B, two-thirds to A', will necessarily create a tenancy in common in equity. The same is true of a conveyance to 'A and B, half each', as this specifies a share. Note, however, that if land is given 'equally' (as in 'to A and B equally'), this can mean either a joint tenancy or a tenancy in common, depending on whether this means 'half each' or 'jointly', although in such cases the next presumption will usually operate.

4   In the absence of an express declaration concerning the equitable interest or words of severance, and if all of the four unities are present, there is a presumption that 'equity follows the law'. Consequently, because the legal title must be a joint tenancy, in the absence of all other evidence, the equitable title 'follows the law' and is deemed to be a joint tenancy also. So, a conveyance 'to A and B' will be taken to be a conveyance to A and B in law as joint tenants (as it must be), and in equity also. However, there are possibly some exceptions to this, being situations in which the

---

20 An oral declaration would not suffice (section 53(1) of the LPA 1925), save only that there is the possibility that it might support a claim in proprietary estoppel.

21 In *Fowler v. Barron* (2008), in which there was no declaration as to the equitable interest, this interest was held 50/50, not because the legal title was held jointly and equity should follow, but because this was the appropriate share, taking account of the entirety of the parties' relationship.

presumption that 'equity follows the law' can be displaced by a counter-presumption, arising from special facts, that a tenancy in common must have been intended. These are cases in which it is recognised that the existence of a joint tenancy may cause hardship to the co-owners, usually because the right of survivorship would be inappropriate. Situations falling into this category include land held by business partners and in related business arrangements,[22] cases in which the co-owned interest is of a mortgage held by co-mortgagees[23] and, most commonly, in which the purchasers have provided the purchase money in unequal shares, which, in the absence of other evidence[24] establishes lack of a unity of interest.[25] In all three of these examples, where equity will not follow the law, the parties are presumed to have preferred a tenancy in common because of the substantial disadvantage of construing the arrangement as a joint tenancy with a right of survivorship that would deprive the dependants of the co-owner of an interest in the property. More controversially, it now also appears from the House of Lords decision in *Stack* v. *Dowden* that equity will not follow the law (i.e. the parties will not be joint tenants in equity) if one of the legal co-owners is able to establish exceptional circumstances such that it is fair in all of the circumstances that they should have a larger share of the equity (i.e. be tenants in common). This is examined in more detail below, and will apply only where there is no express declaration of the equitable interests, but the implications are obvious. While it remains true in principle that absent words of severance and any of the four unities, equity will follow the law and lead to a joint tenancy, the ability of the court to quantify the parties' 'real interests' under *Stack* v. *Dowden* in 'exceptional' cases necessarily means that the distinction between an equitable joint tenancy and a tenancy in common is harder to draw and much less predictable.[26]

4.6   The Statutory Machinery Governing Co-ownership

At first glance, the changes made by the LPA 1925, and then by TOLATA 1996, to the pre-1926 law on co-ownership seem complicated and unwieldy. In fact, as we shall see, the statutory framework for co-ownership established by these statutes is designed to ensure that dealings with co-owned land (particularly sale and mortgage) can be accomplished

---

22 *Malayan Credit Ltd* v. *Jack Chia-MPH* (1986).

23 *Re Jackson* (1887). Thus the death of one mortgagee will not deprive their estate of the security for the loan made because the mortgage will be held under a tenancy in common.

24 For example, that one co-owner was making a gift to another.

25 *Lake* v. *Craddock* (1732). Unusually, in *HSBC* v. *Dyche & Collelldevall* (2009), there was no express declaration of the equitable interest in favour of Mr & Mrs Collelldevall (who were not legal owners), but they were held to be joint tenants in equity because both acquired their equitable interests at the same time for the same reason in the same circumstances.

26 See also *Ritchie* v. *Ritchie* (2007), where there were 'exceptional circumstances' allowing departure from the principle that equity follows the law in a case involving mother and son. Note however, *Jones* v. *Kernott* (2010), where the result was a 50/50 split of the equity, because there was nothing to displace the presumption that equity followed the law.

with more ease than was the case previously. Land is, after all, a prime economic asset. Although complicated as a legal mechanism, the law of co-ownership is now much simpler in practice. We can summarise the situation as follows.

1   It is impossible for a tenancy in common of a legal estate to exist. All legal co-ownership must be by way of joint tenancy.

2   However, the joint tenants are trustees of the legal estate for the equitable owners, holding the property as trustees of land within the LPA 1925 and TOLATA 1996. They hold the property on trust for the equitable owners.

3   The equitable owners are often the same people as the legal owners (the trustees), but there is no necessary reason why this should be so. In equity, the co-owners may be either joint tenants or tenants in common.

4   The number of legal joint tenant trustees is limited to four, usually the first four co-owners named in the transfer to them. The non-legal co-owners remain entitled in equity and the number of potential equitable owners is unlimited.

4.7   The Nature of the Unseverable Legal Joint Tenancy: The Trust of Land

It has already been indicated that the owners of the legal title hold the property as joint tenant trustees of land, with powers specified in the LPA 1925 and TOLATA 1996. This trust is effectively defined in sections 34 and 36 of the LPA 1925 and Part I of TOLATA 1996.[27] The trustees will hold the land for the persons interested in it and, subject to any express terms of the trust and statute, with the powers of an absolute owner.[28] They may delegate any of their functions to the beneficiaries, save that only the trustees may give a valid receipt to a purchaser if the land is sold.[29] In fact, it is unlikely that the provisions of TOLATA relating to trustees' powers and the ability to delegate will be needed in most cases of domestic concurrent co-ownership, certainly if the trustees and equitable owners are the same people. They will be more relevant in cases concerning successive interests in land (Chapter 5) or where the trust of land is used as an investment vehicle rather than as a statutorily imposed device for jointly owning a home.

Perhaps the most important point to grasp when considering the nature of the trust of land is that the trustees are under no duty to sell the land, as was the case before the entry into force of TOLATA 1996.[30] This important change means that the legal mechanism of co-ownership (the trust of land) now more accurately mirrors how most co-owned land is used in practice – not as land to be sold, but as land to be occupied. As we shall see, if the trustees (or equitable owners, if such power has been delegated to them) cannot agree whether to sell the land at an appropriate time (e.g. on divorce or separation of the

---

27 Section 35 of the LPA 1925 is repealed.

28 Sections 6 and 8 of TOLATA and sections 23 and 26 of the LRA 2002 in respect of registered proprietors.

29 Section 9 of the TOLATA.

30 Under the original LPA 1925 scheme, the trustees held the land on a trust for sale, with a power to postpone sale, effectively ensuring that the land could be retained if the trustees agreed (the power to postpone sale) but would be sold if they disagreed (the duty to sell).

co-owners or on bankruptcy), any interested person may apply to the court under section 14 of TOLATA 1996[31] for an order for sale or other order concerning the land. However, there is now no duty to sell the land and the trustees have every right to hold the land for the purpose for which it was acquired, or indeed any other lawful purpose that benefits the equitable owners.

As noted above, TOLATA 1996 came into force on 1 January 1997 and amended the LPA 1925. In fact, most of its provisions are retrospective, in that they apply to co-ownership trusts already in existence on 1 January 1997 and certainly they govern all new instances of co-ownership. Some commentators believe that TOLATA 1996 left much of the pre-1997 law intact and doubt whether much of the legislation was really necessary. Although perhaps an oversimplification, there is merit in this argument, not least because many of the 1996 Act's changes simply brought the legal structure of co-ownership into line with the way in which the courts already had interpreted the 1925 legislation. For example, prior to 1 January 1997, an equitable owner, in theory, did not have an interest in the land itself, but rather had an interest in the proceeds of sale of that land. This arose because of the trustees' duty to sell under the old 'trust for sale' and so the land was treated as having been sold and replaced with money because, in theory, it should have been: 'equity treats as done that which ought to be done'. However, for nearly all practical purposes, such an equitable owner was treated as having an interest in the land itself[32] and now this has been recognised by section 3 of TOLATA 1996. With these considerations in mind, the following are the specific attributes of the unseverable legal joint tenancy under the trust of land established by TOLATA 1996.

1   The trustees (legal owners) are under a duty to hold the land for the persons interested in it (often themselves). Although the trustees must have regard to the wishes of the beneficiaries, TOLATA 1996 gives them the powers of an absolute owner in relation to the land (section 6) subject to any provision in TOLATA itself or the instrument establishing the trust or entries made against the register of title.[33] However, the trustees may delegate 'any of their functions' to a beneficiary of full age (section 9) and the court may intervene by way of an order under section 14 at the request of a trustee or any other person having an interest in the trust property.[34] As noted, the trustees' powers may be restricted by the instrument (the document) creating the trust, except in the case of public, ecclesiastical or charitable trusts (section 8). Note here, however, that not everything done by a trustee will be a 'function relating to' the trust. So in Brackley v. Notting Hill Housing Trust (2001), the giving of notice by one joint-tenant trustee of a lease (thereby terminating the lease) was not such a function, at least in the case of a periodic tenancy.[35]

2   If the trustees do sell the land,[36] they hold the proceeds of sale on trust for the

---

31 Replacing section 30 of the LPA 1925.

32 The seminal example being Williams and Glyn's Bank v. Boland (1981), in which the proprietary nature of Mrs Boland's interest under the (then) trust for sale of land was critical in determining that she had an overriding interest.

33 See section 23 of the LRA 2002.

34 For example, an equitable owner of the land or mortgagee of a co-owner's interest.

35 Consequently, the giving of such notice was not a breach of trust.

36 Either of their own choice or as a result of an order made under section 14 of TOLATA.

equitable owners in the same way that they held the land itself. As discussed in Chapters 2 and 3, the equitable owners' interests are overreached and take effect in the proceeds of sale, if any.[37]

3   As mentioned above, prior to the 1996 Act, the trust was actually a trust for sale and this had the unfortunate consequence that, for some purposes, the interests of the equitable owners were treated as interests in the proceeds of the sale, not as interests in the land itself, even if the land had not actually been sold.[38] Section 3 of TOLATA 1996 abolishes the 'doctrine of conversion' for all new trusts of land and most old ones and so now it is certain that the interests of the equitable owners behind the statutorily imposed trust of land are interests in that land (i.e. proprietary rights) for all purposes.

4   Although the trustees of land now have no duty to sell the land, they do have a power to do so.[39] Given that the trustees are the legal owners of the property, it is their names that will be entered as registered proprietors of the title at HM Land Registry.[40] Consequently, all trustees – as owners of the legal title – must formally join in a conveyance if the land is sold. Not surprisingly, the LPA 1925 foresaw that there might well be disputes between trustees about sale (or the exercise of other powers), so a mechanism was provided for dealing with such disputes. This mechanism is now found in section 14 of TOLATA 1996 and involves an application to the court.[41] It is considered more fully below.

5   A catalogue of the trustees' functions and powers is found in TOLATA 1996 itself. As stated above, most will not be relevant in a 'normal' co-ownership situation in which the co-owners are trustees of land holding for themselves in equity. Similarly, many of these powers will be redundant when there is but one trustee of land holding on trust for himself and for others in equity.[42] However, in those relatively rare cases of residential co-ownership in which the two or more trustees of land are not also the only equitable owners (as in *City of London Building Society* v. *Flegg* (1988), in which daughter and husband held on trust for themselves and one set of parents), the powers and functions of the trustees under TOLATA 1996 may become important if the trustees and equitable owners cannot agree on the future use of the land. Of course, the powers and functions of the trustees remain central when the land is non-residential, as where it is held by trustees as an investment for the equitable co-owners.[43]

6   It is intrinsic in everything we have said so far that the ability to deal with the land lies with the legal owners – the trustees. If, as is often the case in a domestic context, these are the same people as the legal owners, few practical problems arise. However, if the trustees are completely unconnected with the equitable interest (as in an investment situation) or if there are more than four co-owners, or if the legal title was conveyed only to certain of the co-owners, or if some of the co-owners acquired

---

37 This is the balance of funds after paying off any mortgages that had priority to the interests of the co-owners.

38 See, for example, *Perry* v. *Phoenix Assurance* (1988).

39 This may be delegated to the equitable owners.

40 In unregistered land, the trustees would appear as owners under a deed.

41 Replacing section 30 of the LPA 1925.

42 Because, in such a case, there can be no overreaching – section 4.9.8 below.

43 See, for example, *Laskar* v. *Laskar* (2008).

their interests at a later date,[44] there will not be this identity between legal and equitable owners, and problems can occur. We will examine these more closely below, but for now three factors need be noted.

(i)   A sale (including a mortgage) by *all* of the trustees, provided that they are two or more in number, will overreach the interests of the equitable owners (sections 2(1)(ii) and 27 of the LPA 1925).[45] The interests of the equitable owners will take effect in the proceeds of sale, and only a very astute equitable owner even has a chance of stopping this happening.[46]

(ii)   If there is only one trustee of the land, as is likely where the co-ownership has not been created expressly,[47] the interests of the equitable owners cannot be overreached.[48] Consequently, whether the equitable interests can have priority over the interest of a purchaser will depend on the law of registered or unregistered conveyancing (as the case may be).

(iii)   If the trust is created by 'a disposition' (which probably means a trust created expressly in writing, and not one arising informally), the exercise of the trustee's power of sale (among others) can be made subject to an express requirement that the consent of the beneficiaries be obtained.[49] This is an attempt to ensure that a sale does not take place contrary to their wishes or at least of forcing a reference to the court under section 14 of TOLATA 1996.[50]

4.8   The Advantages of the 1925 and 1996 Legislative Reforms

In discussing the property legislation of 1925–96 in general, and the law of co-ownership in particular, it is always important to remember that the wholesale reshaping of English property law was prompted by two fundamental objectives.

1   To ensure that the value of land as an economic asset was utilised to the full and, to that end, to promote the free alienability of land. This would entail both simplifying the conveyancing procedure and providing for the protection of purchasers of land from the myriad rights and interests that might encumber their use of the land.

2   To ensure, as far as was compatible with this first objective, that no owner or occupier of land and no person with any interest in land was unreasonably prejudiced by the procedural and substantive changes that were to be made. It was recognised, however, that some people would find that their rights over the land itself had

---

44 As in HSBC v. Dyche (2009).

45 Provided that the sale is genuine, see HSBC v. Dyche (2009), in which two trustees 'sold' to one of them; see [2010] Conv. 1.

46 See section 4.9 below.

47 See section 4.10.2 below.

48 *Williams & Glyn's Bank v. Boland* (1981).

49 Section 10 of TOLATA 1996.

50 For the position before TOLATA 1996, *Re Herklot's Will Trusts* (1964) suggests that it may have been possible to restrict the powers of the trustees in similar fashion.

diminished, albeit that such rights could now take effect in its exchange product: that is, money.

These two goals remain, but changes in the way in which land was used and the spread of land ownership among all sections of society meant that the machinery of the 1925 legislation was out of date well before 1996. For example, land is no longer owned by a relatively few wealthy families, nor is it used only for investment purposes. The 'property owning democracy' is a clichéd but accurate description for the widespread land owner-ship that exists today. It was almost ludicrous that normal domestic co-ownership should have been forced to operate under a statutory mechanism (the old trust for sale) that was designed to promote the *sale* of land rather than its retention for use by the owners. Hence, the reforms of 1925 were rightly amended by the 1996 Act in order to reflect the reality of property use and ownership in 1997 and beyond. This should be remembered in the following discussion about the advantages of the 1925 and 1996 legislative reforms.

First, prior to 1 January 1926, any person wishing to purchase co-owned land would have to investigate either the one title of the joint tenants or the individual titles of every single tenant in common. Obviously, not only was this time-consuming and expensive, but the objection of just one tenant in common might prevent the land from being sold or mortgaged, even if this would have been for the benefit of every other tenant. By abolish-ing tenancies in common at law, the LPA 1925 has ensured that there is but one title to investigate: the legal joint tenancy. Moreover, the number of legal joint tenants is limited to a maximum of four (irrespective of the number of equitable owners), so that a purchaser need only concern himself with obtaining the consent of, at maximum, four people.[51]

Second, if there are two or more trustees of land (i.e. two or more legal owners), and the purchaser obtains the consent of all[52] to a sale or mortgage, the purchaser safely may ignore all of the equitable owners, subject only to any entries on the register of title restricting the trustees' powers of dealing with the land.[53] This is the magic of statutory overreaching whereby the interests of the equitable owners (be they in equity joint tenants or tenants in common) are transferred from the land to the proceeds of sale arising from the money paid by the purchaser. Indeed, such is the power of overreaching that it will operate even if no money is actually paid over in one large sum, provided that a sum is *payable* should the trustees wish to draw on it. Thus, in *State Bank of India v. Sood* (1997), overreaching occurred by reason of the fact that the trustees had mortgaged the property in return for an overdraft facility rather than receiving a one-off capital payment.[54]

Third, although a tenancy in common cannot exist at law, in equity both this and the joint tenancy are possible. Indeed, in the normal case, the equitable owners are secure in the sense that their interests, however held, will take effect in any proceeds should the property be sold or mortgaged. Moreover, the existence of a trust means that the equitable owners have powerful proprietary remedies in the event of default by the trustees, as where the trustees have spent any money raised by way of mortgage in breach of the terms

---

51 In most cases of residential co-ownership, there will be only two trustees – usually the same people as the equitable owners.

52 Bearing in mind that there may be a maximum of four only.

53 For example, a requirement to obtain a person's consent before sale: a Form N restriction.

54 It would be otherwise if no sum were *payable* at all or if the 'sale' was not genuine: *HSBC v. Dyche* (2009).

of the trust. For example, the beneficiaries may establish ownership of any assets purchased by the trustees with the proceeds of sale or, failing that, may sue the trustees personally if they have spent the money on untraceable assets. After all, the trustees are 'trustees' and subject to the normal core obligations of that office.[55]

Fourth, the existence of a power to sell under the trust of land prevents co-owned land becoming inalienable should there be a dispute between the co-owners (or other interested persons). Although all trustees must agree if the power of sale is to be exercised voluntarily, if the trustees disagree about how the land should be used, application can be made to the court under section 14 of TOLATA 1996 for an order for sale (or other order concerning the property). If sale is ordered, the equitable interests will take effect in the proceeds of sale in the normal way. Consequently, co-owned land will not stagnate through the inability to secure the agreement of all of the legal owners. This is entirely consistent with the general aim of the 1925 reforms, which was to ensure the free alienability of co-owned land through simplifying the conveyancing process and offering protection for the purchaser against any adverse equitable interests (the overreaching machinery). As noted above, the 1996 statute reflects the fact that much co-owned land is not held in order to sell, but in order that it be occupied, but that does not mean that it becomes inalienable. TOLATA's replacement of the old trust for sale with the trust for land, comprising a power (but not a duty) to sell the land, puts this into practice. Thus, the 1996 statute holds more evenly the balance between the needs of the purchaser and the needs of the equitable owners and an application under section 14 can be made when there is deadlock.[56] A synopsis of the effect of the 1996 Act is given below.

4.9 The Disadvantages of the Trust of Land as a Device for Regulating Co-ownership

Given what we have just learnt about purchaser protection through the overreaching machinery, it is not surprising that many of the disadvantages of the current mechanism, even after the 1996 amendments, focus on the other half of the equation: the equitable co-owner – particularly the equitable owner who is not also a trustee of the legal estate. However, as we shall see, not even the legal owners of co-owned land always benefit from the imposition of a trust.

4.9.1 Disputes as to sale

An immediate difficulty of utilising the trust as a mechanism for co-ownership is that there may well be disputes between the co-owners[57] as to whether the property should be sold, retained for occupation by the equitable owners or used to generate income. Admittedly, the difficulty is not as pressing as it was prior to the 1996 Act – the trustees are no longer

---

55 Of course, in many cases in which the trustees have spent any money, their personal liability will be an empty shell and the equitable owners will have been overreached and have no cash share – see e.g. *Flegg*.

56 Although the *express* and deliberate creation of a *trust for sale* is still possible, such trusts will be subject to the strictures of TOLATA 1996 and now carry no advantages.

57 Whether trustees or equitable owners.

under a duty to sell – but the potential remains for disputes and litigation. Indeed, in the normal course of events in respect of residential property, the legal owners and the equit-able owners will be the same people and the property will have been acquired for a purpose (domestic occupation) and both will be happy to retain the property. Yet, should the co-owners' relationship break down, or one of the co-owners go bankrupt, the other co-owner or co-owners[58] or the representatives of the bankrupt co-owner may wish to sell the property to realise its capital value or may be forced to do so to satisfy creditors.

To deal with such disputes, section 14 of TOLATA 1996 provides that any trustee of land, or any person having an interest in land subject to such a trust (e.g. an equitable owner, mortgagee, or trustee in bankruptcy[59]) may apply to the court for an order concerning 'the exercise by the trustees of any of their functions' or declaring the nature and extent of a person's equitable interest. In many cases, the application is for an order for sale or some-times possession and sale. Save in those cases in which the application is made by a trustee in bankruptcy in respect of property in which a bankrupt has an interest,[60] in deciding whether to order a sale (or make some other order), the court is directed to have regard to a number of matters specified in section 15 of TOLATA 1996. These are: the intentions of the persons who established the trust; the purposes for which the property is held; the welfare of any minor who occupies the land as his home (whether or not as a child of the owner); the interests of any secured creditor; and, in most circumstances, the wishes of any equitable owner. Although, as a matter of strict law, this list is not exhaustive of the factors the court should consider (consequently other, novel factors may play a part),[61] in most cases the court will not need to go beyond section 15 in order to reach an appropriate conclusion.

Clearly, section 15 is designed to ensure that a court does not simply order sale of the property as a quick route to a solution, but instead requires it to consider the matter in the round bearing in mind a number of specific matters. Thus, under section 15, it is perfectly possible for an application for an order for sale to be refused,[62] or for sale to be postponed until some date in the future.[63] Importantly, the statutory considerations of section 15 mirror many of the factors developed by the courts when interpreting the now-repealed section 30 of the LPA 1925 – the section that sections 14 and 15 of TOLATA replaced. Thus, it was the Law Commission's view that much of the pre-1996 case law would remain relevant in interpreting sections 14 and 15 of TOLATA 1996.[64] The following are examples of factors considered by the court in deciding whether to exercise its discretion either under the old section 30 or explicitly under the rubric provided by section 15 of TOLATA 1996.

1   Whether the property is needed for the maintenance of a matrimonial home (*Jones v. Challenger* (1961)) or for the home of a stable unmarried couple.

2   Whether the property is required in order to provide accommodation for the lives of the co-owners, or that of the survivor (*Harris v. Harris* (1996)) or until the occurrence

---

58 Meaning whether the legal or equitable co-owners.

59 Being a person appointed by a court to manage the affairs of a person formally declared bankrupt.

60 See section 4.9.3 below.

61 *Putnam & Sons v. Taylor* (2009).

62 For example, *Holman v. Howes* (2007).

63 *Chun v. Ho* (2001).

64 Law Commission Report No. 181, which led to TOLATA 1996.

of any event. Thus, in *Chun v. Ho* (2001), sale was postponed until the completion of the education of one of the co-owners.

3   Whether the property is needed for the provision of a family home for the children of a relationship that has broken down (*Williams v. Williams* (1976)). Under section 15 of TOLATA 1996, the welfare of any minor occupying the land as his home is made relevant expressly, thus resolving the doubts expressed in *Re Holliday* (1981) and *Re Evers' Trust* (1980). This criterion was employed to good effect in *Edwards v. Lloyds TSB* (2004), in which a co-owner was able to postpone a sale for five years in order to safeguard a home for the children of the relationship, even though the application was made by a mortgagee whose mortgage took effect over more than 50 per cent of the value of the property.[65]

4   Whether the property is required in order that a business may continue, the land having been purchased for that purpose, as in *Bedson v. Bedson* (1965).

5   Where the person seeking a sale may be estopped from obtaining an order for sale by their conduct, such conduct having been relied on by the other co-owner: *Holman v. Howes* (2007).[66]

6   Whether there has been any misconduct by the person applying for sale, or his legal advisers, as in *Halifax Mortgage Services v. Muirhead* (1998), in which sale was refused because the claimant's solicitors had wrongly altered relevant documents.

7   The general circumstances of the beneficiaries of the Trust, including age, health, suitability of the premises – *Edwards v. Royal Bank of Scotland* (2010).

8   Finally, and perhaps most importantly, if the request for a sale comes from a creditor – such as a mortgagee – the courts have taken the general view that a creditor should not be kept out of his money unless there are clear reasons to refuse a sale: *Bank of Ireland v. Bell* (2001). Although this is not always the paramount consideration – see *Mortgage Corp v. Shaire* (2001) and *Edwards v. Lloyds TSB* (2004) – there is a trend towards ordering a sale at the request of a creditor even though it will result in the loss of a home for the non-consenting co-owners. So, in *First National Bank v. Achampong* (2003), *Pritchard Englefield v. Steinberg* (2004) and *Putnam & Sons v. Taylor* (2009), a sale was ordered at the request of the mortgagee/chargee even though the interests of the persons in occupation had priority to the mortgagee as a matter of property law.[67] This is considered more fully below.

4.9.2   When is it likely that a court will order sale?

As was the case under the old law of section 30 of the LPA 1925, whether an application under section 14 of TOLATA for a sale will be granted necessarily depends greatly on the particular facts of each case. However, while there is no doubt that the decisions taken under section 30 will remain useful, we must be aware of one very important proviso. As

---

65 The mortgage operated over the former husband's share, but not over the former wife's. But contrast *Edwards v. Royal Bank of Scotland* (2010) where the possibility that a grandchild might visit was not enough.

66 This has echoes of proprietary estoppel. See also *Re Buchanan Wollaston's Conveyance* (1939).

67 This priority would take effect in the proceeds of sale. Thus, the co-owner who is not bound by the mortgage would take their share of the proceeds of sale before any payment to the creditor. Another recent example is *Edwards v. Royal Bank of Scotland* (2010).

we have seen, before the 1996 Act, co-owned land was subject to a trust *for sale* and this carried with it a duty to sell. Thus, in any dispute as to sale, the default position was that a sale must take place and this is reflected in the case law decided under the old section 30. However, under TOLATA 1996, there is no duty to sell the land – it is a trust *of land* – and pre-1996 statements unequivocally favouring a sale of co-owned property in cases of dispute must be read with some care and cannot be applied without thought to applications under section 14 of TOLATA.[68] Thus, in *Banker's Trust v. Namdar* (1997), a sale was ordered under section 30 of the LPA 1925, but Peter Gibson LJ thought that it was 'unfortunate' that TOLATA 1996 was not applicable (the case arose before TOLATA 1996 came into force) 'as the result might have been different'. What this means in practice is hard to predict, but much may turn on precisely who is requesting a sale under section 14. For example, a court is still likely to order a sale when only the co-owners are in dispute and there are no extrinsic factors (e.g. no children), as this supports the alienability of the co-owned land.[69] Again, a sale is likely to be ordered if the land was purchased as an investment, rather than a home, or if it would be inequitable to deny a co-owner their share of the capital value of land.[70] Conversely, a sale may be resisted if there are children living in the property,[71] if the co-owner wanting a sale is not in desperate financial straits or if one co-owner has special reasons for wishing to remain in occupation. So, in *Chun v. Ho* (2001), a sale was postponed until one co-owner completed her studies; the other co-owner had behaved inequitably, there was no real evidence that the money was needed to pay his debts, and the co-owner resisting sale had provided most of the original purchase price. Likewise in *Dear v. Robinson* (2001), in which the wishes of the beneficiaries were critical (even though their consent to a sale was not required formally) and the postponement of sale was in accordance with the original intentions of the creator of the trust.[72] Clearly, then, if the non-trustee equitable owners' consent is *required* before a sale takes place (e.g. where such requirement is imposed in the original instrument creating the trust), a court will be careful before it dispenses with such consent and actually orders a sale against their wishes.

Importantly, case law has not been consistent in those cases (noted above) in which the rights of creditors are in contest with the rights of the innocent co-owner (assuming no bankruptcy[73]). Thus in *Pritchard Englefield v. Steinberg* (2004), a sale was ordered at the request of a creditor holding a charging order[74] despite the objections of an equitable owner and this followed a pattern established by *TSB v. Marshall* (1998),[75] confirmed by *Bank of Ireland v. Bell* (2001) and *First National Bank v. Achampong* (2003), in which even the fact that the non-consenting owner had priority over the creditor could not stave off a sale. Likewise, in

---

68 *Mortgage Corporation v. Shaire* (2001).

69 But see *Holman v. Howes* (2007), in which a sale was refused in precisely these circumstances.

70 See the discussion in *Barclay v. Barclay* (1970).

71 *Edwards v. Lloyds TSB* (2004).

72 Even if the equitable owners' consent is not a *requirement* of a sale or mortgage by the trustees, their wishes are relevant (see section 11 of TOLATA 1996), although it is unlikely that they will be pivotal.

73 The position if one of the co-owners is bankrupt is discussed separately as a different statutory regime applies.

74 Arising from a court judgment securing a debt over land of the debtor.

75 A sale was ordered even though there were children present on the land because there was no realistic prospect of the debt being repaid.

Putnam & Sons v. *Taylor* (2009), a sale was ordered at the request of a claimant with a charging order over H's share of the equitable interest because, generally, a creditor should not be kept out of his money indefinitely, although it may have been relevant in this case that, even after a sale and payment of the debt, there would have been enough money left over to provide a house for H and W.[76] Yet, once again all is not clear-cut. In *Mortgage Corporation* v. *Shaire* (2001), it was made clear that the rights of creditors should not prevail automatically and in *Edwards* v. *Lloyds TSB* (2004), a sale was postponed for five years because of the needs of the children and family even though this would keep the mortgagee out of its security.

As is obvious then, the court's approach to disputed sales will continue to vary with the circumstances, bearing in mind that the default position under section 14 is not sale. Sweeping generalisations about how TOLATA 1996 may have affected the court's view are probably best avoided – for example, in *Shaire* and *Edwards*, there was much about sale no longer being appropriate, and in *Bell* and *Englefield*, there was much about realising the capital value of the land. What is clear, however, is that a properly advised co-owner can act to ensure that they are at least consulted before a sale takes place. In registered land, an equitable co-owner may be able to place a restriction on the title of the co-owned land, which has the effect of limiting the legal owners' (the trustees') powers to act. If an appropriate restriction has been entered, this will ensure that no dealings can take place unless the conditions specified in the restriction are fulfilled: for example, that there are indeed two trustees of the land for overreaching, or that the consents of the equitable owners are required and obtained.[77] Any attempt to deal with the land contrary to the restriction will be discovered by a purchaser and may trigger an application under section 14 of TOLATA 1996 to try to prevent sale, or to ensure that it takes place only on certain conditions.[78] Note finally that a court is empowered under section 14 of TOLATA 1996 to revisit a previous application if circumstances change before a sale actually taking place. So, in *Dear* v. *Robinson* (2001), a previous order for sale was rescinded because circumstances had changed and a majority of the beneficiaries no longer wanted an immediate sale.

4.9.3   The special case of bankruptcy

The list of factors in section 15 of TOLATA 1996 do not apply to disputes concerning sale of co-owned property when an application is made by the trustee in bankruptcy of a

---

76 This was an explicit reason for ordering sale in favour of a non-priority lender in *Edwards* v. *Royal Bank of Scotland* (2010). Neither was a sale in breach of the European Convention on Human Rights as such an order would be in accordance with the law and in the public interest as permitted under Article 1, Protocol 1 to the Convention. See also *Close Invoice Finance Limited* v. *Pile* (2008).

77 Note, however, that in *Coleman* v. *Bryant* (2007), the court decided that it would not order HM Land Registry (after its refusal) to enter a restriction requiring the beneficiaries' consent to a disposition as this would destroy overreaching. Indeed it would. It remains unclear whether HM Land Registry would accept the entry of a restriction requiring the beneficiaries' consent if the requirement for consent was specified expressly in the document establishing the trust. It would be difficult to justify a refusal in such circumstances.

78 The legal owner may also, of course, apply under section 14 of TOLATA for authorisation to conduct a sale contrary to a restriction. In addition, any person interested may apply under section 14 for an injunction preventing an anticipated sale, but this is likely to be granted only in the most unusual and exceptional situations – assuming, of course, that the equitable owner knows of a proposed sale or mortgage before it happens.

person interested in co-owned land. In that case, an application is made under section 14 of TOLATA, but section 335A of the Insolvency Act 1996 provides the list of relevant factors that the court must consider.[79] Note also that, by virtue of the Enterprise Act 2002, a trustee in bankruptcy should apply for sale of the property within three years of the bankruptcy, else he risks the property returning to the bankrupt free from the claims of the creditors.[80]

If one of the persons interested in the co-owned land is made bankrupt (whether they are a legal or equitable owner), their assets vest in a 'trustee in bankruptcy'. The 'trustee in bankruptcy' is simply the name given to the person who administers the bankrupt's assets with a view to paying off his creditors. In a co-ownership situation, a trustee in bankruptcy will step into the shoes of the legal or equitable owner who is bankrupt. Naturally, the trustee in bankruptcy will want to sell the co-owned property to realise some of the bankrupt's assets, and, equally naturally, this will be resisted by the other legal or equitable owners, who is often the bankrupt's intimate partner wishing to stay in the house. If a sale is opposed, the trustee in bankruptcy will apply to the court for an order for sale under section 14 and the court will have to balance the needs of the innocent creditors and the needs of the innocent co-owner within the framework of section 335A of the Insolvency Act 1986. On its face, the section 14/section 335A procedure applies whether or not the co-owners were married, or, indeed, in any emotional relationship. This is different from the now-repealed section 336(3) of the Insolvency Act 1986, which applied only to spouses and only to bankruptcies of the legal owners. However, it is only in the case of spouses (not unmarried couples) that spousal conduct and the needs of children are expressly mentioned as relevant factors for the court's consideration. It is not clear whether this means that the needs of children of non-married couples are irrelevant under the statute (surely not – see section 335A(c)), but in any event the law relating to unmarried couples was declared to be relevant to the old section 336(3) by Re Citro (1991), and this should remain the case for the new section 335A. Section 335A is not to be regarded as an exhaustive list of the factors that the court should consider.

On hearing an application for sale by a trustee in bankruptcy, the court is directed by section 335A to consider the following matters: the interests of the bankrupt's creditors; the conduct of the bankrupt's spouse as a contributing factor to the bankruptcy; the needs of the spouse and the needs of any children; and all other circumstances – but not the needs of the bankrupt.[81] It may then make such orders as it thinks just and reasonable. However, if the application under section 14 of TOLATA 1996 is made more than one year after the bankruptcy, the interests of the creditors are deemed to outweigh the interests of the resisting co-owners unless the circumstances are 'exceptional'. What this means is that, after one year, the court is extremely likely to order a sale of the property in order to satisfy the creditors, but up to then, the court may well delay sale so as to give the 'innocent' occupiers a chance to make alternative arrangements.[82] So, in Harrington v. Bennett (2000), an

---

79 Section 15(4) of TOLATA 1996. Section 335A of the Insolvency Act 1986 replaces the similar, but not identical, section 336(3) of the Insolvency Act 1986.

80 Enterprise Act 2002, section 261, inserting section 283A into the Insolvency Act 1996.

81 See e.g. Everitt v. Budhram (2009). In this context, and probably for all of section 335A, 'needs' does not mean merely financial need but encompasses (among other things) physical and mental welfare.

82 Note that the trustee is generally required to take action for possession and sale within three years of the bankruptcy, (section 383A of the Insolvency Act 1986), else the property revests in the bankrupt to the exclusion of the creditors.

application by the trustee in bankruptcy for sale more than one year after the bankruptcy was granted by the court. It was not an 'exceptional' circumstance that the bankrupt appeared to have a purchaser in view who might pay a higher price than that achievable under a sale by the trustee in bankruptcy.

The overall effect of section 335A was considered at some length by Lawrence Collins J in *Dean v. Stout* (2004). He summarised the position as follows. First, the presence of exceptional circumstances is a necessary condition to displace the presumption that the interests of the creditors outweigh all other considerations, but the presence of exceptional circumstances does not debar the court from making an order for sale. Second, typically the exceptional circumstances relate to the personal circumstances of one of the joint owners, such as a medical or mental condition. Third, the categories of exceptional circumstances are not to be categorised or defined and the court should make a value judgment after looking at all of the circumstances. Fourth, the circumstances must be truly exceptional and, as explained in *Re Citro* (1991), this means matters that are outside the usual 'melancholy consequences of debt and improvidence'. Fifth, it is not uncommon for a partner with children to be faced with eviction in circumstances in which the sale will not produce enough to buy a comparable home in the same neighbourhood or, indeed, elsewhere. Such circumstances cannot be described as exceptional. Sixth, for the purposes of weighing the interests of the creditors, the creditors have an interest in the order for sale being made, even if the whole of the net proceeds will go towards the expenses of the bankruptcy, and the fact that they will be swallowed up in paying those expenses is not an exceptional circumstance.[83]

To conclude then, it is apparent that section 335A of the Insolvency Act 1986 explicitly favours a sale at the request of the trustee in bankruptcy after one year and there may well be sound commercial and equitable reasons why this should be so. Nevertheless, while we know from *Dean v. Stout* what is *not* 'exceptional', it remains uncertain what actually will qualify so as to justify a postponement of sale beyond the one-year period. In fact, until now, very little has satisfied this test, although the fact that the bankrupt or their spouse is terminally or seriously ill has been held sufficiently grave as to justify a postponement of sale.[84] Thus, in *Everitt v. Budhram* (2009), the mental state of the bankrupt's spouse was sufficiently 'exceptional' as to justify a further postponement of sale beyond the one-year period of grace.[85] Of particular interest in this regard is the case of *Barca v. Mears* (2004) in the High Court. In this case, it was argued that a sale should be postponed for longer than one year because of the special educational needs of the son. In the result, and on the particular facts, this was not persuasive, but the Court did make some important observations. First, the Court confirmed that *Re Citro* did assimilate the position of married and unmarried couples and its general approach would apply even if the co-owners stood in no relationship at all. Second, that as the law stood, the pressure for a sale at the request of the trustee in bankruptcy was virtually always overwhelming. Third, however, the Court held that the protection afforded by Article 8 of the European Convention on Human Rights (ECHR),[86] as implemented by the Human Rights Act 1998, might require a rethink. It was

---

83 Neither is it an exceptional circumstance that a creditor would *not* suffer by reason of delaying sale: *Donohoe v. Ingram* (2006). In this case, a sale at a later date would also have achieved payment of creditors.

84 *Claughton v. Charalambous* (1998) and *Re Bremner* (1999).

85 Even so, the house was to be sold when the additional period – a further year – had elapsed.

86 Respect for private and family life and Article 1 of Protocol 1, respect for property.

arguable – indeed likely according to the judge – that the near-*automatic* ordering of sale in bankruptcy cases after one year could contravene the ECHR, the point being that a balance had to be struck between the needs of the creditors and the requirements of Article 8. The presumption of a sale after one year, save in exceptional circumstances, as this had been interpreted, might not represent a sufficient balancing exercise. Consequently, what the judge called a 'shift in emphasis' in the interpretation of section 335A might be necessary to ensure compatibility with the ECHR. This could be achieved by recognising that, in the normal case of 'everyday' bankruptcy, the creditors' interests would outweigh all other interests, but also by accepting that what was 'exceptional' should involve a proper consideration of the facts without the presumption of bias in favour of creditors that was evident in the pre-1998 case law. Unfortunately, subsequent case law has not been as robust in its defence of the rights of innocent co-owners: in *Donohoe v. Ingram* (2006), the court paid lip service to the idea that the test within section 335A might have to be reinterpreted to make it Convention-compliant by simply deciding that, even on that basis, there were no exceptional circumstances. Further, in *Nicholls v. Lan* (2006), the court found no incompatibility *per se* between the provisions of the Insolvency Act 1986 and the Convention,[87] thus neutralising the concerns raised in *Barca*, and in *Everitt v. Budhram* (2009), the human rights point appears not to have been raised at all. Perhaps, therefore, the farthest we can go after *Barca* is to conclude that judicial recognition that the Convention *might* have an impact on the interpretation of section 335A can remind us that 'exceptional' does *not* mean 'nearly never'.

4.9.4   Summary thus far

It is convenient at this stage to summarise the position in respect of the court's approach when an application is made under section 14 of TOLATA 1996. In most cases, the court must consider the factors listed in section 15 of TOLATA 1996 (the intentions of the creator of the trust; the purposes for which the property is held; the welfare of any child who occupies or might occupy the property as his home; the interests of a secured creditor; the wishes of any beneficiaries), but in cases of bankruptcy must consider instead those factors listed in section 355A of the Insolvency Act 1986 (the interests of the creditors; for dwelling houses, the interests and conduct of the bankrupt's spouse; the needs and resources of the spouse; the needs of any children; the requirement to sell after one year barring exceptional circumstances). Importantly, much may turn on who is making the application.

1   In disputes purely between co-owners, without the intervention of any third party, the court may well be happy to postpone sale and make some other order: for example, that one co-owner pays rent to another (or does not have to – *Chun v. Ho* (2001)); or that the land is partitioned (*Rodway v. Landy* (2001)), or that sale is postponed indefinitely to such time as the person in possession does indeed consent (*Holman v. Howes* (2007)). Under TOLATA 1996, the trust of *land* is no longer a trust for *sale* of land and so it is likely that that there will be much less emphasis on a sale in these circumstances. This is even more so if there are children of the relationship or there is some other pressing reason why a sale should be postponed, bearing in mind that this necessarily keeps one co-owner out of their money.

---

87 See above in similar vein *Close Invoice Finance Limited v. Pile* (2008).

2   In disputes between a co-owner and a third-party secured creditor (e.g. a mortgagee), *where there is no bankruptcy*, it is important to assess why the creditor wishes a sale. It is worth noting here that a mortgagee does not have to resort to section 14 for a sale if the mortgagee has overreached the beneficial interests by paying capital money to two or more trustees or otherwise takes free of the mortgage (e.g. having obtained relevant consents). In such cases in which the mortgagee has priority, like *City of London Building Society v. Flegg* (1988) (in which overreaching occurred) and *Le Foe v. Le Foe* (2001) (consent), the mortgagee may sell in virtue of its paramount mortgage powers. Consequently, a mortgagee using section 14 of TOLATA 1996 is by definition a mortgagee bound as a matter of property law by the prior rights of one of the co-owners. This may be important as the court legitimately can ask why it should deprive a co-owner of possession of the land when the co-owner's right is paramount to that of the creditor. Thus, a creditor may not get an order for sale under section 14 where they simply have failed to protect themselves adequately (as in *Boland*). However, we must not think that this is a determining factor because there are a number of cases in which a sale has been ordered in favour of a non-priority creditor where the court determines that it is unjust to keep the creditor out of its funds. This is most marked in those cases in which the 'unjustness' is that the mortgagee believed that all of the co-owners had consented to a mortgage but where this turned out to be untrue because of either fraud by one co-owner in forging the consent of the others (*Bank of Ireland v. Bell* (2001); *Bankers Trust v. Namdar* (1997) *Edwards v. Royal Bank of Scotland* (2010)) or because there was a successful claim of undue influence in relation to the consent (*First National Bank v. Achampong* (2003)). Likewise, a sale might be ordered against the wishes of a beneficiary with priority where, on closer analysis, a sale is actually in their best interests.[88] In those cases in which a sale is ordered at the request of a creditor who does not have priority, the equitable owner will have first call on the sale proceeds to the value of her interest and the creditor will be left to take its funds from the balance of the proceeds of sale.[89] The priority in land is thus reflected in priority over the proceeds of sale. Of course, the court may well conclude that no sale should be ordered, at least not without terms and conditions to protect the innocent co-owners (*Mortgage Corp v. Shaire* (2001)) or where there is a greater need to protect the innocent co-owner and any occupying children (*Edwards v. TSB* (2004)).

3   Where one of the co-owners goes bankrupt and his trustee in bankruptcy applies for an order for sale (within the allotted three years), it will take exceptional circumstances for a sale to be postponed for more than a year. Such a postponement has been rare indeed – for a limited postponement beyond a year, see *Everitt v. Budhram* (2009) – but *Barca v. Mears* (2004) suggests that the need to comply with the Human Rights Act 1998 might force a rethink. This has been sidestepped in *Donohoe v. Ingram* (2006) and flatly contradicted by *Nicholls v. Lan* (2006) and ignored in *Everitt*.

4   It is open to a mortgagee who cannot otherwise obtain a sale under section 14 to make the mortgagor bankrupt. The mortgagor owes a debt that he cannot pay. This

---

88 *Pritchard Englefield v. Steinberg* (2004), in which if there were no sale, the landlord was likely to forfeit the equitable owner's lease, leaving her with nothing.

89 If there is a shortfall, it might then pursue the mortgagor personally for the outstanding balance.

will mean the mortgagee giving up its secured status – and becoming an 'ordinary' creditor losing its proprietary right over the property[90] – but it means that the insolvent co-owner's property passes to the trustee in bankruptcy. This trustee can then apply for a sale under section 14 of TOLATA 1966 and this is likely to be ordered under the more powerful bankruptcy rules just discussed. Although this appears to be allowing the mortgagee to get by the back door what it cannot get by the front – after all, the mortgagee itself could not get a sale under section 14, otherwise it would not resort to this tactic – it is not an abuse of the process and will not be prevented by the court, as made clear in *Alliance & Leicester v. Slayford* (2001). Of course, as a practical matter, the mortgagee would have to be reasonably certain of getting some money as an unsecured creditor in bankruptcy before giving up its protected status as a secured creditor.

4.9.5 The position of a purchaser who buys co-owned land: When overreaching occurs

If a purchaser buys co-owned land from two or more legal owners (i.e. there are two or more trustees of land), then the interests of the equitable owners are overreached. The effect is that their co-ownership interest is transferred from the land and takes effect in the proceeds of sale. The purchaser obtains the land free from their rights, as in *City of London Building Society v. Flegg* (1988), in which the House of Lords confirmed that a mortgage (i.e. a sale) by the two trustees overreached the interests of Mr and Mrs Flegg so as to give the mortgagee a prior right to possession when the trustees defaulted on the mortgage payments.[91] This is the same in registered and unregistered land.

Usually, at least in a residential context, the two trustees will be the couple who together own the home in its entirety, both also being the only equitable owners. In such cases, the power of overreaching causes no difficulty because any 'equitable owner' can object to a proposed sale or mortgage in his or her capacity as a 'legal owner'. However, in some cases, the equitable owners will be different from the legal owners – such as in *Flegg* itself – and if there are two trustees, overreaching will occur. In that situation, the purchaser obtains the land free from the equitable rights, and those equitable rights take effect in the proceeds of sale, even if the equitable owners objected to the sale or knew nothing about it and, in fact, actually get nothing from the proceeds of sale,[92] as in *Flegg*. In other words, overreaching can occur against the wishes of the equitable owners and they could lose their right to occupy the land and must take their 'interests' in the proceeds of sale.[93] This result is not affected by section 11 of TOLATA 1996 whereby the trustees must consult the

---

90 Section 269 of the Insolvency Act 1986.

91 The Fleggs were the parents of one of the trustees (Mrs Maxwell-Brown), had contributed to the purchase price and thus were co-owners in equity, were in actual occupation at the time of the mortgage and knew nothing of it. It was their only home. See also *Birmingham Midshires Building Society v. Saberhawal* (2000).

92 For example, where the mortgage monies have been spent by the trustees, perhaps on the house or on a business venture or just dissipated.

93 Note also that overreaching can occur even if no capital money is actually paid over, provided that it was payable on the sale, as where a mortgage is used to secure a fluctuating overdraft (*State Bank of India v. Sood* (1997) and see Chapter 2).

equitable owners and 'in so far as is consistent with the general interest of the trust' give effect to such wishes. This is because section 11 imposes a duty to consult and pay attention to such wishes, not a duty to follow them slavishly, and overreaching will occur even if the trustees have not consulted at all, although, in such cases, the trustees may be liable personally for breach of trust. We should note, however, that overreaching will occur in 'two trustee' cases only when the sale or mortgage is genuine, in the sense of not being part of a fraudulent design. In HSBC v. Dyche (2009), H and W held on trust for C. H & W 'sold' the land to W alone.[94] As a matter of principle, this could have overreached C, but the judge held that it did not. In the judgment, the judge indicates that overreaching does not work in such circumstances because the purchaser (W) is not in 'good faith' and the sale was not 'authorised' by the equitable owner (C). With respect to the judge, this seems out of place in the law of registered title where the 'good faith' (or otherwise) of a purchaser is largely irrelevant and the trustees have full power to deal with the land and do not need to be 'authorised' by the equitable owners.[95] A better view might be that, on the very particular facts of this case, W was trying to use a statute (section 2 of the LPA 1925 – the overreaching provision) as an instrument of fraud. It is critical, however, that we regard this as wholly exceptional and do not expand our definition of 'fraud' to include situations in which the trustees do something against the interests of the equitable owners. Any wide view of 'fraud' would seriously undermine the integrity of overreaching and would be contrary to the entire philosophy behind the use of a trust in co-ownership.

Of course, we should not underestimate the effect that overreaching has on equitable owners and its powerful effect has caused some concern, for it appears to deprive an equitable owner of their interest in land and substitute instead a monetary claim against the trustee that may in reality be illusory. Indeed, the Law Commission once proposed different ways of combating overreaching and protecting the equitable owner. These proposals – now defunct – are briefly considered below. However, for the moment, let us consider the impact, if any, of other provisions of TOLATA 1996[96] on the effectiveness of overreaching. As we have seen, it is now possible for a settlor (i.e. the person who sets up the trust of co-owned land) to provide that the exercise of the trustees' powers should be subject to the consent of the beneficiaries (section 10 of TOLATA 1996) and further that any interested person (e.g. a non-legal equitable owner) may make an application for an order 'relating to the exercise by the trustees of any of their functions' (section 14). How do these provisions affect the 'trump card' of overreaching when there are two or more trustees of the land?

4.9.6   If consents are required

If the disposition originally conveying the land to the co-owners makes the trustees' powers (e.g. of sale or mortgage) dependent on obtaining the prior consent of the equit-able owners (as envisaged by section 10 of TOLATA 1996), there is a potential conflict with the ability of the trustees to sell the land and overreach the equitable interests. For example,

---

94 W then mortgaged the land and defaulted, hence the claim by HSBC as mortgagee.

95 See section 23 LRA 2002 and note how the reference to 'good faith' echoes the discredited decision in *Peffer v. Rigg* (1978).

96 Section 11 – the duty to consult – is discussed immediately above.

what is the position if the land is sold by the two trustees, but the required consents are not obtained? Is the purchaser bound by the equitable interests, or are they overreached? This is not such an easy question to answer, as the Act is not entirely clear on this point. Although it will be rare for consent requirements to be built into a trust of residential property (because the trustees/equitable owners will usually be the same people), the matter will not be settled conclusively until there has been some case law. Moreover, it should also be remembered that trustees could apply under section 14 of TOLATA 1996 for the removal of a consent requirement in the same way that equitable owners can apply for one to be imposed.

With these qualifications in mind, TOLATA 1996 appears to envisage the following results if land is sold or mortgaged by two or more trustees of land by a proper overreaching transaction yet in violation of a consent requirement. In *registered* land, because the consent requirement is expressed in the 'disposition' establishing the trust (i.e. it will be written in the original conveyance to the two trustees – section 10), the consent requirement is likely to be entered on the register of title in the form of a restriction against dealings.[97] This means that no dealings with the land can occur until the conditions of the restriction have been complied with – that is, consent is obtained. If, by some unlikely chance, no restriction is entered, the better view is that the purchaser obtains a good title to land, the equitable interests are overreached, and the equitable owners are left to sue the trustees for breach of trust.[98] This is despite section 8 of TOLATA 1996, which says that the power of sale 'may not be exercised without that consent'. Although there has been some academic criticism of this view, there is no doubt that TOLATA 1996 was not intended to restrict the power of overreaching. Case law under the Land Registration Act 1925 supported this view,[99] and sections 26, 29 and 30 of the Land Registration Act 2002 settle any doubts in favour of the primacy of overreaching in these circumstances. They stipulate in effect that overreaching is effective save where some restriction is entered on the title, even if a sale by the trustees violates some term of the trust. Note finally that a consent requirement granted by reason of an order of the court following an application made under section 14 of TOLATA 1996 will, of necessity, be registered as a restriction consequent on the court order.[100]

In unregistered land, although any deliberate consent requirement will again be expressly declared in the disposition establishing the trust, there is no mechanism to register it under the Land Charges Act (LCA) 1972. It would not be a land charge within Classes A–F, nor does a consent requirement appear to fall within any of the other registers of the LCA 1972. However, section 16 of TOLATA 1996 (which applies only to unregistered land) says that a purchaser is not affected by the trustees' failure to observe a consent requirement included in a disposition provided that the purchaser had no actual knowledge of the consent requirement. In other words, if the purchaser (or his legal adviser) did not actually know that the land was being conveyed in breach of a consent requirement, then overreaching remains effective. By analogy, the same rule should apply if a

---

97 A Form N restriction.

98 Sections 29 and 30 of the LRA 2002.

99 *Birmingham Midshires Building Society v. Saberhawal* (2000).

100 Note, however, that it now seems unlikely that a court will impose such a requirement, unless the circumstances are exceptional (*Coleman v. Bryant* (2007)).

consent requirement is imposed as a result of an application under section 14 of TOLATA 1996 (although the Act does not address this possibility). This means that the position in registered and unregistered land is broadly similar in effect. Note, however, that the chances of a consent being required in unregistered land are minimal – new trusts will usually take effect in registered land and rare will be the circumstances in which a consent requirement is imposed on an existing trust in unregistered land.

4.9.7   If consents are not initially required

If no consents are required, then clearly the matter is straightforward – overreaching takes its usual course. However, we need to be aware of the possibility that an equitable owner may apply under section 14 of TOLATA 1996 for a court order that the trustees seek his or her consent before a sale or mortgage. This is not precluded by section 14, which says that the court may make any order 'relating to the exercise by the trustees of any of their functions'. It is, however, controversial, for in *Coleman v. Bryant* (2007), the court was not prepared to enter a restriction requiring the consent of the equitable owner before a sale because this would destroy the concept of overreaching. It remains to be seen whether the court will have to develop criteria to determine whether a consent require-ment should be imposed, but if such an order is made, the position is as that described immediately above.[101]

4.9.8   When overreaching *does not* occur

Sections 2(1)(ii) and 27 of the LPA 1925 require money to be paid to at least two trustees[102] in order to overreach the equitable interests behind a trust of land. Consequently, the usual reason why overreaching does not occur is that there is only *one trustee* of the property, as in *Williams and Glyn's Bank v. Boland* (1981), in which Mr Boland was sole trustee holding for himself and his wife in equity. This situation arises most commonly because of a successful claim to an equitable interest in the property by a non-legal owner utilising the rules of resulting or constructive trusts discussed below.[103] A typical example would be where a single woman buys a house (which is conveyed to her name alone) and then she invites her lover to live with her, and the lover acquires an equitable interest under the principles explained in *Pettitt v. Pettitt* (1970) and *Lloyds Bank v. Rosset* (1991). If that happens, a trust of land arises,[104] but there is only one legal owner. If the purchaser buys the property (or a bank lends money on it), but pays the purchase money to the single trustee only, then the purchaser cannot rely on overreaching to protect him from the rights of the equitable owners. The purchaser may be bound by the rights of the equitable owners and his use of the land severely restricted or completely disrupted. In fact, in the absence of overreaching, the normal rules of registered or unregistered land (as the case may be) take over. Thus, in registered land, if the equitable owner is a person in discoverable actual

---

101 Note, however, that section 8 of TOLATA 1996 talks only of a consent requirement imposed by the disposition
      creating the trust. It could be that consent requirements imposed under section 14 will be treated differently.
102 Or a trust corporation.
103 *Pettitt v. Pettitt* (1970); *Lloyds Bank v. Rosset* (1991); *Stack v. Dowden* (2007).
104 *Bull v. Bull* (1955).

occupation of the property at the time of the purchase or mortgage,[105] he will have an interest that overrides the interest of the purchaser or mortgagee under paragraph 2, Schedule 3 of the LRA 2002. However, if this is not the situation – that is, the equitable owner is not in discoverable occupation triggering an interest that overrides – the purchaser or mortgagee will take the land free of the equitable interests even if they are not overreached because this is the normal rule in registered conveyancing (sections 29 and 30 of the LRA 2002).[106]

In unregistered land, these equitable interests *cannot* be registered as land charges (see section 2(4) of the LCA 1972). Consequently, whether they bind a purchaser or mortgagee who has *not* overreached depends on the 'doctrine of notice', this being one of the very few scenarios in which this ancient doctrine is still relevant in modern land law. Usually, if the equitable owner is residing in the property, the purchaser or mortgagee will be deemed to have constructive notice of their interest, and be bound by it, as discussed in *Kingsnorth Trust* v. *Tizard* (1986).

However, in both registered and unregistered land, a purchaser who has failed to overreach, and who is apparently bound by the priority of the equitable interest, nevertheless may be able to plead that the equitable owner has expressly or impliedly consented to the sale or mortgage. In such cases, a court of equity will respect the express or implied consent of the equitable owner with the consequence that the purchaser gains priority over their interest.[107] In order to give the purchaser this relief, the court must be satisfied that the expressed or implied consent is real. Thus, consent does not exist simply because the equitable owner has *knowledge* of the proposed sale or mortgage – *Skipton Building Society* v. *Clayton* (1993) – but rather this knowledge must be combined with circumstances that indicate an acceptance of the priority of the purchaser or mortgagee. Some examples may help to clarify the situation.

First, if the legal owner attempts to mortgage the land to a bank and his lover (the equitable owner) signs a consent form postponing her interest to that of the bank, we can be sure that (in the absence of undue influence) the consent was real for it has been given expressly. The obtaining of such express consent is the safest course of action for a mortgagee dealing with a single legal owner when it suspects that the other person on the land has some equitable interest in it.[108] Second, even in the absence of a signature on a consent form, the equitable owner may have so acted in relation to the mortgage (e.g. attending the bank, explaining the need for a mortgage to the bank's employee) that her consent can be implied from her actions. In such cases, the participation of the equitable owner in securing the mortgage undoubtedly implies consent. Third, if the equitable owner is aware that a mortgage is the only way in which the land can be purchased, he or she must be deemed to have consented to that mortgage. Without the mortgage, there can be no property in which the equitable owner can have an interest and so the equitable

---

105 *Abbey National Building Society* v. *Cann* (1991).

106 As would have been the case in *Thompson* v. *Foy* (2009), see Chapter 2. Note such equitable interests cannot be protected by the entry of a notice against the title: section 33 of the LRA 2002.

107 *Paddington Building Society* v. *Mendelson* (1985), registered land; *Bristol and West Building Society* v. *Henning* (1985), unregistered land.

108 The lender failed to do this in *HSBC* v. *Dyche* (2009) even though it knew of C's interest and when overreaching did not occur, it lost its priority.

owner cannot deny the priority of the mortgage. Importantly, this effectively means that it is near impossible for an equitable owner to claim priority over a mortgagee who provides funds for the original purchase of the land – consent will always be deemed to have been given by reason of the necessity of using a mortgage.[109] Fourth, it is established that genuine consent to one mortgage (mortgage X) will be taken to be effective in favour of a new mortgagee (mortgage Y) if the second mortgagee is providing funds to pay off the first mortgage. This is more properly regarded as a species of subrogation[110] than 'transferred consent' but it is based on the policy that the equitable owner should not benefit (i.e. recover her priority) merely because of a change in the identity of the lender. Consent to one mortgage can be taken to be consent to its replacement.[111] Fifth, by way of contrast, an equitable owner who knows that the legal owner is about to mortgage, but who does not consent expressly or impliedly, *does not* thereby lose the priority of his or her interest – assuming it amounts to an overriding interest under LRA 2002 through (discoverable) actual occupation. It is up to the lender to ensure that it has priority by seeking consent; it is not for the equitable owner to offer it. In practice, of course, most lenders will ensure that all possible or potential equitable owners sign a consent form before the lender agrees to advance the money by way of mortgage, thus securing the priority that may not be available through overreaching.

4.9.9   The position of the equitable owners: Problems and proposals

We have noted above that if a purchaser pays the purchase price to two trustees of the property, the equitable owners' rights are overreached. This means that the equitable rights are automatically transferred to the proceeds of sale – if any – and the trustees hold that money on trust for the equitable owners in the same way as they held the land: that is, as tenants in common or joint tenants. In many cases, of course, the sale will be caused by one or all of the co-owners wishing to realise their investment and it is quite likely that the money will be distributed and the trust brought to an end. Alternatively, where the legal and equitable owners are the same people (e.g. husband and wife), the money may be used to finance the purchase of a new property that could then become co-owned in the same way as the one sold. These are, indeed, the 'normal' cases and the great majority of dealings with residential co-owned land follow this smooth path. Yet there will always be some legal owners who decide to sell without telling the equitable owners, perhaps in order to abscond with the proceeds, or more frequently those who wish to raise a loan by way of mortgage of the property for their own purposes. What happens then?

---

109 *Abbey National Building Society v. Cann* (1991). It might be otherwise if the equitable owner's interest existed in unmortgaged land that was sold to purchase the new land and the equitable owner knew nothing of the need for a mortgage.

110 Generally, where a person (mortgagee Y) discharges an obligation (e.g. a mortgage) owed by person (the borrower) to another (mortgagee X), Y can be subrogated to the 'obligation' and be entitled to enforce the mortgage against the borrower. The person discharging the debt effectively steps into the shoes of the former mortgagee.

111 This consent is effective up to the value of the mortgage that is paid off by the replacement mortgage (*Equity and Home Loans v. Prestige* (1992); *LeFoe v. LeFoe* (2001)).

The first question is always whether overreaching has occurred and, if not, whether the purchaser or mortgagee is bound by the equitable interests. If overreaching has not occurred and the mortgagee/purchaser is bound, from the point of view of the equitable owners, the problem may have gone away. The equitable owners remain in possession of the land, save only that a mortgagee could apply for an order under section 14 of TOLATA 1996 forcing a sale of the land in order to realise its security. Whether the court would order a sale in such circumstances has been discussed above.[112] If overreaching has occurred, the fundamental rule is that the equitable owners have no claim against the purchaser or mortgagee to remain in possession of the land (*City of London Building Society v. Flegg* (1988)). They are overreached and their interests now take effect in the proceeds of sale or mortgage money. If the legal owners have absconded or are unable to pay, the equitable owners will have the normal remedies for breach of trust: for example, a personal action against the trustees or a tracing claim to any assets obtained by use of the trust money. Unfortunately, all of this may be of little comfort to an equitable owner who did not want to have the land sold, especially as their share of the proceeds may not be sufficient to pay for alternative accommodation. This is particularly acute in cases in which the property has been used as a family home. Likewise, the rationale for overreaching disappears completely if no purchase money was actually paid on the transaction, as in *Bank of India v. Sood* (1997).

In response to the decision in *Flegg*, and as a way of limiting the effect of overreaching for an 'unwilling equitable owner', the Law Commission once suggested three alternative reforms to the law (Law Commission Report No. 188). They are discussed briefly below, but are now defunct.[113]

1   That overreaching should not be possible unless one of the trustees is a solicitor or licensed conveyancer. The idea is simply that such a person might offer protection to an equitable owner by looking after their interests and possibly objecting to a sale. However, this is a poor solution, as it would make conveyancing more expensive as well as requiring an 'outsider' to become involved in personal affairs. Moreover, would it work? Would a solicitor have the time or inclination to be the guardian of the equitable owner?

2   That overreaching should not be possible if the equitable owner has registered their equitable interest. This would require an amendment to the LRA 2002 as such interests currently are not capable of protection through a notice – section 33 of the LRA 2002. This is superficially attractive (for the equitable owner) as the register could be relied on by the purchaser to indicate whether it is safe to proceed and the equitable owner would be protected. Unfortunately, however, this 'solution' presupposed that equitable owners would be *prepared* to register, even if they *knew* they should.[114] It is no accident that where there is no overreaching, these equitable rights

112   See section 4.9.

113   It has been accepted that, in fact, *Flegg* was an unusual case and that the need to ensure the alienability of co-owned land has priority over a policy of protecting occupiers.

114   For example, given that many of these equitable interests arise informally without writing or the involvement of solicitors, would a claimant know to register his or her interest 'against' her lover's land? Would she have been prepared to register, especially as this might have been regarded as a hostile act?

are capable of binding the purchaser *without* the need for registration through their potential as overriding interests.

3   That overreaching should not be possible without the consent of all of the equitable owners who are of full age and in possession of the property. The first point is that this would certainly work. An equitable owner's rights to the land would be safe from overreaching under this proposal. However, what this also would do is to destroy the entire overreaching mechanism of the LPA 1925. The whole point behind the abolition of legal tenancies in common, the institution of the joint tenant trusteeship and the concept of overreaching is precisely that a purchaser should be able to buy co-owned land *without* having to search for every legal and equitable owner and obtain their consent. This proposal would return the law to its pre-1926 state. In fact, it would be much easier to reinstate legal tenancies in common if that is what is wanted. That said, it will be obvious from the above discussion of the effect of TOLATA 1996 that some form of 'consent requirement' may now exist. This may not actually prevent a sale by two trustees (see section 4.9.6 above), but it could trigger an application under section 14 of the Act. In essence, then, a partial 'consent bar' may have been created by the 1996 Act, not entirely deliberately, the effect of which is not necessarily to prevent a sale by two trustees, but to trigger the intervention of the court under section 14.

4.9.10   The position of the equitable owners faced with overreaching: The problem in perspective

From the above discussion, we might be left with the impression that the lot of the equitable owner is a poor one. The law appears to favour the purchaser at every turn. However, what is the reality? First, if there is one trustee of the land, overreaching cannot occur. In the very great majority of cases, this will mean that the purchaser is bound by the rights of the equitable owners, both in registered land (as an overriding interest) and unregistered land (through the doctrine of notice). Thus, the equitable owner is secure, save for the possibility of a sale against their wishes if the purchaser or mortgagee applies under section 14 of TOLATA 1996. Even then, the equitable owner would be paid the full value of their share before any claim of the mortgagee or creditor.

Second, if there are two trustees of the land, overreaching can occur, but in most residential property cases, the two trustees will also be the *only* two equitable owners: for example, where man and woman hold the house on trust for themselves. Again, there is no difficulty, because either co-owner can object to a sale in their capacity as legal owner.

Third, it appears then that it is only where there are two trustees of land and *different* equitable owners that problems really occur. Such was the case in *Flegg*. Yet the question the Law Commission did not ask itself when producing its now-defunct report and the question we must ask now is: how often does this factual situation occur in the context of residential property? How often, in a domestic context, will there be two legal owners and *different or additional* equitable owners? The simple fact that the facts of *Flegg* did not arise until some 70 years after the LPA 1925 gives us a clue! There is much to suggest that *Flegg* raises an *exceptional* factual scenario, not a normal one.[115] Should the law be changed to meet the

---

115   Another example is *Birmingham Midshires BS v. Saberhawal* (2000). The point is not that this scenario never occurs, but rather that it is *relatively* rare. See also *HSBC v. Dyche* (2009).

'hard case'? One view is that all that needs to be done is to prevent a *single* trustee from appointing a second trustee (in order to overreach) without the leave of the court or the consent of the equitable owners. Such a move would prevent the artificial creation of a 'two-trustee' situation by a knowledgeable legal owner preparing to sell or mortgage the property. This may be achieved in registered land by the entry of a suitably worded restriction against the title.[116]

4.9.11   The question of possession

Prior to TOLATA 1996, the question of who had a *right* to occupy the co-owned land had caused unnecessary difficulty. There was no doubt that the legal owners had a right to occupy the land, subject to the terms of the trust instrument, for they had a legal estate with all of the rights this entailed. If the land was held for investment purposes, the trustees were likely to have relinquished possession to another (or their possession may have been impliedly or expressly excluded by the original trust instrument), but that would be because of the specific nature of their trust. With residential co-owned land, if all of the co-owners were also legal owners, each could occupy by virtue of their legal estate. Unfortunately, however, problems did arise for non-legal equitable owners. In theory, such persons had only an interest in the proceeds of sale of the land, not the land itself, and consequently could be denied possession. Obviously, this misrepresented the reality of the situation and cases such as *Bull v. Bull* (1955) and then *Williams and Glyn's Bank v. Boland* (1981) ignored the theory and recognised that the equitable owners had an effective right to possess, enforceable against the legal owners and (in the absence of overreaching) against a purchaser. This situation has now been regularised by TOLATA 1996. The Act has not altered the trustees' position as legal owners of the land, as they have all of the powers of an absolute owner unless restricted by the trust instrument or an entry on the register of title.[117] However, not only does the Act abolish the doctrine of conversion and effectively declare that the equitable owners shall be regarded as having rights in the land (section 3), but it also provides in section 12 that an equitable owner has a right to occupy the land if this was the purpose for which the trust came into existence.[118] Such a right can be excluded by the trustees in exceptional circumstances, under section 13, but this will be rare in respect of residential property and cannot, in any event, result in the removal of a person already occupying land unless they consent (section 13(7)). In reality then, TOLATA 1996 has effectively solved any problems that might remain in this regard – as it was intended to do.[119]

---

116   Remember also the *possibility* of using a restriction to prevent a sale of mortgage by two trustees without the consent of some named person – perhaps the equitable owner.

117   See also sections 23, 26 of the LRA 2002.

118   This was enforced in *Chun v. Ho* (2001) against the wishes of the other co-owner who wished the property sold.

119   Note also the court's power to regulate occupation under the Family Law Act 1996 in respect of 'matrimonial home' rights. Such rights of occupation are a creation of statute and do not depend on the claimant owning any interest in the land. They may be entered on the register of title by means of an agreed notice to ensure protection should the land be sold. They may not override.

4.9.12   The payment of rent

Once again, before TOLATA 1996, there were difficulties in requiring one co-owner to pay rent to the other if only one enjoyed occupation of the property. This was because the nature of co-ownership meant that each co-owner was, in theory, entitled to occupy the whole property (not any defined share) and could not be made to 'pay' for enjoying that to which they were already entitled. This is the unity of possession. So, if one co-owner did not occupy, the other could not be forced to pay them 'rent' or 'compensation' by way of recompense for sole use. This could have meant hardship for the 'ousted' co-owner, especially if the reason why only one of them was in possession of the property was because of a breakdown in their domestic relationship. Fortunately, even prior to TOLATA 1996, the courts took a pragmatic view and would order the payment of a monetary sum where it was equitable to do so, irrespective of the theoretical niceties.[120] Now, section 13 of TOLATA 1996 provides that compensation may be paid by one co-owner occupying the land to the exclusion of another if certain conditions are met. Of course, the payment of compensation for sole use by way of occupation rent will not be automatic and it was denied to Mr Stack in *Stack v. Dowden* (2007).[121] Likewise, in *Chun v. Ho* (2001), the co-owner was not required to pay rent to the non-occupying co-owner because the latter had had the benefit of the large amount of money that the occupying co-owner had contributed to the purchase price.

4.9.13   A summary of the Trusts of Land and Appointment of Trustees Act 1996

The effect of TOLATA 1996 has been woven into the preceding text and the picture presented there is of how trusts of land will work from 1 January 1997. The following is a short summary of how the Act changed the original 1925 co-ownership scheme.

1   It is not possible to create new strict settlements of land (see Chapter 5) and the entailed interest is abolished (see section 2 and Schedule 1 of TOLATA 1996). Existing strict settlements will remain valid, but very many will run their course and eventually disappear.

2   The doctrine of conversion is abolished, effective for all new and nearly all existing trusts of land (section 3).

3   Unless a trust for sale has been created expressly, existing trusts for sale of land become trusts of land (sections 4 and 5) and trusts of land will become the model for all future trusts. There is no duty to sell the land. It remains possible deliberately and unequivocally to create a 'trust for sale' of land, but, given that even these deliberate creations are subject to TOLATA 1996, there is very little to be gained practically.

4   The trustees have all of the powers of an absolute owner, but may delegate these to an equitable owner (sections 6–9). They may do this when it is expedient to give the person in possession of the land the power to manage it. However, only the trustees

---

120   *Re Pavlou (A Bankrupt)* (1993). An equitable co-owner could also be made to account for 'rent' in favour of a trustee in bankruptcy who had succeeded to the interest of the other co-owner: *Re Byford* (2003).

121   Lord Neuberger dissented on this point.

can give a valid receipt for purchase money, hence preserving their role in overreaching.

5   The trustees must consult with the equitable owners and give effect to their wishes in so far as is consistent with the purposes of the trust of land (section 11).

6   The trustees' powers may be made subject to the consent of the beneficiaries or some other person, but only if stated in the instrument creating the trust (section 10), or if imposed by the court after a section 14 application. This may have consequences when a sale is proposed.

7   The equitable owners have a right to occupy the property (section 12), which can be modified subject to safeguards (section 13). Compensation may be ordered for exclusive use of the land by one co-owner.

8   Any person with an interest in the land can make an application to the court under section 14 for a variety of orders, based on the criteria identified in section 15: for example, sale, no sale, override consent requirement, impose consent requirement. The criteria specified in section 15 do not apply in cases of bankruptcy because section 335A of the Insolvency Act 1986 applies instead.

4.10   The Express and Implied Creation of Co-ownership in Practice: Express, Resulting and Constructive Trusts

So far, we have considered the nature of co-ownership in general and the statutory machinery that governs it. Much has been said about the existence of two trustees or one trustee and the rights of the equitable owners. Now it is time to examine the way in which this co-ownership can come about. Put simply, how is it that land becomes 'co-owned' so that the panoply of legal rules just discussed come into play?

4.10.1   Express creation

Any land may be deliberately conveyed to two or more people, a typical example being the purchase of a new house by a couple. In such circumstances, the persons to whom legal title is transferred (i.e. by formal conveyance taking effect as a registered disposition under the LRA 2002) will be the legal owners. In the absence of any statement to the contrary, these legal owners will also be taken to be the equitable owners. The result is that land conveyed to A and B as legal owners will be held on trust by them for themselves as either joint tenants or tenants in common. This was effectively the case in *Roy v. Roy* (1996), in which two brothers were held bound by the joint ownership of a house that had been transferred to them both. As we shall see, this presumption that the legal owners (or owner) are also the *only* equitable owners may be challenged by proof of a 'resulting' or 'constructive' trust.

Before we come to that, however, it is important to note that it is quite possible for a conveyance of land expressly to declare who are the equitable owners, and also the nature of their ownership. Thus, land might be conveyed 'to A and B as legal owners on trust for A and B beneficially as tenants in common' or 'to A and B as legal owners on trust for A, B, C and D as tenants in common'. In these cases, both where the legal and equitable owners are the same people, and when they are not, the trust of land and the equitable ownership is 'expressly declared'. Two points are of importance here.

1   In order for an express trust of land to be valid, it must satisfy section 53(1) of the LPA 1925. This means that an express declaration of the beneficial (equitable) interests of the co-owners can only be relied upon to establish ownership if such declaration is 'manifested and proved by some writing'. In other words, as a matter of general principle,[122] a purely oral declaration of co-ownership will not be effective. Usually, the 'writing' is the deed of conveyance to the co-owners, but whatever form it takes, it must amount to a declaration of the equitable interest rather than be for some other purpose. Thus, in *Stack v. Dowden* (2007), the House of Lords held that a statement in the conveyance that a surviving trustee could give a valid receipt for any capital monies could not be taken as a declaration of the nature of the equitable interest.[123] However, there is a vital exception to the requirement of writing: namely, that a person who is not a party to any valid express declaration of trust may establish a beneficial interest in the property by proving a resulting or constructive trust. This is specifically provided for in section 53(2) of the LPA 1925, which exempts resulting and constructive trusts from the need for writing.[124] Importantly, as discussed immediately below, it is only if a person is not a party to a written declaration of trust that they can rely on the doctrine of resulting or constructive trusts. We should also be aware that even in the absence of an express declaration of the beneficial interests in the land (i.e. that no trust is declared), the very conveyance of the land to two or more people will be strong evidence of co-ownership in equity (*Roy*; *Stack*) unless it is clear that the conveyance to two persons was merely administrative in order to enable the single 'true' owner to purchase the land in the first place.[125]

2   If the beneficial interests are expressly declared in writing, this is conclusive as to the beneficial ownership for the parties to that express declaration – *Goodman v. Gallant* (1986). In other words, persons who are parties to the writing that establishes the trust cannot, thereafter, plead a resulting or constructive trust to establish different interests. The only exception to this is if the express declaration has been procured by fraud or some other vitiating factor such as undue influence. Of course, persons not party to the express written declaration of the trust may rely on resulting or constructive trusts. A typical example would be where a claimant to an interest alleges that they have a share by reason of conduct occurring after the legal title was transferred to the registered proprietor – as where a man already owns a house and his new wife or lover claims an equitable share at a later date. Moreover, *Stack* makes it clear that any of the parties to a conveyance that does not actually declare the trusts, but rather merely records the transfer of the land to them, may also rely on resulting or constructive trusts to prove an enlarged share. This seems correct because section 53(1) of the LPA 1925 talks of the express declaration of a trust of land, not merely the normal conveyance of land to two or more people. So, if a conveyance merely records a transfer to A and B without declaring the extent of their equitable ownership, it is

---

122   As ever, there are exceptions.

123   The clause was, simply, to ensure that a surviving joint tenant and so sole trustee could sell when all other trustees had died.

124   See section 4.10.2 below. Consider also the possibility of an interest arising orally through proprietary estoppel, which is not specifically exempted from section 53(1) of the LPA – see section 4.10.7 below.

125   *Goodman v. Carlton* (2001). See also *Abbey National v. Stringer* (2006) and *HSBC v. Dyche* (2009).

possible for either A or B to use resulting or constructive trusts to claim an enlarged or even total share of the equity. Such was the case in *McKenzie v. McKenzie* (2003), in which the father was declared the sole owner in equity under a resulting trust even though legal title was held jointly by both father and son, there being no express written declaration of the extent of the *equitable* co-ownership. Likewise in *Stack* itself, in which where Ms Dowden achieved more than a 60 per cent share of the equitable even though she and Mr Stack were joint legal owners.

4.10.2 Creation of co-ownership even though the legal title is in one name only

It often happens that property is bought by one person and conveyed into their sole name. Of course, this has nothing to do with co-ownership for that person owns the land absolutely. However, what happens if someone else (e.g. a spouse, a lover, a friend, an adult child) comes to live in that property, or makes some contribution to its purchase price? Is it possible that this new person may acquire an equitable interest in the house that is legally owned by the other? To put the question another way, even though legal title to the land is held by its original owner, in what circumstances may some other person gain a share in that ownership, albeit that such a share must necessarily be in the equitable interest given that the original owner is already holding the legal title? The law of resulting and constructive trusts provides the answer.[126] Before considering the matter in detail, however, it is vital to understand why it is so important to determine whether such an equitable interest is created.

In cases in which a claim is successful, although there is only one legal owner (A) (the person who originally purchased the property), the fact that another person (B) has established an equitable interest means that *in equity* the property is co-owned. As made clear by *Bull v. Bull* (1955), this means that a trust of the land comes into existence whereby the original legal owner (A) holds the property on trust for himself and B in equity. In other words, there is *one* trustee of the land, but two co-owners in equity.[127] Because there is only one trustee, a person who wishes to buy the property from the sole legal owner (or a bank that lends money to that owner on the security of the land) cannot rely on overreaching to give them priority over any equitable owner – section 2 of the LPA 1925. Thus, the purchaser/mortgagee may be bound by B's equitable interest according to the rules of registered and unregistered conveyancing.[128] Moreover, because B's equitable interest has arisen *informally* because of a resulting or constructive trust, without writing, the purchaser may be unaware of its existence and may fail to take avoiding action before completing the purchase.[129]

4.10.3 Establishing the equitable interest

The rules considered below are applicable whenever a person seeks to establish a share of

---

126   There may also be an overlap with doctrine of proprietary estoppel – see especially *Oxley v. Hiscock* (2004).

127   The number of potential equitable co-owners is not limited, so, in theory at least, there can be many such claimants!

128   Overriding interests and the doctrine of notice respectively.

129   Of course, to be an overriding interest under paragraph 2, Schedule 3 of the LRA 2002, the equitable interest must be discoverable – but that does not mean that the purchaser or mortgagee necessarily discovered it.

ownership in land, legal title to which is held by someone else. Usually, legal title will be held by one person and the claimant will be their partner or former partner in a domestic relationship, but there is no need for any romantic relationship between the parties for these rules to apply. There is, for example, a growing number of cases in which the claim is by sibling members of the same family against the legal owner.[130] In typical relationship cases, often it is the man who has legal title and the woman who is making a claim, but the law is the same whatever the factual matrix.[131] Likewise, although the disputed property is most often residential property, it need not be, and in Lloyd v. Pickering (2004), the successful claim by Ms Lloyd was to a half-share in a business that was legally in the sole name of Mr Pickering. These rules are also equally applicable when legal title is held by two, three or four people,[132] the only difference being that where there are two or more trustees, the newly established equitable interest would be capable of being overreached.

Bearing these points in mind, it is possible to categorise the methods by which an equitable interest may be claimed. However, it is to be remembered that while these categories are convenient for the purposes of exposition, in reality, the claimant's and defendant's lives tend to be much more complicated and much less susceptible to object- ive, forensic analysis than land lawyers would like! The need to rely on possibly half- remembered conversations or disputed facts makes this area of the law a breeding ground for litigation. In this litigation, it is not always possible or desirable to be as 'black and white' as the rules presented below appear to be. This is, in essence, the thrust of the House of Lords decision in Stack v. Dowden (2007), which emphasises the need for a flexible approach in the light of the complex way in which lives are run.

4.10.4   The express trust

Although it rarely occurs, it is perfectly possible for the legal owner (or owners) delib- erately to generate an interest in the land for another person by means of an express trust. In short, the legal owner (A) may declare expressly and in writing (as required by section 53(1) of the LPA 1925) that he holds the land on trust for the claimant (B), usually in co-ownership with himself. As an express trust, the equitable co-ownership thereby cre- ated is conclusive according to the terms of the written declaration, subject only to rectifi- cation in the event of fraud or forgery. It is also possible for the legal owner actually to convey the legal title to himself and another, in which case there will be co-ownership of the legal and equitable title. This is even rarer, for it involves additional expense and the need to re-register the legal title at HM Land Registry.

4.10.5   The 'purchase money' resulting trust

A second means by which a person may claim an equitable interest in another's property – thereby triggering co-ownership – is by contributing to the purchase price of the prop- erty, despite the fact that their name is not on the legal title. Unless it can be established that the money was given to the legal owner by way of gift or loan,[133] the claimant may

---

130   For example, Hapeshi v. Allnatt (2010).

131   For example, Tinsley v. Milligan (1993), two women; Babic v. Thompson (1999), two businessmen.

132   For example, Grant v. Edwards (1986), in which legal title was held by the defendant and his brother.

133   For example, Bradbury v. Hoolin (1998).

have an equitable interest in the land in direct proportion to their contribution to the purchase price. This is the resulting trust. It is said to arise from an intention to acquire an interest in the property as manifested by the contribution to the acquisition of the property through part-provision of the purchase price.[134] A typical example is where the legal owner has provided some of the purchase price and the balance is provided by a husband, wife or other partner who does not 'go on the title'. In such cases, legal ownership is in one person and equitable ownership is shared among the contributors, usually on the basis of a tenancy in common in proportion to the contribution provided. The principles are the same if all that is provided is the deposit[135] and in certain circumstances may include a notional payment because of a 'right to buy' discount off the purchase price.[136] Note, however, that the contribution must be made to the acquisition of property, not merely to its repair,[137] and it seems that an interest will not arise even if a payment is made if there is positive evidence that intention to acquire an interest in fact existed.[138]

As a variation on this, it is not clear whether an equitable interest may arise if the financial contribution is made to the purchase price over a period of time. The typical scenario would be where the non-legal owner contributes to the repayment or financing of a mortgage that in its turn has been used to purchase the property. Classic theory dictates that a resulting trust can arise only if payments are made *at the time* of the acquisition of the property and post-acquisition mortgage payments appear to fall outside this. Also, it is factually true that repayment of mortgage monies is not a payment to the seller of the property at all; it is a payment to the lender who has already provided the balance of the purchase price in full and, with an endowment mortgage, is not even repayment of the principal sum borrowed.[139] Thus, in Curley v. Parkes (2004), the Court of Appeal denied Mr Curley an interest in the property because such mortgage repayments as he did make were made after the date of acquisition of the property.[140] This is clearly a narrow view of the role of resulting trusts and it is not immediately apparent why repayment of a mortgage (or the financing of its debt if the mortgage is interest-only) that was used to purchase the property cannot be regarded as making a contribution to its acquisition at the relevant time. It takes only a little imagination to regard the mortgagee as the agent of the purchasers, paying at the time of purchase, with the mortgagee being repaid as agent with interest by the contributors. Indeed, cases before Curley have rather assumed that payment of mortgage instalments would suffice. In Carlton v. Goodman (2002) and McKenzie v. McKenzie (2003), both claimants were actually mortgagors, having undertaken mortgage liability in order to secure the relevant finance for the purchase of the property, but because neither

---

134 Tinsley v. Milligan (1993); Laskar v. Laskar (2008).

135 Halifax Building Society v. Brown (1995).

136 Mumford v. Ashe (2000); Laskar v. Laskar (2008).

137 Bank of India v. Mody (1998). If the couple are married, contributions to repairs might squeeze in section 37 of the Matrimonial Proceedings and Property Act 1970 as an 'improvement' generating an interest: see below.

138 First National Bank v. Wadhwani (1998). See also Lightfoot v. Lightfoot Brown (2004), although the cases were argued on the basis of constructive trusts. On the overlap between the resulting and constructive trust, see below.

139 Under an endowment mortgage, the monthly repayments are of only the interest on the debt and the capital is repaid by some other means, usually the cashing in of an 'endowment' or savings plan. A repayment mortgage does include repayment of the capital as part of each monthly instalment.

140 He also claimed to have made some lump-sum payments but these also were post-acquisition.

had undertaken repayment in order to secure an interest in the house,[141] their claims to an interest failed. Indeed, the other party in both cases was held entitled to the entire equitable interest precisely because they *had* paid the mortgage instalments. More importantly, in *Laskar v. Laskar* (2008), the Court of Appeal[142] decided that contributions to mortgage repayments could be treated as a contribution to the purchase price and although in this case the property was purchased for investment purposes – rather than as a home for mother and daughter – there seems no reason to doubt the logic of the decision. It is then now possible to argue that *Curley* is wrong in so far as it decides that mortgage payments can never amount to a contribution to the purchase price so as to trigger a resulting trust. In allowing such contributions, *Laskar v. Laskar* (2005) seems the more pertinent authority, both in terms of principle and precedent.[143]

In *Stack v. Dowden* (2007) – a case concerning quantification of equitable interests rather than their acquisition – the House of Lords also had cause to consider the role of resulting trusts. In the view of the majority – Lord Neuberger disagreeing on this point – resulting trusts should not normally be used as the basis for establishing an interest in another's property, at least in respect of property used as family home. This was because the resulting trust is narrow and focuses on only one aspect of the party's lives – the payment of money. Family relationships are complex and so a better approach – in the sense that it leads to a fairer result – is to use constructive trusts. Many factors can be considered under the rubric of constructive trusts and the courts have considerably more discretion in the quantification of shares (see below). This approach was confirmed by the Privy Council in the later case of *Abbott v. Abbott* (2008) and it looked as if any meaningful role for the resulting trust had disappeared.[144] Lord Neuberger, on the other hand, did not see why the well-understood and relatively certain law of resulting trusts should be so easily abandoned. In his view, it had a role to play in certain circumstances precisely because it led to certain and predictable results. Moreover, as noted above, in the still later case of *Laskar v. Laskar* (2008), Lord Neuberger, sitting in the Court of Appeal, specifically rejected the argument that the *only* route to establishing an equitable interests was by means of a constructive trust. So, in that case, in which the property was purchased not to live in but to use as an investment, the Court applied a traditional resulting trust analysis and quantified the party's shares by reference to the amount of money that each had contributed to the purchase price. This does seem appropriate on the facts of the case. Perhaps, then, a tentative conclusion is that a constructive trust will normally be used in cases in which the property in question is the shared home of the parties,[145] but that either a resulting or constructive trust may be used in cases concerning land purchased for other purposes.

---

141 Such repayments as they had made were made in order to discharge their contractual liability as mortgagors, not in pursuance of an interest in the property.

142 Unusually, Lord Neuberger of the House of Lords chose to sit in this case.

143 Ironically, however, this may not be important given that nearly all of these types of case can be squeezed into the rubric of constructive trusts, as discussed below.

144 The two leading protagonists in *Stack* who favoured the rejection of resulting trusts – Baroness Hale and Lord Walker – also sat in *Abbott*. The advice in *Abbott* was delivered by Baroness Hale. Lord Neuberger – who also sat in both – remained silent in *Abbott*, but see *Laskar v. Laskar* (2005).

145 *Fowler v. Barron* (2008), applying *Stack*.

Finally, before considering constructive trusts, we must consider those cases in which the claimant makes a financial contribution to the cost of running the household, the value of which may have enabled the legal owner to pay the purchase price of the property. An example is where the woman pays all of the regular domestic outgoings and the man pays the mortgage.[146] After *Curley*, it seems unlikely that these can count as an acquisition contribution for the purposes of resulting trusts – even if a resulting trust is the suitable vehicle – and, in truth, it was always doubtful whether they could qualify. *Laskar* has done nothing to change this. Once again, if such indirect financial contributions can be regarded as evidence of an inferred common intention (which, after *Stack*, is very likely) or if they are consequent on a promise made by the legal owner that the claimant is to have a share of ownership, these cases can be dealt with under the rubric of constructive trusts and so the fact that they cannot trigger a resulting trust is immaterial.

4.10.6   The constructive trust

The concept of a 'constructive trust' is used and misused widely in English law, particularly in the field of property law and equity. We must be careful when considering the 'constructive trust' in the present context to appreciate that the role it plays here need not tell us anything about its function or attributes in other areas of the law. It is a term of 'no fixed abode' and much time has been spent examining whether there is any unifying concept that ties together the various uses of it. That is a debate for another day for it goes well beyond the realms of land law.[147]

In order to claim an equitable interest under the rubric of constructive trust, the essence of the matter is that the legal owner and claimant must (expressly or impliedly) share a 'common intention' that the claimant should have some interest in the land, which intention is relied on by the claimant to their detriment. In the normal way, of course, such an intention should be put in writing (section 53(1) of the LPA 1925), but if the intention is supported by acts of detrimental reliance by the claimant, a constructive trust arises whereby the land is held on trust with (in the normal case) the legal and equitable owner sharing the equitable interest.[148] Such constructive trusts do not need to be in, or evidenced in, writing – section 53(2) of the LPA 1925.

The heart of the doctrine is, then, the existence of a common intention, relied on by the claimant to detriment. *Lloyds Bank v. Rosset* (1991), a decision of the House of Lords, provided early guidance, but this may now have been overtaken (or perhaps 'enhanced') by the House of Lords judgment in *Stack v. Dowden* (2007). These two cases need to be

---

146 Even now that it is possible to plead that mortgage payments count as a ground for a *resulting* trust (*Laskar*); it is not enough that financial contributions to the running of the household have been made (*Lloyds Bank v. Rosset* (1991)). They must have been made in order to enable the legal owner to purchase the property. This is very difficult to prove. Such a claim failed in *Burns v. Burns* (1984) and appears to be rejected as a matter of principle in the all-important judgment of Lord Bridge in *Rosset*.

147 A common view is that the various guises of constructive trust all deal with some kind of unconscionability on the part of a person who holds or acquires property, but this is by no means a watertight analysis. A restitutionary approach might stress the use of the constructive trust as a vehicle for reversing unjust enrichment.

148 There is no reason why the claimant should not gain 100 per cent of the equity under a constructive trust. It is more common, however, for the common intention to trigger a share of the equity.

considered together. In *Rosset*, a husband and wife arranged to purchase a derelict farmhouse and legal title was conveyed to the husband alone at the insistence of family trustees who were under a duty under the terms of their trust to ensure that the money for the purchase was given only to the husband. Clearly, however, the renovation was a joint venture with the wife supervising the work. The property was later mortgaged, the repayments could not be met and the bank sued for possession. The wife resisted on the ground that she had an equitable interest in the property by way of constructive trust. In the result, her claim was denied and in the leading opinion, adopted by all of their Lordships, Lord Bridge sets out a framework for the law. Taken as a whole, *Rosset* propounds a fairly narrow view of the law and it has therefore aroused some criticism, criticism that may have led to its refinement in *Stack v. Dowden*. As decided by *Rosset* – confirming a great deal of earlier case law – there are two major fundamental requirements in order to achieve a constructive trust: a common intention plus detrimental reliance. *Stack* does not dispute this statement of general principle, but rather it may have enlarged the circumstances in which a common intention may be established.

4.10.6.1   *Common intention: Three routes*

The claimant must establish a 'common intention' that she was to have an interest. According to *Rosset*, this common intention can be established only in one of two ways, but *Stack* (bolstered by *Abbott v. Abbott* (2005) and applied in *Hapeshi v. Allnatt* (2010)) may have added a third. However, before we consider these routes to a common intention in detail, we must take note of a serious reservation. In *Stack v. Dowden*, the parties already jointly owned the legal title and there was no doubt that Mr Stack had some equitable interest in the land. The narrow point of the case was to determine whether Mr Stack had 50 per cent of the equity on the basis that 'equity follows the law', or whether he had some other, lesser share. Strictly speaking, therefore, *Stack* is a *quantification* case in which the real issue is 'how much' does each co-owner have, rather than whether the claimant has any interest at all. It is not, therefore, strictly about acquisition claims like *Rosset*. It is thus arguable that *Stack* has no application to acquisition claims – being a claim by a non-owner against a legal owner – and if this is correct, the third route to a common intention discussed below does not apply. However, it seems clear from reading the majority opinions in *Stack* that there was an intention that its reasoning should apply to acquisition claims and it was applied as such by the Privy Council in *Abbott v. Abbott*. Again, this is not conclusive (Privy Council authority is persuasive only) and there is a real possibility that the Court of Appeal might refuse to apply *Stack* to an acquisition scenario. At present, there is scant authority either way, but in *Hapeshi v. Allnatt* (2010) in the Chancery Division of the High Court, the claimant was awarded a 25 per cent share of the equity on the basis of *Stack's* holistic approach to proving a common intention and he was not a legal owner. This might prove a powerful authority for using *Stack* in acquisition cases – certainly it appears to be the first – especially as the claimant could not establish one of the *Rosset* routes to a common intention.

Route 1   The first, and established, route to establishing a common intention (*Rosset*), is to determine whether there has at any time prior to acquisition, or exceptionally at some later date, been any agreement, arrangement or understanding reached between the parties that the property is to be shared beneficially. The finding of an agreement or arrangement can only be based on evidence of *express* discussions between the parties, however imperfectly remembered and however imprecise their terms may have been. In other words, there must have been an overt, express statement or agreement, promise or assurance. In many cases, this agreement will be truly express as where A says to B 'Of course half this house is yours', or 'This house is as much yours as mine'. However, promises are also deemed to be made expressly for the purpose of establishing a constructive trust when the legal owner makes a statement reassuring the claimant that they have some sort of stake in the property. This can take many forms and is, ultimately, a matter for construction in each case. For example, does 'This will always be your home', or 'I would never sell without your agreement', imply a promise as to ownership? If it does, a constructive trust is a possibility. Moreover, it appears that such a promise can be enough to trigger a constructive trust even if it is not genuine on the part of the legal owner. So, in *Eves v. Eves* (1975), a promise was held to have been made where the legal owner said, by way of excuse, that the only reason that the property was not conveyed originally to the woman was because she was too young.[149] Likewise, telling the claimant that the property will be conveyed to them in due course can be a relevant assurance, even if it is a lie. The only rule is that an express assurance must be made, in whatever form, and it does not matter that this occurs after the legal owner has acquired the property.[150] However, as shown by *James v. Thomas* (2007), assurances given by the legal owner to the claimant when they were living together that were *neither* intended nor understood as a promise of an interest cannot qualify. It would be otherwise if the landowner did not intend to make such a promise, but it was in fact understood as such by the claimant.[151] To sum up then, the absence of such an *express* promise is fatal to this route to common intention, as it was in *Rosset* itself.

Route 2 Second, if it is not possible to establish the common intention by means of an express assurance, Lord Bridge in *Rosset* notes that, by way of contrast:

> direct contributions to the purchase price by the partner who is not the legal owner, whether initially or by payment of mortgage instalments, will readily justify the inference necessary to the creation of a constructive trust. But, as I read the authorities, it is at least extremely doubtful whether anything else will do.[152]

In other words, according to *Rosset* (but not to *Stack*), the *only* circumstance in which the court may infer a common intention is if there have been direct payments towards the purchase price of the property – such as lump-sum payments or mortgage payments. This is critical for it means that (in the absence of any extension by *Stack*) 'normal' domestic obligations, childcare responsibilities, indirect contributions,[153] payment of household bills and all manner of other conduct that persons sharing a home might engage in cannot

---

149 See also *Grant v. Edwards* (1986), in which a false excuse was given for not including the claimant as legal owner.
150 *Clough v. Kelly* (1996).
151 There are parallels here with the law of proprietary estoppel – see Chapter 9.
152 At p. 8.
153 See *Ivin v. Blake* (1993).

lead to an inference of a common intention. Absent an express agreement, only payments towards the purchase price would do[154] and, even then, clear evidence that no agreement was ever reached – that is, positive proof that the parties *did not agree* – would mean that no common intention could be inferred.[155] After all, this is an inferred common intention, and evidence that no such inference could be made, or would be made, is fatal.

Evidently, the *Rosset* approach is *relatively narrow*: only promises or payments could lead to a common intention. While promoting relative certainty, it excludes the inference of a common intention (absent promises or payments) even though the parties had engaged in the joint enterprise of family life and for all intents and purposes had treated the land as owned jointly, notwithstanding the fact that title was held by only one of them. The classic example of this type is *Burns v. Burns* (1984) – decided before *Rosset* – which is widely castigated as demonstrating the law's disregard for the way in which normal people conduct normal family life.[156] In response to mounting criticism of the narrowness of the *Rosset* approach, the Court of Appeal in *Oxley v. Hiscock* (2004) (which was an acquisition case) attempted to broaden the circumstances in which a person might prove a common intention by allowing such an intention to arise from all of the facts and circumstances of the case. It was essentially an approach seeking to achieve a 'fair' result bearing in mind the realities of modern life, and proved the catalyst for the House of Lords' analysis in *Stack v. Dowden*.

Route 3   In essence, the majority judgment in *Stack* (Lord Neuberger disagreeing as to the reasoning) sets out to make it easier for a claimant to establish a common intention and thereby an equitable interest in land belonging to another. This is done by deciding that it is permissible to find[157] a common intention as to ownership based on the parties' entire relationship with each other. It was not necessary to limit the enquiry to promises or payments – see also *Fowler v. Barron* (2008). The evidence for this common intention could come from a range of factors because, according to Baroness Hale (who gave the leading judgment), 'context is everything' and the domestic context is very different from the commercial world.[158] Thus, to establish a common intention it is possible to rely on:

---

154 Necessarily, of course, because the inference could come only from payments towards the purchase price, there was an overlap with the law of resulting trusts. See, for example, *Oxley v. Hiscock* (2004).

155 For example, *Lightfoot v. Lightfoot Brown* (2004).

156 Mr Burns paid the all of the mortgage monies and never made any promises. Ms Burns (they were not married) looked after the children and ran the home. She lost her claim. It was never quite clear how typical this case was: was it evidence of widespread unfairness, or merely the one 'hard case'?

157 There is some argument as to whether this is inferred, or imputed intention. Lord Neuberger is happy to infer an intention, but not to impute one. An inferred intention is one that arises from the facts; an imputed intention is one that the court thinks the parties would have had, had they addressed the issue, in the light of the facts. Inferred common intention has the approval of precedent, but imputed intentions were rejected by the House of Lords in *Gissing v. Gissing* (1971).

158 *Stack v. Dowden*, at [69].

[m]any more factors than financial contributions . . . These include: any advice or discussions at the time of the transfer which cast light upon their intentions then; the reasons why the home was acquired in their joint names; the reasons why (if it be the case) the survivor was authorized to give a receipt for the capital moneys; the purpose for which the home was acquired; the nature of the parties' relationship; whether they had children for whom they both had responsibility to provide a home; how the purchase was financed, both initially and subsequently; how the parties arranged their finances, whether separately or together or a bit of both; how they discharged the outgoings on the property and their other household expenses.[159]

Clearly, these are wide-ranging factors, and the list is not even meant to be exhaustive.[160] As noted at the outset, the issue arose in *Stack* because of the need to quantify the share of an existing owner, rather than in an acquisition context.[161] But the approval of *Oxley* in *Stack*, and the use of *Stack* in *Abbott* and *Hapeshi* to determine questions of acquisition, suggest that this third route to a common intention really does extend the circumstances in which a claimant may now claim an equitable share.[162] Of course, this represents a move away from the relative strictness of the *Rosset* approach, but as Lord Walker says in *Stack*, and as explicitly approved in *Abbott*, 'in my opinion the law has moved on, and your Lordships should move it a little more in the same direction'.[163] Consequently, there is now a third way in which to establish a common intention in addition to the two routes provided by *Rosset*: it is now possible to find a common intention by examining the whole range of the parties' conduct in relation to the property and, in that context, to each other.

4.10.6.2   *Detrimental reliance*

Once a common intention exists by reason of any of the three routes outlined above, the claimant must then establish that they have relied to their detriment on the existence of such an intention. It is, after all, writ in stone in English law that 'equity will not assist a volunteer'[164] and there is no unconscionability if a promise has been made that has had no impact on the behaviour of the claimant. In this regard, 'reliance' – that is, that the claimant would not have behaved as she did without the common intention – is not difficult to establish and may take many forms. In particular, Lord Denning in *Greasley v. Cooke* (1980) suggests that if there is evidence of 'detriment', there should be a presumption of reliance. Consequently, in the absence of evidence to the contrary adduced by the legal owner, the court is entitled to assume that the claimant did, indeed, rely on the assurance made. This is so even if there is evidence to suggest that the claimant would have

---

159 Baroness Hale at [69].

160 Baroness Hale at [70].

161 Hence the reference in the quotation to a house in joint names.

162 For the relevance of joint-legal ownership on quantification – see below.

163 *Stack v. Dowden,* per Lord Walker at [26].

164 That is, someone who gives nothing or does nothing in response to the promise or assurance of another.

acted as she did for other motives – perhaps out of love for the legal owner. So, in *Chun v. Ho* (2001), the claimant was successful even though her actions were motivated in part by her high regard and affection for the legal owner.[165] This is, of course, a generous presumption and it reverses the burden of proof. Nevertheless, it is wholly necessary in order to prevent the legal owner from denying a constructive trust merely by pleading that the claimant could not actually prove that she had relied on the common intention.

Given this generous approach to the question of reliance, it is clear that 'detriment' is critical in establishing the constructive trust.[166] In cases in which there is an *express* common intention, there is no doubt that detriment may take many forms. It can be in the conduct of the claimant, such as doing extraordinary work about the house as in *Eves v. Eves* (1975) and *Ungurian v. Lesnoff* (1990).[167] The detriment may be financial, such as paying bills or settling other household expenses, provided that the expense is undertaken because an express promise is made. Whatever form it takes, however, the key is that the claimant does something concrete in relation to the express common intention. In this connection, it seems that the 'detriment' does not need to have been detrimental in the sense of harmful. So, giving up existing accommodation in order to move into the legal owner's luxurious property is a 'detriment' (no house to fall back on), as is spending one's life savings on a Porsche in reliance on the legal owner's property that 'you will never have to find another house' (no money to purchase another property). In addition, giving up other opportunities because the legal owner has assured the claimant that her future is secure can count as detriment.[168] As these examples illustrate, it is also true that the detriment need not be made in relation to the property in which the claimant acquires an interest. It often is – for example, renovating the kitchen – but it need not be.

Where the common intention has arisen impliedly as a result of direct contributions towards the purchase price or because of an analysis of the parties' entire course of dealings, there must also be detriment. However, this is not difficult to establish because it is clear from *Rosset* and *Stack* that the actual payments made towards the purchase price or the conduct that gives to the common intention may also qualify as the detriment. In other words, the payments or conduct perform a dual role: they are the reason a common intention can be established in the first place and they can be the detriment consequent on that intention.

---

165 If it were otherwise, the only successful claimants would be those who acted entirely mercenarily simply because they were expressly or impliedly promised something.

166 In *Century UK v. Clibbery* (2004), the acts of alleged detriment were so trivial that, even if there had been an assurance, they would not have generated a constructive trust or estoppel.

167 Note the point is that the claimant undertook work of an extraordinary character, such as doing building work in the garden or renovating the property. It is doubtful whether doing 'normal' domestic obligations can count as a response to an express common intention. In *Rosset*, although Mrs Rosset could be thought of as undertaking extensive renovation work amounting to qualifying conduct, there was (as the law then stood) no common intention – no express promise and no payments. Whether Mrs Rosset would succeed under the more relaxed approach of *Stack* is uncertain.

168 *Chun v. Ho* (2001).

4.10.7 The nature of the interest generated and quantification of share in acquisition cases

If the claimant establishes either a resulting or a constructive trust, she will be entitled to a share of the equitable interest. Legal title will continue to be held by the legal owner, but now as a trustee holding for himself and the successful claimant in equity under the statutory trust of land imposed by the LPA 1925 and regulated by TOLATA 1996. The equitable interest will be held by way of a tenancy in common[169] – only unity of possession is present – and we must ascertain the size of this interest.

If a claimant establishes a resulting trust – by payments to the purchase price – her interest in the property is to be quantified in direct proportion to the amount of the price paid. So, a contribution of 25 per cent made at the time of purchase entitles the claimant to a 25 per cent interest, and so on. This is classical resulting trust theory.[170] Given that use of the resulting trust in these domestic or semi-domestic cases may well now be redundant – see below – there is no reason to disturb this orthodoxy. Cases such as *Midland Bank v. Cooke* (1995) and *LeFoe v. LeFoe* (2001), which appeared to challenge this by suggesting that an interest established under a resulting trust could be expanded beyond a proportional share by taking a broad view of the entirety of the parties' relationship with each other,[171] are now better regarded as cases of constructive trust.[172]

If the claimant establishes a constructive trust, as now is more likely, the matter of quantification is more complex. It might be thought appropriate to quantify the claimant's share in a manner that meets the expectations generated by the common intention or, alternatively, in a manner that compensates for the value of the detriment suffered or the financial contribution made to the purchase price. However, although recent case law has done little to provide us with concrete guidance about how to solve real problems, at least the nature of the enquiry to be undertaken by the courts has been settled. It is clear from *Clough v. Killey* (1996) that if the terms of the express common intention are clear as to both the existence and size of the equitable interest, then the court should not depart from this as the basis for quantification. So, in that case, the promise was that Killey should have a 50 per cent share of the equity, and this is what she received, even though there was evidence that the share 'earned' by her detriment would have been only 25 per cent. This has been confirmed by *Oxley v. Hiscock* (2004) and presents no difficulty. If, however, there is no express discussion or agreement as to the size of the claimant's share,[173] or even if there is positive evidence that no discussions ever took place, the share still needs to be quantified. In *Oxley*, Chadwick LJ reviewed the various possible solutions to this – some based on an imputed intention at the time of acquisition, some on an intention derived from the parties conduct – but in the end made it clear that the court must grasp the nettle and admit that it is exercising a judicial discretion. Consequently, it 'must now be accepted that (as least in this Court and below) the answer is that each is entitled to that share which

---

169 Note, however, the unusual case of *HSBC v. Dyche* (2009), in which two claimants were successful in establishing an equitable interest under a constructive trust and, between themselves, were joint tenants.

170 See, for example, *Springette v. Defoe* (1992).

171 Thus Mrs Cooke was awarded 50 per cent of the equity, having only paid just under 7 per cent of the purchase price.

172 Per Chadwick LJ in *Oxley v. Hiscock* (2004).

173 Whether the common intention arose expressly or impliedly from direct payments is irrelevant.

the court considers fair having regard to the whole course of dealing between them in relation to the property'. This will include all manner of things, including the arrangements the co-owners have made to meet the obligations of normal domestic life, including payments of bills, mortgages, repairs and insurance. This has now been confirmed by the House of Lords in *Stack v. Dowden* (2007) and by the Court of Appeal in *Fowler v. Barron* (2008). It is clear that all types of conduct of a non-financial kind can be included as part of this broad enquiry, so long as it is 'in relation to the property'. This broad-brush approach – the search for a fair and conscionable distribution of the equitable interest – is necessarily fluid and uncertain, but it may nevertheless reflect the reality of what judges have been doing for some time. Certainly, according to Baroness Hale in *Stack*, it is what they should be doing. Moreover, although *Oxley* and *Stack* was decided in the context of a home shared by lovers, it is not the case that this generous approach is restricted to such cases. In *Ritchie v. Ritchie* (2007), the analysis was applied to a property dispute between mother and son.[174]

4.10.8   Quantification when there are two legal owners

Historically, the typical dispute has been between a legal owner and a non-legal owner, the latter claiming a share in the property of the former: for example, *Lloyds Bank v. Rosset* (1991). However, both *Stack v. Dowden* and *Fowler v. Barron* are cases in which the parties are already joint legal owners and they are disputing the size of their shares. Of course, if the parties have expressly declared in writing the nature or size of their shares (e.g. as 'joint tenants in equity' or '50/50' each), they will be held to this agreement (*Goodman v. Gallant* (1986)). Likewise, if there is no express declaration of the beneficial interest, but an explicit verbal agreement as to the size of share, the courts are likely to hold the parties to this, probably on the basis of estoppel (*Crossley v. Crossley* (2005)). Yet, in the absence of an agreement, is it possible for one legal co-owner to argue – on the basis of resulting and constructive trust – that their share is bigger than the other legal owner's? This is important for, as is obvious, both parties are registered as legal owners and third parties might be entitled to assume that equitable ownership follows legal ownership. In fact, as discussed above, there is a presumption that 'equity follows the law' and so, in most cases, we can expect that legal joint tenants will also be equitable joint tenants unless there is an express declaration to the contrary.[175] This re-enforces the security of the title register and allows third parties to deal in confidence with the legal owners knowing that they also own together in equity. However, as both *Stack v. Dowden* and *Fowler v. Barron* demonstrate, it is now possible to challenge the presumption that 'equity follows the law' by using the broad constructive trust to establish a share larger than 50 per cent. Although Baroness Hale in *Stack* says that this can occur only in exceptional cases, the wide range of factors listed in paragraph 69 of her judgment effectively give courts the discretion as to whether to apply the presumption or quantify the parties' interests differently. Thus in *Fowler* and *Ritchie*

---

174 Note *Segal v. Pasram* (2007), in which an almost pre-*Stack* analysis was preferred – possibly because the dispute involved a third party (a trustee in bankruptcy) and the court wished to limit the extent to which the claimant could remove assets from the legal owner's creditors.

175 They would therefore own 50/50 in equity if the joint tenancy were severed (see below) on the occasion of the break-up of their relationship.

v. *Ritchie* (2007) (a mother and son case[176]), the equitable shares differed from the legal title, but in *Segal* v. *Pasram* (2007), the court was happy to follow the 'normal' rule.[177]

The significance of this issue is clear enough. In many cases in which land is conveyed to two or more people as joint tenants at law, there is a failure to declare the equitable interest. We would expect 'equity to follow the law', with the result that the parties are joint tenants in equity, or 50/50 tenants in common after severance. If it is now possible for one party to claim a greater share on the basis of an expanded constructive trust doctrine – albeit in 'exceptional' cases – then there is considerable uncertainty for the parties themselves and any third party (such as a mortgagee) dealing with them.[178]

4.10.9   Resulting trusts, constructive trusts and proprietary estoppel

Although much academic effort has been expended in seeking to differentiate between the concepts of resulting trust, constructive trust and proprietary estoppel (see Chapter 9), this has not been a real problem in the courts – it has been largely ignored. All three concepts have in common the fact that they are a way for a person to obtain a proprietary interest in another's land without the normally required written instrument – they are concerned with the informal creation of property rights. Of course, recent case law with regard to quantification of share reveals a potential difference between pure resulting trusts and constructive trusts, as discussed above. However, given that contributions to the purchase price of property can generate an interest under either a resulting trust (quantified proportionately) or a constructive trust (quantified fairly on the basis of the parties' entire course of dealings) it is probable that most cases will fall under the rubric of the latter. The exception will be, of course, where the claimant has paid the greater part of the purchase price and is using the resulting trust to establish a large share of the equity in direct proportion to such payments – as in *Carlton* v. *Goodman* (2002), in which the person making the payments obtained 100 per cent of the equity. It may therefore come to pass that, save for the odd exceptional case concerning non-residential property, resulting trusts cease to have an effect in the law of co-ownership but return instead to their more limited role in relation to the non-fulfilment of express trusts and similar scenarios. *Oxley* v. *Hiscock* (2004) and *Stack* v. *Dowden* (2007) certainly push the law that way, despite the resistance in *Laskar* v. *Laskar* (2008).

Oxley v. *Hiscock* also brought to a head a similar question: how do constructive trusts and proprietary estoppel fit together? The latter doctrine is also rooted in unconscionable conduct consequent on an assurance, reliance and detriment, and even Lord Bridge in *Lloyds*

---

176 See also the pre-*Stack* case, *Abbey National* v. *Stringer* (2006), in which the mother was awarded 100 per cent of the equity, despite being a legal co-owner with her son. The reasoning in this case is almost non-existent.

177 See also *Jones* v. *Kernott* (2010), where there was a 50/50 split between the legal co-owners because there was nothing to displace the normal presumption that equity followed the law.

178 In *Stringer*, Abbey National's mortgage was effectively destroyed by the finding of 100 per cent equity for Mrs Stringer – a fact that it simply could never have discovered before lending money. It relied – perfectly properly – on the jointly held legal title and was hijacked by the court's decision.

Bank v. Rosset (1991) recognised the overlap between the concepts.[179] In *Oxley*, Chadwick LJ is even more robust, saying that 'the time has come to accept that there is no difference in outcome, in cases of this nature, whether the true analysis lies in constructive trust or in proprietary estoppel'. It is important to realise, however, that he was not saying that the *concepts* are the same; rather that the *outcome* could be the same whichever concept is used. This is a small point, but worth making as many would argue that the concepts are not the same. In fact, in *Stack v. Dowden*, Lord Walker acknowledged that the concepts were different. After noting that he had thought previously that the concepts could be assimilated,[180] he continued: 'I have to say that I am now rather less enthusiastic about the notion that proprietary estoppel and "common interest" constructive trusts can or should be completely assimilated.'[181] This is a view shared by many. A brief assessment of the potential differences between constructive trusts and proprietary estoppel is given at the end of Chapter 9.

4.10.10   Statutory powers

In those cases in which the claimant is unable to prove a constructive trust, resulting trust or estoppel, there will be no interest unless he or she can rely a statutory jurisdiction. If the couple are married or in civil partnership, and then divorce or separate, a 'property adjustment order' can be made in the family court under the Matrimonial Causes Act 1973 and the Civil Partnership Act 2004, but there is no equivalent power if the disputants are unmarried, not civil partners or are just friends or in some other family relationship. Finally, we should also note that the court has a power under section 37 of the Matrimonial Proceedings and Property Act 1970 to award a beneficial interest consequent upon spousal improvements to property. This is a fairly limited power, restricted by definition to married couples and civil partners. It appears that the value of the interest awarded must be commensurate with (i.e. restricted to) the value added to the property by way of the improvement.

The apparently limited circumstances in which a non-owner could claim a proprietary (ownership) interest in another's property under *Rosset* gave rise to much criticism. It seemed unfair that, say, a long-term emotional partner should be unable to claim a share in the family home simply because she could not prove the existence of an express promise or a payment towards the purchase price. Similarly, it appeared as if the law was penalising the stable couple who made a certain kind of life choice. Assuming *Stack* applies to acquisition claims, these criticisms have now disappeared as a result of the widening of the reach of constructive trusts put forward by the majority in that case. In their place, we now have another set of criticisms. After *Stack*, is the law too uncertain? When will a claimant be successful and what factors may count towards proving the common intention? How can third parties such as lenders discover who owns the equitable interest, especially if they

---

179   Per Lord Bridge at p. 8: 'Once a finding [of common intention] is made it will only be necessary for the partner asserting the claim to a beneficial interest against the partner entitled to the legal estate to show that he or she acted to his or her detriment or altered his or her position in reliance on the agreement in order to give rise to the constructive trust or proprietary estoppel.'

180   Indeed, he has a good claim to be the architect of that view – see *Yaxley v. Gotts* (2000).

181   *Stack*, at [37].

cannot even rely on the certainty of a jointly held legal title? Finally, is it really appropriate for judges to be inventing a discretionary-based jurisdiction to do what is fair when, perhaps, these types of judgment about society and families should be left to Parliament?

Above all, however, whether we favour the narrow view of *Rosset* or the new broad approach of *Stack*, there is a need to keep things in perspective. First, as mentioned above, if the couple are married or in civil partnership, the court already has a discretion to readjust property rights on divorce or judicial separation.[182] There is no need to rely at all on the rules of implied trusts. Second, there are relatively few reported cases in which a claimant in a normal domestic context actually failed to secure an interest under the *Rosset* rules (*Rosset* was one) and this is irrespective of whether the couple were married or unmarried, heterosexual or homosexual. The courts were adept at finding some kind of payment to the purchase price and even keener to identify some kind of express agreement about owner-ship. In this sense, it is not clear whether *Stack v. Dowden* really will result in more claimants being successful, rather than the same number of claimants being successful for a different reason. Third, it is now standard practice for persons buying land jointly to indicate the nature and extent of their equitable interest in the property on HM Land Registry's transfer form. This amounts to an express declaration of beneficial entitlement and forestalls any claim of resulting or constructive trust. Fourth, the Law Commission has completed a thorough analysis of the rights of cohabiting couples and its report – *Cohabitation: The Financial Consequences of Relationship Breakdown*[183] – recommends the creation of a statutory, structured discretion whereby courts would have the power to alter the property rights of certain types of unmarried couple who had lived together as a couple. Not all unmarried couples would qualify and there would be safeguards to ensure that the scheme does not catch merely casual relationships. At present, the government has indicated that they do not wish to pursue this proposal, but the recommendations remain the focus of reform in this area. Fifth, while it is true that the courts take a tougher line with property acquired for business purposes – for example, by relying more on a resulting trust – we might argue that this is as it should be. After all, the business partners could have deliberately conveyed the land into joint names. Only rarely might there be the kind of emotional pressures and concerns that require a more generous intervention in the context of family property. Finally, we should always remember that ownership of family property is often of great concern to third parties – banks, lending institutions, creditors, and so on. As we have seen in cases like *Williams & Glyn's Bank v. Boland* (1981) and cases following it, a simple way to keep a mortgagee out of possession of the family home after non-payment of the mortgage is to prove that the non-legal owner has acquired an equitable interest before the mortgage, which then overrides the bank's interest. Sometimes, some cases feel as if the alleged co-owners have manufactured an interest in favour of the non-legal owner precisely (as it turned out) to defeat the claims of a creditor. As Fox LJ said in *Midland Bank v. Dobson* (1985): 'Assertions made by a husband and wife as to a common intention formed 30 years ago regarding joint ownership, of which there is no contemporary evidence and which happens to accommodate their current need to defeat the claims of a creditor, must be received by the courts with caution.'

---

182 We should also recognise that joint ownership of the legal and equitable title is now much more common and is the usual default position when a couple buy a property as their home.

183 Report No. 307 of 31 July 2007.

4.11   Severance

As we saw at the outset of this chapter, co-ownership of the equitable interest in property
may be either as a joint tenancy or a tenancy in common.

A tenancy in common is clearly an 'undivided share' in land, with each co-owner
being able to identify their portion of ownership (e.g. one quarter, one fifth, etc.), even
though there is unity of possession of the whole. Conversely, with a joint tenancy, no co-
owner has a defined share, but each is the owner of the whole and is subject to the right of
survivorship. In practical terms, this means that a joint tenant has no individual share in the
equitable interest in the land that he can sell, give away or leave by will. For some, this may
be perfectly acceptable (e.g. married couples), but for others, it means that they or their
families are denied the opportunity to liquidate the capital value of the land (e.g. business
partners). In order to meet these difficulties, any joint tenant may 'sever' their equitable
joint tenancy, and thereby turn it into a tenancy in common. Of course, because of the
1925 reforms, it is only possible to sever an equitable joint tenancy (not that of the legal
title) because tenancies in common may exist only in equity. That said, there are several
methods by which a joint tenant may sever their interest and thereby constitute themselves
a tenant in common in equity. One is statutory and three arise under common law, as
codified in *Williams v. Hensman* (1861).[184] After severance has occurred, if there were only
two joint tenants, necessarily both are now tenants in common, but if there were three or
more joint tenants, the others can remain as joint tenants between themselves. So, if land is
held by A, B, C and D as legal and equitable joint tenants, and then C and D carry out an act
of severance, legal title remains held by A, B, C and D as joint tenants (it is not severable),
but the equitable title now exists as a joint tenancy between A and B, with C and D as
tenants in common.

4.11.1   Statutory notice: Section 36(2) of the Law of Property
Act 1925

Under section 36(2) of the LPA 1925, any equitable joint tenant may give notice in writing
to the other joint tenants of his intention to sever the joint tenancy. The giving of such
notice results in a severance of that co-owner's interest and they become a tenant in
common.[185] The severance is entirely unilateral and does not require the agreement or
consent of the other joint tenants. Indeed, so long as there is evidence that the written
notice was sent (e.g. by registered post), it seems that it does not have to be received by the
other joint tenants to be effective to sever.[186] So, in *Kinch v. Bullard* (1998), a notice was sent
by one joint tenant to the other and arrived at the receiver's address. He never saw it,
having suffered a heart attack, and the notice was destroyed by the sender in the hope that

---

184 Severance may also result from an unlawful killing of one equitable joint tenant by the other. In such cases, it is a
matter of policy that the killer cannot claim the right of survivorship when he is the reason for the death of his
co-owner.

185 *Burgess v. Rawnsley* (1975).

186 *Re 88 Berkeley Road* (1971).

she benefit from the right of survivorship under the alleged joint tenancy that she had sought to end. Not surprisingly, the court held that the written notice was served effectively by delivery[187] – even if it had not been seen – and that, of course, it could not be withdrawn after service. Severance had occurred and the wife did not succeed to the entire interest under survivorship. Moreover, it is also clear that the notice may take many forms. For example, in *Re Draper's Conveyance* (1969), a summons claiming sale of the co-owned property was held to constitute written notice of severance under section 36(2). Unusually, however, it also seems true that a mere oral agreement *not* to sever can prevent any later act of severance by written notice taking effect (although whether this applies also to the *William v. Hensman* methods is uncertain). In *White v. White* (2001), the property had been conveyed expressly to three people as equitable joint tenants and there had been an oral agreement not to sever. In such circumstances, a clear attempted severance by written notice under section 36(2) was held ineffective on the ground that the oral agreement supported the original declaration of the owners as joint tenants. Of course, the whole point of severance is that it can destroy an expressly declared equitable joint tenancy, so perhaps the case is best explained on the basis that the person wishing to sever was estopped from so doing by their conduct (the oral agreement) because it would have been unconscionable in the circumstances to permit that severance.

There is one possible limitation to statutory severance, and this emerges from the words of section 36(2) itself. The section talks of severance by written notice where land 'is vested in joint tenants beneficially'. This seems to encompass only those situations in which the legal and equitable joint tenants are the same people, and not where, for example, A and B hold on trust for A, B, C and D as joint tenants. Fortunately, this limited interpretation of section 36(2) has not been adopted, and statutory severance is presumed to be available for all joint tenants, whether they are also legal owners or not.[188]

4.11.2   An act operating on his own share

In addition to statutory severance, the common law recognises three other ways in which it is possible to sever the joint tenancy. These were explained in the case of *Williams v. Hensman* (1861), and this case is now regarded as authority for the 'methods' outlined here and below. These three methods may still be used, although it will be appreciated that statutory severance by service of a written notice is by far the most reliable and easily proved.

The first *Williams v. Hensman* method of severance is 'by an act operating on one's own share'. This occurs when one equitable co-owner seeks to deal with 'their share' of the land, so manifesting an intention no longer to be part of the joint tenancy. The very action of dealing with one's own share thereby severs that share. Typical examples are where the equitable owner sells their share to a third party, mortgages it in favour of a bank, or becomes bankrupt, so that their property becomes vested in the 'trustee in bankruptcy'.[189] Likewise, attempting to deal with the legal title by forging the consent of the other legal owners to some purported dealing with that title in fact operates to transfer any equitable

---

187 Section 196(4) of the LPA provides that service is effective if sent by registered post. This letter was sent by ordinary first-class post, but the same result was achieved by analogy.

188 *Burgess v. Rawnsley* (1975).

189 For example, *Re Dennis* (1992).

interest that that person might have, so also effecting a severance. So, an attempted mort-gage by one of two legal owners who forges the signature of the other legal owner cannot actually effect a mortgage of the legal title, but it can effect a mortgage of the fraudster's equitable interest, thereby also severing any joint tenancy.[190] Importantly, however, leaving one's 'share' in a subsisting joint tenancy by will can *never* constitute severance because the right of survivorship operates immediately on death and takes precedence over testament-ary dispositions.[191]

Finally, for this method of severance to be effective, the 'act' operating on the joint tenant's share must be valid and enforceable, unlike the case of 'mutual agreement' con-sidered below. This means that the 'act' that effects the severance must be one that is valid under the general law according to the formality rules for that type of disposition of an interest in land. Therefore, given that nearly all dispositions of an interest in land must be in writing (section 2 of the Law of Property (Miscellaneous Provisions) Act 1989), the 'act of severance' by way of mortgage, sale or lease (if over three years) must be in writing and otherwise enforceable if it is to sever. In other words, this method requires a legally enforce-able 'act' operating on one's own share, not an unenforceable intention to sever. The result of such a severance is, of course, that the 'share' of the person severing passes to the person with whom he has validly contracted: for example, to the mortgagee or purchaser of the share. Necessarily, this must cause a tenancy in common with the remaining co-owners.

4.11.3   Where joint tenants agree to sever by 'mutual agreement'

The second *Williams v. Hensman* method is that, if two or more joint tenants agree among themselves to terminate the joint tenancy, those agreeing are taken to have severed the joint tenancy and constituted themselves as tenants in common. Most importantly, this agreement need not take any specific form and it need not be in writing. It need not be enforceable under the general law and may be inferred from the surrounding circum-stances. The point is simply that the fact of agreement severs the joint tenancy because it indicates an intention to destroy the joint tenancy; there is no need for the agreement to be acted on to effect a severance.[192] For example, severance by this method may occur when the co-owners agree on the precise distribution of property on the breakdown of their relationship.[193] However, the agreement must contemplate an intention to sever the joint tenancy (i.e. the ownership), and not merely amount to an agreement as to the use of the property.[194] It must be an agreement about ownership, not about use.

4.11.4   By mutual conduct

Mutual conduct is a flexible and shifting category that is intended to express the idea that severance may occur because the joint tenants, by their conduct in relation to each other,

---

190 Section 63 of the LPA 1925 and *Banker's Trust v. Namdar* (1997).

191 *Gould v. Kemp* (1834).

192 *Hunter v. Babbage* (1994).

193 *Re McKee* (1975).

194 *Nielson-Jones v. Fedden* (1975).

have demonstrated that the joint tenancy is terminated (*Williams v. Hensman* (1861)). Although very similar to mutual agreement, the point here is that the parties have not agreed to sever – formally or informally – but have so acted that it is clear that the continuance of a joint tenancy would be inconsistent with their intentions. There are many possible examples of mutual conduct, but the most common include physical partition of the land so that each co-owner is barred from the other's portion, the writing of mutual wills and negotiations between the joint tenants as to disposal of the property. The last of these is somewhat controversial, for it is difficult to see why a failed severance under mutual agreement (e.g. because the co-owners disagree about the value of the land) can nevertheless amount to a successful severance under mutual conduct because of severance negotiations. This, however, is the clear inference of Lord Denning's judgment in *Burgess v. Rawnsley* (1975). Essentially, the matter will turn on the facts of each case and whether the court is prepared, as a matter of policy, to extend the circumstances in which severance is possible. The degree of hardship caused by the operation of the right of survivorship might well be relevant in that calculation, as the courts favour severance if this preserves the 'share' of a deceased co-owner for their family.

4.12 Chapter Summary

4.12.1 The nature and types of concurrent co-ownership

'Concurrent co-ownership' of property describes the simultaneous enjoyment of land by two or more persons. Since 1 January 1926, co-ownership of property will either be by way of a *joint tenancy* or a *tenancy in common*. In a joint tenancy, each co-owner is treated as being entitled to the whole of the land and there are no distinct 'shares'. It is characterised by the right of survivorship and the four unities: unity of possession, interest, title and time (PITT). A tenancy in common exists when two or more people own an 'undivided share in land', giving unity of possession, but where no other unities are necessary and where there is no right of survivorship.

4.12.2 The effect of the Law of Property Act 1925 and the Trusts of Land and Appointment of Trustees Act 1996

Before 1926, it was possible for a joint tenancy and a tenancy in common to exist in both the legal and equitable estate in the land. However, after 1925, it is now impossible to create a tenancy in common at law. The legal owners of co-owned property must be joint tenants of the legal estate. They will hold the land as 'trustees of land' for the persons entitled in equity (sections 34 and 36 of the LPA 1925; sections 4 and 5 of TOLATA 1996). Co-ownership of the equitable interest may be by way of either a joint tenancy or a tenancy in common.

4.12.3 The equitable interest: Joint tenancy or tenancy in common?

First, if the unities of interest, title or time are absent, a joint tenancy in equity cannot exist. Second, if the original conveyance to the co-owners stipulates that they are 'joint tenants' or 'tenants in common' *of the beneficial or equitable interest*, this is normally conclusive as to the nature of their co-ownership in equity. Third, if 'words of severance' are used, then a tenancy in common will exist in equity. Fourth, failing any of the above, 'equity follows the law' and there will be a joint tenancy of the equitable interest (as there must be of the legal) unless the co-owners are business partners, co-mortgagees or where they as purchasers have provided the purchase money in unequal shares. However, this presumption can also be rebutted by reliance on the wider constructive trust found in *Stack v. Dowden*.

4.12.4 The nature of the trust of land: The effect of the Trusts of Land and Appointment of Trustees Act 1996

The trustees hold the legal title for the benefit of the equitable owners (who may be themselves), but it is the legal owners who have powers equivalent to those of an absolute owner to deal with the land (section 6 of TOLATA 1996). These powers can be restricted by the document establishing the trust or by order of the court (section 14 of TOLATA 1996) and must be exercised in conformity with the TOLATA regime. The trustees may delegate powers to a beneficiary, except the power to conduct an overreaching transaction. The trustees are not under a duty to sell the land (as was the case with the old trust for sale). Any person interested in the trust of land may apply to the court under section 14 of TOLATA 1996 (replacing section 30 of the LPA 1925) for an order affecting the land, including an order for sale. The powers of the trustees, including sale, may be made subject to the consent of a specified person (e.g. a beneficiary), but only in limited circumstances. Provided that the trustees are two or more in number and are in agreement and are not subject to a protected consent requirement, and that the equitable rights are overreachable, a sale will overreach the equitable interests, sweeping them off the land and into the purchase money so that they do not bind the purchaser.

4.12.5 The advantages of the trust of land as a device for regulating co-owned land

By abolishing tenancies in common at law, the LPA 1925 has ensured that there is but one title to investigate: the legal joint tenancy. The number of potential legal joint tenants is limited to a maximum of four (irrespective of the number of equitable owners). The right of survivorship diminishes the inconvenience and cost if a legal joint tenant dies. If there are two or more trustees of the land, the purchaser may usually ignore all of the equitable owners because of statutory overreaching. The court's powers under section 14 of TOLATA 1996 prevent co-owned land becoming inalienable. TOLATA 1996 gives concrete rights to the equitable owners to possess and enjoy the fruits of the land, subject to the possibility of overreaching.

4.12.6 The disadvantages of the trust of land as a device for regulating co-owned land

There may be disputes between the legal owners as to whether a sale or mortgage, and so on, should take place or whether the land should be retained for the benefit of the equitable owners. The problem is greater if the trustees' powers are subject to the consent of some other person, although disputes may be resolved by application to the court under section 14 of TOLATA 1996. The powerful effect of overreaching may effectively destroy an equitable owner's valuable rights. The ability to prevent overreaching through the imposition of a consent requirement is of limited value only. The trustees' duty to consult the beneficiaries is likely to offer little practical protection. In cases of bankruptcy, it is very likely that the land will be sold, despite any objections by the equitable owners.

4.12.7 The position of a purchaser who buys co-owned land: Overreaching or not?

If a purchaser buys co-owned land from two or more legal owners (i.e. there are two trustees), the equitable interests are transferred to the purchase money and the purchaser obtains the land free from their rights (overreaching). If the purchaser buys the property from a single trustee only, then the purchaser cannot rely on overreaching to protect him from the rights of the equitable owners: he *may* be bound by them according to the normal rules of registered and unregistered conveyancing.

4.12.8 The position of the equitable owners when overreaching occurs

If overreaching has occurred, the fundamental rule is that the equitable owners have no claim against the purchaser (which includes a mortgagee) to remain in possession of the land (*City of London Building Society v. Flegg* (1988)). In order to protect the equitable owner in this position, the Law Commission offered various devices for consideration, none of which were practical or sensible. In any event, it is important to see this 'problem' in perspective. Under TOLATA 1996, the trustees' power to sell or mortgage may be made subject to the consent of another person. In registered land, this will prevent overreaching if the consent requirement is registered as a restriction against the title (assuming consent is not given!), and in unregistered land, a purchaser will not be able to overreach if he has actual notice of the consent requirement.

4.12.9 The question of possession: Who has a right to occupy?

All of the legal owners have a right to occupy the property unless there is something specific to the contrary in the document establishing the trust of land. A purely equitable owner has a right to occupy under section 12 of TOLATA 1996, although this may be excluded or made conditional in the limited circumstances specified in section 13 of TOLATA 1996.

4.12.10 The payment of compensation for exclusive use

Under section 13 of TOLATA 1996, a co-owner enjoying exclusive use of the land (i.e. where the other or others are excluded) can be required to pay compensation for such use. This had been the position under the old trust for sale (*Re Pavlou* (1993)).

4.12.11 The express creation of co-ownership

Any land may be deliberately conveyed to two or more people. In such circumstances, the persons to whom legal title is transferred will be the legal owners (joint tenant trustees) and, in the absence of any statement to the contrary, they will also be the equitable owners. This conveyance may also expressly declare who are the equitable owners and the nature of their ownership, and this is conclusive for those parties (*Goodman v. Gallant* (1986)).

4.12.12   Creation of co-ownership even though the legal title is in one name only

The legal owner (A) may expressly declare in writing (section 53(1) of the LPA 1925) that he holds the land on trust for the claimant (B) or, more usually, a person may claim an equitable interest through the operation of resulting or constructive trusts, as follows:

1   A resulting trust arises where the claimant has contributed to the purchase price of the property. The share of the interest follows the proportion of the purchase price paid.

2   A constructive trust arises either: (i) where the legal owner makes an express oral promise or express oral agreement with the claimant that they 'own' the property or have a share in it, provided that this is relied on by the claimant to their detriment; (ii) a common intention can be implied from direct contributions to the purchase price, such contributions also providing the required detriment; or (iii) assuming *Stack* applies, a common intention is deduced from the whole course of dealings between the parties in respect of their home, such course of dealing also providing the required detriment. The size of the share may be determined by what is fair, taking account of the whole course of dealings between the parties.

4.12.13   Severance

Severance is the process of turning an equitable joint tenancy into an equitable tenancy in common, usually in order to avoid the effect of the right of survivorship (a legal joint tenancy cannot be severed). Severance occurs either by statutory written notice under section 36(2) of the LPA 1925, or by the act of a co-owner operating on his own share (e.g. mortgaging it), or where the joint tenants decide to sever by 'mutual agreement', or where an intention to sever is manifested by the 'mutual conduct' of the joint tenants.

 ## Further Reading

'Constructive trusts: A new model for equity and unjust enrichment' [2008] CLJ 265

'Constructive trusts and proprietary estoppel: The search for clarity and principle' [2009] Conv 104

'Defending *Stack v Dowden*' [2009] Conv 309

Ferris, G and **Battersby**, G, 'The impact of the Trusts of Land and Appointment of Trustees Act 1996 on purchasers of registered land' [1998] Cov 168; see also the reply by Dixon, M, [2000] Conv 267

Glover, N and **Todd**, P, 'The myth of common intention' (1996) 16 LS 325

Hopkins, N, 'The Trusts of Land and Appointment of Trustees Act 1996' [1996] Conv 267

Kenny, P, *The Trusts of Land and Appointment of Trustees Act 1996*, London: Sweet & Maxwell, 1997

Law Commission, *Cohabitation: The Financial Consequences of Relationship Breakdown*, Report No. 307, 31 July 2007

Stack v. Dowden (2007) 123 LQR 511; [2007] Conv 352 et seq

Tee, L, 'Severance revisited' [1995] Conv 105

Chapter 5
Successive Interests in Land

Introduction

In the previous chapter, we examined one way in which two or more people could share in the ownership of land. This was the law of *concurrent* co-ownership, being where all of the co-owners were entitled to the enjoyment of land simultaneously. Typical examples were spouses, civil partners or unmarried couples.[1] However, there is another method by which two or more people can have 'ownership' rights over land at the same time, albeit that only one of them is entitled to the immediate physical possession of the property. This is the law relating to *successive* co-ownership of land, being where one person has an interest in the land for life and another person, or persons, have rights that 'fall into' possession after the 'life interest' has ended.[2] For example, it was once quite common for property to be left by will[3] to one person for their life, then to another, then to another, and so on, as where Blackacre is left to A for life, with remainder to B for life, remainder to C in fee simple. In such a case: A has a life interest in possession (and is known, somewhat confusingly, as the 'life tenant'); B has a life interest in remainder (and will be the life tenant when A dies); and C has a fee simple in remainder (and will become the absolute owner on the death of A and B). As is made apparent by this example, the person who established the successive interests[4] was able to control the destination of the land for a considerable period[5] and often the reason for creating successive interests was 'to keep land in the family' by limiting its ownership to successive generations (e.g. 'my son', 'my grandson', etc.), although it could also be used for business or commercial arrangements. Importantly, even though only one of the co-owners was entitled to the *possession* of the land (the life tenant), all of the other persons interested in 'the settlement' also had property interests that could be dealt with in the normal way. That is why it is a form of co-ownership.

5.1   Successive Interests: In General

The Trusts of Land and Appointment of Trustees Act 1996 (TOLATA 1996) has had a profound impact on the law relating to successive interests in land. Prior to the Act, there were two methods of creating successive interests: first, under a settlement (or 'strict settlement', as it was known) regulated by the Settled Land Act 1925 (SLA); second, under a trust for sale regulated by the Law of Property Act 1925 (LPA). However, since the entry into force of TOLATA 1996 on 1 January 1997, the picture has changed considerably. The purpose of TOLATA 1996 is to simplify the law, to make dealings with land subject to successive interests more transparent and to ensure that the rules by which successive interests are regulated reflects the modern use to which this form of co-ownership can be

---

1   Although, of course, concurrent co-ownership is not confined to persons in intimate family relationships.

2   That is, of course, when the holder of the life interest dies.

3   Or alternatively on the occasion of marriage of the eldest son or other child.

4   Usually called 'the settlor'.

5   The length of time for which the settlor could exercise such control was not unlimited. The 'dead hand' of the settlor was only permitted to exert influence over the destination of the land for that period of time that complied with the 'perpetuity rules'.

put. In essence, TOLATA 1996 changed the way in which successive interests could in future be created[6] and established a much simpler legal mechanism for dealing with all of those people interested in the land than that which existed under the SLA 1925. The principal effects of TOLATA 1996 are as follows.

1   Since 1 January 1997, it has not been possible to create any new settlement within the ambit of the Settled Land Act 1925. The institution of the 'strict settlement' has been abandoned for all successive interests established after that date (section 2 of TOLATA 1996). The obvious consequence is that no new land can be made subject to the regime of the SLA 1925, and, over time, the influence of this creaking statutory regime will diminish.

2   Existing strict settlements will remain effective and be governed by the SLA 1925 – section 2 of TOLATA 1996 – as will resettlements of existing settled land.[7] Inevitably, however, much existing settled land will fall into absolute ownership (i.e. all of the life interests will terminate on the death of the life tenants), and the land will cease to be 'settled land'. Note, however, that if the 'old' settlement is perpetuated by the creation of new life interests *before* the termination of the existing settlement, the land continues to be 'settled land' and remains subject to the SLA 1925 – known as a 'resettlement'. If, by way of contrast, the settlement does indeed terminate, and no land or heirlooms remain subject to it, any subsequent attempt to create a life interest in that land really is a 'new' creation, and will be governed by TOLATA 1996.

3   For those *existing* successive interests *not* governed by the SLA 1925 – being those created deliberately as 'trusts for sale' *prior* to the entry into force of TOLATA 1996 – they will now be governed by the rubric of TOLATA 1996. Technically, if the 'trust for sale' has been created expressly, it will continue to be a 'trust for sale' but once again this is unlikely to have many practical consequences. Moreover, in those rare cases in which the successive interests were governed by a trust for sale that arose by operation of law prior to TOLATA 1996, it is to take effect as a trust of land within that statute.

4   All new attempts to create successive interests in land must take effect under the rubric of TOLATA 1996 (sections 4 and 5 of TOLATA 1996). The normal device will be the standard 'trust of land' instituted by that statute.[8] It will be possible deliberately to establish successive interests under a 'trust for sale of land' on or after 1 January 1997 (but not, of course, a strict settlement), but this will still be governed by TOLATA 1996 and the practical differences between it and the 'trust of land' are minimal.[9] It is very doubtful whether many express trusts for sale will be created after December 1996 as, under TOLATA 1996, very little would be gained by adopting this approach.

Once again, then, the important practical point irrespective of the precise type of trust involved is that successive interests are now governed by TOLATA 1996, save only for that

---

6   From 1 January 1997 and the entry into force of TOLATA 1996.

7   As where a pre-1997 settlement comes to an end only by reason of its replacement with a new set of similar arrangements, a resettlement of existing settled land.

8   Replacing the old 'trust for sale of land'.

9   The definition of a 'trust of land' includes a 'trust for sale of land' (section 1 of TOLATA 1996).

diminishing category of strict settlements that existed before 1 January 1996 that remain within the ambit of the SLA 1925.

5.1.1 Successive interests under the Trusts of Land and Appointment of Trustees Act 1996

As we have seen in the previous chapter, TOLATA 1996 effectively abolished the concept of the trust for sale and replaced it with the trust of land.[10] Furthermore, as noted above, the Act also ensures that all *future* successive interests shall take effect as trusts of land under its rubric. In fact, the great majority of the provisions of TOLATA 1996 were designed specifically with cases of successive ownership of land in mind (rather than concurrent co-ownership). This is because, in cases of successive ownership, it is likely (indeed, almost inevitable) that the trustees of the land will be completely different persons from the person who is to occupy the land for life (the life tenant), or the persons who are entitled in remainder should the life tenant die. The trustees may well be a bank or independent advisers, and the life tenant will be the person most intimately connected with the land – say, the eldest son of the settlor. Necessarily, in such typical cases of successive interests, the life tenant will usually wish to occupy the land,[11] and the life tenant is usually the person best placed to manage the land effectively by exercising the various powers open to either him or the trustees.[12] In their turn, the trustees are likely to prefer to hold a 'watching brief' and allow the tenant for life to use the land as befits his limited ownership.

With this in mind, a summary of the provisions of TOLATA 1996 may be given, remembering that these provisions apply to all new successive interests created on or after 1 January 1997 and for those previously governed by the rubric of the old 'trust for sale'.

1. Save for pre-1 January 1997 strict settlements,[13] there is to be one set of rules governing the creation and operation of successive interests – the trust of land under TOLATA 1996.
2. The doctrine of conversion is abolished, effective for all new and nearly all existing trusts of land (section 3 of TOLATA 1996). The doctrine of conversion was an ancient doctrine applicable to certain property concepts whereby the interest of the persons entitled under the trust (e.g. in our case, the life tenant) was treated not as an interest in the relevant *land*, but as an interest in the proceeds of sale of that land. Hence, the rights were technically 'personalty' and not 'realty'. Thus, a will leaving 'my personal property' to X would actually have passed the testator's interest under a trust to X as potentially converted money, even though it *looked* like an interest in land. Its abolition means, in effect, that the interest of a person under a trust of land[14] is to be regarded as an interest in the land itself, rather than in its monetary

---

10 As noted, it is possible to create an express trust for sale under TOLATA 1996, but this is within the definition of a 'trust of land' and subject to the TOLATA 1996 rules.

11 See section 12 of TOLATA 1996.

12 Hence the trustees' ability to delegate their powers under section 9 of TOLATA 1996.

13 Which will continue to operate under the SLA 1925 until exhausted.

14 Including expressly created trusts for sale of land.

equivalent. Clearly, this accords with the perception of the persons having such interests and, in practice, this change in the law will have only limited consequences.[15] The exception for which the doctrine of conversion may still operate is for trusts for sale of land created by the will of a person dying before 1 January 1997 – such a testator may have ordered his affairs precisely on the basis that the doctrine of conversion was applicable on his death.

3   The legal title to the land will be vested in the trustees of land and they will have all of the powers of an absolute owner (section 6(1) of TOLATA 1996 and section 23 of the LRA 2002). The life tenant and persons entitled in remainder will have equitable interests in the land. However, the trustees' powers are given in virtue of their status as trustees and consequently are subject to the general equitable jurisdiction in relation to the exercise of trustees' powers. In other words, the trustees can be held accountable for the exercise of their powers on normal principles of trustee liability. More specifically, the trustees may delegate certain powers to the life tenant (or other person) and their powers may be restricted by the instrument that establishes the trust.[16] Given that trusts concerning successive interests usually are created deliberately and with considerable formality,[17] it is likely that the trustees will intend from the outset to delegate powers of management of the land to the tenant for life, including the power of sale. However, only the trustees can give a valid receipt for money received on sale ('purchase money') should any of the land be sold, hence preserving their role in overreaching.

4   The trustees must consult with the persons interested in the trust, both the life tenant and persons entitled in remainder. They should give effect to their wishes in so far as is consistent with the purposes of the trust of land (section 11 of TOLATA 1996). This raises similar issues to those considered in relation to concurrent co-ownership considered in Chapter 4.

5   The trustees' ability to exercise their powers, including the power of sale, may be made subject to the consent of the equitable owners (e.g. the life tenant and persons entitled in remainder), but only if stated in the instrument creating the trusts (sections 8 and 10 TOLATA) or if imposed by the court following an application made under section 14 of TOLATA 1996. Given that the creation of successive interests is not usually undertaken lightly, it is quite likely that a consent requirement will be imposed as part of an overall strategy to deal with the land. In relation to registered land, a purchaser will be concerned to comply with the consent requirement if it is imposed by the entry of a restriction against the title to the land, as otherwise the title cannot be conveyed (section 26 of the LRA 2002). The position in

---

15 The courts already treated such interests as 'interests in land' for many purposes irrespective of the doctrine of conversion: see, for example, *Williams & Glyn's Bank v. Boland* (1981) in relation to the overreaching powers of trustees and the concept of overriding interests – Chapter 2.

16 See generally sections 6–9 of TOLATA 1996.

17 It is quite difficult for successive interest trusts of land to be created accidentally, although this can sometimes be the result of a successful claim of constructive trust or proprietary estoppel, as contemplated by *Ungarian v. Lesnoff* (1990) (see Chapter 4, constructive trust) and *Dent v. Dent* (1996) (see Chapter 9, proprietary estoppel).

respect of unregistered land is governed by section 16 of TOLATA 1996, on which see immediately below.[18]

6　The trust of land when it governs successive interests is subject to the same over-reaching machinery as when it governs concurrent co-ownership interests. This is because the interests of the life tenant and persons entitled in remainder are equitable interests, and the legal title is held by the trustees: for example, where Z Bank plc holds land on trust for A for life, with the remainder to B. Necessarily, on sale of the land, it is the trustees who will have to transfer the legal title and it will be the beneficiaries (e.g. a life tenant) who are susceptible to overreaching in favour of a purchaser. If the overreaching process is successful, the equitable interests will cease to give a right to enjoyment of the land but will instead take effect in the purchase money – thus the tenant for life will receive the income from the capital sum for life, with the balance going to the person entitled in remainder on the death of that life tenant. However, should overreaching not occur (as in a rare case of there being only one trustee of a *successive* interest trust for land[19]), whether these equitable interests bind the purchaser is determined by the application of normal principles of registered or unregistered conveyancing as the case may be. In registered land, the interests of the beneficiaries might override if the beneficiaries are discoverable actual occupation of the land[20] but they cannot be protected by an entry of a notice on the register.[21] Consequently, even in the absence of overreaching, the interests of a person not in discoverable actual occupation[22] will not bind a purchaser,[23] and the only way to ensure protection is by the entry of a restriction on the register.[24] In unregistered land, such an interest cannot be a land charge,[25] so in the absence of overreaching may take effect against a purchaser according to the doctrine of notice.

7　In addition to the overreaching provisions, the purchaser of land subject to a successive trust of land is given protection should the trustees sell the land in excess of their powers or in breach of the provisions of TOLATA 1996. In respect of land of unregistered title, the matter turns on the particular violation committed by the trustees. In some cases (e.g. violation of the duty to consult), it seems that the purchaser will obtain a good title from the trustees, assuming overreaching, and the beneficiaries'

18　In the unlikely event of a successive trust of land arising informally, there will be no express requirement that the trustees should seek consent, so an application must be made to the court under section 14 of TOLATA 1996 if one is required.

19　A sole trustee who is a trust corporation (e.g. an authorised bank) is sufficient for overreaching (section 2 of the LPA 1925).

20　Or where, being in actual occupation, the beneficiary's rights are known to the purchaser: see Schedule 3, paragraph 2 of the LRA 2002.

21　Section 33(a)(ii) of the LRA 2002.

22　And not otherwise within Schedule 3, paragraph 2 of the LRA 2002.

23　Section 29 of the LRA 2002.

24　Although there is nothing in the LRA 2002 or the Land Registration Rules to prevent the entry of a restriction requiring consent in order to prevent a sale even if there are two trustees or a trust corporation, HM Land Registry will refuse to enter such a restriction at the request of the equitable on the ground that overreaching should not be rendered ineffective. This has some backing from the courts (*Coleman v. Bryant* (2007)).

25　Section 2 of the Land Charges Act 1972.

remedy lies against the trustees personally. In other cases ,(e.g. non-compliance with a consent requirement), the purchaser will obtain a clean title, assuming over-reaching, provided that he did not have actual notice of the relevant limitation (section 16 of TOLATA 1996). In land of registered title, it is assumed that the limitation on the trustees' powers (if any) will be entered on the register of title by way of restriction, thus preventing any disposition by the trustees unless the limitation is complied with. Necessarily, this will prevent a purchaser buying the land at all until the restriction is complied with. If for some very unusual reason (e.g. a solicitor's failure to act properly), the limitation on the trustees' powers is not entered on the register or the restriction is ignored, it seems likely that a purchaser who can overreach[26] will obtain a clear title free of such interests despite the trustees' non-compliance with the limitation. This is because in registered land, the person entered as proprietor has all of the powers of an absolute owner, subject only to entries on the register,[27] and registration as proprietor (i.e. by the purchaser) is conclusive in his favour.[28]

8   The tenant for life has a right to occupy the property – section 12 of TOLATA 1996. The persons entitled in remainder also may have a right to occupy – sections 12(1)(a) and (b) and section 12(2) – but this would almost certainly be removed or modified under section 12(3) of the Act, which permits the trustees to limit the right of occupation. Note also that section 13 provides that the trustee may impose reasonable conditions on the person occupying the property, including requiring the payment of expenses or outgoings in respect of the land. Likewise, if the trustees have exercised their powers to exclude or limit other beneficiaries' rights to occupy, they may impose a requirement that the occupying beneficiary pay compensation for exclusive use of the land: for example, the life tenant might be ordered to pay a sum equivalent to the market rent of the land, or some proportion thereof, if only the life tenant is in occupation.[29]

9   Lastly, any person with an interest in the land can make an application to the court under section 14 of TOLATA 1996 for a variety of orders in relation to the land. For example, an application can be made for sale, to prohibit a proposed sale, to impose or override a consent requirement or for a declaration of the respective values or shares of the beneficial owners. Generally, such orders are made with reference to the criteria specified in section 15 of the Act, save only that section 15 does not apply in case of bankruptcy, for which section 335A of the Insolvency Act 1986 provides a list of criteria.[30]

---

26 Failure to overreach opens the purchaser to the possibility of being bound by an overriding interest through the discoverable actual occupation etc. of the equitable interest-holder.

27 Sections 23 and 26 of the LRA 2002.

28 Section 58 of the LRA 2002.

29 Section 13(3) of TOLATA 1996.

30 These issues have been discussed at greater length in Chapter 4 in respect of concurrent co-ownership.

5.2 Successive Interests under the Old Regime: The Strict Settlement and the Settled Land Act 1925

As is now clear, the law of strict settlements will apply only to those successive interest trusts created before the entry into force of TOLATA 1996. Necessarily, this means that the complicated rules of the SLA 1925 will become less important. They are discussed below. Points of comparison with the regime of TOLATA 1996 should be kept in mind during this analysis.

The 'strict settlement' is not a creation of the 1925 property legislation and, indeed, one of the reasons for the SLA 1925 was to reform and regulate the pre-1926 rules that had previously governed the creation and operation of successive interests in land. That said, it is to the SLA 1925 that we must look for a comprehensive statement of the pre-TOLATA 1996 law. Unfortunately, the SLA 1925 – and the substantive law – is quite complicated, and it is not an accident that the strict settlement was, for many years, rarely deliberately created or that it has now been abolished for new successive interests. In general terms, a 'strict settlement' exists when land is left on trust (not being a trust for sale) for someone for life, with remainder to another, perhaps also with provision by way of rentcharges for the payment of a regular income to someone else (e.g. the widow of the settlor[31]). However, this is a simplified definition, and sections 1 and 2 of the SLA 1925 define 'settled land' in much more precise terms. Thus, according to the SLA 1925, and bearing in mind that this is not operative for any instrument establishing a new trust on or after 1 January 1997, settled land was either:

1   land 'limited in trust for any persons by way of succession';
2   land 'limited in trust for any person in possession' for an entailed interest (i.e. a fee tail, now abolished by TOLATA 1996) for an infant, for a determinable fee, or for a fee simple subject to an executory limitation;
3   land limited in trust for any person for a legal freehold or leasehold estate that was contingent upon the happening of any event; or
4   land that was charged by way of a family arrangement with the payment of any sums for the benefit of any persons.[32]

There is no denying that this appears to be complicated, but the essential point to remember is that settled land is land for which the estate of the owner in possession is 'limited' in some way. Thus, either the owner's interest is limited to his life, or is tied to the happening of an event, or is charged with the payment of money. Importantly, land that was subject to 'an immediate binding trust for sale'[33] is excluded from the definition of settled land and falls outside the SLA 1925. Such land was already governed by the LPA 1925 and now takes effect under TOLATA 1996 as a trust of land.

---

31 The person that created the trust.

32 For example, *Re Austen* (1929).

33 Section 1(7) of the SLA 1925.

5.2.1   The essential characteristics of settled land

Settled land is land held on trust. Consequently, there will be 'trustees of the settlement', and beneficiaries under the settlement. These beneficiaries may be the owner of a life interest and those persons entitled in remainder – being entitled when the life interest expires. The settlement will have been created by the settlor, by deed, and this deed will usually identify the trustees. Under the SLA 1925, a range of persons are given statutory powers to deal with the land and it is important to remember that the major purpose behind the grant of these powers is to ensure that the land itself can be freely dealt with: in other words, that the land is alienable and does not get tied up in the settlement. As with concurrent co-ownership, if the land is sold, the rights and interests of the beneficiaries will be transferred to the purchase money via the mechanism of overreaching.

5.2.2   The specific attributes of settled land

The person under the settlement who is of full age, and entitled to immediate possession of the settled land (or the whole income from it), is generally regarded as the 'tenant for life' (section 19 of the SLA 1925). The tenant for life is holder of the legal estate in the land, and he holds that legal estate on trust for the beneficiaries under the settlement.[34] In the great majority of cases, this tenant for life is also the person entitled to an equitable life interest in the property. In other words, the tenant for life often has two roles: holder of the legal estate in the land and owner of an equitable, but limited, ownership interest, such as a life interest. It is no accident that the person in possession of the land should have the legal title. Before 1925, that legal title could be vested in several trustees, or split up among several beneficiaries, and this made dealing with settled land a laborious and expensive process. Under the SLA 1925, the legal title is vested solely in the tenant for life, for they are the person in immediate possession of the land, and they are the person who may best judge how to deal with it.

The tenant for life exercises most of the important statutory powers to deal with the settled land. These are found in Part II of the SLA 1925 and effectively place the tenant for life in control of the land. It is in his hands that the power to manage the land for the best interests of all of the beneficiaries is to be found. Thus, the strict settlement was ideally suited to 'family' property arrangements, in which the present occupier of the land could have been expected to manage it for the good of the family with, of course, the ability to deal with the land (and sell it) if the need should arise. The settlement will also encompass 'trustees of the settlement', and although they rarely hold the legal title to the land, they would exercise general supervisory functions over the settlement.[35] Consequently, it is their responsibility to ensure that the rights and interests of all of the beneficiaries under the settlement are protected, especially if the tenant for life misuses his statutory powers. The identity of the trustees is determined according to section 30 of the SLA 1925, although they will usually be named as such in the trust deeds.

If the person with the statutory powers chooses to sell the settled land, the interests of

---

34 Sections 4 and 107 of the SLA 1925.

35 *Wheelwright v. Walker* (1883).

the beneficiaries are overreached if the purchase money is paid to the trustees of the settlement (who must be two in number, or a trust corporation), or into court. If overreaching occurs, the purchaser need not concern himself with the equitable interests, because these take effect in the purchase money. The purchaser obtains a clean and unencumbered title to the land. If overreaching does not occur, the tenant for life cannot make a good title to the purchaser, and the purchaser may be bound by the equitable interests according to the provisions of the SLA 1925.

5.2.3 The creation of strict settlements under the Settled Land Act 1925

Under the SLA 1925, all strict settlements must be created by two deeds: a 'trust instrument' and a 'principal vesting deed' (sections 4 and 5 of the SLA 1925). The trust instrument declares the details of the settlement, appoints the trustees of it and sets out any powers conferred by the settlement that are in addition to those provided automatically in the Act. The principal vesting deed is less comprehensive and describes the settled land itself, names the trustees, states the nature of any additional powers and, most importantly of all, declares that the settled land is vested in the person to whom the land is conveyed (the tenant for life) on the trusts of the settlement. The principal vesting deed is, in one sense, the statement of ownership of the tenant for life and it is with this that any purchaser will be concerned, not least because the equitable interests detailed in the trust instrument will be swept off the land by overreaching.

5.2.4 The position of the tenant for life and the statutory powers

As indicated above, the tenant for life is given statutory powers to deal with the land. These powers are subject to various controls and the tenant for life is overseen usually by the trustees of the settlement in order to prevent him from taking advantage of his dominant position. Certain controls are specific to certain powers, and these are noted below where appropriate. Furthermore, the tenant for life is trustee of his powers and must have regard to the interests of the other beneficiaries when he exercises them (section 107 of the SLA 1925).

1   The tenant for life has power to sell the settled land, or to exchange it for other land (section 38 of the SLA 1925). However, he must obtain the best price that can be reasonably obtained and a court will take action to ensure this.[36] This power is subject to the written notice procedure, as considered below.
2   The tenant for life has power to grant and accept leases of the land, although for certain specific types of lease, the duration of the lease which the tenant for life may grant is limited (sections 41 and 53 of the SLA 1925). This power is also subject to the written notice procedure.
3   The tenant for life may mortgage or charge the land in order to raise money for specific purposes, these generally being purposes that would benefit the land *per se*,

---

36 *Wheelwright v. Walker (No. 2)* (1883).

rather than any individual owner (section 71 of the SLA 1925). This power is also subject to the written notice procedure.

4   The tenant for life may grant options over the land, including granting a person an option to purchase the land, or an option to purchase a lease (section 51 of the SLA 1925). This power is also subject to the written notice procedure.

5   The tenant for life has various ancillary powers in relation to the settled land. This includes the power to dispose of the principal mansion house (section 65 of the SLA 1925), the power to cut and sell timber (section 66 of the SLA 1925), the power to compromise claims concerning the settled land (section 58 of the SLA 1925), and the power to sell and purchase chattels and family heirlooms (section 67 of the SLA 1925). These powers are subject to the tenant for life obtaining, variously, the consent of the trustees of the settlement or the leave of the court.

6   The tenant for life may effect any other transaction for the benefit of the settled land under order of the court (section 64 of the SLA 1925).

7   The trust deeds of the settlement may expressly confer additional powers on the tenant for life.

5.2.5   The role of the trustees of the settlement in regulating the powers of the tenant for life

It has been indicated already that a major role of the 'trustees of the settlement' is to act in a general supervisory function in order to safeguard the rights of all persons entitled to an interest in the land. In addition to this, the most important powers of the tenant for life are subject to the provisions of section 101 of the SLA 1925. Under section 101, a tenant for life who intends to make a sale, exchange, lease, mortgage, or charge in respect of the land, or to grant an option over it, must give written notice to each of the trustees by registered post, and to the solicitor for the trustees, of his intention to exercise one of these powers. Each notice must be posted not less than one month before the proposed disposition and, if there are currently no trustees of the settlement, these powers cannot be exercised.[37]

These provisions are designed to ensure that the trustees are aware of all proposed major dealings with the land and are ready to activate the overreaching mechanism where appropriate. However, although at first sight this notice procedure appears perfectly adequate to protect all beneficiaries, the Settled Land Act itself weakens this protection considerably. Thus, a trustee is under no obligation to interfere with a proposed dealing with the settled land of which he has notice[38] and, except for the power to mortgage or charge the land, the tenant for life may give notice of a general intention to exercise these powers rather than specific notice on each occasion (section 101(2) of the SLA 1925). Furthermore, the trustees may, in writing, waive the notice requirement, or accept less than one month's notice[39] and, importantly, a person dealing with the tenant for life in good faith is not required to inquire whether these procedural safeguards have been observed (section 101(5) of the SLA 1925). Clearly then, much depends on the personal determination and interest of the trustees in supervising the tenant for life.

---

37 *Wheelwright v. Walker* (1883).

38 England v. Public Trustee (1967).

39 Section 101(4) of the SLA 1925.

5.2.6 The fiduciary position of the tenant for life

According to section 107 of the SLA 1925, the tenant for life is trustee of his statutory powers for those entitled under the settlement, and 'shall' have regard to their interests when exercising those powers. This is meant to give further protection to those entitled to either the land or its monetary equivalent. It has some practical consequences, albeit of a limited nature. For example, if the tenant for life sells the settled land, he must sell as fairly as a trustee would sell, which effectively means for the best price reasonably obtainable paying due regard to the interests of the people entitled in remainder.[40] Moreover, the tenant for life cannot accept or keep a payment for exercising the powers because, as a trustee, he is under a duty not to profit from his trust.[41] However, once again, the protection offered by the legislation promises more than it delivers, for it is clear that a court will not invalidate a sale simply because the tenant for life sells the property for a bad motive, or even because he (the tenant for life) is simply uninterested in managing the land.[42]

5.2.7 Attempts to restrict the powers of the tenant for life

It should be apparent from the above that the tenant for life really is in control of the settled land and that the statutory powers he is given are not subject to serious control either by the trustees of the settlement or under the general law of trusts. Consequently, there is a temptation for settlors to attempt to control or restrict the tenant for life in the exercise of his powers by inserting some express limitation in the deeds of the settlement. Unfortunately, this cuts against the philosophy of the SLA 1925 given that the Act was designed to prevent just this sort of control being exercised over the settled land by the 'dead hand' of the settlor. Therefore, according to section 106 of the SLA 1925, any provision inserted in a settlement that purports or attempts to forbid a tenant for life to exercise a statutory power, or any provision that attempts, tends or is intended to induce the tenant for life not to exercise those powers, is void, as in *Re Patten* (1929). Likewise, in *Re Orlebar* (1936), the court discussed a so-called 'residence condition', which stipulated that the tenant for life should lose his interest under the settlement if he ceased to occupy the land, and decided that the tenant for life would not forfeit his interest if he left the land as a result of a proper exercise of a statutory power.[43]

Obviously, section 106 is a very powerful statutory provision and it is largely effective to prevent settlors avoiding the policy of the SLA 1925 by special drafting of the settlement. However, in *Re Aberconway* (1953), a majority of the court held that if that which might be lost to the tenant for life through such a provision was *not* a benefit to him, section 106 did not apply to make that provision void. Taking a different approach, Lord Denning in his dissenting opinion was of the view that anything that even *tended* to restrict the tenant for life in the exercise of his powers was void and this does seem more consistent with the overall policy of the Act than the decision of the majority. Indeed, a simple reading of section 106 appears to confirm Lord Dennings's view and it has an echo

---

40 *Wheelwright v. Walker* (1883).

41 *Chandler v. Bradley* (1897).

42 *Cardigan v. Curzon-Howe* (1885).

43 It would be otherwise if the tenant for life vacated the land for his own private motives.

in section 104 of the same Act, which provides that any contract entered into by the tenant for life himself not to exercise a statutory power is void.

5.2.8 Protection for the beneficiaries

In a very general sense, the beneficiaries under the settlement are protected by the notice procedures discussed above, the general supervisory role of the trustees of the settlement, and the overreaching machinery, especially if all they are concerned with is the income that the land may generate rather than the land itself. More importantly, a very powerful provision is found in section 13 of the SLA 1925. As noted above, when expressly created, each settlement should comprise two deeds: the trust instrument and the vesting deed. Under section 13, if no vesting deed has been executed in favour of the tenant for life, any proposed dealing *inter vivos* by him with the legal estate operates only as a contract to carry out that transaction; it does not transfer the legal title to the prospective purchaser. In other words, in the absence of a vesting deed, dealings with the legal title are paralysed, except in four specified cases, the most important of which is a sale to a purchaser of a legal estate without notice of the absence of the vesting deed. Simply put, the absence of a vesting deed makes it difficult for the tenant for life to deal with the land. However, if he sells that land in violation of the settlement to an innocent purchaser (as most will be), that purchaser will obtain good legal title to the land. The protection of section 13 is thus fragile.

Once a vesting deed has been executed, section 13 no longer applies, and the beneficiaries must look to section 18 of the SLA 1925 for protection in the event of some fraud on the settlement. Under section 18, once a vesting deed has been executed, and until the settlement is discharged, any transaction that is not 'authorised' by the SLA 1925 or other statute is void. Thus, any sale or mortgage, and so on, by the tenant for life that is outside his statutory powers is ineffective to convey legal title to the land. It would operate only in equity to the effect of conveying the tenant's own equitable interest, but no more, to the purchaser.[44] Of course, the existence of a vesting deed normally would inform the purchaser of all material facts in relation to the settlement – or at least indicate areas of concern where further enquiries might be made – and so a purchaser can have little complaint if he purchases the land after inspecting the vesting deed as part of what turns out to be an unauthorised transaction.

5.2.9 Protection for the purchaser of settled land

Once again, in a general sense, the purchaser of settled land is protected by the overreaching machinery. He need be concerned only with the vesting deed and can rely on the interests of the beneficiaries being overreached. However, things can, and do, go wrong. To meet this situation, section 110 of the SLA 1925 provides that a purchaser who deals in good faith with the tenant for life is, as regards the beneficiaries, deemed to have paid the best price and to have complied with all of the requirements of the Act. Although it is sometimes thought that this provision sits uneasily with section 18 (which voids all unauthorised transactions), it seems that section 110 is concerned with matters

---

44 *Weston v. Henshaw* (1950).

of detail, not of principle. Thus, section 110 will not protect a purchaser if the transaction with the tenant for life is wholly unauthorised (for this falls within section 18), but it will protect him if there are omissions of detail in an otherwise authorised transaction.[45]

5.2.10 The overreaching machinery

Equitable interests under strict settlements are capable of being overreached on a sale of the settled land (section 2 of the LPA 1925). If successful, overreaching will confer legal title on a purchaser free of all equitable interests under the settlement. Of course, no legal rights are capable of being overreached and with three minor exceptions (annuities, limited owner's charge, general equitable charge), neither are any equitable interests created prior to the settlement. As with all overreaching, the capital purchase money must be paid to at least two trustees of the settlement or a trust corporation. In unregistered land, failure to overreach may result in the equitable interests binding the purchaser through the doctrine of notice because such interests cannot be registered as a land charge.[46] In land of registered title, when overreaching fails, the position is more complex. Equitable interests under an SLA 1925 settlement cannot be overriding interests[47] nor may they be protected by the entry of a notice against the title.[48] In consequence, the beneficiaries must either be content to rely on the protective sections of the SLA itself (sections 13 and 18 above) or have had the foresight to enter a restriction against the title effectively preventing a sale of the land at all unless the conditions for overreaching are in fact complied with.[49]

5.2.11 The duties of the trustees of the settlement

The supervisory duties of the trustees of the settlement, and their role in regulating the tenant for life in the exercise of his statutory powers, have been mentioned already. In addition to this, the SLA 1925 gives the trustees other responsibilities, not least receipt of the capital sum in order to facilitate overreaching. More specifically, the trustees may actually act as 'statutory owner' (with all of the powers of a tenant for life) if there is no tenant for life, or the tenant for life is an infant and, under section 24 of the Act, the court may authorise the trustees to exercise the powers of the tenant for life (in his name) if the tenant has ceased to have a substantial interest in the land, or has refused (but not merely neglected) to exercise those powers.[50]

---

45 *Re Morgan's Lease* (1972).

46 Section 2 of the Land Charges Act 1972.

47 Schedule 3, paragraph 2 of the LRA 2002.

48 Section 33(a)(ii) of the LRA 2002.

49 The entry of a restriction preventing sale unless there are two trustees or a trust corporation would have been normal when the strict settlement was created deliberately. Note that the effect of such a restriction is to ensure that overreaching occurs – thus forcing the equitable owners to take their interests in money.

50 As explained in *Re 90 Thornhill Road* (1970).

5.3   The Trust for Sale of Land: Pre-TOLATA 1996

The second method of regulating successive interests in land *before* the entry into force of TOLATA 1996 was the *trust for sale* of land. Although trusts for sale expressly created before or after 1 January 1997 may continue to exist in name, they will take effect under the regime of TOLATA 1996 and there will be little practical difference between these and the more common *trust of land*.[51] Further, any trusts in relation to land that had been, or will be, imposed by statute will take effect as a simple trust of land subject to TOLATA 1996. This will include any trusts created impliedly by reason of the application of the principles of resulting or constructive trusts. Consequently, in terms of pre-1997 law, the other method of creating a trust for successive interests (the old trust for sale) comes under the TOLATA 1996 regime and is, for all practical purposes, equivalent to a trust of land. The principal features of this regime have been discussed above.[52]

5.4   A Comparison between the Strict Settlement under the Settled Land Act 1925 and the Regime of the Trusts of Land and Appointment of Trustees Act 1996

As noted at the outset of this chapter, pre-1997 existing successive interest trusts for sale, and all new attempts to create successive interests in land, will take effect under TOLATA 1996. This is regardless of whether they take effect as a *trust of land*, or whether they retain their *trust for sale* label (having been created as such expressly). Again, as noted above, the difference between the two types of trust is minimal, as it is the provisions of TOLATA 1996 that are important. These apply equally to the trust of land and the trust for sale of land. Consequently, in order to appreciate more fully the difference that the obligatory application of TOLATA 1996 has made to the law of successive interests, a comparison with the 'old' law of strict settlements of the Settled Land Act 1925 is appropriate.

1   Settled land is governed by the complicated provisions of the SLA 1925. The trust of land under TOLATA 1996 is relatively easy to understand and operate (and this includes expressly created trusts for sale). The abolition of the strict settlement for new successive interests should mean less litigation and less cost.

2   The strict settlement was ideally suited to keeping land 'in the family', especially where the tenant for life may have wished to occupy the land and consequently declined to exercise his power of sale. This was perfectly legitimate, even if those entitled on his death saw the value of their prospective interests dwindle. The

---

51   Above section 5.2.

52   Section 5.2.1 above.

machinery of TOLATA 1996 can ensure occupation by interested persons (i.e. the tenant for life), but also has the flexibility to ensure that the land is sold if this is in the best interests of every equitable owner (see section 14 of TOLATA 1996).

3   Under a strict settlement, the tenant for life has legal title and is in effective control of the land. Under TOLATA 1996, the trustees have legal title, and have all of the powers of an absolute owner. They will control the land unless they choose to delegate powers to the person with the life interest or other person interested. They will not divest themselves of legal title unless the land subject to the trust is sold.

4   The tenant for life under the SLA 1925 is constrained by the fact that his powers and the legal estate are held on trust. Moreover, certain powers are subject to notice procedures or the consent of the trustees of the settlement. The trustees of land under TOLATA 1996 are obliged to consult the beneficiaries (e.g. the person with a life interest), and should endeavour to give effect to his wishes. However, they are not bound to do so. Under TOLATA 1996, the trustees may have delegated their powers irrevocably, and the exercise of the powers by the trustees may be made subject to the consent of some other person interested in the land.[53]

5   On the death of a life tenant under a strict settlement, the legal estate can be transferred only by means of the expensive and time-consuming process of obtaining a vesting deed. On the death of a trustee of land under TOLATA 1996, legal title simply accrues to the remaining trustees (being joint tenants of the legal estate) under the right of survivorship. No cost, no documents and no fuss.

6   The position of a purchaser of land subject to a strict settlement was not always clear, but was generally quite favourable. Under TOLATA 1996, a purchaser may be bound by equitable interests taking effect as overriding interests, but only if overreaching does not occur. In both the strict settlement and the trust of land, a restriction may be placed on the register of title restricting the ability of the registered proprietor in his dealings with the land unless the conditions for overreaching are complied with.

5.5   Chapter Summary

5.5.1   What is successive ownership of land?

Successive ownership of land occurs when one person has an interest in the land for life and another (or others) has (have) rights that 'fall into' possession after the 'life interest' has ended. There are two ways in which land can be held subject to successive interests. First, for successive interests created before 1 January 1997, a settlement (or 'strict settlement') may be used. Such land is called *settled land* and falls within the machinery of the SLA 1925. Second, for successive interests created on or after 1 January 1997, TOLATA 1996 requires that a trust of land be used. No new strict settlements can be created after this date, save for resettlements of existing settled land.

---

53 For example, the life tenant to whom delegated powers have not been given.

5.5.2   The strict settlement and settled land

A 'strict settlement' will exist in a number of (complicated) circumstances, but the most common are where land is 'limited in trust for any persons by way of succession' or where land is charged by way of a family arrangement with the payment of any sums for the benefit of any persons.

5.5.3   The essential characteristics of settled land

The person under the settlement who is of full age and entitled to immediate possession of the settled land (or the whole income from it) is generally regarded as the 'tenant for life' (section 19 of the SLA 1925). The tenant for life is holder of the legal estate and holds that estate on trust for the beneficiaries under the settlement (sections 4 and 107 of the SLA 1925). The tenant for life exercises most of the important statutory powers to deal with the settled land. These effectively place the tenant for life in control of the land. There are also 'trustees of the settlement' and they exercise general supervisory functions over the settlement. Where the person with the statutory powers chooses to sell the settled land, the interests of the beneficiaries are overreached if the purchase money is paid to the trustees of the settlement (who must be two in number or a trust corporation) or into court.

5.5.4   The position of the tenant for life and the statutory powers

The tenant for life will usually have various powers to deal with the settled land, including the power to sell it, grant a lease of it and mortgage it for specific purposes. These powers are subject to the consent of the trustees of the settlement or the leave of the court, although the tenant for life may effect any other transaction for the benefit of the settled land under order of the court (section 64 of the SLA 1925). The trusts of the settlement may expressly confer additional powers on the tenant for life. Under section 106 of the SLA 1925, any provision inserted in the settlement that purports or attempts to forbid a tenant for life to exercise a statutory power, or any provision that attempts, tends or is intended to induce the tenant for life not to exercise those powers, is void.

5.5.5   The role of the trustees of the settlement in regulating the powers of the tenant for life

Under section 101 of the SLA 1925, a tenant for life who intends to make a sale, exchange, lease, mortgage, or charge in respect of the land, or to grant an option over it, must give written notice to each of the trustees by registered post and to the solicitor for the trustees of his intention to exercise one of these powers.

5.5.6   The fiduciary position of the tenant for life

Under section 107 of the SLA 1925, the tenant for life is trustee of his statutory powers for those entitled under the settlement and 'shall' have regard to their interests when exercising those powers.

5.5.7 Protection for the beneficiaries

In addition to the notice procedure, the general supervisory role of the trustees of the settlement and the overreaching machinery, the beneficiaries are protected by sections 13 and 18 of the SLA 1925. These sections can paralyse dealings with the land in certain circumstances.

5.5.8 Protection for the purchaser of settled land

Section 110 of the SLA 1925 provides that a purchaser who deals in good faith with the tenant for life is, as regards the beneficiaries, deemed to have paid the best price and to have complied with all of the requirements of the Act. This is concerned with matters of detail and section 110 will not protect a purchaser if the transaction with the tenant for life is wholly unauthorised (section 18).

5.5.9 The overreaching machinery

Equitable interests under strict settlements are capable of being overreached on a sale of the settled land (section 2 of the LPA 1925). No legal rights are capable of being overreached.

5.5.10 The trust for sale of land and TOLATA 1996

TOLATA 1996 regulates all successive interests of land (except resettlements) created on or after 1 January 1997. Legal title is vested in the trustees who have all of the powers to deal with the land. The life tenant and others entitled will have equitable interests. The trustees may delegate their powers (except the power to overreach) to any person and may well give some powers to the person in occupation of the land, usually the tenant for life. The trustees must consult the beneficiaries before dealing with the land, but only in limited circumstances will they have to obtain the consent of the beneficiaries before exercising their powers. The tenant for life (and other beneficiaries) has a right to occupy the land, although this can be excluded. Usually, only the tenant for life will occupy. A sale (including a mortgage) by the trustees will overreach the equitable owners, provided that the conditions for statutory overreaching are met. Any person interested in the trust of land may apply to the court under section 14 of TOLATA 1996 for an order concerning the land.

Chapter 6
Leases

6.1   The Nature of a Lease

The leasehold is one of the two estates identified in section 1 of the Law of Property Act (LPA) 1925 as capable of existing as either a 'legal' or 'equitable' interest. As we shall see, whether any given lease is legal or equitable will depend primarily on the way in which it has been created. However, irrespective of whether a leasehold is legal or equitable, there is no doubt that it is one of the most versatile concepts known in the law of real property. Even the terminology of leases reflects the many purposes to which they may be put. The 'term of years', 'tenancy', 'sublease' and 'leasehold estate' are all terms in common use, and all of them describe the existence of a 'landlord' and 'tenant' relationship. For example, a 'lease' or 'term of years' is most often used to describe a commercial or long-term letting, whereas the description 'tenancy' is often used for residential or short-term lets. This variety does not mean that different substantive rules apply to different types of lease (although this may be the case where a statute applies only to one kind of lease), but it does indicate the importance that the leasehold plays in the world of commercial and residential property management and investment. In this respect, three fundamental features of the leasehold should be noted at the outset.

First, the leasehold allows two or more people to enjoy the benefits of owning an estate in the same piece of land at the same time: the freeholder will receive the rent and profits, and the leaseholder will enjoy physical possession and occupation of the property. Indeed, if a 'subtenancy' (also known as an 'underlease') is created, being where a shorter lease is carved out of the 'headlease', the number of people enjoying the land or its fruits increases further. For example, if a freeholder (A) grants a 99-year lease to B, and B grants a 50-year subtenancy to C, then A receives rent from B, B receives rent from C and C enjoys physical possession of the land. In theory, there is no limit to the number of underleases that can be created out of a freehold estate, and each intermediate person will be the tenant of their superior landlord and the landlord of their own tenant. It is the ability of the leasehold to facilitate this multiple enjoyment of land that gives it its unique character. It allows the landlord to generate an income through rent (thus employing land as an investment vehicle), while at the same time the tenant is a 'purchaser' of an estate in land through the payment of that rent.

Second, it is in principle inherent in the leasehold estate that both the landlord and tenant (and all subtenants) have a proprietary right in the land.[1] Thus, the tenant owns the lease, and the landlord owns the 'reversion expectant on the lease' – that is, the right to possession of the property when the lease ends. Importantly, both of these proprietary rights can be sold or transferred while the lease is in existence. The tenant may sell his lease to a person who becomes the new tenant (an 'assignee' of the lease), and the landlord may sell his reversion to a person who becomes the new landlord (an assignee of the reversion). Likewise, the assignees of the lease and reversion may assign (i.e. sell or transfer) their interests further. The result is that the current landlord and current tenant under a lease may be far removed from the original landlord and tenant who actually negotiated its creation. Nevertheless, as explained below, the landlord and tenant currently 'in possession'

---

1   But note *Bruton v. London and Quadrant Housing Trust* (1999), below.

may well be bound by the terms of the lease as originally agreed. Figure 6.1 represents this diagrammatically.

Third, all leases will contain covenants (promises) whereby the landlord and tenant promise to do, or not to do, certain things in relation to the land. These may either be 'express covenants', as where they are agreed between landlord and tenant and written deliberately into the lease, 'implied covenants', being covenants read into the lease as a matter of law (e.g. the repairing covenant implied in certain leases by section 11 of the Landlord and Tenant Act 1985), or 'usual' covenants, being those that are not expressly mentioned but are so common in the landlord and tenant relationship that they are taken to be part of the lease unless clearly excluded: for example, the tenant's obligation to pay rent under an equitable lease (*Shiloh Spinners v. Harding* (1973)). Typical examples of express covenants are the landlord's covenant to repair the buildings and the tenant's covenant to pay rent or not to carry on a trade on the premises. All of these types of covenant are enforceable between the *original* landlord and tenant and, as we shall see, in many circum-stances are also enforceable between assignees of the lease or reversion. The particular rules concerning the enforceability of leasehold covenants are discussed below in section 6.4, but the important point is that the ability to make rights and obligations 'run' with the land is a special feature of the landlord and tenant relationship. It is the reason why the leasehold estate is a particularly useful investment vehicle because the freeholder can generate an income while, at the same time, preserving the value of the land through properly drafted covenants (e.g. that the tenant must repair, may not keep pets, etc.), which will bind the original tenant *and* any subsequent assignees. Moreover, given that both the benefit of a leasehold covenant (the right to enforce it) and its burden (the obligation to observe it) can run with the land, the use of a leasehold with appropriate covenants can achieve what covenants affecting freehold land cannot: that is, with a landlord and tenant relationship, even positive obligations can be made to run with the burdened estate.[2]

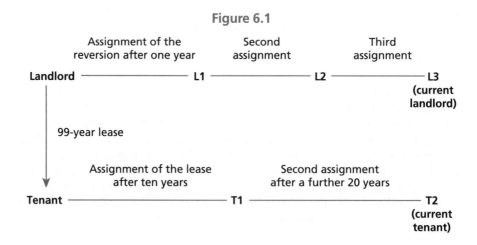

Figure 6.1

———————————

2   Contrast the position in respect of freehold covenants in Chapter 8.

6.2   The Essential Characteristics of a Lease

There are various definitions of a lease, both in statute[3] and in common law, but probably the most commonly cited is that of Lord Templeman in *Street v. Mountford* (1985). In his now famous judgment, Lord Templeman identifies the essential qualities of a lease as that arrangement that gives a person the right of exclusive possession of land, for a term, at a rent. These three elements are commonly regarded as the *indicia* of a leasehold estate, irrespective of the purpose for which the estate is created.[4] They have been affirmed many times in a residential context,[5] a commercial context,[6] where the landlord is a private individual[7] and where the landlord is a public or semi-public authority.[8] These three *indicia* will be examined in turn.

6.2.1   Exclusive possession

A lease is an estate in the land; it signifies a form of 'ownership' of the land for a stated and defined period of time. However, there are many other ways in which a person may enjoy a limited right to use or occupy land owned by another person and it is sometimes necessary to distinguish these relationships from the leasehold estate. For example, a person may be given a 'licence' to occupy the land of another that, in many ways, might resemble a lease.[9] Yet a licence is a mere personal right, binding only the parties that created it – *Lloyd v. Dugdale* (2001). A lease, on the other hand, is properly regarded as a proprietary interest in the land itself and it may be assigned to, and become binding on, any subsequent owner of the reversion. Moreover, 'leases' (but not licences) fall within the statutory regulatory machinery of the Rent Act 1977 and the Housing Act 1988, so restricting the ability of landlords to remove tenants and set rent.[10] There are other differences too. For example: a tenant may sue any person in trespass (including his landlord), but a licensee enjoys only a very narrow right;[11] a tenant may sue in nuisance, but a licensee may do so only in exceptional circumstances;[12] and only a landlord may avail himself of the remedy of forfeiture (and hence only a tenant may claim 'relief'). In fact, in years past, these differences, particularly the absence of statutory protection and rent control for licensees, prompted landowners to attempt to draw up agreements with potential occupiers of the land that gave mere licences and not leases. In most cases, this was attempted by seeking to

---

3 For example, section 205 of the LPA 1925.

4 Note the absence of an obligation to pay rent does not necessarily imply that there is no lease: see section 6.2.5 below.

5 *Aslan v. Murphy* (1989).

6 *Clear Channel UK v. Manchester City Council* (2004); *Vandersteen v. Angus* (1997).

7 *Antoniades v. Villiers* (1990); *AG Securities v. Vaughan* (1988).

8 *Westminster City Council v. Clarke* (no lease); *Bruton v. London & Quadrant Housing Trust* (lease).

9 The occupier may pay a regular 'licence fee' and treat the land as their home (*Ogwr Borough Council v. Dykes* (1989)) or use it as a business (*London Development Agency v. Nidai* (2009)).

10 Note, however, that the relaxation in the regulation of leases means that the majority of leases no longer fall within the protective ambit of these statutes.

11 *Manchester Airport v. Dutton* (1999).

12 *Hunter v. Canary Wharf* (1996).

deny the grant of 'exclusive possession' to the occupier, thereby removing a vital element in the creation of a lease. Consequently, a series of cases in the House of Lords and Court of Appeal sought to draw a legal and practical distinction between a 'lease' and a 'licence', and this battle was fought largely over the concept of 'exclusive possession'. Indeed, although legislative changes have made the distinction between a lease and a licence less critical,[13] these important cases still provide the basic tools for identifying whether a right to occupy amounts to a 'lease' or whether instead it amounts to some other arrangement between the parties.

As a basic proposition, a lease will exist when the occupier of land has been granted exclusive possession of the premises. This is a question of fact, to be decided in each case by reference to the surrounding circumstances, the course of any negotiations prior to the grant of the right of occupation, the nature of the property and the actual mode of occupation of the occupier. Further, the landowner cannot avoid granting a lease by merely calling the arrangement between the parties 'a licence', even if this is expressly stated. Labels are not decisive. Generally, it is not the parties' intentions (whether expressly stated or not) that are relevant, but the substance of the rights they have created by their agreement (*Street v. Mountford* (1985), overruling *Somma v. Hazlehurst* (1978)). However, Lord Templeman in *Street* also accepted there are certain exceptional situations in which the occupier of land may have exclusive possession of the property but, for special reasons, no lease will exist. These are cases in which the grant of exclusive possession is referable to some other *bona fide* relationship between the parties. Examples given in *Street* include a mortgagee going into possession of the property under the terms of a mortgage, usually where the borrower cannot repay the loan,[14] the occupancy of the purchaser under an enforceable contract for the sale of the land[15] and where the occupation is based on charity[16] or friendship, when there is no intention to create legal relations between the owner and the occupier.[17] In fact, these special cases were explained at length by Denning LJ in *Facchini v. Bryson* (1952) and also include situations in which the occupier is a 'service occupier', being a person who occupies property for the better performance of his duties under a contract of employment with the landowner.[18] Although such an occupier may have exclusive possession of the property, that occupation feeds off his employment contract and does not exist because of a landlord and tenant relationship. Thus, they are a licensee, as in *Carroll v. Manek* (1999), in which a hotel manager was held to have a licence of a hotel room (despite being in exclusive possession) because the possession was entirely referable to this employment relationship. The effect is, then, that as well as having only a personal right in the land, the exclusive possession of the employee must end when the employment ends.

According to Lord Templeman in *Street*, the practical effect of the principle that an occupation agreement is to be assessed according to its substance, not its label, is that a genuine licence can exist in only very limited circumstances. In fact, apart from the *Facchini*

---

13 For example, because of the removal of rent control and security of tenure under various Housing Acts.

14 See Chapter 10.

15 *Bretherton v. Paton* (1986).

16 For example, *Gray v. Taylor* (1998).

17 *Marcroft Wagons v. Smith* (1951).

18 *Norris v. Checksfield* (1991).

exceptions, Lord Templeman's view is that an occupier of premises must be either a 'tenant' or a 'lodger'. This is another way of saying that the only genuine occupation licence that can exist is that held by a lodger. In law, a lodger is someone who receives services and attendance from the landlord, such as room cleaning or meals. Moreover, as *Markou v. Da Silvaesa* (1986) illustrates, a mere promise by the landowner to provide such services is *not* sufficient to generate a lodging agreement (i.e. a licence); they must actually be provided. What this means, then, is that it should be a relatively straightforward task to distinguish between a lease and a licence: if the occupier receives 'board and lodging', he holds a mere personal licence; otherwise, he must be a tenant, unless one of the exceptional *Facchini* situations exists. Unfortunately, however, things are never this simple, for if it is true that an occupier is *either* a lodger or a tenant, this implies that no other kind of 'occupation licence' can exist. There can be no intermediate category of licensee who, while not a lodger, is still not a tenant. Obviously, this has far-reaching consequences, for it restricts the options open to a landowner when seeking to make use of his property. It is the triumph of property law over freedom of contract, and it is precisely this legal straitjacket that cases subsequent to *Street* found difficult to accept. Indeed, many of the apparently inconsistent decisions of the Court of Appeal that followed *Street* have resulted from attempts to identify some middle way, some form of occupation that can still give rise to a licence, but where the occupier is not a lodger. For example, *Hadjiloucas v. Crean* (1988) and *Brooker Estates v. Ayers* (1987), both decisions of the Court of Appeal quite soon after *Street*, are of this type. In fact, although the primacy of the lease/licence distinction based on exclusive possession has been preserved by the House of Lords in cases such as *Antoniades v. Villiers* (1990) and *Bruton v. London & Quadrant* (1999), and by the Court of Appeal in *Aslan v. Murphy* (1989) and *Mikeover v. Brady* (1989), there has been an acceptance that property rights, or rights to use property, are not as black and white as the tenant/lodger distinction suggests. Necessarily, this has resulted in a certain refinement of the principles, and some other guidelines have emerged.

First, it is now clear that a licence (as opposed to a lease) may exist in cases in which two or more people occupy the same property, as in shared houses. It is not that the people occupying the property under a 'multiple occupancy agreement' *cannot* be lease-holders; rather it is that to be leaseholders of the entire property the 'four unities' must be present so as to support a joint tenancy of the leasehold estate.[19] Therefore, the issue turns on the nature of the multiple occupancy agreement. For example, if four people occupy a four-bedroomed house, but each signs a different agreement, on different days and for different rents, there can be no 'exclusive possession' of the *entire* premises, because there is no unity of interest, title or time. The house, as a whole, cannot be held on a lease because the necessary conditions for a joint tenancy of a leasehold estate do not exist. Of course, each occupier may have a lease of his individual room, with a licence over the common parts, but this is very different from a single, jointly owned leasehold estate of the whole premises. Note, however, that while it is perfectly under-standable and indeed practical that no joint leasehold should exist in respect of a property occupied by a shifting population of previously unrelated persons (e.g. house-sharing in London), the same considerations do not apply where the 'multiple' occupancy is that of a romantically linked couple who, for all intents and purposes, are living in the

---

19 *AG Securities v. Vaughan* (1988).

property together, not as separate individuals. In such cases, as explained below, the court might well regard the existence of an alleged multiple occupancy licence as a deliberate and artificial (and hence disallowed) attempt to avoid the grant of a joint leasehold interest.

Second, some cases also suggest that there are certain types of public sector landlord who *may* be able to grant licences in circumstances in which a private landlord could only grant leases. Examples are *Westminster CC v. Basson* (1991), *Ogwr BC v. Dykes* (1989) and the decision in *Westminster CC v. Clarke* (1992). In these situations, the landowner may be able to deny exclusive possession to the occupier (and hence deny a lease) because to do otherwise would be to hinder it in the exercise of its statutory housing duties. In other words, the denial of exclusive possession with all that this entails, is necessary if local authorities and the like are to be able to carry out their duty to accommodate the homeless and provide temporary accommodation to the needy. Such landlords should be able to grant personal licences in order to be able to manage their housing stock more effectively without being 'caught' by the greater obligations owed by landlords to their tenants. Seen in this light, the privileged position of public sector landlords is justified by policy rather than principle, but, of course, that does not make it any less sensible. A similar view was taken in *Gray v. Taylor* (1998), in which one ground for denying that the occupier of a charity almshouse was a tenant was that it would be inconsistent with the duty of the particular trustees of the charity to have granted a tenancy and with it, a measure of residential security. Importantly, however, this view of the *Westminster* cases (i.e. that the identity of the landlord can be a decisive factor in drawing the lease/licence distinction) has been challenged. In *Bruton v. London and Quadrant Housing Trust* (1999), the House of Lords was considering the status of Mr Bruton, who held a property on an express 'licence' from the Trust. The Trust itself held a licence from the freeholder, Lambeth London Borough Council, and was acting in support of Lambeth's housing functions. In deciding that Mr Bruton held a lease (on which, see immediately below), Lord Hoffmann noted (*obiter*) that the law does not accept that the identity or type of landlord is relevant in determining the existence of a lease or licence. This does seem to shut down this line of argument but it is not immediately apparent why, as the earlier Court of Appeal cases demonstrate, the identity of the landlord cannot help to establish whether the giving of a licence to an occupier was a *genuine* response to the unique circumstances of a case rather than an attempt to avoid the grant of a lease *per se*. So, the fact that Westminster Council had statutory housing functions must impact on the genuineness of its attempt to give some of its occupiers 'mere' licences, just as in *Mehta v. Royal Bank of Scotland* (1999), in which the Court of Appeal decided that a hotel occupier had 'only' a licence as against the hotel owners (as made clear in his agreement) because this was the only sensible interpretation of the relationship between the particular parties. In fact, as discussed below, *Bruton* is a case that raises other concerns when considering the distinction between a lease and a licence and it is not certain that it is the most reliable authority in this area.

Third, in *Bruton v. London & Quadrant Housing Trust* (1999), Mr Bruton contended that he held a lease from London & Quadrant on the basis that he enjoyed exclusive possession. However, the Trust itself held only a licence from the freeholder, not because of some clever draughtsmanship by the freeholder, but because any grant of a lease by Lambeth LBC (the freeholder) would have been *ultra vires* its powers under section 32 of the Housing Act 1985. Naturally (one might think), the Trust resisted the claim that Bruton held a lease on the simple ground that it (the Trust) held no estate in the land and so could not grant such an estate in the land to Mr Bruton: *nemo dat quod non habet*.[20] This was accepted by a majority of the Court of Appeal but, somewhat surprisingly, was rejected by the House of Lords. According to Lord Hoffmann, giving the leading judgment and deciding in favour of the existence of a lease for Mr Bruton, the test of whether an occupier held a lease was simply that of 'exclusive possession' as laid down in *Street*. Bruton had exclusive possession, so he had a lease and it did not matter that London & Quadrant held no estate because it was the agreement between the parties that created 'a lease', not the prior existence of an estate in the 'landlord'. Unfortunately, this deceptively simple (and, with respect, simplistic) reasoning has far-reaching consequences. It means, as acknowledged by Lord Hoffmann, that a lease is not always a proprietary right in the land. Apparently, it is a contractual state of affairs between 'landlord' and 'tenant' and whether it is also proprietary in the sense of being capable of binding third parties depends on the circumstances in which the 'lease' arises. To put it another way, apparently there is, in English law, the 'normal' proprietary lease that has been with us for centuries and also the 'non-proprietary lease' or 'contractual tenancy', being a 'lease' between the parties, but not 'a lease' in a proprietary sense. It is an understatement to say that this muddies the waters. The decision in *Street* itself is premised on the assumption that a lease is proprietary and that is why it must be distinguished from a licence! To take the *ratio* of *Street* and apply it to *Bruton* in the manner suggested by Lord Hoffmann does great violence not only to established principles of property law, but also goes against the very purpose of Lord Templeman's judgment in the earlier case. Exclusive *possession* signifies exclusive control in virtue of an estate in land granted by the landlord; exclusive occupation signifies exclusive control in virtue of other arrangements and it might be thought that the occupier in Bruton had the latter, but not the former. No doubt, the decision in *Bruton* was convenient in that it enabled Mr Bruton to compel the Trust to perform the repairing obligations that are implied into a 'lease' under section 11 of the Landlord and Tenant Act 1985. On the other hand, the 'non-proprietary lease' is a strange creature in English property law and, we might suggest, it already has a name: that is, it is a licence! Subsequent to *Bruton*, the reasoning has been applied in two cases, *Kay v. London Borough of Lambeth* (2006) and *London Borough of Islington v. Green* (2005), both of which involved 'Bruton tenants' seeking a remedy against the freeholders of the land. However, while in both cases the Court of Appeal adopts the reasoning of the House of Lords (as it must) that the absence of an estate in the intermediate 'landlord' is not destructive of the occupier's 'non-proprietary lease', in both cases the Court decides that the occupier's 'lease' is purely a contractual arrangement between the intermediate licensor and the occupier that is without proprietary effect against the freeholder or any other third party. Indeed, when *Kay v. Lambeth* (2006) was appealed to the House of Lords (partly on other grounds[21]), Lord Scott (with whom all six other Lords agreed), made it clear that the 'Bruton tenancies' had no proprietary character at all and were not governed by any of the principles relevant to leasehold estates.[22] So it is then, that the 'Bruton tenancy' is 'a lease' without meaning as an estate in the land. In such circumstances, we might ask

---

20 In this context, meaning that a person cannot grant what they do not own. The Trust had no lease, so it could not carve one for Mr Bruton.

21 Questions arose as to the occupiers' right to a home under Article 8 of the European Convention on Human Rights.

22 For example, the agreements were not governed by the leasehold estate principles concerning surrender of the estate by a tenant to his landlord.

legitimately why this is a 'lease' at all, as opposed to perhaps a contractual licence.[23] It remains to be seen whether the 'Bruton tenancy' gains any further credibility but it seems likely that the case will come to be regarded as decided 'by reference to its own special facts', as seems inherent in Lord Scott's unsympathetic analysis of it in *Kay*. In *LDC v. Nidai* (2009), it was conceded that the occupier held a licence in the land because the 'landlord' held only a licence. The striking thing is that *Bruton* was not raised by counsel and does not feature in the judgment. On balance, it would be a mistake to regard *Bruton* as an authority for the destruction of one of the most fundamental distinctions in property law: that is, the distinction between proprietary leases and personal licences.

Fourth, continuing this analysis of cases after *Street*, Lord Oliver in *Antoniades v. Villiers* (1990) suggests that there may be circumstances in which a landowner can genuinely reserve to himself a right to make use of the premises that they have given over to an occupier and, if such use is made, no exclusive possession will be given and a lease will not exist. An example might be where a landowner grants occupation of her house to a student for £50 per week, but reserves a right (subsequently used) to enter at any time and make use of the study. In effect, this is no more than a restatement of the distinction between exclusive *possession* and exclusive *occupation*: the former establishing the legal relationship of landlord and tenant; the latter describing a factual situation, devoid of proprietary effect. However, the ability of a landowner to reserve a right to himself that effectively destroys the grant of exclusive possession is controversial because it appears to offer landowners a way out of the rigours of *Street v. Mountford* (1985). For that reason, it must constitute a rare exception to the *Street ratio*, and the 'pretence' rule (discussed below) may invalidate most attempts by landowners to achieve such an outcome. In any event, this 'exception' would not be applicable if the right reserved by the landowner were consistent with the grant of a lease. For example, a landowner may reserve the right to enter the premises, in order to inspect and carry out repairs, but such a right actually confirms the grant of a tenancy rather than denies it, for this is just the sort of right a landlord would expect to have under a lease.

Finally, the cases also establish that these glosses on the strictness of the *Street v. Mountford* analysis are applicable only if genuinely employed for legitimate reasons. Consequently, attempts by the landlord (or tenant[24]) to deny the grant of exclusive possession are subject to the court's powers to ignore 'pretences' (or 'sham devices'). According to *Antoniades v. Villiers* (1990), a 'pretence' exists where a clause in an agreement for the occupation of land is inserted into that agreement deliberately in order to avoid the creation of the lease that would otherwise arise and where either party does not intend to rely in practice on the clause. A pretence may be established from an examination of the surrounding circumstances of the case and may be confirmed by the parties' subsequent practice. For example, in *Antoniades*, an unmarried couple each signed a separate agreement for the occupation of a single-bedroom flat that was clearly going to be their joint home.

---

23 One reason might be that a 'Bruton tenancy' as between the parties to it, but only those parties, partakes of the normal obligations of 'landlord and tenant', such as repairing obligations and the like. In this sense, although the 'Bruton lease' has no proprietary effect, it would be different from a pure contractual licence. To the present author, this appears as a sleight of hand, not justifiable as a matter of property law, but to be seen as a device to give certain contractual licensees rights as if they were tenants.

24 For example, where there is a dispute over the rent of property.

These agreements gave the landowner certain rights over the property that were unlikely to be enjoyed in practice – for example, the right to nominate another occupier. This was an attempt by the landowner to avoid the grant of a tenancy by artificially destroying the 'four unities' necessary to give the couple a joint tenancy of the leasehold estate and by reserving to himself some power over the property that might be thought to destroy exclusive possession. This was held to be a pretence, created only to deny artificially the grant of a lease. The objectionable clauses had no merit or purpose other than to prevent the occupiers from obtaining a lease. Hence, the clauses were struck out and the agreements given effect without the offending clause – the couple held a joint lease.

6.2.2   For a term certain

Another essential ingredient in a lease is that the exclusive possession granted to the tenant must be for a defined and certain period of time: for example, one year, one month, seven years, 99 years, and so on. This means not only that the lease must start at a clearly defined moment, but also that the length of the term granted must be certain. At the commencement of the lease, it must be possible to define exactly the maximum duration of the lease, even if it is possible to end the lease at some time before this. So, a lease for 3,000 years is perfectly valid, even if the lease contains 'break clauses' entitling the landlord and tenant to terminate the lease by notice on, say, every tenth anniversary. Any lease, or rather any intended lease, that fails to satisfy this condition is necessarily void, because it does not amount to a 'term certain'. Of course, in the great majority of cases, this condition is easily satisfied, as in the above example, because the landlord and tenant will state clearly the duration of the lease. However, problems can arise where the term of the lease is set by reference to some other criteria, such as the happening of an uncertain event. For example, in *Lace v. Chandler* (1944), an alleged lease for the duration of the Second World War was held void as being of uncertain maximum duration. In recent years, the principle of term certain has been under attack, and there was an attempt to accept as leases arrangements that, on a proper construction, could not be said to create a certain term. So in *Ashburn Anstalt v. Arnold* (1989), an arrangement whereby a tenant occupied property indefinitely until the landlord gave three months' notice was said to be a lease on the ground that the term *could* be rendered certain by action of one of the parties. In reality, of course, this does not comply with the spirit of the rule that a lease must be certain *at the date* of its commencement and it came as no surprise when the House of Lords in *Prudential Assurance v. London Residuary Body* (1992) reaffirmed the rule that a leasehold term must be certain from the outset and overruled this aspect of the *Ashburn Anstalt* decision. Consequently, it is not enough that an uncertain term can, in fact, be rendered certain by action of either the landlord or the tenant *after* the lease has commenced.[25] This is a significant and welcome return to the orthodox position. Both landlord and tenant will know the maximum duration of their obligations and it will be easier to place a monetary value on both lease and reversion should either wish to assign their rights to a purchaser.

---

25 Note, however, that a lease for 2,000 years, terminable on notice by the landlord or tenant, would be legitimate, if unusual.

6.2.3   Periodic tenancies

In a great many cases concerning residential property, a tenant may occupy premises and pay a regular sum in rent to the landlord, but there may not be an express agreement (written or oral) regulating the occupation. In these circumstances, a tenancy of a certain duration will be implied from the facts. Thus, if money is paid weekly in respect of a week's occupation, a *periodic tenancy* of one week will be implied. Likewise, if rent is paid with reference to a monthly or quarterly period, a monthly or quarterly periodic tenancy will result. Obviously, if a further weekly, monthly or quarterly payment is made, the lease will continue for a further period. In this sense, the lease can continue indefinitely and the *total* period of the tenancy will not be known in advance. However, although this appears to give rise to a lease of uncertain duration, in fact there is a succession of periodic tenancies, all of which are of a certain term: that is, one week after one week, or one month after one month, and so on.[26] The validity of periodic tenancies was confirmed by *Prudential*, with the court explaining that there is a clear conceptual distinction between a succession of certain periods with simple uncertainty about how many more periods there will be (a periodic tenancy), and a 'term' that, from its outset, is defined by reference to uncertainty (e.g. a tenancy 'until the good weather ends'). As discussed below, because the great majority of periodic tenancies are for individual periods of three years or less (e.g. a month), they will be legal interests.[27]

6.2.4   Statutory provisions concerning certain terms

There are a number of statutory provisions that are related to the principle of 'term certain' and the general effect of which is to convert uncertain periods into certain terms or to invalidate certain types of arrangement.

1   A lease for the duration of the life of any person, or which is due to end with expiry of any life, or on the marriage of the lessee (all being uncertain terms), which is granted for a rent or a premium, is converted into a lease for 90 years, subject to determination (i.e. ending) if the death or marriage occurs before this (section 149(6) of the LPA 1925). So, a lease of a cottage granted to me by my parents 'until I marry', for £60 per week, or for an initial capital sum of, say, £45,000 (a premium), will take effect as a lease for a certain period of 90 years, determinable when (if) I marry.

2   A lease that is perpetually renewable is converted into a lease for 2,000 years (Schedule 15, section 145 of the LPA 1922). So, a lease for 40 years, containing a clause whereby the tenant has the right to renew the lease for a further 40 years at the expiry of *every* period, is perpetually renewable and will take effect as a lease for 2,000 years. This, of course, is tantamount to the grant of a freehold. Note, however,

---

26 Thus a monthly periodic tenant who has been in occupation for, say, ten years, has had 120 separate monthly tenancies.

27 For example, as a matter of practice, rent is not usually calculated by reference to a period any longer than a quarter, and yearly periodic tenancies are in practice the longest periodic tenancies under this principle.

that a lease for 40 years that is renewable only for one further period of 40 years is not perpetually renewable and takes effect in the normal way.

3   A lease that is intended to start more than 21 years after the instrument that creates it is void (section 149(3) of the LPA 1925). So, if Z, by contract with X dated 1 January 2010, attempts to grant a lease of land to start after 1 January 2035, the intended lease is void. The commencement of the lease is postponed for longer than the law allows.

6.2.5   Rent

One of the main motives for the letting of property is the desire to generate income through the payment of rent. Even where the tenant pays a large premium or fine (a capital sum) at the start of the lease, there is usually provision for a 'ground rent' payable annually.[28] Indeed, as noted above, Lord Templeman, in *Street v. Mountford* (1985), included 'rent' as part of the definition of a tenancy. However, strictly speaking, the existence of a lease does not depend on a provision for the payment of rent. Section 205(1)(xxvii) of the LPA 1925 provides that a term of years means a 'term of years . . . whether or not at a rent'. As it happens, certain types of lease (such as those within the Rent Acts and early Housing Acts) must be supported by rent in order to qualify for statutory protection and this is why Lord Templeman in *Street* refers so explicitly to 'rent' as part of the definition of a tenancy.[29] However, it is clear that, as a matter of law, a lease may exist where there is no rent payable.[30] Of course, in reality, the existence of an obligation to pay rent as an adjunct to a lease is so likely that, in the absence of an express promise by the tenant or an express exclusion of rent, a covenant by the tenant to pay rent will be readily implied from the words of a deed. Moreover, although the landlord and tenant can *deliberately* exclude the rent obligation and still create a lease, an explicit exclusion of rent (or other clear evidence that rent is not to be paid) may suggest that the parties did not intend to create a lease at all. Necessarily, this will depend on the peculiar facts of each case, but the absence of a rent obligation, if not counteracted by the existence of any of the other hallmarks of a lease (e.g. a repairing obligation), can indicate that no landlord and tenant relationship was intended. In such cases, the occupier may have a mere licence. Note, however, that, as discussed above, the fact that the parties choose to describe the periodic payment as an 'occupation fee', a 'licence fee' or some such similar phrase does not prevent it amounting to 'rent' in law. Again, it is a matter of substance, not form.

Finally, it is a common misconception that rent has to be in monetary form. It can be in goods, services, or payable in kind. The only requirement is that the amount of rent must be capable of being rendered certain. Thus, in *Bostock v. Bryant* (1990), the obligation to pay fluctuating utility bills (gas, electricity, etc.) could not be regarded as rent, being an

---

28 There is likely also to be an annual service charge to meet the cost of running and maintaining any common parts of the building, such as lifts, stairways, and shared paths.

29 It was a Rent Act case.

30 See the discussion in *Ashburn Anstalt v. Arnold* (1989), overturned on other grounds. Note also that if rent is payable, its non-payment does not mean there is no tenancy. It means, simply, that the tenant is in arrears of rent and may be subject to remedies by the landlord for non-payment.

ever-changing sum. On the other hand, an annual rent of 'a peppercorn' or 'five tons of flour' is perfectly acceptable.

6.3   The Creation of Legal and Equitable Leases

The existence of a 'term certain', the granting of exclusive possession, and (subject to the reservations just discussed) the payment of rent, are the hallmarks of a tenancy. Of course, in most cases, the parties will have agreed a web of other rights and obligations extending beyond acceptance of this bare legal framework: for example, the lease may contain covenants to repair, options to renew the lease, obligations relating to the use of the premises and the like. Generally, the more complicated or extensive these other matters, the more likely it is that the 'lease' itself will be embodied in a formal document, such as a deed or written instrument. Moreover, while there are very few legal rules concerning the precise words or phrases that must be used to create a valid lease or the obligations therein (although certain 'precedents' or standard wordings have been developed and HM Land Registry requires certain standard clauses for registered leases[31]), there are a number of legal formalities that must be observed before the arrangement agreed by the parties will be enforced as a lease by the courts. These 'formality' requirements generally are required by statute. They relate to the manner in which a lease may be created, rather than to what a lease must contain. In essence, they are the embodiment of a legislative policy that seeks certainty about dealings with land. So, these statutory rules determine whether an arrangement between owner and occupier that otherwise satisfies the inherent requirements of a lease can nevertheless be enforced as a lease and, if it can, whether the lease so created is legal or equitable.

6.3.1   Introductory points

A lease is a legally binding agreement between landlord and tenant. As such, the creation of a lease amounts to both a contract between them *and* the creation of a proprietary right that exists beyond the mere contract. It can give rise to contractual remedies (such as an action for damages), but it can affect 'third parties' to whom the reversion or lease is assigned.[32] Furthermore, in some cases, the creation of a lease will occur in two stages: the conclusion of a 'contract to grant a lease' between prospective landlord and tenant, and the later execution of the contract by the 'grant' of the lease by deed. This is important in understanding how equitable leases are created. However, even where a lease is created without first concluding a separate contract to grant it (e.g. the parties simply execute a deed or agree to a written lease[33]), the lease itself will always amount to a contract between

---

31 The prescribed clauses relate to such matters as identification of the parties, commencement, and identification of the land and are mandatory for certain registrable leases. They are designed to aid the process of registration, particularly under e-conveyancing: see *HM Land Registry Practice Guide No. 64*.

32 With the exception of 'Bruton tenancies'.

33 The creation of leases without first concluding a contract is becoming much more common.

them. So, 'the lease as a contract' refers either to an aspect of the landlord and tenant relationship (its contractual aspect), or to the manner in which the lease was created originally.

6.3.2   Legal leases: Creation

The creation of legal leases depends on rules laid down by statute and, as with all legal rights, there is an emphasis on formality.

1   Leases for three years or less that give the tenant an immediate right to possession of the land without the payment of an initial capital sum (i.e. a premium) will be legal whether created orally, by written contract, or by deed (sections 52(2)(d) and 54(2) of the LPA 1925). Into this category will come many residential or domestic leases, and, significantly, most 'periodic tenancies' created in the way described in section 6.2.3 above. This is simply because the 'period' for which rent is paid and accepted will usually be three years or less (e.g. a week, month, quarter, etc.).

2   Leases for more than three years, and those of three years or less that do not fall within point 1 above,[34] are required to be made by deed to have any prospect of taking effect as a legal estate (section 52(1) of the LPA 1925). A 'deed' is, in essence, a more formal written document and, prior to the Law of Property (Miscellaneous Provisions) Act 1989, such a document had to be 'signed, sealed and delivered' before it could be regarded as 'a deed'. Now, by virtue of section 1 of the 1989 Act, a document is a deed if it declares itself to be such (e.g. it says 'this is a deed made between X and Y'), it is signed as a deed, and is witnessed as a deed by one other person. It can be seen, therefore, that the execution of a deed remains a relatively formal process and most leases by deed are drawn up by solicitors or licensed conveyancers. However, the execution of a deed is straightforward and now relatively inexpensive. Note also that, in the future, it may be possible – perhaps mandatory – to execute a 'deed' in relation to registered land in electronic form. This will be no less a deed than its paper counterpart and will necessarily satisfy the rules relating to the creation of legal leases (sections 91 and 93 of the Land Registration Act (LRA) 2002).

3   Currently, if the lease is granted by deed out of *registered land* (i.e. where the freehold or superior leasehold is a registered title) and it is for a term *over* seven years, it must also be registered as a title at HM Land Registry (section 27(2) of the LRA 2002). This means it must be entered for registration with its own title number at the appropriate district office of HM Land Registry and so becomes substantively registered in its own right. Failure to so register means that the lease takes effect only as an equitable estate (section 27(1) of the LRA 2002).[35] It should be remembered, however, that the very great majority of these long legal leases will have been negotiated and executed with professional advice and so there is every likelihood that they will be appropriately registered. Certain other special shorter-term leases also require

---

34 For example, where a premium – an initial capital payment – is charged.

35 For an example of how this worked under the LRA 1925, see *Brown and Root v. Sun Alliance* (1995).

36 Section 27(2), including timeshare leases, special Housing Act leases and leases where possession is postponed for more than three months after the lease is granted.

such registration[36] and it is anticipated that, in due course, this 'registration trigger' will shorten to encompass leases for over three years, thus ensuring that the need for a deed is synonymous with the need for registration.[37] If the legal lease falls outside of the registration triggers (i.e. is a normal lease of seven years or less), it takes effect as a legal estate without title registration and, in fact, amounts to an unregistered interest that overrides under Schedule 3, paragraph 1 of the LRA 2002.

4   Currently, if the lease is granted by deed out of *unregistered land* (i.e. where the freehold or superior leasehold is not a registered title) and it is for a term of *over* seven years, it must also be registered as a title at HM Land Registry (section 4(1) of the LRA 2002). The grant of such a lease is a trigger for first registration of title of the leasehold.[38] Failure to so register means that the lease takes effect only as an equitable estate (section 7 of the LRA 2002). Certain other special shorter-term leases also require such registration[39] and, once again, it is anticipated that, in due course, this 'registration trigger' will shorten to encompass leases for over three years.

5   If the lease is to take effect in land of unregistered title and the lease is outside the first registration trigger (i.e. when it is for seven years or less), the grant by deed (where required) is all that is needed to convey the legal leasehold estate to the tenant from the date specified in the deed. Moreover, following the general rule in *unregistered* land that 'legal rights bind the whole world', a legal lease will automatically bind any subsequent purchaser or transferee of the land out of which it is created (i.e. of the landlord's reversion) and when the purchaser of the reversion applies for compulsory first registration of his title, the lease will override under Schedule 1, paragraph 1 of the LRA 2002.[40]

6   For the future, it is likely that the grant of certain leases will be made subject to compulsory e-conveyancing. This aspect of the LRA 2002 is not yet active, but it will mean that the grant of a qualifying lease (i.e. one specified in the Land Registration Rules) will be required to be made by an electronic entry on the register and in no other form (section 93 of the LRA 2002). Failure to electronically create and register the lease (for these will be synonymous) will mean that the purported lease is without effect.

6.3.3   Legal leases and third parties

As far as the effect of legal leases on third parties in *registered* land is concerned (i.e. purchasers and other transferees of the reversion), the current position is governed by the specific provisions of the LRA 2002. First, legal leases that are registered as titles in their

---

37 As yet, there is no indication of when this will be.

38 But not necessarily of the superior unregistered freehold or leasehold out of which it is granted.

39 See section 4 of the LRA 2002 – timeshare leases, special Housing Act leases and leases where possession is postponed for more than three months after the lease is granted.

40 At first registration of the superior title, the lease may also be entered against that title by means of a notice. This would, of course, supersede its protection as an overriding interest.

own right under the LRA 2002[41] clearly will bind a transferee of the reversion.[42] In the very unlikely event that a registrable lease has not actually been registered, it will take effect as an equitable lease only and its position in respect of third parties is governed by the principles applicable to equitable leases. Secondly, legal leases for seven years or less[43] are interests that override within paragraphs 1 of Schedules 1 and 3 of the LRA 2002.[44] Consequently, they bind subsequent purchasers and transferees of the reversion automatically under sections 28, 29 and 30 of the LRA 2002.

In respect of legal leases granted out of *unregistered* land that do not trigger compulsory first registration of the lease (i.e. generally when the lease is for seven years or less), the situation is governed by the long-established rules of unregistered conveyancing.[45] Thus, 'legal rights bind the world' and the lease is effective against any transferee of the reversion. Of course, on such transfer, the reversion will become subject to first registration and thereafter the legal lease will take effect as an interest that overrides under Schedule 1, paragraph 1 of the LRA 2002.[46]

6.3.4 Equitable leases: Creation

While it is true that the Law of Property (Miscellaneous Provisions) Act 1989 simplified the requirements for the execution of a deed, nevertheless many leases are created in the absence of a deed. The majority of these are for three years or less and qualify as legal interests under the 'short lease exception' discussed above. Moreover, in practice, it is unusual for a lease of over three years' duration to be created without the use of a deed – primarily because the parties routinely use lawyers who proceed to execute the lease by deed without first concluding a contract. However, there will be situations in which the parties do not use a deed to create a lease longer than three years: for example, if a written contract is used, the parties may be content to rely on it rather than execute a deed, or the parties may not use property professionals and so not realise that a deed is required at all. In such cases – that is, where there is an intended lease of over three years not executed by deed – if there is a written contract (or a written record of an agreement that can be treated as if it were a contract), the parties may be taken to have created an equitable lease. In simple terms, an equitable lease arises from an enforceable contract between landlord and tenant to grant a lease, but where no grant of a lease by deed has in fact occurred. There are a number of distinct steps in this process.

---

41 This includes leases registered as titles in their own right under the LRA 1925 where the registration trigger was for leases granted for more than 21 years, and also existing legal leases that were assigned when there was more than 21 years left to run.

42 Sections 28, 29, 30 of the LRA 2002.

43 Save those special short-term legal leases that must be registered as titles.

44 For an example under the LRA 1925, see *City Permanent Building Society v. Miller* (1952). Such leases, if granted for more than three years, may voluntarily be entered on the register by means of a notice against the registered title out of which they are granted, but it is not critical to do so.

45 Such situations will become increasingly uncommon. Even now, they are not prevalent.

46 Or it may be entered on the register by means of a notice.

1   The contract between prospective landlord and tenant must be enforceable: that is, since 27 September 1989, the contract must be in writing, containing all of the terms and signed by both parties (section 2 of the LPA 1989), replacing section 40 of the LPA 1925.[47] In this connection, 'written contract' means either a written document clearly expressed to be a contract, or a written record of agreement that the law is prepared to treat as a contract. A good example of the latter is where A and B set down in writing (and sign) the terms on which A will let her house to B. A and B may not intend to take any further steps to create the lease, perhaps believing they have done all that is necessary, but their written agreement will be treated as a 'written contract to grant a lease', so as to give rise to an equitable lease.[48]

2   The remedy of specific performance must be available, should either party to the contract actually wish to enforce the contract and compel the grant of a legal lease (*Coatsworth v. Johnson* (1886)). Specific performance will be available if the person seeking to enforce the contract has given valuable consideration, damages would be an inadequate remedy (as they nearly always are with contracts for land) and if the person seeking to enforce the contract comes to equity with 'clean hands'.[49] If all of these conditions are fulfilled – which will be true in most cases – a court of equity will treat the unenforced (but enforceable) contract to grant the legal lease as having created an equitable lease between the parties on the same terms as the potential (but ungranted) legal lease (*Walsh v. Lonsdale* (1882)).[50]

The contract/lease analysis discussed above is the usual way in which an equitable lease comes into existence: it arises out of a written, enforceable contract. However, it is also possible for an equitable lease to arise out of the operation of the doctrine of proprietary estoppel. Proprietary estoppel leases will arise where the 'landlord' has promised some right to the 'tenant' in writing *or* orally, and this is relied on by the prospective tenant to his detriment. The court may then 'satisfy' the estoppel by giving the promisee a tenancy, albeit an equitable one that has arisen out of the informal dealings between the parties.[51] Such a situation will be rare, but cannot be discounted completely.[52] It is discussed in more detail in Chapter 9. For now, the important point is that proprietary estoppel may result in the generation of an equitable lease out of a purely oral agreement. Similarly, if a party to an agreement seeks to use section 2 of the 1989 Act as a vehicle for unconscionable conduct – for example, by pleading that the contract is not in writing and so not valid when that very person had assured the other party that the contract need not be written – the agreed lease might be enforceable under a constructive trust or property (*Yaxley v. Gotts* (1999)).[53]

---

47 Before 27 September 1989, the contract was enforceable even if oral, so long as it could be supported by part performance (see the now-repealed section 40 of the LPA 1925).

48 The provisions on e-conveyancing, when they come into operation, will supersede this.

49 Specific performance is an equitable remedy, and so may be denied if the claimant has behaved unconscionably or otherwise inequitably.

50 Of course, there is nothing to stop one of the parties going ahead to actually compel the grant of the legal lease.

51 See generally *Taylor Fashions v. Liverpool Victoria Trustees* (1982). Specifically for an estoppel lease see *Lloyd v. Dugdale* (2001).

52 Usually, if the court is minded to award the claimant a lease as a means of satisfying the estoppel, it will order the landowner to formally grant a lease by deed.

53 The extent to which this is different from a claim in estoppel is a matter of debate: see Chapter 9.

It will be appreciated from the above that the circumstances in which an equitable tenancy can arise can be distinguished from those concerning the creation of a legal lease by the *relative* informality of the former. However, in one set of circumstances this is not true: that is, the creation of a legal periodic tenancy where the 'period' is three years or less, as these may be 'legal' whether created by deed, in writing or orally. Consequently, it can happen that the same set of facts can presumptively give rise to either an equitable tenancy or a shorter, legal periodic tenancy. For example, in those cases in which the equitable tenancy has sprung from a written contract (or a document taken to be a written contract), the tenant may well have entered the premises and be paying rent to the landlord. It is easy to see that this could be taken to have given rise to the creation of a periodic tenancy in favour of the occupier because of the payment and acceptance of rent. This periodic tenancy will usually be legal, as the period for which rent is paid and accepted will be three years or less. Potentially, then, there is a conflict between the equitable lease arising from the enforceable written contract (which will be of the same duration as the original intended lease), and the implied short-term, legal periodic tenancy. According to *Walsh* v. *Lonsdale* (1882), the equitable lease will prevail (despite the problems encountered by equitable leases – see below), not least because it will contain all of the terms originally found in the contract between the parties and is likely to be of longer certain duration. Of course, if the equitable lease does not arise (e.g. because of a failure to conclude an enforceable contract, or where the contract is not specifically enforceable), the implied legal periodic tenancy can take effect to provide some comfort for the tenant.

6.3.5   Equitable leases and third parties

The above principles concerning the creation of equitable leases apply whether the land is registered or unregistered. However, bearing in mind that one of the main purposes of the 1925 and 2002 reforms was to bring clarity to dealings with equitable interests in land, it is not surprising that the effect of an equitable lease on a third party (i.e. a transferee or purchaser of the reversion from the current landlord) differs according to whether title has been registered or remains unregistered.

6.3.5.1   *In registered land*

Equitable leases are capable of being entered on the register of title of the land over which they take effect. This would be through a notice.[54] If registered, they are protected by such registration and are effective against later transferees of the reversion (sections 28 and 29 of the LRA 2002). However, even if not registered in this way (and many will not be) most equitable leases will take effect as an interest that overrides a transferee and thus be binding on the new landlord. This is because the equitable tenant will almost certainly be a person in discoverable actual occupation within the meaning of Schedule 3, paragraph 2 of the LRA 2002. Here, then, is virtually automatic protection for the equitable tenant in registered land, for the tenant need do nothing – except remain in occupation – to be secure. Such leases may, of course, be brought on to the title through disclosure and

---

54 Usually an agreed notice because, after all, the landlord has granted the lease!

registration by means of a notice, but that is not necessary even under the LRA 2002 to secure their protection.[55]

6.3.5.2   *In unregistered land*

Equitable leases that arise from enforceable contracts are registrable as Class C(iv) land charges ('estate contracts'). Consequently, they must be registered against the appropriate name of the estate owner (i.e. the freeholder or superior leaseholder) in order to bind a purchaser of a legal estate in the land. Failure to register means that the equitable lease is void against such a purchaser.[56] This can mean the ejection of the equitable tenant if the superior interest is sold (*Hollington Bros v. Rhodes* (1951)). Of course, even an unregistered equitable lease is binding against a non-purchaser (e.g. an adverse possessor, devisee under a will, donee of a gift), or against someone who purchases only an equitable interest. Importantly, these rules mean that there is no protection for an equitable tenant in unregistered land merely because they occupy the land. This should be contrasted with the position in registered land. As a further complication, equitable leases arising from proprietary estoppel (which are very rare) may not be registrable as land charges at all, and would bind a subsequent transferee of the reversion through the equitable doctrine of notice (*Ives v. High* (1967)).

6.3.6   The differences between legal and equitable leases

As noted above, legal and equitable leases are created in different ways, with legal leases generally requiring more legal formality and many also requiring substantive registration as titles. In a similar vein, the existence of an equitable lease depends on the availability of the remedy of specific performance of the enforceable contract out of which it arises.[57] The following further points of difference should also be noted.

First, equitable leases *appear* vulnerable to a sale of the freehold or leasehold estate out of which they are created. So, it *is possible* that a purchaser of the land may not be bound by an existing equitable lease according to the rules of registered and unregistered conveyancing. However, as noted above, the problem is likely to be more acute in unregistered land for which there is no protection *per se* for the rights of persons in actual occupation. Equitable tenants in registered land need hardly fear this in practice because they are likely to have an interest that overrides.[58] Currently, legal leases do not suffer from this problem and are fully protected in registered and in unregistered land. Significantly, however, the entry into force in full of the electronic conveyancing provisions of the LRA 2002 may produce a curious effect for land of registered title. If it becomes the case that certain legal leases and equitable leases must be 'completed' by electronic entry on the register (section 93 of the LRA 2002), they will not exist at all as proprietary rights until such registration, even if

---

55 The position was the same under the LRA 1925, save that the actual occupation need not have been discoverable: section 70(1)(g) of the LRA 1925.

56 Land Charges Act 1972, sections 2 and 4.

57 With the exception of the rare estoppel lease.

58 It is, of course, possible that an equitable tenant might not be in discoverable actual occupation under the LRA 2002 and so be denied an overriding interest, but such a situation will be rare.

'created' by deed or written contract. Of course, neither will they be capable of binding a purchaser if they are not so registered. This illustrates very clearly that the brave new world of electronic conveyancing under the LRA 2002 is going to affect fundamentally the way in which we think about legal and equitable proprietary rights in registered land.

Second, as we shall see below, the ability of covenants in leases granted before 1 January 1996 to 'run' to (i.e. bind) purchasers of the tenant's interest (the lease) depends on the existence of 'privity of estate' between the claimant and defendant. As a general principle, 'privity of estate' exists between the current landlord and the current tenant of a *legal* lease only. Thus, the lack of privity of estate in equitable leases makes it difficult for all leasehold covenants to bind purchasers of the lease. Fortunately, however, the position is different for equitable leases granted on or after 1 January 1996 because of the Landlord and Tenant (Covenants) Act 1995.

Third, as demonstrated in Chapter 7, easements may be created by the operation of section 62 of the LPA 1925 on the occasion of a conveyance by deed of an estate in the land, either freehold or leasehold. In other words, this section applies only to legal leases, so a tenant under an equitable lease cannot claim the benefit of any potential section 62 easements.

Finally, when the tenant under an equitable lease first enters into the lease, he is 'only' a purchaser for value of an *equitable* estate in the land. Consequently, the tenant is not a purchaser of a legal estate for the purposes of unregistered land nor is he treated as having made a registrable disposition for the purposes of section 29 of the LRA 2002 in registered land. This means that the equitable tenant cannot avoid being bound by pre-existing property rights even if those rights do not comply with the relevant protective mechanisms of the Land Charges Act 1972 (unregistered land) and the LRA 2002 (registered land) respectively.[59]

6.4   Leasehold Covenants

Nearly all leases contain 'covenants' whereby the landlord and tenant promise each other to do, or not to do, certain things in relation to the land and its environment. For example, the landlord may promise to keep the premises in repair and the tenant may promise not to use the premises for any trade or business. Necessarily, these covenants are binding between the original landlord and the original tenant – being contained in a deed or binding contract to which they are party – and they can be enforced by either of them using a normal contractual or proprietary remedy.[60] However, one of the great advantages of the leasehold estate is that these covenants are *capable* of running to both purchasers of the original landlord's reversion and to purchasers of the original tenant's lease. In other words, both the right to sue on the leasehold covenants, and the obligation to perform them, can be passed on to successors in title of the original parties.

---

59 In unregistered land, the equitable tenant is not a purchaser of the legal estate for the purposes of the doctrine of notice and the enforcement of Class C(iv) and Class D land charges. In registered land, they cannot rely on section 29 of the LRA 2002 and so are bound by all pre-existing property rights under section 28 of the LRA 2002.

60 For example, an action on the contract for damages, or an action on the lease for forfeiture.

Figure 6.2

6.4.1   The separate nature of the 'benefit' of a covenant and the 'burden' of a covenant

In order to understand the law of leasehold covenants, it is first necessary to appreciate that the right to sue on a covenant (the benefit) and the obligation to perform or observe a covenant (the burden) must be treated separately. For example, it may well be true for pre-1996 leases (see below for the relevance of the date) that the current tenant under a lease (not being the original tenant) has the benefit of covenants, but is not subject to the burden of them: that is, the tenant has the right to enforce a covenant, but cannot be compelled to observe any obligation the lease imposes. Consequently, in any 'real life' problem, there are always two distinct questions to be answered. First, has the benefit of the particular covenant in issue run to the claimant? Second, is the defendant subject to the burden of it? Only if both of these questions can be answered positively can there be an action 'on the covenant' between claimant and defendant.

6.4.2   Two sets of rules concerning the enforceability of leasehold covenants

The rules relating to the enforceability of leasehold covenants have undergone a radical transformation in recent years. As we shall see, the common law/pre-1996 statutory rules were unsatisfactory in many respects and this prompted the Law Commission to propose wholesale reform of the law of leasehold covenants.[61] Although the Law Commission's proposals were not enacted as originally conceived, they did provide the impetus for reform. After much consideration and consultation, a private member's Bill was presented to Parliament and this became the Landlord and Tenant (Covenants) Act 1995 (LTCA 1995). This reforming statute applies to all leases – legal and equitable – that are granted

---

61 Law Commission Report No. 174.

on or after 1 January 1996, and it establishes a code for determining the enforceability of leasehold covenants in all such leases. However, for leases granted before 1 January 1996, the old common law/statutory rules still apply, save only that sections 17–20 of the 1995 Act operate retrospectively and apply to them. In due course, the 1995 Act and cases decided under it will come to govern the great majority of leases, but for now it is necessary to be aware of both the pre-1996 principles and those of the 1995 Act. This is all the more important when we remember that many pre-1996 leases will have been granted for terms in excess of 90 years and will have decades left to run.

6.5   Rules for Leases Granted before 1 January 1996

These rules are found in both common law and statute. They are complicated, often inconsistent and may produce injustice. They were ripe for reform.

6.5.1   Liability between the original landlord and original tenant: The general rule

In any action on a leasehold covenant between the *original* landlord and the *original* tenant in a pre-1996 lease, *all* covenants are enforceable.[62] This is simply because the liability of these original parties to the lease is based squarely in contract: that is, the contract between them, which is also the lease. Liability is said to be based on 'privity of contract'. Importantly, as noted, *all* covenants are enforceable, whether or not they relate to the leasehold land or to a personal obligation undertaken by either party. For example, between the original parties, a tenant's covenant to provide the landlord with a free pint of beer (personal) is just as enforceable as a landlord's covenant to repair the premises (proprietary).

6.5.2   The continuing liability of the original tenant throughout the entire term of the lease

The fact that the liability of the original tenant is founded in contract has important consequences. Even though the original tenant may assign (i.e. sell or transfer) his lease to another, he will remain liable on the leasehold covenants in a pre-1996 lease throughout the entire term of the lease (*Allied London Investments Ltd v. Hambro Life Assurance Ltd* (1984)). This liability will be enforceable by whomsoever has the benefit of the covenants. So, if the current tenant violates any of the covenants (e.g. the covenant to pay rent), the landlord may look to the original tenant to perform the covenant (pay the rent), even though the original tenant may have actually left the land many years ago and had nothing to do with the breach. A typical example is where the original tenant took a 99-year lease in, say, 1950, but the current tenant (say, the fifth assignee) defaults on the rent in 2010.

---

62 'Original' here means the landlord and tenant that were the first parties to the lease, it having been granted between them.

The original tenant remains liable for this rent, despite having parted with possession years before and in ignorance of the identity of all assignees apart from the very first person to whom he assigned. It should come as no surprise that this continuing liability attracted considerable criticism and, as we shall see, it has been abolished by the 1995 Act for leases granted on or after 1 January 1996. For leases granted prior to the Act, the original tenant remains liable throughout the term of the lease, subject only to the following exceptions and mitigating factors.

1   The liability of an original tenant will not continue after an assignment of a perpetually renewable lease.[63] If it were otherwise, the original tenant would forever be liable and there would be no limit or certainty to his obligation.

2   The lease between the original landlord and original tenant may stipulate expressly that the tenant's liability is to end when the lease is assigned. This is unusual in pre-1996 leases, but perfectly possible due to the contractual nature of a lease.[64] It depends on the original tenant having, and using, a dominant bargaining position. It can occur on a more widespread scale when there is an oversupply of premises for rent, such as during a recession in the commercial property market.

3   The original tenant will not be liable for breaches of covenant committed by an assignee where the original term of the lease has been statutorily extended under the Landlord and Tenant Act 1954 (and, by analogy, under the Housing Act 1988) and the breach occurs during the statutory extension (*City of London Corp v. Fell* (1993)). This is because the original tenant's liability is to be construed, as a matter of contract, as relating to the period of time as originally agreed, and not to the subsequent legislative extension of that term. The counterargument – that the original parties should have contemplated the risk of a statutory extension when they signed the lease – was not accepted in *Fell*.

4   The original tenant will not be liable if a subsequent assignee of the lease and landlord agree to surrender the old lease and carry out a 'regrant' of the lease on new terms. Simply put, the 'original' lease has ended and the original tenant's liability with it. In most cases, this surrender and regrant will be explicit, but it can be presumed if current landlord and tenant so vary the terms of the 'old' lease that, in reality, it ceases to exist. This is a more extreme version of the principle noted below, that an original tenant may not be liable if subsequent tenant and landlord vary the terms of individual leasehold covenants.[65]

5   If the original tenant is made liable on a covenant through the actual breach of that covenant by an assignee, the original tenant under a pre-1996 tenancy may have a right to recover any damages or rent paid by them under an indemnity obligation. A right to claim an indemnity[66] may be in the form of an express or implied obligation undertaken by an assignee of the original tenant, and any subsequent assignee, to reimburse any monies paid by the original tenant where the actual acts of default are attributable to that assignee. An indemnity obligation can take one of

---

63 Section 145, Schedule 25 of the LPA 1922.

64 As explained, in the context of the landlord's position, in *London Diocesan Fund v. Avonridge Property Company Ltd* (2005).

65 *Friends Provident Life Office v. British Railways Board* (1996).

66 Effectively, recovery of sums paid.

three forms. First, each assignee in turn may have made an express covenant of indemnity with their assignor, promising to indemnify the assignor in respect of liabilities arising post-assignment. So a 'chain' of indemnity covenants may exist, stretching from original tenant to current tenant. If, then, the original tenant is forced to pay, he may claim an indemnity from his assignee, who may pass that liability to their assignee, and so on, until the current (and defaulting) tenant is reached. As can be seen, however, a chain of indemnity is only as strong as its weakest link and the original tenant may find that the chain is broken before the defaulting tenant is reached. Second, in the absence of an express indemnity covenant, the original tenant may be able to rely on the covenant of indemnity that is implied under section 77 of the LPA 1925. However, this covenant may – and often is – expressly excluded by the terms of the original lease. Third, the original tenant may be able to rely on an action in 'restitution' against the person (i.e. the defaulting tenant) whose liability has been discharged by the original tenant but, of course, only to the extent that the defaulter was actually liable.[67] This will occur where it can be shown that the defaulting tenant has been unjustly enriched at the expense of the original tenant and so will be required to reverse the unjust enrichment. It has been held that an express exclusion of the section 77 indemnity covenant does not also exclude the implied indemnity available under the rule in Moule v. Garrett (1872).[68]

6   The original tenant will not be liable for any increased rent resulting from a variation of the terms of the lease. In the case of variations effected on or after 1 January 1996, section 18 of the LTCA 1995 applies retrospectively and it means that the original tenant's liability for rent cannot be increased by any variation to the lease after it (the lease) has been assigned. Note, however, that the original tenant escapes liability only for the increased rent attributable to the variation. Liability remains for the originally agreed rent. Further, section 18 does not affect the operation of rent review clauses. So, if a tenant's rent is increased because of the effect of a rent review clause that was itself a term of the original lease (e.g. a clause that says the rent may be adjusted every five years in line with inflation), the original tenant is liable for this increased rent if the current tenant defaults, because this increase is contemplated by the lease itself. It does not matter that the increased rent may be far in excess of what the original tenant paid when he actually occupied the premises, because the increase has not been caused by a variation to the terms of the lease, but by the lease itself. A 'variation' (i.e. a change in rent for which the original tenant is not liable under section 18) is where the current tenant and current landlord effectively alter the terms of the lease between themselves and it is quite right that the original tenant should not be liable for any increased rent flowing from this later agreement to which he is not a party. Indeed, such is the common sense embodied in section 18 that the court in Friends Provident Life Office v. British Railways Board (1996) had already decided, prior to the entry into force of the LTCA 1995, that privity of contract meant privity to the original contract, and not some later variation of it.[69] As it turns

---

67 Moule v. Garrett (1872). The action was formerly said to arise in 'quasi-contract' but English law's recognition of a general principle of restitution has made this fiction unnecessary.

68 Re Healing Research Trustee Co (1992).

69 See also Beegas Nominees Ltd v. BHP Petroleum Ltd (1998).

out, then, section 18 of the LTCA 1995 was not actually needed. This means that no original tenant will be liable for an increased rent due to a variation, even if that variation occurred before 1 January 1996 and the entry into force of the LTCA 1995.

7   Under section 17 of the 1995 Act, although a pre-1996 original tenant's liability continues throughout the term of the lease, a landlord may only enforce a liability against this tenant for a 'fixed charge' – for example, rent, a service charge or liquidated damages for breach of covenant – by serving a statutory notice (a 'problem notice') within six months of the charge becoming due. This ensures that the original tenant is warned early of the potential liability and, in effect, ensures that only a maximum of six months charge (i.e. rent, etc.) can be claimed without the tenant being able to take action to minimise its liability. Failure to serve a notice relieves the original tenant of all liability for that breach of covenant.[70] Moreover, as noted immediately below, the payment by an original tenant of a fixed charge in consequence of receiving a problem notice gives the original tenant certain additional rights in relation to the land that he may utilise in an attempt to recover the sum paid.

8   If an original tenant is served with a problem notice under section 17 of the LTCA 1995 and pays the charge in full (e.g. the rent owed), the original tenant becomes entitled to the grant of a lease of the property (called an 'overriding lease') (section 19 of the LTCA 1995). This effectively inserts the original tenant back into possession of the property as 'tenant' of the current landlord, but as 'landlord' of the defaulting tenant.[71] The advantage of this is that it enables the original tenant – now back in possession – to take action against the current tenant, perhaps by forfeiting (terminating) his lease and thereby to use the land to meet the rental liability. He becomes the tenant of the current landlord but also the landlord of the defaulting tenant. Consequently, the original tenant who takes an overriding lease[72] can then pursue action against the defaulting tenant to recover the monies they have paid: for example, suing for the rent or forfeiting the lease and then assigning it for value to another person. This is the third provision of the 1995 Act that applies to pre-1996 tenancies. The tenant called on to pay the 'fixed charge' may opt for an overriding lease within 12 months of making the payment, and this overriding lease itself is either a pre-1996 or post-1996 tenancy, depending on the nature of the lease that it overrides.[73] It contains the same covenants as the overridden lease, except covenants 'expressed to be personal'. This right to call for an overriding lease against a landlord who claims payment of the fixed charge is itself an interest capable of protection by means of a notice against a registered title under the LRA 2002 and as a Class C(iv) land charge in unregistered land.[74] Finally, for completeness, we should remind ourselves that the problem notice/overriding lease system applies only when

---

70 If, however, the current tenant fails to pay rent in the future, the original tenant's liability arises for that rent and the landlord has six months from that liability arising to serve a problem notice.

71 It is as if the original tenant has created a subtenancy for the defaulting tenant.

72 Despite the similarity of name, this has nothing to do with 'overriding interests' under the LRA 2002.

73 Note, as we shall see, that the same scheme applies where the landlord seeks to enforce a liability for a fixed charge against an 'AGA tenant': see section 6.6.2 below.

74 Sections 19 and 20 of the LTCA 1995.

the original tenant is liable for a 'fixed charge'. So, the original tenant's liability under other covenants, such as the covenant to repair, remains unaltered unless and until that liability is crystallised by a liquidated damages clause.[75]

6.5.3 The continuing rights and obligations of the original landlord throughout the term of the lease

As with the original tenant, the original landlord remains liable on all of the leasehold covenants throughout the term of the lease, even after assignment of the reversion – *Stuart v. Joy* (1904) – and even to assignees of the tenant if they have the right to enforce the covenants (*Celsteel v. Alton (No. 2)* (1987)).[76] However, the original landlord may well have specified in the lease that his liability is to end on assignment and this contractual limitation would be effective to prevent continuing landlord liability.[77] In similar fashion, as a matter of principle, the ability of the original landlord under a pre-1996 lease to sue for breaches of covenant should remain for the full duration of the lease. However, if and when the landlord assigns the reversion, he will, in effect, pass the benefit of covenants (the right to sue) to the assignee. This is the effect of section 141(1) of the LPA 1925 for pre-1996 leases because the section operates to transfer the benefit of all proprietary leasehold covenants to the assignee and, following *Re King* (1963), this means that the original landlord's right to sue passes to the assignee even if that right existed in respect of a breach of covenant occurring before assignment. So, if, in 1989, L has the right to sue T for (say) non-payment of rent, an assignment of the lease by L to L1 in 1990 will pass not only L's right to sue on the benefit of leasehold covenants from thenceforward, but also L's accrued right to sue T for the rent owed in 1989. If L wishes to retain this right, it will have to be reconveyed back explicitly by L1 to L at the time of the assignment.[78]

6.5.4 The assignment of the lease to a new tenant for pre-1996 leases

The question here is whether the benefit *and* burden of any of the covenants in the lease made between the original landlord and the original tenant can 'run' with the land automatically when the *lease itself* is assigned. In simple terms, do the leasehold covenants (benefit and burden) pass automatically to a new tenant on assignment of the lease? In essence, this depends on two factors: first, does 'privity of estate' exist between the landlord and tenant so as to allow enforcement of the covenants; and second, do the covenants 'touch and concern' the land (*Spencer's Case* (1583))?

6.5.5 The claimant and defendant must be in 'privity of estate'

It is intrinsic to the enforcement of leasehold covenants under pre-1996 tenancies by, and against, the assignee of the lease (the new tenant) that he must stand in the relation of

---

75 A clause fixing the amount of damages in advance of a breach and triggering the 'fixed charge' procedure.

76 This position is modified for tenancies granted on or after 1 January 1996, and is discussed in section 6.6.3 below.

77 For why this remains important under the LTCA 1995, see section 6.6.3 below.

78 *Kataria v. Safeland* (1997).

'privity of estate' with a landlord who is also subject to the benefits and burdens of the covenants. In general terms, privity of estate exists where the claimant and defendant in an action on a leasehold covenant currently stand in the relationship of landlord and tenant under a legal lease. This can be broken down into two parts.

1   The claimant and defendant must stand in the relationship of landlord and tenant. Hence, there is the potential for privity of estate between the original landlord and an assignee of the lease, between an assignee of the reversion and the original tenant, and between assignees of the reversion and the lease while they are sharing the estate in the land. Significantly, however, there is no privity of estate between a landlord and a subtenant, as they are not each other's landlord and tenant. So, the simple point is that, in order for the benefit and burden of leasehold covenants to run to an assignee of the original tenant, that assignee must be 'the tenant' of the landlord who is suing or being sued.

2   The claimant and defendant must be landlord and tenant under a legal lease. Despite some dicta to the contrary,[79] it is clear that 'privity of estate' can exist only in respect of a legal lease. This means not only that the original lease must be legal in character,[80] but also that any assignment of the reversion or the lease (as the case may be) must be in the form prescribed for legal interests: that is, by deed in compliance with section 52 of the LPA 1925. In this respect, it is important to note that, even if the original lease is created as a legal estate without the need for a deed – for example, it is for three years or less – if the 'legal' character of it is to be maintained, any assignment of it must be effected by deed (Julian v. Crago (1992)). The insistence that privity of estate can exist only when the assignee tenant and his landlord are tenant and landlord under a legal lease is an historical anomaly generated by the now-defunct distinction between courts of law and courts of equity, but it is a distinction at the heart of the pre-1996 law. Of course, in practice, leasehold covenants are likely to be of importance in long leases where an effective web of transmissible leasehold covenants will be crucial – as in long leases of residential flats. Such leases are very likely to have been granted on legal advice and, as such, will be made by deed and any assignment of them is equally likely to be effected by deed. For leases granted on or after 1 January 1996, the rules concerning the transmissability of leasehold covenants make no distinction between legal and equitable leases and so this condition is not relevant.

6.5.6   The covenant must 'touch and concern' the land

In order that the benefit and burden of a leasehold covenant can pass to an assignee of the lease, it is not enough that the tenant stands in a relationship of privity of estate with the claimant/defendant landlord under a legal lease. In addition, for pre-1996 tenancies, only those covenants that 'touch and concern' the land are capable of being enforced by, and against, the assignee of a lease. The purpose of this requirement is to distinguish 'proprietary' covenants from merely 'personal' covenants. Proprietary covenants are those that

---

79 Famously, Lord Denning, in Boyer v. Warby (1953).

80 See section 6.3.2 above.

attach to the land and affect its use, while personal covenants are those that were intended to confer an individual benefit on the original tenant alone. In practice, it can be difficult to distinguish between those covenants that do, and those that do not, 'touch and concern' the land, although considerable help has been provided by the guidelines put forward by Lord Oliver in *Swift Investments v. Combined English Stores* (1989). Although this test is not to be applied mechanically (i.e. each case depends on its own facts), it is of considerable assistance. In determining the nature of a covenant, the following points are to be considered. First, could the covenant benefit *any* owner of an estate in the land as opposed to the particular original tenant (indicates a proprietary covenant)? Second, does the covenant affect the nature, quality, mode of use or value of the land (indicates a proprietary covenant)? Third, is the covenant expressed to be personal? Examples of covenants that, by this test, would 'touch and concern the land' are covenants to repair, covenants restrictive of use of the premises,[81] covenants not to assign or sublet without consent and, of course, the tenant's covenant to pay rent. Covenants imposing an obligation to pay money have, in the past, caused some concern, but it is now clear from *Swift* that a 'monetary covenant' that underpins the performance of covenants that touch and concern the land will itself 'touch and concern'. For example, a covenant by a third party promising to underwrite the performance of the covenants (a 'surety covenant') does touch and concern the land – it underpins proprietary obligations – so that it may be enforced by a person other than the original party to whom it was made. Note, however, the anomalous position with respect to one particular type of covenant that should by any measure 'touch and concern' the land but is in fact treated differently. A landlord's covenant to renew the lease (i.e. to give the tenant a new lease at the tenant's option when the old lease expires through time) clearly fulfils the *Swift* test, but it is not capable of being passed (i.e. binding a new landlord) under leasehold covenant rules. Following *Phillips v. Mobil Oil* (1989), such covenants must be treated as typical third-party interests under the Land Charges and Land Registration Acts. Hence, in unregistered land, the tenant must ensure that the covenant to renew is registered against the landlord as a Class C(iv) land charge if it is to bind a purchaser of a legal estate in the land (i.e. a new landlord under a legal lease), and, in registered land, the covenant should be registered by means of a notice against the burdened title, unless it can take effect as an interest that overrides under the 'actual occupation' provisions of Schedule 3, paragraph 2 of the LRA 2002. Albeit illogical, this position is now well established (i.e. property professionals know about it) and has been continued under the system for post-1996 leases. To sum up then, if the covenants touch and concern the land, they may be enforced by, or against, an assignee of the lease (a new tenant) by or against a landlord with whom the tenant then stands in the relationship of privity of estate under a legal lease or legal assignment thereof.

6.5.7   Special rules

As noted above, even if the assignee of the lease is liable under the leasehold covenants, the liability of the original tenant under a pre-1996 tenancy continues throughout the entire term and, given that this is a primary liability, a landlord may resort to him immediately

---

81 For example, not to carry on a trade or business, or not to grow trees over a certain height.

without resort to the assignee. Hence, it is always in the original tenant's interest to ensure that any assignee of the lease is able and willing to fulfil all covenants. In contrast, the liability of an *assignee* of the lease extends only to breaches committed while the lease is vested in them. Therefore, an assignee is not liable for breaches of covenant committed before assignment of the lease (*Grescot v. Green* (1700)) unless these are of a continuing nature.[82] Likewise, there is no liability for breaches committed after the lease has been assigned (*Paul v. Nurse* (1828)), for that liability must fall on the new tenant. Also, under pre-1996 tenancies, the original tenant is able to sue for breaches of covenants committed while he was in possession of the property, even though the lease may have been assigned subsequently (*City and Metropolitan Properties v. Greycroft* (1987)). The same is probably true for all subsequent assignees. Finally, in contrast with the position of original landlords, we may note that an original tenant does not lose the right to sue for breaches of covenant occurring before assignment.

6.5.8 The assignment of the reversion to a new landlord under pre-1996 tenancies

The question to be considered here is the mirror image of that considered above: that is, whether an assignee of the reversion (the 'new' landlord) is able to enjoy the benefits of the covenants in the original lease and whether he is subject to the burdens they impose. However, although the issue is the same, the relevant conditions are slightly different from those concerning assignment of the lease, primarily because of the intervention of statute.

6.5.9 Section 141 of the Law of Property Act 1925: The benefit of the original landlord's covenants

For pre-1996 tenancies, section 141(1) of the LPA 1925 provides that an assignment of the landlord's reversion carries with it the benefit (the right to sue) of all covenants that 'have reference to the subject matter of the lease'. In essence, this is a statutory transfer of the benefit of all covenants that 'touch and concern' the land (*Hua Chiao Commercial Bank v. Chiaphua Investment Corp* (1987)). Importantly, this means that the benefit of all 'touching and concerning' covenants are transferred to an assignee of the reversion, irrespective of whether privity of estate exists, although, of course, the defendant in an action must still be liable on the covenants and privity of estate may be necessary to establish this. It also means (because of the clear words of the section) that the 'new' landlord acquires the right to sue in respect of breaches of covenant that occurred before assignment and that the 'old' landlord loses this right (*London and County (A and D) Ltd v. Wilfred Sportsman Ltd* (1971)). The test of covenants that have 'reference to the subject matter of the lease' (i.e. 'touch and concern') is that specified by Lord Oliver in *Swift*. In practical terms, then, the transfer of the benefit of all proprietary covenants to an assignee of the landlord is a simple matter: statute ensures that they pass automatically with the lease. Note that, under the LTCA 1995, section 141(1) has no application to leases granted on or after 1 January 1996. It is replaced by a provision having wider effect.

---

82 For example, continuing non-payment of rent after assignment.

6.5.10   Section 142 of the Law of Property Act 1925: The burden of the original landlord's covenants

For pre-1996 leases, section 142(1) of the LPA 1925 provides that an assignment of the landlord's reversion carries with it the burden of (the obligation to perform) all covenants that also 'have reference to the subject matter of the lease'. In essence, this is a statutory transfer of the burden of all covenants that 'touch and concern' the land. Again, this means that the obligation to perform these covenants passes to an assignee of the reversion, irrespective of privity of estate, although the claimant (e.g. the current tenant) may need to plead such privity in order to prove that the benefit of the covenant has run to him. In this respect, the *Swift* test of 'touching and concerning' is again relevant, although, as discussed below, some problems have emerged. Note that, under the LTCA 1995, section 141(1) has no application to leases granted on or after 1 January 1996. Again then, in practical terms, the position for pre-1996 leases is relatively simple: the burden of all proprietary covenants passes to an assignee of the reversion automatically. However, for reasons that are not particularly cogent or convincing, there are some exceptions to this simple rule.

1   It is clear that a landlord's covenant to renew the lease at the tenant's option when the original term expires does 'have reference to the subject matter of the lease' and hence is *capable* of being enforced against assignees of the reversion (*Simpson v. Clayton* (1838)). However, according to *Beesly v. Hallwood Estates* (1960) and *Phillips v. Mobil Oil* (1989), the burden of this covenant does *not* pass automatically on assignment of the reversion, despite the clear words of section 142(1) of the LPA 1925. According to the judge in that case, such a covenant is registrable as a Class C(iv) Land Charge in unregistered land, and must be so registered in order to bind the assignee of the reversion; it will not pass automatically. This does seem a strange decision, and has been roundly criticised as being inconsistent with section 142. Indeed, in *Armstrong and Holmes v. Holmes* (1993), the judge criticised *Hallwood* and pointed out that it had been disapproved of by the Court of Appeal in *Greene v. Church Commissioners* (1974). However, even under the new regime of the LTCA 1995, these covenants will continue to be registrable in both registered and unregistered land (section 3(6)(b) of the LTCA 1995) rather than automatically binding under leasehold covenant rules. Fortunately, however, in respect of registered land, if the burden of such a covenant cannot pass automatically under 'leasehold covenant rules' (as *Mobil Oil* implies[83]), it is likely to constitute an interest that overrides under Schedule 3, paragraph 2 of the LRA 2002 and be binding on the assignee of the reversion because the tenant who can enforce it will be in actual occupation of the land to which the covenant relates.

2   In contrast to a surety covenant that underpins the performance of leasehold obligations (see above), a covenant by the landlord to repay a deposit given by the tenant does not 'touch and concern' and cannot, therefore, be enforced against an assignee of the landlord who actually received the money under a tenancy granted before 1 January 1996 (*Hua Chiao Commercial Bank v. Chiaphua Investment Corp* (1987)). This changes for tenancies subject to the LTCA 1995.

---

83 But note the words of section 29(2)(b) of the LRA 2002, that a disposition of a registered leasehold estate is subject to the burden of an interest that is an incident of the estate. Thus, the burden might bind in all cases.

3   A landlord's covenant to sell the freehold to the tenant does not 'touch and concern' the land, and cannot be enforced against an assignee of the reversion (*Woodall v. Clifton* (1905)). It is not entirely clear why this covenant should be regarded as personal, whereas the landlord's covenant to renew the lease is regarded as proprietary. Again, this changes for leases subject to the LTCA 1995.

6.5.11   Special rules

As noted above (and in contrast to the position with the original tenant), the ability of the original landlord to sue for breaches of covenant ceases after assignment of the reversion, even if the breach was committed before that assignment. This is because section 141(1) of the LPA 1925 transfers *all* of the assignor's rights to the assignee whenever they accrue (*Re King* (1963)). Second, the liability of an assignee of the reversion ceases when he assigns the lease to another assignee. However, it is uncertain whether an assignee of the reversion is liable for breaches of covenants committed by the original landlord before assignment. As a matter of principle, it would seem that he should not be so liable, but *dicta* in *Celsteel v. Alton* (1985) suggest otherwise. Third, the benefit and burden of leasehold covenants under pre-1996 tenancies pass to the assignee of the reversion by statute, not by the doctrine of privity of estate. Therefore, benefits and burdens pass, and may be sued on, in circumstances in which there is no privity of estate, as in the case of equitable leases/equitable assignments, or where the assignee of the reversion sues the original tenant even though the original tenant had never been *that* assignee's tenant (e.g. because the lease was assigned before the reversion – *Arlesford Trading v. Servansingh* (1971)). Fourth, rights of re-entry are special rights reserved by a landlord to 're-enter' the property and terminate the lease as a result of a tenant's breach of covenant. Importantly, every assignee of the reversion under a pre-1996 tenancy obtains the benefit of this right if it was included in the original lease (section 141 of the LPA 1925) and every tenant will be subject to the right of re-entry even if they are not actually liable on the covenants that have been broken (*Shiloh Spinners v. Harding* (1973)). This is because the right of re-entry operates against the land, whoever is in possession and irrespective of whether that person was actually the person whose actions breached the covenants. The position is the same for tenancies operating under the LTCA 1996 (see section 4). Finally, by way of confirmation of the special position of rights of re-entry, we can note *Kataria v. Safeland plc* (1997). In that case, the reversion was assigned together with a right of re-entry, but the 'old' landlord was granted by contract the right to recover rent owed prior to the assignment.[84] The new landlord was not owed rent but, nevertheless, was permitted to enforce his right of re-entry because rent was owing on the land and the right of re-entry stands separately from the covenants that it underpins.

6.5.12   Equitable leases and equitable assignments of legal leases

As far as pre-1996 tenancies are concerned, all that has been said above about the running of leasehold covenants to successors in title of the original landlord and original tenant

---

84 In effect, the parties contracted out of *Re King* (1963).

apply when both the original lease was legal and the assignment of it was made in the way appropriate to legal interests: that is, by deed. If, however, the original lease is equitable, or if a legal lease is imperfectly assigned (by written contract, not deed), then for pre-1996 tenancies, different considerations apply, primarily because, as explained above, 'privity of estate' does not exist under equitable leases or equitable assignments of legal leases.

6.5.13   The original landlord and tenant

The majority of equitable leases arise from a specifically enforceable written contract between the prospective landlord and prospective tenant.[85] Consequently, the original parties are bound in contract to perform all of the obligations of the lease, even those that are purely personal in nature.

6.5.14   The assignment of the reversion of an equitable lease to a new landlord

The intervention of statute means that, where the reversion of an equitable lease is assigned from landlord to landlord (or a legal reversion is imperfectly assigned[86]), the absence of privity of estate does not seriously prejudice the assignee's position. This is because sections 141 and 142 of the LPA 1925 ensure the transmission of the benefit and burden of leasehold covenants irrespective of the nature of the lease in which they are contained. Therefore, for pre-1996 tenancies, by virtue of section 141(1) of the LPA 1925, the assignee of the reversion of an equitable lease will be entitled to enforce all leasehold covenants (the benefit) that 'have reference to the subject matter of the lease'.[87] Likewise, under section 142(1), the obligation to perform similar covenants (the burden) will pass to the assignee. In short, the position is very similar to that operating for legal leases granted before 1 January 1996.

However, for a pre-1996 tenancy, the position is not quite as straightforward as this first appears. In order for the passing of the 'benefit' or 'burden' to have any practical meaning, the landlord must have someone to sue, or someone who can sue him. If the land is still held by the original tenant, there is no problem, as this will be the original contracting party and he will be subject to the terms of the lease, both as to benefits and burdens. But if the original tenant has also assigned the equitable lease, two further issues must be resolved. First, does the lease itself bind the purchaser of the reversion, so that the new landlord takes the land subject to the equitable tenancy? This falls to be determined by the normal rules of registered or unregistered conveyancing.[88] Second, and more importantly for present purposes, before the new landlord can actually rely on the leasehold covenants or be accountable under them, it is also necessary to show that the assignee of the equitable tenant is subject to the burden, or enjoys the benefit of

---

85 *Walsh v. Lonsdale* (1882). Or a written instrument that is treated as if it were a contract.

86 That is, where a written instrument is used instead of the required deed.

87 *Rother District Investments Ltd v. Corke* (2004), in which the assignee of the landlord was entitled to forfeit prior to his lease being registered and having, in consequence, an equitable title.

88 See Chapters 2 and 3 and the position is noted briefly above.

those covenants (as the case may be). For pre-1996 tenancies, this turns on the rules discussed below.

6.5.15   The assignment of the equitable lease to a new tenant

The ability of the benefit or burden of the original tenant's covenants in a pre-1996 tenancy to run with the assignment of an equitable lease (or an imperfect assignment of a legal lease) is complicated. The first point is that traditionally this situation is regarded as lacking the necessary 'privity of estate' and so *Spencer's Case* (1583) does not apply and the covenants cannot pass automatically.[89] However, it is well established that the *benefit* (but not the burden) of any contract can be expressly assigned. Consequently, an equitable tenant is perfectly free to transfer the benefit of every covenant (including personal ones) to the assignee *expressly* when the lease is itself assigned. Indeed, this is normal conveyancing procedure, and has the consequence that most equitable assignees will have the right to enforce the original tenant's covenants against whomsoever is subject to their burden. The reason is, quite simply, that the original contracting party has passed the benefits under the contract (the right to sue) to the person to whom he has also assigned the lease.

Unfortunately, however, there are no parallel rules concerning the passing of the burden of the original equitable tenant's leasehold covenants. In fact, as *Purchase v. Lichfield Brewery* (1915) illustrates, an equitable assignee of the lease may not be liable to perform *any* of the original tenant's covenants, including the obligation to pay rent. This is the combined effect of the rule that no privity of estate exists between landlord and tenant under an equitable lease (or equitable assignment of a legal lease), so preventing automatic passing of the burden of the covenants, and the rule that burdens of a contract cannot be assigned, so preventing the express *inter partes* transfer of leasehold obligations. So, while benefits may run under an equitable lease (because of express assignment), and the new tenant may sue the landlord, the landlord cannot sue the tenant. Obviously, this can cause considerable hardship to the landlord who may find the value of his reversion substantially diminished through an assignment of the lease over which he had little control and where the land is now possessed by a tenant whom he cannot control. Consequently, a number of alternative, or 'indirect', methods of enforcing the burden of leasehold covenants against equitable assignees of the lease have been developed. These are considered below. For the most part, they will be redundant for tenancies granted on or after 1 January 1996 because of the statutory magic of the LTCA 1995.

First, in *Boyer v. Warby* (1953), Denning LJ held that the burden of leasehold covenants that 'touched and concerned' the land *could* pass to the assignee of a lease for three years or less (which is legal without a deed), even though the assignment itself was not by deed. On one view, this could be taken to mean that *Purchase v. Lichfield Brewery* (1915) has been overruled, and that burdens (and so benefits) can pass automatically, as with legal leases. However, this wide interpretation is very doubtful, and no conclusive reasons were given in *Boyer* other than that 'law' and 'equity' were now fused. Unfortunately, this merely assumes what it has to prove. In other words, *Boyer* should be limited to its own facts: that

---

89 Whether this be a defensible position is beside the point. The rule is well established and has governed conveyancing practice.

is, because the lease was originally legal, even though not made by deed (being for three years or less), its assignment without deed may be treated as an effective transfer of the legal estate, so preserving the required 'privity of estate' necessary to make leasehold covenants run.

Second, even if the covenants themselves are not binding on the equitable assignee, they can be enforced against that assignee indirectly by means of a right of re-entry (a forfeiture clause) in the original lease. As we shall see, the right of re-entry allows a landlord to recover premises after a breach of covenant and thereby terminate the lease. Such rights of re-entry stand alone, and may be relied on by a landlord if a covenant is broken, even though the covenant itself was not binding on the tenant (*Shiloh Spinners v. Harding* (1973)) or, indeed, even if a previous landlord enjoys the personal right to enforce the covenant, as in *Kataria v. Safeland plc* (1997). This may seem odd because the right of re-entry is usually seen as a remedy for breach of covenant and thus appears to require that a covenant has been broken by the person subject to the remedy of forfeiture. However, land law is more inventive than this. A proprietary ('touching and concerning') leasehold covenant attaches to the land, even though the current tenant (as an equitable assignee) may not be bound by it. Consequently, if actions take place on the land that contravene the covenant, the covenant has been broken. Admittedly, direct action against the defaulting tenant is not possible (e.g. no action in damages), but action against the land is. So, if the landlord has the benefit of a right of re-entry, the landlord can 're-enter', take possession and bring the lease to an end. Although there are statutory controls on the exercise of the right of re-entry,[90] it will be appreciated that the possibility of re-entry is very persuasive in ensuring that the tenant does, in fact, observe the leasehold covenants. Would the tenant be happy to lose his lease through forfeiture, or instead actually perform the leasehold obligations? We must note, however, that the efficacy of this indirect enforcement method is constrained by the following requirements: that a right of re-entry must exist and its benefit have been passed to the current landlord (this is most likely); that the leasehold covenant is proprietary in nature; and that the tenant is bound by the right of re-entry, even though not bound by the actual covenants. This last restriction operates differently, depending on whether the land is registered or unregistered. In unregistered land, rights of re-entry in an equitable lease are not land charges and are binding on a tenant (and any other person in possession) according to the doctrine of notice. A tenant will be deemed to have notice of all terms of the original lease, including the right of re-entry, and hence the condition is satisfied easily. In registered land, the right of re-entry is likely to bind automatically under the express provision in section 29(2)(b) of the LRA 2002.[91]

Third, even though the landlord and equitable assignee do not stand in a relationship of privity of estate, any 'restrictive covenants' (i.e. those preventing the assignee of the lease from doing something on the land) may be enforced by virtue of the principle of *Tulk v. Moxhay* (1848). This is discussed further in Chapter 8 (the law of freehold covenants), but, in essence, the rule in *Tulk v. Moxhay* permits the enforcement of any restrictive proprietary covenant against a person in possession of the land over which the covenant takes effect. This may be an adverse possessor, freeholder or, as here, an equitable tenant. So, if an

---

90 See section 6.7.5 below.

91 That a disposition of a registered leasehold estate is subject to the burden of an interest that is an incident of the estate.

equitable lease contains a restrictive covenant and the benefit of that covenant has passed to the current landlord (as is most likely – section 141(1) of the LPA 1925), that covenant can be enforced against the equitable tenant by means of an injunction preventing any continuation of the activity that is prohibited.[92] The conditions for this means to enforcement are that the covenant is proprietary ('touches and concerns'), that it has become attached to the land (achieved through section 79 of the LPA 1925[93]); and that it is binding on the tenant. In unregistered land, the restrictive leasehold covenant cannot be a land charge, and so will be binding according to the doctrine of notice (*Dartstone v. Cleveland Petroleum* (1969)). Again, the tenant will be deemed to have notice of all covenants contained in the lease. In registered land, the restrictive covenant will be binding because of the effect of section 29(2)(b) of the LRA 2002.

Fourth, it may be possible to argue that a new legal tenancy comes into existence between the landlord and the equitable assignee when the assignee pays rent and this is accepted. Such a periodic tenancy will usually be legal (because it will be for three years or less and no formality is required) and leasehold covenants will be directly enforceable. However, it is not clear why the covenants implied into the 'new' legal periodic tenancy between landlord and equitable assignee should be the same as those contained in the original equitable lease, and there remains the difficulty that the parties will have intended and believed that their relations are governed by the old equitable lease, not some new artificial creation.

Fifth, it may be possible to imply new contractual obligations on the part of the equitable assignee in favour of the landlord that will then create a direct contractual nexus between those parties. This is similar to the implication of a new periodic tenancy considered above, except that in this case it is simply new obligations that are being implied, not an entirely new lease. The occasions when this implication may be made are a matter of some debate and much will depend on the circumstances under which the assignee has taken the lease. Proprietary estoppel could come to the aid of the landlord, although it will be difficult to prove that there is unconscionability simply because the landlord has been denied the benefit of the covenants.

Finally, if the equitable assignee enters into new *express* covenants directly with the landlord, then these are enforceable as a matter of contract. In fact, the possibility of new, direct covenants between the intended assignee and the landlord is a real option if the landlord has the right to withhold consent to assignment of the lease. In such a case, the insistence on new direct covenants between assignee and landlord will be the price extracted for the landlord's agreement to the assignment and occurs frequently in practice.[94]

The efficacy of these methods of enforcement against the assignee should not be underestimated. The threat of re-entry, the enforcement of restrictive covenants by injunction and the ability of the landlord to extract new direct covenants can prove just as effective in ensuring that the equitable assignee observes the leasehold covenants as

---

92 For example, that the tenant may not carry on a trade or business.

93 See Chapter 8.

94 A landlord will wish to have some control over any new tenant (the assignee) and while consent to an assignment cannot usually be refused unreasonably, the insistence by the landlord of a direct contractual relationship with the intended assignee reflecting the original covenants is not unreasonable.

would have been the case had the covenants passed automatically. Consequently, the 'new' statutory rules of the LTCA 1995, discussed below in section 6.6, should not be seen as directed primarily at the 'evils' associated with equitable leases. These 'evils' could be countered and usually were.

6.5.16   The position of subtenants

As was indicated at the very outset of this chapter, a tenant may create out of their interest a 'shorter' tenancy for another person. The original tenant under the 'headlease' then becomes the landlord of his own tenant, often called the 'subtenant'. Of course, the sub-tenancy may contain its own covenants, and often these will be identical to those contained in the headlease. However, it may well happen that it is the subtenant (the actual occupier of the land) who so acts as to cause a breach of a covenant that was made between the original landlord and original tenant. An example is where the original tenant has prom-ised not to carry on any trade or business, but then a sublet is established, and the subtenant does just that. Once again, the head landlord has a problem, as he does not stand in the relationship of privity of estate or privity of contract with the subtenant and cannot enforce leasehold covenants against him directly. There are, however, a number of possibilities that may assist the landlord in this situation, assuming that the current tenant is not prepared to act against the subtenant under the lease (the sublease) that exists between them.

1   The head landlord may enforce a right of re-entry against the current tenant. This is because, in absolute terms, the acts of the subtenant have caused a violation of the covenant whose performance is owed by the tenant to the landlord. Hence, the landlord has at his disposal the remedy of forfeiture. As is explained below, successful forfeiture of a lease automatically terminates any subleases.[95] Necessarily, this is an effective, but drastic, remedy. It results in the landlord having no tenant and hence no income from the land unless a new lease can be arranged. It may not be a remedy of first choice.

2   The head landlord may be able to use the *Tulk v. Moxhay* rules to enforce restrictive covenants directly against the subtenant. The situation is effectively the same as that discussed in relation to the position of equitable assignees and subject to the same limitations, both legal and practical.

3   The subtenant may enter into direct covenants with the head landlord. These can again be enforced directly as a matter of contract. The landlord may be able to insist that these covenants are entered into as a condition of his consent to such sub-tenancy, if that power has been retained in the lease between the landlord and tenant.

6.5.17   The Law Commission and proposals for reform

Prompted by some of the uncertainties, inconsistencies and perceived injustices of the pre-1996 rules, the Law Commission proposed a number of changes to the law of leasehold covenants.[96] The Commission believed that the continuing liability of the original tenant

---

95 *Pennell v. Payne* (1995).

96 Report No. 174.

throughout the entire term of the lease both distorted the public perception of the nature of the landlord and tenant relationship,[97] and caused unwarranted and unfair hardship to tenants who found themselves liable to perform rental or other obligations undertaken some time ago and now broken by some tenant over whom they had no control: for example, where the tenant in breach was the third or fourth assignee. Consequently, it proposed that when a tenant assigned a leasehold interest, he should be released automatically from all liability in respect of any future breaches of the covenants. The only exception would be where an assignment by the tenant was conditional on the landlord's consent, in which case the landlord could impose a condition whereby the original tenant would guarantee the performance of the covenants by the immediate assignee. However, any continuing liability imposed in this manner could not extend beyond one assignment and it would truly be a guarantee so that the landlord would have to look to the assignee first in the event of any breach.

Somewhat controversially, however, the Law Commission did not feel it necessary to protect the landlord from continuing liability under his covenants. Thus, under the original proposals drafted by the Law Commission, a landlord would remain liable for breaches of covenant committed by his successors unless he served a notice on the tenant indicating his desire to be released. Should the tenant disagree with the proposed release, the matter would be resolved in court, with the landlord seeking to establish that it would be reasonable to release him from continuing responsibility.[98] However, as discussed below, the tenant's apparent position of strength in this regard has been mitigated by the House of Lords decision in *London Diocesan Fund v. Avonridge* (2005). The Law Commission also proposed a much more radical reform: the abandonment of the requirement of 'touching and concerning' as the touchstone for the transmissibility of the benefits and burdens of leasehold covenants. As we shall see, this has now been done for leases granted on or after 1 January 1996, even though most of the problems with the 'touching' principle appear to have been generated more by the fact that it is difficult to define in advance what the concept requires, rather than by an analysis of whether the rationale behind the requirement is still compelling.

6.6   The New Scheme – The Law Applicable to Tenancies Granted on or after 1 January 1996: The Landlord and Tenant (Covenants) Act 1995

The Law Commission's proposals generated much public interest and resulted eventually in the presentation of a private member's Bill to Parliament. It may seem surprising that

---

97 The perception being that the liability of landlord and tenant was co-extensive with their possession.

98 One reason may have been to prevent landlords assigning the lease to a 'shell' company with which they were associated and thereby obtaining release from the covenants for themselves. If the 'shell' were then to prove empty, this would effectively strip the tenant of any remedy. This may now be possible after *London Diocesan Fund v. Avonridge* (2005).

such a 'technical' item of legislation should be presented to Parliament under the cumbersome private member's Bill procedure instead of being guided through smoothly as an uncontroversial government Bill. In fact, opposition to the Law Commission's proposals by landlords' pressure groups, such as the British Retail Consortium, and pressure on the legislative timetable, meant that the private member's Bill procedure was, at the time, the only hope of securing reform of leasehold covenant law. Even then, the strength of this opposition, when combined with the absence of government protection in the legislature, nearly destroyed the Bill and resulted in the new Act being much more of a compromise between tenants' and landlords' interests than was envisaged originally by the Law Commission. As we shall see, one view of the legislation is that the improvement in the position of tenants secured by the LTCA 1995 is effectively countered by the corresponding advantages secured for landlords, at least in respect of commercial leases.

The Landlord and Tenants (Covenants) Act 1995 came into force on 1 January 1996. Save for those sections of the Act mentioned above that apply to all tenancies, the Act regulates the transmission of the benefit and burden of leasehold covenants in all new leases (legal or equitable) granted on or after that date. Consequently, for such leases, reference must be made to the Act to determine whether a landlord or tenant is bound by, or may enforce, leasehold covenants relating to the land demised in the lease (*Oceanic Village* v. *United Attractions* (2000)).

6.6.1   General principles of the 1995 Act

This section indicates in very brief terms the general effect of the LTCA 1995 and the principles on which it is based. The sections following will discuss the position in more detail, although it must be remembered that case law on the 1995 Act is still relatively sparse.

First, the Act applies to tenancies granted on or after 1 January 1996, and it applies in the same way to legal and equitable tenancies. The old rules that differentiated between these types of lease are no longer relevant (section 28(1) of the LTCA 1995). Second, the tenant (whether original or an assignee) is released automatically from the burden of leasehold covenants when he assigns the tenancy (section 5 of the LTCA 1995), subject only to the possibility that he might be required to guarantee performance of the leasehold covenants by the next (but only the next) immediate assignee (section 16 of the LTCA 1995). There is an exception for assignments made in breach of covenant, or assignments made by operation law, when the assigning tenant remains liable (section 11(2)). Third, the original landlord is not released automatically from the burdens of leasehold covenants,[99] but may serve a notice on the tenant applying for such release (section 6). Release will occur if the notice is not answered within a specified time, or if the landlord's application to the county court in the event of objection by the tenant is successful (section 8). A landlord assigning this reversion in breach of covenant, or by operation of law, cannot serve such a notice (section 11(3)). In any event, a successful notice relieves the original landlord from liability arising only under 'landlord' covenants. It does *not* relieve liability under personal covenants that, because they are expressed to be personal (see below), have not passed to the assignee (*BHP Petroleum* v. *Chesterfield Properties* (2001)). However, a

---

99 Assuming the original landlord would have been liable after assignment under the terms of the lease – see section

   6.3.3 above and the effect of *London Diocesan Fund* v. *Avonridge* (2005).

landlord is able to limit contractually the period of their liability to the period for which they are in possession (thus avoiding the notice procedure), as decided by the House of Lords in *London Diocesan Fund v. Avonridge* (2005). Fourth, the rule that covenants must 'touch and concern' the land or 'have reference to the subject matter of the lease' before the benefits and burdens can pass to assignees of the lease or the reversion is abolished (sections 2 and 3 of the LTCA 1995). Fifth, the benefit and burden of all leasehold covenants pass *automatically* to assignees of the lease and of the reversion so that an assignee may enforce, and will be subject to, any covenant contained in the lease (section 3). This means that there is no need to show 'privity of estate' and that sections 141 and 142 of the LPA 1925 are no longer applicable to tenancies granted on or after 1 January 1996. Only those covenants that are 'expressed to be personal', that are not actually binding on the assignor, or that do not relate to the premises subject to the lease will not so pass.[100] Note also that, unlike the 'old' law, the transfer of the benefit of a covenant to an assignee of the landlord does not deprive the assignor of the right to sue in respect of breaches occurring before the assignment, so reversing *Re King* (1963) for 'new' leases (section 24(4) of the LTCA 1995). Sixth, the provisions relating to 'problem notices' and over-riding leases, discussed above in relation to pre-Act leases, also apply to tenancies falling under the Act. For example, if an assigning tenant is called on to pay a sum under his guarantee of the next immediate assignee's liability, then a 'problem notice' must be served within the proper period (six months from the liability arising[101]) for the guarantee to be enforceable. Likewise the guarantor has the option of securing an overriding lease.

6.6.2   The tenant's position in more detail

The 1995 Act has modified considerably the position of tenants under leasehold covenants. The two most important reforms are the statutory release of *all* tenants, including the original tenant, from the burden of all covenants when they assign the lease, and the rule that the benefit and burden of covenants in most cases will pass automatically to an assignee of the lease. Gone are the worries about the continuing liability of an original tenant throughout the entire term of the lease, but no longer does a landlord have to prove 'privity of estate' and 'touching and concerning' before he can enforce leasehold covenants against a tenant in possession. All current tenants under legal or equitable leases granted on or after 1 January 1996 will be bound by the leasehold covenants. For example, an assignee under an equitable lease will be bound to carry out the original tenant's covenant to repair, even though no privity of estate exists with the current landlord. Similarly, the original tenant will be released from this liability, save only that he may have been required to enter an authorised guarantee agreement (AGA) to guarantee performance of the obligation by the tenant to whom he assigns.

Although the Act has entered into force, and applies to leases granted on or after 1 January 1996, case law remains relatively scarce. The statute itself can be difficult to interpret,[102] and the diverse uses of the leasehold estate are sure to generate unforeseen

---

100   Section 3(1)(a) and 3(2) of the LTCA 1995.

101   And see *Scottish & Newcastle plc v. Raguz* (2008) for when liability arises.

102   In *First Penthouse v. Channel Hotels and Properties* (2003), Lightman J, when construing section 3 of the Act, noted that '[t]he Act is the product of rushed drafting and its provisions create exceptional difficulties'.

difficulties and anomalies. It will be some time yet before the precise operation of the statute is clear, although there has been some important guidance. What follows, then, is an outline of the effects of the legislation on both a legal and equitable tenant under a lease to which the statute applies. It is important to note at this early stage that the statute says very little about the position of subtenants in their relation with landlords. The Act is concerned with the 'assignment' of a lease of a reversion: a subtenant takes a new lease from his landlord and is not an assignee.[103]

6.6.2.1   *Release of tenants and authorised guarantee agreements*

First for consideration is the principle encapsulating one of the fundamental motives for the legislation: that the original tenant and all subsequent tenants will be released from the obligation to perform the covenants (and lose the right to enforce them) on assignment of the lease, provided that such assignment is not itself in breach of covenant, or otherwise excluded by operation of law (sections 5 and 11 of the LTCA 1995). Necessarily, the release of the original tenant from liability on assignment deprives the landlord of an effective remedy if the tenant currently in possession defaults on the lease. For this reason, a landlord may require the original tenant to enter into an AGA as a condition of the assignment of the lease (section 16). Such an agreement will oblige the assigning tenant to be guarantor of the tenant's leasehold covenants for the next immediate assignee. So, if T wishes to assign to T1, the landlord may be able to require T to guarantee the performance of the covenants by T1. Under the Act, it is only permitted to require an AGA in order to guarantee performance for the next immediate assignee. Thus, on an assignment by T1 to T2, T's guarantee agreement is no longer effective.[104] This procedure is a necessary counterbalance to the release of the tenant on assignment, and was proposed by the Law Commission in its original report.

The circumstances in which a landlord may require a tenant to enter into an AGA are found in section 16(3) of the 1995 Act and their meaning is not altogether free from doubt. The issue is best considered first in relation to the original tenant and then any assignee.

6.6.2.1.1   *When may the original tenant be required to enter into an AGA?*

In considering this issue, it must be remembered that the ability of a landlord to require the original tenant to enter into an AGA is closely connected to the landlord's ability to control assignment by requiring the tenant to seek his (the landlord's) consent before assignment. Clauses requiring a tenant to seek the landlord's consent before assignment are very common in commercial and long-term residential leases.

1   If the lease contains an absolute covenant against assignment, then the landlord is entitled without more to require the tenant to enter into an AGA as a condition to giving his consent (section 16(3) of the LTCA 1995). This is as it should be, given

---

103   Of course, the Act will apply separately to the lease between the tenant and subtenant, but not between landlord and subtenant.

104   See *Good Harvest Partnership LLP* v. *Centaur Services Ltd.* [2010 EWHC 330 (Ch)]. Although it may be possible to require T1 to enter into an AGA to guarantee performance by T2: see below.

that an absolute covenant against assignment means that the landlord can simply refuse permission to assign without reasons. Some commercial leases will contain such a covenant but they are unattractive to tenants for obvious reasons and are unlikely to be agreed when there is an ample of commercial property for rent.

2   If the lease contains a qualified covenant against assignment – meaning that the landlord's consent to assignment may be withheld only in certain circumstances – and it is a lease of commercial premises and the lease itself stipulates that the giving of an AGA can be a condition of the landlord's consent to assign – then the landlord may require an AGA. This is so whether or not it is reasonable to impose an AGA (section 16(3) of the LTCA 1995 and section 22 of the LTCA 1995).[105] Most leases of commercial premises will fall into this category and, in consequence, the imposition of an AGA will be possible in the majority of cases.[106]

3   If the lease contains a qualified covenant against assignment and is of residential or agricultural premises, or of commercial premises where the lease contains no specific obligation to enter into an AGA, then the landlord can require an AGA only if it is reasonable to do so (section 16(3)(b) of the LTCA). It is not yet clear when it will be 'reasonable' to do so, although landlords would argue that it is always reasonable to do so provided that no other conditions are attached to the consent to assign.

4   If the lease (of any kind) contains no covenant against assignment – meaning that the tenant can assign irrespective of the landlord's wishes – then the landlord cannot insist on an AGA. However, it is most unlikely in practice that a lease will omit to give the landlord the right to control assignment either by an absolute or qualified covenant.

6.6.2.1.2   *When may an assignee be required to enter into an AGA?*

This is the situation in which T (the original tenant) has assigned to T1 and T has been required to enter into an AGA guaranteeing T1's performance of the covenants in the lease. If T1 then assigns to T2, it is absolutely clear that T is released from the AGA, for the original tenant can only ever be required to guarantee performance by the next immediate assignee. But can T1 be required to enter into an AGA to guarantee performance by T2? The position is unclear. The difficulty arises because the LTCA 1995 appears to say that an AGA may be required by a landlord only when a tenant is released from liability on covenants by virtue of the Act itself (section 16(1) of the LTCA). This is certainly the original tenant, but an assignee (T1) was never, under the old law, liable after he had assigned to another (T2). The assignee's liability ended when he assigned and did not continue in the same way as that of the original tenant. Hence the assignee (T1) is not released

---

105 Section 22 inserts a provision in section 19 of the Landlord and Tenant Act 1927 allowing AGAs in 'unreasonable' circumstances. The section also permits other objective conditions to be attacked to consent to assign and these also may not be attacked on the ground of unreasonableness: for example, the potential assignee company has a certain level of capital reserves, or is publicly quoted, or is fully insured, or is backed by appropriate guarantees.

106 That is not to say that one will be insisted on in practice – a landlord may regard an AGA as unnecessary to protect its position, given the remedy of forfeiture and there are disadvantages attendant on enforcing AGA liability (i.e. that the former tenant liable under an AGA may be entitled to an overriding lease).

from liability *by the Act* and so it appears cannot be required to enter into an AGA to guarantee T2.

If this were the final word, it might pose serious difficulty for landlords as they would lose the ability to sue another person as soon as the first assignee assigned to a second assignee.[107] Consequently, there are three arguments countering this possibility. First, if the assignee (T1) enters into direct covenants with the landlord on assignment, these would have continued to bind throughout the entire term of the lease, so T1's release is caused by the Act and so he can be required to enter into an AGA in exactly the same circumstances as the original tenant. This is because, in effect, the assignee has become the original tenant by making direct covenants with the landlord. Given that this will occur in most assignments concerning commercial premises, perhaps there will be few difficulties in practice. Second, if the lease itself contains a covenant requiring a tenant to enter into an AGA, this is itself a tenant's covenant that will run to all assignees under the rules of the LTCA providing for the automatic transmission of benefits and burdens. In other words, if the requirement to enter an AGA is treated as a 'normal' covenant, it will run to assignees and is not required by the landlord *per se* under the Act but was freely agreed in the terms of the lease.[108] However, this might contravene the anti-avoidance provisions of the LTCA and so it remains to be seen how the courts resolve this contradiction in the effect of the LTCA 1995 in those cases in which the assignee has not been required to enter into direct covenants with the landlord. Third, controversially, it could be argued that because the benefit and burden of leasehold covenants now pass to assignees under the Act, their release from those covenants on assignment is, after all, caused by the Act. Hence, the assignee can be required to enter into an AGA after all. This is in effect an argument that the Act has entirely replaced the old law and so any reference to it – by saying that assignees are not released by the Act but by the old law – is misplaced and inaccurate.

Obviously, these provisions are complicated, not least because of the elliptical statutory language, but the crucial point is that if a lease granted on or after 1 January 1996 contains a promise by the original tenant not to assign without the landlord's consent, and the landlord requires an AGA before he will give such consent, the assigning tenant will be required to enter an AGA in order to assign if that is reasonable or, for leases of commercial premises, simply if the need for an AGA was stated expressly as a condition on which consent to assignment could be refused by the landlord. For assignees, if the assignee has made direct covenants, he will be an 'original' tenant for these purposes. If he has not, then his position is uncertain, but there are good arguments why he too should be subject to the AGA regime. Importantly, if a landlord seeks to enforce a (lawful) AGA liability against the last immediate tenant (the 'AGA tenant'), the 'problem notice' procedure of section 17 of the LTCA is applicable. This means that the guaranteeing tenant must be given at least six months' notice of any liability arising under the AGA[109] and, if the liability

---

107 Where the lease is assigned by the original tenant, ignoring guarantors, the landlord has two potential defendants: the current tenant and the original tenant under an AGA. If the assignee then assigns, the landlord would 'lose' a defendant, now having only the current tenant (T2) and not the original tenant (the AGA lapses) and not the first assignee (T1) as he (on one view) cannot be required to enter into an AGA.

108 This contractual approach may find favour, given that *Avonridge* makes clear that the LTCA 1995 has not ousted the parties' ability to regulate their own liability.

109 Of course, the actual default is by the tenant to whom he assigned.

is met, of claiming an overriding lease under section 18 of the LTCA 1995.[110] So to sum up this point, although landlords have lost the right to sue the *original* tenant throughout the entire term of the lease, all professionally drafted leases are likely to contain a provision enabling the landlord to impose an AGA on the original tenant (and possibly later assignors). It can happen, therefore, that each assignee will have to guarantee performance of the covenants by the tenant to whom they assign (but only that tenant). In effect, the landlord retains a second defendant as 'compensation' for losing the original tenant as a second defendant.[111] Seen as such, it seems that the Law Commission's aim of relieving the original tenant of continuing liability has been achieved at the price of transferring that liability 'down the chain' of assignments to each assigning tenant in turn. Undoubtedly, this is fairer because it equates liability with possession and liability for the assignee who the assignor has chosen, but it should not be thought that the 1995 Act has diminished to any great extent the totality of rights available to a landlord when default occurs.

6.6.2.2   *Automatic transfer of benefits and burdens*

Second, and as a corollary to the above, the other major effect of the LTCA is that assignees of the current tenant will acquire the benefit and burden of leasehold covenants relating to the demised premises, save only that benefits and burdens of covenants that are 'expressed to be personal to any person' will not pass (section 3(6)(a) of the LTCA 1995).[112] However, this does not deprive the assignor of the right to sue for pre-assignment breaches, so reversing *Re King* (1963) (section 24(4) of the LTCA 1995). As noted above, the decision to ensure that the benefit and burden of all leasehold covenants relating to the demised premises pass on assignment was taken in response to concerns over the adequacy of the 'touching and concerning' test. Under the new law, it appears that we need not attempt to differentiate between 'proprietary' and 'personal' covenants, because all pass unless 'expressed to be personal' (*BHP Petroleum v. Chesterfield Properties* (2001)). It is not at all clear that this was a wise reform because the distinction between obligations attaching to the land (e.g. 'the tenant must repair') and obligations attaching only to the person (e.g. 'the tenant must walk the landlord's dog') is at the heart of property law: see, for example, the distinction between leases and licences. If it is argued that very few 'personal' covenants are found in leases anyway, so implying that making all covenants run will cause little practical hardship, surely that also demonstrates that the occasions for applying the allegedly fickle 'touching and concerning' test were also rare and caused little practical hardship! In fact, much will turn on how the courts interpret the statute when it says that

---

110 If the overriding lease is claimed, it will have the effect of propelling the AGA tenant back into possession 'in between' the landlord and the current (defaulting) tenant. It will thus give the AGA tenant the opportunity of forfeiting the lease of the defaulting tenant and either taking beneficial possession himself or assigning the lease for value to a new tenant. This might be worth more money than the liability he has paid.

111 The first defendant is the current tenant whose actions have actually breached the terms of the lease: for example, by not paying rent.

112 There is an exception because the anomalous rule in *Phillips v. Mobil Oil* (1989) that covenants to renew a lease required separate registration in order to bind an assignee of the reversion remains intact (section 3(6)(b) of the LTCA 1995). Consequently, the tenant will not be able to exercise the benefit of the covenant unless its burden has been entered on the register of title by means of a Notice; but see also LRA 2002 s. 29(2)(b).

a covenant that '(in whatever terms) is expressed to be personal' will not run. In this regard, it seems that the courts are reluctant to turn away from old – and logical – distinctions. In *First Penthouse v. Channel Hotels and Properties* (2003), Lightman J was considering whether a covenant was 'expressed to be personal' within the meaning of the statute. As well as noting that the statute generally was of low quality, he decided that a covenant is expressed to be personal 'in whatever terms' if either it says so in words (e.g. 'this is personal') or if its *substance* is such that its personal character is expressed through the nature of the obligation it imposes.[113] In other words, that a covenant is expressed to be personal either expressly or impliedly. Of course, to say that the covenant may be 'expressed to be personal' explicitly or impliedly is but a small step from the old 'touching and concerning test', but then again many commentators could not understand why the LTCA 1995 ever thought that it was sensible to make *all* covenants run unless they were 'expressed to be personal'. After all, property obligations *are* different from personal ones, even if not 'expressed' to be so.

6.6.3   An assessment of the landlord's position

The landlord may, at first, appear to have lost most by the passing of this new Act. After all, the original landlord is not automatically released from performance of his covenants, but apparently has to serve a notice on the tenant requesting this, and the landlord has lost the right to sue the original tenant throughout the term of the lease. However, as intimated already, all is not as it seems.

First, following the House of Lords decision in *London Diocesan Fund v. Avonridge* (2005), it is now clear that a landlord can stipulate in the original lease that his liability ceases when he assigns the reversion. In other words, provided that the lease contains a clause limiting the landlord's liability to the period of his possession, when L assigns to L1, all liability for L will cease and he does not have to serve a notice on the tenant requesting release from liability for future breaches of covenant. According to the majority in the House of Lords (Lord Walker dissenting), this is perfectly possible because the LTCA 1995 was not intended to do away with the parties' freedom of contract. So if a landlord can negotiate an '*Avonridge* clause', all liability for future breaches ceases on assignment and L1 becomes the only person liable. Of course, as pointed out by Lord Walker in his dissent, this effectively makes the notice procedure in sections 5 and 8 entirely redundant and amounts effectively to an avoidance device. As anticipated, most professionally drafted commercial leases now contain an *Avonridge* clause, thus rendering the original landlord immune from liability after he has assigned the reversion and, more importantly, placing the tenant in a position in which he has limited remedies for future breaches of covenant. This is exactly what the LTCA 1995 was intended to avoid.[114]

---

113   '[T]he tenancy does not have to spell it out in terms that the covenant is to be personal. The intention may be expressed explicitly or implicitly. The intention may be stated in terms or it may be deduced from the language used in its proper context' – at [49].

114   All that need happen is that the original landlord deliberately assign to L1, under an *Avonridge* clause, thus ensuring its release from liability. If L1 is a mere 'shell' company, then T's remedies are worthless. Indeed, L may assign to L1 – a company set up just for this purpose – deliberately to relieve itself of liability.

Second, the benefit and burden of all landlord's covenants will pass automatically to an assignee of the reversion, unless expressed to be personal and with the exception of the landlord's covenant to renew the lease at the tenant's option (section 3(6)(b) of the LTCA 1995). With the passing of the benefit and burden of all of the tenant's covenants – even to an equitable tenant and equitable assignee – every landlord can now be certain of having a remedy against the tenant in possession of the land. Although landlords acting against assignees of equitable leases did have ways of ensuring that leasehold obligations were observed, the simplification of the rules concerning enforceability brought about by the Act is a definite advantage for landlords.

Third, the ability to require the original tenant and, with careful attention, all assigning tenants[115] to enter into an AGA places the landlord in a strong position – the more so in commercial leases, where, with careful drafting, there is no requirement of reasonableness.

Fourth, the 'problem notice' procedure is tiresome, but will not hinder a careful landlord. The landlord – or, more realistically, his legal advisers – will simply have time limits to observe, and this is already a common feature of the landlord and tenant relationship.[116] Moreover, if the tenant called to account under the AGA chooses to take up the option of an overriding lease, this is unlikely to disturb the landlord. After all, the landlord knows that the tenant under the overriding lease is solvent, as they have just paid the sum demanded.[117]

Fifth, the benefit of a landlord's right of re-entry is automatically annexed to the land, thus giving all assignees of the reversion the opportunity to forfeit the lease if the current tenant defaults (section 4 of the LTCA 1995), or, indeed, if there is any default on a covenant affecting the land irrespective of whether the covenant binds the defaulter.[118]

6.6.4   To sum up

It is tempting to shy away from the law of leasehold covenants because of its complexity. Admittedly, this is understandable when dealing with the law applicable to tenancies granted before 1 January 1996 where the old common law/statutory rules still hold sway and where it is vital to distinguish between different types of covenant and different types of landlord and tenant. However, for leases granted on or after 1 January 1996, the position is relatively simple.

1   All leasehold covenants relating to the demised premises bind assignees of the landlord and tenant (including equitable lessees/assignees) unless expressed to be personal (and excluding the landlord's covenant allowing the tenant to renew). There is no need to worry about 'touching or concerning', privity of estate, or

---

115 By making all assignees covenant directly with the landlord and so become as original tenants.

116 And see *Scottish & Newcastle plc v. Raguz* (2008) for a flexible interpretation of when the time limit for serving a notice commences.

117 However, the landlord should stop to consider whether he wishes to forfeit the lease of the tenant in possession and thereby regain control of the land and its capital value. If he sues the AGA tenant, the landlord takes the risk that this tenant will opt for an overriding lease and himself resume possession and thereby have the opportunity of cashing in on the value of the land by selling it to a new tenant.

118 As section 6.5.5 above and see *Kataria v. Safeland plc* (1997).

sections 141(1) and 142(1) of the LPA 1925. The same is true of the benefit of such covenants.

2   An original tenant is released from liability throughout the term of the lease, but an original landlord must serve a notice requesting such release unless they have the benefit of an *Avonridge* clause.

3   A landlord can require the original tenant to guarantee the next immediate assignee's performance of covenants by means of an AGA (but only the next immediate assignee), and can enforce this liability subject to the problem notice/overriding lease procedure. It is possible to ensure that all assigning tenants come under an obligation to enter an AGA if they assign, thus always giving the landlord a guarantor.

4   The LTCA does not affect significantly the position of subtenants, which continues to be governed by the principles discussed above (see section 6.5.16). Note in particular that restrictive covenants will continue to bind subtenants, subject to registration requirements under the *Tulk v. Moxhay* rules (section 3(5) and (6) of the LTCA 1995).

6.7   The Landlord's Remedies for Breach of Covenant

After having established that a particular landlord has the right to sue on a covenant *and* that the particular defendant tenant is subject to the burden of it, the next matter is to consider the nature of the remedies available to the landlord. These will be considered in turn, although there is no doubt that the remedy of forfeiture is the most important for our purposes.

6.7.1   Distress and Commercial Rent Arrears Recovery

At the current time, landlords are able to use the ancient feudal remedy of distress. However, legislation is in place to abolish this remedy and replace it for commercial leases only with a new scheme – the scheme for Commercial Rent Arrears Recovery (or CRAR). This legislation is not yet in force and it is not clear when this will occur.

The remedy of distress allows a landlord to enter the land of his tenant (any tenant) and seize goods found there in order to sell them for the purpose of paying any arrears of rent. It is a feudal remedy, grounded in self-help, and is available only to a landlord proper, and not a licensor (*Ward v. Day* (1864)). It requires no court proceedings but is subject to many restrictions, both under common law and imposed by statute. For example: distress must be levied between sunrise and sunset; entry must not be forcible (unless the landlord has already gained entry and is forcibly ejected – *Khazanchi v. Faircharm* (1998)); and certain goods are exempt, especially the tenant's 'tools of the trade' and goods in actual use. Likewise, a subtenant's property may not be seized by a head landlord, although an innocent stranger's goods may be seized, subject to the right of the owner to claim their return. Importantly, resort to distress by the landlord is a clear affirmation of the continuation of the landlord and tenant relationship and, therefore, excludes the remedy of forfeiture (which seeks to end that relationship). Action by way of court proceedings to recover arrears of rent also precludes distress.

The Law Commission proposed the abolition of this remedy,[119] not least because of the potential for abuse and the lack of regulation by the courts. On the other hand, landlords' interests groups pointed out that it was useful in difficult situations: for example, when a landlord anticipates a tenant's bankruptcy and acts to seize goods before the tenant becomes insolvent and recovery of rent arrears becomes unlikely. The compromise solution is found in Part 3 of the Tribunals, Courts and Enforcement Act 2007, although this is not yet in force. Under this reform, the remedy of distress will be abolished. However, in respect of leases of commercial premises only, the 2007 Act will introduce a statutory scheme for recovering rent arrears without resort to the courts.[120] This will be the CRAR scheme. As noted, it will apply only to leases of commercial premises (and never to oral leases of any type of premises) and is, in effect, distress in all but name. The procedure is laid down in some detail in Schedule 12 of the 2007 Act and depends on notice being given in accordance with the procedure. As with the current remedy of distress, it will provide an effective remedy for landlords faced with defaulting tenants,[121] especially where the tenants' bankruptcy is anticipated. Like distress, the result will be that the landlord (effectively a bailiff acting as his agent) will be able to enter premises, seize certain goods[122] and sell them in order to satisfy arrears of rent. It is not clear when CRAR will be brought into effect, and so the position at the time of writing is that distress is available for all leases, both commercial and residential.

6.7.2   Action for arrears of rent

The landlord can enforce the covenant to pay rent by bringing an action to recover arrears of rent either in the High Court or county court, depending on the amount owed. By virtue of section 19 of the Limitation Act 1980, a maximum of six years' rent may be recovered in this way. The limitation also applies to guarantors of the tenant's promise to pay rent (*Romain v. Scuba* (1996)). It often happens that one reason why a tenant has not paid rent is a real (or perceived) failure by the landlord to perform his covenants, often the landlord's covenant to repair. Usually, leasehold covenants are not interdependent, so that non-performance by the landlord of his obligations is not an excuse for non-performance by the tenant. For example, the landlord's failure to honour his promise to repair is not usually a lawful reason to withhold rent, and the tenant can be vulnerable to landlord's remedies for non-payment of rent unless the tenant can show that the withheld rent was actually used to pay for repairs for which the landlord was liable, and which fell due after the disrepair occurred. Note, however, if the landlord does bring in an action for recovery of rent, a tenant may claim to 'set off' a sum representing damages for breach of covenant, unless such right is expressly excluded (*Lee-Parker v. Izzet* (1971)). Thus, although the tenant has broken his covenant (and importantly opened himself to other remedies), the result can take account of the context of the claim.[123]

---

119 Law Commission Report No. 194 (1991).

120 For residential leases, the landlord will either have to sue for the rent or forfeit.

121 It remains to be seen whether tenants on whom the notice will be served under CRAR will remove their goods before the bailiffs arrive.

122 The goods may be physically removed or be secured on the premises itself.

123 See also *Smith v. Muscat* (2003), in which set-off against rent for breach of a repairing obligation was permitted when the landlord had assigned his right to sue for the rent to the current claimant.

6.7.3   Action for damages

The landlord may sue for damages for breach of every covenant other than the covenant to pay rent. Except in the case of covenants to repair, the measure of damages will be that necessary to put the landlord in the same position as if the covenant had not been broken. By virtue of the Landlord and Tenant Act 1927, damages for a tenant's breach of a covenant to repair are limited to the amount by which the landlord's interest (the reversion) has diminished in value through the lack of repair, and although this may be the amount necessary to carry out proper repairs (*Jones v. Herxheimer* (1950)), there is a very real likelihood that the amount will be less than this, due to uncertainties about how much the reversion really has declined in value (*Crewe Services and Investment Corp v. Silk* (1997)). Note also that, for leases of seven years or more (with at least three years left to run), the procedure relating to 'notices' set down in the Leasehold Property (Repairs) Act 1938 must be followed before a claim in damages can be made.[124]

6.7.4   Injunction and specific performance

At the discretion of the court, a landlord may obtain an injunction to prevent the breach of a restrictive covenant by the tenant, as where the landlord secures an injunction against the keeping of animals on the land contrary to a leasehold covenant. However, the orthodox view is that a landlord cannot obtain specific performance of the majority of tenants' covenant (an exception is a covenant to build), as this would generate problems about how the court could supervise the tenant in execution of the covenant, as well as raise general issues of equity and fairness. So, in *Co-op Insurance Society v. Argyll Stores* (1997), the House of Lords refused to order specific performance of a tenant's covenant to keep open retail premises for a specified time. Likewise, *Hill v. Barclay* (1811) was thought to be clear authority that a landlord could not obtain specific performance of a tenant's repairing obligation, even though in fact this point was not critical to the decision in the case. Yet, in a novel judgment, Lawrence Collins QC (sitting then as a deputy judge of the High Court) held in *Rainbow Estates v. Tokenhold* (1998) that a landlord could obtain specific performance of a tenant's repairing obligation in special and exceptional circumstances, particularly where the landlord had no other remedy and the court's order could be defined with precision and hence was capable of supervision. It now appears that this has become the new orthodoxy (in the sense that it has not been judicially disapproved), but we might wonder why a landlord who has failed to include a right of re-entry in the lease, or a right to enter and repair and recover the costs from the tenant, should be sent the lifeboat of an order for specific performance. It might be thought that these 'exceptional' circumstances were all of the landlord's own making.

6.7.5   Forfeiture

By far the most powerful weapon in the armoury of the landlord in the event of a breach of covenant is the remedy of forfeiture. In principle, this remedy is available for breaches of all

---

124   This is relevant in cases of forfeiture.

covenants, including the covenant to pay rent, and the effect of a successful forfeiture of the lease is to bring the lease to an end. It is a remedy that can result in the tenant's estate in the land being terminated, even if the loss to the landlord because of the breach is small, and even if the ejection of the tenant will give the landlord a windfall gain (by reacquiring the unencumbered freehold) out of all proportion to that loss. The drastic consequences of a successful forfeiture have always attracted the attention of the courts, and it is not surprising that both the opportunity to forfeit and the effect it has on the tenant are now strictly controlled by statute. In fact, the Law Commission has proposed wholesale reform of the law of forfeiture in its numerous reports on termination of tenancies,[125] and other changes in procedure have occurred as a result of the entry into force of the Commonhold and Leasehold Reform Act 2002.

6.7.5.1   *General considerations*

In general terms, in order for forfeiture to be available at all, the lease must contain a *right of re-entry*. This is a stipulation that the landlord is entitled to re-enter the premises should the tenant fail to observe his covenants. All professionally drafted leases will contain such a right, and one will be implied in all equitable leases (*Shiloh Spinners v. Harding* (1973)). By section 4 of the LTCA 1995, the benefit of the landlord's right of re-entry will pass automatically to assignees of the reversion for a legal or equitable lease. Subject to what will be said below about statutory safeguards, which are particularly strong in the context of long residential leases, the existence of a right of re-entry gives the landlord two potential paths to a successful forfeiture. First, the landlord may physically re-enter the property by obtaining actual possession of it, a typical example being the changing of locks, provided that this demonstrates an unequivocal intention to take possession. So, in *Charville Estates Ltd v. Unipart* (1997), the landlord's entry to carry out works that the tenant had covenanted (but failed) to undertake was not a physical re-entry, and the lease remained alive, permitting the landlord to continue to claim rent and, in *Cromwell v. Godfrey* (1998), there was neither evidence of a manifest intention to forfeit, nor the retaking of possession. Second, and more frequently, a landlord may seek to exercise his right of re-entry through an action for possession brought against the tenant in the courts. At one time, a landlord had a free choice about which path to take, but this is now modified by statute, mainly to protect the tenant from an overzealous landlord. The limitations on forfeiture by physical retaking of possession are noted below.

1   The enforcement of a right of re-entry in a residential lease 'while any person is lawfully residing in the premises' must take place through court action (section 2 of the Protection From Eviction Act 1977). Any attempt physically to re-enter such premises without a court order is without legal effect and will result in criminal liability.

---

125   See, for example, Report No. 142 (1985), Report No. 221 (1994), Report No. 254 (1998), Consultation Paper No. 174 (2004) and the most recent Report No. 303 (2006), *Termination of Tenancies for Tenant Default*. The latest report contains a draft Bill establishing a new scheme for termination of a lease on the grounds of tenant default instead of forfeiture (a 'termination order scheme') and this has a reasonable chance of reaching the statute book in due course.

2   Even if the lease is non-residential (or otherwise outside the scope of section 2 above), it is only *peaceful* physical re-entry that is permitted and effective, and the landlord must avoid committing offences under the Criminal Law Act 1977. The use or threat of violence for the purpose of gaining entry when there is someone on the premises opposed to the entry may be a criminal offence and render the forfeiture ineffective.

3   After the decision in *Billson v. Residential Apartments* (1992), even a lawful physical re-entry may be set aside some time later if the tenant applies for 'relief' from forfeiture.[126]

The net result of these provisions is that physical re-entry is *possible* only when the tenant is holding the premises under a business lease *and* those premises are unoccupied. Further, it may not be *desirable* even then, due to the court's willingness to grant relief from forfeiture after such physical re-entry has occurred.

6.7.5.2   *Forfeiture for non-payment of rent*

Forfeiture of the lease for the tenant's non-payment of rent stands apart from forfeiture for breaches of other covenants, although both physical re-entry and an action for possession are available (where lawful). In all cases, there must be a right of re-entry (forfeiture clause) in the lease, and the landlord must make a formal demand for rent unless the forfeiture clause dispenses with the need for such a demand (most do), or the rent is six months or more in arrears. In addition, however, as a result of the Commonhold and Leasehold Reform Act 2002 (CLRA 2002), certain additional safeguards exist for tenants under long leases of a dwelling.[127] In such cases, not only is a tenant *not* liable to make a payment of rent (and so is not in arrears so as to trigger forfeiture) unless the landlord has given him a notice concerning payment and the date on which it is to be made,[128] but section 167 of the CLRA 2002 also provides that the landlord may not forfeit *at all* unless the amount owed exceeds a statutory prescribed sum (currently £350) or has been unpaid for more than a prescribed period (currently three years).[129] Of course, in most cases, these are not burdensome conditions and the new provisions of the CLRA 2002 in relation to long leases of dwellings are a much overdue measure of tenant protection that will prevent unexpected forfeiture or forfeiture for trivial debts.

Having surmounted these hurdles, the landlord then may proceed to forfeit the lease either by physical re-entry or a possession action in the county court. In either case, however, the general rule applies that the 'law leans against forfeiture'. Thus, in suitable circumstances, a tenant will be granted 'relief from forfeiture' if he pays all of the rent due plus all costs within the appropriate time.[130] In the county court, a tenant has a right to

---

126 See section 6.7.5.3 below.

127 Being a lease of over 21 years (section 76 of the Commonhold and Leasehold Reform Act 2002).

128 Section 166 of the CLRA 2002.

129 These provisions also apply to attempts to forfeit for non-payment of a service charge, a much more likely event in these long leases. Moreover, a landlord may not forfeit for non-payment of a disputed service charge until a Leasehold Valuation Tribunal has determined the amount of the charge – section 81 Housing Act 1996, as amended by the CLRA 2002.

130 The application for relief will be either in the landlord's possession action or by direct application to the court by the tenant.

stop the possession proceedings on the payment of arrears and costs at any time up to five days before the trial (section 138(2) of the County Courts Act 1984). Further, the county court will postpone execution of a possession order for four weeks (or more if warranted), during which time a tenant has an automatic right to relief on payment of outstanding amounts (section 138(3) of the County Courts Act 1984). Obviously, because the tenant in these circumstances has a right to have the proceedings stayed, it is important to know what sums must be paid to secure relief. Clearly, these include all of the landlord's costs and it is now clear, following *Maryland Estates v. Joseph* (1998), that the amount of arrears is calculated up to the date for possession specified in the court order and not the earlier date on which the tenant was served with the summons for possession. This is perfectly consistent with the concept that a lease remains in existence up until such time as it is actually forfeited, being when the landlord has taken possession and all hopes of relief from forfeiture are gone.[131] In the normal course of events, failure to pay by the date specified in the order will bar the tenant from further relief, and the landlord's possession order becomes enforceable, save only that a tenant may apply for *discretionary* relief within six months of the landlord taking possession under the court order (section 138(9A) of the County Courts Act 1984).

If the landlord lawfully re-enters physically (i.e. without a court order), the High Court[132] has a discretionary power to grant relief under its inherent equitable jurisdiction (*Howard v. Fanshawe* (1895)) although only in favour of someone entitled to claim possession of the land by virtue of a legal or equitable proprietary right.[133] The county court also has a discretionary jurisdiction to grant relief in the event of physical re-entry, although it is founded on statute. It exists only if the application for relief is made within six months of the re-entry occurring (section 139(2) of the County Courts Act 1984).

6.7.5.3   *Principles for granting discretionary relief for non-payment of rent*

It will be apparent from the above that there are circumstances in which the tenant may claim relief from forfeiture as of right. Where these circumstances exist, relief must be ordered because, in essence, they cover those cases in which the tenant pays all necessary sums before the landlord recovers possession. However, in those cases in which the right to relief does not arise, there remains the court's discretionary jurisdiction to grant relief

---

131 For example, see *Ivory Gate Ltd v. Spetale* (1998).

132 Forfeiture proceedings for on-payment of rent generally start and finish in the county court. In the event that a matter is transferred to the High Court, a tenant has a statutory right under section 212 of the Common Law Procedure Act 1852 to have the possession proceedings stopped if he pays all of the rent due plus costs before the date of the judgment against him, although this right is available only if at least six months' rent is in arrears. Even if the landlord has obtained and executed a possession order, the tenant may apply for relief if he then pays all arrears and costs, provided that the application is made within six months of the possession order being executed (section 210 of the Common Law Procedure Act 1852) and the premises have not been let to a third party. In those cases in which this statutory relief is not available, the tenant may fall back on the High Court's general equitable jurisdiction to grant relief from forfeiture if the tenant pays all outstanding amounts (*Howard v. Fanshawe* (1895)) and this may be useful where the tenant seeks relief more than six months after the landlord has regained possession (*Thatcher v. CH Pearce* (1968)).

133 *Bland v. Ingram's Estate* (2001).

that it will seek to exercise in the tenant's favour, even in some cases in which the landlord has relet the premises.[134] The underlying rationale for this generosity is the simple point that the purpose of forfeiture in 'rent cases' is to secure the sum owed, and once this has been achieved, forfeiture is no longer appropriate and relief should be granted (Gill v. Lewis (1956)). This means that it will be rare for a tenant offering full payment within the period in which relief can be claimed to be denied that relief, even if they are a persistently late or bad payer, even if the breach was wilful, and even if prospects for payment of future rent appear bleak. However, relief will be granted only if the rent is paid or will be paid, so a claim that related legal action will secure enough funds to pay the rent is not sufficient to trigger relief (Inntrepreneur Pub Co. v. Langton (1999)). On the other hand, it is now clear that this generosity should extend to all covenants aimed at securing a liquidated sum from the tenant. So, in Khar v. Delbounty (1996), the landlord claimed to forfeit for non-payment of quantified service charges and, although this was a 'section 146 case',[135] the court held that the same principles of generosity should apply as would in rent cases and the tenants were granted discretionary relief.

6.7.5.4   Forfeiture for breach of covenants other than to pay rent

In all cases in which the landlord is seeking to forfeit the lease because of breach of covenant, other than a breach of the covenant to pay rent (and 'rent' includes a covenant to pay a service charge if the lease declares that the charge is to be treated as rent, as was not the case in Delbounty), the procedure specified in section 146 of the LPA 1925 must be strictly followed, together with additional procedural safeguards introduced in the case of long leases of dwellings by section 168 of the CLRA 2002. Also, of course, the lease must contain a right of re-entry.

In general terms, a landlord may serve 'a section 146 notice' when he believes a breach of covenant has occurred and there is no doubt that this can concentrate the mind of a tenant on observing the obligations of a lease. Less commendable is the occasional practice of serving section 146 notices to threaten or cajole tenants when there is no real evidence of a breach or of only a trivial or technical breach. One response to this is the provision in section 168 of the CLRA 2002 that a landlord of a long lease of a dwelling[136] may not serve a section 146 notice for breach of covenant unless the tenant has admitted the breach or a period of 14 days has passed since a Leasehold Valuation Tribunal has decided that a breach has occurred. The aim is once again to prevent unexpected or unjustified forfeitures. Assuming then that a section 146 notice is capable of being served lawfully, the notice must:

1   specify the breach of covenant of which complaint is made;
2   request compensation for breach of covenant if desired and also advise the tenant of their rights under the Leasehold Property (Repairs) Act 1938 if appropriate;[137]

---

134   For example, Bank of Ireland Home Mortgages v. South Lodge (1996).

135   See section 6.7.5.4 below.

136   As before, a lease over 21 years.

137   If three or more years of the lease are unexpired, the section 146 notice must alert the tenant to the protection available under this Act. This is to serve a counternotice on the landlord claiming the benefit of the Act and so ensuring that no forfeiture may proceed without a court order.

3   request that the breach of covenant be remedied, if that is possible; and
4   if the forfeiture is in respect of a service charge (not being a charge to be treated
     as rent), the landlord must inform the tenant of the safeguards established by
     section 81 of the Housing Act 1996 and now enhanced by the CLRA 2002.[138]

This procedure is designed to give the tenant every opportunity to remedy the alleged
breach of covenant and to avoid the serious consequences of forfeiture. Indeed, any
attempt to forfeit the lease in violation of these provisions is void (*Billson v. Residential
Apartments* (1992)). After the service of a valid section 146 notice, the landlord may be able
to proceed to forfeit the lease, either by a court action for possession, or by physical
re-entry (if that is available). However, whether the landlord can, in fact, proceed to forfeit,
and how long they must wait before doing so after the service of the notice, depends on
whether the specified breach of covenant is 'capable of remedy'. The section 146 notice
must request that the breach of covenant be remedied if that is possible. If the covenant is
capable of remedy (i.e. it is 'remediable'), then the landlord must give the tenant 'a
reasonable time' (e.g. three months) to effect such remedy, and will not be allowed to
forfeit during this period. Of course, if the tenant then remedies the breach of covenant,
the question of forfeiture no longer arises, although there may be claims for damages for
past breaches. If, however, the covenant is not capable of remedy, then the landlord may
proceed to forfeit relatively quickly, normally after 14 days, again by action or physical
re-entry.[139] Necessarily, it is vital to know whether the covenant is 'capable of remedy', as
this will dictate both the contents of the section 146 notice and the speed with which the
landlord may proceed to forfeit, if at all. The basic test of remediability was put forward in
Expert Clothing Service and Sales Ltd v. Hillgate House Ltd (1986), which in essence recognised that a
covenant was 'capable of remedy' if the *damage* the breach had caused could be rectified.
Thus, breaches of most positive covenants can be remedied (*Expert Clothing*) because
the tenant can do that which they have not done: for example, by carrying out repairs.
Conversely, it is commonly thought that breaches of negative covenants are more likely
to be incapable of remedy, thus permitting early forfeiture. This may well be true in cases
in which the breach is 'once and for all', such that doing the prohibited action is irre-
coverable (an example is breach of a covenant against subletting[140]) and likewise with a
breach that taints the land so that no amount of effort on the part of the tenant can remedy
the stigma.[141] Yet it is not simply the case that breaches of all restrictive covenants should
be regarded as incapable of remedy, for if the breach is 'ongoing and continuous', the
tenant can effect a remedy by ceasing the prohibited activity (*Cooper v. Henderson* (1982)), as
where the tenant remedies breach of a covenant against keeping pets by no longer keeping
them. Moreover, in *Savva and Savva v. Hussein* (1996), the Court of Appeal held that there was
nothing in logic to differentiate between positive and negative covenants in this regard

---

138 As above, that no forfeiture may occur unless the arrears of a disputed service charge have been established by a
     Leasehold Valuation Tribunal and that they exceed the statutory minimum or have been in arrears longer than the
     statutory period.
139 *Scala House and District Property Co Ltd v. Forbes* (1974). *Courtney Lodge v. Andrew Blake* (2004) decided that four working
     days is not sufficient time to respond to a section 146 notice.
140 But see the doubts about such breaches in *Bass Holdings v. Morton Music Ltd* (1988).
141 As where, in breach, a tenant opens a sex shop (*Dunraven Securities v. Holloway* (1982)) or keeps a brothel (*Kelly v. Purvis*
     (1983)).

because the *Expert Clothing* test required that each breach of covenant be taken on its own merits. So, in that case, breach of a covenant against alterations was not, in principle, incapable of remedy.

Having surmounted the hurdle of remediability, the landlord may proceed to forfeit by an action for possession or by physical re-entry. However, the tenant still has the ability to apply for relief from forfeiture, as stipulated in section 146 of the LPA 1925, either in an action for possession by the landlord, or by an independent application to the court. Indeed, one purpose of the section 146 notice procedure is to alert the tenant to the possibility of forfeiture and the opportunity to apply for relief. Relief from forfeiture will be granted if the tenant has performed the covenants, or if the court considers that it would be just and reasonable to allow the lease to survive despite the breaches of covenant (*Shiloh Spinners v. Harding* (1973)). Several matters will be relevant in determining whether relief should be given: for example, the drastic effect that a successful forfeiture has *per se*; the value of the lease when compared with the damage caused by the breach; the seriousness or triviality of the breach; whether the landlord has relet the premises to an innocent third party;[142] whether the breach was wilful, negligent or innocent; and the past performance of the tenant in performing the covenants. Importantly, relief will not be refused just because the tenant breached a negative covenant, or because the breach was itself irremediable, as in *Mount Cook Land v. Hartley* (2000) and *Amana Holdings Ltd v. Fakhir Shatub al-Darraji* (2003), in which tenants were given relief after breaking a covenant against subletting. However, a court is entitled to refuse relief because of the conduct of the tenant or those standing behind it. So, in *Shirayama Shokusan v. Danovo Ltd* (2005), the tenant (D) was refused relief after breaking covenants concerning use of the premises because of its own inequitable conduct and those standing behind it. As the court said, the jurisdiction to grant relief under section 146 was unlimited, but it had to be exercised equitably. Under section 146(4) of the LPA 1925 (and probably the wider section 146(2)[143]), a subtenant or mortgagee[144] of the original tenant may also apply for relief from forfeiture even though the breaches of covenant were committed by the tenant, as in *Bank of Ireland Home Mortgages v. South Lodge* (1996), in which relief was granted to the tenant's mortgagee.

6.7.5.5 *Availability of relief when the landlord proceeds to forfeit by an action for possession*

The position here is effectively governed by section 146 of the LPA 1925, as interpreted by the House of Lords in *Billson v. Residential Apartments* (1992). As that case makes clear, an action for possession will be the normal method by which the landlord attempts to forfeit the lease. A tenant may apply for relief as soon as the landlord serves a section 146 notice and up to the moment at which the landlord actually recovers possession under an order of the court (i.e. the moment when the order is executed). Thus, although the landlord is subject to a claim for relief after the court has granted the order, prompt

---

142   There is a tendency to deny relief in such cases, but see *Delbounty and Bank of Ireland Home Mortgages v. South Lodge* (1996), in which relief was granted with special provision for the innocent third party now in possession.

143   *Escalus Properties v. Robinson* (1995).

144   Including a chargee: *Croydon (Unique) Ltd v. Wright* (1999).

action to enter into possession will defeat relief once and for all (*Rogers v. Rice* (1892)). In most cases, the denial of a right to claim relief under section 146 where forfeiture has been by court proceedings and the landlord has actually recovered possession causes little hardship. It also encourages landlords to use the courts for forfeiture, because the same restriction does not apply to forfeiture by peaceful re-entry (see below). However, there will always be cases in which a tenant will wish to apply after the landlord has executed the possession order, and, indeed, such is quite possible if it is a tenant's mortgagee claiming late relief, having been unaware of the forfeiture proceedings. This potential cause for hardship has generated some discussion as to whether the court's inherent equitable jurisdiction to grant relief has survived the enactment of section 146. The strongest authority is against the survival of such a jurisdiction – *Smith v. Metropolitan City Properties* (1986) – but it has been asserted *obiter* (*Abbey National Building Society v. Maybeech Ltd* (1985)) and academically. Technically, *Billson* leaves the matter open to argument, and although the legislative intention probably was the removal of the inherent jurisdiction in non-rent cases, no doubt a 'hard case' would find a court open to persuasion. In *Bland v. Ingram's Estate* (2001), the court (uncontroversially) noted the existence of an inherent jurisdiction in respect of non-payment of rent but said nothing about such a jurisdiction in non-rent cases.

6.7.5.6   *Availability of relief when forfeiture is by physical re-entry*

Prior to *Billson*, forfeiture by re-entry held some attractions for a landlord in that it was thought that the tenant had lost all rights to apply for relief once the landlord had actually entered the premises. So, for example, a landlord who was forfeiting for breach of an irremediable covenant might serve a section 146 notice and physically re-enter and terminate the lease, all within the space of 14 days. In *Billson*, however, the House of Lords adopted a purposive approach to section 146 and held that a landlord was 'proceeding to forfeit' within that section, so giving the tenant a right to apply for relief, even if he (the landlord) had actually entered on the land. Consequently, a tenant who suffers physical re-entry may apply for relief against a landlord in possession of the property for a 'reasonable time' after that possession has occurred. Necessarily, this will make the possession of a landlord who has physically re-entered somewhat fragile, and liable to be defeated by a claim for relief, although it is unlikely that relief will be granted if the landlord has since transferred the land to an innocent third party. In other words, the decision in *Billson* encourages landlords to forfeit leases by action in the courts, as no relief is available then, when the landlord has finally secured possession under a valid court order.

6.7.5.7   *Waiver*

A landlord attempting to forfeit the lease must ensure that he has not waived the right to forfeit the lease for the tenant's breach of covenant. The essence of the matter is that there will be a waiver of forfeiture if there is any act that amounts to an affirmation of the continuing validity of the lease, as this is inconsistent with forfeiture. In the typical case, waiver will exist where a landlord has knowledge of a prior breach of covenant and then does an act that manifests an intention to regard the lease as still in existence (*Matthews v. Smallwood* (1910)). The most obvious example is where the landlord, or his duly authorised agent, accepts or demands rent after the breach of covenant has occurred, provided that he also knew (or ought to have known) of that breach (*David Blackstone v. Burnetts* (1973)). This principle is applied strictly, as the courts are astute to ensure that the landlord does not gain the double advantage of forfeiture and rent recovery; after all, the purpose of forfeiture in rent cases is the payment of rent, and with such payment, forfeiture abates (*Gill v. Lewis* (1956)). So a 'without prejudice' demand for rent does not preserve forfeiture, and the landlord has the relevant degree of knowledge if he is aware that a breach has occurred, even if he did not know the legal consequences of such a breach. However, it remains true that all cases are decided on their own facts, and, for example, in *Yorkshire Metropolitan Properties v. CRS Ltd* (1997), the landlord's demand for payments towards insurance costs did not amount to a waiver. Similarly, a landlord's express or implied waiver relates only to a particular breach of covenant, and not to any future breaches. Thus a waiver of a breach of a restrictive covenant may be taken as a waiver of only the initial breach and not of any continuing breach.

6.7.5.8   Breaches of repairing covenants

All that has been said so far about forfeiture for breach of covenants other than to pay rent applies in equal measure to breaches of the tenant's covenant to repair, save that the tenant is given additional protection because of the propensity of some landlords to use minor breaches of repairing covenants as a means of ending an otherwise valid lease. Under the Leasehold Property (Repairs) Act 1938, the landlord must serve the section 146 notice in the normal way, but this triggers the tenant's right to serve a 'counternotice' claiming the protection of the 1938 Act. If this counternotice is served, the landlord may not forfeit the lease without the permission of the court, and such permission may be given only if one of the grounds specified in section 1(5) of the 1938 Act is established. The Leasehold Property (Repairs) Act 1938 applies to leases of seven years or more that have at least three years left to run.

6.7.5.9   Reform

There has been pressure for reform of the law of forfeiture for some time.[145] The remedy is seen as disproportionate to the loss to the landlord caused by the breach as well as being capable of misuse in the hands of an unscrupulous landlord who might use the remedy to threaten or cajole an unsuspecting tenant. This is particularly true in those cases in which forfeiture by physical re-entry remains possible. Current statutory controls on forfeiture are effective to meet some of the more serious concerns, but in its 2006 report entitled *Termination of Tenancies for Tenant Default*,[146] the Law Commission make a case for wholesale reform of the law. In essence, the Commission proposes the abolition of forfeiture and its replacement by a statutory scheme. Under the scheme, a tenancy could be terminated for breach of covenant by a tenant only as a result of the landlord pursuing a termination action, to which there would be only limited exceptions. There would be no need for a lease to contain a right of re-entry. A 'termination action' would be either a 'termination

---

145   See for example, Report No. 142 (1985), Report No. 221 (1994), Report No. 254 (1998), Consultation Paper
No. 174 (2004) and the most recent Report No. 303 (2006), *Termination of Tenancies for Tenant Default*.

146   Report No. 303.

claim' or the swifter 'summary termination procedure', but both would depend on the landlord serving a notice on the tenant. The procedures would be mutually exclusive and the landlord would have to decide which method to adopt. Necessarily, the scheme incorporates opportunities for the tenant to remedy any default and to seek what is currently known as relief. The court would have discretion to make such order as it thought appropriate and proportionate, based around a number of specified criteria, and these would include a termination order, an order for sale, an order for a new tenancy or an order transferring the tenancy. Likewise, those persons with derivative interests in the land – for example, subtenants and mortgagees – would also have an opportunity to respond to the landlord's termination action. These proposals have not yet been enacted, but they enjoy widespread support. They appear to offer good protection for the tenant while at the same time preserving a landlord's ability to recover the land in the face of a defaulting and carefree tenant. The law would be improved significantly by their enactment.

6.8   The Tenant's Remedies for Breach of Covenant

The tenant's remedies for breach of covenant by the landlord are less extensive than those of the landlord and are based on the normal contractual remedies available to any person who has suffered loss by reason of a breach of a binding legal obligation. Importantly, breach by the landlord of his covenants does not generally entitle the tenant to ignore their own obligations under the leasehold covenants (the covenants are not interdependent), subject only to the limited right to deduct future rent payments, as noted below.

6.8.1   Damages for breach of covenant

The tenant may sue the landlord for damages at common law for any breach of covenant that causes loss, and the measure of damages is that which puts the tenant in the same position as if the breach had not occurred (*Calabar* v. *Stitcher* (1984)). In the context of damages for breach of the landlord's repairing obligations, this means the tenant should be compensated for the loss of comfort and convenience that they would have enjoyed had the repairs been undertaken. This can sometimes be reflected in a reduction in rent, having regard to the diminution in the value of the tenancy (*Wallace* v. *Manchester CC* (1998)).

6.8.2   Action for an injunction

The tenant may sue for an injunction to stop a continuing or threatened breach of covenant by the landlord. As with all equitable remedies, this lies at the discretion of the court.

6.8.3   Action for specific performance

It is clear that the tenant may claim specific performance of a landlord's covenant where this is consistent with the supervisory jurisdiction of the court. Such an order has been granted to enforce performance of a landlord's repairing covenant (*Jeune v. Queens Cross Properties* (1974)) and particular covenants such as the landlord's covenant to employ a resident porter (*Posner v. Scott-Lewis* (1986)). Under section 17 of the Landlord and Tenant Act 1985, there is a statutory jurisdiction to order specific performance of a landlord's repairing covenant in respect of a dwelling house. This position should be contrasted with that of the landlord where, until recently, a landlord was denied the reciprocal right specifically to enforce the tenant's repairing obligations.

6.8.4   Retention of future rent

Following *Lee-Parker v. Izzet* (1971), if the landlord is in breach of a covenant to repair, the tenant may carry out the necessary repairs and deduct the cost thereof from *future* payments of rent. However, the tenant must be careful not to withhold rent already due, as this will trigger liability to the landlord and perhaps the remedy of forfeiture. In a similar vein, if the landlord is in breach of a repairing covenant, and the tenant therefore refuses to pay rent, the tenant may 'set off' any damages they would have received for the landlord's breach if the landlord should bring an action for arrears of rent. It is only in these two limited circumstances that performance of the tenant's covenants (i.e. to pay the full rent) are modified in the face of a breach of covenant by the landlord.

6.9   Termination of Leases

There are several ways by which the landlord and tenant relationship may come to an end. When it does, possession of the land reverts to the freeholder or other person (e.g. headlessee) entitled on expiry of the term.

6.9.1   By effluxion of time

The most obvious way in which a lease will end is when the contractual term has expired. However, some leases may give the tenant the right to extend the lease at the end of the initial period and, of course, this must be honoured. Likewise, the tenant may be able to claim a statutory extension of the tenancy under the Landlord and Tenant Act 1954 (business tenancies), Agricultural Holdings Act 1986, the Rent Act 1977 or the early Housing Acts (residential tenancies).

6.9.2   By forfeiture

This is considered above where it is made clear that a successful forfeiture by the landlord necessarily terminates the lease early.

6.9.3   By notice

Leases sometimes give either or both the landlord and tenant the right to terminate the lease before the end of the contractual period by giving 'notice' to the other party. These 'break clauses' are common in long leases and are intrinsic in periodic tenancies. Importantly, if a *periodic tenancy* is held by two persons as joint tenants, the notice of only one of them is required to terminate the tenancy, irrespective of the other's wishes

(*Hammersmith and Fulham LBC v. Monk* (1992)) and the giving of such notice is not a 'function relating to land' within section 11 of TOLATA 1996 so as to require any tenant who is also a trustee to consult any beneficiary before giving notice (*Brackley v. Notting Hill Housing Trust* (2001)).[147] Although this may seem startling, we should remember that a periodic tenancy is in reality a succession of individual tenancies and each new period is in reality a new tenant. Thus any one of the joint tenants can refuse a new tenancy and so break the chain. In addition, the essence of a periodic tenancy is that it is implied from the circumstances surrounding the occupation. Thus, in the case of a periodic tenancy, the continued occupation of the remaining tenant and acceptance of rent by the landlord will generate a new periodic tenancy with a sole tenant only (*Burton v. Camden LBC* (1997)). Critically, however, where there is a fixed-term lease (i.e. not a periodic tenancy) containing a break clause, all joint tenants must concur in exercising the break clause for it to be effective.[148]

A notice to quit given by a tenant will automatically terminate any subtenancies that that tenant may have carved out of their own interest – *Pennell v. Payne* (1995) – even if the lease appears to stipulate otherwise because this is the proprietary essence of the leasehold estate.[149] However, subtenancies will survive if the head tenancy is terminated by a consensual surrender between landlord and tenant, for a subtenant is not party to this bilateral arrangement (*Barrett v. Morgan* (2000)).

6.9.4   By merger

The tenant may acquire his landlord's interest in the land and thereby 'merge' the lease and reversion, as in *Ivory Gate v. Spetale* (1998).

6.9.5   By surrender

The tenant may surrender his lease to his landlord, and, if accepted, this will terminate the lease. Surrender may be either expressed or implied by operation of law, this being an example of estoppel (*Mattey v. Ervin* (1998)), but in either case, there must be an intention to terminate the lease (*Charville Estates Ltd v. Unipart* (1997)). As noted above, a surrender, being a consensual act between landlord and tenant, will not thereby determine any subtenancies.

6.9.6   By enlargement

Under section 153 of the LPA 1925, a tenant of a lease of more than 300 years, of which at least 200 years are left to run, has a right, in some circumstances, to enlarge their leasehold interest into the freehold.

---

147   Moreover, the Court of Appeal has decided that the giving of notice by just one tenant under a periodic tenancy (so as to terminate it for both) is not a breach of the other tenant's human rights under the ECHR: *Wandsworth LBC v. Dixon* (2009). That is, that *Hammersmith and Fulham LBC v. Monk* (1992) is not invalidated by human rights considerations, even though the tenant not giving notice is deprived of their home (and property) without any opportunity for consideration of their position. There is a respectable body of opinion that argues that *Monk* would not survive a human rights challenge if the matter were to go to the Supreme Court: see [2010] Conv 57 and note *McCann v. UK* (2008) in the ECHR.

148   *Crawley LBC v. Ure* (1996).

149   *PW v. Milton Gate Investments*. Note that this is entirely at odds with the philosophy of *Bruton v. London & Quadrant* (1999).

6.9.7 By disclaimer

A lease may come to an end because the tenant denies the landlord's superior title to the land, and thereby disclaims the lease.

6.9.8 By frustration

Since the decision in *National Carriers Ltd* v. *Panalpina* (1981), it has been accepted that the normal law of frustration of contract applies to leases. Thus, a fundamental change of circumstance after the commencement of the lease may so alter the rights and obligations of the parties that the original lease (contract) between them in no sense represents their original bargain and is frustrated.

6.9.9 By repudiatory breach of contract

Somewhat illogically, although leases could be frustrated, the availability of the other great contractual remedy of repudiation of the lease, because of a fundamental breach of covenant (contract) by the other party, was once not readily accepted in English law. However, in *Hussein* v. *Mehlman* (1992), the High Court took the first steps to recognise this remedy, on the ground that there is no reason in principle why leases should be regarded as different from other types of contract; the availability of repudiatory principles was confirmed in *Chartered Trust* v. *Davies* (1997). This may well prove a valuable 'remedy' for a tenant as it could provide a method by which a tenant can 'terminate' a lease because of a landlord's refusal to perform critical leasehold covenants. As will be apparent from the above, no such right exists under the 'pure' law of landlord and tenant as there is *no* tenant's right of forfeiture. So it is that contract law may come to a tenant's aid.

6.10 Chapter Summary

6.10.1 The nature of a lease

The leasehold allows two or more persons to enjoy the benefits of owning an estate in the land at the same time. Both landlord and tenant retain a proprietary right in the land and both of these proprietary rights can be sold or transferred after the lease has been created. All leases will contain covenants (or promises) whereby the landlord and tenant promise to do – or not to do – certain things in relation to the land. These rights and obligations may 'run' with the land on a transfer of the lease or of the landlord's 'reversion'. The essential qualities of a lease are that (a) it gives a person the right of exclusive possession of land (b) for a certain term (c) at a rent (*Street* v. *Mountford* (1985)), although the last of these is not strictly necessary as a matter of law. Leases may be legal or equitable.

6.10.2 The creation of legal and equitable leases

As a general rule, legal leases must be created by deed. Currently, leases for over seven years, even if created by deed, will not take effect as a legal estate until registered with their own title number. Leases for three years or less that take effect immediately in possession where the tenant does not pay an initial capital sum will be legal, however created (orally, in writing or by deed). Most periodic tenancies are legal leases under this exception.

As a general rule, equitable leases must derive from a written contract (or written document equivalent to a contract). This written agreement will create an equitable lease if it is specifically enforceable (as most are). As an exception, an equitable lease can be generated purely orally via the principles of proprietary estoppel.

6.10.3   Leases in registered and unregistered land

Currently, in registered land, the majority of legal leases for seven years or less are overriding interests (paragraph 1 of Schedules 1 and 3 of the LRA 2002) and legal leases created for more than seven years are registrable as titles in their own right. (If they are not so registered, they will take effect as equitable leases only.)

Equitable leases can be registered as a protected interest by notice, although most equitable leases will be overriding interests and automatically binding against a subsequent purchaser because the equitable tenant will be a person in 'actual occupation' of the land, within paragraph 2 of Schedules 1 and 3 of the LRA 2002.

In unregistered land, a legal lease will bind automatically any subsequent purchaser or transferee of the estate out of which it is created. An equitable lease arising from an enforceable written agreement is registrable as a Class C(iv) land charge (and void against a purchaser if not so registered). Estoppel equitable leases probably bind a subsequent transferee of the freehold land through the doctrine of notice. For registered land, rules concerning electronic conveyancing may mean that certain types of lease do not exist at all until registered.

6.10.4   The differences between legal and equitable leases

Legal and equitable leases are created in different ways. Equitable leases are potentially very vulnerable to a sale of the freehold or leasehold estate out of which they are created. For leases granted before 1 January 1996, leasehold covenants will 'run' with the land in a legal lease more easily than in an equitable one. For leases granted on or after 1 January 1996, leasehold covenants will 'run' in legal and equitable leases identically, thanks to the LTCA 1995. Easements may be created by section 62 of the LPA 1925 on the occasion of a grant of a legal lease only. The equitable tenant is a purchaser of an *equitable* estate in the land and therefore cannot be a purchaser of a legal estate so as to avoid being bound by those equitable rights in unregistered land that still depend on the doctrine of notice. Neither could an equitable tenant in unregistered land avoid being bound by an unregistered Class C(iv) or Class D land charge, both of which are void only against a purchaser of a legal estate.

6.10.5   Leasehold covenants in leases granted before
            1 January 1996

In any action on a leasehold covenant between the original landlord and the original tenant, *all* covenants are enforceable: liability of these original parties is based in *contract*. Both original parties will remain liable on the leasehold covenants throughout the entire term of the lease, even after they have assigned their interests. The liability is to any person having the right to enforce the covenant. The position of an assignee of the lease (i.e. the tenant's interest) depends on whether 'privity of estate' exists between the landlord and tenant so as to allow enforcement of those covenants that 'touch and concern' the land. The position of an assignee of the reversion is governed by the application of sections 141 and 142 of the LPA 1925. 'Privity of estate' does not exist in respect of assignees of an equitable lease (although the original parties remain bound in contract). Consequently, although the benefits and burdens of leasehold covenants will be passed to the assignee of the reversion in an equitable lease (because sections 141 and 142 of the LPA 1925 still apply), the benefits and burdens will not pass automatically to an assignee of the tenant.

6.10.5.1   *Note 1*

An assignee of an equitable lease may obtain the benefit (but not the burden) of the covenants by express assignment, but the lack of privity of estate means that the burdens cannot run.

6.10.5.2   *Note 2*

There may be indirect enforcement of the burdens of leasehold covenants against an equitable assignee: for example, by use of the landlord's right of re-entry and the rules relating to restrictive covenants.

6.10.5.3   *Note 3*

Subtenants do not stand in privity of estate with the head landlord, so are treated vis-à-vis that landlord in the same manner as equitable tenants. A subtenant is in privity with his or her own immediate landlord.

6.10.6   Leasehold covenants in leases granted on or after 1 January 1996: The Landlord and Tenant (Covenants) Act 1995

The LTCA 1995 applies to all leases granted on or after 1 January 1996 whether legal or equitable. The original tenant is released from liability under leasehold covenants on assignment, subject only to the possibility of guaranteeing the next immediate tenant's performance of the covenants under an authorised guarantee agreement (AGA). The original landlord is not automatically released on assignment, but may apply to the court for such release or may rely on an *Avonridge* clause. The rule that covenants must 'touch and concern' the land in order to run to new landlords and tenants is abolished. *All* covenants will run unless they 'are expressed to be personal'. By statute, the benefit and burdens of leasehold covenants pass automatically to assignees of the landlord and the tenant without the need to show privity of estate or to rely on sections 141 and 142 of the LPA 1925. A tenant is liable on the leasehold covenants only while in possession of the land, subject only to the possibility that he may be required to guarantee performance of the covenants by the next immediate assignee under an AGA. The rules concerning the imposition of AGAs are very favourable to landlords, particularly landlords of commercial premises.

6.10.6.1   *Note*

The provisions of the LTCA 1995 relating to 'problem notices' to enforce liability against a tenant not in possession (e.g. under an AGA) apply to leases granted before 1 January 1996. Hence, the procedure is applicable to the enforcement of original tenant liability in pre-1996 leases. The same is true of the provisions relating to overriding leases.

6.10.7   The landlord's remedies for breach of covenant

Distress allows a landlord to enter the land and seize goods found there in order to sell them to pay rent arrears. This feudal remedy may be replaced by the Commercial Rent Arrears Recovery (CRAR) scheme in respect of most commercial leases. CRAR would allow a landlord of commercial premises to achieve the same result as distress currently allows, but subject to regulation (although no court order would be required). CRAR is not yet in force and distress remains available for both commercial and residential leases.

The landlord can enforce the covenant to pay rent by bringing an action to recover arrears of rent either in the High Court or county court, depending on the amount owed.

The landlord may sue for damages for breach of every covenant other than the covenant to pay rent.

At the discretion of the court, a landlord may obtain an injunction to prevent the breach of a restrictive (negative) covenant by the tenant. It may now be possible to get specific performance of a tenant's repairing obligation.

The most powerful weapon in the armoury of the landlord in the event of a breach of covenant is the remedy of forfeiture. The lease must contain a right of re-entry. Re-entry may be by peaceful physical re-entry or through court action, although the former is not possible in all cases. Forfeiture for non-payment of rent depends on the landlord making a formal demand for rent and the court not being prepared to grant the tenant relief from forfeiture under its various inherent and statutory jurisdictions. The matter has been further regulated by the CLRA 2002 in respect of leases of dwellings for over 21 years. Forfeiture of the lease because of a breach of any other covenant is governed by section 146 of the LPA 1925, with additional procedural changes made by CLRA 2002. After the service of a 'section 146 notice', the landlord may be able to proceed to forfeit the lease, either by physical re-entry or by a court action for possession. The tenant may apply for relief from forfeiture, as stipulated in section 146 of the LPA 1925, whether the re-entry is by court order or by physical re-entry. Also, a landlord attempting to forfeit the lease must ensure that they have not waived the breach, so losing the right to forfeit for that particular breach.

6.10.8   The tenant's remedies for breach of covenant

The tenant's remedies for breach of covenant are: to sue the landlord for damages at common law; to sue for an injunction to stop a continuing or threatened breach of covenant by the landlord; to sue for specific performance of the landlord's covenants, particularly the landlord's covenant to repair; or to deduct the cost of carrying out the landlord's repairs from future payments of rent. The law of contract may also provide remedies in 'frustration' or repudiatory breach.

6.10.9 Termination of leases

The landlord and tenant relationship may come to an end in several ways: by effluxion of time (the term ends); by forfeiture; by serving notice if the lease contains a break clause; by merger with the superior estate out of which it is carved; by surrender to the landlord; by enlargement into the superior estate; by disclaimer; by frustration; or by repudiatory breach of contract.

 ## Further Reading

Bridge, S, 'Former tenants, future liabilities and the privity of contract principle: The Landlord and Tenant (Covenants) Act 1995' [1996] 55 CLJ 313

Bridge, S, 'Landlord and tenant law', in Tee, L (ed.) *Essays in Land Law*, Devon: Willan, 2002

Bridge, S, 'Putting it right: The Law Commission and the condition of tenanted property' [1996] Conv 342

Dixon, M, 'The rise of the feudal phoenix' [2000] CLJ 22

Hill, J, 'Intention and the creation of proprietary rights: Are leases different?' (1996) 16 LS 200

Smith, PF, '*Billson v Residential Apartments Ltd*' [1992] Conv 273

Sparkes, P, '*Prudential Assurance Co Ltd v London Residuary Body*' (1993) 108 LQR 93

Thornton, R, 'Enforceability of leasehold covenants: More questions than answers' (1991) 11 LS 47

Walter, P, 'The Landlord and Tenant (Covenants) Act 1995: A legislative folly' [1996] Conv 432

Chapter 7
The Law of Easements and Profits

7.1   The Nature of Easements as Interests in Land

Easements are incorporeal hereditaments. They comprise limited certain rights that one landowner may enjoy over the land of a near neighbour. Common examples are the right of way and the right of light, but easements are not limited to these two ancient rights. The right to use a neighbour's land in connection with the movement of aircraft,[1] the right to park on land[2] and cross it with shopping trolleys,[3] and the right to the enjoyment of lighting and exit signs[4] are more recent examples. As we shall see, the 'definition' of an easement cannot be expressed in simple terms – it is a recipe of many ingredients – but, at the outset, it is vital to realise that every easement will involve two separate pieces of land.[5]

First, an easement confers a benefit on the *dominant tenement* (i.e. benefited land) enabling the owner for the time being of that land to use the easement: for example, to walk across a neighbour's land, or to receive light or to use a drainage channel. Second, an easement places a burden on the *servient tenement* (i.e. burdened land), requiring the owner for the time being of that land to suffer the exercise of the easement: for example, to allow a neighbour to walk across it, or not to interfere with the passage of light to a neighbour or to permit the drainage of water.[6] Moreover, as implied by the above analysis, the easement once created confers a benefit and burden *on the land itself*, so that in principle it may be enjoyed or suffered by any *subsequent* owner of the dominant or servient land. In other words, the easement is not merely personal to the persons who originally created it. It is a proprietary interest in land, so that (subject to the rules of registered and unregistered conveyancing) the benefit of it passes with a transfer of the dominant tenement and the burden of it passes with a transfer of the servient tenement.

---

1   *Dowty Bolton Paul Ltd* v. *Wolverhampton Corp* (No. 2) (1976).

2   *Moncrieff* v. *Jamieson* (2007). This may be in a single space: *Virdi* v. *Chana* (2008).

3   *London and Blenheim Estates Ltd* v. *Ladbroke Retail Parks Ltd* (1992).

4   *Bratt's Ltd* v. *Habboush* (1999).

5   This is different from profits, which do not require dominant land, although such land may exist (see e.g. *Polo Woods* v. *Shelton-Agar* (2009)). A profit à prendre is a right to take something from another's land, such as wood, pasture, turf or fish: see section 7.13 below.

6   Generally, however, an easement does not require the owner of the burdened land to expend money in order that the easement may be exercised. Thus, the servient owner need not pay the cost of the upkeep of a right of way or drainage channel or take other positive steps to facilitate the easement: *William Old International* v. *Arya* (2009). However, the owner of the dominant land is usually permitted to enter the servient land and maintain the easement and may well be under a positive obligation to pay for its upkeep as a condition of exercising it: *Changeinvest Ltd* v. *Rosendale-Steinhusen* (2004).

7.2   The Essential Characteristics of an Easement

The essentially proprietary nature of an easement, which allows its benefit and burden to be passed to whomsoever comes to own an estate in the land, means that care must be taken in defining the types of right that may be recognised as an 'easement'. For example, if too many rights, or rights that are vague and uncertain, can amount to easements, the owner of the servient tenement might find the use and enjoyment of his own land seriously disrupted. Conversely, if the law recognises too few easements, or is stagnant in the face of economic and social change, it would be impossible for the owners of dominant tenements to safeguard the value and amenity of their property.[7] A balance has to be struck. The law of easements must accommodate the needs of the dominant tenement, while at the same time ensuring that the servient tenement does not become overburdened and inalienable, all in the context of a modern society. For this reason, there are established criteria for determining whether an alleged right is capable of amounting to an easement, although it is also clear that these encompass a certain amount of judicial discretion. These four 'essential characteristics' of an easement are taken from the judgment of Evershed MR in Re Ellenborough Park (1956),[8] itself an adoption of the criteria put forward by Cheshire in Modern Real Property (7th edition). They represent the distillation of much case law, but they are not to be treated as if they were a statute. In addition, it must be appreciated that if these criteria are satisfied, it means that the claimed right is *capable* of being an easement. Satisfaction of the criteria is not enough to ensure that an easement actually exists. As well as being inherently 'easement-like', the right must be created *as an easement* using the proper formalities applicable to proprietary rights.[9] Failure to use the appropriate formalities means that the potential easement will not exist and will take effect only as a personal licence.

7.2.1   There must be a dominant and a servient tenement

The first of the traditional conditions for the existence of an easement is that there *must* be a dominant and a servient tenement. This criterion lies at the very heart of the nature of an easement. Easements are rights that exist for the benefit of one piece of land and are exercised over another. This means that there must be land that is benefited (the dominant tenement), and land that is burdened (the servient tenement). In technical terms, the easement cannot exist 'in gross'[10] and both the dominant and servient land must be identifiable at the time the easement is created. The creation of easements for the benefit of

---

7 There is an element of public policy in regard to the granting of easements: see *Smith v. Muller* (2008), in which it was held that an easement must have been contemplated, otherwise the claimant's land would have been inalienable.

8 The claimed easement, which was held to exist, was the right to use a private garden for the benefit of certain surrounding houses.

9 Generally, for legal easements, this means a deed (plus registration in some cases), or long use through prescription. For equitable easements, it means an enforceable written instrument or a claim of proprietary estoppel.

10 *Hawkins v. Rutter* (1892). As noted, this differs from *profits à prendre*, which, while always being a burden on some land, may be enjoyed by a person who owns no land himself: see section 7.13 below.

land not yet identified is not possible.[11] Although there are some statutory exceptions to this rule, as where utility companies are given easement-like rights over land despite not owning any land of their own,[12] the need for a dominant and servient tenement limits both the impact of easements on the servient land – so that not everybody is able to enjoy rights over the servient land, just the owner of the dominant tenement[13] – and confines the ambit of easements to those rights that truly benefit other land, as opposed to merely benefiting a particular person.[14]

7.2.2   The separation of the dominant and servient tenement

The second condition is that the creation and continued existence of an easement is dependent on the dominant and servient tenements being owned or occupied by different persons. An easement is essentially a right in another's land: for example, to walk over it, or to enjoy the passage of light or right of drainage across it. For that reason, the dominant and servient tenements must not be both owned and occupied by the same person.[15] Moreover, should the dominant and servient tenements come into the ownership and possession of the same person, any easement over the servient land will thereby be extinguished: a person cannot have an easement against themselves. Note, however, that there is nothing to stop a tenant enjoying an easement over land retained by the landlord, and vice versa, because in that situation the land is not owned and occupied by the same person.[16] In the landlord and tenant situation, each party owns an estate in the land to which the benefit and burden of the easement attach and so the proprietary status of the easement is assured. However, should the occupier be only a licensee,[17] no easement can be created between that person and the licensor, since a licensee owns no estate in the land.[18] Finally, if the dominant and servient tenements come into the same occupation, but not also the same ownership (as where the freehold owner of the servient tenement takes a lease of the neighbouring dominant tenement in order to enlarge his premises), the easement is suspended for the duration of the common occupation and may be revived thereafter.[19]

---

11 *London and Blenheim Estates Ltd v. Ladbroke Retail Parks Ltd* (1992).

12 For example, to run water pipes or electricity cables under a person's land, although such companies prefer to obtain the owner's consent: see e.g. *William Old International v. Arya* (2009).

13 And, of course, his agents and *bona fide* guests.

14 In this regard, note *Wall v. Collins* (2007). In that case, an easement was granted for a leasehold estate and the leaseholder subsequently acquired the freehold. The servient landowner alleged that because the leasehold had become extinguished (it had merged with the freehold), therefore the easement had been extinguished because the dominant estate to which it was attached had ceased to exist. The Court of Appeal wished to avoid this unpalatable result and decided that it was enough if there was a dominant tenement now benefiting from the easement, rather than the original dominant tenement.

15 *Roe v. Siddons* (1888).

16 *Wright v. Macadam* (1949); *Bratt's Ltd v. Habboush* (1999).

17 See Chapter 6 for 'occupation licences'.

18 A 'Bruton tenant' (see Chapter 6) has no estate and so any rights that this occupier might enjoy over the land of their 'landlord' (who may also have no estate – as in *Bruton v. London & Quadrant* (1999) itself) can only be licences effective in contract between the parties.

19 *Canham v. Fisk* (1831).

The alleged easement must accommodate (benefit) the dominant tenement

The third requirement attempts to limit 'easements' to those substantive rights that affect land *as such*. Thus the alleged easement must 'accommodate' (i.e. confer a benefit on) the dominant tenement. This is an important requirement because it circumscribes easements to those rights that attach *to land* and not 'merely' to that person who currently owns or occupies the land. The general idea is that the easement must benefit the user of the land, the value of the land or the mode of occupation of the land (like the idea of 'touch and concern' in restrictive covenants), but there are no set criteria for judging whether an alleged easement is sufficiently proprietary in nature and each case must be decided on its own facts. The following guidelines give a flavour of what is required, but they may wilt in the face of peculiar or special facts.

1   The servient tenement must be sufficiently proximate (i.e. near) to the dominant tenement to be able to confer a benefit on it.[20] For example, only in unusual circumstances can an alleged right of light over land that does not border the alleged dominant tenement actually be said to 'benefit' that tenement. Of course, the two tenements need not be adjacent, or share a common boundary to satisfy this requirement, but in general, the more physically separate the two properties, the less likely it is that a court would regard an alleged easement over one as benefiting the other. For example, it would be difficult to establish a right of way over Blackacre in favour of Whiteacre when the two plots are at opposite ends of the village.

2   The alleged right must not confer a purely personal advantage on the owner of the dominant tenement. This is a necessary but sometimes elusive criterion because, in a very general sense, a benefit to 'the land' necessarily benefits the person currently occupying it. Nevertheless, it is firmly fixed in the case law. For example, in *Hill v. Tupper* (1863), the owner of a canal granted the claimant the right to put pleasure boats on the canal for profit, but this was held to be a personal advantage, not a right attaching to the claimant's land. The right was not sufficiently connected with the claimant's land so as to amount to an easement as he would have benefited from the right whatever land he had owned, or even if he had no land at all. There was no sense in which this particular right conferred a proprietary benefit on the claimant's particular piece of land; there was no connection between the alleged easement and the dominant tenement. However, it is a mistake to think that rights cannot be easements simply because they confer a commercial or business advantage on the alleged dominant tenement. It is not the commercial nature of the right granted that is important, but whether the commercial advantage endures as an aspect of the benefited estate or, in contrast, whether it is given to a person irrespective of whether he owns an estate in the land. So, in *Moody v. Steggles* (1879), it was accepted that there could be an easement to hang a sign advertising a pub on neighbouring land because this benefited a trade or occupation taking place on the dominant tenement as such. Likewise, in *London and Blenheim Estates Ltd v. Ladbroke Retail Parks Ltd* (1992), it was accepted that a right to park on adjoining land and to walk across it with shopping

---

20 *Bailey v. Stevens* (1862).

trolleys was capable of existing as an easement for the benefit of the dominant tenement on which there was a supermarket, and in *Platt v. Crouch* (2003), the right to moor boats at a riverbank was capable of subsisting as an easement for the benefit of a hotel on the dominant land. In both of these cases, there was a connection between the substance of the right claimed and the alleged dominant land: the right was for that land. Indeed, if it were true that easements could not accommodate a commercial activity on the dominant land, then much of their usefulness would dissipate. Consequently, the issue is not whether a commercial use is being facilitated by the easement, but whether the alleged easement is so connected with the land that the 'benefit' accrues to the current owner *because* he owns an estate in the land.

3   It is unlikely that a right that confers a purely 'recreational use' on the dominant tenement will be accepted as an easement. For example, a right to wander over open countryside or parkland is unlikely to be accepted as an easement. Given that the law of easements exists to enhance the social and economic value of land, by giving benefits and imposing burdens on the land as such, it is not to be used for the provision of public amenities. However, the point to remember is that only a *pure and undefined* recreational use is suspect. So, in *Re Ellenborough Park* (1956) itself, a defined right to enjoy an enclosed private park was capable of existing as an easement because the park was created for the very purpose of enhancing the utility of the few private houses that had access to it. The law of easements can accommodate recreational use that confers a benefit in clear and defined circumstances, especially if it enhances the value of the dominant land, but it cannot be used to provide benefits for the public at large, or for ill-defined recreational uses. Once again, however, it must be a defined use that benefits the dominant tenement as such rather than satisfying the personal tastes of the owner at the time the 'easement' was created.

4   In order for an alleged easement to 'accommodate' the dominant tenement, it does not have to be 'needed' by the dominant tenant. The claimant does not have to prove that the alleged right is beneficial in the sense of conferring a distinct advantage that the land would not otherwise enjoy. It is enough if the alleged right has a sufficient connection with the dominant land and enhances its utility even though the dominant owner had other means of achieving the same advantage. This emerges from *Polo Woods v. Shelton-Agar* (2009), and although, strictly speaking, this analysis is made in the context of *profits à prendre* (rather than easements),[21] the same test of 'accommodate' applies to both types of incorporeal right.

7.2.4   The alleged easement must 'be capable of forming the subject matter of a grant'

The fourth condition identified in *Re Ellenborough Park* (1956) is that the alleged easement must be *capable* of forming the subject matter of a grant. This is an all-embracing criterion and one over which the court enjoys considerable discretion in deciding whether any right

---

21 An alleged profit of pasturage that the alleged dominant tenement did not actually need but which still 'accommodated' that land.

is capable of being an easement. Technically, the point is that every easement must be *capable* of being expressly conveyed by deed (even if it is created in some other way) and so must 'lie in grant'. The creation of rights by deed – by grant – was once a laboured process where every particular had to be described with clarity and certainty. After the Law of Property Act 1925, this is no longer true of deeds in practice, but the criterion remains that to be an easement, a right has to meet the standard of clarity and certainty such that it could have been 'granted'. Today, this criterion has generated a number of subrules, and while previous case law is of considerable help in identifying 'easement-type' rights, there is no doubt that the principles are flexible and there is much room for judicial inventiveness. The following points arise from the case law.

1   *An easement cannot exist unless there is a capable grantor*: that is, somebody legally competent to create an easement (being the person in possession of an estate in the intended servient tenement). For example, no easement can exist where the purported grantor is a limited company having no power to grant easements under its articles of association.

2   *An easement cannot exist unless there is a capable grantee*: that is, somebody in whose favour an easement may be legally granted (being the person in possession of an estate in the intended dominant tenement).

3   *All rights that are capable of forming the subject matter of a grant must be sufficiently certain*, and this applies just as much to alleged easements as to other types of proprietary right. In the case of an easement, the right must be capable of clear description and precise definition, principally so that the servient owner (and any purchaser from him) may know the extent of the obligation. For example, in *Re Aldred* (1610), a right to 'a good view' could not exist as an easement, as 'a good view' was simply too indefinite to exist as a property right. Similarly, there is no easement of privacy[22] and no easement to receive light generally as opposed to a right to receive light through a defined window. Given the proprietary status of easements – that is, that they may endure through changes in ownership of both the dominant and servient tenements – this requirement of exactness is no surprise. Easements affect land both as a benefit and a burden, and so it is vital to ensure that the scope of the right granted and the burden of the obligation imposed is clear and unambiguous.

4   For a right to be capable of being an easement, it must be within the general nature of rights recognised as easements and this encompasses a reluctance to accept positive or burdensome obligations. Although 'the general nature' of an easement is not cast in stone and may change over time as the use and occupation of land changes, it remains true that certain types of obligation cannot qualify as easements because they impose too heavy a burden on the servient landowner. For example, it is unlikely that a court will recognise new easements that require the servient tenement owner to spend money because such a positive obligation is not generally consistent with the limited nature of easements.[23] Easements are designed to allow the owner for the time being of the dominant tenement to gain an advantage from the servient

---

22 *Browne v. Flower* (1911).

23 *Phipps v. Pears* (1965), no easement of weatherproofing as servient owner would have to have maintained the buildings providing the weatherproofing.

land, rather than imposing positive obligations on the servient tenement owner.[24] Thus, in *William Old International v. Arya* (2009), the judge held expressly that easements generally could not impose a positive obligation on the servient owner to do something, but rather operated negatively to prevent the servient owner from interfering with a permitted use.[25] Such exceptions as existed were confined to limited and special circumstances. One recognised exception is the 'easement of fencing', whereby the servient tenement owner is required to maintain a boundary fence.[26] That said, there are some cases in which the court has come close to recognising other forms of 'positive' easement that require expenditure and action on the part of the servient owner. So, in *Cardwell v. Walker* (2003), Neuberger J appears to accept that a servient owner can be under an obligation to provide electricity to the dominant land from a private supply,[27] although this does not establish a general easement concerning the supply of electricity (*William Old International v. Arya* (2009)) and is justified by the special conveyancing history of the land in that case.

5   For a right to be capable of being an easement, it must be within the general nature of rights recognised as easements and this encompasses a reluctance to accept undue restrictions on the servient land. In a similar vein to the general disapproval of positive obligations, a court will only reluctantly allow an easement that gives the dominant tenement owner a right to prevent the servient tenement owner from doing something on their own land (*Phipps v. Pears* (1965)), as opposed to allowing the dominant owner also to do something. Any other view would affect the future use and enjoyment of the servient tenement in an unwarranted manner and such obligations fall more properly within the realm of restrictive covenants than of easements where they are subject to tighter controls. However, some traditional easements clearly do have a restrictive effect, as where the easement of light effectively prevents the servient owner from building on parts of his land, and there is a need to accept that pragmatism may take priority over logic. Similarly, there is a reluctance to recognise an easement that gives the dominant tenement owner a large measure of occupation or control of the servient tenement. An easement is a right over the servient land for a defined purpose; it is not equivalent to a right of ownership of that land, and if the dominant owner had desired a greater degree of use of the servient land, he should have bargained for a lease. For example, in *Copeland v. Greenhalf* (1952), no easement could exist to store tools of the trade on the servient land; in *Grigsby v. Melville* (1974), a right of storage in a cellar could not be accepted; and in *Hanina v. Morland* (2000), the alleged right to use the flat roof of neighbouring land could not be an easement because it was equivalent to ownership. Likewise, in *Batchelor v. Marlowe* (2001) and *Central Midlands Estates v. Leicester Dyers* (2003), a right to

---

24 Thus, in *Moncrieff v. Jamieson* (2007), Lord Scott notes in passing (the case was about an alleged easement to park) that it is unlikely that the right to use a swimming pool could ever qualify as an easement because it would impose an unacceptable burden of maintenance on the alleged servient owner.

25 He also made the more general point, that in principle, property law rarely allowed positive obligations to run with the land. See for example Chapter 8, freehold covenants.

26 *Crow v. Wood* (1971).

27 As opposed to merely allowing the transmission of electricity across his land. The dominant owners would pay for the electricity.

park several cars on the alleged servient land could not be an easement by analogy with *Copeland* as the impact on it was too great and was inconsistent with the limited nature of easements. In other words, it is a question of degree in each case whether the dominant rights are so extensive as to prevent them being recognised as easements. In essence, the question is whether the alleged easement would leave the servient owner a reasonable use of his own land – *London and Blenheim Estates Ltd v. Ladbroke Retail Parks Ltd* (1992).

Recently, this aspect of easement definition has been examined in greater detail due to issues raised by the House of Lords in *Moncrieff v. Jamieson* (2007), a case concerning an alleged easement to park. In *Moncrieff*, Lord Scott suggested a more radical approach to the problem. In his view, the relevant question is not whether the alleged easement permits the servient owner a reasonable use of their land, but rather whether the alleged easement leaves the servient owner in possession and control of their land. On this view, even very extensive use of the servient land might amount to an easement, provided that the servient owner retained possession and control, and on this basis Lord Scott doubts whether *Batchelor v. Marlowe* (in denying an easement because the alleged right would interfere with the servient owner's reasonable use) was rightly decided.[28] However, not all of their Lordships in *Moncrieff* went as far as Lord Scott[29] and certainly it did not overrule *Batchelor*. In simple terms, the question is whether the relevant test (sometimes known as the 'ouster rule') is whether the servient owner retains possession and control, or whether the servient owner retains reasonable use. The former would allow more extensive easements, the latter less so.[30] At present, it may be safer to rely on the 'reasonable use' test, bearing in mind that the law must be flexible in the face of changing patterns of land use. Indeed, in *Virdi v. Chana* (2008), the trial judge makes the point that *Batchelor* has not been overruled and that he is required to follow it. Fortunately for the claimant, however, the judge in *Chana* is also able to decide that the alleged easement of parking on land where there is only space for one car does not prevent the servient owner from enjoying reasonable use of that space (the *Batchelor* test) because, on the rather unusual facts, the servient owner already had real practical difficulties in accessing that portion of her land. This willingness to seek a pragmatic solution is not new. Thus, in *Wright v. Macadam* (1949), the tenant successfully claimed an easement of storage of coal in a small part of the landlord's coal shed and there is perhaps little to distinguish this case from *Copeland* and *Melville*, save only that the court's assessment of the impact of the alleged easement on the servient land in *Wright* revealed that the servient owner would not thereby be deprived of substantial use of his own property.[31]

It is apparent, then, that flexibility is inherent in the *Ellenborough* conditions, especially in respect of the fourth criterion, and it would be unfortunate if the development of the law of easements were circumscribed by too exacting and rigorously applied conditions. Fortunately, there is no evidence that this is the case and new easements can be accepted if

---

28 Lord Scott also has doubts about *Copeland v. Greenhalf*, but is prepared to uphold the decision on its facts.

29 Lord Neuberger in particular was not convinced.

30 The Law Commission, in its March 2008 Consultation Paper on *Easements, Covenants and Profits à Prendre* (CP No. 186), takes the view that Lord Scott's new test is not particularly helpful.

31 It may be that, in *Wright v. Macadam*, the court felt disposed to protect the tenant in the full enjoyment of his rights against an ungenerous landlord.

this is consistent with precedent and policy. While the title to servient land should not be 'clogged' by haphazard acceptance of new easements, the law of easements must develop in tune with changing social, economic and technological circumstances.[32]

7.2.5 Public policy

Public policy is not mentioned expressly in *Re Ellenborough Park* (1956) as a factor in deciding whether a right may exist as an easement. In any event, as noted above, that case attempted to define the intrinsic characteristics of an easement, rather than laying down comprehensive rules about when the courts would accept that a specific easement actually existed. To put it another way, the *Ellenborough* conditions tell us when a right is *capable* of being an easement; they do not necessarily tell us when that right will be recognised as an easement in a specific case. However, we must proceed with considerable caution when suggesting that considerations of public policy might have an impact on whether a right that qualifies in principle as an easement will in fact be recognised as such in a concrete case. Rarely are questions of 'public policy' openly discussed in the cases, although one does find references to ensuring that land is freely alienable – either by giving easements that promote this or denying onerous ones.[33] That said, and despite a natural reluctance to appeal overtly to public policy, the flexible nature of the *Ellenborough* conditions means that there is always scope for public interest arguments to play a part. For example, in *Hill v. Tupper* (1863), it may well have been against the public interest for a particular individual to have exclusive rights to a waterway, and the absence of any similar problem in *Moody v. Steggles* (1879) might explain the acceptance of a 'commercial' easement in that case. Likewise, was the easement of storage accepted in *Wright v. Macadam* (1949) to protect a vulnerable tenant against a powerful landlord? And in *Platt v. Crouch* (2003), did the court accept the existence of the easements of mooring and signage because otherwise the claimant's land, which he had purchased from the defendant, would have been rendered commercially unviable?[34]

7.3 Legal and Equitable Easements: Formalities

As noted above, in order to exist in *fact* as an easement, the right must be created with a sufficient degree of formality. Like a number of other proprietary rights, an easement may be either legal or equitable[35] depending on the type of instrument used to create it. Failure to use formality when required means that no easement will exist at all.[36] Further, the distinction between 'legal' and 'equitable' easements remains important in modern land

---

32 For example, it is clear that it would be possible to create easements to place a television satellite dish on a neighbour's land and to run fibre optic cables beneath it.

33 *Smith v. Muller* (2008).

34 The claimant had purchased the land to run a hotel – the same hotel run by the defendant before he sold the land to the claimant.

35 Section 1 of the LPA 1925.

36 In such cases, the claimant will be a mere licensee.

law despite the entry into force of the Land Registration Act 2002 and will continue to do so until e-conveyancing becomes widespread.[37]

7.4   Legal Easements

In order for an easement to be a legal interest, there are a number of essential conditions that must be met. These appear to be quite complicated, but it must be noted that they are satisfied in the great majority of cases. Normal conveyancing practice on the transfer of land usually ensures that the appropriate formalities are completed.

An easement can qualify as a *legal interest* only if it is held as an adjunct to a fee simple absolute in possession or as an adjunct to a term of years (section 1 of the Law of Property Act (LPA) 1925). Quite simply, this means that an easement is only capable of being a legal interest if it is attached to a dominant tenement that is held under a normal freehold or leasehold estate.[38] Of course, most are.[39] Second, and more importantly from a practical point of view, easements are legal only if they are created by statute, by deed or registered disposition, or by the process of prescription (long user). All other easements created by different means, even if held for a legal freehold or legal leasehold, must be equitable (if they exist at all).

7.4.1   Easements created by statute

Occasionally, an Act of Parliament may determine that a local authority, a corporation, or even a private individual shall be entitled to the benefit of an easement. This is usually for some public purpose such as, for example, to facilitate the completion of a high-speed rail link or enhancement of electricity distribution networks. Such easements will be legal. Note, however, that creation by statute *does not* refer to the creation of easements by the action of section 62 of the LPA 1925 (on which, see section 7.9.4. below). Here, we are concerned with easements deliberately created by a specific Act of Parliament.

7.4.2   Easements created by prescription

Easements created by the process of prescription are also legal. Prescription signifies the acquisition of a right by long use: for example, where a person has enjoyed a right of way for many years. Prescription is discussed in more detail below, but for now we may note that prescription takes three forms: common law prescription; 'lost modern grant'; and prescription under the Prescription Act 1832.

---

37 Even then, the continued importance of 'implied' easements (being those not created electronically by entry on the register) will mean that the distinction cannot be abandoned altogether.

38 Note that, in *Wall v. Collins* (2007), there is a suggestion that an easement can attach to the land itself, independent of any estate in it. This novel doctrine was important to the result in that case (because the dominant leasehold estate had been terminated through enlargement into a freehold), but it is not clear that it is correct outside of the special facts of that case.

39 Easements held for other periods, for example, with a life interest or a surviving fee tail, must be equitable, but they are quite rare.

7.4.3 Easements created by deed (unregistered land) or registered disposition (registered land)

The great majority of legal easements are created by deed (in the case of unregistered land), or by registered disposition entered on the register of titles (in the case of registered land). Easements created by this method are necessarily encompassed in a formal document (the deed or registered disposition) and rightly are regarded as legal rights. Indeed, the manner of their creation by formal documents ensures that their existence is more readily discoverable by a prospective purchaser of the servient land. As we shall see below, the creation of legal easements by deed or registered disposition may occur in a wide range of circumstances, and may be either express or implied. Note, however, that whether the easement is *expressly* or *impliedly* created by a deed or registered disposition does not affect its quality as a legal interest. Thus, in unregistered land, the mere fact that an easement has been granted (expressly or impliedly) over an unregistered estate by deed is sufficient to constitute it as a legal interest. In registered land, however, the position is more complex.

Under the Land Registration Act 2002, an easement *expressly* granted[40] out of a registered estate – that is, where the servient land is a registered title – *must* be entered on the title of the servient land in order to take effect as a legal interest.[41] Failure to do so renders the easement equitable.[42] This is so whenever title to the servient land is registered.[43] Moreover, if the dominant land is registered, the benefit of the easement must also be noted against its title.[44] In other words, registration of the burden of an expressly granted easement against the title of the burdened land is a precondition to its 'legal' status and, at the same time, ensures that any purchaser of the burdened land both knows about and is burdened by the easement. However, for *impliedly* granted easements affecting registered land, and easements burdening servient land that is not registered (for example, where the servient estate is a lease for seven years or less), the easement is legal if created by deed in the normal way. Importantly, however, because legal easements arising in these circumstances are by definition not noted on the title of the servient land,[45] they take effect against a purchaser under the complex provisions relating to easements and overriding interests under the Land Registration Act 2002.[46] Finally, although the current position is as just described, come the advent of e-conveyancing, the creation of expressly granted easements[47] will occur simultaneously with their registration and this will be done electronically. This means that eventually an expressly created easement will not exist at all

---

40 An easement is not 'expressly' granted by reason of the operation of section 62 of the LPA – see LRA 2002, section 27(7).

41 Sections 25 and 27 of the LRA 2002 and Schedule 2, paragraph 7.

42 Section 27(1) of the LRA 2002.

43 Thus, even if the grant took place in the context of a transaction that itself is not registrable – such as the grant of a lease for seven years or less which becomes the dominant title – the easement must still be registered against servient land of registered title even though the lease itself need not.

44 Schedule 2, paragraph 7 of the LRA 2002.

45 Either because they were not expressly created and so no opportunity for registration arises or because there is no registered title to register them against.

46 See below.

47 Assuming that expressly created easements are specified for e-conveyancing under section 93 of the LRA 2002.

until entered on the title register of the servient land and this entry must be done electronically. Hence, when the full system of e-conveyancing under the 2002 Act comes into force, it will not be possible to create easements expressly in registered land by a material (i.e. non-electronic) deed or written contract. Easements will exist only if entered on the register, and this will be capable only by electronic entry. At that (still distant) time, deeds and written agreements will create nothing at all.

7.5   Equitable Easements

Easements held for periods less than a fee simple absolute in possession or a term of years (leasehold) must be equitable. They are not included in the definition of legal estates and interests found in section 1 of the LPA 1925. However, most easements are created for these two estates, and the equitable quality of easements more usually derives from the fact that they have not been created in the manner appropriate for the creation of legal rights. Consequently, an easement will be equitable even if held for a legal freehold or leasehold if it is not created by statute, nor by prescription, nor by deed/registered disposition (which includes the registration requirements noted above), provided that either the easement is embodied in a written contract that equity regards as specifically enforceable[48] or the easement is generated by proprietary estoppel. These two alternative conditions are the 'formality' requirements for the creation of equitable interests and mean that the easement must be created by signed writing, or fall within the limited exception of easements generated by proprietary estoppel. If even these more relaxed formality requirements for the creation an equitable easement are not met, then the right cannot be regarded as an easement at all. It may then amount to a licence to use land, but of course this is a mere personal right unenforceable against a purchaser or other transferee of the 'servient' land. Indeed, we should remember that irrespective of the manner in which an equitable easement comes into existence – and they are rare in practice – they also are vulnerable on a sale of the servient land and must be protected in the appropriate manner in the systems of registered and unregistered conveyancing if they are to remain enforceable after the sale.

1   *Creation of equitable easements by written instrument* – Under section 2 of the 1989 Law of Property (Miscellaneous Provisions) Act 1989, a contract for the creation of an interest in land (e.g. an easement) must be in writing, incorporating all of the terms and be signed by both parties, if it is to be enforceable. So, rather as is the case with equitable leases, if the parties have entered into a written agreement (i.e. instead of a deed or registered disposition) that purports to create an easement, and if this agreement can be regarded as specifically enforceable under the rule in *Walsh* v. *Lonsdale* (1882), a court of equity will treat the contract as having been performed (even though it has not), and an equitable easement will be the result. It should be noted, however, that come the advent of e-conveyancing such a paper contract will create nothing at all; the easement will be required to be created by an electronic instrument that will both create the right and register it at the moment of its e-registration.[49]

---

48 Section 2 of the Law of Property (Miscellaneous Provisions) Act 1989 and *Walsh* v. *Lonsdale* (1882).

49 In this context, then, the distinction between legal and equitable easements will disappear.

2   *Operation of proprietary estoppel* – The above explanation makes it clear that it is no longer true (since the 1989 Act) that mere oral agreements as such can create equitable easements.[50] However, as discussed in Chapter 9 in detail, an equitable easement may be created through the process of proprietary estoppel. Thus, in *Ives v. High* (1967), an oral promise, relied on by the promisee to their detriment, generated an equitable easement against the promisor because it was unconscionable to deny it.

7.6   The Significance of the Distinction between Legal and Equitable Easements in Practice: Easements and Purchasers of the Dominant or Servient Tenement

The most important reason for distinguishing between legal and equitable easements at the current time is because of the effect that easements may have on subsequent purchasers of the dominant and servient tenements. We know that easements are proprietary: thus the benefit of the easement is *capable* of running with the dominant tenement, and may be enforced by any owner for the time being of an estate in that tenement; and the burden of the easement is *capable* of running with the servient tenement, and may be enforced against any owner for the time being of an estate in that tenement.[51] However, just as with other interests in land, whether an easement does *in fact* run with the land depends crucially on its legal or equitable status *and* the mechanics of the systems of registered and unregistered title. In practice, it is usually a potential purchaser of the servient tenement that is most concerned with this issue, simply because it is they who will have to allow the dominant tenement owner to exercise the easement. After all, the existence of a binding easement may well affect a purchaser's view of the desirability or value of the servient land.

7.6.1   Registered land

With regard to registered land, the *benefit* of an easement becomes part of the dominant tenement and automatically passes to a purchaser or transferee of it. This is so whether the easement is legal or equitable. In fact, in practice, the register of title of a dominant tenement often may note the existence of the benefit of a legal easement and under the Land Registration Act (LRA) 2002, if at the time the easement is expressly created the dominant land comprises a registered estate, the benefit of an expressly created easement must be noted on the register of title of the dominant land.[52] However, this will occur

---

50 Prior to the entry into force of the 1989 Act, easements could be created by oral contract if supported by 'acts of part performance' under section 40 of the LPA 1925, as in *Thatcher v. Douglas* (1996). Section 40 is now repealed and mere oral contracts (i.e. where no estoppel is involved) cannot create equitable rights.

51 Note also that persons present on the servient land with no estate – such as adverse possessors and licensees – can be compelled to permit enjoyment of the easement (although they cannot create one) precisely because the easement binds the land, not simply the people occupying it.

52 Schedule 2 of the LRA 2002.

automatically as a result of the conveyancing transaction in which the easement is expressly created and thus ensures for the most part that purchasers of benefited land are aware of the easements that exist for the benefit of the land they are purchasing.[53]

By way of contrast, the position in respect of the servient land is more complicated and depends on whether the easement is legal or equitable and whether it was expressly or impliedly granted and on the scope of the LRA 2002. However, in all cases we must remember that should the easement fail to be protected in the appropriate manner, then a purchaser of the servient land will take the servient land free from the easement and so cannot be required to permit its exercise by the dominant owner.[54]

7.6.1.1   Legal easements in existence before 13 October 2003 (the date of entry into force of the LRA 2002)

The great majority of these legal easements will be registered against the title of the servient land (because of the way in which they were created) and will, therefore, be binding against a subsequent purchaser of it. However, those legal easements created before first registration of title, or which are not registered because they were impliedly created before the entry into force of the LRA 2002 (or which for some other reason were not registered against the servient land), qualified as overriding easements under the LRA 1925.[55] They continue to qualify as interests that override under the LRA 2002 and thus bind the servient land automatically.[56]

7.6.1.2   Legal easements in existence at first registration of title under the LRA 2002

These legal easements, whenever created and whether arising expressly or impliedly, qualify as interests that override under Schedule 1, paragraph 3 of the LRA 2002. Consequently, they bind the servient land automatically. This is as it should be, because such easements would have bound the applicant for first registration immediately before such an application.[57] However, such easements are likely to be brought on to the register of title in due course when the first registered proprietor disposes of the land because the new owner would come under a duty to disclose such interests by reason of section 71 of the LRA 2002. If registered as a result of this disclosure, they will then bind by reason of their registration.[58]

---

53 If the benefit is not noted on the title – perhaps because it was impliedly granted or pre-dated the LRA 2002 – the person entitled to the benefit of the easement in respect of his dominant tenement may apply to have that benefit noted on his title (Land Registration Rules 2003, Rules 73 and 74).

54 Section 29 of the LRA 2002. If the transferee of the servient land is not a purchaser, the transferee is bound by the easement whether appropriately protected or not (section 28 of the LRA 2002).

55 Under the old section 70(1)(a) of the LRA 1925.

56 Schedule 12, paragraph 9 of the LRA 2002. Such easements may be brought onto the register of title in due course when a person makes an application to register a disposition of a registered estate by reason of the duty to disclose such interests under section 71 of the LRA 2002. They will then bind by reason of their registration.

57 Because 'legal rights bind the whole world' in unregistered conveyancing and the land was transferred as an unregistered title and then first registered.

58 If they are not disclosed and registered, they remain as overriding interests.

7.6.1.3 *Legal easements expressly created over a registered estate on or after 13 October 2003: Those governed entirely by the LRA 2002*

Under sections 25, 27 and Schedule 2 of the LRA 2002, a legal easement expressly created on or after the entry into force of the Act does not actually qualify as a legal interest unless and until it is entered against the title of the servient land.[59] Thus, for these easements, both their status as a legal interest and their ability to bind a purchaser of the servient land depends on their registration. In fact, this will occur as a matter of course if the easement is created during a conveyance of a registered estate, although it will require a deliberate act of registration if the easement is contained in a deed of grant not tied to a sale or transfer of land.[60] Under this provision, the great majority of expressly granted easements will take effect as legal interests binding the servient land. However, failure to register when required means that the easement can qualify only as an equitable interest.[61]

7.6.1.4 *Legal easements impliedly created over a registered estate or where the servient land is not a registered estate,[62] on or after 13 October 2003: Those governed entirely by the LRA 2002*

These legal easements cannot be registered automatically against the servient land either because they are created impliedly and thus the conveyance contains no express mention of them that would trigger their registration, or because the servient land is carved out of a registered estate but is not itself a registered estate and so there is no registered title that can be burdened. For practical purposes, this means legal easements created by reason of prescription, necessity, common intention, the rule in *Wheeldon* v. *Burrows* (1879), under section 62 of the LPA 1925,[63] or where the easement (however created) takes effect over a lease for seven years or less. In all of these cases, because the legal easement cannot be registered, it falls to be protected as an overriding interest. However, it will qualify as an overriding interest only if it falls within the complex provisions of Schedule 3, paragraph 3 of the LRA 2002. If it does not so fall within Schedule 3, it will not override and will not bind a purchaser of the servient title unless it has otherwise been entered on the register.[64] As discussed in Chapter 2, Schedule 3, paragraph 3 is not the easiest statutory provision to understand, but in essence it stipulates that a legal easement of this type (i.e. impliedly granted or taking effect over a non-registered estate) will take effect as an overriding interest if, but only if:

(a)   it is registered under the Commons Registration Act 1965; or
(b)   it would have been obvious on a reasonably careful inspection of the land; or
(c)   it was known about the purchaser of the servient land; or
(d)   it has been used within one year immediately prior to the transfer in question.

---

59 If the dominant land is also registered, the benefit should be entered against the dominant title also.

60 For example, where two existing neighbours agree to grant mutual easements to each other.

61 Section 27(1) of the LRA 2002.

62 For example, in the case in which the servient estate is a lease for seven years or less – this is not registrable with its own title.

63 These cases of implied grant are considered below.

64 They would, of course, bind a non-purchaser (section 28 of the LRA 2002).

Clearly, the point of these provisions is to give the purchaser of the servient land every opportunity of discovering the easement before he buys the land while at the same time seeking to preserve the overriding status of those important easements that, even though undiscoverable, are actually used for benefit the dominant land. In fact, in practice it is difficult to imagine how any implied legal easement could fail to qualify as an overriding interest under these wide-ranging provisions, and at this early stage in the life of the LRA 2002, we might venture the tentative conclusion that virtually all legal easements in principle falling within the schedule (i.e. impliedly granted or over an unregistered estate) will qualify as overriding despite the obvious intention that some at least should be excluded. Once again, many of these easements are likely to be brought onto the register of title in due course when the registered proprietor disposes of the land because the new owner is under a duty to disclose such interests by reason of section 71 of the LRA 2002. If so registered, they will then bind by reason of their registration.

7.6.1.5   *Equitable easements that were overriding prior to 13 October 2003*

The original scheme of the LRA 1925 envisaged that the great majority of equitable easements (if not all) would need to be registered if they were to bind a purchaser of the servient tenement. However, according to *Celsteel v. Alton* (1986), as followed by the Court of Appeal in *Thatcher v. Douglas* (1996), equitable easements that were 'openly exercised and enjoyed' within the meaning of the old Rule 258 of the Land Registration Rules 1925 qualified as overriding interests under section 70(1)(a) of the 1925 Act. Where such easements did qualify as overriding because of this provision, they will continue to override under the LRA 2002.[65] Although there is no doubt that this interpretation of the 1925 Act subverted the registration system, the LRA 2002 cannot remove the overriding status of those equitable easements that did qualify and so the anomaly must remain. However in reality, cases are likely to be few and far between and will relate only to equitable easements that had overriding status on 13 October 2003.

7.6.1.6   *Equitable easements at first registration of title under the*
LRA 2002

Immediately prior to first registration of title, the land is (of course) unregistered. An equitable easement will be binding on the owner of the unregistered servient land (assuming they were a purchaser of it and not the grantor of the easement[66]) only if it is registered as a Class D(iii) land charge under the Land Charges Act 1972. If it is so registered, its registration will be transferred to the register of title of the servient land when the servient land is first registered. If it is not so registered as a land charge, it could not have bound the owner of the servient land (assuming he was a purchaser for money of money's worth of a legal estate[67]) and so should not bind at first registration of title. After all, the first registered proprietor was the previous owner of the unregistered estate and the

---

65 Schedule 12, paragraph 10 of the LRA 2002.

66 The grantor is bound by the easement as a matter of contract.

67 If the servient owner created the easement himself, he will be bound to respect it in favour of the grantee irrespective of registration.

mere act of registration cannot make him bound by something that he was not previously bound by. Thus, equitable easements at first registration are not interests that override and can bind the new registered proprietor only if they are entered on the register of title by reason of a transfer of a previous entry as a land charge in unregistered conveyancing.[68]

7.6.1.7 New equitable easements and dealings with land already registered

The rationale of the LRA 2002 is to bring as many rights onto the register as possible. Consistently with this, equitable easements created over registered land after the entry into force of the LRA 2002[69] cannot qualify as interests that override under Schedule 3 of the Act. Paragraph 3 of Schedule 3 is limited to certain types of *legal* easement and it is most unlikely that an equitable easement could qualify as an overriding interest by reason of 'discoverable actual occupation' within paragraph 2 of the schedule because, by definition, the dominant owner merely uses the servient land, he is not in actual occupation of it. Consequently if an equitable easement created after the entry in to force of the LRA 2002 is to survive a transfer of the servient land to a purchaser, it must be protected by the entry of either an agreed or unilateral notice on the register of title of the servient land. Failure to so register would make it unenforceable against a purchaser of the servient land (section 29 of the LRA 2002), although it would be enforceable against a non-purchaser, such as a donee of a gift or a devisee under a will (section 28 of the LRA 2002).

At this point, because of the complex nature of the provisions concerning easements under the LRA 2002, a summary may be helpful.

1   All easements (legal or equitable) that were overriding before the entry into force of the LRA 2002 continue to be overriding.
2   All legal easements expressly or impliedly granted will override a first registration.
3   Legal easements expressly granted over a registered estate after the entry into force of the LRA 2002 must be entered on the register against the servient land to exist at law and so cannot be overriding. In fact, they are protected by such entry and binding for this reason.
4   Impliedly granted legal easements and legal easements over an unregistered estate carved out of registered land created after entry into force of the LRA 2002 will override against a purchaser provided that they are either known to the purchaser, or are patent on a reasonably careful inspection of the servient land, or have been exercised within one year before the sale to the purchaser, or are entered (if permitted) on the special register maintained under the Commons Registration Act 1965.
5   Equitable easements will not override at first registration but will bind only if previously registered as a land charge in unregistered land and such registration is transferred to the register of title of the servient land.

---

68 It is most unlikely that an equitable easement could qualify as an overriding interest by reason of 'actual occupation' because, by definition, the dominant owner merely uses the servient land, he is not in actual occupation of it.

69 Those that existed prior to entry into force of the LRA 2002, and which overrode under the LRA 1925, continue to do so – see section 7.6.1.5 above.

6   New equitable easements will not override a purchaser of an already registered title (provided that they did not override under the old LRA 1925, being in existence before 13 October 2002) and so must be protected by the entry of a notice in order to bind a purchaser of the servient land.

7   Non-purchasers of a registered title take the land subject to all pre-existing easements, whether overriding or registered or neither.

7.6.2   Unregistered land

With regard to unregistered land, the *benefit* of both legal and equitable easements becomes part of the dominant tenement and automatically passes to a purchaser or other transferee of it. The position is similar to that found in registered land. Once again, questions concerning the *burden* of the easement are best considered by separating legal and equitable easements. Note, however, that these rules will determine whether the purchaser of the servient land is bound by the easement immediately prior to compulsory first registration of title following the purchaser's acquisition of the land. At first registration, the effect of the easement is determined by the LRA 2002, although in reality those provisions effectively ensure that the applicant for first registration is in the same position they were in immediately prior to such first registration.

7.6.2.1   *Legal easements*

As with all legal rights in unregistered land (except the *puisne* mortgage – see Chapter 3), legal easements 'bind the whole world'. They are automatically binding on a purchaser (or other transferee[70]) of the servient land, who must allow the owner of the dominant tenement to exercise it.

7.6.2.2   *Equitable easements*

Most equitable easements are Class D(iii) land charges under the Land Charges Act 1972. As such, they must be registered in order to bind a subsequent purchaser for money or money's worth of a legal estate in the land. If an equitable easement is not registered as a Class D(iii) land charge, it will be void against such a purchaser, but will remain enforceable against others: for example, a squatter or person inheriting under a will.[71] The single exception to this need to register may be equitable easements created by proprietary estoppel. According to Lord Denning in *Ives v. High* (1967), equitable easements created by estoppel are not within the statutory definition of Class D(iii) land charges, apparently because that category includes only those equitable easements that could once have been legal but are rendered equitable by the 1925 legislation. Estoppel easements are, of course, purely equitable, and always will be. Therefore, equitable estoppel easements will be binding against a purchaser of the servient land according to the old 'doctrine of notice'. This means that an equitable estoppel easement will be valid against everyone except a *bona*

---

70 For example, a person inheriting under a will.

71 See generally *Midland Bank v. Green* (1981).

fide purchaser for value of a legal estate in the servient land who has no notice (actual or constructive) of the easement.[72]

7.7   The Creation of Easements

We have noted above that currently there are various ways in which a legal or equitable easement may come into existence.[73] To sum up, they are: by statute (legal easement); by prescription (legal easement); by deed or registered disposition (legal easement); by a specifically enforceable written contract, not amounting to a deed or registered disposition (equitable easement); and by estoppel (equitable easement). The creation of easements by statute for particular and special circumstances need not be considered in any detail, and prescription is considered in section 7.10 below. The operation of the doctrine of proprietary estoppel is considered in Chapter 9, where it will be seen that it is a general doctrine under which the emergence of an easement is only one in which a court might choose to 'satisfy' the estoppel. It is best considered separately. The following section therefore considers the creation of easements by deed, registered disposition or by written contract. However, although the use of one of these three methods of creating an easement may give rise to a different quality of easement (i.e. a legal or equitable easement), it should be appreciated that all three 'methods' will operate against the same factual background. Whether the parties to a transaction choose, or are required to use, a deed, a registered disposition or a written contract to carry out their intentions will depend on the nature of the land (unregistered or registered) and their own appreciation of the needs of the situation at the time. What is important, therefore, is to analyse the factual scenarios in which easements may be created, and only after that ascribe a legal or equitable status to the easement thereby created according to the actual formalities used by the parties. To put it another way, these three methods of creating easements (deed, registered disposition and written contract) simply reflect the level of formality used by the parties; they are not intrinsically different. What is important is the different factual situations (excluding statute, prescription and estoppel) in which easements may be created. These are described immediately below.

7.8   Express Creation

Easements may be created expressly, either by express *grant* or express *reservation*.

7.8.1   Express grant

An easement is expressly granted when the owner of the potential servient tenement gives (i.e. grants) an easement over that land to the owner of what will become the dominant tenement. This may occur in two principal ways.

---

72 But it would not bind at first registration without an entry being made against the title by means of a Notice.

73 This will change under e-conveyancing.

1   Where the servient and dominant tenements are already in separate ownership, the servient tenement owner may grant an easement over his land to his neighbour: for example, A grants B (a neighbouring landowner) a right of way over A's land in return for a one-off payment, or simply to be neighbourly. This is relatively un-common,[74] but might occur when a landowner proposes to change the use of his or her land and requires an easement over a neighbour's land in order to accomplish it.[75] If the grant is by deed or registered disposition[76] (as the case may be for unregistered or registered land), the easement will be legal, and if it is by enforceable written contract, the easement will be equitable.

2   Where land is owned by a potential servient owner and he then sells or leases a piece of that land to another, the potential servient owner (and seller) may include in that sale/lease a grant of an easement to the purchaser. The land remaining in the seller's possession becomes the servient tenement and the piece sold/leased becomes the dominant tenement. The seller has granted an easement over his own land along with the sale/lease of the dominant part and the easement is mentioned expressly in the conveyance of the dominant part to the purchaser. If that conveyance is by deed or registered disposition (as the case may be), the easement is legal;[77] if the transfer is by written contract, the easement is equitable. An example is where a person sells part of his land and includes in that sale the right to lay water pipes under his retained land for the benefit of the part sold: an easement has been expressly granted. This is a very common way of easements being created, an example being *Hillman v. Rogers* (1998), which concerned an easement to cross a road at a defined point.

7.8.2   Express reservation

An easement is expressly reserved when the owner of the potential dominant tenement keeps (i.e. reserves) an easement for the benefit of the land kept, operating over other land. In practice, this is the opposite of express grant by sale or lease, considered above. For example, where land is owned by the potential dominant owner, and he then sells or leases a piece of that land to another, the potential dominant owner may include in that sale/lease a reservation of an easement for himself. The land remaining with the seller becomes the dominant tenement, and the piece sold/leased becomes the servient tenement. The seller has reserved an easement for the benefit of his own land in the sale/lease and the easement is expressly reserved in the transfer of the servient part to the purchaser. If that conveyance is by deed or registered disposition (as the case may be), the easement is legal; if the transfer is by written contract, the easement is equitable. An example is where a person sells part of his land to a builder, but reserves a right of way over the land sold: an easement of way has been expressly reserved. Note, however, that there is a general rule that a seller must not derogate from his conveyance.[78] Consequently, any attempt to reserve for oneself

---

74 See *CP Holdings v. Dugdale* (1998) for an example.

75 For example, the building of an extension might require an easement of drainage through pipes over a neighbour's land.

76 Plus completion of registration as required in registered land.

77 Plus registration as required in registered land.

78 For an example, see *Donnington Park Leisure v. Wheatcroft* (2006).

a right over the land conveyed by one to another must be clearly and unequivocally expressed.

7.9   Implied Creation

The above section dealt with the express creation of easements, either by grant from the owner of land on a sale/lease of part of it, or by reservation of an easement by that person for the benefit of his retained land. In either case, the point is that the easement is expressly mentioned in the transfer of the dominant tenement (grant) or servient tenement (reservation). Furthermore, the easement is legal or equitable depending on whether the transfer of the land is by deed/registered disposition, or specifically enforceable written contract. Of course, given that a transfer of an estate in land is involved, the use of a deed/registered disposition is very probable. It may happen, however, that a transfer of land does not expressly mention an easement, even though this would have been expected or desirable in the circumstances. What if, for example, a seller of part of land meant to grant an easement of way to a purchaser or to keep an easement of drainage for himself but the conveyance was silent on the matter? In some of these situations, an easement can be implied into a transfer of the relevant land, so creating an easement in a similar manner as if it had been expressly created. These situations are noted below, and again encompass situations of implied *grant* and implied *reservation*. In either case, however, if the easement is implied into a deed/registered disposition, the easement will be legal, and if it is implied into a specifically enforceable written contract, it will be equitable. The easement takes the character of the document into which it is implied.[79]

7.9.1   Implied by necessity: Grant and reservation

An easement may be impliedly granted, and occasionally impliedly reserved, because of necessity. The most common example is where the land sold (grant) or land retained (reservation) would be useless without the existence of an easement in its favour. Although the implication of an easement by necessity can be prevented by clear words in the relevant conveyance, the courts will not readily reach such a conclusion.[80]

7.9.1.1   *Grant*

Although it is perfectly possible for any type of easement to be implied into a conveyance for reasons of necessity, easements of necessity arise most frequently in connection with easements of way or light. So, if A sells part of his land to B, but it is impossible for B to gain access to his new land without walking over the land retained by A, an easement of way by necessity will be impliedly granted in favour of B's land over A's retained land: that is, the grant of an easement will be implied into the transfer of the dominant part to B. Another example is provided by *Wong v. Beaumont* (1965), in which an easement of

---

79 Note, however, that impliedly created legal easements operate differently under the LRA 2002 to those that are expressly created; see above in respect to registration requirements and overriding status.

80 *Hillman v. Rogers* (1998).

ventilation by necessity was held to exist when the land sold to the purchaser was intended to be used as a restaurant, but could not be so used without an easement permitting a ventilation shaft to be constructed over the land retained by the seller.[81] Generally, it is easier to claim an implied grant of an easement of necessity than it is an implied reservation but, in all cases, as *Re MRA Engineering* (1988) shows, a real necessity must exist. We are considering easements of necessity, not of convenience. So, in *Manjang v. Drammeh* (1990), an easement of way by necessity could not exist over the alleged servient land, because the owner of the alleged dominant tenement could access his land by boat along a navigable river. This is similar to *Re MRA Engineering* (1988), in which access to the land by foot was possible, and so excluded an alleged implied easement of way by reason of necessity for vehicles.

7.9.1.2   *Reservation*

Again, using an easement of way as an example, if A sells part of his land to B, but it is impossible for A to gain access to the land he has retained without walking over the land sold to B, an easement of way by necessity can be said to be impliedly reserved in A's favour: that is, the reservation of the easement will be implied on the occasion of the transfer of the servient part to B.[82] Note, however, that the reservation of easements by necessity will happen only rarely because it must be clear that the land retained by the seller would be unusable without the easement claimed. For example, no easement of way will be allowed where it is merely inconvenient to use another route, as in *Re Dodd* (1843), although recently, in *Sweet v. Sommer* (2004), an easement of way was impliedly reserved because the alternative access could be achieved only by the destruction of a physical barrier that both seller and purchaser agreed had to remain in place. *Sommer* is, perhaps, one of the more generous applications of this doctrine and the court adopted a slightly less rigid concept of 'necessity' than had been apparent previously. Indeed, we must remember the alleged dominant tenement owner (i.e. the seller) had it in his power expressly to reserve an easement when he sold part of his land. Consequently, the law 'leans against' the seller,[83] and he will have to discharge a heavy burden of proof before the court will agree that an easement of necessity should be impliedly reserved in his favour.

7.9.2   Implied by common intention: Grant and reservation

Easements may be impliedly incorporated into sales of land, either in favour of the purchaser (grant), or in favour of the seller (reservation), if this is required to give effect to the common intention of the parties. The result of such a doctrine is identical to the implied grant and reservation of easements by necessity, considered above, except that the easement does not have to be *necessary* for the use of the land. The point is, rather, 'whether there was a common intention of the parties that the land granted [or reserved] should be

---

81 It is uncertain whether this situation is more properly to be regarded as an example of an easement granted by reason of common intention, on which, see below.

82 *Pinnington v. Galland* (1853).

83 Often expressed in the idea that a person 'may not derogate from their grant', meaning that the seller cannot easily claimed to have retained some right over land when granting it to another.

used in some definite or particular manner and, secondly, whether the grant [or reserva-
tion] of the easement is necessary to give effect to that intention'.[84] Clearly, the acceptance
of such a doctrine facilitates the implied creation of easements in a much wider range of
circumstances than that of 'necessity', and what is required is proof that the parties shared
an intention as to a definite use of the land and that the easement is required in order to
facilitate that purpose. A clear example is provided by *Stafford v. Lee* (1993) in the Court of
Appeal, in which Nourse LJ makes it clear that 'common intention' is distinct from
necessity *per se*. So, in *Stafford*, the claimant (the purchaser) wished to build a house on his
own land, when the only practical access for construction purposes was over the defendant's land. As the land had been sold to the claimant by the defendant with a view to the
construction of a house, an easement of way for the purpose of construction was held to
have been granted. Similarly, in the admittedly exceptional case of *Peckham v. Ellison* (1998),
an easement of way was held to be impliedly *reserved* in favour of the seller, on the basis of
common intention. Of course, the implied creation of easements by way of common
intention is not lightly to be presumed, the more so in cases in which it is alleged to be
reserved in favour of the seller, because once again the parties could have (perhaps should
have) specified for express easements. So in *Chaffe v. Kingsley* (1999), the Court of Appeal
refused to impliedly reserve an easement by way of common intention, distinguishing
Peckham on the ground that the alleged easement in its case was too unspecific and imprecise to justify such a step. It seems then that implied creation by reason of common
intention is possible, but not always permissible. After all, we must not forget that if the
alleged easement was so crucial to the parties' common intention, why was it not
expressly inserted in the relevant conveyance?

7.9.3   Easements implied under the rule in *Wheeldon* v. *Burrows:* Grant only

The rule in *Wheeldon v. Burrows* (1879) may appear complicated at first, but it is only a
variant of the situation considered above where a person sells/leases part of his land and
thereby grants to the purchaser an easement for the benefit of the part sold, burdening the
part retained. The difference is that, under *Wheeldon*, the easement is not *expressly* granted,
but is deemed to be implied into the sale of the land. Note, however, that easements may
only be *granted* by this method: that is, granted for the benefit of the land sold to the
purchaser (which becomes the dominant tenement) to take effect over the land retained
by the seller (which becomes the servient tenement). The rule in *Wheeldon* may not be used
impliedly to reserve an easement for the benefit of the land retained.[85]

    The rule in *Wheeldon* provides that, where a person transfers part of his land to another,
that transfer impliedly includes the grant of all rights in the nature of easements (called
'quasi-easements') that the seller enjoyed and used prior to the transfer for the benefit
of the part transferred, provided that those rights are either 'continuous and apparent'
and/or 'reasonably necessary' for the enjoyment of the part transferred. As we know, no
easement can exist where the dominant and the servient tenement are owned and occupied by the same person. However, it often happens that a landowner will use one part of

---

84 *Davis v. Bramwell* (2007), applying *Pwllbach Colliery v. Woodman* (1915).

85 Confirmed in *Peckham v. Ellison* (1998).

his land for the benefit of another, as where a landowner walks across his own field to get to his house. These are so-called 'quasi-easements', because they would have been easements had the plots been in different ownership or possession. Thus, under the rule in *Wheeldon*, if the owner of the entire plot of land sells or leases the 'quasi-dominant' part of his land to another (being the land benefited by the right – in our example, the house), the purchaser is taken to have been impliedly granted the right previously used for the benefit of that part (in our case, a right of way over the retained field). The purchaser's land then truly becomes the dominant tenement, and the land retained by the seller (in our example, the field) is truly now the servient tenement. Clearly, this is a remarkable rule for it might operate unexpectedly to impose a proprietary burden on the land retained by a seller simply because he made use of that land for the everyday benefit of the part he has just sold or leased. It is no surprise, therefore, that this potentially injurious rule is subject to a number of conditions.

1   The rule can be expressly excluded, as where a seller stipulates that the only easements granted to the purchaser are those expressly provided for in the sale or lease. This is a most important point and it is standard conveyancing practice to exclude the implied grant of easements when an owner sells or leases part of their land. However, as Millman v. Ellis (1996) shows, the exclusion of the rule in *Wheeldon* must be clear and the express grant of a lesser (but similar) easement does not exclude the implied grant of a wider easement. So, in that case, the express grant of an easement of way over a road did not exclude the implied grant, under *Wheeldon*, of an associated easement of way over an adjoining lay-by. Likewise, in Hillman v. Rogers (1998), the express grant of an easement to cross a road did not exclude the implied grant of a right of way over the road under *Wheeldon*. It is apparent then that the clearest words should be used to exclude the rule for there is no certainty that a court will agree that it has been excluded simply because the conveyance contains complimentary express easements.

2   Only those rights that are *capable* of being easements within the *Ellenborough* criteria may become easements by operation of the *Wheeldon* rule. This is self-evident. If a right is not capable of amounting to an easement, it is irrelevant how it is created. Such a non-proprietary right will be a licence.

3   The rule applies to those quasi-easements that are used by the *owner* of the whole land for the benefit of the part sold *before* the lease or sale of the alleged dominant part. It does not appear to be enough that some other person used the quasi-easement, save only if this other person can be regarded as the original owner's agent or *alter ego*. So, if the owner of land always flew by helicopter to his house, but all visitors approached the house by walking across his adjoining field, it is debatable whether sale of the house to a third party would carry with it an easement of way over the field; the right alleged to be an easement was not used by the owner of the common part for the benefit of the land sold. It would be otherwise if any of those using the field could be regarded as the owner's agent, *alter ego*, or with his permission, as in Hillman v. Rogers (1998), in which the owner of the whole land had given permission for others to use the right of way that was subsequently impliedly created when he sold the dominant part.

4   The quasi-easement must have been 'continuous and apparent' and/or 'necessary for the reasonable enjoyment' of the part granted. As matters stand currently, it is not clear whether these conditions are alternatives or whether both are required. *Wheeldon*

itself is equivocal, and some case law suggests that both are needed (e.g. Millman), while others imply that either will do (e.g. Rogers). This apparent uncertainty may exist because, in the majority of cases, the alleged easement will be both 'continuous and apparent' as well as 'necessary for the reasonable enjoyment' of the dominant part. Of course, it remains open to the House of Lords to clarify the situation by reaching a firm conclusion, although given the paucity of cases applying Wheeldon [86] this seems unlikely. A quasi-easement is 'continuous and apparent' if it is visible on inspection of the servient land over which it exists, or so obvious that its use for the benefit of the part sold is beyond doubt. In Millman, the fact that the lay-by was covered in tarmac was evidence that it was used as part of a right of way and was proof that it was 'continuous and apparent'. Similarly, the passage of light through a defined window would be continuous and apparent, even though the window itself is the only outward sign of the right. Moreover, 'continuous' does not mean 'in continuous use', in the sense that the owner continuously used the right now alleged to be an easement (e.g. there is no need to walk over the field every day); rather, it is that the right was constantly *available* for use by the owner and was, in fact, used when appropriate before the sale to purchaser.[87] The requirement that the quasi-easement must be 'necessary for the reasonable enjoyment' of the dominant part, can cause greater difficulties. Strictly speaking, the requirement is *not* that the easement is 'necessary' for the enjoyment of the land – these are not easements of necessity; rather, it is that the easement is necessary for the 'reasonable enjoyment' of the land. The emphasis is on reasonable enjoyment, not necessity. In Millman, therefore, the fact that use of the lay-by as part of the easement of way made access to the property considerably safer was enough to establish its contribution to the reasonable enjoyment of the land. By no stretch of the imagination was this lay-by actually 'necessary' in order to access the land; it merely facilitated its reasonable use. However, in Wheeler v. JJ Saunders (1995), decided before Millman, and also in the Court of Appeal, it was held that a proposed easement of way was not 'necessary for the reasonable enjoyment' of land because other access to the property existed. While, on a simple view, this could be correct – that is, the existence of another access can mean that the proposed easement of way adds nothing to the reasonable enjoyment of the land and is not, therefore, 'necessary' for its reasonable enjoyment – the judgment in Wheeler comes close to equating this criterion with the much stricter test for easements of necessity. This is unfortunate, as the rationale for the two methods of easement creation are different. Easements of necessity do not depend ultimately on the express or implied intentions of the parties but are 'granted' in order to ensure that use of land can be maximised: it is almost policy-based.[88] Easements created by Wheeldon are much more clearly rooted in the parties' intentions, as demonstrated by their actions prior to sale of the dominant part. The decision in Wheeler was subjected

---

86 Because the rule is usually expressly excluded.

87 It may be that the rule in Wheeldon can be displaced by the common owner ceasing the activity at some time before selling the alleged dominant part. The owner would not then have been using the land before the sale. Indeed, this might be done deliberately to prevent any chance of Wheeldon applying, although what amount of time would have to elapse before a subsequent sale cannot be identified with certainty.

88 Thus it may not be possible to exclude the implied grant of easements of necessity.

to close analysis in *Hillman v. Rogers* (1998), and this later case makes it clear that 'necessary for reasonable enjoyment' should not be equated with 'necessity'.

5   Although the most common example of the application of *Wheeldon* is where the common owner keeps the potential servient land, having sold the potentially dominant, it seems that the rule also operates where the original landowner grants the quasi-dominant part to X, and, at the same time, grants the quasi-servient part to Y. According to *Swansborough v. Coventry* (1832) and *Hillman v. Rogers* (1998), this double conveyance would operate to give X an easement over Y's land. In other words, the rule will operate for simultaneous transfers of the prospective dominant and servient parts even though (in our example) X and Y had not been dealing with each other and were in neither privity of contract nor privity of estate. So, if A (original landowner) walks across a field to get to his house, and then sells the house to X and the field to Y, X enjoys the right of way across Y's land. In respect of Y, this is *not* a case in which the burden of an *existing* easement is passing to Y. This is a case of a new easement being created over Y's land, so Y is, in fact, the first owner of the servient tenement. For the purposes of this principle, transactions will be regarded as 'simultaneous' if clearly part of a design to deal with all of the land.[89]

As in the case of easements of necessity and common intention, the character of the easement implied by *Wheeldon v. Burrows* follows the character of the document into which it is implied. So, a sale or lease of the dominant part by means of a deed (or registered disposition in registered land) means that the easement will be legal, and a sale or lease of the dominant part by an enforceable written contract (as in *Borman v. Griffiths* (1930)) means that the easement will be equitable. Finally, although the rule in *Wheeldon* does appear complicated, its operation is well established and well known. It is a trap for the unwary conveyancer and should be excluded by clear words in the conveyance to the purchaser. Its justification is that a person (the seller) cannot 'derogate from their grant' when transferring land unless there are clear words to the contrary. So, unless specific provision is made, a seller must transfer his land with all of the rights attaching to it, even if this means that 'new' easements are created over his retained land.

7.9.4   Easements implied by reason of section 62 of the Law of Property Act 1925: Grant only

The final method by which easements may be impliedly created arises because of the effect of section 62 of the LPA 1925. Once again, the situation in which this occurs is where an owner of land sells or leases part of it to another, and that sale or lease impliedly carries with it certain easements for the benefit of the part sold, burdening the part retained. In this respect, the operation of section 62 is similar to *Wheeldon v. Burrows* (1879), especially as easements may only be granted to the purchaser by this method (not reserved for the seller). However, as we shall see, despite some judicial suggestions that the rules are near identical,[90] the better view is that there are some crucial differences between the creation

---

89 *Hillman v. Rogers* (1998).

90 'Somewhat similar but more extensive in effect is s. 62 Law of Property Act 1925' *per* Nourse LJ in *P & S Platt v. Crouch* (2003).

of easements via section 62 of the LPA 1925 and their creation under the rule in *Wheeldon v. Burrows*.

At first glance, section 62 appears to have little to do with easements, and especially little to do with the creation of *new* rights over land where none existed before. The material part says that:

> a conveyance of land shall be deemed to include and shall by virtue of this Act operate to convey, with the land, all buildings, erections, fixtures . . . liberties, privileges, easements, rights, and advantages whatsoever, appertaining or reputed to appertain to the land, or any part thereof.

So, in simple terms, if a landowner has two or more plots of land and then conveys a legal estate[91] in one of those plots to a purchaser, the purchaser will be granted, by the automatic action of section 62 of the LPA 1925, all those rights that were previously enjoyed with the land. This is straightforward enough, but section 62 is a powerful statutory provision. Its importance lies in the fact that it will convert into easements (for the benefit of the land sold, to the burden of the land retained) all of those rights that were previously enjoyed for the benefit of the land sold (or leased), even though, prior to sale, they were merely 'precarious': that is, they were exercised over the land now retained by the seller only by virtue of his permission, and not as of right. An example will be given shortly, but first we must note the conditions that must be fulfilled before section 62 can create new easements in favour of the purchaser.

1   Section 62 LPA 1925 applies only to sales or leases that are made by 'conveyance', and a conveyance means the grant or transfer of a legal estate. In all cases, save for leases for three years or less, this means that a deed or a registered disposition must be used. Consequently, section 62 will create easements only when the sale or lease to the purchaser is made by a deed or registered disposition as the case may be, not when it is made by written contract. Consequently, section 62 creates only legal easements, because the easement will be implied into the transfer of a legal estate.

2   The operation of section 62 can be excluded by the conveyance to the purchaser, either expressly by clear words, or where the circumstances existing at the time of the conveyance show that the parties intended to exclude the section.[92] In fact, most professionally drafted conveyances will exclude section 62, as this prevents the seller of land creating new easements burdening any land that they might retain. Consequently, many cases in which section 62 operates today are the result of some conveyancing blunder or result from some other entanglement between the parties where they were uncertain about the need for easements (and hence implied

---

91 A 'conveyance of land' within the section means the grant of a legal estate and includes a legal freehold and legal leasehold. Thus, the section is triggered by the use of a deed (except for leases three years or less, etc.) and not a 'mere' written instrument. A 'registered disposition' is a deed and thus a 'conveyance' in registered conveyancing and thus is within the section.

92 *Birmingham, Dudley and District Banking Co. v. Ross* (1888); *Hair v. Gillman* (2000), confirmed in *Platt v. Crouch* (2003). Implied exclusion will be difficult to prove when the alleged rights are so obviously for the benefit of the land conveyed, as in *Platt*. Consequently, a well-drafted conveyance will expressly exclude the operation of section 62 and *Wheeldon v. Burrows*.

creation was not excluded). P & S Platt v. Crouch (2003), considered below, is of this type.

3   Like the rule in *Wheeldon*, only those rights that are intrinsically capable of being easements may be impliedly created by virtue of section 62. So, even though the 'right' over the land that is then turned into an easement by a conveyance under section 62 is not (prior to that conveyance) an easement (because, for example, the landowner merely a limited, verbal and temporary permission), it must fall within the general nature of rights recognised by easements under the law. A mere permission to park a car can turn into an easement of way by section 62 (as in *Hair v. Gillman* (2000)), but a mere permission to play football somewhere on the land never can.

4   Most importantly, and in complete contrast to the rule in *Wheeldon*, it may be essential for the operation of section 62 that the plots of land owned by the seller were in separate *occupation* (but not ownership) before the sale or lease. This is what is called 'prior diversity of occupation' and is explained more fully below. This limitation on section 62 is found in the important cases of *Long v. Gowlett* (1923) and appears to have been confirmed by the House of Lords in *Sovmots v. Secretary of State for the Environment* (1979), although it seems not to apply in respect of easements of light.[93] However, that said, it is true that the need for this 'prior diversity of occupation' has been controversial and there is both ancient and recent judicial authority that it is not *always* required (P & S Platt v. Crouch (2003) – see below). If 'prior diversity' is needed, it means in practice that, before the potential dominant tenement is sold, different persons must have been occupying that land and the land retained by the seller (the potential servient tenement). Effectively, this means that the seller will have been occupying the potential servient land and the potential dominant tenement will have been occupied by his tenant or licensee. It is this classic 'landlord and tenant' scenario that gives rise to many cases concerning section 62. Indeed, usually this tenant or licensee will be the person who then purchases or leases the property by conveyance and thereby obtains the easement under section 62, but it is not essential that this be so (as in *Hillman v. Rogers* (1998)), provided that such diversity did exist prior to the conveyance of the dominant plot to the purchaser.[94]

5   As an alternative to 'prior diversity', the Court of Appeal in *Platt v. Crouch* decided that section 62 also will operate provided that the alleged easements were 'continuous and apparent' prior to the conveyance and that it is only if such continuity and apparentness does *not* exist that 'prior diversity' comes into play. If this is the correct analysis, then section 62 overlaps considerably with *Wheeldon v. Burrows*, without the need to show (as there is for *Wheeldon*) 'necessity for reasonable enjoyment'. Thus, in *Platt*, the claimant established easements of mooring, of way and of signage over the servient land, having purchased this land from the defendant, the defendant previously owning and occupying the whole property and using these rights for the benefit of the part sold to the claimant on which stood an hotel (now owned by the claimant). Peter Gibson LJ was clear on this point, stating explicitly that 'the rights were continuous and apparent, and so it matters not that prior to the sale of the hotel

---

93 *Broomfield v. Williams* (1897).

94 Hence the purchaser may be some unconnected person, or be the original occupier whose prior lease or licence has come to an end.

there was no prior diversity of occupation of the dominant and servient tenancies'. Assuming this is accurate, this breathes fresh vigour into section 62 and takes it out of the narrow field of operation to which it had been confined. It means, in essence, that it can take over from *Wheeldon* in most cases because the requirement that the right be 'continuous and apparent' appears to be identical to that required for *Wheeldon*.[95] Even then, should the right not be continuous and apparent, the claimant will succeed if he can show 'prior diversity of occupation' without having to show 'necessity for reasonable enjoyment'.

If the above conditions are fulfilled (bearing in mind the uncertainty of the approach adopted in *Platt*) and a conveyance of the potential dominant tenement is made (e.g. a sale, a lease, a renewal of a lease), then the purchaser will be impliedly granted as legal easements those rights that were previously enjoyed for the benefit of the land sold. Clearly, however, it will be apparent from the above explanation that the operation of section 62 is dependent on the existence of the proper factual background and the fulfilment of appropriate legal formalities for a 'conveyance.' It is also important to remember that, once again, this is the creation of an easement where none existed before; it is not the purchase of already burdened land by the purchaser and so questions of registration are not relevant. The following example demonstrates how section 62 might operate in practice.

7.9.5   An example of the creation of easements by section 62 of the Law of Property Act 1925

Smith owns two houses, one of which she occupies herself and one of which she lets by lease or licence to Jones (therefore the land is in 'prior diversity of occupation'). Smith allows Jones to walk over the garden of the house that Smith occupies as a short cut to the road. This is a mere licence, being an informal personal permission. Smith then grants a new lease by deed to Jones (or sells him the house). The effect of section 62 of the LPA 1925 is to turn the mere permission to walk over the garden into an easement of way. An easement has been implied into the conveyance of part of the land from Smith to Jones. Note, also, the result would be the same if Jones had vacated the property and Smith had conveyed it by deed to Xavier; Xavier would then have been impliedly granted the same easement with and for the benefit of the land he had purchased. The crucial elements in this example are as follows:

1   Both plots of land were owned by the seller originally (Smith), but that there was diversity of occupation (Smith and Jones on separate plots). The status of Jones (tenant or licensee) prior to the 'easement creating' conveyance is immaterial.
2   Smith then sells that part of the land that enjoys the benefit of the right by a conveyance (transfer of a legal estate) without excluding section 62. The sale will often be to Jones (the person previously on the land), but may be to a completely new person.

---

95 In respect of easements of light, section 62 certainly operates without the need for prior diversity of occupation, but it is not clear whether this is because such easements are always 'continuous and apparent' or because this a unique rule applicable only to easements of light (*Broomfield v. Williams* (1897)).

3   The 'precarious' right is inherently capable of being an easement because section 62 of the LPA 1925 may only generate easements where the previous right is capable of being an easement.

4   Note also, as an alternative, if Smith simply owned and occupied both houses, using a path over the first house to access the second, but then conveyed the second house to Jones, *Platt* decides that section 62 would again operate to create easements in favour of Jones's land over Smith's retained land if the alleged easement was 'continuous and apparent'.[96]

As you will see on reading section 62 of the LPA 1925, it has many uses, but the creation of easements by implied grant is one of its most startling. Obviously, a seller of land that has been occupied by some other person prior to the sale (or where some use has been continuous and apparent) must be very careful not to grant new easements in favour of a purchaser. For example, in *Goldberg v. Edwards* (1950), a licensee enjoyed a limited access by permission over her 'landlord's' land, and when a new tenancy by deed was granted to her, that permissive right was transformed into an easement,[97] and in *Hair v. Gillman* (2000), the seller inadvertently granted a legal parking easement to a former tenant when the tenant purchased the freehold of what became the dominant land.

7.9.6   A comparison between the rule in *Wheeldon* v. *Burrows* and section 62 of the Law of Property Act 1925

The circumstances in which *Wheeldon v. Burrows* (1879) and section 62 operate are so similar – even more so after *Platt v. Crouch* (2003) – that they are often regarded as interchangeable, as in *Hillman v. Rogers* (1998) and *Platt*. This may be true, and there is no doubt that they have the same origin in the rule that a person must not derogate from their grant on the conveyance of land. However, their assimilation is not yet certain. Thus, while section 62 and the rule in *Wheeldon* operate against the same factual background, the conditions on which they depend *may* be different in detail.

1   *Wheeldon* operates where the common seller was in occupation of all of the land before the sale of the dominant part and he (or his *alter ego*) used the potential easement. Section 62 certainly operates where the land was in separate occupation (albeit single ownership) before the sale of the dominant part, and the right was enjoyed by the other occupier against the owner. However, *Platt* decided that section 62 may also operate in circumstances of single ownership and occupation.

2   *Wheeldon* creates easements only where the right is 'continuous and apparent', or 'necessary for the reasonable enjoyment of the land'. Section 62 has no limitation as to necessity of reasonable enjoyment. However, in cases of no 'prior diversity of occupation', *Platt* decides that section 62 may also operate also where the alleged easement is continuous and apparent.

3   *Wheeldon* can imply easements into a legal or equitable sale or lease and may, therefore, create legal or equitable easements. Section 62 operates only where the sale or lease is a conveyance and can create only legal easements.

---

96 *Wheeldon* would produce the same result.

97 See also *Wright v. Macadam* (1949).

4   Both *Wheeldon* and section 62 of the LPA 1925 can be excluded by clear words in the conveyance of the alleged dominant tenement. Section 62 can be impliedly excluded by circumstances existing at the date of the conveyance and it would be surprising if this were not also the case for *Wheeldon*.

7.10   Easements Resulting from Prescription

Another method of creating easements is by 'prescription'. To be more precise, we should say easements are 'generated' by prescription, rather than 'created', because 'prescription' is more a process than a deliberate act. In general terms, 'prescription' occurs when the owner of what will be the dominant tenement establishes long use of a 'right' over what will be the servient land. If, then, the 'right' so used is capable of being an easement (i.e. if the *Ellenborough* conditions are satisfied), the long use can mature into an easement proper. All easements created in this fashion will be legal. As we shall see, the period for which the use must be established may vary from case to case (depending on which of the three 'methods' of prescription is used), but the essential point is that easements generated by prescription are easements created through the very use of the right itself. So, if the owner of Pinkacre has walked across Blueacre for the required period of time in the appropriate circumstances, an easement of way by prescription (long use) may be established.

Before going on to consider the conditions for the acquisition of an easement through prescription, it is important to appreciate the basis of this doctrine. After all, it seems strange that one person can acquire a powerful right over their neighbour's land in the absence of any written document or express grant of the right. In fact, the rationale for prescription is a subtle one. The essential point is that the fact of long use of the 'right' by the owner for the time being of the dominant tenement gives rise to a presumption that a grant of the right was actually made. This is so even though there clearly is no grant at all! In this sense, prescription is not 'adverse' to the owner of the servient tenement, for the fact of long use is taken to be conclusive evidence of the servient owner's grant of the right.[98] Unlike the law of adverse possession (Chapter 11), the owner of the dominant tenement is taken to have acquired the easement through the acquiescence of the servient owner. Also, again unlike the law of adverse possession, the effect of a successful prescriptive claim is to create a new right for the dominant tenement owner, not merely to extinguish the rights of the owner on whose land the long use occurs.[99] Consequently, the law of prescription is sometimes known as the law of 'presumed grant': the grant of the easement is presumed in favour of the dominant tenement owner from the fact of long use. Of course, there is also policy at play here, and in R. v. *Oxfordshire County Council, ex p Sunningwell Parish Council* (2000), Lord Hoffmann made the point with the utmost clarity by noting that 'any legal system must have rules of prescription which prevent the disturbance of long-established de facto enjoyment'.

---

98 *Neaverson v. Peterborough Rural District Council* (1902).

99 We might note, however, that where an adverse possessor is registered as the proprietor of land, this looks very much like the creation of a new title in his favour.

7.10.1   General conditions for obtaining an easement by prescription

As mentioned already, there are three 'methods' or 'routes' to a successful claim of prescription. They are: common law prescription; common law prescription under the rules of 'lost modern grant'; and prescription under the Prescription Act 1832. However, these methods are not inherently different, but simply describe the three different ways by which the person claiming the prescriptive right may establish that the long use was, indeed, long enough to mature into an easement. All three take the same common thread, that long use presumes a grant of the easement in favour of the dominant tenement. Therefore, the following sections discuss the general conditions for establishing an easement by prescription and, where the different methods have different requirements, this will be noted.

7.10.2   Easements of prescription lie in fee simple only

Although it may now appear to be somewhat anomalous, the origin of prescriptive easements is that they are presumed to 'lie in grant', meaning that they are presumed to have arisen by a grant from the fee simple owner of the servient tenement (absolute in possession) to the fee simple owner of the dominant tenement (absolute in possession). Consequently, easements of prescription are always legal, and always attach to the fee simple estate: they are 'permanent' in the same sense that a fee simple is permanent. There can be no easement by prescription in favour of, or against, a leaseholder or an estate that exists in equity only, such as a life interest.[100] This has certain consequences that limit the circumstances in which a prescriptive easement can arise.

1   The long use must be by a fee simple owner of the alleged dominant tenement. This is not necessarily a serious problem, because if the dominant land is possessed by a tenant, the tenant's use of the alleged easement (i.e. by walking across a neighbour's land) can be held to be on behalf of his landlord: that is, on behalf of the fee simple owner. So, provided that the tenant is not asserting that the alleged easement should endure only for so long as the tenancy, this requirement can be met, as explained in *Hyman v. Van den Bergh* (1907).

2   The long use must be against a fee simple owner of the servient tenement. This is the converse of the above and means that easements by prescription cannot exist against tenants (however long their lease) or any equitable estate-holder. Moreover, there are further difficulties here, because if the long use occurs at a time when a tenant is on the alleged servient land, it might be difficult to prove that the long use was against the fee simple owner – after all, at the time of the long use, a tenant was on the land. However, as *Williams v. Sandy Lane (Chester) Ltd* (2006) makes clear, there is no rule of law that prevents an easement from arising simply because the servient land was in the possession of a tenant at some time during the use. Prescriptive easements rest on acquiescence, not on the fact of whether there was, or was not, a lease. Two different situations need to be distinguished. First, there is no objection to the presumption of

---

100   For example, *Kilgour v. Gaddes* (1904).

an easement from long use if the fee simple owner was in possession of the servient land at the commencement of the long use, but then subsequently leased the land to a tenant.[101] This is because, at the time the long use started, it is possible to presume that the grant was made by the fee simple owner – the fee simple owner had the power to terminate the use before the tenancy took effect. Second, where a tenant is in possession of the alleged servient land *before* the long use commenced, it remains possible to presume a prescriptive easement against a freeholder, albeit that it might be difficult to establish on the facts. This is because the generation of an easement by prescription rests on the acquiescence of the freeholder and it is perfectly possibly for a freeholder to acquiesce in the long use (so as to burden the freehold) even though the land was in the possession of his tenant when the use commenced. If, however, the long use commenced while a tenant was on the land *and* the freeholder had no power to exclude the long use while his tenant was in possession,[102] it would be almost impossible to establish a prescriptive easement against the freeholder because a person (the freeholder) cannot be taken to acquiesce in something that they cannot prevent.

3   The above rules have additional practical implications. It is impossible for a tenant to claim a prescriptive easement against his own landlord and vice versa. If L (landlord) occupies Plot 1, and leases Plot 2 to T (tenant), T can never claim an easement by prescription against L, and L can never claim an easement by prescription against T. In both cases, the fee simple owner cannot be presumed to have granted an easement against himself. Likewise, if L leases both plots to different tenants, the tenants cannot claim an easement by prescription against each other, since neither is a fee simple owner.

4   It has been confirmed, in *Simmons v. Dobson* (1991), that the above limitations apply to both common law prescription proper and common law prescription under 'lost modern grant'. In principle, they should apply in the same measure to prescription under the Prescription Act 1932. However, it seems that the words of this statute may have modified the position. Thus, if the 40-year period of the Act is applicable (see section 7.11.3 below), it may well be that objections based on the lack of a fee simple owner fall away. This is because, under section 2 of the Act, a claim to an easement based on 40 years' use (without consent) is said to become 'absolute and indefeasible' and, according to *Wright v. Williams* (2001), this is enough to oust objections based on (at least) the lack of a fee simple servient owner.[103] Likewise, under section 3 of the Act, it is clear that claims to easements of light do not have to fulfil all of the common law conditions. One of the consequences is that there is no objection, if relying on the Prescription Act 1832, to prescriptive easements of light in favour of, or against, land held for the leasehold or life interests. Under the Prescription Act 1832, a tenant may acquire an easement of light by prescription against his landlord (and vice versa), and two tenants of the same landlord may acquire such easements for and against each other.

---

101   *Pugh v. Savage* (1970).

102   For example, because the right to control the land had been given to the tenant exclusively for the duration of the lease.

103   *Davies v. Du Paver* (1953) appears to doubt this proposition.

7.10.3   Use must be 'of right', so as to presume the grant

A second general requirement for the acquisition of an easement by prescription is that the long use must be 'as of right'. To some extent this is circular. An easement is only truly 'a right' after it has been acquired, but in order to be generated by prescription, the requirement is that the long use must already be 'as of right'! What is meant, then, is that the dominant tenement owner's use of the servient tenement owner's land must be in the character of a use as of right, and not be explicable for any other reason. As is sometimes said, the use must be *nec clam* (without secrecy), *nec vi* (without force) and *nec precario* (without permission).[104] Thus, in *Odey v. Barber* (2007), a claim to a prescriptive right of way failed because use of the track had been with the permission of the alleged servient owner. Indeed, it does not matter whether that permission is express, implied, solicited or unsolicited. In *Odey*, the claimants had never sought permission, but it had been given and they were aware of it; hence, their use was not 'of right'. *Odey* is, perhaps, generous to the defendant and is explicable only on the ground that the claimants had effectively accepted the unsolicited permission. In most cases, an unsolicited permission will not suffice to defeat a prescriptive claim because the claimant's assertion as to use by right cannot be defeated unilaterally by the acts of the landowner offering a permission. Indeed, as *R v. Redcar and Cleveland* (2010) makes clear, a claim "of right" is not denied simply because the claimants are solicitous in allowing others to use the same easement. The key is whether a reasonably alert landowner would have recognised a claim "as of right".

7.10.3.1   *Use without secrecy*

No easement can be acquired by prescription unless it arises in circumstances in which a grant can be presumed. Consequently, a secret, hidden use by the owner of the alleged dominant tenement is not sufficient because it demonstrates that no grant can be presumed: a grant presumes a degree of awareness on the part of the servient owner. In practice, this now means that prescriptive easements can be generated only if the use has been 'open' – that is, 'of such character that an ordinary owner of land, diligent in the protection of his interests, would have, or must be taken to have, a reasonable opportunity of becoming aware' of the use (*per* Romer LJ in *Union Lighterage Co v. London Graving Dock Co* (1902)). For example, the wearing of a path on the servient land, or the open use of an existing path, are not secret, but the hidden discharge of water onto a neighbour's land would be.

7.10.3.2   *Use without force*

No easement can be acquired by prescription if the owner of the alleged dominant tenement must use 'force' to accomplish the use. Again, the need to use force shows that no grant can be presumed. 'Force' in this situation means either forcible assertion of the use (e.g. breaking down a fence), or continued use in the face of protests by the alleged servient owner. The latter is a forcible assertion of a use, even though no violence is used. A typical example of

---

104 *Solomon v. Mystery and Vintners* (1859). See now *R (on the application of kevin Lewis) v. Redcar and Cleveland BC* (2010) [2010] UKSC 11; [2010] 2 WLR 653.

use 'with force' is continued use after the alleged servient owner has threatened to take, or has taken, legal proceedings (provided, of course, that this does not occur *after* the completion of the period of use sufficient to establish the prescriptive claim).

7.10.3.3   *Use without permission*

As we have seen, the acquisition of an easement by prescription assumes the grant of a right to the dominant tenement. The crucial matter, then, is the servient tenement owner's acknowledgment of the dominant tenement owner's 'right' to the use, not the servient owner's consent to it. The servient owner must acquiesce in the right, not give his permission for the use, because 'consent' implies that the dominant owner has no right. Consequently, evidence that the alleged servient owner has consented to the use, perhaps by giving a licence, will bar a prescriptive claim, as in Hill v. *Rosser* (1997), and this may be effective even where the permission is unsolicited – *Odey v. Barber* (2007). Necessarily, however, the line between acquiescence (the claim to an easement succeeds) and consent (the claim fails) is a thin one. Generally speaking, the servient owner cannot argue that their mere knowledge of the use amounts to implied consent so as to defeat the claim[105] and the dominant and/or servient owner's belief that consent has been given, when it has not, does not defeat prescription.[106] A good checklist for determining whether the use has been without consent (but with acquiescence), and, therefore, may generate a prescriptive easement, is provided by Fry J in *Dalton v. Angus and Co* (1881).

1   Is there a use of the servient owner's land?
2   Is there an absence of a strict right to carry on the use?
3   Does the servient owner have knowledge (actual or constructive) of the use?
4   Does the servient owner have the ability to stop the use, either practically or legally?
5   Has the servient owner abstained from stopping the use for the period required for a successful prescriptive claim?

If these can be answered positively, the prescriptive claim is likely to succeed, although one must be wary of dismissing claims simply because they fail to meet these criteria in some small way. Finally, it is in the nature of many prescriptive easements that they start out as being exercised with the servient owner's consent and then cease to be consented to at a later date: for example, where a neighbour is given permission to walk across land for one month, but continues after that time. If it can be established that the use became without consent, the prescriptive claim can succeed, with the period of use being calculated by reference to the moment the consent ended.

7.10.3.4   *A limited exception*

As we have seen above, claims to easements of light under section 3 of the Prescription Act 1832 do not have to fulfil all of the common law conditions. A further consequence is that

---

105 Mills v. *Silver* (1991), and see R v. *Redcar*.

106 Bridle v. *Ruby* (1989).

the long user does not have to be 'as of right', in the sense just discussed. Therefore, under the Act (but only the Act), easements of light may be established even if it is clear that the servient owner was consenting to the right of light.

7.10.4   Use must be in the character of an easement

This is an obvious condition because, after all, we are discussing the generation of a proprietary right that will affect the dominant and servient tenements, irrespective of who later owns the land. Thus, no 'easement' by prescription can arise unless the 'use' itself satisfies the inherent characteristics of an easement. For example, no easement to wander over land can arise by prescription, because such a right can never be an easement and no prescriptive easement of drainage for the benefit of 'higher' over 'lower' land can exist, because the drainage is natural and not in the way of a right that the owner of the lower land could ever have prevented – *Palmer v. Bowman* (1999). Again, if both the dominant and servient tenements have come into common ownership at some time during the period of long use, there may be difficulties in establishing a prescriptive claim. In such cases, there is a union of the two tenements, and a landowner cannot have a true easement against himself. The period of long use would, therefore, be terminated and would have to recommence if the tenements later separated.

7.10.5   Use must be lawful

It is also the case that long use may mature into an easement by prescription only if the use itself is lawful. In general terms, easements may not exist for unlawful purposes and no servient owner can be presumed to grant one. However, it is clear from more recent authority that this is a limited objection to the prescriptive grant of an easement. In *Bakewell Management Ltd v. Brandwood* (2004), the question arose whether the defendants had acquired prescriptive vehicular rights of way over common land. If they had not, Bakewell Management, as owner of the common, could charge a large fee. Under statute,[107] a person who drives a vehicle on common land without lawful authority commits a criminal offence and Bakewell argued that no vehicular prescriptive right could have arisen because the alleged use was unlawful as contrary to the criminal law.[108] The issue, being one of national as well as individual importance, found its way to the House of Lords. In the result, their Lordships overruled prior authority and upheld the prescriptive grant of the easement. While it was true that no easement could be acquired by prescription that involved a substantively unlawful purpose, that did not prevent the acquisition of easements the substance of which would be lawful but for the lack of lawful authority that is alleged to deny the easement. Thus, a vehicular easement of way was, in itself, a perfectly lawful purpose, and it was only the lack of 'lawful authority' that rendered it unlawful, but this was the very reason why the easement was claimed in the first place. So, the alleged easement was not inherently unlawful, but was made unlawful by reason of the very facts that required an easement to be granted. While this distinction between a purpose that is substantively unlawful (no prescription) and one that would be lawful but for the denial of

---

107 See section 14(1) of the Road Traffic Act 1930 and section 193(4) of the LPA 1925.

108 See *Hanning v. Top Deck Travel Group Ltd* (1993), overruled by this case.

right by the landowner (prescription possible) may seem a fine one, it is submitted that it is perfectly in keeping with the rationale of prescription to preserve the quiet enjoyment of those who have exercised otherwise perfectly rights undisturbed for many years. Thus mere 'unlawfulness' will not always prevent a successful claim of prescription.

7.11 Methods of Establishing an Easement by Prescription

As indicated at the start of this section, there are three recognised varieties of prescription: prescription at common law; prescription at common law utilising the doctrine of 'lost modern grant'; and prescription under the Prescription Act 1832. We have seen, also, that the inherent nature of a prescriptive claim is the same under all three methods, save that prescription under the Prescription Act 1832 has less rigid requirements in matters of detail, due to the wording of that statute. In fact, when it comes to making a prescriptive claim, the owner of the potential dominant tenement may rely on any or all three methods.[109] This illustrates more than anything their common origin. As we shall see, the methods differ essentially in the way in which the claimant must establish the long use and the length of time for which he must have used the 'right' before it can mature into an easement proper. In essence, the methods are about how the long use is to be proven, not primarily about the quality of the long use. In all three methods, even though the period of long use required for a successful claim can vary, the claimant must establish that the use has been 'continuous' throughout the relevant period.

'Continuous user' (sometimes referred to as 'continuity of user') does not mean that the claimant must use the 'right' incessantly, never stopping. It denotes, rather, that there is a regular, consistent use of the right for the relevant period, commensurate with the nature of the right. This means that 'regular' use will be a question of fact. The exercise of a right of way might be 'continuous' in one case if it is exploited only two or three times a year but, in another set of circumstances, monthly use might be required. Again, some easements are, by nature, more obviously exercised 'continuously' – such as an easement of way – while others (an easement to enter and cut obstructing trees) are not. The continuity of some easements is often completely hidden – as with the easement of support offered by a wall on the servient owner's land. Likewise, unimportant inconsistencies in the long use cannot defeat a claim, as where the route of a path deviates over time, or a replacement sign is hung in a slightly different position on the servient owner's land. For example, in *Propertypoint Ltd v. Kirri* (2009), an easement of way by prescription was established even though the exact manner in which the servient land had been used (in respect of turning vehicles) had varied over the years. Assuming, then, that the claimant can establish that he is a continuous user, what period of time is necessary to propel this into an easement proper?

7.11.1 Prescription at common law

At common law, long use could mature into an easement if it could be shown to have occurred since before 'legal memory'. According to the Statute of Westminster 1275, legal

---

109 In *Brandwood*, the claim rested on either the Act or lost modern grant.

memory was fixed (rather arbitrarily) at 1189, so a claim of prescription could succeed at common law if it could be shown that the use existed before then. Obviously, this was well nigh impossible, so it became accepted that use for 20 years raised a presumption that use commenced before 1189.[110] Unfortunately, however, this did not mean that 20 years' use generated a prescriptive easement. It remained the case that the claim could be defeated by any evidence that the use could not, in fact, have started before 1189. So, for example, a claim to a right of light, even if used for 150 years, could be defeated by showing that the building so benefited was built 'only' in the year 1190. The ease with which an alleged servient owner can defeat the 20-year presumption effectively ensures that this form of common law prescription is hardly ever successful.

7.11.2   Prescription at common law: Lost modern grant

The doctrine of lost modern grant developed as an antidote to the manifest deficiencies of 'pure' common law prescription. In fact, this doctrine is really no more than a fictional gloss on the old common law rules. As we know, the rationale for prescription is a presumed grant of the right by the servient owner. Under 'lost modern grant', the law assumes that 20 years' use of the right is conclusive evidence of such a grant being made by the servient owner. The grant is 'modern', because it is assumed to have been made at some time after 1189, and it is 'lost', because it cannot now be produced – of course, it does not actually exist, but this is the convenient fiction. Stripped of its trappings, the doctrine means that 20 years' continuous use by the owner of the dominant tenement is sufficient to establish an easement by prescription (*Dalton v. Angus* (1881)). This is so even if the servient owner produces evidence that no grant had been made – which, of course, is true. Indeed, it seems that the one way in which the servient owner can defeat the claim (apart from the absence of other requirements mentioned above) is if he shows that the servient owner who is assumed to have made the grant (i.e. the owner at the commencement of 20 years' use) was legally incompetent at the time, being a minor or lunatic. Even then, although there is authority to support this limitation,[111] it seems strange to deny a prescriptive claim on the ground that the person supposed to have made the fictitious grant was unable to do so, when everybody knows that he never made the grant at all. Why is legal incapacity a bar, when actual non-existence of the grant is not? Be that as it may, the doctrine of lost modern grant is sufficient in most cases to ensure that long use, as of right, matures into an easement.

7.11.3   The Prescription Act 1832

The Prescription Act 1832 is not a replacement for the common law (especially lost modern grant) and, considering some of its mystifying language, this is just as well. It is intended to bolster the common law principles, supplementing them where necessary, with the general aim of making it easier to establish an easement by prescription. It is doubtful whether it does this, but that is its purpose. The Act divides easements into two classes: easements of light and all other easements.

---

110   *Dalton v. Angus* (1881).
111   *Oakley v. Boston* (1976).

7.11.3.1 *All easements except easements of light*

Under section 2 of the Act, a period of 20 years' use is sufficient to establish a prescriptive claim, provided that the 'right' was enjoyed 'without interruption' for that period (e.g. the successful claim of way in *Denby v. Hussein* (1999)). Evidence that the 'right' was not enjoyed, or lacked some other quality, in the period *before* commencement of the 20 years, cannot defeat the claim. Moreover, an interruption by the servient owner during the 20 years is sufficient to defeat the claim only if the alleged dominant owner tolerated the interruption for one year or more. However, the Act does not remove the need to satisfy the conditions for prescription *during* the 20-year period. Thus, any inability to meet the common law conditions during the 20 years' use is fatal to the claim. Finally, there is a further practical limitation in that the alleged dominant owner cannot pick any 20 years' use: the 20 years' use must be calculated by reference to the 20 years immediately prior to 'some suit or action'. This has the unfortunate consequence that no easement of prescription can arise if, say, the use has been enjoyed for 100 years, but no 'suit or action' is brought, or if the easement was enjoyed for 200 years in conformity with the common law conditions, but at some time in the last 20 years before a suit, one of the common law conditions was not met (e.g. the dominant and servient tenements came into common ownership).

In contrast to this, section 2 provides as an alternative that 40 years' use without interruption ensures that the right is 'absolute and indefeasible' unless exercised with the consent of the servient owner. This effectively eases the conditions imposed by section 2 for 20 years' use. It remains the case (with the same problems) that the 40 years' use must be that which is immediately prior to a 'suit or action', and the same principles of 'interruption' apply. However, because 40 years' use makes the right 'absolute and indefeasible', it seems that it does not matter that someone other than the fee simple owner (e.g. a tenant) was in possession of the land at the start of the period, provided that the period is completed. On the other hand, the remaining common law conditions appear to apply, save only that if the servient tenement's consent is given at the start of the use (or possibly the start of the 40-year period – the Act is unclear), it must be in writing or by deed to negate the prescriptive claim. The issue of 'consent' occurring at any other time during the 40 years is determined by reference to the common law.

7.11.3.2 *Easements of light*

Under section 3 of the Act, use of light for a period of 20 years (probably that period prior to any 'suit or action' – again, the Act is unclear) 'without interruption' becomes 'absolute and indefeasible' unless the servient owner consents in writing or by deed. In particular, there is no provision in section 3 that preserves the conditions of the common law, so uninterrupted use for 20 years without written consent will mature into an easement even if there is some defect that would have defeated a common law claim. Whether there has been written consent is, furthermore, a matter of construction of any agreement, and so, in *Salvage Wharf Ltd v. G & S Brough Ltd* (2009), an agreement concerning aspects of a building project and *existing* rights to lights did not amount to an agreement within section 3. On the other hand, a written agreement need not specifically refer to 'light' in order to qualify under section 3, provided that its effect necessarily implies exclusion of a right to a light, as in *RHJ v. F T Patten* (2007). Note, however, that there can be 'an interruption' of light for the purposes of section 3 by the alleged servient owner without that owner actually physically blocking the light. The servient owner can take steps to register a notice in the local land charges register as provided by the Rights of Light Act 1959. This notice acts in law as an interruption and may prevent the acquisition of a right of light under section 3. Its purpose is to remove the need for the erection of numerous anti-light structures by potential servient owners as the end of a 20-year period approaches.

7.12   The Extinguishment of Easements

Given that an easement is essentially a right enjoyed by one landowner over the land of another, it is vital to its existence that the dominant and servient tenements are in separate ownership or occupation. Thus, the most common reason why easements cease to exist is that the dominant and servient land comes into the ownership and possession of the same person. Note that there must be unification of both ownership and possession, for it is perfectly possible for a tenant to enjoy an easement against their landlord and vice versa,[112] although, as just noted, one such cannot be generated through prescription. Importantly, there is no statutory mechanism by which a person may apply for the judicial termination of an easement, unlike the position with restrictive covenants. Consequently, failing extinguishment through unification of the tenements, easements may only be terminated by a release of the easement by the current owner of the dominant tenement (express or implied through conduct), by abandonment (mere non-use is not abandonment – *Benn* v. *Hardinge* (1992)), or by a specific Act of Parliament. Equitable easements may also become void and unenforceable against subsequent purchasers of the servient tenement by reason of a failure to register (if required) in registered or unregistered land.

7.13   A Note on *Profits à Prendre*

Profits à prendre are often considered alongside easements, not least because they also give rights over land belonging to another. The essential nature of a profit is that it is a proprietary right to enter upon another's land and take for oneself the profits of the land. For example, the profit of piscary entitles a person to enter another's land and take fish, likewise with the profits of turbary (turf) and estovers (wood). Profits may also be legal or equitable and fall within the regime of the LRA 2002 in similar fashion to easements. Again, with the possible exception of the rule in *Wheeldon* v. *Burrows* (1879), profits may be created in the same ways as easements. However, there is one important difference that is worthy of note: whereas an easement can exist only if there is a dominant and a servient tenement, a profit may exist in relation to a dominant tenement or 'in gross'. A profit 'in gross' exists over servient land, but the person entitled to the benefit of it does not have to own land of their own. The burden of a profit attaches to land (hence its proprietary status), but the benefit may be held by any person or indeed any number of persons.[113] Profits can be commercially important, as with profits of piscary in salmon-

---

112 For example, *Wright* v. *Macadam* (1949).

113 Of course, many profits are attached to dominant land – see the discussion in *Polo Woods* v. *Shelton-Agar* (2009).

rich waters. For this reason, the LRA 2002 enables legal profits to be registered with their own title.[114]

7.14   Reform

In March 2008, the Law Commission issued a consultation paper on *Easements, Covenants and Profits à Prendre*.[115] Much of the paper is taken up with proposed reform to the law of covenants, as these present more pressing problems.[116] In respect of easements and profits, the proposals are modest and sensible and are directed more to ironing out the wrinkles in the law rather than to wholesale reform. Some are more tentative than others. The main proposals for consultation in respect of easements are: the abolition of the existing methods of prescription and their replacement with a single, statutory method; the ration-alisation of the law on extinguishment of easements including the creation of a statutory jurisdiction to discharge or modify easements and profits in similar fashion to that obtain-ing for covenants; the acceptance that an easement could still exist where the dominant and servient land was owned by the same person provided that benefit and burden of the easement were registered against the respective titles; and the possibility that the rules on implied creation might be amalgamated and replaced by a single rule based on what is necessary for the reasonable use of the land. There are no proposals to change the essential definition of easements, although the need for the right to be clearly defined and *not* to involve unrestricted use of the servient land could be made statutory.

7.15   Chapter Summary

7.15.1   The essential characteristics of an easement

The traditional criteria for determining whether a right amounts to an easement are found in *Re Ellenborough Park* (1956).

1   There must be a dominant and a servient tenement (easements cannot exist in gross).
2   The dominant and servient tenements must be owned or occupied by different persons.
3   The alleged easement must accommodate (i.e. benefit) the dominant tenement, meaning that: the servient tenement must be sufficiently proximate (i.e. near) to the dominant tenement; the alleged easement must not confer a purely personal advan-tage on the owner of the dominant tenement; and the alleged easement must not confer a purely 'recreational use' on the dominant tenement.
4   The alleged easement must 'be capable of forming the subject matter of a grant', meaning that: an easement cannot exist unless there is a capable grantor; an easement

---

114   Section 3 of the LRA 2002.

115   Consultation Paper No. 186.

116   See Chapter 8.

cannot exist unless there is a capable grantee; an easement cannot exist unless the right is sufficiently definite; and the right must be within the general nature of rights recognised as easements.

5   Public policy may also be relevant, although it is not mentioned in *Re Ellenborough Park* (1956).

7.15.2   Legal and equitable easements: Formalities

An easement can qualify as a legal interest only if it is held as an adjunct to a freehold or leasehold estate and if it is created by statute, by prescription, or by deed (unregistered land) or registered disposition (registered land).

Easements held for less than a freehold or leasehold must be equitable. Even easements held for these estates will be equitable if not created properly (or registered appropriately under the LRA 2002 on express creation). In that event, the easement may be equitable, provided that it is embodied in a written contract or instrument that equity regards as specifically enforceable or it arises orally through proprietary estoppel.

7.15.3   The significance of the distinction between legal and equitable easements in practice: Third parties

In *registered land*, the benefit of an easement becomes part of the dominant tenement and automatically passes to a purchaser, whether legal or equitable. The burden of a legal easement in registered land currently will either be registered against the title of the servient land or be an overriding interest under Schedules 1 and 3 of the LRA 2002, depending on when the easement came into existence and whether its expressly or impliedly created. In order for new equitable easements (those arising after the entry into force of the LRA 2002) to bind a purchaser of the servient land, the easement must be registered by means of a notice.

In *unregistered land*, the benefit of an easement becomes part of the dominant tenement and automatically passes to a purchaser, whether legal or equitable. The burden of a legal easement in unregistered land will 'bind the whole world'. The burden of an equitable easement in unregistered land must be registered as a Class D(iii) land charge under the LCA 1972 in order to bind a purchaser, save that estoppel easements bind according to the doctrine of notice.

7.15.4   The express creation of easements

An easement may be expressly granted by the potential servient owner to the potential dominant owner: for example, where the servient and dominant tenements are already in separate ownership and a grant is made, or where land is owned by a potential servient owner, and he then sells or leases a piece of that land to another and includes an express grant in the sale.

An easement may be expressly reserved by the potential dominant owner when that owner sells or leases a piece of that land to another and includes in that sale a reservation of an easement for themselves.

7.15.4.1 *Note*

The easement is legal or equitable depending on the character of the document in which it is contained. A legal conveyance creates a legal easement and transfer of an equitable estate creates an equitable easement.

7.15.5 The implied creation of easements

7.15.5.1 *Necessity*

An easement may be impliedly granted, and occasionally impliedly reserved, because of necessity, as where the land sold (grant) or land retained (reservation) would be useless without the existence of an easement in its favour.

7.15.5.2 *Common intention*

An easement may be impliedly incorporated in a sale of land either in favour of the purchaser (grant) or exceptionally in favour of the seller (reservation) if this is required to give effect to the common intention of the parties as to the use of the land.

7.15.5.3 Wheeldon *v.* Burrows *(grant only)*

Where a person transfers part of their land to another, that transfer impliedly includes the grant of all rights in the nature of easements (called 'quasi-easements') that the seller enjoyed and used prior to the transfer for the benefit of the part transferred, provided that those rights are either 'continuous and apparent' or 'reasonably necessary for the enjoyment of' the part transferred.

7.15.6 Implied under section 62 of the Law of Property Act 1925 (grant only)

If a landowner has two or more plots of land and then conveys, by deed, one of those plots to a purchaser, the purchaser will be granted, by section 62 of the LPA 1925, all of those rights that were previously enjoyed with the land. This is so even if before the sale the 'rights' were enjoyed purely by permission and not as of right. Section 62 applies only to conveyance of a legal estate.

7.15.6.1 *Note*

In cases of implied creation, the easement is legal or equitable depending on the character of the document into which it is implied.

7.15.7 Easements by prescription

Prescription occurs when the owner of what will be the dominant tenement establishes long use of a 'right' over what will be the servient land. If, then, the 'right' so used is inherently capable of being an easement, the long use can mature into an easement proper.

All easements created in this fashion will be legal. The period for which the use must be established will vary from case to case, depending on which of the three 'methods' of prescription is used.

7.15.8 General conditions for obtaining an easement by prescription

* Easements of prescription lie in fee simple only. There can be no easement by prescription in favour of, or against, a leaseholder or an estate that exists in equity only, such as a life interest. So, the long use must be by a fee simple owner of the dominant tenement and it must be against a fee simple owner of the servient tenement. It is impossible for a tenant to claim a prescriptive easement against his own landlord and vice versa (or against another tenant). These rules have been modified for claims made under the Prescription Act 1832.
* The use must be 'of right'. The long use must be *nec clam* (without secrecy), *nec vi* (without force) and *nec precario* (without permission).
* The use must be in the character of an easement, as satisfying the criteria of *Re Ellenborough Park* (1956).

7.15.9 Methods of establishing an easement by prescription

For all 'methods' of establishing an easement by prescription, the claimant must establish first that the use has been 'continuous' throughout the relevant period. The length of the required period varies with each method.

* *Prescription at common law* – The use must have occurred since before 'legal memory', that being before 1189. Use for 20 years raises a presumption that use commenced before 1189, but the claim can be defeated by any evidence that the use could not, in fact, have started before then. Such claims hardly ever succeed.
* *Prescription at common law – lost modern grant* – The law assumes that 20 years' use of the right is conclusive evidence of a grant of the easement being made by the servient owner. This means that 20 years' continuous use by the owner of the dominant tenement is sufficient to establish an easement by prescription, even if the servient owner produces evidence that no grant had ever been made – which of course is true.
* *Prescription Act 1832* – For all easements – except easements of light – a period of 20 years' use is sufficient to establish a prescriptive claim, provided that the 'right' was enjoyed 'without interruption' for that period. Alternatively, 40 years' use without interruption ensures that the right is 'absolute and indefeasible', unless exercised with the consent of the servient owner. For easements of light, a period of 20 years' use 'without interruption' becomes 'absolute and indefeasible', unless the servient owner consents in writing or by deed.

7.15.10 The extinguishment of easements

This can occur in a variety of ways. For example: the dominant and servient land may come into the ownership and possession of the same person; the dominant owner may 'release' the easement, expressly or impliedly through conduct; or the easement may be terminated by Act of Parliament.

7.15.11 *Profits à prendre*

A 'profit' is a proprietary right to enter upon another's land and take for oneself one of the 'profits' of the land. Profits may be legal or equitable. With the possible exception of the rule in *Wheeldon v. Burrows* (1879), profits may be created in the same ways as easements. Note, however, that profits may exist 'in gross': that is, they may exist over servient land even if the person entitled to the benefit owns no land himself. Examples are the profit of piscary (to take fish), the profit of turbary (to cut turf) and the profit of estovers (to cut wood). Under the LRA 2002, legal profits are capable of being registered with their own title.

 Further Reading

Barnsley, DG, 'Equitable easements 60 years on' (1999) 115 LQR 89

Law Commission, *Easements, Covenants and Profits à Prendre*, Consultation Paper No. 186, *March 2008*

Luther, P, 'Easements and exclusive possession' (1996) 16 LS 51

'Prescriptive easements: Capacity to grant' [2009] CLJ 40

Tee, L, 'Metamorphoses and s 62 of the Law of Property Act 1925' [1998] Conv 115

Chapter 8
Freehold Covenants

Chapter Contents

Introduction

The law concerning covenants made between freeholders ('freehold covenants') repre-sents yet another way by which one landowner may control or affect the use of neighbour-ing land.[1] In some respects, the principles discussed below are similar to those seen in respect of leasehold covenants (Chapter 6) and easements (Chapter 7), in that a binding freehold covenant entails both a benefit and a burden in respect of two estates in land held by different people. Similarly, covenants represent another species of proprietary obligation, albeit one that owes its origin to the remedial jurisdiction of the courts of equity.[2]

In simple terms, 'freehold covenants' are, as their name implies, promises made by deed ('covenants') between freeholders,[3] whereby one party promises to do or not to do certain things on their own land for the benefit of neighbouring land. Thus, the owner of house no. 1 may promise the owner of house no. 2 not to carry on any trade or business on his (no. 1's) land, or the owner of house no. 3 may promise the owner of house no. 4 not to build above a certain height or without first obtaining the agreement of the owner of house no. 4.[4] Consequently, the landowner making the promise on behalf of his land is the covenantor (where the burden lies), and the landowner to whom the promise is made is the covenantee and his land is where the benefit lies. As in these examples, the great majority of covenants between freeholders are 'restrictive' (negative) in nature, in that they prevent a landowner from doing something on his own land, as opposed to requiring him to take positive action. Of course, that is not to say that 'positive' covenants cannot exist (e.g. a covenant to erect and maintain a boundary fence[5]), but, as we shall see, the enforcement of a positive covenant between persons other than the original covenantor and covenantee currently is extremely difficult.[6] Consequently, much of the law in this area has concentrated on restrictive covenants, and many textbooks refer to this topic as 'the law of restrictive covenants'. Similarly, 'freehold covenants' may be contrasted with 'leasehold covenants', the latter being promises taking effect as a term of a lease made between a landlord and a tenant and usually (but not necessarily) referring to the land that is the subject matter of the lease.

---

1 Technically, this is the law concerning covenants made between persons who are not in privity of estate. In the main, this means covenants affecting freehold land, but it also includes the enforcement of covenants between head landlords and subtenants. In addition, for reasons that will become clear, sometimes these rules are described as the law relating to restrictive covenants, a convenient but inaccurate description.

2 Thus, covenants as proprietary obligations – as opposed to mere personal contractual obligations – developed because courts of equity were prepared to grant a remedy against a landowner who acquired land in the knowledge that it was affected by a covenant. The court of equity could not, in conscience, allow a landowner to escape an obligation affecting the land of which he was aware, even though it has been created by some other person – see Tulk v. Moxhay (1848).

3 Or other persons who do not stand in relationship of privity of estate: above fn.1.

4 For example, Margerison v. Bates (2008).

5 For example, Norwich City College of Further & Higher Education v. McQuillin (2009).

6 The Law Commission is in the process of considering the law of covenants and whether the enforcement of positive covenants between persons other than the original parties should be made possible – Consultation Paper No. 186, March 2008, Easements, Covenants and Profits à Prendre.

8.1   The Nature of Freehold Covenants

A covenant is a promise made in a deed[7] and, as such, is enforceable as a contract between the covenantor (promisor) and covenantee (promisee) irrespective of whether contractual consideration is given. The covenant may be given in a stand-alone transaction by one neighbour to another, but is more likely to arise when a person sells part of their land to another and either gives (or extracts) covenants as part of the bargain. Thus, a landowner might agree to sell part of his land to X, but X will covenant as part of the transaction that he (X) will not build more than one dwelling on the land, or will not carry on a trade or business or undertake some other obligation of importance to the seller. In this sense, covenants can be an important source of private planning law because they may be used to preserve the character of a neighbourhood by preventing activity contrary to the *status quo* (e.g. 'no trade') or by limiting the impact of development ('not more than one dwelling'). This is particularly important in large-scale developments where a web of interlocking covenants and easements can be used for the benefit of all future purchasers of land within the development.[8] Moreover, if covenants are able to 'run' with the land in the sense of conferring proprietary benefits on one plot of land and proprietary burdens on another, these obligations may assume a permanence than endures irrespective of who comes to own the benefited and burdened plots in the future. With this in mind, the nature of freehold covenants can be analysed in the following way.

8.1.1   Positive and negative covenants

Covenants between freeholders may be either positive or negative in nature. Positive covenants require the owner of the burdened land to take some action on their own or adjoining property, usually requiring the expenditure of money. An example is a covenant to keep one's own property in good external repair in order to maintain the character of a neighbourhood. Negative or restrictive covenants require the owner of the burdened land to refrain from some activity on his own land. An example is a covenant not to carry on any trade or business perhaps because it is intended to preserve the residential character of a neighbourhood.[9]

8.1.2   Covenants as contracts

Covenants are promises made by deed by one person to another to do, or more usually not to do, something on their own or adjoining land. The covenant is made between the *covenantor* and the *covenantee*. Covenants are binding and enforceable as a matter of contract law between the parties to it, irrespective of the presence or absence of consideration. Consequently, the original covenantor must do, or refrain from doing,

---

7   Consequently, it must comply with the formalities required of deeds found in section 1 of the Law of Property (Miscellaneous) Provisions Act 1989.

8   Commercial, as well as residential, developments may benefit. Thus, restrictive covenants may be used to limit the type of products that are sold on individual premises, thus preserving a diversity of local shops in a high street.

9   For example, *Gafford v. Graham* (1998).

that which he promised (and, therefore, is subject to a burden), and the original covenantee has the right to sue for performance of the covenant (and therefore enjoys a benefit).

8.1.3   Covenants as interests in land

Most importantly, covenants are now clearly regarded as proprietary interests in land, albeit equitable in nature.[10] This means that they have the following attributes.

8.1.3.1   *The covenantor's land: The burden of the covenant*

The contractual nature of a covenant means that the original covenantor (he who made the promise) is under the burden of the covenant. He must refrain from doing something on his own land if the covenant is restrictive (negative), or he must carry out the terms of the promise if the covenant is positive. As we shall see, however, performance of this burden is not limited to the original covenantor, but may (if certain conditions are fulfilled) pass or 'run' with the land itself. In other words, any person who subsequently comes into possession of the original covenantor's land may be subject to the burden of the covenant and be required to observe its terms. So, if Mr Smith, the owner of Pinkacre, covenants with Mr Jones, the owner of Blackacre, that he (Smith) will not carry on a trade or business on Pinkacre, it is perfectly possible for any future owner (or, indeed, a mere occupier) of Pinkacre to be bound to observe the covenant, whether or not that new owner specifically agrees to the covenant. The burden of the covenant may 'run' with the land.

8.1.3.2   *The covenantee's land: The benefit of the covenant*

Likewise, there is no doubt that the original covenantee (the person to whom the promise was made) has the 'benefit' of the covenant and may enforce it as a matter of contract. He has the right to sue for performance of the covenant and may be awarded damages (for past breaches of covenant), an injunction (to prevent impending breaches of covenant), or a decree of specific performance (to compel performance of a positive covenant). Once again, however, in certain circumstances, the ability to enforce the covenant may 'run' with the land benefited by the covenant and pass to any subsequent owner of it, giving that person the ability to obtain the appropriate remedy. So, adopting the above example, if Mr Jones, the owner of Blackacre (the land having the benefit of the covenant) sells that land to another person, the new owner may obtain the benefit of the covenant as being attached to the land he acquires, and may sue the person now subject to the burden of it. As can be seen, this means that the landowners who are parties to 'an action on the covenant' may, or may not, be the original covenantor and original covenantee. Assuming the requisite conditions are satisfied (on which see below), the parties to an action can be the current owners of the burdened and benefited land.

---

10 They may not subsist as legal property interests (section 1 of the LPA 1925), although the covenant may create
    obligations at law as a matter of contract between the original parties. In its final report on this subject, the Law
    Commission may propose that covenants do become enforceable at law – but that is not yet certain.

8.1.3.3   *The duality of benefit and burden*

In practice, what we have just discussed is the proprietary nature of covenants: that is, their ability to impose benefits and burdens on land so that any owner or occupier of the land may be affected by the covenant, either as to burden or as to benefit. In short, the covenant has been attached to the land itself. Obviously, in practice, the person claiming the benefit of a covenant usually will be the owner for the time being of the benefited land, and the person allegedly subject to the burden usually will be the owner for the time being of the burdened land. Indeed, it is important to realise that in all cases in which a person is seeking to enforce a freehold covenant, it must be possible to show both that the benefit of the covenant has run to the claimant *and* that the burden has run to the defendant. In the following sections, we shall see that the rules or conditions for the transmission of the benefit and then of the burden of a freehold covenant are different. However, the essential fact remains that before any covenant can be enforced, it must be shown separately that the benefit has passed to the claimant (under the appropriate rules) and that the burden has passed to the defendant (under the appropriate rules). Without this duality, there can be no action 'on the covenant'.[11]

8.2   The Relevance of *Law* and *Equity* and the Enforcement of Covenants

The history of land law is replete with references to the differences between 'common law' and 'equity' and this is one area in which the old distinctions still have some relevance today. Historically, this distinction resulted from the different types of remedy available in a court of law or in a court of equity and particularly because of the latter's willingness to allow the covenant to 'run' with the land more easily. It was, in essence, the willingness of courts of equity to give a remedy against a person other than the original covenantor that caused the evolution of the covenant from a purely contractual animal (giving a remedy 'at law') to a proprietary animal (giving a remedy at first in equity and now also occasionally at law). This duality – that a covenant is both a contract and a proprietary obligation – persists to this day and the distinction between enforcement *at law* (whether contractual or proprietary) and enforcement *in equity* can still have consequences, although there is a tendency to downplay these, save where this is impossible.[12]

8.2.1   Suing at law

If a person sues on a covenant at law, he will be claiming that the defendant is subject to the burden of the covenant at law and should pay damages. If successful, the claimant has a right to those damages, which the court cannot refuse. As we shall see, the circumstances

---

11 *Thamesmead Town v. Allotey* (1998).

12 For example, in *Gafford v. Graham* (1998), the court observed that the defence of acquiescence (usually an equitable defence) should operate identically whether the claimant was claiming suit at law or in equity.

in which a remedy lies at law (i.e. for damages) are narrower than the situations in which a remedy lies in equity.

8.2.2   Suing in equity

The story of the courts of equity is that they would always act to mitigate the harshness of the common law and this is amply reflected in the modern rules concerning the enforcement of freehold covenants. Consequently, not only is it easier to enforce a covenant in equity, but the range of potential defendants is much greater because the *burden* of a covenant may run with the land in equity in a way that is impossible at law. Moreover, because enforcement of the covenant is in equity, equitable remedies are available, although unlike remedies at law they are subject to the discretion of the court and may be withheld in an appropriate case. These remedies are the injunction (for restrictive covenants) and the decree of specific performance (for positive covenants).[13] Finally, and perhaps most importantly of all, if the claimant sues in equity, either because they are required to (as where the defendant is not the original covenantor) or out of choice (because they do not want 'mere' damages), then the normal principles of registered and unregistered conveyancing come into operation. These will be considered below, but for now, the point is that a restrictive covenant[14] may need to be registered in the manner appropriate to either registered or unregistered land (as the case may be) in order to be enforceable against certain kinds of defendant.

To sum up then, in any concrete case involving the enforcement of freehold covenants, there are always two issues of primary importance: first, has the benefit of the covenant run to the claimant in law or equity; and second, has the burden of the covenant also passed to the defendant in law or in equity? Importantly, it also seems that there must be symmetry about the running of the benefit and burden. So, if the claimant is suing at law, he must establish that the defendant is subject to the burden at law and if the claimant is suing in equity, he must establish that the burden has passed to the defendant in equity.

8.3   The Factual Context for the Enforcement of Freehold Covenants

As the title of this chapter makes clear, the rules about to be discussed operate when one freeholder has the right to enforce a covenant against another freeholder. This may be when the claimant and defendant are the original parties to the covenant or where the claimant/defendant has acquired the benefited/burdened land from the original parties and the covenant has 'run' with the land. However, it is not only in actions between freeholders that these rules may be relevant. In fact, they may be applicable between any claimant and defendant who do not stand in a relationship of 'privity of contract' or

---

13 In appropriate cases, damages may be awarded in lieu of an injunction (see e.g. *Small v. Oliver & Saunders* (2006)), but usually the claimant wants to compel the defendant to perform the covenant or to desist from some activity that breaches it.

14 As we shall see, the burden of positive covenants cannot pass at all, either at law or in equity.

'privity of estate'. Consequently, as well as regulating actions on the covenant between freeholders, these rules also will be relevant when a landlord seeks to enforce a covenant contained in a lease against a subtenant and where a landlord seeks to enforce a leasehold covenant against a person who has taken only an equitable lease or an equitable assignment of a lease under an assignment taking effect on or before 1 January 1996.[15] Finally, the rules may also be relevant where the claimant is seeking to enforce a restrictive covenant (but not a positive one) against someone whose claim to an estate in the burdened land is merely possessory: for example, an adverse possessor.

8.4   Principle 1: Enforcing the Covenant in an Action between the Original Covenantor and the Original Covenantee

A covenant is equivalent to a legally binding contract between the covenantor and the covenantee. As such, the covenantee may sue the covenantor for damages at law for breach of covenant or, in appropriate circumstances, obtain one of the equitable remedies of injunction or specific performance. This is straightforward, and is a reflection of the 'privity of contract' that exists between the original covenantee and original covenantor. However, because the benefits and burdens of certain types of covenant are transmissible to subsequent purchasers of both the original covenantor's and original covenantee's land, a number of different situations must be identified.

8.4.1   Both original parties to the covenant in possession of their respective land

If the original covenantor and original covenantee are still in possession of their respective land, the matter is relatively straightforward. *All* covenants between them are enforceable and the covenantee may obtain damages, an injunction (to prevent breach of a restrictive covenant), or specific performance (to ensure compliance with a positive covenant) against the covenantor. This is a matter of contract. For example, in an action between original covenantor and original covenantee, the claimant can enforce a covenant to maintain a boundary fence and a covenant prohibiting the carrying on of a trade or business on the land. Both positive and negative covenants are enforceable between the original parties in possession of their lands.

---

15 For equitable leases/assignments taking effect on or after 1 January 1996, the Landlord and Tenant (Covenants) Act 1995 generally ensures the enforcement of a restrictive covenant against the owner or occupier of land (sections 3(5) and 3(6) of the Act and see Chapter 6). In respect of actions against a subtenant or other occupier of leasehold land, it is not clear whether section 3(5) of the Landlord and Tenant (Covenants) Act 1995 means that restrictive covenants contained in a lease always will be enforceable against subtenants (assuming registration, section 3(6)), or whether the conditions about to be discussed must continue to be fulfilled. The second view is more likely, given the focus of the Act.

8.4.2 After the original *covenantor* has parted with the burdened land

If the original covenantor has parted with the land that was subject to the covenant, he remains liable on all of the covenants to whomsoever has the benefit of the covenant. This is because of the contractual nature of the covenant. However, in most cases, a claimant will want to enforce the substance of the obligation (i.e. making sure the covenant is actually performed) and so will take action against the person currently in possession of the burdened land. Consequently, a remedy against the original covenantor who is no longer in possession of the land is of little practical use unless this is the only person against whom there is a realistic chance of a remedy and where damages are acceptable.

8.4.3 After the original *covenantee* has parted with the benefited land

If the original covenantee has parted with the land that had the benefit of the covenant, he *may* still be able to enforce a covenant against whomsoever has the burden of it. However, when suing at law (i.e. claiming damages), this right will almost certainly have been given up due to an express assignment of the right to sue when the land was transferred to the new owners.[16] In any event, any damages are likely to be only nominal because the real loss has fallen on the person who is actually in possession of the land rather than the original covenantee who is no longer in possession. In addition, when suing at equity (i.e. for an injunction or specific performance), the court is likely in its discretion to refuse to grant an equitable remedy to an original covenantee who no longer is in possession of the benefited land, because, in reality, such a person suffers no loss.[17]

8.4.4 Original *covenantor* having had no land at all at the time the covenant was given

It has always been the case that a covenantor is liable on a covenant at law (but *not* in equity), even if he never had any land burdened by the covenant. This is because the contractual nature of the obligation is not dependent on the existence of any estate in land held by the original covenantor. Therefore, in *Smith and Snipes Hall Farm Ltd v. River Douglas Catchment Board* (1949), the defendant was liable on its positive covenant to repair and maintain river banks even though it had no land burdened by the covenant.

8.4.5 Defining the original covenantee and covenantor

It goes without saying that it is vital to be able to determine exactly who is an 'original' covenantor or covenantee, particularly if either is still in possession of the land, and so able to sue effectively and easily. Usually, of course, this is quite simple, they being the parties to the deed of covenant and identified as such, having signed the deed in the presence of a

---

16 See section 8.8.2 below.

17 *Chambers v. Randall* (1923).

witness: as where the deed recites that 'Mr Smith, freehold owner of Pinkacre, hereby covenants with Mr Jones, freehold owner of Blackacre', and both sign the deed in the presence of a witness. However, it is possible under section 56 of the Law of Property Act 1925 to extend the range of original covenantees (but not covenantors) beyond those persons who are actually parties to the deed in the sense just described. By virtue of section 56, a person may enforce a covenant (i.e. be regarded as an *original* covenantee), even if they are not actually a party to it (i.e. have not signed it under witness), provided that the covenant was intended to confer this benefit on the person *as a party* and the person is in existence and identifiable at the date of the covenant.[18] What this means in practice is that far more people may have the right to the benefit of a covenant as an original covenantee (which may then be transmitted on a sale of *their* land) than simply the person who signs their name to the deed, provided only that the deed does not purport to confer these benefits on 'future' owners of land or persons who cannot be identified. A good example is where A covenants with B 'and with the present owners of Plots 1, 2 and 3' not to carry on any trade or business on his (A's) land. Here, A is the original covenantor, B is an original covenantee and party to the deed, and the owners of Plots 1, 2 and 3 are also original covenantees, by virtue of section 56, provided that they are intended to be treated as parties. Thus the 'benefit' of the covenant is enjoyed originally by four persons, each of whom may pass that benefit with their land if the conditions discussed below are satisfied. Note, however, that it now seems established that section 56 only has this effect when the persons identified in the covenant as being entitled to its benefit are intended to be treated as *parties*, not simply additional persons to whom the benefit has been given.[19] This is a fine distinction, and although it can be crucial (as in *Amsprop Trading Ltd v. Harris Distribution* (1996)), the difficulty can be avoided by careful drafting. Simply put, the point is that section 56 is intended to ensure that specific, identifiable persons are treated as parties to the covenant, and is not intended to confer the benefit of the covenant on hoards of landowners simply because they fall within the literal ambit of a particularly boldly drafted covenant.

8.5   Principle 2: Enforcing the Covenant against Successors in Title to the Original Covenantor – Passing the Burden

One of the great steps forward in English property law was the transformation of freehold covenants from purely personal obligations governed by the law of contract to proprietary obligations governed by the law of real property. This is generally regarded as having been achieved by the landmark case of *Tulk v. Moxhay* (1848), in which a covenant not build on open land in Leicester Square, London, was enforced against the defendant when the defendant was not the original covenantor but a purchaser from him. What this means in simple terms is that if the various conditions discussed below are satisfied, a covenant can

---

18 *White v. Bijou Mansions* (1938).

19 *Amsprop Trading Ltd v. Harris Distribution* (1996). The point is that it is not enough that the persons are intended to take a
    benefit; they must be intended to be parties. Thus, the covenant should be made 'with' them, not merely 'for' them.

be enforced not only against the original covenantor, but also against anyone who comes in to possession of the land burdened by the covenant (i.e. the land over which the covenant operates). Obviously, this might be a severe limitation on the uses to which the burdened land can be put by a successor in title to the original covenantor (e.g. if the land is subject to a covenant against business use, as in *Re Bromor Properties* (1995), or against building, as in *Tulk* itself), and so it is not surprising that there are strict limitations defining the precise circumstances in which the burden of a covenant may 'run' with the land under the *Tulk* principle.

First, it is not possible for the burden of a covenant between freeholders to run *at law* in any circumstances.[20] There can be no claim at law against a successor to the original covenantor. This is simply not possible.[21] However, as noted above, equity is not as strict as the common law and it *is* possible for the burden of *some* (but not all) covenants to run with the land in equity. In short, if a burden is to run at all, it must be in equity. This has its own consequences – in particular, that a claimant relying on the equitable claim takes the risks associated with the enforcement of all equitable rights over land. These are dealt with below, but importantly encompass the rule that the award of a remedy is discretionary (even if the burden has actually run to the defendant) and that the covenant must have been registered appropriately in the systems of registered and unregistered land to be enforceable against purchasers of the burdened land.

Second, even in equity, it is not the burden of every covenant that is capable of passing on transfer of the covenantor's land. The rule is simple – some would say simplistic – and is that only the burden of restrictive covenants are capable of passing.[22] This means that it is not possible for the burden of a positive covenant to be enforced against a successor to the original covenantor, and so only the original covenantor can be liable on positive covenants. For example, if the original covenantor and owner of Plot X has made a covenant with the owner of Plot Y (the original covenantee) not to carry on a trade or business and a covenant to maintain a fence, and then Plot X is sold to a third party, the new owner *could* be liable on the covenant restricting use but *cannot* be liable on the covenant to maintain the fence. Positive burdens cannot pass. This is vitally important. What it means in practice is that, as soon as the land has passed out of the hands of the original covenantor, only restrictive covenants can be enforced against the land, and then only in equity. Indeed, although the claimant may well have the benefit of both positive and restrictive covenants, the defendant can only be liable for breaches of the restrictive ones. Despite some criticism of this rule, there is no doubt that it remains the law. It has been reiterated by House of Lords in *Rhone v. Stephens* (1994) and applied (albeit with considerable reluctance) by the Court of Appeal in *Thamesmead Town v. Allotey* (1998).[23] In both cases, there was distinct judicial criticism of the rule, but the fact that conveyancing practice has developed around it (and because of it!), and the reluctance of the House of Lords to intervene, means that it can be changed only by Act of Parliament. This course of action was urged strongly by the Court of Appeal in *Thamesmead Town*, but there is little hope of legislation in the short term,

---

20 As we have seen, however, the burdens of positive and negative *leasehold* covenants can run with the lease and the reversion in law and in equity – Chapter 6.

21 *Rhone v. Stephens* (1994).

22 *Hayward v. Brunswick Building Society* (1881); *Thamesmead Town v. Allotey* (1998).

23 See also, more recently, *Cantrell v. Wycombe DC* (2009).

despite the fact that the burden of positive *leasehold* covenants is easily transmissible.[24] Note, however, that the Law Commission has argued persuasively that there is no reason of principle why the burden of positive obligations should not run with freehold land and has produced a comprehensive consultation document seeking views on the best way to amend the law.[25] For now, it remains vital to be able to distinguish between those freehold covenants that impose on the covenantor an obligation to act (positive), and those that impose an obligation to refrain from acting (negative). The precise conditions for the passing of the burdens of restrictive covenants are discussed below.

8.5.1   The covenant must be restrictive or negative in nature

As noted immediately above, and mentioned here for the sake of completeness, it is vital that the covenant be restrictive (or negative) in nature. Importantly, this is a question of substance, not of form, and it is irrelevant how the covenant is actually worded – as in *Tulk v. Moxhay* itself, in which a covenant expressed in terms of the need to keep land as an open space was rightly held to be negative in substance because, in reality, it was a covenant not to build. The essence is that a covenant is negative if it prevents the land-owner from doing something on his own land, however it may be worded. Typical examples include a covenant not to carry on any trade or business, a covenant not to build and a covenant not to sell certain types of product. In this sense, a covenant that compels the owner of land to spend money on his property will usually be regarded as positive, and hence unenforceable against successors to the original covenantor. A covenant to maintain a boundary fence is a good example,[26] as is the covenant to repair a roof considered by the House of Lords in *Rhone v. Stephens* (1994).

8.5.2   The covenant must touch and concern the land

It is axiomatic that only a covenant that relates to the use or value of the land should be capable of passing with a transfer of it. The law of property is generally concerned with proprietary obligations, not personal ones. Consequently, only the burden of restrictive covenants that 'touch and concern' the land are capable of being enforced against successors in title to the original covenantor.[27] There is one possible exception to this rule, being the case in which a head landlord attempts to enforce a leasehold restrictive covenant against a subtenant. Such parties do not stand in either privity of contract or privity of estate, so, as noted above, the 'freehold covenant rules' are applicable. However, according to section 3(5) of the Landlord and Tenant (Covenants) Act 1995, 'any' landlord or tenant's restrictive covenant contained in a lease to which the Act applies[28] 'shall' be capable of being enforced against any owner or occupier of the land, subject to requirements of

---

24 Especially for leases granted on or after 1 January 1996 – see Chapter 6.

25 See Law Commission Report No. 127, *Transfer of Land: The Law of Positive and Restrictive Covenants* (1984), and Law Commission Consultation Paper No. 186, *Easements, Covenants and Profits à Prendre* (2008).

26 For example, *Norwich City College of Further & Higher Education v. McQuillin* (2009).

27 The original covenantor is, of course, liable on all covenants. Thus, as explained above, it is not even necessary for the original covenantor to have land in order to be liable on the covenant at law.

28 Leases granted on or after 1 January 1996.

registration.[29] There is nothing in this section that requires a leasehold restrictive covenant concerning the demised land to 'touch and concern', and it may be that this requirement has been abolished (possibly accidentally?) in those cases in which the burden of a *leasehold* restrictive covenant is being enforced under the 'freehold covenants' rules.

The above point aside then, there is no doubt that for restrictive covenants between freeholders,[30] the requirement of 'touching and concerning' still applies.[31] Indeed, given that the Tulk principle is applicable most frequently in disputes concerning freeholders, the importance of the requirement is apparent. In practice, assessment of whether the covenant 'touches and concerns' usually occurs in relation to the question whether the *benefit* of a covenant has passed with the land, rather than the burden. This is simply because it is axiomatic that if a covenant confers a proprietary *benefit* on land, it necessarily involves a proprietary burden on the land once owned by the original covenantor. Lest we think, however, that the lack of explicit mention of a 'touching and concerning' requirement means that it is not required when considering the passing of the burden, we should remember that the additional requirement of registration when considering the running of the burden – discussed below – necessarily assumes that the burden is proprietary in nature. It is generally impossible to protect by registration a burden against land that is merely personal.

In essence, whether any particular restrictive covenant does 'touch and concern' will depend on the facts of each case, but a general test has been laid down by Lord Oliver in *Swift Investments v. Combined English Stores* (1989).[32] This test, which is not rigid in its application, but is a valuable guide, requires us to ask a number of questions. First, could the covenant burden *any* owner of an estate in the land as opposed to the particular original owner? If it could, it may 'touch and concern', as this shows that the covenant has meaning even though the original covenantor is no longer in possession of the estate. Second, does the covenant affect the nature, quality, mode of user or value of the land?[33] Again, if the covenant affects how the land may be utilised or its value to *any* purchaser, it is likely to touch and concern. Third, is the covenant expressed to be personal so that, irrespective of its substance, it is meant to operate only as a promise binding the original covenantor?[34]

Consideration of these issues should be enough to determine whether the restrictive covenant 'touches and concerns' the land and they will be applied with reference to the mass of case law on this point. Perhaps the safest route for a conveyancer when attempting

---

29 See sections 8.5.5–8.5.6 below.

30 And in other situations in which the 'freehold rules' are relevant save, possibly, in a lease granted on or after 1 January 1996.

31 See, for example, *Robins v. Berkeley Homes* (1996).

32 Although developed in the context of leasehold covenants, this test applies with equal force to freehold covenants.

33 For example, the classic user covenants, such as that not to carry on a trade or business, or a certain trade, not to build, not to keep any animals.

34 An example is *Margerison v. Bates* (2009). Express words may be used, as where a covenant is expressed 'to be enforceable only against the person hereinafter named as the original covenantor' or this may arise from construction of the covenant, as in *Margerison*, in which the covenant was limited to 'the vendor', thus indicating that it was not intended to operate as a proprietary obligation. It seems then that, unlike issues concerning the existence of a lease (*Street v. Mountford* (1985) – Chapter 6), the parties' intentions can undo what might otherwise be a proprietary obligation. See also *Sugarman v. Porter* (2006).

to ensure that a covenant 'touches and concerns' is to follow the advice of Wilberforce J in *Marten v. Flight Refuelling* (1962) that a covenant that expressly states that it is imposed for the purpose of affecting land will normally be taken by the court as being capable of doing so. Assuming, then, that this hurdle has been cleared, the remaining conditions must be met.

8.5.3 The covenant must have been imposed to benefit land of the original covenantee

This condition is one that expresses most clearly the nature of a covenant as affecting both benefited and burdened land. It means that the burden cannot pass at all unless the *covenantee* had land at the time the covenant was made *and* that that land was capable of benefiting from the covenant *and* that the burden was imposed in order to benefit that land.[35] In other words, the covenant must have been made to benefit *land* and if there is no benefit or no such land, the covenant is unenforceable other than against the original covenantor. In the language of easements, there must be a 'dominant tenement' that could benefit from this restrictive covenant,[36] although the condition is satisfied if the covenant was made to benefit the proprietary interest of the covenantee, such as that held by a lessor or a mortgagee.[37]

A common reason why there may have been no land owned by the covenantee that was intended to benefit from the covenant at the time it was given is the simple one that the original covenantee may not have retained any such land at that time. For example, if Smith sells Blackacre to Jones, and in the sale Jones (as original covenantor) covenants with Smith (as original covenantee) not to build on Blackacre, the burden may run to Jones' successors in title only if Smith retained some land at the time the covenant was executed.[38] If Smith sold everything at that time (i.e. he kept no portion of Blackacre), he remains the original covenantee, but has no benefited land, and so the burden cannot pass to successors of the original covenantor. Likewise, the covenant must have been undertaken in order to benefit the land and be capable of so benefiting. Thus the substance of the covenant must be such that it confers a proprietary advantage on the covenantee's land[39] and the relationship between the plots of land must be such that a benefit does indeed accrue. So, like

---

35 *Whitgift Homes Ltd v. Stocks* (2001).

36 *London and South Western Railway v. Gomm* (1882).

37 There is no separate physical land in these cases, but there is a separate benefiting estate. There are also statutory exceptions in favour of local authorities under the Town and Country Planning Acts and Housing Acts, and in favour of certain other bodies such as the National Trust. So, contrary to the general rule, a restrictive covenant may be enforced against a landowner by a local authority, even if it (the authority) did not own land at the time of the covenant – see *Cantrell v. Wycombe DC* (2009), applying section 609 of the Housing Act 1985, but where it is made clear that all of the other conditions must still be met. See also the last sale by a developer under a 'building scheme' – the developer retains no land, but the covenant is still effective.

38 *Formby v. Barker* (1903).

39 This appears to be equivalent to the touching and concerning requirement. 'Land' here means the estate of the covenantee, so a covenant specifically imposed to benefit a tenant's leasehold interest only may be enforced only by the holder of the lease (*Golden Lion Hotel v. Carter* (1965)). Absent a specific limitation to a particular estate, the benefit may then be enforced by the holder of any estate in the land and, in the case of restrictive covenants, by an adverse possessor (section 78 of the LPA 1925).

easements, it would be unusual for a covenant to be transmissible if it were to impose a burden on one plot of land for the alleged benefit of land that was not reasonably geographically close.

8.5.4   The burden of the restrictive covenant must be intended to run with the land

A further condition is that the burden of the restrictive covenant must have been intended to run with the land of the original covenantor: that is, there must be evidence to establish that the 'burden' was intended to be enforceable whomsoever came into possession of the burdened land. However, this is not difficult to establish because, in the absence of a contrary intention, the burden of a restrictive covenant is deemed to be attached to the land by virtue of section 79 of the LPA 1925. According to section 79(1):

> A covenant relating to any land of the covenantor . . . shall, unless a contrary intention is expressed, be deemed to be made by the covenantor on behalf of himself, his successors in title and the persons deriving title under him.

By virtue of this section, the burden of a covenant is deemed to be made by the original covenantor on behalf of himself and all future owners of the land, thereby annexing the burden of the covenant to that land because of a statutory presumption of an intention that it shall run.[40] The burden may then become enforceable against such successors. A 'successor' is someone with a legal or equitable estate in the land[41] and, for restrictive covenants only, includes any person in occupation of the land without an estate, such as an adverse possessor (section 79(2) of the LPA 1925). Of course, this statutorily assisted annexation of the burden occurs 'unless a contrary intention appears', and it is clear that the covenant does not have to recite specifically that section 79 is inapplicable to exclude its effect.[42] A 'contrary intention' will 'appear' from the instrument creating the covenant if there is anything in it indicating that successors in title or assigns of the original covenantor would not be bound, as in *Morrells v. Oxford United FC* (2000), in which section 79 was found to be excluded by the whole tenor of the arrangement between the parties. Clearly, whether section 79 of the LPA 1925 is so excluded is a matter of construction, and so the safest course for someone wishing to exclude statutory annexation of the burden would be to say so in clear terms in the deed of covenant.

8.5.5   Registration

The fifth and final condition that must be satisfied before the burden can be enforced against a successor to the original covenantor arises because such burdens may be enforced only in equity. In short, restrictive covenants are equitable interests in another's land, and in consequence must comply with the rules of registered and unregistered conveyancing relating to such interests.

---

40 *Tophams Ltd v. Earl of Sefton* (1967).

41 *Mellon v. Sinclair* (1996).

42 *Re Royal Victoria Pavilion, Ramsgate* (1961).

8.5.5.1   *In registered land*

If the person against whom the restrictive covenant is being enforced is a purchaser of a registered title under a properly registered disposition (which includes a mortgage), the covenant must have been protected by the registration of a notice against the burdened title in order to be enforceable.[43] Should it not be so registered, it loses its priority and cannot be enforced against the purchaser (section 29 of the LRA 2002).[44] Of course, most transferees of the burdened land will be purchasers and registered as title-holders in this way[45] and most restrictive covenants will have been protected by registration of a notice at the time they were created. However, even if not protected by the entry of a notice, a restrictive covenant will nevertheless remain enforceable against a transferee in two cases (section 28 of the LRA Act 2002). First, it will remain enforceable (whether registered or not) against a registered proprietor who is not a purchaser of the burdened land for valuable consideration: for example, the donee of a gift, a devisee under a will or an adverse possessor. Second, it will remain enforceable (whether registered or not) against someone who purchases only an equitable interest in the land: for example, an equitable tenant or a purchaser who fails to register his or her disposition.[46]

8.5.5.2   *In unregistered land*

If the person against whom the restrictive covenant is being enforced is a purchaser of a legal estate in the burdened land for money or money's worth, the covenant must have been registered against the name of the original covenantor as a Class D(ii) land charge under sections 2(5) and 4(6) of the Land Charges Act (LCA) 1972 in order to be so enforceable. Of course, most transferees will be purchasers of this type and most covenants will be registered in this way. However, if the restrictive covenant is not registered in this way, it will be void and unenforceable forever if the land is sold to a purchaser[47] and cannot be revived by subsequent registration when the land becomes land of registered title. Note, however, that even an unregistered restrictive covenant can be binding in unregistered

---

43 Given that registration will occur normally when the covenant is made, registration is likely to be with the agreement of the registered proprietor of the burdened plot (the original covenantor) and thus an agreed notice may be used. However, a unilateral notice may be used if such agreement is not forthcoming or indeed if it is desired to keep specific details of the covenant away from public inspection.

44 Such a covenant would have been registrable as a minor interest under the LRA 1925 and void against a purchaser (section 20 of the LRA 1925).

45 Or treated as such, as with lessees under a legal lease that cannot be substantively registered (section 29(4) of the LRA 2002).

46 Such a purchaser does not take under a registered disposition. In addition, it is plausible that a purchaser under a registered disposition might agree expressly to give effect to an unprotected covenant in return for paying a lower price for the land. In such a case, the purchaser may be required in equity to give effect to the unprotected covenant by means of a personal constructive trust (*Lyus v. Prowsa Developments* (1982); *Binions v. Evans* (1972)).

47 Such a purchaser will purchase under the rubric of unregistered conveyancing and will apply for first registration of title. If the covenant was registered as a Class D(ii) land charge, it will be transferred to the new registered title and a notice will be entered against the newly registered title. If it is not so registered, it would have become void on the sale and remains void at first registration (section 11 of the LRA 2002).

conveyancing in some circumstances: first, against someone who is not a purchaser – for example, the donee of a gift, the devisee under a will or an adverse possessor; second, against someone who does not give 'money or money's worth' – for example, the recipient of land under marriage consideration; and third, against someone who purchases only an equitable estate – for example, an equitable tenant.[48]

8.5.6   The equitable nature of the remedy

To conclude, then, the burden of a restrictive covenant may run in equity to successors of the original covenantor if certain conditions are met. In the great majority of cases, the conditions will be met, and the only real issue is likely to be whether the covenant was appropriately registered. Assuming that it was – and the other conditions are satisfied – the burden runs and the defendant is liable. Even then, however, the award of equitable remedies is discretionary, and the claimant may not get what he asked for. For example, in *Thamesmead Town v. Allotey* (1998), damages were awarded instead of the desired injunction.[49] In the worst possible scenario for the claimant, the court might decide that he has behaved so inequitably that neither an injunction nor damages should be awarded, despite the fact that the burden of the covenant has run to the defendant. This might occur in cases in which there has been unreasonable delay on the part of the person seeking to enforce the covenant or where the claimant has stood by while the defendant has breached the covenant. So, in *Gafford v. Graham* (1998), the claimant was denied both an injunction and damages in respect of the breach of one covenant because he had acquiesced in the conduct that was in breach and was granted only damages in respect of another breach. Importantly, however, it is now clear that the denial of a remedy depends on the claimant having behaved unconscionably (*Harris v. Williams-Wynne* (2006)). For example, in *Williams-Wynne*, the defendant had never believed that he was bound by the covenant against building and thus the claimant's acquiescence in the breach was not the reason why the defendant had gone ahead. Consequently, the claimant was not denied a remedy as his actions had produced no effect on the defendant, and so it was not unconscionable to seek to enforce the covenant. Damages were awarded.[50] Although one can see the logic of this position – that if a defendant would have behaved as they did in any event, then the claimant's acquiescence is not the reason for the breach of covenant – the decision here might well be as far as we can go. We might argue that the relevant point is not whether the claimant's acquiescence caused the defendant's breach of covenant, but whether the claimant should have done something to stop the defendant breaching the covenant. Thus, if the claimant knew that the covenant was binding, and knew that the defendant incorrectly believed that it was not, then perhaps the claimant is behaving unconscionably by allowing the defendant to continue in his mistaken belief, such unconscionability becoming crystallised as an estoppel when detriment is incurred?[51]

---

48 Note also the possibility put forward in *Lyus v. Prowsa Developments* and *Binions v. Evans*, noted above fn. 46.

49 See also *Small v. Oliver & Saunders* (2006).

50 There was no claim to an injunction or order of specific performance and, of course, it is likely that these remedies would have been denied.

51 See Chapter 9 on proprietary estoppel.

8.6   Principle 3: Passing the Benefit of a Covenant to Successors in Title to the Original Covenantee

As indicated at the beginning of this chapter, in all cases in which it is proposed to enforce a covenant, it must be possible to show both that the defendant has the burden and that the claimant has the benefit of the covenant. There must be correlative rights and obligations. Before dealing with the matter in detail, a number of preliminary points relating to the passing of the benefit should be noted.

First, the benefit of a covenant may be passed at law or in equity (unlike the burden, which passes only in equity). The conditions for the transmission of the benefit in equity are slightly easier to satisfy than those needed to pass the benefit at law. Also, the benefit of both positive *and* restrictive covenants may pass at law and in equity, although the fact that only the burdens of restrictive covenants may pass means that, if the original covenantor has parted with the land, only restrictive covenants are in issue. Second, given again that only the burden of restrictive covenants may pass, and then only in equity, in practice the claimant usually pleads that the benefit has also passed in equity (as explained in *Gafford* v. *Graham* (1998)). This will give us our claimant (benefit) and defendant (burden) suing in equity. In effect, then, this means that the passing of the benefit of covenants *at law* and the passing of the benefit of *positive* covenants are relevant in practice only when the claimant is suing the original covenantor as this is the only person liable in such cases.

8.6.1   Passing the benefit of positive and negative covenants at law

To reiterate, passing the benefit of positive and negative covenants at law will be relevant only when the claimant – the successor to the original covenantee – is claiming the benefit of such covenants in order to sue the original covenantor. If any other person is the defendant, the claimant must sue in equity, and on a restrictive covenant, as it is only the burdens of these that are capable of passing. With that practical limitation in mind, the conditions for the passing of the benefit of a freehold covenant at law are as follows.

1   The covenant must 'touch and concern' the land of the original covenantee (*Rogers* v. *Hosegood* (1900)). In other words, as before, the covenant must relate to use of the land and not be merely personal in nature. The test of 'touching and concerning' is the same as that discussed above. In essence, we are searching for a covenant that could benefit *any* estate owner as opposed to the particular original covenantee, or for a covenant that affects the nature, quality, mode of user or value of the land, not being one that is expressed to be personal to the original covenantee.[52]

2   The claimant must have a legal estate in the land, although, by virtue of section 78 of the LPA 1925, the claimant does not have to have the *same* legal estate as the original covenantee. Thus, the original covenantee may have been the freeholder, but the

---

52 *Swift Investments* v. *Combined English Stores* (1989) and see *Sugarman* v. *Porter* (2006).

claimant will succeed even if they have 'only' a legal lease. Importantly, however, any occupier (including an adverse possessor) may enforce the benefit of a restrictive covenant. This is because section 78 of the LPA 1925 deems 'the owners and occupiers for the time being' to be successors in title for the purpose of enforcing restrictive (but not positive) covenants. This mirrors the position in respect of the burden of restrictive covenants.[53]

3   The benefit of the covenant must have been annexed to a legal estate in the land, either expressly or by implication. A covenant may be annexed expressly by words that make it clear that the covenant is for the benefit of certain land, or by words that make it clear that the covenant is intended to endure for successive owners of the land: for example, where a covenant is with the 'heirs and successors of X, the owner for the time being' of Plot 2. In either case, however, the land must be readily identifiable, and capable of benefiting from the covenant (*Re Gadd's Transfer* (1966)) and this must be possible at the time the covenant is executed, rather than the (later) time when the title to which it relates (i.e. on which the benefit is conferred) is presented for registration.[54] This has the happy side-effect that the benefit of a freehold covenant still annexes to the estate in the land even if the first owner of the benefited land (i.e. the original covenantee) delays or forgets to apply for registration as proprietor. This is to be contrasted with the unhappy side-effect produced by *Brown and Root v. Sun Alliance* (1996) in the law of leasehold covenants in pre-1996 leases, where lack of registration of the lease seriously disrupts the passing of the leasehold covenant.[55] A covenant will be assumed to benefit land where it affects the value, method of enjoyment or mode of user of the land to which it is annexed. Importantly, however, as well as annexation by the act of the parties, a covenant[56] may be annexed by virtue of section 78 of the LPA 1925, as discussed in *Federated Homes v. Mill Lodge Properties* (1980), *Whitgift Homes v. Stocks* (2001) and *Crest Nicholson Residential v. McAllister* (2004). According to the Court of Appeal in *Federated Homes*, section 78 of the LPA 1925 has the effect of statutorily annexing the benefit of every covenant – both positive and negative – to each and every part of the benefited land. The only conditions are that the land is capable of benefiting from the covenant and that the land can be easily identified from the deed. This second condition – that the land to be benefited must be easily identified from the deed for statutory annexation to apply – once generated some uncertainty, for it was not clear whether the covenant itself had to describe the land in such a way that it was identifiable (albeit with the aid of some extrinsic evidence) or whether it was sufficient (on a more generous view) for the land to be identified even if it was not described in some way in the deed. Now, however, *Crest Nicholson* has settled the matter. In that case, McAllister was seeking to enforce covenants that had not been expressly annexed and Chadwick LJ was faced with the puzzle posed by *Federated Homes*. In essence, his Lordship applied the test put forward in the earlier case of *Marquess of Zetland v. Driver* (1939) and decided

---

53 See section 79(2) of the LPA 1925 and section 8.5.4 above.

54 *Mellon v. Sinclair* (1996).

55 See further Chapter 6.

56 That is, covenants entered into on or after 1 January 1926. For pre-1926 covenants, express or implied annexation by act of the parties is required.

that, in order for statutory annexation to apply, the covenant must describe the land in such a way that it is easily ascertainable *from the covenant*, albeit with the assistance of some extrinsic evidence. This is, then, broadly in line with the narrower of the two possible interpretations of *Federated Homes* and it accords with the principle that the benefit is being attached to land by the covenant and so the covenant itself must identify the land.[57] Extrinsic evidence will thus be available to bring clarity to the description provided by the covenant, but not to identify the land when the covenant itself is silent. In practice, this means that, unless a contrary intention is clearly shown,[58] the benefit of most covenants will now be annexed to the covenantee's land and be available to a purchaser of it, or part of it, provided that the covenant itself identifies the land in such a way that the benefited land is easily ascertainable.[59] The decision in *Federated Homes* was of considerable interest and this is not lessened by the clarification provided by *Crest Nicholson*. The overall effect is to ensure that the benefit of covenants (created after 1925) will attach to each and every part of benefited land, and (subject to the other conditions) will run to successors in title of the original covenantee, even if the original benefited land is subsequently sold off in parts. So, if X (original covenantor) covenants with Y that no trade or business is permitted on X's land, the benefit of that covenant will attach to each and every part of Y's land, and subsequent purchasers of the whole, or part of it, will obtain the benefit of the covenant.[60] If we then imagine that Y is a property developer, selling off individual plots on a housing estate, the wide impact of section 78 is obvious, as apparent from very similar facts in *Whitgift Homes* (2001). However, although much has been written about *Federated Homes* – for example, whether section 78 of the LPA 1925 was ever intended to have this wide effect – it is not at all clear that the interpretation has had much effect on the practical realities of freehold covenant disputes. In most cases, the covenant will have been drafted expressly with annexation in mind – either expressly to exclude it[61] or expressly to include it. This means that practical impact of *Federated Homes* will be felt most readily in those less frequent cases in which the covenant is silent or ambivalent about its intended effect on purchasers of the benefited land (usually as a result of inattentive drafting), in which case statutory annexation to each and every part may follow. *Whitgift Homes* v. *Stocks* (2001) is just such a case, concerning a dispute over a housing development completed in the 1920s and 1930s and in which statutory annexation was central to the question whether certain covenants were now enforceable.

4   As an alternative to annexation, it is possible for the benefit of a covenant at law – the right to sue – to be assigned expressly to another person. This is in essence the assignment of a 'chose in action' within section 136 of the Law of Property Act 1925 and must be in writing, with written notice being given to the covenantor. It is not a very common method of passing the benefit at law, especially given the impact of the *Federated Homes* case discussed above.

---

57 This was effectively the position adopted in *Whitgift Homes* v. *Stocks* (2001).

58 *Roake* v. *Chadha* (1984), confirmed in *Crest Nicholson*.

59 It may therefore require care when drafting covenants.

60 For example, *Robins* v. *Berkeley Homes* (1996).

61 And possibly to provide for express assignment of the benefit instead – see section 8.6.2 below.

So, to conclude this analysis, if the above conditions are satisfied, the claimant, being a successor to the original covenantee, may sue any person *at law* who is subject to the burden of the covenant. However, in practice, because of the limited ability of burdens to pass and then only in equity, the defendant to an action on the covenant *at law* is going to be the original covenantor. No other person can be liable at law and the same is true if the covenant is positive.

8.6.2   Passing the benefit of covenants in equity

This brings us to consideration of the principles concerning the passing of the benefit in equity. The rules about to be discussed apply equally to positive and negative covenants, but (once again) because the burden of a positive covenant cannot run, the principles have developed primarily in the context of restrictive covenants and their enforcement against successors of the original covenantor. With that significant point in mind, there are a number of conditions to be satisfied in order to establish that the benefit of a covenant has passed in equity.

1   The covenant must 'touch and concern' the land of the original covenantee (*Rogers v. Hosegood* (1900)). This is identical to the position 'at law' discussed above. We might note, however, that if the claimant is trying to use the 'freehold' rules to enforce a leasehold restrictive covenant against, say, a subtenant or adverse possessor (i.e. *not an assignee* of the original tenant), it is arguable that the Landlord and Tenant (Covenants) Act 1995 has removed the 'touching and concerning' requirement for a restrictive covenant contained in a lease granted on or after 1 January 1996. So, for example, if the head landlord is attempting to enforce a restrictive covenant prohibiting 'any occupier wearing brown shoes' – which clearly does not touch and concern – it is arguable that the benefit of this covenant runs to a new landlord because of the 1995 Act. We shall probably never know whether this is correct, because, in practice, it is unlikely that a landlord would ever wish to enforce such a clearly personal leasehold restrictive covenant against an occupier.

2   The claimant must have a legal or equitable estate in the land of the original covenantee. Again, this is similar to the position 'at law' and, by virtue of section 78 of the LPA 1925, the claimant does not have to have the same estate as the original covenantee. For example, the claimant may be the equitable tenant of the original covenantee. Moreover, it remains true that *any* occupier (including an adverse possessor) may enforce the benefit of a restrictive covenant because section 78 deems 'the owners and occupiers for the time being' to be successors in title for the purpose of enforcing restrictive (but *not* positive) covenants. It will be appreciated that this is particularly important given that a claim in equity will usually be to enforce a restrictive covenant against a successor of the original covenantor in a situation in which the burden of a restrictive covenant may well have passed.

3   The benefit of the covenant must have been transmitted to the claimant in one of three ways.

     (i)   *Annexation: express and statutory* – The benefit of a covenant can be expressly annexed to the land in equity in exactly the same way as at law. Indeed, the same words will, in most cases, annex the benefit of the covenant at law and in equity simultaneously. Again, it is important that the words establish that the covenant is for the benefit of certain land, or make it clear that the covenant is intended to endure for successive owners of the land. This was not the case in the marginal decision in *Lamb* v. *Midas Equipment* (1999), in which the Privy Council held, on appeal from Jamaica, that a covenant to X and 'his heirs, executors, administrators, transferees and assigns' (surprisingly) did not result in express annexation to the land but was meant to describe the covenantee personally. Moreover, the land must be readily identifiable at the time the covenant is executed – *Mellon* v. *Sinclair* (1996) – and be capable of benefiting from the covenant, according to the general test laid down in *Re Gadd's Transfer* (1996). Once again, however, it is the effect of section 78 of the LPA 1925, as discussed in *Federated Homes* and clarified by *Crest Nicholson*, that is most important here. As already explained in the context of covenants running at law, according to section 78, '[a] covenant relating to any land of the covenantee shall be deemed to be made with the covenantee and his successors in title and the persons deriving title under him or them, and shall have effect as if such successors and other persons were expressed'. Although this was thought to be a 'word-saving' provision that simply ensured that 'successors', and so on, were deemed to be included in the deed, but without doing away with the necessity of finding the relevant express intention to annex, Brightman LJ, in *Federated Homes*, makes it clear that the effect of section 78 (by including these words in the deed) is to annex automatically the benefit of the covenant to the covenantee's land. Again, of course, the land has to be readily identifiable from the deed as explained in *Crest Nicholson* and capable of benefiting from the covenant, but, if these conditions are satisfied, the benefit of the covenant is annexed to each and every part of the land. It will, therefore, be available to a purchaser of the whole or any part of it. Again, as noted, 'automatic statutory annexation' can be avoided by an express contrary intention (*Roake* v. *Chadha* (1984))[62] and the doubts expressed earlier about the practical impact of *Federated Homes* are equally applicable here. However, as a consequence of the combination of better drafting skills (to ensure express annexation) and *Federated Homes*, it now seems that the other two methods of passing the benefit of a covenant in equity are now less important, although, as we shall see, the 'scheme of development' does give some additional advantages.

(ii) *Assignment: express or implied* – As an alternative to annexation, the claimant may rely on the general rule that the benefit of a contract may be assigned expressly to another person. This means that it is perfectly possible for the original covenantee expressly to assign the benefit of a covenant to the transferee at the same time as he transfers the land.[63] Again, the land must be capable of benefiting from the covenant, and must be readily identifiable and, if the claimant is suing someone other than the original covenantor, the assignment must be made together with a transfer of the benefited land.[64] It is important to note here that

---

62 See also *Sugarman* v. *Porter* (2006), in which there was an intention to benefit only the original covenantee, thus providing a sufficient contrary intention to prevent the operation of section 78 of the LPA 1925.

63 The assignment would normally be clearly expressed, but it is sufficient if there were a clear intention to assign.

64 *Chambers* v. *Randall* (1923). The original covenantor is, of course, liable on the covenant and so the claimant under an assignment need not establish that he (the claimant) has land.

this is an assignment of the benefit of the covenant *inter partes*; it is not an annexation of the covenant to the land (*Marten v. Flight Refuelling* (1962)). Theoretically, therefore, if the purchaser of the land, who has had the benefit of the covenant assigned to them, transfers the land again, there should be another assignment of the benefit to the second purchaser. So, if the benefit is to be transmitted with the land in perpetuity, a 'chain of assignments' appears to be necessary, as held in *Re Pinewood Estates* (1958). However, some earlier cases suggest that once the benefit has been assigned with the land initially, it thereafter becomes annexed to the land,[65] although this does appear an illogical conclusion if one has chosen the express assignment method precisely because the benefit was not annexed! Thus, although some doubt remains, the better view is that put forward in *Re Pinewood Estates*.[66] Note, however, that there is a further untested argument that if there has been an initial express assignment of the benefit, future transfers of the land will include an *implied* assignment of the benefit of the covenant to the purchaser under section 62 of the LPA 1925,[67] although *obiter dicta* in *Kumar v. Dunning* (1989) that restrictive covenants are outside the scope of section 62 would seem to tell against this.[68]

(iii) *A scheme of development: a 'building scheme'* – A third alternative is to establish that the benefit of the covenant has passed in equity under a 'building scheme'. The ability of the benefit of covenants to pass under a 'scheme of development' derives from a rule based on 'common intention' and practicality. In simple terms, it allows a common vendor of land (such as a property developer or builder) to transfer the benefit of any covenants received by him from the purchasers of a plot of the land to every other purchaser of a plot of that land. Thus it represents an attempt to create mutually enforceable obligations by giving the benefit of every covenant, made by every purchaser, to every other purchaser. (The burdens, of course, pass in the normal way, if possible.) In itself, there is nothing unusual about a building scheme, as it is perfectly possible for a common vendor of land to transfer the benefit of covenants already made by previous purchasers (and, therefore, attaching to his remaining land) to subsequent purchasers of parts of it under the rules of annexation or assignment considered above. However, the advantage of a building scheme is that it allows the benefit of later purchasers' covenants to be annexed to the land *already* sold (i.e. to that owned by previous purchasers), notwithstanding that this should not be possible because the covenantee (the builder) no longer owns *that* land. Thus, despite the fact that previous purchasers bought their land before later purchasers had made their covenants, the benefit of those later covenants still passes; the benefit of every covenant is available to all purchasers within the scheme of development, irrespective of the time of their purchase. For example, if Bloggs & Bloggs own 20 plots of land on which they have built

---

65 *Renals v. Colishaw* (1878).

66 In *Sugarman v. Porter* (2006), Peter Smith J declined to decide the point as it was no longer relevant.

67 This section, relevant also in the law of easements, transfers the benefits of all rights *relating to the land* to a transferee of it.

68 In *Sugarman v. Porter* (2006), Peter Smith J tends to support the doubts expressed in *Kumar*.

houses, they may extract a covenant preventing use for a trade or business from any person who buys a house, say, Mr A. The burden will follow the plot purchased by Mr A in the normal way, and the benefit will pass to all land then owned by Bloggs & Bloggs. When Bloggs & Bloggs sell a second plot to Mr B on the same terms, Mr B's land comes under a burden (i.e. he is an original covenantor) and, because he has purchased *part* of the land that was owned by Bloggs & Bloggs at the time of their sale of another plot to Mr A, Mr B gets the benefit of Mr A's covenant. Alas, however, under the normal rules, Mr A cannot get the benefit of Mr B's covenant, because Mr A already owns his land. Mr B made the covenant *after* Mr A had purchased a plot. A 'building scheme' ignores this problem of timing and permits the passing of the benefit of every pur-chaser's covenant to every other purchaser. It also permits benefits to pass even though, on the occasion of a sale of the last plot, the covenantee (e.g. Bloggs & Bloggs) no longer owns any land to be benefited. However, in order to generate this effect, it must be clear that the entire land was intended to fall within a common scheme of covenants, and be governed by similar rules. The necessary factual conditions for a scheme of development were laid down in *Elliston v. Reacher* (1908). These are, generally: that there must be a common vendor; that the land must be laid out in identifiable plots; that the benefit of every pur-chaser's covenants must be intended to be mutually enforceable (i.e. to pass to every other purchaser); that the purchasers must have bought the land on condition that this was intended; and that the area subject to the scheme must be well defined. Of course, as one might expect with a rule of equity, these conditions are not inflexible and, on one view, the *Elliston* conditions are not conclusive or mandatory but merely evidence of a more general rule stemming from common intention. So, a 'scheme' has been accepted where there was no lotted plan (*Baxter v. Four Oaks Properties* (1965), approved in *Whitgift Homes v. Stocks* (2001)), where there was no common vendor (*Re Dolphin's Conveyance* (1970)), where the property was laid out in subplots (*Brunner v. Greenslade* (1971)), and even following the demerger of separate plots that had been 'joined' after the scheme had come into existence. However, recognition of a building scheme has been rightly refused when it was clear that each purchaser's covenants were different in substance, and therefore lacking the element of mutuality of purpose (*Emile Elias v. Pine Groves* (1993)). More importantly, it is clear from *Whitgift Homes* that it is crucial for the existence of a building scheme and the generous rules it brings that the area subject to the scheme be defined with sufficient certainty – that is, sufficient certainty to ensure that *all* purchasers of plots know the extent both legally and physically of their mutual obligations. In that case, a housing development had been completed in the 1920s and 1930s and there was no doubt that a mutually enforceable scheme had been contem-plated at the time the site was developed. However, there was real uncertainty as to the physical reach of the alleged scheme, and although one could say that certain plots in the development may have been within a scheme, there were a number of areas of the estate of which one could not be certain whether they were included or excluded. Consequently, a scheme could not operate even for those areas that appeared to have mutually enforceable obligations because there was fatal uncertainty as to the physical (and hence legal) reach of the alleged mutual obligations. No purchaser could be certain of the extent of his benefits and burdens.

Finally, we should note, for the avoidance of doubt, that a successful 'building scheme' does not affect the running of the burden of covenants and if the obligations are to be truly mutually enforceable, the normal steps for transmitting the burden of restrictive covenants must be followed. Usually, this will mean registration of the covenants against the title of all purchasers. That said, however, it is also clear that the courts are very reluctant to disturb the 'local law' established by a building scheme, and once one has been validly created, the courts will not readily refuse a remedy to a claimant seeking to enforce the benefit that he has been given. Neither will the Lands Tribunal easily agree to the discharge (i.e. destruction) of building scheme covenants under the procedure for the modification or discharge of covenants laid down in section 84 of the LPA 1925.[69]

8.7 Escaping the Confines of the Law: Can the Burden of Positive Covenants be Enforced by Other Means?

The position, as it stands so far, can be summarised quite easily; first, the benefit of positive and negative covenants can run with the land at law or in equity; second, only the burden of negative covenants may run, and then only in equity; third, therefore, the great majority of disputes involve a triple claim that the benefit has passed in equity, that the covenant is negative and that the burden has passed in equity. Naturally enough, this is not an entirely satisfactory position, as both *Rhone v. Stephens* (1994) and *Thamesmead Town v. Allotey* (1998) illustrate, because in both cases the claimant was denied the enforcement of a positive covenant against a successor to the original covenantor when it was clear both that the successor knew of the obligation and that it was of real benefit to the original covenantee's land. Indeed, there seems no reason why, in principle, the burden of positive covenants should not be able to run with the land and it is difficult to find such a restriction in *Tulk v. Moxhay* (1848) itself, even though it appears clearly in later cases.[70] Moreover, it is not unknown for the law to allow positive obligations, including those requiring expenditure of money, to pass as proprietary obligations in other contexts – see, for example, the law of leasehold covenants, the easement of fencing[71] and the feudal chancel repair liability.[72] Given that any such burden would need to be registered to be binding (as currently with negative burdens), any prospective purchaser of affected land would be well warned that they were accepting such a liability and could act accordingly – they could walk away from the purchase, offer a lower price or take out insurance. This is, in essence, the substance of the Law Commission's criticism of the current law and the reason why it has tentatively

---

69 See *Re Bromor Properties' Application* (1995); *Re Lee's Application* (1996).

70 *Austerberry v. Oldham Corporation* (1885).

71 *Crow v. Wood* (1977). Note also the seemingly positive easement to actually supply electricity in *Cardwell v. Walker* (2003).

72 *Aston Cantlow v. Wallbank* (2003).

proposed that the law be amended to allow positive obligations to run with freehold land, subject to registration requirements.[73] Nevertheless, be that as it may, the current rule is that the burden of positive covenants cannot run and any claimant under a positive coven-ant is limited to suing the *original* covenantor in damages if they want any remedy at all. This has led to the development of a number of indirect methods of enforcing positive coven-ants, none of which is entirely satisfactory.

8.7.1   A chain of covenants

A chain of covenants is common in practice, although it only gives a remedy in damages. In essence, each purchaser of the burdened land covenants separately with their immedi-ate predecessor in title (their seller) to carry out the positive covenant. Thus, if the original covenantor is sued on the covenant, he (the original covenantor) will be able to recover any damages paid from the person to whom he sold the land (and who cov-enanted with him directly to perform the positive covenant), and so on down the chain. The well-known defect is that the chain is 'only as strong as its weakest link', so that (for example) the death, insolvency or other circumstance affecting any person in the chain may render the device useless. After all, personal liabilities such as these are not as robust as proprietary obligations. A variation on this is to ensure that each successive purchaser of the burdened land covenants directly, at the time they purchase the land, with the person entitled to the benefit of the covenant. In *Thamesmead Town*, for example, the original covenantor had covenanted with the claimant (the person entitled to the benefit) to pay certain charges relating to the maintenance of the common parts of a housing estate. When the defendant purchased the land from the original covenantor, it was intended that he should then make a covenant with the claimant to like effect; in fact, the original covenantor had promised the claimant that, when they sold the land, they would require their purchaser to make such a covenant. This was, therefore, an attempt to create a series of covenants, with each new owner of the burdened land promising separately to pay the charge. It failed miserably because when the defendant purchased the land, he was not asked to make this new covenant! Here, the chain broke the first time it was tested. Note, however, that if the land burdened is of registered title, it is possible to register a restriction against that title requiring the purchaser of the burdened land to enter into the positive covenant as a condition of the purchase. This would have been effective in *Thamesmead Town* to ensure that the positive obligation was undertaken when the land was sold to a new purchaser. The entry of such a restriction is the most effective way of ensuring that positive burdens are undertaken by purchasers of the original covenantor's land.[74]

---

[73] See Law Commission Consultation Paper No. 186, March 2008, *Easements, Covenants and Profits à Prendre*. Such a reform would also mean that covenants became legal interests in land, because the benefit would be noted against the registered title of the benefited land, as well as the burden being noted against the obligated land. There seems to be no reason why this should not occur (subject to amendment of section 1 of the LPA 1925), provided that the availability of the flexible equitable remedies is preserved.

[74] Assuming, of course, that HM Land Registry requires evidence that the restriction is complied with before registering the sale and the relevant legal advisers carry out their professional duties properly.

8.7.2   The artificial long lease

As seen in Chapter 6, positive covenants in leases are quite capable of binding successive owners of the land. Thus, by artificially creating a long lease containing the desired positive covenant, and then 'enlarging' the lease into a freehold under section 153 of the LPA 1925, the positive covenant will bind successive owners of land, because the 'leasehold rules' remain applicable.

8.7.3   Mutual benefit and burden

It is a general principle of equity that a person who takes the benefit of a deed of covenant must also share any burden inherent in it. Thus, if a landowner enjoys the benefit of a covenant to use a private road or sewer, they must also take the burden of the upkeep of the road or sewer. They may take the benefit of the covenant only if they share its burden (*Halsall* v. *Brizell* (1957)). Consequently, any later owner of the land will also be subject to the burden of the positive covenant, if they wish to enjoy the benefits it offers. The proper ambit of the 'benefit and burden' principle has been the subject of judicial consideration, and a number of uncertainties about its scope have now been resolved. In *Thamesmead Town*, the claimant alleged that the defendant was liable to pay maintenance charges (i.e. liable to observe a positive covenant), because those charges related to facilities from which the defendant took a benefit. In fact, the charges related to two distinct 'benefits': a charge for the upkeep of roads and sewers, and a charge for the maintenance of common parts, such as walkways, open spaces, and so on. The Court of Appeal decided that the benefit and burden rule allowed recovery of the charges in respect of roads and sewers, but not in respect of the 'general facilities'. In the court's view, a person could be liable on the burden of a positive covenant only if the burden was intrinsically related to the benefit gained. It was not enough that the documents of title said that a person could take a benefit from the land only if they accepted an attached burden: the mere linking of a benefit with a burden was insufficient. What was required was that the burden be the 'flip side' of the benefit: the burden had to be inherent in the benefit obtained. So, if a landowner wanted to use sewers and a private road, he had to pay for those sewers and that road. This was mutual benefit and burden, the mutuality being that the benefit and burden were simply two halves of the same coin.[75] However, if a landowner was required to pay a sum towards the upkeep of open spaces, and this was linked on paper to the benefit of not having his neighbours carry on a trade or business, this was not mutual benefit and burden. The benefit would run, but the burden would not, because the burden was not inherently connected to the benefit: it was not mutual, but merely reciprocal. The benefit and burden rule allows the enforcement of a positive covenant if it conforms to 'if you want to use X, you must pay for it'; it does not allow the enforcement of a positive covenant in terms that 'I will give you X, if you will give me Y'. This must be correct. Otherwise, careful drafting of covenants could utilise the 'benefit and burden' principle to circumvent almost entirely the rule against the transmission of the burden of positive covenants. What is not so clear is why the Court of Appeal in *Thamesmead Town* further limited the principle. In its view, a

---

75 See also *Changeinvest Ltd* v. *Rosendale-Steinhusen* (2004), in which the owner of dominant land was required to pay for the cost of upkeep of the road that comprised his easement over the servient land.

person was liable on the burden of a truly mutual positive covenant only if that person chose to exercise the corresponding benefit. The contrary view, that such a person is liable to the burden if they are entitled to the benefit, whether they use it or not, has much to commend it, for (as counsel for the claimant put it) it does not confuse the acquisition of a right with its exercise. In truth, the court was persuaded by this argument but felt compelled by authority to adopt the former view. So, for the present, the principle of mutual benefit and burden will permit the enforcement of a positive covenant when the burden is intrinsic in the benefit, and if the defendant has actually partaken of the benefit.

8.7.4   Construing section 79 of the Law of Property Act 1925

It has been noted that section 79(1) of the LPA 1925 is taken to annex the burden of restrictive covenants to land so that, other things being equal (e.g. registration), the burden passes to a successor in title. In fact, a careful reading of section 79(1) reveals that it is not in terms limited to restrictive covenants, and there is nothing in the statute itself that prevents it being interpreted as annexing the burden of positive covenants as well. Indeed, the fact that it was felt necessary deliberately to confine the effect of section 79(2) to restrictive covenants[76] surely implies that the general principle of section 79(1) is not so limited. Be that as it may, the argument is all but over. Section 79(1) has been interpreted narrowly for reasons of policy rather than necessity: that is, that section 79(1) not change substantive principles of law, but merely facilitates the passing of that which could already pass, being burdens of restrictive covenants.

All in all, of course, none of these devices are satisfactory and it would make far greater sense to allow the burden of positive covenants to run in much the same way as the burden of restrictive ones. This has been proposed many times, but unless there is a revolutionary House of Lords decision, the matter will have to wait for legislation. In 2008, the Law Commission published a Consultation Paper on *Easements, Covenants and Profits à Prendre* (CP No. 186) in which it asked for views on reform of the law of covenants.[77] The Commission itself proposed replacement of the current law with a scheme of 'land obligations', although it now seems that the terminology of 'land obligation' is to be dropped and instead we should continue to refer to these obligations as 'covenants'.[78] Under the proposed scheme – which may well be fine-tuned as a result of the consultation process – a covenant could be enforceable whether positive or negative. The new-style covenant would be a legal interest requiring registration against the title of both the benefited and burdened land in order to be effective,[79] and so could exist only where both the burdened and benefited land were of registered title.[80] Consequently, a legal covenant could only be created expressly, but if registered, any owner of the benefited land could sue any owner of

---

76 That is, when adverse possessors are in possession.

77 Consultation Paper No. 186, March 2008. This builds on its earlier 1984 report, *Transfer of Land: The Law of Positive and Restrictive Covenants*, Report No. 127. The 2008 paper also proposed some changes to the law of easements and profits (see Chapter 7).

78 This is appropriate as it reminds us that we would not be creating a new obligation, but merely reforming existing law. Thus, existing rules about remedies and interpretation would remain relevant.

79 It would be capable of being equitable, but this would arise only because of a failure to observe proper formalities.

80 The current law would remain for unregistered titles, but no new covenants could be created.

the burdened land in respect of positive and restrictive covenants. If adopted, this proposal would, in essence, allow the benefits and burdens of both types of covenant to run at law and in equity. However, pending such reform, the law of freehold covenants remains restricted: the benefit of any covenant can pass, in law or in equity – but only the burden of restrictive covenants can pass, and then only in equity.

8.7.5   Rentcharges and rights of re-entry

A rentcharge is a periodic payment charged on land[81] and it may be annexed to a right of re-entry – that is, a right to enter the burdened land and forcibly terminate the landowner's estate unless the sum is paid. It is possible to use the combination of a rentcharge (to secure a sum of money) and the right of re-entry (to force payment) to support a positive covenant. The right of re-entry is itself an interest in land that can bind purchasers of the burdened land even though it supports a positive obligation. Consequently, careful drafting of these 'estate rentcharges', as they are known, can indirectly ensure performance of a positive obligation because non-payment of the charge supporting the positive obligation means loss of the defendant's estate in the land!

8.7.6   Discharge and modification of restrictive covenants

As noted briefly above, section 84 of the LPA 1925 contains a jurisdiction to discharge or modify restrictive covenants affecting freehold land. In fact, section 84(1) gives the court a useful power to declare whether any land is subject to the burden of a restrictive covenant – thus providing a simple method of determining whether a burden has 'run' – and section 84(2) gives the Lands Tribunal power to discharge or modify restrictive covenants. The power contained in section 84(2) is critical, for the enduring nature of restrictive covenants means that they can impose restrictions on the use of land that simply become outdated or even positively detrimental. For example, a restrictive covenant against building may impede the development of land for social housing or may obstruct the economic regeneration of a depressed industrial area. Conversely, one landowner may seek the discharge of a covenant against building, in order to build a second house in his capacious garden that he wants to sell for a large capital gain. The Lands Tribunal will exercise its jurisdiction in all of these cases, but no discharge or modification will occur unless the claimant can make out one of four general grounds: first, that the covenant is obsolete by reason of changes in the property or the neighbourhood; second, that the continuance of the covenant would obstruct the reasonable use of the land for private or public purposes; third, that the person entitled to the benefit has agreed to the discharge or modification; or fourth, that the discharge or modification would cause no loss to the person entitled to the benefit.

---

81 By way of contrast, 'rent' in a landlord and tenant context – technically *rent service* to distinguish it from a *rentcharge* – is a periodic payment in respect of a lease.

8.8   Chapter Summary

8.8.1   Positive and negative freehold covenants

Covenants between freeholders may be either positive or negative. Positive covenants require the owner of the burdened land to take some action on his own property or property related to it, usually requiring the expenditure of money. An example is a covenant to pay for the upkeep of a private road. Negative (or 'restrictive') covenants require the owner of the burdened land to refrain from some activity on his own land. An example is the covenant against carrying on any trade or business on the land.

8.8.2   Covenants as contracts

Covenants are promises by one person to another contained in a deed to do, or more usually not to do, something on their own or related land. The covenant is made between the *covenantor* and the *covenantee* and is enforceable like any other contractual obligation between these original parties.

8.8.3   Covenants as interests in land

Covenants comprise both a benefit (the right to sue) and a burden (the obligation to perform). Both the benefit and burden may be 'attached' to the benefited and burdened land respectively, so that they pass to later purchasers or transferees of it. Although the benefit and burden of each covenant may pass independently, before a covenant can be enforced, in practice, the claimant must prove they have the benefit and the defendant must be fixed with the burden.

8.8.4   The relevance of 'law' and 'equity' in the enforcement of covenants

If a person sues on a covenant *at law*, he will be claiming that the defendant is subject to the burden of the covenant under the common law and should pay damages. The remedy is as of right. If a person sues on a covenant *in equity*, he will be claiming that the defendant is subject to the burden of the covenant under the rules of equity and susceptible to the discretionary equitable remedies of injunction and specific performance and to rules of registration. Note that if the burden has passed to the defendant in equity, so must the benefit have passed to the claimant in equity.

8.8.5   Principle 1: Enforcement between the original covenantor and the original covenantee

If the covenantor and covenantee are still in possession of their respective land, all covenants are enforceable and the covenantee may obtain damages, an injunction or specific performance (i.e. they may sue at law or in equity). If the original *covenantor* has parted with the land (or never had land) that was subject to the covenant, he remains liable on all of the covenants to whomsoever has the benefit of them, although damages are available only because the covenantor has no land on which to perform the covenant. If the original *covenantee* has parted with the land that had the benefit of the covenant, he may still be able to enforce a covenant against whomsoever has the burden of it. However, at law, this right could easily have been given to another by an express assignment of the right to sue and, in equity, the court is likely in its discretion to refuse to grant an equitable remedy to such a claimant as he has no land capable of benefiting. Note that it is important to identify exactly who are the *original* covenantees and covenantors, especially as this may go beyond the actual signatories to a deed (section 56 of the LPA 1925).

8.8.6 Principle 2: Enforcement against successors to the original covenantor (passing the burden)

It is not possible for the burden of *any* covenant to run at law. In equity, the burden of restrictive covenants *only* may pass, provided that:

1   the covenant is restrictive in nature;
2   the covenant touches and concerns the land (except possibly where the Landlord and Tenant (Covenants) Act 1995 applies to a leasehold covenant not enforceable under 'leasehold rules');
3   at the date of the covenant, the covenant actually did confer a benefit on land owned by the original covenantee;
4   the burden of the restrictive covenant must have been intended to have run with the land of the original covenantor (section 79 of the LPA 1925);
5   in registered land, the covenant must be registered by means of a notice against the burdened land in order to bind a purchaser for value who becomes registered proprietor (section 29 of the LRA 2002);
6   in unregistered land, the covenant must be registered as a Class D(ii) land charge to bind a purchaser of a legal estate who gives money or money's worth; and
7   the claimant is granted a remedy by virtue of the court's discretion.

8.8.7 Principle 3: Enforcement by successors to the original covenantee (passing the benefit)

The benefit of both a positive and restrictive covenant may be passed at law or in equity. However, given that only the burden of a restrictive covenant may pass, and then only in equity, most practical examples concern the passing of the benefit of a restrictive covenant in equity. This will give us our claimant (benefit) and defendant (burden) in suit in equity.

If it is necessary to consider passing the benefit of a covenant *at law* (e.g. the original covenantor may be the defendant), then:

1   the covenant must 'touch and concern' the land of the original covenantee;
2   the claimant must have a legal estate in the land, although not necessarily the same legal estate as the original covenantee: for restrictive covenants only, this may include an 'occupier' – for example, an adverse possessor (section 78 of the LPA; 1925);
3   the benefit of the covenant must have been annexed to a legal estate in the land either expressly or by implication or by statute – that is, by express words or necessary implication from express words or by statute under section 78 of the LPA 1925.

In order to pass the benefit of a covenant in *equity*, then the following must be true.

1   The covenant must 'touch and concern' the land of the original covenantee.
2   The claimant must have a legal or equitable estate in the land of the original covenantee, although not necessarily the same estate as the original covenantee. For restrictive covenants only, this may include an 'occupier': for example, an adverse possessor (section 78 of the LPA 1925).
3   The benefit of the covenant must have been transmitted to the claimant in one of three ways.

   (i)   By annexation: express, implied or by statute – The benefit of a covenant can be expressly annexed to the land in equity in exactly the same way as in law: that is, by express words or by statute under section 78 of the LPA 1925.
   (ii) By assignment: express or implied – Following the general rule that the benefit of a contract may be assigned to another, the original covenantee may expressly assign the benefit of a covenant at the same time as he transfers the land. For future sales of the land, an assignment of the benefit of the covenant may be implied by section 62 of the LPA 1925, subject to criticism in *Kumar v. Dunning* (1989).
   (iii) By a scheme of development (building scheme) – This allows the benefit of later purchasers' covenants to be passed to the land already sold by a common vendor (i.e. to previous purchasers), notwithstanding that this should not be possible because the original covenantee (the common vendor) has already parted with the land. The conditions are that: there must be a common vendor; the land must be laid out in definable plots; the benefit of every purchaser's covenants must be intended to be mutually enforceable (i.e. to pass to every other purchaser); the purchasers must have bought the land on condition that this was intended; and the area of the scheme must be well defined.

8.8.8   Devices that may allow the passing of the burdens of positive covenants in practice

These include: a chain of covenants; the artificial long lease; mutual benefit and burden; reinterpreting section 79 of the LPA 1925; restrictions on the title of registered land; and the use of rentcharges, coupled with a right of re-entry.

Further Reading

Law Commission, *Easements, Covenants and Profits à Prendre*, Consultation Paper No. 186, March 2008

Martin, J, 'Remedies for breach of restrictive covenants' [1996] Conv 329

Scamell, EH, *Land Covenants*, London: Butterworths, 1996

'To restate or not to restate? Old wine, new wineskins, old covenants, new ideas' [2009] Conv 448

Chapter 9
Licences and Proprietary Estoppel

9.1   Licences

In Chapters 7 and 8, we examined in some detail two important ways in which one person could enjoy limited rights over the land of another. In many respects, these easements (Chapter 7) and freehold covenants (Chapter 8) were seen to be similar, especially where the effect on the 'servient' or 'burdened' land was restrictive in that it prevented the current owner from engaging in some activity on their own land. Of course, both easements and restrictive covenants are proprietary in nature; they are interests in land that may 'run' with the benefited and burdened land and are not personal to the parties that created them. However, a moment's thought will reveal that easements and freehold covenants can cover only a small fraction of the situations in which one person may wish to use the land of another. For example, what is the position where I ask my neighbour if I can park my car on his land, or my children play football there? Again, what are my rights if I pay an entrance charge to go to a play or a film on someone else's land, or use neighbour's garden for the day for a party, or wish to store something on his land or in his outbuildings? All of these are activities undertaken on another person's land, but they may not fall within the realm of easements or freehold covenants.[1]

This is where the 'licence' to use land comes into play. 'Licences' are a third way in which a person may enjoy some right or privilege over the land of another person. However, as we shall see, they are fundamentally different in nature and effect from both easements and freehold covenants. In essence, they are personal rather than proprietary.

9.2   The Essential Nature of a Licence

Licences involve a permission from the owner of land that is given to another person (who may or may not own land themselves) to use that land for some specific purpose. The permission (or 'licence') can be to do anything from attending a cinema (Hurst v. Picture Theatres Ltd (1915)), to parking a car (Colchester & East Sussex Co-op v. Kelevedon Labour Club (2003)),[2] erecting an advertising hoarding (Kewall Investments v. Arthur Maiden (1990)), running a school (Re Hampstead Garden Suburb Institute (1995)), using buildings as a social club (Onyx v. Beard (1998)), or allowing children to play in your garden. Licences can even give a limited right of occupation as with the 'occupation licences' that can be difficult to distinguish

---

1   There is, in practice, a potential overlap between licences and easements and it is clear that, in some cases, the same type of use may qualify as either a licence or an easement depending on the manner and circumstances in which it arose. In Batchelor v. Marlowe (2001), for example, a right to park a number of cars was held to be a licence, even though a similar right may in the appropriate circumstances be an easement: see Moncreiff v. Jamieson (2007), in which the House of Lords also expressed doubts whether Batchelor was rightly decided. Likewise, absence of the proper legal formalities for the creation of an alleged easement will mean that the claimant obtains only a licence, as where no deed or written instrument is used.

2   This was the express intention of the parties. It is clear that the right to park a car may also qualify as an easement: Moncreiff v. Jamieson (2007).

from leases.[3] Indeed, the range of activities that can be covered by the giving of 'a licence' is virtually limitless simply because it is impossible to foresee all of the circumstances in which one person may wish to use the land of another! With this in mind, the following points about licences should be noted.

1   A licence is given by the owner of land (the licensor) to some other person (the licensee), permitting him to do something on the owner's land. They are classically defined, in *Thomas v. Sorrell* (1673), as a *personal* permission to use land belonging to another that, without such permission, would amount to a trespass. As such, licences may cover any activity – long or short term – that may be undertaken on land. This versatility means that licences can arise in all manner of situations, and consequently it is crucial to be able to distinguish licences from proprietary rights such as leases, easements and freehold covenants, all of which also allow one person to use another's land but which have the essentially different quality of being 'real property'.

2   There are no formal requirements for the creation of a 'licence' as such, although occasionally a licence may depend on the fulfilment of conditions imposed by some other branch of the law; for example, with contractual licences an 'offer and acceptance' is as essential as for any other type of contract. Consequently, licences may be created orally, in writing, or even be found in a deed or registered disposition if they are ancillary to the grant of some right or interest in land. A good example of a licence found in a registered disposition is on a conveyance of a house from A to B, wherein B is given a personal right to park his car on land retained by A. As is obvious, however, where licences are found in formal documents (and sometimes where they are not!), there is always the danger that they will be confused with true proprietary rights, especially if the substantive right granted (e.g. to park a car) is, in fact, capable of being either a licence or a proprietary right such as an easement. Importantly, if the formalities required by statute for the creation of a proprietary right are not satisfied – for example, if the required written instrument or deed is not used – the right thereby given to the claimant cannot amount to a proprietary right but it may still result in the claimant having a licence. For example, if A were to verbally permit B a right of passage across A's land, this *could have been* a legal easement had it been properly granted by deed and correctly registered against the burdened title, but failing this, it amounts to a licence such that B does not commit a trespass when he uses the right of way.[4]

3   It follows from the above that a licence is a right to use the land of another that is *either* inherently incapable of being a proprietary right – for example, it does not fit within the definition of any known proprietary right (e.g. a right for my children to play in your garden) – or one that arises because the parties have deliberately or

---

3   Chapter 6 and see *Street v. Mountford* (1985) and *Ogwr BC v. Dykes* (1989). See also the distinction between licences and life interests in Chapter 5, as in *Dent v. Dent* (1996). Note also the decision in *Bruton v. London & Quadrant Housing Trust* (1999), discussed in Chapter 6, which suggests that 'a lease' is not always proprietary, but may give rise to a merely contractual landlord and tenant relationship. Whether this legal creature – the non-proprietary lease – really exists or is in fact just a licence by another name – is a matter of controversy.

4   Of course, being now only a licence, it cannot bind a successor to A's land.

accidentally failed to use the proper formalities for the creation of a proprietary right, with the result that the claimant has merely a licence. This failure will be accidental where, as in the example above, the parties unwittingly omitted to use a deed or written instrument, but it can be deliberate, as in *Colchester v. Kelevedon Co-op*, (2003), in which the parties' express written intention was to create a parking licence even though that right could have been created as an easement. In this regard, it is noteworthy that the parties' intentions are apparently permitted to play a vital role when distinguishing an easement from a licence, but not (as we have seen in Chapter 6) when distinguishing between a lease and a licence.[5]

4   A licence may be given to any person for any lawful purpose, not only to someone who also owns land. In this respect, licences are different from easements and most freehold covenants. In other words, there is no *need* for a 'dominant tenement', although it is perfectly acceptable if the licensee does own adjoining or other land. So, using the example above, when A conveys land to B, he may grant a parking licence over his retained land to B (who is a landowner). But A may also decide to give or sell a parking licence to X, a person with no land, who simply wants somewhere to park his car.

5   The orthodox (and correct) view of licences is that they are *not* proprietary in nature. As Vaughan CJ makes clear in *Thomas v. Sorrell* (1673), the traditional analysis of licences is that they 'properly passeth no interest nor alter or transfer property in any thing'. A licence is not an interest in land, but rather a right *over* land, and one that is personal to the parties who created it (the licensor and licensee). This is so whether the licence is inherently non-proprietary in substance or arises because of failure to create a proprietary right. As a consequence, the right conferred by a licence can be enforced only against the person who created it. It does not 'run' with the land, and unlike easements and freehold covenants, cannot be enforced against a purchaser or transferee of the land over which it exists. The licence is not within the realm of 'real property', and is incapable of binding third parties when the licensor transfers the 'burdened' land. So, assuming A has indeed granted a parking licence over his retained land to B, if A then transfers (by sale or gift) the 'burdened' land to P, P is under no obligation whatsoever to continue to allow B to park his car. The point is, simply, that a licence is incapable of binding land: it is personal to licensor and licensee. In recent years, this fundamental theoretical distinction between 'interests in land' and 'licences' has been attacked unsuccessfully (thus generating much needless comment), and we shall consider the matter in more detail when examining 'contractual licences' and so called 'estoppel licences'.

6   If the relationship between the licensor and the licensee is based in contract – a permission given in return for a counterbenefit such as payment of money – then obviously the parties are susceptible to normal principles of contract law concerning remedies and damages for breach of the contractual licence. The fact that the subject matter of the contract is land does not elevate the status of the licence to anything more than a personal relationship between licensor and licensee. However, given that the licensor and licensee are likely to have been in close contact over the use of the land, it is possible that their relations with each other may have generated

---

5   *Street v. Mountford* (1985), see Chapter 6.

a *separate and independent* claim in proprietary estoppel. The existence of such an estoppel – considered later in this chapter – is not dependent on any prior relationship of licensor and licensee, but many successful claims of estoppel have arisen out of such a relationship precisely because the parties are already dealing with each other concerning the use of land. An example is *Parker (9th Earl of Macclesfield) v. Parker* (2006), in which according to the court the claimant's entitlement to use land arose either under a licence or out of estoppel, depending on how one viewed the facts. Given that the nature of proprietary estoppel as a property right has now been settled[6] and that a licence is clearly personal, it is important to know which of these solutions is correct.

9.3 Types of Licence

Although a licence to use land may be given for any lawful purpose, it is possible to classify types of licence according to the functions they serve, the circumstances in which they arise, or the way in which they are created. The following classification draws the traditional distinctions between different types of licence. However, it is important to remember that the real issues concerning licences revolve around practical matters, rather than some artificial classification of licences. Thus, although the following analysis will proceed on the basis that there are different types of licence, the critical issue is to determine how each 'type' deals with the following four practical matters.

1   What is the nature of the licence and how is it created?
2   What are the obligations of the licensor to the licensee, and vice versa?
3   Is the licence in any sense an 'interest in land'?
4   Are there any circumstances in which a licence can take effect against a third party: that is, can a person who purchases land over which a licence already exists ever be bound to give effect to that licence?

9.3.1 The bare licence

A bare licence is probably the most common form of permission that a landowner gives to another person to use his land. It is, in essence, permission to enter upon the land, given voluntarily by the owner, who receives nothing in return. The giving of the licence is 'gratuitous' in that it is not supported by 'consideration' moving from the licensee. There is no contract between the parties, merely a bare permission to do that which the landowner has allowed and which otherwise would be a trespass. Typically, such licences allow the licensee to carry on some limited activity on the licensor's land, as where permission is given to use a garden, to deliver some previously ordered goods or to enjoy a limited and revocable right of access. Necessarily, these bare licences can be given in any shape or form, and many are oral or implied from the landowner's lack of objection to the activity taking place. It is also inherent in a bare licence that it lasts only for so long as the licensor wishes.

---

6   Section 116 of the LRA 2002 and see below.

Thus, the licensor may terminate the licence by giving reasonable notice to the licensee (*Robson v. Hallet* (1967); *Re Hampstead Garden Suburb Institute* (1995)), and the licensee has no claim in damages or specific performance should this happen. Importantly, there is no doubt that a bare licence is *not* an interest in land; it is personal only to the original licensor and licensee. Such a licence *per se* is incapable of binding a third party and any person who subsequently acquires the licensor's land may disregard the bare licence with impunity.

9.3.2   Licences coupled with an interest (or 'grant')

This is a rather loose category of licences covering a range of activities that are grouped together because the licences are said to be 'coupled' with an interest in land or with the grant of an interest in land. As discussed in Chapter 7, a landowner may grant another person a profit *à prendre* over their land: that is, a right to take from the land some natural resource, such as fish, pasture, wood or turf. Necessarily, in order to exercise this 'profit', the grantee must be able to enter upon the land and remain there for an appropriate time. This is achieved by means of a licence attached (or 'coupled') to the profit, as in *James Jones and Son v. Earl of Tankerville* (1909). To some extent, of course, to call this a 'licence' at all is misleading for the licence is merely incidental and ancillary to the right that has actually been granted over the land (the profit). The licence merely facilitates the achievement of the primary purpose; it is not a purpose in itself. So where, as is the case with profits, the right granted is proprietary in nature (i.e. it is an interest in land), the licence that attaches to it *appears* also to be proprietary, because it lives or dies with the profit. The licence will last for as long as the profit exists and will be enforceable against whomsoever the profit is enforceable against because it is an inherent component of the greater right. Likewise, should the grantee of the profit be unlawfully denied the right granted, the normal remedies will be available to prevent interference with it or to compensate for its denial. Nevertheless, the licence only has these characteristics because it is coupled with the grant of an interest; it has no proprietary status of its own.

9.3.3   Contractual licences

Contractual licences are, in nature, similar to bare licences with the important difference that contractual licences are granted to the licensee in return for valuable consideration. Two examples are the purchase of a cinema ticket and the 'occupation licence' discussed in Chapter 6. Simply put, there is a contract between the licensor and licensee, the subject matter of which is the giving of a licence to use land for a stated purpose. Crucially, there-fore, contractual licences are governed by the ordinary rules of the law of contract, and like most contracts, do not need to be created with any particular formality. Indeed, although they are contracts concerning the use of land, they are not contracts for the *disposition of an interest in land* (they are not proprietary) and so need not meet the requirements of section 2 of the Law of Property (Miscellaneous Provisions) Act 1989. They may be oral or written. The characteristics of contractual licences are discussed below.

9.3.4   Remedies and contractual licences

As these licences are founded in contract, both licensor and licensee may rely on the normal remedies for breach of contract in the event of a failure to carry out the terms of the licence. Thus, either party may sue for damages for breach of contract, although it is usually the licensee that needs such a remedy when the licensor fails to allow him to use the land for the purpose for which the licence was purchased. More importantly, it is now clear that, as with other contracts, an injunction or a decree of specific performance may be obtained by the licensee in appropriate circumstances. An injunction can be obtained to prevent the licensor from revoking the licence before its contractual date of expiry,[7] or a decree of specific performance may be awarded requiring the licensor to permit the activity authorised by the licence to take place.[8] Indeed, the effect of the availability of these last two remedies can be to make the licence *de facto* irrevocable between the *original* parties throughout the contractual period of the licence. In this respect, a contractual licence is vitally different from a bare licence and can assume the character of an unbreakable arrangement between the original parties lasting for the agreed duration of the licence. So, if A gives B a parking licence for three years, at £100 per year, this is a contractual licence of three years' duration. If A should then seek to deny the right, A may be liable in damages for breach of contract or held to the licence for the three years by injunction. Note, however, that if A breaks the contract because he has sold the land to P within the three years and simply has no land on which B can now park, A will remain liable in damages, but, of course, P cannot be subject to an injunction because the licence is not proprietary and cannot 'bind' a third party. The liability of P in these circumstances (if any) is discussed in section 9.3.7 below.

9.3.5 Are contractual licences interests in land? Can they affect purchasers of the licensor's land?

The above is clear enough, for there is no reason why a contractual licence should not be irrevocable between the *original* parties for the duration of the licence in the same way as many other contracts. However, there are lingering problems. For example, if A grants a contractual licence to B allowing B to park her caravan in his garden for five years, a court may well enforce this by injunction for five years *against* A. Yet, what if, after three years, A sells his land to P? Is P bound to give effect to the licence for two more years, or can P ignore it, even though A would have been bound? In other words, does the irrevocability of some contractual licences between the original licensor and licensee mean that a purchaser of the licensor's land is also bound to give effect to the licence for the remainder of the contractual term? In essence, this boils down to two very important questions: first, is a contractual licence an 'interest in land' so that it may bind a purchaser of land in the normal way according to established principles of registered or unregistered conveyancing? And second, even if contractual licences are not interests in land, can they take effect against a purchaser of the licensor's land for any other reason?

9.3.6 Are contractual licences interests in land? Are they proprietary?

The starting point for a discussion of this question must be the famous *dictum* in *Thomas v. Sorrell* (1673) that a licence 'properly passeth no interest nor alters or transfers property

---

7 *Winter Garden Theatre v. Millennium Productions Ltd* (1948).

8 *Verrall v. Great Yarmouth BC* (1981).

in any thing'. This states that, as a matter of principle, a licence operates merely personally between the parties and creates no interest in land that might be enforceable against a third person. Indeed, as much has been confirmed by the House of Lords in *King v. David Allen and Sons, Billposting* (1916), which decided expressly that contractual licences were not proprietary and thus could not bind third parties. Nevertheless, despite this clear and principled position, the many uses to which licences could be put generated academic and judicial discussion as to whether this orthodox view should prevail in all circumstances. Were there, perhaps, circumstances in which a 'contractual licence' could be regarded as a new species of property right in much the same way that restrictive covenants became proprietary after *Tulk v. Moxhay* (1848)? In particular, the widespread use of 'occupation licences' as a deliberate alternative to leases[9] meant that some licensees were occupying their homes under a 'mere' licence that could be defeated simply by a sale of the land from licensor to a new owner. For example, could it be 'equitable' that a landowner might allow a person to occupy their property under a licence for an agreed period of (say) five years, but, just one month after completing the deal, sell their land to P and thereby defeat the licence, with the result that the occupier would be turned out onto the street? Of course, in these circumstances, the licensee might well be able to claim damages for breach of contract from the licensor, but this is not the same as enjoying the benefits of occupation. Likewise, an injunction or decree of specific performance as a remedy for breach of a contractual licence against the licensor are not much use once the land has been sold.

This was the apparent problem facing the courts, especially pressing in the case of occupation licences before *Street v. Mountford* (1985) revealed their true character as leases. In typical fashion, it was addressed squarely by Lord Denning in *Errington v. Errington* (1952). In that case, Lord Denning regarded a contractual licence granted to the claimant as binding on a wife who had received land under a will, her husband being the original licensor. His reasoning was that, as the licensee could restrain revocation of the licence by the licensor for its agreed duration (i.e. by injunction), there was no reason why the licence could not continue against a third party in appropriate circumstances. The 'appropriate circumstances' seemed to be when the contractual licence was 'supported by an equity' (for this gave it proprietary status), and an 'equity' would exist where it would be unjust to deny the continued existence of the licence. Unfortunately, however, all of this simply assumes that which must be established: that is, it assumes without reasons that contractual licences are *per se* interests in land that are *capable* of binding third parties. In reality, however, the real question is not *when* can a contractual licence bind a third party? It is, rather, whether it is *possible* that a contractual licence can do this? If it is *possible* in principle, then the circumstances *when* it may happen in practice can be identified. If it is not possible, then the 'when' becomes irrelevant. Lord Denning in *Errington* never got to the heart of this problem, preferring (no doubt with good cause) to concentrate on the result rather than the reasoning. Moreover, Lord Denning did not attempt to explain why the House of Lords' seemingly binding decision in *King* could be ignored by his Court of Appeal – or perhaps he knew that in truth it should not be? Neither is Lord Denning's appeal to 'justice' very persuasive, because it may always be 'unjust' in one sense to deny

---

9   See Chapter 6.

the continuing validity of a licence against a purchaser of the licensor's land. It can be very 'unjust' for a landowner to be able to ignore an unregistered option to purchase the land, even though such options really are proprietary interests, but as we have seen in *Midland Bank v. Green* (1981), this is the principled answer and the House of Lords in that case did not contemplate the judicial repeal of the Land Charges Acts simply because, on a populist view, the result appeared 'unjust'. After all, even if we put aside the powerful arguments of principle and policy that should have led Lord Denning to the opposite conclusion in *Errington*, it is not necessarily 'unjust' to allow a purchaser of land to escape from a valid licence granted previously by the seller, even if he knew of its existence, because this possibility may have been the very reason why the seller gave 'a licence' to the claimant in the first place. Perhaps the seller deliberately chose to limit the claimant's rights to those of a merely personal character to enable him to sell the land quickly and unburdened at a moment of his choosing. Put another way, the whole purpose behind the identification of a group of rights to use land as 'licences' instead of 'property rights' is precisely to ensure that they are not interest in land. In terms of a general theory of land law then, the very definition of, and the role for, 'licences' is that they are not proprietary.

Despite these powerful arguments, and despite the existence of the House of Lords decision in *King*, *Errington* was followed by a number of decisions involving the Court of Appeal and the High Court and these appeared to be generating a head of steam that might result in recognition of the proprietary status of contractual licences. Even then, however, the matter was not clear, for many of these apparently rogue decisions – albeit purportedly following *Errington* – can be explained on the simple grounds that the claimant never really had a contractual licence at all, but on a true analysis had a proprietary right within the accepted categories of such right (e.g. a lease, life interest, easement or equitable co-ownership right). Naturally, such substantive rights, although mislabelled by the courts as 'contractual licences', should be binding on third parties in the normal way and the error lay in calling them 'licences' in the first place. Yet, be that as it may, on the question of principle, the Court of Appeal in *Ashburn Anstalt v. Arnold* (1989) re-examined the matter afresh and reasserted the orthodox view. In that case, Fox LJ relied on the House of Lords' decisions in *King* and in *National Provincial Bank v. Ainsworth* (1965) to confirm unequivocally that licences were not, and could not be, interests in land. They were personal rights between licensor and licensee, and nothing more. Furthermore, in so far as *Errington* decided otherwise, it was *per incuriam* (being decided without reference to *King*) and could in any event be explained on other grounds. For example, perhaps the claimant in *Errington* did not have a contractual licence at all but an estate contract binding a non-purchaser, or perhaps there was a *Lloyds Bank v. Rosset* (1991) type of equitable right of ownership, or perhaps the third party was bound by an estoppel. However, whatever spin we place on *Errington* to justify its result, Fox LJ's judgment in *Ashburn* makes it clear that, *as a matter of principle*, licences are not interests in land and cannot bind third parties for that reason. This view has been confirmed now on many occasions, but none with more force than Mummery LJ in *Lloyd v. Dugdale* (2001), who noted that '[n]otwithstanding some previous authority suggesting the contrary, a contractual licence is not to be treated as creating a proprietary interest in land so as to bind third parties who acquire the land with notice of it'. This is, of course, a thoroughly orthodox and convincing approach to the problem and it serves to highlight the fundamental distinction between interests in land and purely personal interests, even those that just happen to relate to property. It is submitted that the contrary view now is unarguable.[10] Indeed, if one takes Lord Wilberforce's definition of an interest in land, in *National Provincial Bank v. Ainsworth* (1965), that

> Before a right or interest can be admitted into the category of property, or of a right affecting property, it must be definable, identifiable by third parties, capable in its nature of assumption by third parties and have some degree of permanence or stability,

it is obvious that licences *per se* have no claim to proprietary status. Of course, this does mean, as noted above, that courts must be very careful to categorise rights correctly. This is not always easy, but it is easier than floundering in the chaos created by dissolving the distinction between personal and proprietary rights.[11]

9.3.7 Can the personal contractual licence take effect against a purchaser despite not being an interest in land?

Following the decision in *Errington*, a second, related attempt was made by Lord Denning's Court of Appeal to explain why a contractual licence could affect a purchaser of the licensor's land. In *Binions v. Evans* (1972), a purchaser of land subject to what looked like a contractual licence *expressly agreed* to purchase the land *subject to* that licence. The purchaser then sought to evict the licensee and he was prevented from doing so. In fact, two judges in the Court of Appeal actually decided that no licence was involved at all; rather, the occupier had a life interest under a strict settlement (a true proprietary right) that was protected under the Settled Land Act 1925.[12] Lord Denning, however, took a different view and decided that the purchaser was bound to give effect to the contractual licence because he had purchased the land expressly subject to it. As Lord Denning explained it, the licensee was protected against eviction by the purchaser because equity would impose a constructive trust on the purchaser behind which the licence could take effect. Subsequent decisions, such as *Re Sharpe* (1980), have followed this reasoning. The net result is that the contractual licence is said to take effect against a purchaser because that *particular purchaser* is bound by a constructive trust because of that *particular purchaser's* conduct. It will be apparent from this explanation that the words and deeds of the particular purchaser are crucial here. Importantly, the licence takes effect only against the particular purchaser, and then only because of his conduct. The licence is not, in fact, an interest in land but is merely protected from revocation by that particular purchaser. It still remains incapable of binding the land as such, even though it may take effect personally against one particular purchaser of it.

---

10 Now that the House of Lords has asserted in *Street v. Mountford* (1985) that residential occupation usually gives rise to a lease and not a licence, many of the practical concerns about the non-binding status of contractual licences have been removed. It was, after all, these 'licences' that appeared to deserve protection against third parties. In fact they did, but that was because they were really leases.

11 We are not yet free of confusion. In *K Sultana Saeed v. Plustrade* (2001), the Court of Appeal, following a concession from counsel, expressed the view that it did not matter whether the claimant had a licence to park or an easement to park as either was enforceable against a third party as an overriding interest if actual occupation existed. Like Lord Denning in *Errington*, this begs the question whether a right to use land can amount to an overriding interest only if it is, in the first place, an interest in land. Overriding status may be given only to interests in land.

12 See Chapter 5.

The 'constructive trust' idea was also re-examined by Fox LJ in *Ashburn Anstalt v. Arnold* (1989) and he accepted that, in appropriate cases, a contractual licence may take effect behind a constructive trust and be enforceable against a purchaser. However, it was not enough that the purchaser simply *agreed* to buy the land subject to the licence for that would be to repeat the heresy of *Errington*; rather, the purchaser must have so conducted himself that it would be inequitable and unconscionable for the licence to be denied. An example would be where the purchaser promised to give effect to the licence, obtained the land from the vendor for a lower price in consequence of that promise, and then refused to honour the licence.[13] Moreover, as Fox LJ makes absolutely clear, the licence is only pro-tected behind a *personal* constructive trust binding on this particular purchaser because of his particular conduct: the licence has not thereby assumed the status of an interest in land. It 'takes effect' against a particular purchaser and, in strict terms, is not 'binding' on the land. So, if the first purchaser is bound to give effect to the licence by means of a personal constructive trust because of his conduct, but then sells the land to a second purchaser, the second purchaser takes free of the licence (it is only a personal right) unless he also becomes personally affected through unconscionable conduct.

The limits of this special intervention by equity have been examined again by the Court of Appeal in *Lloyd v. Dugdale* (2001), in which among other things it was claimed that a purchaser of land was obliged to give effect to the claimant's otherwise void interest because of a personal constructive trust. On the facts of the case, it was clear that Mr Dugdale had some kind of interest in the property (possibly a proprietary one), but equally clear that he had neither registered it as a protected interest nor was he in actual occupation of the property so as to gain an overriding interest under the old rules of the Land Registration Act 1925.[14] In such circumstances, his interest could not bind Lloyd (the purchaser) in the normal manner for one of two alternative reasons: either the interest was merely personal or, even if it was proprietary, it had no protection in the system of registered land. Lloyd had, however, purchased the property apparently subject to such rights that Dugdale could claim. In rejecting the submission that Lloyd was thus bound by a personal constructive trust, Mummery LJ summarised the relevant principles: first, that even where a seller has stipulated that the purchaser shall take the land subject to potential adverse rights, there is no general rule that a constructive trust is to be imposed on the purchaser to give effect to those rights; second, a constructive trust will not be imposed unless the court is satisfied that the purchaser's conscience is so affected that it would be inequitable to allow him to deny the rights of the claimant; third, the critical question in deciding whether the purchaser's conscience is bound is to assess whether the purchaser has undertaken some new obligation, not merely offered to give effect to a pre-existing obligation; fourth, a contractual licence is not to be treated as creating a proprietary interest in land; fifth, evidence that the purchaser has paid a lower price can indicate the acceptance of a new obligation so as to trigger the constructive trust; and finally (and perhaps most import-antly), 'it is not desirable that constructive trusts of land should be imposed on inferences from slender materials'. Clearly, this is an orthodox and, it is submitted, entirely cogent explanation of the relevant principles. It highlights the need to protect a claimant where

---

13 Note there is no estoppel in favour of the licensee directly because the purchaser makes his promise to the seller, not the claimant.

14 The now repealed section 70(1)(g) of the LRA 1925.

appropriate but also reminds us that the courts will not sidestep 'normal' property law principles by unwarranted use of the constructive trust.

9.3.8   A summary

To summarise the above position regarding contractual licences, first, given that they arise through a binding contract, the availability of normal contractual remedies may make them irrevocable between the licensor and licensee for the agreed duration of the licence; second, however, licences are not, as a matter of principle, interests in land. They are not proprietary and cannot be registered within the system of registered or unregistered land. If they are so registered (assuming they get past the scrutiny of the registrar), the registration is of no effect, for it cannot confer a status that the right does not have.[15] As licences, they cannot bind third parties who purchase the licensor's land. Third, licences can 'take effect' against a particular purchaser if it is possible to impose a constructive trust on that purchaser. This can occur in limited circumstances, and is personal to the individual whose conscience is bound. It would not affect a second or third purchaser unless that purchaser were also personally affected. Finally, we must also note that, following the general rule that the 'benefits' of a contract may be assigned to another (i.e. transferred), the right to enjoy a contractual licence may be expressly transferred by the original licensee. This is purely a matter of contract and has nothing to do with property law. So, if B enjoys a licence to park his car on A's land, B may transfer ('assign') that benefit to P expressly, provided that the licence does not expressly, or by implication, prohibit such assignment. In fact, the benefit of many licences (i.e. the right to exercise the right) is indeed declared to be available only to the original licensee and this is why many contractual licences such as theatre, sporting and car park tickets are said to be 'non-transferable'.

9.3.9   The operation of proprietary estoppel: So-called estoppel licences

As we shall see in the discussion below, proprietary estoppel may be pleaded by any person claiming that they have an interest in land or a right to use land for some specific purpose. This claim arises from an assurance made to them, upon which they have relied to their detriment. This is considered in greater detail shortly, but it is a basic rule of the law of proprietary estoppel that the court may 'satisfy' the estoppel in any way it chooses, at least up to the maximum extent of the right assured to the claimant[16] and, as a minimum, in such a way as to do justice between the parties.[17] This may, in fact, result in the award of a 'licence' to the successful claimant, as may have occurred in *Binions* v. *Evans* (1972) and *Bibby* v. *Stirling* (1998). The same issues that are raised in connection with other licences are relevant here also, especially whether the 'estoppel licence' is an interest in land and

---

15 For example, see section 32(3) of the LRA 2002 (registration does not validate an otherwise invalid interest) and note *Nationwide* v. *Ahmed* (1995), in which it was held that a contractual licence could not be an overriding interest under the then operative section 70(1)(g) of the LRA 1925 even if the licensee were in actual occupation, precisely because a licence is not proprietary. The same must be true under Schedules 1 and 3 of the LRA 2002.

16 *Orgee* v. *Orgee* (1997).

17 *Crabb* v. *Arun DC* (1976); *Jennings* v. *Rice* (2002).

whether it has any impact on a third-party purchaser of the land over which it is said to exist. However, these are large questions that cannot be considered fully without an analysis of the nature of proprietary estoppel itself. For that reason, consideration of the nature of so-called estoppel licences (and every other right created through the process of proprietary estoppel) must be deferred to section 9.7 below. Bearing that in mind, it is important to realise, in the context of licences, that the term 'estoppel licence' can describe rights arising in a number of different situations and that these situations may not share common attributes. In the light of this, it is not clear that the term 'estoppel licence' is helpful or indeed meaningful in modern land law.

The first, and most usual, scenario for the existence of an 'estoppel licence' is where a person is already enjoying some access to another's land by means of a genuine licence and then the owner makes some assurance (e.g. that the right shall continue or be enlarged) that is relied upon in such a way as to generate an estoppel in favour of the promisee. An example is where B enjoys a right to park his car on A's land for two years, and A then encourages B to believe that B can always park his car on the land, in reliance on which B turns down the offer of another permanent parking space elsewhere. It is obvious why this is called an estoppel licence – because it arose in the context of a pre-existing licence. However, this label can be misleading. Clearly, as between the landowner (A) and the promisee (B), the effect of the estoppel is to prevent the former from going back on his promise: A is estopped from denying his assurance; in our example, the assurance of a permanent right to park. However, if A then sells the land to a purchaser, it is by no means clear that the purchaser will be bound to give effect to the estoppel. This depends crucially on the nature of proprietary estoppel itself, particularly whether it gives rise to, or is itself, an interest in land. Moreover, just because the estoppel arose out of a situation in which a licence already existed, that does not mean that the 'right' generated by the estoppel is actually a licence. It could be a lease, or an easement, or some other proprietary right. In other words, an 'estoppel licence' as used in this scenario may not be a licence at all (it merely arose out of a licence situation), and, even if it is, its proprietary status and its ability to affect third parties depends on a wider question about the nature of proprietary estoppel.

Second, a so-called 'estoppel licence' may arise when a landowner and the promisee had no previous arrangement concerning the land in question. Thus, it is perfectly possible for a landowner (A) to make an assurance to any person (B) that they shall enjoy some right over A's land, which is relied on in such a way as to give rise to an estoppel. It does not matter that they did not stand in any prior legal relationship. If then the court chooses to 'satisfy' the estoppel by awarding the claimant (B) a licence, an 'estoppel licence' in its purest form has been created. Moreover, it is a licence that has been created entirely informally – that is, by the oral promise of A – and clearly the landowner will be compelled to give effect to the licence for so long as the court orders (which may be the period that A originally had promised). An example is where A orally promises B that B can use A's land as a short cut, and, in reliance, B spends money improving access to A's land. However, whether this estoppel licence is binding on a third-party purchaser of the 'burdened' land depends, again, on whether 'proprietary estoppel' is itself an interest in land, so that once it has arisen it can bind third parties irrespective of how the court chooses to satisfy it.

The third scenario in which the term 'estoppel licence' may be used is where a landowner (A) grants a licence over her land to another person (B), but then sells the land to a purchaser (P), and P then assures B that he may continue to enjoy the licence. An example is where A has granted B a licence permitting B's children to play on A's land, A sells to P, P assures B that the children can continue to play, in reliance on which

B purchases a new climbing frame to build on P's land. This will generate a new 'estoppel licence' between P and B. Note that there is not an estoppel between A and B (merely the licence they had previously created), but there is an estoppel directly between P and B due to the former's assurance to the latter. In consequence, it is important to realise that this is not an example of an existing licence (between A and B) becoming binding on a third party (P). It is the creation of a new 'estoppel licence' between two new parties (P and B). The estoppel licence (if that is how the court chooses to satisfy the estoppel) might be irrevocable by P, but whether it can be binding on a further purchaser (Z) depends, once more, on the crucial question about the nature of proprietary estoppel.

9.4   Proprietary Estoppel

Land law is the study of proprietary rights, being estates or interests in land. Generally, when discussing the creation, operation or transfer of these rights, we have seen that a certain amount of formality is required. Usually, 'interests in land' can be created only by deed, registered disposition or a specifically enforceable written contract (or, in due course, electronic versions of the same). Similarly, a will is needed to transfer land on death and the absence of a valid will is usually fatal to a person's claim to own land that they allege has been promised orally during the deceased's life. Of course, there are exceptions to this, such as certain leases for three years or less (Chapter 6), or rights in unregistered land acquired through adverse possession (Chapter 11) or easements acquired by prescription (Chapter 7), but the overall picture is clear enough. Further, the reason why formality is required is also obvious: proprietary rights become part of the land itself and may endure through successive changes in ownership of the land, so it is imperative that their existence and scope is certain and well defined both for the immediate parties and any intending purchasers or mortgagees. Necessarily, there is a price to pay for this certainty, especially if it is secured through the use of formality requirements. In land law, that price is flexibility, and occasionally fairness. A person may claim that they have a right in land, and it may be 'fair' or 'just' that this be recognised but, nevertheless, their right could be denied because it was not created with due regard to the formality requirements laid down by statute.

Importantly, the Law of Property (Miscellaneous Provisions) Act 1989 was passed in order to bring more clarity and more certainty to the creation and disposition of interests in land. It requires more formality for dealings with land than was the case under the old section 40 of the Law of Property Act (LPA) 1925 by which purely oral contracts could generate an interest in land if 'partly performed'.[18] A direct and intended consequence is that informal arrangements that once would have generated an interest in land for the claimant are now invalid, as with the once valid informally created mortgage by deposit of title deeds.[19] This emphasis on the need for formality in dealings with land continues today under the Land Registration Act (LRA) 2002. When the full weight of e-conveyancing

---

18 In effect, section 2 means that oral contracts for the disposition of an interest in land are invalid, save in exceptional cases and it abolishes the doctrine of part-performance: *Singh v. Beggs* (1996).

19 The deposit of title deeds was evidence of an oral contract that was 'partly performed' when the money was paid over by the lender. A mortgage must now be created by deed and appropriately registered (legal) or be made in writing (equitable), or else it is void as a mortgage: *United Bank of Kuwait v. Sahib* (1995).

comes into force, any transaction specified under section 93 of the Act as requiring electronic execution 'only has effect'[20] if it is so electronically executed. In other words, for those events – for example, the grant of mortgages or long leases[21] – that might fall within section 93, not even a deed or a written contract will be enough to generate an interest in land. The use of electronic means will be mandatory and exclusive. This is not a lessening but an increase in formality requirements and will bring with it an inevitable increase in claims in which one party alleges that it is 'unfair' that they have been denied a proprietary interest because of lack of compliance with formality requirements.

Fortunately, the difficulties that can flow from an over-rigorous reliance on formality are mitigated in English and Welsh property law by the doctrine of proprietary estoppel. Proprietary estoppel is the name given to a set of principles whereby an owner of land may be held to have conferred some right or privilege connected with the land on another person, despite the absence of a deed, registered disposition, written contract or valid will. It will also be applicable in cases of failure to comply with electronic formalities when they are introduced under the LRA 2002. Typically, the right or privilege conferred will arise out of the conduct of the parties, usually because of some assurance made by the land-owner, which is relied upon by the person claiming the right. In this sense, proprietary estoppel is to be understood as a mechanism whereby rights in, or over, land can be created informally. This is important in two principal ways.

First, proprietary estoppel can provide a defence to an action by a landowner who seeks to enforce his strict rights against someone who has been informally promised some right or liberty over the land. For example, an action in trespass by the landlord can be met by a plea of estoppel, in that the landowner had assured the 'trespasser' that they could enjoy the right now being denied. The landowner is not permitted to plead the lack of formality in the creation of the defendant's rights if this would be inequitable. This is proprietary estoppel as a defence or shield. So, in *Wormall v. Wormall* (2004), the defendant successfully pleaded estoppel to an action in trespass brought against her by her father. Second, as indicated already in this chapter, proprietary estoppel can have a much more dramatic effect. There is no doubt that, if successfully established, it can generate new property interests in favour of a claimant. As is commonly stated, proprietary estoppel can be a sword in the hands of a claimant who has relied on an assurance by a landowner that they will be given some right or privilege over the land.[22] A court of equity will 'satisfy' the estoppel by awarding the claimant that right or interest that they deem appropriate, although the court will rarely, if ever, go beyond the maximum the claimant was informally promised[23] and will seek to do that which remedies the unconscionability suffered by the claimant.[24] This means that proprietary estoppel can result in the creation of an interest in land without the need for any formality in the dealings between landowner and claimant. It represents the creation of rights arising from the action of equity on an individual's conscience and is the antidote to unconscionable reliance on formality rules.

---

20 Section 93(2) of the LRA 2002.

21 No transactions have yet been specified under section 93, so these two events represent an educated guess at what might be specified in the first instance.

22 *Crabb v. Arun DC*(1976).

23 *Orgee v. Orgee* (1997).

24 *Jennings v. Rice* (2002).

9.5   Conditions for the Operation of Proprietary Estoppel

Proprietary estoppel has had a role in English property law for many decades, being another example of the intervention of equity to mitigate the consequences of lack of compliance with the formality requirements of the common law or statute. At one time, the conditions for the operation of proprietary estoppel were fairly strictly drawn and these were codified by Fry LJ in *Willmott v. Barber* (1880). He identified the so-called 'five probanda' of proprietary estoppel and, as can be seen, they required the claimant to jump a high hurdle to be successful. As Fry LJ specified, the following had to be established.

1   The claimant must have made a mistake as to their legal rights over some land belonging to another.
2   The true landowner must know of the claimant's mistaken belief.
3   The claimant must have expended money or carried out some action on the faith of that mistaken belief.
4   The landowner must have encouraged the expenditure by the claimant, either directly, or by abstaining from enforcing their legal rights.
5   The owner of the land over which the right is claimed must know of the existence of their own rights, and that these are inconsistent with the alleged rights of the claimant.

Perhaps we should not be surprised that these conditions were onerous because a successful claim of proprietary estoppel could result in the creation of an interest in land that not only affected the immediate estate owner in his current or planned use of the land, but also future purchasers or transferees of the land. Indeed, the informal way in which the estoppel by definition arises means that it is not certain that any intending purchaser or mortgagee would or could be aware of the existence of the estoppel-generated adverse right. After all, the right would have been created without a deed or written instrument or registration. However, since these early days of estoppel, there have been many social and economic changes in the use of land and in the structure of land ownership,[25] and when combined with a tightening of the formality rules themselves (e.g. section 2 of the Law of Property (Miscellaneous Provisions) Act 1989), it was perhaps inevitable that proprietary estoppel would grow in importance and its defining features would change.

In the result, and as a reflection of modern conditions, the original criteria for establishing an estoppel have been largely abandoned and the modern approach is to be much more flexible about the way in which an estoppel can arise. According to Oliver J in *Taylor Fashions v. Liverpool Victoria Trustees* (1982), a claimant will be able to establish an estoppel if they can prove an assurance, reliance and detriment in circumstances in which it would be unconscionable to deny a remedy to the claimant. This has confirmed that the emphasis in cases of proprietary estoppel has shifted away from an examination of the actions of the landowner and has become more focused on the behaviour of the claimant. Moreover, as we shall see, *Gillett v. Holt* (2002) and *Jennings v. Rice* (2002) make it clear that these four features of estoppel – assurance, reliance, detriment and unconscionability – are

25 For example, shared family ownership of property; occupation by extended family groups.

not to be seen as isolated features, but that each case must be looked at 'in the round'[26] in order to determine whether the landowner should be able to go back on his assurance to the claimant about the use of land. We are to adopt an holistic approach to establishing proprietary estoppel, a point reiterated by a majority of the House of Lords in *Thorner v. Majors* (2009).[27]

Before examining in more detail the conditions necessary to establish an estoppel in modern land law, it is important to appreciate that it is not a universal remedy that can cure every defect in formality. If it were, there would be little point in having formality rules at all. As the court of first instance emphasised in *Prudential Assurance v. Waterloo Real Estate* (1998), estoppel is a drastic remedy and it is a major step for a court to award a claimant a proprietary right over another's land in the absence of due formality, even more so if the effect of the estoppel is to compel a transfer of ownership of the land itself. So, in *Taylor v. Dickens* (1997) and *Uglow v. Uglow* (2004), the claimant had been promised property in a will, but when the promise was not honoured, the court rejected the claim that the property should be transferred under proprietary estoppel; in *Evans v. James* (2000), proprietary estoppel did not cure the absence of a valid contract between the parties relating to the transfer of land; in *Slater v. Richardson* (1980), the claimants were unable to rely on estoppel after having failed to observe the formalities of the Agricultural Holdings Act 1986; in *Canty v. Broad* (1995), the claimants, having failed to conclude a contract for the sale of land in accordance with section 2 of the LP(MP)A 1989, were unable to claim the land by estoppel; and in *Cobbe v. Yeomans Row Management* (2008), the House of Lords refused to allow estoppel to effectively enforce an oral agreement that both parties knew was only 'binding in honour' until it was reduced to writing.[28] By way of contrast, the claimant was partially successful in *Matharu v. Matharu* (1994), using estoppel as a means to live in a property for the rest of her life; in *Wayling v. Jones* (1993), *Gillett v. Holt* (2000), *Jennings v. Rice* (2002), *Ottey v. Grundy* (2003) and *Thorner v. Majors* (2009), the claimants established a right to particular land promised by the deceased, but not left to them by will (but not in *McDonald v. Frost* (2009)); in *Sleebush v. Gordon* (2004), the claimant had succeeded to half the interest in a property on the death of her husband but was successful in recovering the other half by way of estoppel even though it had been left by will to another; in *Bibby v. Stirling* (1998), the claimant used estoppel to establish a right to use a greenhouse erected on the defendant's land; in *Flowermix v. Site Developments* (2000), a contract that was void for uncertainty (as to the extent of land concerned) was nevertheless effectively enforced by reliance on the estoppel rules; in *Joyce v. Rigolli* (2004), the Court of Appeal was prepared to use estoppel to enforce a contract for the disposition of land that was completely devoid of writing; and in *Kinane v. Alimamy Mackie-Conteh* (2005), the Court of Appeal used proprietary estoppel and constructive trust[29] to validate a mortgage that failed completely to meet any of the formality requirements usually required for either legal or equitable mortgages.

These are just a sample of the numerous cases in which estoppel is pleaded. Of course,

---

26 See also *Ottey v. Grundy* (2003) for a successful claim on this basis and *Murphy v. Burrows* (2004) for an unsuccessful claim on this basis.

27 It is not clear whether Lord Scott in that case shares this view, but it is affirmed by Lords Neuberger and Walker, with the agreement of Lord Rodger. Lord Hoffmann does not dissent from it.

28 Applying *AG for Hong Kong v. Humphreys* (1987).

29 On which, see below.

many of the cases in which the plea was unsuccessful can be explained on the basis that, say, the assurance was never made or not made clearly enough (e.g. *McDonald v. Frost*) or the alleged detriment was never suffered or too minimal (e.g. *Century UK v. Clibbery* (2004)) or there was no unconscionability (e.g. *Cobbe*). However, to apply the *Taylor Fashions* criteria mechanically is to miss the point. Estoppel is available to cure absence of formality when, but only when, it would be unconscionable for the defendant to rely on the lack of formality to defeat the claimant – see, for example, *Hopper v. Hopper* (2008). Unconscionability is at the heart of the doctrine and the existence of unconscionability is the reason why the lack of formality can be excused. This is examined in more detail but it is mentioned at the outset to reinforce the link between formality and the plea of estoppel.

9.5.1   The assurance

Proprietary estoppel is a flexible doctrine that acts on the conscience of a landowner. Accordingly, the landowner must have made some kind of assurance to the claimant that either he would refrain from exercising his strict legal rights over his own land or, more commonly, that the claimant might have some present or future right or use over that land. While, in many cases, the assurance will be as to some specific property right over the land (e.g. 'you can have a lease'), it is clear from the House of Lords' decision in *Thorner v. Majors* (2009) that this is not necessary in order for proprietary estoppel to be established. In that case, the landowner had never promised the claimant any specific right, or even made any express promises (the assurance was implied), but the claim of estoppel was upheld. According to Lord Walker, the assurance had to be 'clear enough' and this would depend hugely on context. In the context of a family arrangement concerning a farm (*Thorner*), it might be enough for some general assurance to have been made concerning the future ownership of the land; in the context of a commercial arrangement, however, it was likely that a much more specific assurance would be needed (*Cobbe*). Thus, according to *Thorner*, the House of Lords' earlier decision in *Cobbe* was not to be taken as always requiring an assurance of a specific property right, although that conclusion was justified on the facts of that case. Importantly, this is not simply a matter of distinguishing between 'family' and 'commercial' cases, for everything depends on context. Thus, in *McDonald v. Frost* (2009), a typical family dispute, the court found that no adequate assurance had been made in the context of the parties' complex relationship.[30] Consequently, the important point is that the House of Lords in *Thorner* did not adopt the strict approach put forward earlier in *Cobbe*, essentially because it was recognised that this would have reduced successful estoppel cases to a trickle.[31] Instead, the majority in *Thorner*[32] maintained the flexible, holistic approach that had developed in the Court of Appeal, particularly in *Gillett*, and accept that estoppel responds to a 'certain enough' assurance that must depend on the context in which it is given. In addition, and to be clear, there is no doubt that the

---

30   For example, In *Slater v. Richardson* (1980), a statement by the landowner that he would welcome the claimant as his tenant was not an 'estoppel generating assurance' that a tenancy would be given. See also *Lissimore v. Downing* (2003).

31   That, of course, may have been the point behind Lord Scott's analysis in *Cobbe*, and it seems to have been a position that his colleagues in *Thorner* were not prepared to endorse.

32   Lord Scott did not recant from the view of estoppel he put forward in *Cobbe*, but instead chose to regard *Thorner* as an example of a remedial constructive trust.

assurance must be about, or relate to, some reasonably identifiable land – *Thorner*. However, it does not matter if the exact scope of the land is uncertain, or even if over time some land is sold and other purchased, provided that it is reasonably clear which land the assurance relates to at the time the claim of estoppel falls to be considered – *Thorner v. Majors* (2009).[33]

This analysis of estoppel necessarily means that the form that the assurance takes is irrelevant and it may be given orally, arise from conduct, or even be in the form of a written instrument that is not itself enforceable as a contract to transfer an interest in land (as apparently in *Flowermix v. Site Developments* (2000)). The assurance may be 'unilateral' in that it was offered freely by the landowner, but it might also arise from a mutual under-standing between the parties about the use of the land. The assurance may be express[34] or implied, as where a landowner refrains from preventing the claimant using his land in a particular way,[35] or the landowner by actions rather than words effectively assures the claimant about use or ownership of the land. *Thorner v. Majors* is of this type. However, the assurance must be such as to generate unconscionability if withdrawn, so in *Murphy v. Burrows* (2004), the fluid and uncertain nature of the parties' relationship meant that the assurances did not give rise to estoppels as it was unclear whether they were given, or reasonably understood, as assurances about property. By way of contrast, and somewhat remarkably, it seems from *JT Developments v. Quinn* (1991) that an estoppel can arise even though the assurance was given in circumstances in which there was clearly no intention to create binding obligations between the parties at all, as where the parties had attempted to negotiate a contract governing use of the land, but had failed. Again, in *Lim Teng Huan v. Ang Swee Chuan* (1992) and in *Flowermix*, a written, although unenforceable agreement was held to constitute the requisite assurance, with the consequence that the unenforceable agreement was indirectly given effect through the intervention of proprietary estoppel, even though this appears to be enforcing a contract that the parties have not put into effect properly through their own fault. Similarly, in *Kinane v. Alimany Mackie-Conteh* (2005), the borrower had agreed by letter to charge his land as security for a loan, but the written instrument did not meet with the formality requirements of section 2 of the 1989 Act as both borrower and lender did not sign it. It failed, therefore, as an equitable mortgage, but the Court of Appeal was prepared to use estoppel to support the creation of the mortgage and so give the lender his proprietary remedies when the loan was not repaid.

The *Kinane* case is, perhaps, the most extreme example of a very liberal approach to proprietary estoppel that developed in the years following the tightening of the formality rules by the Law of Property (Miscellaneous Provisions) Act 1989. In it, and in *Lim Teng Huan*, it is difficult to see why the formality rules could be ignored just *because* the claimant had partly performed the unenforceable contract. In both cases, there is a need to demonstrate why it would be unconscionable to apply the formality rules that apply to other trans-actions and this is not clear from the judgments. Indeed, in *Cobbe v. Yeomans Row* (2008), the

---

33 'The owl of Minerva spreads its wings only with the falling of the dusk' – *per* Lord Hoffmann in *Thorner*. 'It would represent a regrettable and substantial emasculation of the beneficial principle of proprietary estoppel if it were artificially fettered so as to require the precise extent of the property the subject of the alleged estoppel to be strictly defined in every case' – *per* Lord Neuberger in the same case.

34 For example, in *Ottey v. Grundy* (2003), in a letter of intent or *Gillett v. Holt* (2000) repeated publicly on many occasions. See also *Salvation Army Trustees v. West Yorkshire CC* (1981).

35 *Ramsden v. Dyson* (1866).

House of Lords made it clear that it is not permissible to use proprietary estoppel to circumvent the formal requirements of section 2 of the 1989 Act and this is not challenged by Thorner.[36] Consequently, in Cobbe, the claim of estoppel failed because both the parties knew that they should have entered into an enforceable contract if they wanted to create a legal obligation between them and they had chosen not to.

Finally, it is clear that an estoppel can succeed provided that the claimant reasonably believes that an assurance has been made, even if the landowner did not intend to make an assurance by words or deeds – Thorner. The landowner cannot defeat the estoppel merely by claiming that he did not intend an assurance, if any reasonable claimant would have believed that one had been made. However, we must be careful here. If the landowner knows nothing (and could not reasonably be expected to know) of the claimant's belief that he (the claimant) has been promised some right in or over the land, and the land-owner has done nothing to encourage the claimant's belief, then it is going to be difficult to establish an estoppel. For example, if A promises B the right to park a car on A's land, but B takes this as a promise to give him the land, which belief is neither encouraged nor acquiesced in by A nor reasonably held by B, no estoppel involving transfer of the land can arise (although a right to park the car might). So, in Slater v. Richardson (1980), the defend-ants were wholly unaware of the claimant's belief and had done nothing to encourage it and no estoppel arose.

What we need to remember is that we should adopt an holistic approach to estoppel, and should not be tied to a mechanical application of the requirement for an assurance. A forensic dissection (and limitation) of the 'assurance' requirement is unlikely to be in keeping with the inherently equitable nature of the doctrine. All depends on context. Thus, it will be rare for the court to find that an assurance has been made in the context of negotiations between parties intending to complete a fully binding contract, especially if the negotiations are expressly 'subject to contract'.[37] But, even general words, or a general understanding implied from the parties' behaviour, may well be enough in other cases, especially if the litigants acted without the benefit of legal advice. The cases tell us that the assurance must be in the way of an understanding or unilateral promise between claimant and defendant, but not necessarily amounting to the promise of some specific right in property. The assurance must be clear enough in context. It should be given to the claim-ant personally and must relate to land that is readily identifiable at the time the estoppel is crystallised. It is sufficient, save for exceptional circumstances,[38] if the claimant reasonable believes that an assurance has been made.

9.5.2   The reliance

As we have seen, the 'assurance' may be entirely informal, but whatever form it takes, it is essential that it produces an effect on the claimant. The claimant must 'rely' on the assurance, in that it must be possible to show that he was induced to behave differently because the assurance had been given. It is sufficient if the claimant reasonably relies on the assurance, even if the landowner did not intend that he should so rely – Thorner.

---

36 There was no attempted contract in Thorner, and hence section 2 of the LPA 1989 was not in play. An estoppel may exist independently of the failed contract – see 9.5.4 below.

37 Edwin Shirley Productions v. Workspace Mana Ltd (2001).

38 Regarded by Lord Neuberger as a possibility in Thorner, but not elaborated.

Of course, in practice, reliance can be very difficult to prove and a court may well be prepared to infer reliance if that is a plausible explanation of the claimant's conduct. Thus, in *Greasley v. Cooke* (1980), the Court of Appeal held that, if clear assurances have been made and detriment has been suffered, it is permissible to assume that reliance has occurred. Likewise, in *Wayling v. Jones* (1993), the Court of Appeal looked only for a 'sufficient link' between the assurance made and the detriment incurred by the plaintiff, the existence of which would throw the burden of proof onto the defendant to show that there had, in fact, been no reliance. The crucial point seems to be that there will be no reliance only when it can be shown that the claimant would have incurred detriment completely irrespective of the defendant's conduct. In *Orgee v. Orgee* (1997), for example, it was clear that much of the plaintiff's alleged detriment was ordinary expenses that would have been incurred normally and in any event. However, even this must not be taken too far. In *Campbell v. Griffin* (2001), the claimant had been a lodger in the landowner's house and over time had taken on the responsibility of caring for his 'landlords', an elderly couple. There was clear evidence of relevant assurances about the property. At trial, the claimant admitted that he would have assisted his landlords out of ordinary human compassion rather than in clear reliance on their promises. Nevertheless, the Court of Appeal upheld the estoppel claim, noting that a dual motive for action (the assurance plus normal human compassion) does not thereby diminish the fact that reliance has occurred. This might seem overly generous, but it would be harsh indeed to dismiss a claim simply because the claimant was not, after all, a thoroughly selfish individual who was prepared to help only because of what was on offer. A further example of this is provided by *Chun v. Ho* (2001), in which Miss Chun successfully established a claim in estoppel[39] to a share in a business and its property because her actions in giving up her career and establishing a life with the landowner to the disgust of her family[40] could not be explained solely on the basis of her love for him. There must have been some reliance on his clear assurances about the business. Evidently, then, the existence of reliance is critically dependent on the peculiar facts of each case and is not to be discounted merely because of family or emotional ties between claimant and landowner that might otherwise explain a course of action. Equally clear is the point made by the Court of Appeal when upholding the estoppel claims in *Gillett* and *Jennings*: assurance, reliance and detriment are necessarily interwoven and the court should not approach them forensically as if they were entirely separate requirements. The case must be viewed in the round.

9.5.3 The detriment

Equity has always been wary of 'volunteers': that is, claimants who seek to enforce a promise even though they have given nothing in return. Similarly, proprietary estoppel cannot be established unless the claimant can prove that he has suffered some detriment in reliance on the assurance. Not surprisingly, so long as the detriment is not minimal or trivial, it may take any form. For example, it may be that the claimant has spent money on the land or advanced money to the landowner in reliance on the assurance,[41] or has

---

39 She also claimed constructive trust and the court drew no distinction between the claims.

40 He was serving a prison sentence in Hong Kong.

41 *Kinane v. Alimany Mackie-Conteh* (2005).

physically improved the land in some way, or has devoted time and care to the needs of the landowner,[42] or has forsaken some other opportunity.[43] Indeed, as *Campbell v. Griffin* and *Jennings v. Rice* show, it is not necessary that the detriment be related to land at all, or the land in dispute.[44] It may be, for example, that the claimant has spent their money in other ways, on the faith of an assurance that they would have somewhere to live or an inheritance to enjoy. It is even true that detriment in this technical sense can exist even though the claimant has derived some benefit from his association with the landowner. In *Gillett v. Holt* (2002), Mr Gillett might be thought to have done rather well out of his relationship with Mr Holt as the former now owned valuable shares in the farm company and held property in his own right. Nevertheless, he still incurred the detriment of lost opportunities. The point is simply that an estoppel cannot be established unless there has been some detrimental reliance, for that is what makes a retraction of the assurance potentially unconscionable.[45] Sufficient detriment is always a question of fact and many claims fail because there was neither an assurance nor detriment. This should be no surprise as people do not usually act to their detriment unless they are certain that they have been promised something concrete. Consequently, detriment itself, however extensive, is not enough. In *Taylor v. Dickens* (1997), the plaintiff worked for a number of years without pay in the expectation that he would inherit from the deceased. The deceased changed her will and left everything to another. Detriment was clear enough but, according to the trial judge, there was no assurance that the deceased would *never* change her will and so the claim failed for lack of an enforceable assurance. This case was settled before an appeal but now looks harsh in the light of the decisions in *Gillett, Grundy, Jennings* and *Thorner*. Even so, it remains the case that an unencouraged detriment is not sufficient to found an estoppel. Finally, in case there is doubt, *Lloyd v. Dugdale* (2001) makes it clear that the detriment must be incurred by the person to whom the assurance is made. There is no concept of 'derivative detriment' and so Mr Dugdale had to prove (as he did successfully) that the detriment was incurred by him personally and not on behalf of his company (a separate legal entity).

9.5.4   Unconscionability

It is clear that Oliver J in *Taylor Fashions* regarded unconscionability as the very essence of a claim of proprietary estoppel. Indeed, in the great majority of cases, the simple fact that the landowner is seeking to retract an assurance given and relied upon will be unconscionable. In *Gillett*, at first instance, Carnwath J put the matter succinctly by noting that '[n]ormally it is the promisor's knowledge of the detriment being suffered in reliance on his promise which makes it "unconscionable" for him to go back on it' and this was reiterated by the Court of Appeal in the same case. As noted above, it is this unconscionability that frees the court from the strictures of the formality requirements imposed by statute[46] and allows the claimant to succeed. So, an oral agreement deliberately made 'subject to contract', as in

---

42 *Campbell v. Griffin* (2001).

43 *Ottey v. Grundy* (2003); *Lloyd v. Dugdale* (2001); *Thorner*.

44 In *Ottey*, one disputed property was in Jamaica and see *Wayling v. Jones* (1993).

45 *Gillett v. Holt* (2000).

46 This may well include the e-conveyancing provisions of the LRA 2002.

Canty v. Broad (1995),[47] or a void executory contract (i.e. one that might never be binding as to substance),[48] or a conditional assurance the conditions of which are not fulfilled[49] cannot be enforced via estoppel, because there is no unconscionability in relying on the absence of formality in these circumstances, even if there has been reliance and detriment. This may be a better explanation of why the claim failed in Cobbe – in which both parties knew that an enforceable contact was required – rather than dismissing the claim because of a lack of a specific assurance. So, also, the common understanding that a person is free to change their will makes it difficult to plead unconscionability when a will is changed or property left to another in a new will,[50] although unconscionability may exist if the assurance is withdrawn after it is repeated so often and so loudly that no one could doubt that the landowner meant what they said about the destination of their property on their death, as in Gillett v. Holt and Ottey v. Grundy. In Gillett itself, Mr Holt had promised Mr Gillett over a 40-year period that he (Gillett) would be the beneficiary of Holt's will. When Holt changed his will to exclude Gillett, a claim based on estoppel was successful, the Court of Appeal noting that the mere withdrawal of the assurance after such detriment (that is, 40 years of work at less than the market wage) was sufficient to establish unconscionability. A similar result is reached in Thorner, although the period of detriment in that case was shorter.

The analysis in Gillett is driven by the understanding that estoppel claims should not be dissected too closely by analysis of the three 'ingredients' but should be looked at in total to see if the denial of the claimant's right is unconscionable. Of itself, this formula presents certain difficulties for it appears to define unconscionability purely in terms of assurance, reliance and detriment (i.e. unconscionability exists when the assurance is withdrawn after detrimental reliance) and so the 'all-important' criterion of unconscionability, the raison d'être of estoppel,[51] becomes a mere shadow of the other three components. The case itself can be justified on the ground that (as noted above) the repeated assurances implied that Mr Holt would not exclude Mr Gillett from the will and hence the unconscionability lay in the attempt to plead the formality of the new will in defiance of Gillett's claim. This might also be the reason why the claimant succeeded in Thorner, even though the period of detriment was shorter than that found in Gillett. Clearly, the law must be astute to protect a claimant when there is genuine estoppel, but should not permit estoppel to be an easy way of avoiding the formalities normally required for conducting dealings with land. Thus, the common understanding that there is no contract for the sale of a house until formalised in writing explains why a house owner may accept and reject offers for the house at any point up to exchange of (written) contracts without behaving unconscionably. In the final analysis, unconscionability is, by its nature, a fluid concept and much depends on the facts of each case. It does not mean that the claimant must prove 'fraud' by the defendant, although there are elements of fraud in the concept.[52] It means, simply (and unhelpfully!),

47 Also AG for Hong Kong v. Humphreys (1987); Secretary of State for Transport v. Christos (2003). See also Yeoman's v. Cobbe (2008), which confirms that void oral contracts cannot be enforced by estoppel.

48 Ravenocean v. Gardner (2001).

49 Uglow v. Uglow (2004).

50 Taylor v. Dickens (1997); Murphy v. Burrows (2004); Driver v. Yorke (2003).

51 Taylor Fashions (1982).

52 Orgee v. Orgee (1997).

whether, in all of the circumstances, the landowner can resile from the assurance he has given and on which the claimant has relied to detriment (*Hopper v. Hopper* (2008)). Crucially, even if the claimant has relied to detriment on an assurance, there can be no proprietary estoppel without unconscionability.

Importantly, however, it is clear from the House of Lords' decisions in *Cobbe* and *Thorner* that it is not the purpose of estoppel to remedy unconscionable conduct *per se*. Estoppel is a response to an assurance about land, relied on to detriment, where it would be unconscionable for the assurance to be withdrawn. Unconscionability is necessary, but it operates within the parameters proved by assurance, reliance and detriment. In *Cobbe*, many observers might well regard the behaviour of the defendant as being 'sharp', unfair or even unconscionable in a general sense. But lacking the factual basis of a claim – that is, a clear enough assurance in context – there could be no estoppel. *Thorner* does nothing to depart from this, save only to remind us 'that focussing on technicalities can lead to a degree of strictness inconsistent with the fundamental aims of equity'.[53]

9.6   What is the Result of a Successful Plea of Proprietary Estoppel?

The myriad circumstances in which proprietary estoppel can be established necessarily means that the remedy for each successful claimant will vary. Broadly speaking, however, two possibilities are available. First, if the proprietary estoppel is established by a defendant in an action by the landowner for recovery of the land or exclusion of the defendant or denial of some right alleged by the defendant, the landowner's claim will be dismissed and the defendant will be left to enjoy the right that the landowner was seeking to deny. This is estoppel as a shield, and is illustrated by *Gafford v. Graham* (1998), in which the landowner entitled to the benefit of a restrictive covenant was estopped from enforcing it due to his acquiescence in conduct contrary to the covenant by his neighbour. Second, and more importantly for our purposes, if the estoppel is established by a claimant seeking to enforce a right or use against a landowner in consequence of an assurance, the court can award the claimant such remedy as it deems appropriate, save only that *Orgee v. Orgee* (1997) suggests that the court cannot award more than the claimant was ever assured. In fact, as is made clear by *Jennings v. Rice* (2002), the precise reach of the remedy awarded should be tailored to remove the unconscionability suffered by the claimant.

As explained in *Crabb v. Arun DC* (1976), on a practical level, this means that the court can 'satisfy' the equity in any manner that is appropriate to the case before it, provided that it does the minimum to achieve justice between the parties.[54] The remedy may be 'expectation-based' (the claimant gets that which was promised), 'reliance-based' (the claimant gets a remedy commensurate with extent of their detrimental reliance) or a mixture of the two provided that the unconscionability is remedied. Crucially, therefore, a

---

53 Lord Neuberger, in *Thorner*.

54 In *Wormall v. Wormall* (2004), the successful claimant was granted a right to occupy the land for a stated period, but on appeal to the Court of Appeal, her claim to additional monetary compensation was dismissed. The time-limited right to occupy was the minimum necessary to do justice between the parties.

court can award the claimant any proprietary *or* personal right over the defendant's land, or no substantive remedy at all. For example, in *Dillwyn v. Llewellyn* (1862) and *Pascoe v. Turner* (1979), the claimant was actually awarded the fee simple in the land; in *Celsteel v. Alton* (1987), *Bibby v. Stirling* (1998) and *Sweet v. Sommer* (2004), there appears to have been the award of an easement; and in *Voyce v. Voyce* (1991), there was a complete readjustment of the parties' rights over the property. Yet although in all of these cases the successful claimant was awarded a proprietary right in the land, it is possible that he will be given only a personal right (a licence) to use the land. On one view, this occurred in *Inwards v. Baker* (1965), in which a father had encouraged his son to build a bungalow on his (the father's) land, and when the son went ahead, the court appeared to grant the son a licence to use the land for life. Likewise, in *Matharu v. Matharu* (1994), the claimant's claim for a share of beneficial ownership was rejected, but she was awarded a licence to occupy for life, and in *Parker v. Parker* (2004), a licence appears to have been awarded as a result of estoppel. Again, there is no reason why any right *over land* – proprietary or personal – should be awarded at all. For example, in *Wayling v. Jones* (1993), the claimant was awarded compensation in lieu of a proprietary interest because the relevant land had been disposed of previously, and in *Campbell v. Griffin* (2001), the claimant was given a charge to the value of £35,000 over the property and was not permitted to remain in possession.[55] Similar results were achieved in *Jennings* and in *Ottey* and this would have been the judge's solution in *Murphy v. Burrows* (2004) had he believed that the estoppel was made out in the first place. Interestingly, in *Murphy*, the judge regards the monetary award as a *lesser* form of relief – justified in that case by the weak acts of detriment. Certainly, in both *Jennings* and *Campbell*, it seems clear that the claimant would have preferred a proprietary stake in the property.

As one can see, the range of remedies available to the court is open-ended, and, importantly, does not necessarily have to result in the grant of a traditional proprietary interest at all, as where a licence is granted or a money award made. Of course, this flexibility does produce a measure of uncertainty, both for the claimant and any potential purchaser of the land over which the estoppel is asserted. In fact, the most difficult problems in practice occur when the 'burdened' land is sold to a purchaser *before* the estoppel has been crystallised by decision of the court, as in *Bibby v. Stirling* (1998) and *Lloyd v. Dugdale* (2001). Naturally, the purchaser is likely to deny that the claimant has any right over the land – after all, there is no written evidence of the right and the purchaser is not responsible for generating the estoppel. In these circumstances, the court is faced with the classic property law issue: whose right to the land should have priority, that of the person alleging the estoppel who by definition has been treated unconscionably, or that of the purchaser who has paid value for land that now might be burdened by an adverse right? In fact, this dilemma hides layers of further questions. First, does the claimant benefit from an estoppel; and second, does that estoppel bind the purchaser? In turn, this second question will depend on both the nature of proprietary estoppel itself *and* (assuming estoppel is 'proprietary' in character) whether the appropriate rules of registered and unregistered land have been observed.

---

55 The house was to be sold and the claimant paid out of the proceeds.

9.7　The Nature of Proprietary Estoppel and its Effect on Third Parties

Prior to the Land Registration Act 2002, the nature of proprietary estoppel was not easy to determine and there were two major strands of thought. On one view, proprietary estoppel was itself an interest in land, although necessarily an equitable interest because of the informal way it arose. In other words, it was irrelevant how the court satisfied the equity (e.g. by easement, fee simple or licence), because the *estoppel* was proprietary in nature and itself capable of binding a purchaser of the land. Thus, a purchaser buying land over which there was a potential estoppel could find the land subject to an adverse right if the claimant could prove that the *former* owner had 'created' an estoppel in his favour. Support for this view was derived from the argument that 'estoppel licences' were interests in land and from cases such as *Ives v. High* (1967) and *Inwards v. Baker* (1965), in which the 'bindingness' of estoppel appears to be accepted. In the latter case, the court indicated that the claimant should be awarded a licence to occupy the land as a result of an estoppel, which could then bind a third party and the same solution was adopted in *Greasley v. Cooke* (1980) and in *Re Sharpe* (1980).[56] Likewise, in *Habermann v. Koehler* (1997) and *Birmingham Midshires v. Saberhawal* (1999), the Court of Appeal intimated, without deciding, that if the claimant could establish an estoppel, it might amount to an overriding interest under the then applicable section 70(1) of the LRA 1925, thus indicating its proprietary status.[57] However, it is also true that both *Inwards* and *Cooke* could have been justified on other grounds (i.e. that the claimant should have had a life interest under a settlement[58]) and *Bibby v. Stirling* (1998) is probably an example of an *existing* easement binding the burdened land. Likewise, in *Williams v. Staite* (1979), another case often cited in support of this view, the matter was assumed, rather than argued. Significantly, however, in *Lloyd v. Dugdale* (2001), the Court of Appeal took the view that if the claimant had been in actual occupation of the property, his right arising by estoppel would have bound the purchaser (Lloyd) as an overriding interest under the then applicable section 70(1)(g) of the LRA 1925.[59] This was, prior to the Land Registration Act 2002, the clearest evidence that estoppels were themselves proprietary.

The second view did not see proprietary estoppel as a right in itself, but rather as a method of creating rights: a means to an end, not the end itself. On such a view, the estoppel was regarded as a process whereby rights in, or over, land were created, rather like a contract or a deed but much less formal. Consequently, it was not the fact of estoppel that was relevant, but the right that was created by the court when it satisfied the estoppel. So, for example, if the estoppel gave rise to a lease, a freehold, an easement or any other proprietary right, then there was no doubt that a third person buying the land over which the right took effect might be bound by it, being bound in the same way that any lease,

---

56　In *Re Sharpe*, the court accepted that the estoppel (the 'equity') could bind a trustee in bankruptcy.

57　The argument would be equally applicable to paragraphs 2 of Schedules 1 and 3 of the LRA 2002.

58　*Dodsworth v. Dodsworth* (1973).

59　Consequently, were it not for the unfortunate circumstance that Mr Dugdale's company was in actual occupation rather than he personally, he would have succeeded in his claim against the purchaser because his estoppel would have bound as an overriding interest.

freehold or easement would bind. The essence of the matter was that the estoppel had generated a proprietary right and it was the right that was binding, not the estoppel. The obvious consequence of this was, however, that if the estoppel generated a personal right (i.e. a licence or a money award) that licence or award was incapable of binding a purchaser, simply because it was personal and the method of its creation (estoppel) was irrelevant. For some commentators, this alternative view of proprietary estoppel had much to commend it, not least that it maintained a clear distinction between proprietary and personal rights and did not fetter a court in its discretion. If, for example, the court wished to ensure that a future purchaser of the 'burdened' land was bound by an estoppel, it could have awarded the claimant a proprietary right arising from it. If the court wished to ensure that the estoppel was effective only against the maker of the assurance, it could have awarded a personal remedy. However, it is true that there was little judicial support for this theory, and not only because the effect of an estoppel on a third-party purchaser was rarely a live issue in the courts. It had the great disadvantage that a right so painstakingly established by the claimant, stemming from the landowner's unconscionability could be defeated pro tanto by the simple device of conveying the land to another.

9.7.1   Estoppels after the Land Registration Act 2002

While there may have been doubts and arguments about the nature of proprietary estoppel before the entry into force of the Land Registration Act 2002, these doubts have been resolved by express provision in the Act itself. Section 116 provides that:

> [F]or the avoidance of doubt that, in relation to registered land . . . an equity by estoppel . . . has effect from the time the equity arises as an interest capable of binding successors in title (subject to the rules about the effect of dispositions on priority).

This import of this section is clear enough and is spelled out in the Law Commission report on which the Land Registration Act 2002 is based. It means that an *uncrystallised* estoppel (the 'equity by estoppel') has proprietary character, with the consequence that if the normal priority rules of registered conveyancing are satisfied ('rules about the effect of dispositions on priority'), the estoppel will bind a third party. In practice, this means that we must examine the precise circumstances in which it is alleged that an estoppel is alleged to bind a third party. There appear to be three possibilities.

1   The landowner (A) generates an estoppel in favour of B. Before B can sue A to determine the precise remedy he will receive, A sells the land to P. The uncrystallised estoppel – the equity by estoppel – is declared by section 116 to be proprietary and so it has the potential to bind P. Whether in fact it binds P depends on the normal rules of registered conveyancing. Thus B would either have to have entered the estoppel against A's registered title by means of a notice[60] or, as is more likely, claim an overriding interest by reason of actual occupation. If neither are true – as of Mr Dugdale in *Lloyd v. Dugdale* (2001) – the purchaser takes the land free of the uncrystallised

---

60 Probably, a unilateral notice. A well advised claimant might try to register their estoppel as a means of crystallising their claim. The entry of the notice is likely to be challenged by the landowner, thus requiring the estoppel claim to be judicially determined. See also *Henry v. Henry* [2010] UKPC 3, where the bindingness of an estoppel was confirmed in the context of an appeal from St. Lucia.

estoppel, as provided by section 29 of the LRA 2002, even though it is proprietary. Of course, if the transferee is not a purchaser – perhaps A gifts the land to his daughter or leaves it by will – then the transferee is bound by the estoppel because it is a proprietary right and has priority (section 28 of the LRA 2002). This is simply the application of normal rules of registered conveyancing to a property right – the uncrystallised estoppel.

2   The landowner (A) generates an estoppel in favour of B. B sues A and the court awards an estoppel remedy in the nature of an orthodox proprietary right, such as a lease, easement, or the like. It is highly likely in such a case that the order of the court will be carried out by the formal grant of the right so awarded: for example, A grants a formal lease or easement to B or conveys the freehold and the register of title of the burdened land will be amended accordingly. In such cases, the formal grant of the right will be registered and so the claimant will be protected against any future transferee of the land. If by some rare chance the land is transferred by A to a purchaser (P) before the court order is carried out, B nevertheless has a proprietary right that might bind P. This is because B has a specific proprietary right arising from the claim in estoppel (e.g. a lease etc.), and if this is to bind P, the right must be protected in the manner appropriate to registered title as specified by the LRA 2002.[61] Note, however, that the fact that a court has ordered that B should be given a specific property right makes it highly unlikely that a transfer would take place before this right is formally granted.

3   The landowner (A) generates an estoppel in favour of B. B sues A and the court awards an estoppel remedy in the nature of a personal remedy against A, such as a money award or a licence. In such cases, the estoppel has been crystallised and A is under an obligation to ensure that B receives that which the court has ordered. If A then sells to P, a strict reading of section 116 means that P cannot be bound by 'the equity by estoppel' because the 'equity by estoppel' no longer exists. It has been satisfied by the court order. This is, indeed, perfectly understandable if the award against A was a money award; after all, why should P have to pay out the award when it was ordered against A? The issue appears more troublesome if B is given a licence over A's land, for on this reasoning the licence will be defeated by a transfer to P – the estoppel is satisfied and a licence is personal. In fact, however, this is not a surprising result and should not cause eyebrows to be raised. If the court has seen fit to crystallise the estoppel by means of a licence – after all, it had free choice as to remedy – it may well be because B's claim was not regarded as of sufficient merit to justify the potential carry-over of that remedy against P. The licence or money award might have been chosen deliberately to ensure that no purchaser could be bound. Of course, if this is a true interpretation of section 116,[62] then what is most needed is for a court to consider carefully the precise remedy it gives to a successful claimant.[63]

---

61 Again, usually this will be because the right qualifies as an overriding interest by reason of actual occupation.

62 Currently, there are no cases that raise this issue.

63 An example of this is *Parker (9th Earl of Macclesfield)* v. *Parker* (2004), in which it is not clear whether the claimant is awarded a licence or some other estoppel-based right. Consequently, in the unlikely event (on the facts) that the property would be sold, it would not have been clear whether the purchaser would have been bound by the claimant's interest.

9.7.2   Estoppel and e-conveyancing

It has been noted above that the Land Registration Act 2002 has confirmed that estoppel rights are proprietary from the moment the equity arises. There is, however, another way in which the LRA 2002 may affect proprietary estoppel. As discussed in Chapter 2, an important element in the scheme of electronic conveyancing is to ensure that the creation of rights in registered land occurs simultaneously with their entry on the register. In essence, for rights subject to electronic conveyancing, the right or interest will not exist at all until it is electronically entered on the register – see section 93 of the LRA 2002. The necessary consequence is that paper deeds and written contracts will be a nullity. They will create nothing at all. Of course, this system will not come into effect overnight, but when it does operate (perhaps within the next five years for some interests), it is a fair bet that people will still attempt to create rights by deed or by written contract believing that they are doing all that the law requires. If the land is registered land, they will fail: creation will be possible for specified interests only by electronic entry on the register. Given, then, that proprietary estoppel is a way to create property rights without the normally required formality, it takes no foresight at all to realise that claims in estoppel are likely to boom when the mandatory electronic formality rules take effect. Proprietary estoppel might well become the antidote to a failure to use the e-formalities that are at heart of the 2002 Act.

9.7.3   Estoppel in unregistered land

Although section 116 of the LRA 2002 necessarily applies only to registered land, the balance of the case law before the 2002 Act was in favour of the proprietary status of estoppel. It is certain, therefore, that estoppels are now to be regarded as proprietary in unregistered land. Again, this means that they would be capable of binding a third party on a transfer of an unregistered title.[64] As noted, estoppel interests are necessarily equitable. Equitable interests in unregistered land usually must be registered as land charges under the Land Charges Act (LCA) 1972. However, 'estoppels' are not within any of the statutorily defined classes of land charge. Consequently, whether an estoppel binds a purchaser of the 'burdened' unregistered land will depend on the old 'doctrine of notice'. For example, in *Ives v. High* (1967), the Court of Appeal held that an estoppel easement was binding on a third party through the doctrine of notice. Necessarily, this will now be a rare event given that the overwhelming majority of transferable titles are already registered.

9.7.4   An apparently similar, but very different, situation

In the above sections, we have been considering the situation in which A's actions are such that they generate an estoppel interest in favour of B over A's land, and then A sells that land to a purchaser, P. The issue then is, clearly, whether the right existing between A and B can be binding on P, a third party. However, another possibility exists that appears to be very similar, but which is logically and legally different. Thus, A may act so as to generate

---

64 That transfer will, of course, trigger compulsory registration of the title, but the position of the new owner (and potential first registrant) will be judged according to the principles of unregistered conveyancing and then, on first registration, by the LRA 2002.

an estoppel in favour of B over A's land, and A again may sell the land to P. Yet this time, after the sale, P may confirm by words or conduct the continuance of B's right and so a new estoppel between P and B comes into existence. This is not a case of a pre-existing right binding P, but the generation of a new right by P's own conduct in favour of B. Indeed, one explanation of *Ives v. High* (1967) is that A and B had, by their action, created an easement binding on A's land, and, when the land was sold to P, P so acted as to be estopped from denying the continuance of the right. In effect, this has nothing to do with the transfer of *existing* rights against a third party, because the alleged 'third party' transferee is bound by estoppel due to their own actions: P is bound by his own estoppel, not that which existed between A and B.

9.8   Proprietary Estoppel and Constructive Trusts

It will be apparent from the above analysis of the principles of proprietary estoppel that the doctrine has much in common with that branch of constructive trusts considered in Chapter 4 – that is, constructive trusts concerning the acquisition of an equitable interest in another person's land. As we know, an estoppel is triggered by an assurance, relied on to detriment where it would be unconscionable for the assurance to be withdrawn, and a 'common intention' constructive trust is triggered by an express promise or assurance as to ownership that is relied on to detriment. The similarities are obvious and in a number of cases such as *Ottey v. Grundy* (2003), *Oxley v. Hiscock* (2004) and *Kinane v. Alimamy Mackie-Conteh* (2005), the court was content to rely on either (or both) doctrines in pursuit of a just outcome. This tendency was always latent in constructive trust cases,[65] but it was given prominence by the Court of Appeal in *Yaxley v. Gotts* (1999).

In *Yaxley*, the claimant originally alleged an estoppel against Mr Gotts because of an agreement between them concerning ownership of land and its redevelopment. The Court of Appeal allowed the claim, but on the basis that Mr Yaxley was the beneficiary under a common intention constructive trust that was in some way linked to the estoppel. The case clearly raised questions concerning the relationship between the doctrines – questions that the judgments themselves do not answer. However, in *Stack v. Dowden* (2007), the House of Lords reconsidered the role of constructive trusts in co-ownership cases[66] and Lord Walker – who had given the leading judgment in *Yaxley v. Gotts* – noted that he was 'now rather less enthusiastic about the notion that proprietary estoppel and "common interest" constructive trusts can or should be completely assimilated'. Bearing that warning in mind, the following is a very tentative attempt to compare and contrast the two doctrines. However, it should be noted at the outset that some of these comparisons and contrasts are not certain, not logical and not necessarily justifiable. They are a template for discussion.

1   Both constructive trusts and proprietary estoppel are triggered by an assurance (express promise), reliance and detriment. In consequence, there are many cases in which a claimant could plead either doctrine and in many cases they do. It is generally thought, however, that estoppel is available in a wider range of

---

65 See the remarks in *Grant v. Edwards* (1986), *Re Basham* (1986) and *Lloyds Bank v. Rosset* (1991).

66 See Chapter 4.

circumstances because constructive trusts leading to the acquisition of an interest in land tend to arise in the context of disputes between persons who once stood in an intimate relationship.[67] Indeed, there is the sense in *Stack v. Dowden* (2007) that it is because of this intimate relationship that the parameters of constructive trusts should be widened. It is clear that there is no such factual limitation in estoppel cases, although many cases do involve disputes between family members.

2   The constructive trust is often said to arise from a 'common intention' between the parties, whereas an estoppel can arise from a 'unilateral' assurance. This is the basis of Arden LJ's distinction between the doctrines in *Kinane*, in which she emphasised the mutually shared nature of the common intention constructive trust. However, it is not at all clear that constructive trusts really do result from a shared intention relating to the land – in what sense did Mr Stack and Ms Dowden ever have a shared intention?[68] Conversely, there are cases in which an estoppel arose from a common intention that once existed – see, for example, *Gillett v. Holt* (2002). We can only conclude, therefore, that the theory that constructive trusts are 'mutual', whereas estoppel is 'unilateral', is not proven, albeit that it is superficially attractive.

3   The constructive trust tends to be relied on in matrimonial or quasi-matrimonial disputes concerning the family home. Proprietary estoppel tends to be used for all other cases, both as between strangers and between persons in other family or friendship arrangements. This may be merely historical or traditional and without any logical base. Alternatively, it may not. In *Oxley v. Hiscock* (2004), Chadwick LJ came close to stating that proprietary estoppel was a better ground for deciding the shared home cases, but this has been overtaken by the clear view of the House of Lords in *Stack* that a broad-based concept of constructive trust is more appropriate.

4   Both the constructive trust and proprietary estoppel are a means of enforcing an 'informal' promise by a landowner made in favour of a claimant. They are methods by which a person may acquire an interest in land without having been granted that interest in writing or by deed and hence are exceptions to the need for 'formality' in land transactions.

5   The constructive trust is statutorily exempt from the normal formality requirements for transactions involving land – section 53(2) exempts it from the requirements of section 53(1) of the LPA 1925 and section 2(5) exempts it from the requirements of section 2 of the Law of Property (Miscellaneous Provisions) Act 1989. There is no statutory exemption for proprietary estoppel. In consequence, courts may feel on safer ground when relying on constructive trust, as, for example, in *Yaxley* and *Bright-lingsea Haven v. Morris* (2008). Likewise, there is a need to explain why claims of proprietary estoppel are exempt from these formality requirements (there is no statutory approval) and this is usually done by reference to the criterion of 'unconscionability'. This may explain why 'unconscionability' is more overtly central in estoppel claims.

6   The lack of statutory approval for proprietary estoppel has led some courts to suggest that, when an estoppel is made out, it is supported or protected behind a constructive trust. This suggested in *Yaxley* and appears also in *Ottey, Jiggins v. Brisely*

---

67 But, of course, not always, as in *Yaxley* itself.

68 See Chapter 4.

(2003) and *Brightlingsea Haven*. However, it appears an unnecessary and confusing addition to an already confused debate and may have been rejected by Lord Walker in *Stack*. If proprietary estoppel can generate property rights without formality – as it patently and historically obvious – then it has no need of the shelter of a constructive trust to explain its validity. Its validity is justified because it prevents unconscionability. It is a creature of equity and needs no statute to validate it.

7   A successful plea of constructive trust results in an equitable share of ownership for the claimant with the legal owner holding the land under a 'trust of land' governed by the Trusts of Land and Appointment of Trustees Act 1996. A successful proprietary estoppel may be 'satisfied' by the award of any proprietary right, any personal right (including a money award) or no right at all. In this sense, proprietary estoppel is more flexible and this understandably holds attraction for some judges. This difference in the outcome of each claim seems to have been at the heart of Lord Walker's acceptance in *Stack* that they should not be assimilated.

8   A constructive trust is certainly proprietary (it gives an equitable interest behind a trust of land), and now, following *Lloyd v. Dugdale* (2001) and section 116 of the LRA 2002, so is the uncrystallised estoppel.

9   It is sometimes said that a successful claim to a constructive trust is akin to a claim of right (i.e. an interest will be awarded), whereas a successful claim of estoppel is more discretionary (i.e. an interest may be awarded). However, such a distinction may be more apparent than real. Both are equitable doctrines and a court may refuse to grant relief (or will modify the quantum) where it is not 'deserved'. It may be simply that courts are more open about their discretion in estoppel cases. Indeed, the decision in *Oxley* that the court should strive to reach a fair and reasonable quantification of a beneficial interest under a constructive trust, now confirmed by *Stack* and put into practice in *Jones v. Kernott* (2009), illustrates clearly that constructive trusts also contain a large element of discretion.

10   It has been said that the evidentiary requirements for the two concepts are different, in that a constructive trust can be more difficult to prove. Rarely is this acknowledged but it may be a sensible deduction from the results in cases. On the other hand, it could be (merely) a reflection of the fact that a constructive trust usually leads to the award of a proprietary right, whereas estoppel does not always have this outcome – thus courts may require more proof where the result of a successful claim will be the award of a proprietary interest in the land.

Clearly, it is dangerous to draw firm conclusions from these arguments. Many academics see the concepts as virtually indistinguishable as *concepts* while recognising that in practice they are used in different types of case. Other academics maintain that the concepts are inherently different, albeit that in some cases they overlap. The latter view appears to have been adopted by Lord Walker in *Stack v. Dowden*.

9.9   Chapter Summary

9.9.1   The essential nature of a licence

There are no formal requirements for the creation of a 'licence' as such. A licence is given by the owner of land (the licensor) to some other person (the licensee), permitting them to do something on the owner's land. Without such permission, the activity would amount to a trespass. A licence may be given for any lawful purpose and not only to someone who also owns land. Crucially, the traditional view of licences is that they are not proprietary in nature.

9.9.2 Types of licence

A bare licence is a permission to enter upon the land given voluntarily by the owner who receives nothing in return. A bare licence lasts only for so long as the licensor wishes, terminable on reasonable notice.

A 'licence coupled with a grant' is a permission that enables a person to exercise some other right connected with the land, usually a profit à prendre. A contractual licence is granted to the licensee in return for valuable consideration. It is founded in contract and the normal remedies for breach are available in the event of a failure to carry out its terms. The effect of these remedies can be to make the licence *de facto* irrevocable between the parties throughout the contractual period of the licence. Contractual licences are not interests in land. Notwithstanding this, a contractual licence can take effect against a purchaser of land by means of a *personal* constructive trust.

An estoppel licence may arise out of a successful plea of proprietary estoppel. It is an interest in land *only* if 'the estoppel' itself is regarded as a new species of property right. This appears to be the predominant view and is given effect to in section 116 of the LRA 2002 when the estoppel is uncrystallised.

9.9.3 The role of proprietary estoppel

Proprietary estoppel can provide a defence to an action by a landowner who seeks to enforce his strict rights against someone who has been informally promised some right or liberty over the land. Proprietary estoppel can also generate new property interests in favour of a claimant. It can be a shield or a sword.

9.9.4 Conditions for the operation of proprietary estoppel

The modern doctrine of *Taylor Fashions* v. *Liverpool Victoria Trustees* (1982) is that there must be the following.

1   *An assurance* – The form of the assurance is irrelevant and it may be implied from conduct so long as the landowner is aware, or ought to have been aware, that the claimant is relying on the assurance. It need not amount to the promise of a specific property right, so long as the assurance is 'certain enough'. Everything depends on the context in which the assurance is given. Contrast *Thorner* v. *Majors* (2009) with *Cobbe* v. *Yeoman' Row* (2005).

2   *Reliance on the assurance* – This can be assumed from the fact that the claimant acted to his detriment. The assumption can be rebutted by evidence that the claimant would have behaved the same way irrespective of the landowner's assurance.

3   *Detriment* – This may take many forms, provided that it is not minimal. It may involve expenditure on the land, work undertaken in connection with the land or work undertaken for the landowner without pay or at less than market pay, or lost opportunities.

4   *Such circumstances that it would be unconscionable to allow the landowner to escape from his promise* –
      Unconscionability is the reason why oral assurances can be enforced despite
      non-compliance with normal formality requirements. If the facts do not reveal
      unconscionability, then a simple assurance, reliance and detriment on their
      own cannot generate an estoppel. Similarly, estoppel is not available to remedy
      unconscionability *per se* if the factual prerequisites are not established.

9.9.5 What is the result of a successful plea of proprietary estoppel?

If a defendant establishes the proprietary estoppel in an action by the landowner, the
landowner's claim will be dismissed and the defendant will be left to enjoy the right that
the landowner was seeking to deny. If the estoppel is established by a claimant seeking to
enforce a right against a landowner in consequence of an assurance, the court can award
the claimant any remedy it deems appropriate, although probably not in excess of that
which was actually promised. The aim of the award is to remedy the unconscionability and
to do the minimum necessary to satisfy the equity.

9.9.6 The nature of proprietary estoppel and its effect on third parties

This has now been settled by section 116 of the LRA 2002. If the estoppel is uncrystallised
before the transfer of the burdened land, then it is a property right capable (subject to
registration principles) of binding a third party. If the right is crystallised in a proprietary
way before such transfer, the same is true. If the right is crystallised in a personal way
before transfer, it remains a personal right.

Further Reading

'Apocalypse averted: Proprietary estoppel in the House of Lords' [2009] LQR
535

Battersby, G, 'Contractual and estoppel licenses as proprietary interests in land'
[1991] Conv 36

Battersby, G, 'Informal transactions in land: Estoppel and registration' (1995)
58 MLR 637

Baughen, S, 'Estoppels over land and third parties: An open question?' (1994) 14
LS 147

Bright, S, 'Bright: The third party's conscience in land law' [2000] Conv 388

Cooke, E, 'Estoppel and the protection of expectations' (1997) 17 LS 258

Dixon, M, 'Proprietary estoppel and formalities in land law and the Land Registration Act 2002: A theory of unconscionability', in Cooke, E (ed.) *Modern Studies in Property Law*, Vol. 2, Oxford: Hart, 2003, pp. 165–182

Dixon, M, Defining and confining estoppel (2010) 30 LS.

Howard, M and Hill, J, 'The informal creation of interests in land' (1995) 15 LS 356

'Proprietary estoppel: A return to principle?' [2009] Conv 260

Chapter 10
The Law of Mortgages

Chapter Contents

Introduction

A mortgage is an extremely versatile concept in the law of real property. For most people, a mortgage signifies the method by which they may raise enough capital to purchase a house or other property. However, the use of a mortgage to finance the purchase of property is a relatively recent phenomenon, and mortgages have been used as security for the repayment of a loan, or for the performance of some other obligation, for much longer.

10.1 The Essential Nature of a Mortgage

There are several different aspects to a mortgage, the most important of which are discussed below. As we shall see, a mortgage is a concept that partakes both of the law of contract and the law of real property. This duality provides the basis for the versatility of the mortgage in the modern world of property ownership, property investment and capital finance. It gives the mortgagee – the lender – a proprietary right that it can shape to its own use depending on its particular requirements and it provides the mortgagor – the borrower – with a relatively economic and efficient way of turning an immoveable asset (their land) into a liquid one (its cash value).

10.1.1 A contract between borrower and lender

Like many other concepts in the law of real property, a mortgage is also a contract, this time between the borrower and the lender. Usually, this contract is express – as where the parties negotiate and execute a mortgage by deed based on the standard terms and conditions of the lender – but sometimes it is implied, as where the court decides that the conduct of the parties in relation to an asset (i.e. land) amounts to a mortgage (or 'charge'), whether or not this was the intention of the parties or spelt out in their agreement. In the typical mortgage of land, with which this chapter is concerned,[1] the borrower of money (the mortgagor) will enter in to a binding contract with the mortgagee (the lender, for example a merchant bank, high street bank or building society), whereby a capital sum will be lent on the security of property owned by the mortgagor. Indeed, as a matter of contract, the mortgagor and mortgagee are free to stipulate whatever terms they wish for repayment of the loan, the rate of interest and so forth. Consequently, one of the remedies available to a mortgagee, when faced with a mortgagor who will not or cannot repay the loan, is to sue the mortgagor personally on the contract for repayment of the sum borrowed, plus interest and costs.[2] On the other hand, and as we shall see, the contractual nature of a mortgage is not always consistent with its status as a proprietary interest in land under the control of the court exercising its equitable jurisdiction. Of course, these two dimensions of a mortgage often complement each other,[3] but it is possible for the

---

1 Mortgages of ships and aircraft, which are common, are outside the scope of this chapter.

2 *Vedalease Ltd v. Cascabel Investments Ltd* (2009). See also the discussion in *Alliance & Leicester v. Slayford* (2001).

3 For example, in *Alliance & Leicester v. Slayford* (2001), the mortgagee pursued its contractual remedies against the mortgagor after its proprietary remedies proved ineffective.

contractual obligations freely undertaken by the parties to be in conflict with the essential nature of a mortgage as a proprietary concept, and it is then for the court to assess which will gain the upper hand – the contractual terms of the mortgage or the proprietary aspects of the mortgage security.[4]

10.1.2   An interest in land in its own right

Although a mortgage is a contract, and the parties to it are subject to contractual rights and obligations, a mortgage is also a proprietary interest in the land over which it takes effect. Thus, under a mortgage, the mortgagee obtains a proprietary interest in the land of the borrower with all that this entails, and the borrower retains an 'equity of redemption' – itself a proprietary right – which encapsulates his residual rights in the property.[5] In fact, both mortgagee and mortgagor may transfer their respective property interests under the mortgage to third parties and this often occurs when a bank transfers its 'mortgage book' to another lender. In addition, the proprietary nature of a mortgage brings with it the intervention and attention of equity and, as noted above, this can result in a conflict between the mortgage as an interest in land and the mortgage as the creation of a contract.

10.1.3   The classic definition of a mortgage

At its root, a mortgage is security for a loan. The inherent attribute of a mortgage of real property is that it comprises a transfer (conveyance) of a legal or equitable interest in the borrower's land to the mortgagee, with a provision that the mortgagee's interest shall end upon repayment of the loan plus interest and costs. The lender's contractual rights (including the right to sue for the debt) are thus supported by a proprietary interest in the land.[6] However, it is a fundamental principle of the law of mortgages that 'once a mortgage, always a mortgage', even if this contradicts the terms of the contract between the parties. In other words, the borrower has the right to have their property returned in full once the loan secured on it has been repaid and any clause of the mortgage that destroys that right will be struck out as inconsistent with the essential nature of a mortgage.[7] Consequently, the proprietary nature of the mortgage lasts only for so long as the debt remains outstanding, and the mortgagee's remedies (which can be proprietary or contractual in nature) endure only so long as the borrower owes money or the mortgage still exists.

---

4 See, for example, *Jones v. Morgan* (2001), section 10.9.3.1 below.

5 Today, the modern method of creating mortgages – the use of 'a charge' – does not actually transfer an interest in the land to the mortgagee. However, the legal mortgagee under 'a charge by deed by way of legal mortgage' is treated as having such a right for all purposes (section 87(1) of the LPA 1925) and such charges are registrable under the Land Registration Act 2002.

6 *Santley v. Wilde* (1899). Even though all modern mortgages are created by a 'charge by deed by way of legal mortgage', the mortgagee is treated as if he has acquired such an interest and gets 'the same protection, powers and remedies' as a mortgagee who does in fact take conveyance of an estate – section 87(1) of the LPA 1925.

7 *Jones v. Morgan* (2001).

10.1.4 The mortgage as a device for the purchase of property

In recent years, the mortgage has come to the fore as the major device by which individuals may finance the purchase of property. Of course, the mortgage is still security for a loan, but now the purpose of the loan is to purchase the very property over which the security is to take effect. Necessarily, this has given rise to some conceptual problems, not least that the purchaser must actually own the property before he can create a mortgage over it, but, of course, he cannot own it until he has the money to pay for it and this is what the mortgage will provide! In formal terms, this problem is dealt with by the transfer (i.e. the completed sale) of the estate in the land to the new owner, followed immediately thereafter by the execution of a mortgage over that property and a transfer of the purchase price to the vendor. This is simple enough, but it does mean that *logically* there is a 'time gap' between the purchaser acquiring the property and the execution of the mortgage over it. This is known as a *scintilla temporis* – a sliver of time. In practice, this *scintilla temporis* may only be a matter of a few minutes or moments, but it has the potential to create problems. For example, if the new owner holds the land on trust for another person (e.g. their spouse or partner[8]), the moment that the new owner acquires title, the equitable owner's interest also springs into life. Such an equitable interest would, therefore, come into existence a few moments before the mortgage takes effect and thus apparently have the potential to take priority over the mortgagee's interest (because it arose first).[9] Figure 10.1 will make this clear.

Fortunately, this logical problem has now been solved in a practical way. According to the House of Lords in *Abbey National Building Society v. Cann* (1991), as a matter of law, there is no *scintilla temporis* between a purchaser's acquisition of title to a property and the subsequent creation of a mortgage over that property that has enabled the purchase to take place. Consequently, any potential equitable interest held by another person must always rank second in time to the mortgage, and cannot take priority over the mortgagee.[10] For all

Figure 10.1

---

8 For example, because the equitable owner has contributed to the purchase price, or contributed to the purchase price of a previous property the proceeds of the sale of which are being used to buy this one – see generally *Stack v. Dowden* (2007) and Chapter 4.

9 For example, as an interest that overrides through discoverable actual occupation: Chapter 2.

10 See for example, *Leeds Permanent Building Society v. Famini* (1998).

practical purposes, this must be correct, for not only does it reflect the reality of conveyancing practice, but it also corresponds to the reality of the parties' situation: that is,
that the property would not have been purchased at all without the mortgage and, therefore, the interests of all of the owners of the property (legal and equitable) should give way
to the rights of the mortgagee.[11] However, it is important to note that the lender only
obtains priority over equitable interests the very existence of which depends on the acquisition of the land that is financed by the mortgage – as in Figure 10.1. If the property is
already held on trust for a claimant and the mortgage is not the reason why the claimant has
an interest, then a mortgagee cannot rely on the *Cann* principle, and priority is determined
by the application of the normal rules.[12]

10.1.5   Types of mortgage

The contractual nature of a mortgage means that each mortgage is potentially unique
depending on the needs of the particular mortgagor and mortgagee. The following is
a non-exhaustive list of the different types of mortgage in general use, although it must
be remembered that all are 'mortgages' within the Law of Property Act (LPA) 1925 and
are governed by that Act and the principles of registration found in the Land Registration
Act 2002.

1   The 'repayment mortgage' is used frequently for the purchase of residential property and to finance commercial activities. The mortgagor borrows a capital sum
and agrees to pay back that sum plus interest over a fixed period of time. The capital
and interest are paid back in instalments, with (usually) the early instalments representing pure interest, and the later instalments comprising a greater and greater
capital element. At the end of the period, the mortgage has been redeemed (paid
off), the registered charge is discharged and the mortgagor owns the property
absolutely.

2   The 'endowment mortgage' is also used for the purchase of residential property,
though less frequently in commercial transactions. The mortgagor borrows a capital
sum for a fixed period (usually 25 years). This accumulates interest and the mortgagor repays that interest in regular monthly instalments. No part of the instalments
goes towards repaying the capital sum. However, the mortgagor also enters into an
'endowment policy' (i.e. a savings plan), whereby he pays a regular sum towards the
purchase of an 'endowment', which will mature (become payable) at the same time
as the mortgage period ends. The endowment should generate a large enough capital
sum to pay off the capital mortgage debt at the end of the period and, possibly, leave
a sum of 'spare' money for the mortgagor. However, if, when the endowment policy
matures, it does not realise enough to pay off the capital debt, the mortgagor must
provide the balance from other funds or remortgage and continue to pay instalments.

---

11 Even if it were otherwise, it would be arguable that the equitable owner had impliedly consented to the mortgage,
this being necessary for the very acquisition of 'their' interest in land (*Cann*).

12 That is, whether there has been overreaching or whether the claimant's interest binds the mortgagee as an overriding
interest (in registered land) or through the doctrine of notice (unregistered land) – see e.g. HSBC v. *Collelldevall* (2009)
and the analysis in Chapter 4.

3   The 'current account mortgage' is a relatively new type of mortgage that may be advantageous to borrowers whose only or principal debt is a mortgage. The lender will agree an overdraft facility on a bank current account to the value of the mortgage. The lender will provide these monies for the purchase of property in the normal way (or for other property-related purposes such as extension) and interest will be charged at the prevailing rate. The borrower will pay funds into the mortgage current account (e.g. a monthly salary) and some of these funds will pay the interest and/or capital repayments and will be taken by the lender. Any surplus funds will go towards paying off the debt. This has the advantage that the mortgage debt decreases the more that surplus funds are paid into the account. Further, given that interest will be payable only on the actual mortgage debt, the borrower pays less interest over the period of the mortgage (assuming the capital debt is decreasing) than with a conventional repayment/endowment mortgage. This is even more the case if the borrower overpays the agreed instalments, as this further reduces the capital debt and the interest. Moreover, as the lender has promised an overdraft facility to the level of the original mortgage, the borrower can draw on the current account up to this limit (in effect recover any surplus paid) should the need arise.

4   The secured overdraft is common where funds are required for commercial purposes, as where an entrepreneur uses the family home to raise finance for his company. In essence, the lender promises to make an overdraft facility available and the borrower may draw monies up to this agreed overdraft limit as and when they are needed. No lump sum is paid, interest is charged on the amount of the actual debt and the total amount owed varies according to the level of current indebtedness. Hence the value of the mortgage secured over the land fluctuates (or 'floats') in line with the indebtedness, as in *State Bank of India v. Sood* (1997).

5   The 'charge': as we shall see, mortgages are commonly created by the use of a charge;[13] a 'charge' does not refer to a specific type of mortgage, but rather to the manner in which *any* type of mortgage may be created. It is mentioned here because many judicial decisions refer to a mortgage of land as a 'charge over property' or 'a charge by deed by way of legal mortgage', irrespective of whether the actual mortgage is a repayment, endowment or other type of mortgage.

10.2   The Creation of Mortgages before 1925

Although it is uncommon for mortgages to exist today that were created *before* the Law of Property Act 1925, a brief discussion of how these mortgages were created will help understand why modern mortgage law is constructed as it is. Before 1 January 1926, if an owner of a legal or equitable estate in land wished to raise money on the security of that land, the borrower's entire interest in the property was usually conveyed in full to the lender. In other words, the borrower divested themselves entirely of their interest in return for the loan. Of course, the mortgagee promised to reconvey the land on repayment of the principal (i.e. the capital sum), interest and costs but, importantly, the mortgage contract allowed the mortgagee to keep the borrower's land if he failed to repay the loan on the date

---

13 This method is now mandatory for legal mortgages of registered titles: see section 23(1) of the LRA 2002 and below.

stipulated in the mortgage contract. This date, known as the 'legal date of redemption', was crucial, and the consequences for the borrower of missing payment on that date were theoretically severe. To a large extent, however, the position was mitigated by the intervention of equity. Applying the policy that 'once a mortgage, always a mortgage', an 'equity of redemption' was held to exist, whereby the borrower was entitled to a reconveyance of his property should he pay the full sums due under the mortgage, even though the 'legal date' for redemption had passed. This was simply an aspect of the rule that a mortgage really was security for a loan and did not represent an opportunity for the mortgagee to obtain the property of a solvent mortgagor if the debt could be repaid. Importantly, however, because the mortgagor conveyed everything to the mortgagee, there was no estate remaining in the borrower that could be used to create second or subsequent mortgages and the mortgagor had to take positive steps to recover their estate should it not be reconveyed on redemption of the mortgage.

10.3   The Creation of Legal Mortgages on or after 1 January 1926

The LPA 1925 made significant changes to the ways in which mortgages could be created. The overall intent was to ensure that a mortgagor retained the fullest interest possible in their own property, even when seeking a mortgage of it, provided that the mortgagee had suitable remedies in the event of failure to repay the loan. In general terms, as a consequence of the reforms of the LPA 1925, a mortgage of a legal estate does not occur through the transfer of the mortgagor's entire interest in the land to the mortgagee. However, the mortgagee is given some lesser proprietary right in the mortgagor's land appropriate to the type of mortgage created. Furthermore, since 13 October 2003 – the date of entry into force of the Land Registration Act 2002 – mortgages of registered titles may be created only by the use of a 'charge' and thus the long leasehold method described below is available only for land of unregistered title.[14]

10.4   Legal Mortgages of Freehold Property: Unregistered Land and Registered Freehold Titles Mortgaged before 13 October 2003

Under section 85(1) of the LPA 1925,[15] there are two methods of creating a legal mortgage of an unregistered freehold estate and these two methods also could have been used to create a mortgage of a registered title before the entry into force of the LRA 2002. For the

---

14 In fact, mortgages of unregistered titles will almost invariably take the form of a charge and, of course, trigger compulsory first registration of title. Even for registered land mortgaged before the entry into force of the 2002 Act, the 'long lease' method would rarely have been employed.

15 This does not apply to mortgages of registered land executed on or after 13 October 2003.

avoidance of doubt, section 85(2) also provides that these two methods cannot be circumvented (where they are still available) and this it is impossible to create a mortgage by a conveyance of the mortgagor's entire interest to the mortgagee.

10.4.1 The long lease method

The first method is where the mortgagor grants the mortgagee a long lease over the land with a provision for the termination of the lease on repayment of all sums due under the loan. In technical terms, the mortgagor will 'demise a term of years absolute' to the mortgagee 'subject to a provision for cesser on redemption'. In the typical case, the mortgagee's lease is usually for 3,000 years, although the mortgage contract will fix an earlier contractual date for repayment and redemption. This earlier date comprises the legal right to redeem and may be a mere six months after the date of execution of the mortgage. However, as was the case before 1926, the mortgagor has an equitable right to redeem the mortgage, and thereby to terminate the long lease, on the payment of all sums due at any time after this legal date has passed. Indeed, this may be recognised explicitly by the inclusion of a right to pay by instalments that necessarily postpones the legal date for redemption. Of course, the grant of the exceptionally long lease to the mortgagee is something of a fiction, but it does have a number of important consequences.

First, the mortgagor retains the legal fee simple throughout the term of the mortgage. The borrower always retains an estate in their own land and the mortgage is more accurately shown to be what it really is – the security for a loan. Second, the mortgagee acquires a proprietary interest in the land, being the leasehold granted to them. This preserves the efficacy of their remedies in the event of non-payment of the mortgage debt. It also means that, as a leaseholder, the mortgagee has a right to possession of the property although, in most cases, this will not be exercised and the mortgagor will be allowed to remain in occupation. Third, it means that the mortgagor may create further legal mortgages of his land in order to raise further sums. For example, because the mortgagor retains his legal fee simple, it is perfectly possible to obtain another mortgage from another mortgagee by granting a second leasehold over the property for a period longer than the first lease, say, 3,001 years. The term granted to the second mortgagee will necessarily always be longer than that granted to the first, as this gives the second mortgagee a notional legal interest in the property distinct from that of the first mortgagee – in our example, one year more. Of course, the actual sum lent on the second mortgage will be calculated by reference to the value of the land taking account of the debt owed under the first mortgage, but again the mortgagor retains the ultimate fee simple and the second mortgagee also receives a proprietary interest in the land. For example, if land is worth £100,000, the freehold owner (A) may seek a mortgage from XYZ Bank plc in the sum of £45,000. XYZ Bank will be granted a mortgage by way of a 3,000-year lease (with provisions for termination on repayment), and A retains the freehold. A may then seek a second mortgage from PQR Bank plc, which may be willing to lend anything up to £55,000, taking a 3,001-year lease by way of mortgage (with provisions for termination on repayment), A still retaining the freehold. As noted above, however, this method is not available for mortgages of registered titles taking effect after the entry into force of the Land Registration Act 2002.

10.4.2   The charge

The second method of mortgaging unregistered titles (and also registered titles) is the charge by deed. Instead of the relative formality involved in granting the mortgagee a long lease over the land, the mortgagor may create a mortgage by executing 'a charge by deed' (sections 85(1) and 87 of the LPA 1925). This is a much simpler method of creating a mortgage than executing a long leasehold. It is, in fact, the common form of mortgaging land and is by far the most predominant method. More importantly, since the entry into force of the LRA 2002, it is the only method of mortgaging registered titles. Consequently, it is dealt with more fully below.[16]

10.5   Legal Mortgages of Leasehold Property: Unregistered Leases and Registered Leasehold Titles Mortgaged before 13 October 2003

For unregistered leasehold land (and pre-LRA 2002 registered leasehold titles), there are also two methods of creating legal mortgages, and these are substantially similar to that used for the freehold. Once again, before 1 January 1926, the leaseholder (the tenant) would assign his entire lease to the mortgagee but, once again, this is not now possible (section 86 of the LPA 1925).

10.5.1   Long subleases

As with freeholds, the first method of creating a legal mortgage of an unregistered lease-hold (and a mortgage of a registered leasehold taking effect before the LRA 2002) is to grant the mortgagee a lease over the property. Of course, given that the mortgagor himself is a leaseholder, the 'mortgage-lease' will actually be a sublease (a 'sub-demise'). This sublease will necessarily be shorter than the lease that the leaseholder has, simply because the mortgagor cannot grant a greater term than they have. In practice, the mortgagee's term will be ten days shorter than that of the original leaseholder. For example, if the mortgagor has a lease of 100 years, a first mortgage will operate by the grant of a legal lease to the mortgagee of 90 years. In turn, this will ensure that the leaseholder can grant second and subsequent legal mortgages of the leasehold property by creating further subleases. These additional subleases will be longer than the first mortgagee's lease (so as to give the second mortgagee a separate interest in the property), but shorter than the mortgagor's own lease. Using the above example, the second mortgagee will be granted a legal lease of 91 years. Any mortgage that attempts to avoid these provisions, by providing that the leaseholder's entire term should be assigned to the mortgagee, will operate only as a sublease for a term shorter than that of the mortgagor.[17]

---

16 Section 10.6 below.

17 *Grangeside Properties v. Collingwood Securities Ltd* (1964).

10.5.2   **The charge**

The second method of creating a legal mortgage of an unregistered leasehold (and pre-2002 Act registered leasehold) is to use the 'legal charge by deed' under section 87 of the LPA 1925 and referred to above. This is substantially the same as for freeholds, and is the common form. It is discussed immediately below because, once again, it is the only permissible form of mortgaging registered leasehold titles under the LRA 2002.

10.6   Legal Mortgages of Registered Titles under the Land Registration Act 2002

Although, before the entry into force of the LRA 2002, it was possible to create legal mortgages by the long lease method, almost invariably the common form was the legal charge. Now, by virtue of section 23(1) of the LRA 2002, the legal charge is the only permissible method of creating a legal mortgage of a registered freehold or leasehold estate. In fact, section 23(1) contemplates two ways in which a registered title may be 'charged' so as to create a legal mortgage: the first is the usual 'charge by deed expressed to be by way of legal mortgage'; and the second is the less common method of simply charging the land with the payment of money.[18] However, in practice, it makes little difference which version of the charge is used because, under section 52 of the LRA 2002, a charge on the land (the second version) is to take effect as a 'charge by deed by way of legal mortgage'.

As noted above, the charge by deed by way of legal mortgage is the standard and widespread method of mortgaging legal estates. Under section 87 of the LPA 1925, the charge must be made by deed, and it must be expressed to be by way of legal mortgage: that is, it must declare itself to be a 'legal mortgage made by charge'. Technically, the charge[19] does not confer any proprietary interest on the mortgagee (the 'chargee') but section 87 of the LPA 1925 also makes it clear that a chargee obtains 'the same protection, powers and remedies' as if the mortgage had been created by a long lease of 3,000 years in the old way.[20] This means that, for all practical purposes, the legal charge is as effective as if a proprietary right had actually been conferred on the mortgagee and nothing turns on the issue. Indeed, for both borrowers and lenders, the charge represents a quick, easy, economical and simple way of mortgaging land and it is no surprise that the Land Registration Act 2002 provided that it should be the only method of creating mortgages of registered estates on or after 13 October 2003.

---

18 Section 23(1)(b) of the LRA 2002; *Cityland and Property (Holdings) Ltd v. Dabrah* (1968).

19 In both versions.

20 *Regent Oil Co v. Gregory* (1966).

10.7   Registration of Legal Mortgages under the Land Registration Act 2002

Before a legal mortgage actually can take effect as a legal interest over a registered title, it must be registered as a 'registrable charge' against that title.[21] This registration will show the mortgagee as the proprietor of the charge and will ensure both that it takes effect as a legal interest and that it amounts to a 'registered disposition' for the purpose of obtaining priority for the mortgagee over prior rights – except registered interests and overriding interests (section 29 of the LRA 2002). Consequently, in the absence of such registration, the mortgagee only has an equitable interest and may lose its right to priority over the land in the event that the mortgagor disposes of the legal title by a registered disposition.[22] This is the natural consequence of the registration system: properly created legal mortgages need registration to ensure their existence and priority as a legal interest.[23]

Of course, in the normal course of events, the mortgagee will ensure that the mortgage is registered and such registration is no more than an administrative act for institutional lenders.[24] Indeed, come e-conveyancing, the registration of mortgages will occur simultaneously with their creation and this will be done electronically so streamlining the procedure and ensuring that mistakes in the registration process become even less likely.[25] It will also eliminate any lingering issues that remain over the 'registration gap' – that is, the possibility that an interest adverse to the mortgagee will be created and gain priority in the time it takes for the mortgagee to send in its mortgage for registration.

10.8   Equitable Mortgages

The above sections have discussed the creation of mortgages where the borrower owns a legal estate in the land and it is this that is mortgaged formally in return for a loan. The result is a legal mortgage. By way of contrast, it is perfectly possible to create equitable mortgages of land and these may arise in a variety of circumstances. In simple terms, a

---

21 Sections 25 and 27 of the LRA 2002.

22 This might be a registered sale of the land or a properly registered legal mortgage under section 29 of the LRA 2002. See *Halifax plc v. Popeck* (2009), in which, in the result, the transaction by the registered proprietor did not amount to a transfer for value within section 29 of the LRA 2002 and thus Halifax's unprotected equitable charge did not lose its priority.

23 See, for example, *Barclays Bank v. Zaroovabli* (1997), in which failure to register the mortgage meant that it lost its priority to a subsequently created legal lease of the land. In *Leeds Permanent Building Society v. Famini* (1998), the mortgagee was more fortunate in that although it had failed to register its mortgage, the later lease was itself equitable and so the rule that 'the first in time prevails' became operative and the prior equitable mortgage prevailed. A similar result to *Famini* is found in *Popeck*.

24 In *Popeck*, failure to register Halifax's mortgage over the primary land was due either to the incompetence of a solicitor's conveyancing clerk or his willing participation in the borrower's fraud.

25 Section 93 of the LRA 2002. It is likely that the creation of legal mortgages will be one of the first transactions specified for e-conveyancing under the Land Registration Rules.

mortgage may be 'equitable' either because the borrower originally has only an equitable interest in the land, or because the borrower has a legal interest and the mortgage is not executed with the formality required by statute for the creation of a 'legal' interest.

10.8.1 Mortgages of equitable interests

It may well be that the potential mortgagor only has an equitable interest in the land, as where they are an equitable owner behind a trust of land,[26] or have only an equitable lease.[27] Necessarily, it follows that any mortgage of that equitable interest will itself be equitable. The mortgagor can mortgage only that which they own. The Law of Property Act 1925 and the Land Registration Act 2002 have not affected this matter to any great extent and mortgages of equitable interests are still carried in to effect by a conveyance of the whole of the mortgagor's equitable interest to the mortgagee. This will, of course, be accompanied by a provision for retransfer of the equitable interest when the loan is repaid (*William Brandt v. Dunlop Rubber* (1905)). Importantly, however, given that a mortgage of an equitable interest is achieved through a transfer of it (a 'disposition') to the mortgagee, there are still certain formalities to be met. There is no need to use a deed,[28] but because the mortgage will be a 'disposition of a subsisting equitable interest' (i.e. the equitable interest of the mortgagor), it must comply with section 53(1)(c) of the LPA 1925. This requires the mortgage of the equitable interest to be in writing, on penalty of voidness.[29]

10.8.2 'Informal' mortgages of legal interests

As we have noted above, a legal mortgage of a freehold or leasehold is usually accomplished by the execution of a legal charge by deed that must then be registered. It is perfectly possible, however, for the mortgagor and mortgagee to create a mortgage of a legal interest by 'informal' means: in other words, either by not using a deed or by failing to register the deed that they do use. In the former case, the parties might choose deliberately (but usually unwisely) not to use a deed, and in the second example, registration may be omitted by error, negligence or fraud. However, whatever the reason for failure to comply with the various formalities for the creation of a legal mortgage, these 'informal' mortgages can, in appropriate circumstances, take effect as an equitable mortgage of the legal estate.

---

26 For example, *Banker's Trust v. Namdar* (1997) and see Chapter 4.

27 A lease of sufficient length to be a good security is likely to have been created with professional advice and thus likely to be legal. Consequently, equitable mortgages of equitable leases will be a rarity.

28 However, a deed will often be used so as to import the power of sale in the event of default by the mortgagor: section 101(1) of the LPA 1925.

29 In *Murray v. Guinness* (1998), the court appears to have held that the creation of an equitable charge (as distinct from an equitable mortgage proper) did not have to be in writing under section 53(1)(c) of the LPA 1925, because technically no interest in land is actually transferred to the chargee under a charge. However, even if this is accurate, it may well be that an equitable charge will be caught by section 2 of the LPA 1989 as equivalent to a contract for the disposition of an interest in land – a security interest and require writing for that reason: see *Kinane v. Alimamy Mackie-Conteh* (2004).

Where the 'informality' arises because of a failure to register the mortgage as required, the mortgage is equitable by force of statute (section 27 of the LRA 2002).[30] Where no deed has been used at all, the mortgage will be equitable only if it complies with the less stringent requirements for the creation of equitable interests – that is, there must be a written instrument within section 2 of the Law of Property (Miscellaneous Provisions) Act 1989. This is because the written instrument is treated as a valid contract for the creation of a mortgage within section 2, which, if specifically enforceable, can take effect as an equitable mortgage under *Walsh v. Lonsdale* (1882).[31] Of course, if either the requirements of a written contract or specific enforceability are not met, the mortgage will be void at both law and in equity, unless it can be saved by the doctrine of proprietary estoppel.[32]

10.8.3   Mortgages by deposit of title deeds

Before the Law of Property (Miscellaneous Provisions) Act 1989, it was also possible to create an equitable mortgage by depositing the title deeds of the property with the mortgagee. The deposit of the mortgagor's title deeds was treated as both evidence of a contract (as above) and 'part-performance' of that contract under the then operative section 40 of the LPA 1925.[33] This was, of course, a very informal but relatively efficient way of creating a mortgage, and the mortgagee was protected because it held the documents of title, so preventing the mortgagor from further dealing with the land. After 1989, however, contracts for the disposition of any interest in land (including therefore to create a mortgage) must be in writing and this cannot be presumed to exist from the deposit of title deeds. Consequently, although some commentators have argued that the enactment of section 2 of the 1989 Act was not intended to do away with this informal method of creating equitable mortgages, the Court of Appeal in *United Bank of Kuwait v. Sahib* (1996) has confirmed that deposit of title deeds is an attempt to create a mortgage by unwritten contract and is therefore void. No such mortgage can be created. This is unfortunate and makes matters much less convenient for both borrower and lender – especially for short-term loans – but at least it is consistent with the policy behind the 1989 Act of bringing more formality to dealings with interests in land. Of course, if the mortgage was created by deposit of title deeds before 27 September 1989,[34] it remains a valid equitable mortgage.

10.8.4   Mortgages by estoppel

As we have seen in Chapter 9, proprietary estoppel may operate to give a claimant an interest in land even though the claimant cannot produce the deed or written instrument that is normally required to establish a proprietary right. Moreover, we also know from *Jennings v. Rice* (2002) and cases before it that the court has an equitable jurisdiction to grant the remedy that is necessary to remove the unconscionability that triggered the

---

30 In *Cheltenham & Gloucester plc v. Appleyard* (2004), the mortgagee was unable to register its mortgage because of difficulties with a prior lender and so was effectively forced to take an equitable mortgage.

31 For example, *Parker v. Housefield* (1834).

32 See section 10.8.4 below and then Chapter 9 generally.

33 *Re Wallis* (1974).

34 The date on which the LPA 1989 entered force.

estoppel – sometimes described as 'the minimum equity to do justice between the parties'.[35] There is no reason why this remedy should not be such so as to give the claimant an equitable mortgage over the defendant's land, even despite the absence of formality. This is unlikely to be the case where the defendant landowner has made some unspecific promise to the claimant,[36] but what if the defendant has done some act that leads the claimant to believe they actually have a mortgage and the claimant acts on that belief?

As we know from *Taylor Fashions v. Liverpool Victoria Trustees* (1982), if one person promises an interest in land to another, and that is relied upon to their detriment, equity will enforce the promise and can give effect to the claim of the promisee. So, if a lender has actually advanced money on the basis of a promise (either given orally or represented by the deposit of title deeds), it is possible that the mortgage will be enforced despite the absence of any formality. The difficulty is, of course, that to use estoppel in these circumstances appears to be sidestepping the statutory imposed requirement of formality – after all, the lender will have an action in debt for recovery of the money and why should estoppel be used to create a proprietary claim simply because the parties failed to use the proper formalities? The answer is that estoppel can operate in these circumstances not simply because formalities were not used, but because it would be unconscionable in the circumstances to deny the mortgage. Thus, in *Kinane v. Alimamy Mackie-Conteh* (2005), the Court of Appeal accepted that the claimant had a mortgage by estoppel because he had lent money to the claimant on the faith of an assurance that a valid mortgage would be forthcoming. When that mortgage did not materialise – the written agreement attempted by the parties did not comply with section 2 of the 1989 Act[37] – estoppel stepped in. In particular, the Court specifically decided that a failed contract could indeed form the basis of the assurance necessary to support an estoppel. Critically, this was not to be regarded as the avoidance of statutory formalities, because there was nothing to prevent a failed contract from forming an assurance if there was unconscionability.[38] Thus, in the words of the Court, 'The cause of action in proprietary estoppel is thus not founded on the unenforceable agreement but on the defendant's conduct which, when viewed in all relevant aspects, is unconscionable'. In this case, then, a mortgage created by estoppel was accepted by the court because of the unconscionability of the borrower in leading the lender to believe that a valid mortgage did exist.[39] Another example is provided by *Halifax plc v. Popeck* (2008), in which Halifax's charge appears to have arisen by estoppel because it lent money on the faith of an assurance by the borrowers that it would be granted a legal mortgage over the whole of the borrower's land. When it transpired that Halifax only had a registered charge over a narrow strip of land – because of fraud perpetrated by the borrowers – it was saved by estoppel and in the result its equitable estoppel charge prevailed over other claimants to the proceeds of sale of the land.

---

35 *Wormall v. Wormall* (2004).

36 It might still generate an estoppel, and some other remedy, but the recognition of a mortgage is most unlikely.

37 It was signed by the mortgagor, but not also by the mortgagee.

38 Thus the court was able to distinguish the House of Lords decision in *Actionstrength Ltd v. International Glass Engineering SpA* (2003).

39 If the estoppel mortgagee brings a claim based on the estoppel itself (rather than seeking to enforce the equitable mortgage), the court might order the borrower to grant a formal mortgage to the lender – thus the estoppel is crystallised by the grant of a legal mortgage.

10.8.5   Equitable charges

Finally, mention must also be made of the equitable charge, a completely informal way of securing a loan over property. This requires no special form of words, only an intention to charge property with a debt.[40] Such a method is extremely precarious, and is not often used deliberately for either commercial or residential mortgages. As noted above, however, there is a doubt as to what type of formality is required for such a mortgage. *Murray v. Guinness* (1998) suggests that, because such a charge does not technically involve a disposition of an interest in land, it need not comply with section 53(1)(c) of the LPA 1925. However, whether this means that no written formalities are required at all has been questioned – without any conclusive answer – in *Kinane v. Alimamy Mackie-Conteh* (2005), in which Arden LJ ponders whether such a charge might nevertheless fall within section 2 of the LPA 1989 and thus require a written instrument under this statute.

10.8.6   A problem with equitable mortgages and equitable charges over land

An equitable mortgage suffers from the same vulnerability that affects all equitable rights in land: that is, the equitable mortgagee may lose his priority over the land because of a subsequent sale or properly registered disposition for value of a legal estate within section 29 LRA 2002.[41] Therefore, the equitable mortgagee must act to protect his interest.

1   If the equitable mortgage exists over unregistered land, it is registrable as a Class C(iii) land charge under the Land Charges Act 1972. If then so registered against the name of the estate owner who granted it (i.e. the mortgagor), it is binding on all subsequent transferees of the land over which the mortgage exists. This means, of course, that the mortgagee will be able to exercise his rights against the land in priority to the new owner. However, if not so registered, the mortgage will be void against any purchaser for valuable consideration of a legal or equitable interest in the land.[42] It will remain valid against someone who does not 'purchase' the land, such as the donee of a gift, devisee under a will or a squatter.

2   In registered land under the Land Registration Act 2002, the equitable mortgagee should seek to protect his mortgage by means of the entry of a notice against the mortgaged registered title.[43] This will ensure its protection against any later registered disposition for value of the legal estate, including a later legal mortgage (sections 29 and 30 of the LRA 2002). Failure to enter a notice will cause the equitable mortgagee to lose priority in favour of a properly registered purchaser of the land or later legal mortgagee unless the equitable mortgagee happens to be able to claim an

---

40 *National Provincial and Union Bank of England v. Charnley* (1924).

41 Before the LPA 1989, an equitable mortgagee by deposit of title deeds was in practice protected because no other dealings with the legal title could be carried out while the deeds were in the mortgagee's possession.

42 Land Charges Act 1972, sections 2 and 4.

43 Given that the mortgage will usually have been granted by the mortgagor deliberately, an agreed notice may be used. A restriction may also be entered and this will alert the mortgagee to any proposed dealings with the legal title by the mortgagor.

overriding interest under paragraph 2, Schedule 3 to the Act, perhaps through being in actual occupation.[44] Although not impossible, this last is unlikely and it would be unwise for an equitable mortgagee to rely on being able to claim an overriding interest. Note, however, that when full electronic conveyancing is in force, the equitable mortgage of registered land could be one of those interests specified under section 93(1)(b) of the LRA 2002 that will not exist at all unless it is entered electronically on the register of title. Thus the existence of an equitable mortgage will coincide with its protection.

3   In registered land, even an unregistered equitable mortgage will retain priority over a transferee who does not give valuable consideration, such as the donee of a gift or person who inherits under a will or on intestacy – section 28 of the LRA 2002. An example is provided by *Halifax v. Popeck* (2008), in which the transferee was held not to be a 'purchaser' and thus Halifax's equitable charge retained its priority as being first in time.

10.9   The Rights of the Mortgagor: The Equity of Redemption

The fact that a mortgage is both a contract between lender and borrower and amounts to the grant of a proprietary right by the mortgagor to the mortgagee means that both parties may have rights in contract and rights in property. For example, a court of equity is always willing to protect the mortgagor's property rights in the face of unconscionable dealing by the mortgagee. Indeed, we should remember that, whatever the contract says, a mortgagor under a legal mortgage always retains paramount legal title to the estate they are mortgaging. The owner of a legal freehold or leasehold never conveys all that they have to the lender when the mortgage is created.[45]

10.9.1   The contractual right to redeem

As a matter of contract, the mortgagor has a contractual right to redeem the mortgage on the date specified in the mortgage contract. This is the legal date for redemption. Where it is still employed,[46] this is usually six months from the date of execution of the mortgage, although it may be any date specified by the parties, subject to the 'clogs and fetters' rules discussed below.[47] Obviously, it is rare for a mortgagor to redeem on the legal date for redemption: after all, the parties expect the mortgage to endure for some time and for interest to be paid on the capital debt outstanding. In any event, due to the intervention of equity, the mortgagor has the right to redeem the mortgage at any time after the legal date

---

44 For example, where the equitable mortgagee is a family member living in the property who lent money to the registered proprietor.

45 However, as we shall see, default by the borrower may well result in him losing his paramount legal title.

46 Many modern mortgages no longer employ the device, being content to contract for repayment by instalments whereby one missed instalments makes the borrower liable to repay the entire loan.

47 Section 10.9.3 below.

for redemption has passed simply by paying the principal debt, interest and costs. This right to redeem beyond the date fixed by the contract is known as the 'equitable right to redeem'. Of course, the relevance of the passing of the contractual date for redemption – whether fixed or determined by reference to the payment of instalments – is that its passing can trigger the availability of the mortgagee's contractual remedies under the mortgage. As we shall see when considering the remedies of the mortgagee, the actual date on which the monies become owed under the contract is important for setting the limitation period within which the mortgagee can sue on this contract for recovery of the debt.[48]

10.9.2   The equitable right to redeem

At one time, if the mortgagor did not redeem on the legal date for redemption, the property was lost. A few days or even hours late entitled the mortgagee to keep the property even if its value was far greater than the loan secured on it. Obviously, here was great opportunity for abuse and unfairness. In consequence, the court of equity, acting under the maxim 'once a mortgage, always a mortgage', would allow redemption of the mortgage after this date – *Thornborough v. Baker* (1675). This became known as the 'equitable right to redeem'. The equitable right to redeem is the epitome of the property lawyer's approach to a mortgage – the mortgage is a security for a loan, not an opportunity for the mortgagee to obtain the mortgagor's property or impose any other burden upon him. It meant, in effect, that payment of principal, interest and costs even after the contractual date for redemption would free the land of the mortgage.

10.9.3   The equity of redemption

The equitable right to redeem the property at any time after the legal date for redemption has passed is certainly one of the most valuable rights that a mortgagor has. If it were otherwise, mortgage lending in England and Wales would be wholly different from that which now exists. In fact, however, the intervention of equity goes further than this because the equitable right to redeem is just part of the wider rights that a mortgagor enjoys under the mortgage. These wider rights are collectively known as 'the equity of redemption'. The equity of redemption represents the sum total of the mortgagor's rights in the land that is subject to the mortgage. In essence, it comprises the residual rights of ownership that the mortgagor has, both in virtue of their paramount legal estate in the land, and the protection that equity affords them.[49] Indeed, the equity of redemption is itself valuable, and is a proprietary right, which may be sold or transferred in the normal way. It represents the mortgagor's right to the property (or its monetary equivalent) when the mortgage is discharged (redeemed) or the property sold, and its existence is the reason why second and third lenders are willing to grant further loans. As noted above, equity regards the mortgage as a device for the raising a loan, secured on property, which can be redeemed once the debt is repaid. Fundamentally, a mortgage is not seen as an opportunity for the lender to acquire the mortgagor's property. For this reason, a court of equity will

---

48 *Wilkinson v. West Bromwich Building Society* (2004).

49 See, for example, *Re Sir Thomas Spencer Wells* (1933).

intervene to protect the mortgagor and their equity of redemption against encroachment by the mortgagee. This protection manifests itself in various ways.

10.9.3.1 *The rule against irredeemability*

It is a general principle that a mortgage cannot be made irredeemable. It is a security for a loan, not a conveyance, and the right to redeem cannot be limited *pro tanto* to certain people or certain periods of time (*Re Wells* (1933)). Thus any provision whereby the mortgagor is said to forfeit his property on the expiry of the legal right to redeem is void, and any undue postponement or limitation on the mortgagor's right to redeem thereafter will not be enforceable (*Jones v. Morgan* (2001)). However, this does not mean that the parties' hands are always tied, especially in cases of mortgages negotiated between commercial corporations at arm's length. Consequently, a provision postponing the date of redemption may be valid where the mortgage is not otherwise harsh and unconscionable, so long as the right to redeem is not made illusory. In such cases, the mortgagor might be held to his bargain by being compelled to pay all of the interest that would accrue up to the lawfully postponed date of redemption if he wishes to redeem early.[50] For example, a provision in a mortgage of residential property that the borrowers cannot redeem for 20 years unless they pay an additional percentage (say 15 per cent) as a 'redemption fee' might well be void as tending towards irredeemability. A similar provision in a mortgage between Powerful Industries plc and MegaBank plc may not.

10.9.3.2 *The mortgagee and attempts to purchase the mortgaged property*

A provision in a mortgage contract that provides that the property shall become the mortgagee's or which gives the mortgagee an option to purchase the property is void. It is not necessary to show in addition that either the mortgage itself or the offending term is unconscionable (*Samuel v. Jarrah Timber* (1904)). Such a term is repugnant to the very nature of a mortgage and is offensive both to the legal and equitable right to redeem and is void both at law and in equity (*Jones v. Morgan* (2001)). The rationale is thus part contractual (it offends against the essence of a mortgage) and part equitable (that the vulnerable mortgagor should not be forced into a conveyance when he requires only a loan). Importantly, however, it is clear that it is necessary to determine, first, that the transaction really is a mortgage, and second, that the offending term is part of that mortgage transaction. So, in *Warnborough Ltd v. Garmite Ltd* (2003), the court made it clear that the true nature of the agreement between the parties must be determined by reference to its substance rather than the label given to it. Thus, in that case, what appeared at first to be a mortgage with a provision permitting the mortgagee to purchase the property (which would have been void) was in fact a complex sale and repurchase transaction that did not attract the intervention of the court. Second, an option to purchase the property given to the mortgagee in a *separate and independent transaction* can be valid, provided that it does not *de facto* form part of the mortgage itself (*Reeve v. Lisle* (1902)). A mortgage is a mortgage, but separate agreements will be enforced in the normal way. Of course, there may be some doubt as to whether the option to purchase is truly a separate transaction, and its artificial divorce

---

50 *Knightsbridge Estates v. Byrne* (1940); *Fairclough v. Swan Breweries* (1912).

from the mortgage is not enough. So, in *Jones v. Morgan* (2001), a clause in a document executed in 1997 whereby the lender became entitled to a 50 per cent share of the borrower's land after the borrower had redeemed the mortgage was held void and this was so even though the document was executed some three years later than the mortgage. The 1997 document was treated as a variation of the original mortgage and as part of it, and so the clause was unenforceable as being repugnant to the very nature of a mortgage. Finally, it should also be noted, for the sake of clarity, that the rule prohibiting the mortgagee from having a right to purchase the land as a term of the mortgage does not prevent the mortgagee exercising its normal rights over the land in the event of the mortgagor's default on the loan: for example, its power of sale. Purchase by the mortgagee is repugnant to the very nature of the mortgage; sale by the mortgagee in the event of default is the enforcement of the security that they have been given.

10.9.3.3　*Unfettered redeemability: Collateral advantages*

As a matter of principle, the mortgagor should be able to redeem the mortgage and have the mortgagee's rights extinguished on the payment of the principal debt, interest and costs. There should be no other conditions attached to the right of redemption because a mortgage is merely the security for a loan that ends when its reason – the money – has been repaid. Consequently, on several occasions, a court has struck down 'collateral advantages' made in favour of a mortgagee, as where the mortgage contract stipulates that the mortgagor should fulfil some other obligation as a condition of the redeemability or continuation of the mortgage. An example is where the mortgagor promises to buy all of his supplies from the mortgagee, or to give the mortgagee some other preferential treatment. Typical cases would be brewery/mortgagees requiring pub landlords/mortgagors to take only the brewery's beer, or similar arrangements between oil companies and the owners of petrol stations. At one time, such collateral advantages were uniformly struck down as being a 'clog' or 'fetter' on the equity of redemption (*Bradley v. Carrit* (1903)). They were seen as striking at the essence of the mortgage as only security for a loan. However, it is now clear that there is no objection to a collateral advantage that ceases when the mortgage is redeemed. This is a matter of contract between the parties, and provided that the terms of the collateral advantage are not unconscionable, or do not in fact restrict the right to redeem,[51] they will be valid.[52] This is a fair outcome given the reality of many commercial mortgage transactions, which are more in the nature of a comprehensive tie between mortgagor and mortgagee than simply about a loan. Indeed, with commercial mortgages made between equal parties at arm's length, *Kregliner v. New Patagonia Meat Co* (1914) suggests that a collateral advantage that *does* continue after redemption (e.g. a continuing obligation to take supplies from the mortgagee even though the mortgage has ended) may be acceptable, so long as the mortgagor's land returns to them in the same form that it was mortgaged. It seems that such commercial arrangements are acceptable because they neither restrict the former mortgagor's use of the land as such, nor hinder the redeemability of the mortgage. They are truly 'collateral' and, therefore, not objectionable.

51　For example, a contractual clause that provided that the mortgagor had to buy such a great amount of oil before he could redeem that in fact redemption was practically impossible would be void.

52　See the earlier cases of *Santley v. Wilde* (1899) and *Biggs v. Hoddinot* (1898).

It is apparent that this is one area in which the 'contractual' nature of a mortgage may be in conflict with its 'proprietary' nature. As we have been discussing, the extent to which the parties to a mortgage should be able to modify the essential nature of a mortgage and provide additional benefits to the mortgagee is a matter for argument. Does it matter if the parties are commercial organisations, and should the same considerations apply to residential mortgages? How far may the parties to a mortgage – especially those with whole batteries of legal advisers and accountants – be permitted to change the essential nature of a mortgage from a security for a loan to something outside the realm of property law altogether?

10.9.3.4   Unconscionable terms and unreasonable interest rates

It is also clear that a court has the power to strike down any term of a mortgage – or indeed the whole mortgage – where it is the result of an unconscionable bargain and irrespective of whether it also amounts to a clog or fetter on the equity of redemption. The basic proposition is that found in the judgment of Browne-Wilkinson J in *Multiservice Bookbinding Ltd v. Marden* (1979) to the effect that a term will be unconscionable (and hence unenforceable) where it is in substance objectionable and has been imposed by one party on the other in a morally reprehensible manner.[53] This means, in essence, that there must be some impropriety both in the substantive term and the conduct of the party imposing the term that, taken together, 'shocks the conscience of the court'. An example is an interest rate at such a high level that it renders the equity of redemption valueless, as explained in *Cityland Properties v. Dabrah* (1968).[54] However, in exercising this jurisdiction, the court is not concerned with excusing a mortgagor from the consequences of a bad bargain, especially if they have had the benefit of legal advice. Such a deal is the mortgagor's own affair and a bad bargain, or hard terms, do not necessarily make an unconscionable mortgage. Thus, in *Jones v. Morgan* (2001), the mortgagor had the benefit of legal advice and was able to evaluate the options presented to him and so, even though aspects of the mortgage were struck down on other grounds, the mortgage itself was not unconscionable.

In similar vein, it also seems from *Nash v. Paragon Finance* (2001) that a mortgagee – at least a commercial mortgagee – is under an implied contractual obligation (a 'limited duty') not to set interest rates dishonestly, for an improper purpose, capriciously or arbitrarily and not in a manner that no reasonable mortgage lender would countenance (so-called '*Wednesbury* unreasonableness'). However, with due respect to the Court of Appeal in *Nash*, it is not immediately clear where such a wide principle comes from, even though Paragon Finance did fall foul of it in this case. A commercial mortgagee is not in any sense a public authority (for *Wednesbury* unreasonableness) and the Court gives little authority for the proposition that these implied terms can be imported in to the mortgage contract. Indeed, in *Paragon Finance v. Pender* (2005), a later Court of Appeal accepted the *Nash* argument in principle, but noted that it did not prevent a lender, for good commercial reasons, from raising interest rates to such a level that borrowers, or a class of borrowers, might be forced to seek refinancing elsewhere. Consequently, it remains to be seen how far the *Nash* argument can run. If the 'implied term' argument gains momentum – as it may well do in

---

53 Confirmed in *Jones v. Morgan* (2001).

54 In this case, the interest rate amounted to the equivalent of 57 per cent and was held unconscionable.

times of economic slowdown – this will add another string to the bow of the mortgagor in trouble.

10.9.4   Undue influence

There have been many cases in which a mortgagor has claimed that the mortgage is void (i.e. unenforceable against them in whole or in part) because of 'undue influence'. In general terms, a mortgage may be struck down on the ground that it was obtained by the undue influence of the mortgagee directly, or by the undue influence of a third party that is attributable to the mortgagee: for example, a husband inducing his wife to sign a mortgage over the jointly owned matrimonial home.[55] In either case, if the plea is successful, the mortgagor (or guarantor of the mortgagor[56]) who is released from the mortgage because of the undue influence might nevertheless be required to repay part of the sums lent if she derived some material benefit from it, but the mortgage itself may be unenforceable.[57] We should note, however, that the law in this area has undergone several transformations in recent years, not all of which are consistent with each other or earlier authority. However, the following is an attempt to highlight the basic principles of undue influence after the House of Lords' decisions in *Barclays Bank* v. *O'Brien* (1992), *CIBC Mortgages plc* v. *Pitt* (1993), and *Royal Bank of Scotland* v. *Etridge* (No. 2) (2001).

A mortgage will be set aside for undue influence in so far as it binds the 'victim' when either there is 'actual undue influence' or 'presumed undue influence'. Actual undue influence arises where the claimant (i.e. the mortgagor or guarantor) proves affirmatively that undue influence has been exerted. This will be established from the facts of the case, ranging from a husband standing over his wife with a shotgun threatening her unless she consents to the mortgage, to a woman threatening to leave her lover unless he signs. The possibilities are endless. However, the influence must be both 'actual' and 'undue'. Persuasion after full explanation of what was involved is not undue, even though the influence may have been actual (in the sense of causative of the consent). Walking, eyes wide open, into a bad bargain, having made an informed choice, is unfortunate, but it is not the result of undue influence.[58] However, as *Steeples* v. *Lea* (1998) illustrates, it is the *consent* of the claimant that must be given freely. So, being aware of the nature of a mortgage, after having received advice as to its effect, does not mean an absence of undue influence if the claimant can prove that she was not making a 'free' choice at the time. As the Court of Appeal emphasised in *Stevens* v. *Leeder* (2005), the critical point is not only that the claimant knew what she was doing, but also why she was doing it, for only then could she genuinely consent. A similar approach is evident in *Burbank Securities* v. *Wong* (2008), in which the victim understood generally that she was borrowing money but had no

---

55 For example, *Castle Phillips Finance* v. *Pinnington* (1995).

56 This is the person who promises the lender to meet the obligations under the mortgage should the mortgagor default.

57 *Allied Irish Bank* v. *Byrne* (1995). Thus, the mortgagee would lose its proprietary claim to the land in priority to the victim of the undue influence and may have to resort to other means of recovery, as in *Alliance & Leicester* v. *Slayford* (2001).

58 See the forceful judgment of Scott VC, in the context of presumed undue influence, in *Banco Exterior Internacional* v. *Thomas* (1997) and note also *Bank of Scotland* v. *Bennett* (1998).

conception as to the import of a mortgage transaction in the light of the actual undue influence exercised over her. Importantly, if 'actual' undue influence is proved, it is not necessary for the 'victim' to establish that the transaction was to their 'manifest disadvantage', meaning a transaction obviously not to their benefit. It is enough in such cases that the victim was persuaded to enter into a transaction that they would not otherwise have entered into.[59]

By way of contrast, presumed undue influence arises where the relationship between the person who is alleged to have exercised undue influence (e.g. the claimant's spouse or partner) and the victim is one of trust and confidence, so making it likely that unacceptable influence has been exerted. After the House of Lords decision in *Barclays Bank v. O'Brien* (1992), presumed undue influence cases were subdivided into class 2A and class 2B-type cases. Class 2A cases were where the relationship between persons was of such a nature that the presumption existed independently of the facts of the case. Typical examples are the relationships of doctor/patient, solicitor/client and parent/child,[60] but do not include the bank/customer and husband/wife relationship. These class 2A cases are rare in mortgage transactions, not least because patients and clients do not normally lend money to doctors or solicitors and rarely go into business with them. On the other hand, class 2B cases of presumed undue influence were where, although the relationship *per se* was not one of the 'special' cases, nevertheless the substance of the relationship between the parties was such that one person placed so much confidence in the other that the presumption of undue influence should arise. Clearly, husband/wife or lover/lover could fall within this class, as might employer/employee.[61]

In fact, the difference between class 2A 'presumed' cases and class 2B 'presumed' cases has been explored again by the House of Lords in *Royal Bank of Scotland v. Etridge (No. 2)* (1998) and this long and impressive judgment sheds much light on the issue. As is made clear in *Etridge*, if the case is not one of actual undue influence, it is indeed possible that undue influence may be 'presumed'. However, this presumption is properly to be regarded as an evidentiary presumption that simply shifts the burden of proof from the victim to the alleged wrongdoer (the influencer).[62] In other words, for presumed undue influence to exist, it is necessary for the claimant to show a relationship of trust and confidence that, if established, requires the alleged wrongdoer to explain the impugned transaction. So, in *Turkey v. Awadh* (2005), there was no presumed undue influence because although there was a relationship of trust and confidence, the transaction was easily explicable; in *Popowski v. Popowski* (2004), the relationship of trust and confidence did not lead to a transaction that was manifestly disadvantageous to the claimant, thus displacing the presumption of undue influence; and in both *De Wind v. Wedge* (2008) and *Thompson v. Foy* (2009) the impugned transactions were explicable as exactly the sort of transactions family members might enter into, even if they were unwise. In other words, the alleged wrongdoer may still dispel any whiff of undue influence by producing evidence as to the propriety of the transaction, based in part on producing a credible reason for it. Importantly, when viewed in this light, *Etridge* makes it clear that there is no real merit in adopting the *O'Brien* categories of 'class

---

59 *Barclays Bank v. O'Brien* (1992).

60 For example, *Langton v. Langton* (1995).

61 *Steeples v. Lea* (1997).

62 *Turkey v. Awadh* (2005).

2A' and 'class 2B' presumed undue influence. There are some relationships, such as parent/child and doctor/patient (the old 'class 2A' cases), which necessarily and irrebuttably establish a relationship of trust and confidence and if the transaction called for an explanation (was 'manifestly disadvantageous'), this shifts the burden of proof to the alleged wrongdoer to explain the transaction. Failure to do so necessarily leads to a finding of undue influence. There are other cases in which the claimant can demonstrate on the evidence that a relationship was one of trust and confidence (the old 'class 2B' cases) and, if the transaction called for an explanation (was 'manifestly disadvantageous'), this then shifts the burden of proof to the alleged wrongdoer to explain the transaction.

Consequently, two things are now clear. First, the 'presumption' of undue influence is no more than a tool to explain the shift of the evidentiary burden from the claimant and so 'manifest disadvantage' is necessary as it explains why the burden should shift. The 'presumption' is not that undue influence exists, but that it will exist if the wrongdoer cannot explain the transaction (i.e. discharge the burden of proof). Thus, as noted above, manifest disadvantage (meaning a transaction that needs explaining) is not needed in 'actual undue influence' cases, because the claimant has already established undue influence on the facts. Second, the difference between the now defunct class 2A and class 2B cases is simply that, in the former, the fact of trust and confidence could not be disputed by the wrongdoer, whereas in the latter, it could. So, in the second type of case (class 2B), the wrongdoer could adduce evidence to show that no such relationship existed and hence avoid even having to explain the transaction. In the former case, a disadvantageous transaction always needs an explanation. Although this seems complicated, *Etridge* has made the matter rather straightforward, and certainly more straightforward than was the case under O'Brien. In cases of actual undue influence, any transaction (disadvantageous or not) can be attacked if the victim has shown by positive proof that they have been unfairly persuaded to enter a mortgage. In cases of a successful plea of presumed undue influence, only transactions that are 'manifestly disadvantageous' to the victim can be impugned (being transactions that on their face appear not to be for the benefit of the victim), because it is the existence of this disadvantage that, if not explained away, permits the court to infer that undue influence has occurred.

With this matter now clarified by *Etridge*, we must consider the circumstances in which a mortgage actually can be voided as a result of proven actual or presumed undue influence. Of course, in reality, there are few cases in which the mortgagee itself exerts the undue influence over the victim and the usual scenario (considered below) is that the victim claims, first, that they were unfairly induced (actual or presumed) to enter the mortgage by another person (usually the victim's domestic or business partner who co-owns the property and who is pressing for the mortgage), and second, that this undue influence taints the mortgagee. According to O'Brien, there are two sets of circumstances in which a mortgagee will not be able to enforce the mortgage against the victim, even though the mortgagee itself has not exercised undue influence: first, where the real inducer (the husband/wife, lover, etc.) was acting, in a real sense, as agent of the mortgagee (this is quite unlikely in the majority of cases); or, second, where the mortgagee has actual or constructive notice of the inducer's unfair conduct, and has not taken steps to ensure that the claimant has been independently advised. Moreover, a mortgagee will be deemed to have notice of the unfair conduct (and therefore risk losing the security unless they have offered independent advice) when the transaction is *prima facie* not to the advantage of the mortgagor, and the transaction itself is of such a kind that there is a substantial risk that undue influence may have been exerted. Such a risk, and therefore notice to the mortgagee, will be present when a person signs a mortgage as guarantor (surety) for the debts of their domestic partner (O'Brien), although such a risk may not be present, and therefore no notice to the mortgagee, when a person signs a mortgage as joint mortgagor for a loan made to the mortgagors jointly for their joint benefit (Pitt). In the end, however, as explained in O'Brien, the existence or absence of such notice very greatly depended on the particular facts and, following *Barclays Bank v. Boulter* (1997), it was clear that the burden is on the mortgagee to prove that it is not tainted by the undue influence (or misrepresentation) of the actual inducer. So, the claimant may raise undue influence as a defence to an action on the mortgage instigated by the mortgagee, and the burden of proof then shifts to the lender.[63]

As expected after O'Brien and Pitt, there was a wave of claims of 'undue influence' by mortgagors/guarantors/sureties facing repossession of their property or a demand for payment of monies owed. Unfortunately, a consistent approach was not possible and two powerful difficulties emerged. First, if the mortgagee is to avoid being fixed with notice of another person's undue influence (e.g. that of the husband/wife, lover, etc.), the mortgagee must ensure that the mortgagor is 'independently advised'. Does this mean advised independently from their partner (the undue influencer), independently of the mortgagee, or both? Some cases suggested that the mortgagee escaped liability by ensuring that the claimant was advised by someone other than its own staff,[64] and conversely did not escape when the adviser was closely linked with the mortgagee (*Allied Irish Bank v. Byrne* (1995)), save only that a mortgagee did not seem to incur liability simply because the same solicitor acted for both wrongdoer and victim.[65] Other cases suggested that such advice must also be given independently from that given to the wrongdoer.[66] Second, given that the mortgagee must take steps to see that the claimant has been independently advised, what steps are sufficient? Can the mortgagee avoid its potential liability by merely recommending the mortgagor to take independent advice? The decision in *Crédit Lyonnais Bank v. Burch* (1997) (*contra* to the tenor of *Albany Home Loans v. Massey* (1997)) suggested that merely advising the claimant to seek advice may not be sufficient if the claimant did not then seek or receive such advice. Does this mean that the claimant must be led like a horse to water to a solicitor's office and be 'made' to listen? Again, *Parker-Tweedale v. Dunbar* (1991) and *Midland Bank v. Kidwai* (1995) made it clear that, having received advice, the mortgagee is not tainted if the claimant then chose to ignore it. So why cannot a claimant legitimately choose to ignore the advice to seek advice? May the mortgagee avoid liability by relying on a solicitor's certificate (a formal letter) that the claimant has been given advice – even if this is not true? *Banco Exterior Internacional v. Mann* (1995) suggests that reliance may be placed on a solicitor's certificate that independent advice has been given, even if this is not the case. *TSB v. Camfield* (1995) suggests that the mortgagee may not avoid liability if, in fact, no proper advice has been given, even if the mortgagee was misled by a solicitor's certificate into believing that it had been.

Clearly, this was an unsatisfactory state of affairs and it became apparent that O'Brien had failed in its attempt to clarify the law. In fact, there was a litigation industry and the result

---

63 For a recent example see *Burbank Securities v. Wong* (2008).

64 *Midland Bank v. Massey* (1995), *Banco Exterior Internacional v. Mann* (1995) and *Scottish Equitable Life v. Virdee* (1998).

65 *Bank of Scotland v. Bennett* (1998).

66 *TSB v. Camfield* (1995).

of O'Brien *appeared* to be that mortgagors merely had to raise the plea of undue influence to propel the mortgagee into a (usually forlorn) attempt to explain why undue influence had not in fact incurred.[67] Indeed, after O'Brien, there were still many cases going to the Court of Appeal, not all taking a consistent approach to the problem, and in consequence, there was considerable uncertainty among lenders and borrowers alike. It was thus no real surprise when the House of Lords reconsidered the issue in *Royal Bank of Scotland v. Etridge* (and seven other co-joined appeals). In that case, if any reminder was needed, Lord Bingham, leading the House, put [the matter succinctly and his words bear repetition and need no elaboration:

> The transactions which give rise to these appeals are commonplace but of great social and economic importance. It is important that a wife (or anyone in a like position) should not charge her interest in the matrimonial home to secure the borrowing of her husband (or anyone in a like position) without fully understanding the nature and effect of the proposed transaction and that the decision is hers, to agree or not to agree. It is important that lenders should feel able to advance money . . . on the security of the wife's interest in the matrimonial home in reasonable confidence that, if appropriate procedures have been followed in obtaining the security, it will be enforceable if the need for enforcement arises. The law must afford both parties a measure of protection . . . The paramount need in this important field is that these minimum requirements should be clear, simple and practically operable.[68]

This concern, echoed by Lord Nicholls in the leading judgment,[69] led the House of Lords to lay down a set of procedures that, while not being cast in stone, would bring certainty and stability to this sector of the mortgage market. Sometimes known as 'the *Etridge* protocol' these steps (or a tailored version to same effect) are now followed as a matter of routine by most institutional lenders.

First, it is necessary to prove actual or presumed undue influence by the 'wrongdoer' over the claimant. This has been discussed above and the impact of *Etridge* on the law of presumed undue influence should be noted here. In particular, the House of Lords explains the role of 'manifest disadvantage' and how the mortgagee can dispel the presumption of undue influence by producing an explanation for the impugned transaction.

Second, we must determine whether the mortgagee is put on inquiry as to the existence of the undue influence: in other words, assuming no agency,[70] does the lender have notice of the undue influence so as to put its mortgage at risk? In this connection, the first point is that the House makes it clear that 'notice' does not mean that the lender is in some

---

67 One wonders how many of these O'Brien cases really involved undue influence or were rather the clever tactical deployment of the undue influence plea by mortgagors who saw the O'Brien defence as the way out of an onerous mortgage.

68 At para. 2.

69 Lord Nicholls noted that couples should not be restricted in using the matrimonial home to raise finance for small businesses or any other purposes and that '[t]hese businesses comprise about 95 per cent of all businesses in the country, responsible for nearly one-third of all employment. Finance raised by second mortgages on the principal's home is a significant source of capital for the start-up of small businesses'.

70 As noted above, it will be rare for a mortgagee to have formally appointed one borrower to act as its agent in securing the consent of the other.

way being bound by a proprietary right of the claimant. This is not property law notice of some equitable interest; rather, it is a loose description of the idea that the lender can be affected by undue influence in certain circumstances and that, if so affected, it must take steps to prevent its mortgage being tainted.[71] More importantly perhaps, the House then adopts a robust and blunt approach to the question of when such 'notice' exists. Recognising that there are difficulties, and that its approach is 'broad-brush' rather than precisely analytical, the solution is that a lender will always be put on inquiry if a person is standing surety for another's debts,[72] provided that such surety is not offered as a commercial service.[73] This is both clear and an extension of the pre-existing law, for now there is always 'notice' when one person is a non-commercial surety for another and this has the great merit of ensuring that lenders do not have to probe the relationship of the parties in order to assess whether they are on notice. Thus, it is not the relationship between the parties that triggers the 'notice', but rather the very nature of the transaction irrespective of the relationship. The principle is not relationship-specific and may apply equally to married and unmarried couples, same-sex couples or persons in no emotional relationship at all. If, however, the loan is made to the parties jointly for their joint purposes (i.e. the claimant is not merely guaranteeing the wrongdoer's borrowing but is also taking a benefit from the mortgage[74]), then the lender is not put on inquiry unless it is aware (or possibly 'ought to be aware') that in reality the money is for the wrongdoer's purposes alone. An example is provided by *Chater v. Mortgage Agency Services* (2003), in which a joint loan to mother and son did not, on the facts, put the lender on notice of the undue influence that had occurred. However, as one would expect, the court will examine carefully whether the victim really obtains a benefit from the mortgage or whether the transaction is simply cast that way in order to mask the fact that the real benefit is being taken by the wrongdoer – as in *Burbank Securities v. Wong* (2008).

Third, there remains the question of what the mortgagee must do in order to avoid being tainted by the undue influence of which it has notice, for failure to take appropriate steps could result in the loss of its security. Indeed, it is this aspect of the *Etridge* decision that is of the greatest practical importance. Lenders are not in the business of taking chances so, undue influence or not, they will adjust their lending practices just in case there is the possibility of the transaction being attacked. In fact, it seems that the judgment in *Etridge* is not principally concerned with preventing the occurrence of undue influence over a claimant at all, but rather with identifying what a lender must do to avoid being tainted by it if such influence occurs. Fortunately, the steps that a lender must now take are such that the chances of undue influence occurring will be much reduced, but it is important to appreciate that the primary purpose of these steps is protect the bank, not to stop the undue influence. Thus, for past cases – that is, mortgages executed prior to the *Etridge* decision – the lender must take steps to ensure that the wife understands the risk she is running and should advise her to seek independent advice. For future cases – that is, mortgages executed post-*Etridge* – the lender must insist that the wife attend a private

---

71 This confirms *Barclays Bank v. Boulter* (1997).

72 That is, mortgaging their own property, or share of property, to guarantee a loan that benefits the other party.

73 For example, a bank might stand as guarantor for a fee.

74 For example, the mortgage is to fund a company jointly owned by the parties.

meeting with the lender at which she is told of the extent of her liability, warned of the risk she is running and urged to take independent legal advice.

How this will operate in practice for 'past cases' is still open-ended, although it does seem that it is not the lender's responsibility to see that no undue influence has been exercised, nor necessary that the lender seeks confirmation from a solicitor that no such influence exists (as opposed to confirmation that advice has been given). This is because the solicitor will be acting for the claimant and the lender can expect the solicitor to act properly for his or her client. Consequently, if a solicitor gives inadequate advice, the lender is not affected, provided that the lender does not know (or ought to have known) that no advice was received or that it was inadequate. After all, the claimant can sue the solicitor. In reality, then, the past practice of relying on solicitor's certificates will suffice, unless the lender knows or ought to have known that the claimant was not thereby properly warned of the nature of the transaction or of the risks it posed.[75] In this sense, *National Westminster Bank v. Breeds* (2001) is rightly decided as the lender should have known that the advice given to the claimant was defective despite receiving a certificate from the advising solicitor. Likewise, in *National Westminster Bank v. Amin* (2002), a decision on a pre-*Etridge* claim, the House of Lords sent a case back for retrial on the basis that the bank might have known that the solicitor had not given appropriate advice (e.g. the bank knew that the mortgagors could not speak English and the solicitor could not speak Urdu) and that it was not clear in any event whether the solicitor was acting for the mortgagors or for the bank when giving advice.

For future transactions – that is, those taking place after *Etridge* – the practical steps indicated by the House in *Etridge* will give the lender the security they have bargained for and will essentially reduce the risk of a mortgage being set aside for undue influence to a minority of cases – cases that will only arise because of the lender's failure to follow the simple guidelines. First, the lender should check directly with the potentially vulnerable party for the name of the solicitor who is acting for her or him, advising that it will seek written confirmation that advice about the proposed transaction has been given. The potentially vulnerable party should be told that this is because the lender does not intend that he or she should be able to dispute the mortgage later. The potentially vulnerable party should also be told that he or she may (but not must) use a different solicitor from that which his or her partner uses. The lender must await a response from the potentially vulnerable party before it proceeds. Second, the lender should provide the advising solicitor with all of the necessary financial information required for the solicitor to give proper advice: for example, level of total indebtedness of the husband and a copy of the application form. This usually will require the consent of the other proposed mortgagor, failing which the mortgage is unlikely to go ahead and of itself will give a pause for thought as to the wisdom of the mortgage. Third, the lender must inform the solicitor of any concerns it has over the genuineness of the potentially vulnerable party's consent or understanding and, of course, this will vary from case to case and often be non-existent. Fourth, the lender should obtain written confirmation from the solicitor that all of these steps have been complied with and that appropriate advice has been given. If, after taking such steps, the lender is provided with a written certificate from the advising solicitor, the lender will be protected against a claim of undue influence even if it transpires that such influence did

---

75 *Bank of Scotland v. Hill* (2002).

in fact occur. Consequently, the lender's mortgage will be secure unless it knew, or ought to have known, of some defect in the advice or some material untruth in the solicitor's certificate of compliance.[76] In this sense, the purpose of the Etridge guidelines is to provide a firm base for institutional lending that might also prevent undue influence being practised on the unwary.[77] It is, however, the first of these results that is the avowed aim of the Etridge protocol. Protection of the potential 'victim' is perhaps more than a happy coincidence, but this benefit is more because the interests of the lender and the potential victim coincide rather than an a priori desire to protect the financial naive.

Such evidence as does exist – for example, the reduction in claims of undue influence in post-Etridge cases seems to indicate that the House of Lord's decision has provided the certainty that was so desired.[78] Undoubtedly, it has forced a change in lending practices, but this has been absorbed into the administrative practices of the competent lending institutions and does not appear (so far as one can tell) to have increased lending charges.[79] Of course, some lenders will fail to observe the new procedures and they are likely to get short shrift from the courts. After all, it is not that difficult to understand what must be done. As for the law, we now know that the 'presumption' of undue influence is really a presumption that reverses the burden of proof and is not a presumption that such influence really exists. Hence it can be met with an explanation of why the transaction is undue influence free.[80] We also know that 'manifest disadvantage' in the weak sense of a transaction that on its face needs explaining is still an element in 'presumed' cases because it (merely) helps to prove the presumption to reverse the burden of proof: that the class 2A and 2B dichotomy in presumed cases is not helpful; that 'notice' does not really mean property law notice; that a lender will always be on inquiry ('have notice') in non-commercial surety cases; that, in other cases, the lender will be on inquiry only in exceptional cases because it is entitled to assume that a person knows what he or she is doing when the loan is for their own benefit; that, for past cases, reliance on a solicitor's certificate will normally protect a lender; that, for future cases, the steps a lender must take are greater than before, but not onerous and may both protect the lender and prevent any undue influence from arising in the first place; and finally, that a lender can never be protected when it knows, or ought to know, that the claimant has not received the guidance and counsel he or she needed to judge the appropriateness of the transaction. Of course, we also know that in reality Etridge has shifted the risk. The risk of being sued by a claimant because of undue influence can now be deflected by a bank onto the shoulders of the solicitor that advises the potentially vulnerable party. Failure to give advice, or the giving of negligent advice, will no longer result in the

---

76 As in National Westminster Bank v. Amin (2002).

77 The risk of litigation, therefore, passes to the advising solicitor.

78 Recent cases in which undue influence has been established have not involved mortgagees, but other transactions set aside for undue influence. In these cases, the Etridge rules were applied, so demonstrating the importance of this case beyond the sphere of mortgages. But see Abbey National plc v. Stringer (2006), in which the finding of undue influence in a mortgage situation was catastrophic for the lender.

79 However, it may well have increased overall costs to the borrower because the solicitor's mandatory advice will not be free and someone has to pay for the increased risk of solicitor's liability.

80 For example, Turkey v. Awadh (2005).

81 Which, as noted above, may well involve transactions other than mortgages, because mortgagees learn quickly.

mortgagee losing its security. However, it may well result in the solicitor being sued by the victim.

Finally, and for the sake of those cases in which, despite *Etridge*, undue influence can be established,[81] we must consider the effect of a successful plea of undue influence on the mortgagee. For example, is the mortgagee's entire security voided completely (*Camfield*; *Castle Phillips Finance* v. *Pinnington* (1995)), or is it voided only to the extent that the undue influence was operative, as where the claimant genuinely agreed to a mortgage of £X, but in fact signed a mortgage for £X + Y?[82] In *Barclays Bank* v. *Caplan* (1998), the court held that if a claimant could establish that only part of the mortgage transaction was void for undue influence, that void part could be severed, with the balance of the mortgage remaining valid. This might arise, for example, where the original mortgage was validly consented to, but a 'top-up' sum was secured from the mortgagee only after undue influence. It is submitted that this is, indeed, the correct approach. The purpose of the undue influence rule is to ensure that mortgagors enter mortgages freely; it is not to give them a windfall by voiding an entire mortgage if only part is tainted by undue influence.[83] Another way of apparently achieving the same result is to void the entire mortgage on condition that the claimant gives credit to the mortgagee (i.e. pays them) for any sums advanced that resulted in a benefit to that claimant (*Allied Irish Bank* v. *Byrne* (1995)). However, although this seems attractive, in fact there is no necessary correlation between the extent of the undue influence and the benefit received by the victim. To put it differently, should the victim be made to account for a benefit they may not have wanted, and which was given in a transaction already held to have been procured by undue influence? Seen in this light, whether the claimant secured a benefit or not is not the real issue. A better view might be that either the entire mortgage is void for undue influence, or it remains valid in part to the extent of the borrowing to which the claimant really did consent.[84]

10.9.5   Unlawful credit bargains

Mortgages are contracts for the provision of credit. As such, they may be subject to statutory controls similarly imposed on other types of credit relationship: controls that are designed to protect an impecunious borrower from the unfair practices of unscrupulous lenders. Thus a mortgage may fall within the provisions of the Consumer Credit Act 1974 (as amended by the Consumer Credit Act 2006) as a regulated credit agreement. However, it is unusual for a mortgage to be regulated in this fashion, not least because this part of the Consumer Credit Act 1974 (as amended) does not apply to mortgages offered by building societies, local authorities and institutions regulated by the Banking Act 1987.[85] These are 'exempt agreements' and the practical effect of these provisions is that most normal 'land

---

82 Of course, the undue influence may be operative to void the entirety of a charge, or number of charges – see *Burbank Securities* v. *Wong* (2008).

83 In the same vein, if an initial mortgage is void for undue influence, a replacement mortgage that paid off that mortgage is also void: *Yorkshire Bank* v. *Tinsley* (2004).

84 This is a property-based approach. A restitutionary analysis would require the victim to account for benefits received, save to the extent that she could claim to have changed her position in reliance on such receipt.

85 Note that there is now no upper limit on the amount of credit caught by these provisions. Section 2 of the CCA 2006 abolishes the £25,000 limit that applied previously.

purchase' mortgages will not be caught by the main provisions of the Consumer Credit Act 1974 (as amended). For those mortgages caught by the Act – such as second mortgages securing loans for other purposes – they may not be enforced without a court order.

In addition to the above protection, under the Consumer Credit Act 1974, it was possible for any mortgage to be set aside, or its terms adjusted, if it was found to be an 'extortionate credit bargain' within the meaning of sections 137–140 of the Consumer Credit Act 1974. This power was used sparingly and the courts were reluctant to interfere with the bargain struck by the parties except in the clearest cases of abuse of a dominant position by a lender – *A Ketley Ltd* v. *Scott* (1980).[86] Thus, in *Paragon Finance* v. *Nash* (2002), the court held that whether a mortgage was 'extortionate' was to be judged by reference to the 'total charge for credit' as determined at the *start* of the mortgage under its original terms and so a mortgage could not become 'extortionate' merely because, at some time after its commencement, the lender legitimately varied the interest rate so that the charge for credit became greater. However, by virtue of the Consumer Credit Act 2006, since April 2008, the 'extortionate credit bargain' test has been replaced with a test of whether there is an 'unfair relationship' between creditor and debtor.[87] This test now applies to all mortgages (including mortgages already in existence) *except* a first legal mortgage over residential land that is regulated under the Financial Services and Markets Act 2000. (Of course, many mortgages are exactly this: see below.)[88] The 2006 Act provides guidance as to what is 'unfair'[89] and the court has broad powers in relation to repayment, redemption, variation of terms and may set aside the mortgage in whole or in part.

10.9.6   Restraint of trade

A mortgage that attempts to tie a mortgagor to a particular company or mortgagee may well fall foul of the contractual rules prohibiting contracts in restraint of trade. Typical examples include brewery mortgagees using the mortgage to tie the pub landlord to the brewery as sole supplier of beer, and oil company mortgagees using the mortgage to tie in the owner of a petrol station.[90] However, once again, the unwillingness of the courts to interfere unduly with contractual relationships must be remembered, and in the same way that the courts have become more relaxed about collateral advantages, so these 'solus' agreements are less likely to be disturbed.

10.9.7   Financial Services and Markets Act 2000

Mortgages entered into on or after 31 October 2004 are likely to fall within the consumer protection regime of the Financial Services and Markets Act (FSMA) 2000. This umbrella statute, which seeks to regulate many aspects of financial services, requires providers of 'regulated mortgage contracts' to ensure that the 'consumer' is treated fairly and is not

---

86 In this case, the borrowers had known exactly what they were doing and an *annualised* interest rate of 48 per cent was not extortionate.

87 Consumer Credit Act (CCA) 2006, sections 19–22.

88 See CCA 1974, section 16(6C).

89 See CCA 1974, section 140A(1), inserted by CCA 2006.

90 See, for example, *Esso Petroleum* v. *Harpers Garage* (1968).

open to excessive or hidden charges. It is, essentially, an early warning system that is designed to alert the borrower as to the full extent of their liability in the worst possible case. The provision of mortgage business must thus confirm to the good practices of the FSMA 2000, as detailed in the Financial Services Authority (FSA) Handbook. It has led primarily to the adoption of pre-mortgage administrative practices by lenders whereby warnings about the nature and extent of liability follow a ritualised pattern, which in many cases is understood neither by person providing the advice (the employee of the lender) nor the borrower to whom the advice is given. Whether this regulatory framework does indeed ensure that borrowers are treated fairly – or whether borrowers in need of finance simply carry on regardless – remains to be seen. Crucially, however, the FSMA does not interfere with the mortgagee's extensive remedies should the mortgagor enter into the mortgage and then default.[91]

10.9.8   Powers of the mortgagor

As well as benefiting from the protective mechanisms outlined above, the mortgagor also has certain powers and rights under the mortgage or by statute. In outline, these are: the power to redeem the mortgage, which may be enforced by action in the courts (section 91 of the LPA 1925); the power to lease the property for certain limited purposes and the power to accept surrenders of existing leases (section 99 of the LPA 1925), but not if this is contrary to the terms of the mortgage;[92] the power to claim possession where this is not claimed by the mortgagee (section 98 of the LPA 1925); and the ability to apply for an order for sale of the property under section 91 of the LPA 1925, even in the teeth of objections by the mortgagee. On this last point, the court's discretion to order sale on an application by the mortgagor is now thought to comprise a power to order sale even if the proceeds of sale will not pay off the mortgage debt – *Palk v. Mortgage Services* (1993)[93] – and possibly even if the mortgagee is seeking possession of the property because of the mortgagor's inability to pay any sums due.[94] Indeed, the right to ask the court for sale under section 91, and to have it granted against the wishes of the mortgagee, is particularly valuable to a mortgagor whose debt is increasing because of his inability to meet interest payments. Sale in such circumstances stops the debt increasing further, and the mortgagor remains liable only for outstanding sums. If this jurisdiction exists in the wide form advocated by *Palk*, it will be used sparingly because of the adverse effect on the mortgagee and the value of its security.[95]

---

91 The FSMA 2000 appears to regard mortgages as consumer items, like loaves of bread, which carry a list of ingredients and suitable health warnings. Most consumers of bread do not read the labels, and this author doubts whether most 'consumers' of mortgages take any notice of the formalised warnings adopted by mortgagees because of the Act. By the time a borrower has secured the offer of a mortgage, they are likely to be strongly emotionally connected to the purpose for which the loan is desired (a new home, business, or financial salvation) and it must be rare indeed for a borrower to pull out at this stage after having been advised of the risks involved.

92 *Leeds Permanent Building Society v. Famini* (1998).

93 See also Lloyds Bank v. Polonski (1999).

94 *Palk*, but see contrary to this view *Cheltenham and Gloucester plc v. Krausz* (1997) and *Scottish & Newcastle v. Billy Row Working Men's Club* (2000). See also section 10.10.3 below and *State Bank of New South Wales v. A Carey Harrison III* (2002).

95 *Cheltenham and Gloucester v. Pearn* (1998).

10.10 The Rights of the Mortgagee under a Legal Mortgage: Remedies for Default

A mortgage is as valuable to a mortgagee as it is to a mortgagor. Obviously, the main benefit is that a rate of interest can be charged for the money lent and an income is generated for the mortgagee on the security of what is, in all but the most severe economic conditions, an asset that is not going to depreciate significantly in value. However, just as the property owner uses the mortgage to liquidate his assets, the mortgagee uses the mortgage to capitalise his income. As is apparent from all that has gone before, the essential characteristic of a mortgage is that it is security for money lent, and the ultimate goal of any mortgagee will be to recover payment of the principal debt, plus interest and related costs. As we shall see, this can be achieved in a number of ways, some of which spring from the nature of a mortgage as a contract, and some of which spring from the fact that the mortgagee has a proprietary interest in the land. Note, in this respect, that a mortgagee under a mortgage created by 'a charge by deed expressed to be by way of legal mortgage' – the only way now to create legal mortgages of registered estates – obtains the same powers and remedies as if the mortgage actually had involved the grant of a proprietary right to the mortgagee.[96]

The particular remedy employed by the mortgagee will depend on the precise nature of the default of the mortgagor and the particular requirements of the mortgagee. So, some remedies are more suitable for the recovery of unpaid interest, while others are more suitable for recovery of the entire loan and the termination of the mortgage, or even the termination of the mortgagor's rights over the property. Moreover, whereas the mortgagee can never recover more than the principal debt plus interest and costs,[97] it is clear that the mortgagee's remedies are cumulative and the mortgagee may deploy them in combination or successively until the debt is repaid. Where one fails, another might be employed until the mortgagee is successful or all remedies are exhausted.[98]

10.10.1 An action on the contract for recovery of the debt

It is in the very nature of a mortgage as a contract of loan between the parties that the mortgagee has an action on the mortgagor's express contractual promise to repay the money owed. Such a contractual term forms part of every mortgage. In short, the mortgagor will promise to repay the sum due on a certain date plus accrued interest. This is the legal date of redemption (encapsulating the mortgagor's legal right to redeem), and as soon as this date has passed, the mortgagee has a personal action on the contract for repayment of the sum owed, unless the mortgagee has also promised to defer the remedy

---

96 Sections 85(1) and 87 of the LPA 1925 and *Regent Oil Co v. Gregory* (1966). The assumption is that the mortgagee is treated as if they had been given a long lease by deed – importantly, this ensures that the right of possession still exists.

97 Or the secured property itself (by foreclosing) where its value is less than the entirety of the debt. Foreclosure is rare.

98 For an exceptional example, see *Alliance & Leicester v. Slayford* (2001).

pending the payment of instalments.[99] If the mortgagor fails to repay (or fails to pay a due instalment), the mortgagee can have the personal judgment debt satisfied in the normal way, including execution against the property of the mortgagor or by making the mortgagor bankrupt: *Alliance & Leicester v. Slayford* (2001). It may seem surprising that the mortgagee has a remedy as soon as the legal date for redemption has passed (or an instalment is missed), but this flows naturally from the mortgage as a contract, wherein each party has promised to fulfil certain obligations. Of course, in the normal course of events, the mortgagee will not sue for the money owed immediately the date for redemption has passed (nor indeed until instalments are significantly in arrears), but instead will be happy to collect the outstanding interest and continuing repayments. However, an action on the contract always remains a possibility, and may be used whenever the mortgagee wishes to recover the full amount of the debt, often in conjunction with other remedies.

It is particularly useful if a sale of the mortgaged property fails to realise enough money to pay off the debt and the mortgagor has sufficient additional assets to meet their mortgage liability. Of course, being a personal remedy against the mortgagor (that is, not against the land itself), it may be valueless if the mortgagor is bankrupt.[100] On the other hand, being an action in debt (and not for breach of contract *per se*), the mortgagee is under no duty to mitigate its loss, and, therefore, cannot be compelled to exercise any of its other remedies (*Lloyds Bank v. Bryant* (1996)). Moreover, it is clear, that in most cases, the mortgagee has 12 years from the date of default in which to sue the mortgagor for the principal sum owed under the mortgage, rather than the usual six years on a 'normal' contract. This is because the right arises under a 'speciality' (i.e. a deed) and so benefits from a longer limitation period than other contractual debts.[101] However, should the mortgagee fail to commence proceedings during this period, the debt will be unrecoverable (*Wilkinson v. West Bromwich BS* (2004)), although any acknowledgment of the debt due by the borrower during this time will restart the 12-year period (*Bradford & Bingley plc v. Rashid* (2006)). Although most lenders have voluntarily agreed (via the Council of Mortgage Lenders[102]) that they will not enforce a claim to the principal debt beyond six years from the date of default, it remains a valuable weapon and allows a mortgagee to return to a defaulting mortgagor many years after the property has been sold if that sale did not pay off the entire debt. If money is owed, therefore, a mortgage does not end with the disposal of the mortgaged property unless the mortgagee forecloses on the mortgage and itself takes the land.[103]

10.10.2 The power of sale

Another remedy that is designed to recover the whole sum owed, and also thereby to terminate the mortgage if the loan is fully repaid, is the mortgagee's power of sale of the

---

99 *Wilkinson v. West Bromwich BS* (2004). The date of default is usually the date on which the first instalment is missed as this is when the mortgagee's right to receive the money accrues.

100 In such a case, the lender would share *pro rata* in the bankrupt's assets along with other unsecured creditors.

101 Sections 8 and 20 of the Limitation Act 1980. The mortgagee has the normal six years to recover any unpaid interest.

102 The representative body to which most institutional lenders belong.

103 See below. A foreclosure necessarily brings the mortgage to an end in its entirety and kills even the personal obligation to pay. Foreclosure is rare to the point of extinction.

mortgaged property. In most cases, a mortgage will contain an express power of sale, but if not, a power of sale will be implied into every mortgage made by deed by virtue of section 101(1)(i) of the LPA 1925, unless a contrary intention appears.[104] This means that, subject to any express provision in the mortgage itself, a mortgagee will be able to sell the mortgaged property and use the funds to satisfy the mortgage debt if two conditions are fulfilled. First, the power of sale must have arisen. A mortgagee's power of sale will *arise* as soon as the legal (contractual) date for redemption has passed or, in the case of instalment mortgages, usually when one instalment is in arrears (*Twentieth Century Banking v. Wilkinson* (1977)). Once again, this reflects the contractual nature of a mortgage and the liability of the mortgagor in debt when the stipulated date for redemption has passed. Second, the power of sale must have become exercisable. The mortgagee's power of sale becomes *exercisable* when the conditions specified in section 103 of the LPA 1925 are satisfied. These require either that notice requiring payment of the whole of the mortgage money has been served by the mortgagee, and the mortgagor is three months in arrears with such payments since the notice was served, or the interest under the mortgage is in arrears and unpaid for two months after becoming due, or that the mortgagor has breached some provision of the mortgage deed (other than the covenant to pay the sum due), or a relevant provision of the LPA 1925.[105]

10.10.2.1 *The consequences of a sale*

The point of the above provisions is that they give the mortgagee an effective power of sale of the mortgaged property should the mortgagor be in serious default, either because of a breach of the promise to repay the debt with interest, or breach of any other promise.[106] The consequences of a sale are that the proceeds of sale are applied to meet the mortgage debt and associated liabilities according to the priority specified in section 105 of the LPA 1925: that is, first, in payment of the costs and charges incurred by the sale; second, in satisfaction of the principal debt, interest and costs, with the aim of discharging the mortgage; and third, if there is any surplus, to the person entitled under the mortgage, usually being the mortgagor, as in *Halifax Building Society v. Thomas* (1995).

Necessarily, a successful sale by a mortgagee with priority extinguishes the mort-gagor's equity of redemption and transfers the land to the *purchaser* free of any claim of the mortgagor. The mortgagee has the right to transfer legal title to the purchaser by the proper exercise of the power of sale – the borrower's legal title is technically over-reached[107] – because the mortgagee has the right to the economic value of the land that has been used as security for his loan. If it were otherwise, the mortgage as a *secured* debt would be meaningless. In addition, the purchaser takes the land free of any *subsequent mortgages*: that is, those granted later than the mortgage under which the sale has taken place,[108] but

---

104 This is why it is good practice to execute equitable mortgages by deed, even though a deed is not required for their validity.

105 For example, the mortgagor may have let the premises without permission, or failed to insure the property.

106 For example, to insure the property.

107 Section 2(1)(iii) of the LPA 1925.

108 Sections 88 and 113 of the LPA 1925.

subject to any previous mortgages. All subsequent mortgagees will be entitled to the balance of any money left after discharge of the mortgage under which sale has occurred in the order in which those mortgages were made, but before payment of any balance to the mortgagor. In other words, subsequent mortgagees are 'persons entitled' to the proceeds of sale of the mortgaged property under section 105 of the LPA 1925, as noted above. What this means in practice is that, provided that property values have not fallen too far, and that subsequent mortgagees operated a sensible lending policy, there should be enough money to pay off the debt of the selling mortgagee and that arising under the later mortgages. For example, if a property worth £100,000 were subject to a first mortgage of £85,000, a second mortgage of £5,000 and a third mortgage of £7,000, a sale at £100,000 by the first mortgagee would enable payment of all three mortgagees plus some balance (if any, after costs) to the mortgagor. Similarly, if the second mortgagee were to exercise their power of sale, a purchaser would buy the land subject to the first mortgage, probably paying only £15,000 (£100,000 – the value – minus £85,000 – the first mortgage), and the second and third mortgagees would be paid.

10.10.2.2   *Regulating the power of sale*

It is clear that a sale of the mortgaged property is a calamitous event for the mortgagor. Essentially, it means forced loss of the land – often the home – with only the balance of the purchase price (if any) as a comfort. Not surprisingly, therefore, in addition to the limitations on the circumstances in which a sale by the mortgagee may be undertaken at all, the mortgagee is placed under common law and statutory obligations with respect to the conduct of the sale.

First, if a mortgagee sells the property *before* the power of sale has arisen, the purchaser obtains only the mortgagee's interest, and the mortgagor remains unaffected. It is as if the mortgagee had transferred only the mortgagee's rights to the purchaser. Second, if a mortgagee sells after the power has arisen, but before it has become exercisable, the purchaser takes the land free of the mortgage, save that the mortgagor may be able to set the sale aside if the purchaser had notice of the mortgagee's fault – section 104 of the LPA 1925 and see *Cuckmere Brick Co v. Mutual Finance* (1971).

Third, and most importantly in practice, in cases in which the power of sale has both arisen and become exercisable,[109] the mortgagor must rely on the intervention of equity to protect his position. This intervention is premised once again on the fundamental point that a mortgage is security for a debt and that a mortgagee is entitled to his remedies in such a way that ensures fair payment of the debt and nothing more. In essence, a 'selling mortgagee' is under a duty of care to the mortgagor to obtain the best price reasonably obtainable (*Standard Chartered Bank v. Walker* (1982)). This has a number of different facets. The primary duty is, of course, to get the best price *reasonably* obtainable, so a sale by open public auction, even when prices are low, satisfies this duty (*Cuckmere Brick Co v. Mutual Finance* (1971); *Wilson v. Halifax plc* (2002)). Where this course is not pursued and a number of offers are made for the property, the court will consider the steps the mortgagee took to sell the property and then consider whether, in accepting the offer to contract at a price,

---

109   Of course, this is nearly always the case.

this was within an acceptable bracket for the property.[110] However, the mortgagee is not obliged to take those steps that an owner might take in selling the property, so there is no obligation on the mortgagee to pursue planning applications or the grant of leases that might make the property more valuable (*Silven Properties v. Royal Bank of Scotland* (2003)) or to sell certain fixtures separately in the hope of raising more money.[111] Neither is the duty owed to any person other than the mortgagor – particularly, it is not owed to a person with an equitable interest in the property[112] – and so the mortgagor may agree specifically to a sale by a mortgagee at a price lower than the market price and, in that way, become estopped from relying on any breach of the duty of care.[113] Similarly, the mortgagee is not a trustee of the power of sale – he is exercising it for himself, not for the mortgagor – and therefore his motives in choosing to exercise the power of sale are generally irrelevant, although it would be a breach of duty if *no* part of his motive in selling was to recover the debt (*Meretz Investments v. ACP Ltd* (2006)).

It should not be thought, however, that the general duty is without substance. In particular, the mortgagee may not sell the property to himself or his agent or his employee[114] (*Williams v. Wellingborough Council* (1975)) and if a mortgagee sells to a company in which he has an interest, or is even associated with, the burden of proof of establishing that the sale was at the best price reasonably obtainable lies with the mortgagee, and if he cannot discharge it, he is liable.[115] Likewise, the mortgagee fails to discharge this duty if he chooses a method of achieving a sale that is not likely to achieve the best price reasonably obtainable. In *Bishop v. Blake* (2006), the mortgagee failed to put the property up for auction and failed to advertise it sufficiently and then sold the property to a tenant of the mortgagor with whom the mortgagee was developing a commercial relationship, leaving the conduct of the sale in the hands of the purchaser's solicitors. The mortgagor was able to recover some £115,000, being the difference between the price actually paid and the price reasonably obtainable. In general, failure to discharge this duty will result in the award of damages – as in *Blake*, the difference between the price obtained and the true price reasonably obtainable[116] – but if the sale was to a connected person, it may be set aside completely, and may even be set aside against an unconnected purchaser, but only if the purchaser had actual knowledge of the impropriety surrounding the sale at an undervalue.[117]

---

110 *Michael v. Miller* (2004), in which the initial offer was perfectly acceptable, being within the values specified by professional valuers, but the failure to fulfil the duty was caused by the last minute reduction in the price of some £25,000.

111 *Michael v. Miller* (2004) – no obligation to sell commercially grown lavender plants separately.

112 *Parker-Tweedale v. Dunbar* (1991).

113 This appears to be the *ratio* of *Mercantile Credit Co v. Clarke* (1997), although it does assume that the mortgagor's agreement to sale at a lower price was not tainted by undue influence or unconscionable action on the part of the mortgagee.

114 In *Halifax v. Corbett* (2002), the mortgagee was held liable in damages for sale at an undervalue. In fact, it had been purchased by an employee of the mortgagee acting deceitfully, but this was unknown to the mortgagee.

115 *Mortgage Express v. Mardner* (2004); *Bradford & Bingley v. Ross* (2005). If he so desires the property, the mortgagee may apply to the court under section 91 of the LPA 1925 for authority to sell to himself, in which case the propriety of the transaction will be assessed by the court.

116 *Corbett v. Halifax* (2002).

117 Ibid.

10.10.2.3 *Judicial sales*

Although generally it is the mortgagee who will choose to sell the mortgaged property, a mortgagor may apply to the court under section 91 of the LPA 1925 for an order requiring a sale. As noted above, this is particularly beneficial to a mortgagor whose outstanding mortgage is greater than the value of the property because a sale in these circumstances will crystallise the mortgagor's liability.[118] Of course, in such circumstances, the mortgagor will still be liable on their personal contractual promise to repay the whole sum borrowed, although insurance can be obtained for this eventuality.

10.10.2.4 *Sale before possession*

A selling mortgagee will normally seek possession prior to sale.[119] This minimises the risk of the mortgagor sabotaging the sale and usually will lead to a higher price, especially as purchasers tend to want vacant possession. However, it is clear that a mortgagee is not bound to take possession before sale because a selling mortgagee has the power to convey the legal estate to the purchaser even if the mortgagor remains in possession.[120] The effect of such a sale is illustrated clearly by *Horsham Properties v. Clarke and Beech* (2009), in which the mortgagee sold the property to Horsham, which became registered proprietor, and effectively rendered the mortgagors trespassers in their 'own' home. As such, Horsham was entitled to possession of the property as of right as against the mortgagors/trespassers. This had the further unhappy consequence that the mortgagors could not rely on the statutory protection given to mortgagors of dwelling houses when facing an action for possession by a mortgagee (being section 36 of the Administration of Justice Act (AJA) 1970[121]) because such protection was available only when a *mortgagee* sought a possession order. It is not clear in *Horsham* whether the sale by the mortgagee without first taking possession was undertaken deliberately to sidestep the protection given to mortgagors of dwelling houses, but it certainly had that effect. Further, Briggs J in *Horsham* held that such a manoeuvre did not entail an infringement of the mortgagors' rights under the European Convention on Human Rights[122] and there appears to have been no suggestion that a mortgagee selling in such circumstances might not have obtained the best price reasonably obtainable.[123] Indeed, such was the alarm caused by this case – given that it highlights an easy route for mortgagees needing to sell in a flagging market and with no risk to their purchasers – that there was a proposal to amend section 36 of the AJA 1970 through clauses in the draft Banking Bill, but these were withdrawn.[124] Instead, a private member's Bill – the Home Repossession (Protection) Bill – was introduced in February 2009 to remedy the situ-

---

118　*Mortgage Services Funding v. Palk* (1993).

119　This is easy to achieve, see section 10.3.3 below.

120　Section 2(1)(iii) of the LPA 1925; section 101(1)(i) of the LPA 1925.

121　Considered in detail below.

122　As he was bound to do, given *Doherty v. Birmingham City Council* (2008).

123　While a selling mortgagee is under no obligation to take steps to improve the value of the property – *Silven Properties v. Royal Bank of Scotland* (2004) – have they obtained the best price 'reasonably' obtainable if not selling with the benefit of vacant possession, given that such possession is not difficult to achieve?

124　I am grateful to Gary Webber of Property Law UK (www.propertylawuk.net) for this information.

ation,[125] but this was later dropped due to lack of parliamentary time and support. However, as a response to these initiatives – and because of the furore cased by *Beech* – the Ministry of Justice has published a Consultation Paper that contains the tentative proposal that the law should be amended so as to provide that a mortgagee of a dwelling house should not be able to exercise its power of sale without either the consent of the borrower or an order of the court. Under these proposals, the court's discretion would be exercisable on the same basis as that found in section 36 of the AJA 1970 in relation to orders for possession.[126] Thus while, at present, a mortgagee's exercise of the power of sale does not first require possession to be obtained, and does not need a court order, this may change. It may well be that the existence of such capacity is eminently sensible in relation to commercial mortgages, but it can operate significantly to the detriment of mortgagors of dwelling houses.

10.10.3   The right to possession

The most effective way for the mortgagee to realise its security, in the event of default by the mortgagor, is to sell the property in the manner explained above. In most cases – see above – for sale to achieve its aim of maximising the chances of the mortgagee recovering its loan in full, the mortgagee will want the property to be put on the market with vacant possession: that is, after having ejected the mortgagor from the premises. In practice, therefore, it is still usual for the mortgagee to exercise his right to possession of the mortgaged property before attempting to sell. Moreover, although possession is often a prelude to sale, it can also be used as a method of securing recovery of the outstanding interest on a loan. For example, the mortgagee may take possession of the premises and manage them in such a way so as to generate income that can then be used to satisfy the mortgagor's obligations. Possession, then, does not necessarily mean the end of the mortgage, although realisation of the security through a sale may follow.

The mortgagee's right to possession is *exactly* what it says. By virtue of the way in which legal mortgages are created, the mortgagee is regarded as having an estate in the land and this gives the mortgagee an immediate right to possession the moment the ink is dry on the mortgage.[127] It is important to realise, then, that the mortgagee may take possession of the property at any time, *even if the mortgagor is not in default*, subject only to any provision to the contrary in the mortgage itself or in statute. Of course, in the normal course of events, the mortgagee will not exercise this right, and will be content to allow the mortgagor to remain in possession so long as the terms of the mortgage are observed and agreed payments are made. Indeed, the mortgagee may have contractually promised not to seek possession unless the mortgagor defaults on the repayments or breaches some other obligation but, if this occurs, possession may then be obtained in virtue of the right of the mortgagee, not in virtue of a remedy to be asked for from the court.[128]

---

125   By requiring mortgagees to obtain a possession order from the court in all cases involving dwelling houses.

126   Ministry of Justice *Mortgages: Power of Sale and Residential Property*, Consultation Paper, 29 December 2009. The consultation period ended on 28 March 2010. See also the Mortgage Repossessions (Protection of Tenants etc) Act 2010 giving limited protection to tenants occupying land likely to be re-possessed.

127   *Four Maids v. Dudley Marshall* (1957); *Ropaigelach v. Barclays Bank* (1999).

128   See section 98 of the LPA 1925.

10.10.3.1 *The consequences of the mortgagee taking possession*

Although the mortgagee has a right to possession, subject only to self-limitation as expressed in the contract, it is not always productive to exercise this right. A mortgagee in possession of the mortgaged premises will be called to account strictly for any income generated by their possession (*White v. City of London Brewery* (1889)). This means that the mortgagee will be taken to have received not only the actual income generated by their management of the property (which can go towards repayments), but also any income that should have been received assuming the property had been managed to the high standard required. Any shortfall between the actual income and the reasonably expected income will have to be made up by the mortgagee, who may find that he actually owes money to the mortgagor if the income that should have been received is greater than the money owed. This is why most commercial mortgagees desist from seeking possession, and why most residential mortgagees seek possession only as a prelude to sale.[129]

10.10.3.2 *Statutory restrictions on the right of possession*

In the residential context, where the mortgage may well have been used to finance the purchase of the property in the first place, it is rare for the mortgagee to seek possession other than as a prelude to sale. The mortgagor will occupy the property unless there is a problem with mortgage repayments and the mortgagee is likely to have contractually bound themselves not to seek possession unless this occurs. Moreover, if a mortgagee[130] brings an action to recover possession of land 'which consists of, or includes, a dwelling house', whether as a prelude to sale or not, the mortgagor may avail themselves of the protection afforded by section 36 of the AJA 1970 (as amended by section 8 of the AJA 1973). Under section 36 (as amended), an application by a mortgagee for possession of a dwelling house may be suspended, adjourned or postponed by the court, in its discretion, if it appears that the mortgagor would be likely to be able to pay within a reasonable period any sums due under the mortgage. Whether a property is a 'dwelling house' for the purpose of section 36 is to be determined by reference to the state of the premises at the time the order for possession was sought, not by reference to their use at the time the mortgage was executed.[131] By virtue of the section 8 amendment,[132] 'any sums due' may be treated only as those instalments that have not been paid by the mortgagor as they fell due and not, as most mortgages provide when one mortgage payment is missed, the whole mortgage debt. Likewise, the statutory relief is available for endowment mortgages, despite the elliptical wording of the statute,[133] although there is some doubt whether

---

129 A notable exception was *Mortgage Services Funding v. Palk* (1993), in which the mortgagee wished to take possession in order to keep the mortgage alive in the hope that property prices would rise and wipe out some of the escalating debt. In effect, this was the mortgagee gambling at the mortgagor's expense, for while the mortgagee was in possession, the interest would accumulate faster than any reasonably expected income from the property. This explains why the mortgagor was successful in obtaining an order for sale under section 91 of the LPA 1925.

130 But only a mortgagee – see *Horsham Properties v. Clarke* (2009), section 10.10.2.4 above.

131 *Royal Bank of Scotland v. Miller* (2001).

132 Effectively reversing *Halifax Building Society v. Clark* (1973).

133 *Bank of Scotland v. Grimes* (1985).

the statutory discretion is available if the mortgagor is not actually in default under the mortgage.[134] The statutory discretion is not available once a warrant for possession has been executed: that is, if the mortgagee has actually recovered possession (*Mortgage Agency Services v. Ball* (1998)).

It is important to realise the precise limitations and effect of section 36 of the AJA 1970 (as amended), for although it clearly benefits mortgagors in general, in reality it comprises a fairly limited power. First, as noted above, it is available only in respect of dwelling houses. Second, the court's discretion is triggered by an application for *an order* for possession. If the mortgagee, in exercise of its right to possession, takes possession without a court order – as it is perfectly entitled to do – then the court has no jurisdiction to control or suspend the possession (*Ropaigelach v. Barclays Bank* (2000)). Third, as noted above, the jurisdiction is available when a mortgagee seeks a possession order, not a purchaser from the mortgagee – *Horsham Properties v. Clarke* (2009). Fourth, the mortgagor must be likely to be able to pay any sums due within a reasonable period. While it is clear that a 'reasonable period' in which to repay the arrears might actually be the rest of the mortgage term,[135] the court has no discretion to make an order if there is no prospect of the mortgagor making a reasonable attempt actually to repay the accumulated arrears, let alone meet future repayments.[136] Thus the court must embark on a fairly detailed analysis of the mortgagor's overall income and outgoings in order to see if even the rescheduled arrears can be paid back alongside future obligations. Of course, an intended sale of the property by the mortgagor is a factor that could justify suspension of a possession order under section 36, as this might mean that the mortgagor is likely to be able to pay all monies due within a reasonable period (*National and Provincial Bank v. Lloyd* (1996)), but it is clear that there must be firm evidence that a sale is likely, not merely that it might occur or that the mortgagor will now takes steps to secure a sale. Mortgagees are rightly worried that mortgagors will attempt to use the section 36 discretion to stay in their homes while the debt mounts without any real prospect of arrears or capital ever being paid.

Prior to the important Court of Appeal decision in *Cheltenham & Gloucester Building Society v. Norgan* (1996), the practice relating to a mortgagor's request to suspend or dismiss a possession application by reason of section 36 had become somewhat rigid, with the courts (especially the county court where most of these applications are heard) generally suspending possession for an 'automatic' two years, so that the mortgagor had to make up the arrears in that time. As noted above, however, section 36 itself lays down no such time limit and *Norgan* contemplates a 'reasonable period' for repayment as being the whole of the remaining mortgage term. Clearly, the thrust of *Norgan* is that section 36 should be used more effectively to protect mortgagors of residential property, and, to that end, the case established that a court should address a number of issues before deciding whether to exercise its discretion. These considerations are designed to ensure that the particular

---

134 *Western Bank v. Schindler* (1977). Section 36 does not say in terms that it applies only when the mortgagor is in default, so it is arguable that it is applicable whenever the mortgagee seeks possession by court order. However, if the mortgagor is not in default, it will be a rare mortgage that has not curtailed the right to possession in this circumstance.

135 *Middlesbrough Mortgage Corp v. Cunningham* (1974); *Cheltenham and Gloucester Building Society v. Norgan* (1996). Thus the arrears effectively may be rescheduled to be repaid alongside future scheduled repayments.

136 *First National Bank v. Syed* (1991); *Bristol & West Building Society v. Dace* (1998); *Barclays Bank v. Alcorn* (2002).

circumstances of each mortgagor are given due weight. They include consideration of: how much the mortgagor can afford to pay given his other commitments; whether the mortgagor is in temporary difficulty, or his problems are more enduring; what were the reasons for the arrears; how long of the original mortgage period is left; what are the contractual terms relating to repayment of the capital sum – in particular, was this an instalment mortgage; over what period is it reasonable to expect the mortgagee to wait for repayment of the arrears, bearing in mind that the mortgagee could be asked to wait even longer than the original mortgage term; and, finally, how the value of the land relates to the amount borrowed and now owed.

Obviously, these considerations represent an attempt to cover all eventualities and the Court of Appeal is essentially advising county courts to take more care to assess individual circumstances rather than adopt an institutional, unthinking approach to its discretion. Even then, however, we must recognise section 36 for what it is. It is a great advantage to borrowers in short-term difficulty who are now able to cope after an unexpected disaster or whose fortunes are likely to improve. For these homeowners, a temporary setback will not mean loss of the family home. However, for those borrowers who are simply over-committed, section 36 offers no comfort. It is a temporary fix for a temporary problem; it does not allow the borrower to escape from an unwise bargain. Indeed, let us not think that mortgagees find section 36 necessarily troublesome: mortgagees do not want posses-sion, or the expense of a sale; they want the mortgage repaid according to its terms. A possession order under section 36 gives the mortgagee all it could ask for: an order for possession, albeit suspended, *and* an order requiring the borrower to repay the arrears and to stick to a schedule for future payments. This might explain why so many section 36 applications are not resisted by mortgagees.

We should also note in this connection that there is some control on a mortgagee's ability to commence possession proceedings in the first place. Where a court order for possession of a dwelling house is sought (but not in respect of other land), a lender should first comply with the procedures established by the Pre-action Protocol for Possession Claims based on Mortgage or Home Purchase Plan Arrears in Respect of Residential Property.[137] The central thrust of the Protocol is to ensure that lenders follow a uniform, clear and structured approach to dealing with mortgage arrears leading to possession claims of residential properties. It provides a series of steps that are designed both to keep the borrower fully informed of their indebtedness and to ensure that lenders give borrowers every opportunity to avoid repossession by rescheduling the debt, utilising State support or selling the property. The emphasis is on contact and communication between borrower and lender – within defined time limits – and is designed to reduce the circum-stances in which a mortgagee is driven to take possession. In fact, where the borrower intends to deal with the debt by selling the property himself, the Protocol provides: 'If a borrower can demonstrate that reasonable steps have been or will be taken to market the property at an appropriate price in accordance with reasonable professional advice, the lender should consider postponing starting a possession claim. The borrower must con-

---

137 http://www.justice.gov.uk/civil/procrules_fin/contents/protocols/prot_mha.htm. See also the Mortgage
     Reposessions (Protection of Tenants etc) Act 2010. This is not yet in force, but it gives a court the power to
     postpone possession for up to 2 months where possession of a dwelling house is sought against a landlord who has
     let the property to an unauthorised tenant.

tinue to take all reasonable steps actively to market the property where the lender has agreed to postpone starting a possession claim.'[138] In this respect at least the Protocol goes a little further in the borrower's favour than section 36 of the AJA 1970, which usually requires the borrower to be able to demonstrate a very real likelihood of a sale before the mortgagee can be kept out of possession.[139] The Protocol is enforced through a Practice Direction issued by the Head of Civil Justice, and non-compliance by a mortgagee can be penalised by case management orders and in costs. Significantly, however, non-compliance does not result in the loss of the right of possession[140] but, that said, most major lenders will adhere to its very modest requirements.[141] Indeed, most responsible lenders will already have had similar mechanisms in place as part of their own internal enforcement processes.

Finally, to return to a matter touched on briefly above, it is important to appreciate that a mortgagee does not actually need a court order to secure possession. The mortgagee's ability to possess arises *as of right* by virtue of the interest they have or are deemed to have in the land. Possession may then be taken peacefully through self-help without any application to the court. In most cases, of course, a lender will not pursue this option, not least because there is a real risk of committing criminal offences in the act of taking possession if there should be any person lawfully residing on the premises at the time. Moreover, the lender may well want the security that a court order brings and the assurance that the mortgagor is not trying to defeat the mortgage (and hence the right to possession) on other grounds (e.g. undue influence). Importantly, however, as just discussed, if a lender does take possession of a property without a court order, the court then has no power to suspend the possession under section 36 of the AJA 1970. Clearly, this may well represent a considerable advantage for a lender, as exemplified by *Ropaigelach v. Barclays Bank* (2000), in which the lender took peaceful possession without a court order while the habitually defaulting mortgagee was elsewhere. Although this is perhaps not the first option for an institutional lender operating under the Council of Mortgage Lenders Code of Practice and the FSMA 2000, it is an effective and inexpensive way of realising the security of those mortgagors who appear to have no real intention or ability to repay the debt.[142]

10.10.3.3 *Other possible limitations on the right to possession*

The nature of possession as a right, rather than as a remedy, means that the court only has such powers to keep a determined mortgagee out of possession as are given it by statute or which arise out of the conscience of equity. Of course, many would argue that this is just as it should be: after all, what use is a security if the creditor cannot realise it easily? Nevertheless, the widespread use of the mortgage not only as a means of raising capital on the security of land, but also as a means of buying that land in the first place means that the taking of possession has a disruptive influence on more than simply the finances of the

---

138 Protocol, paragraph 6.2.

139 Often the real issue in section 36 proceedings is whether the borrower or lender should have charge of the sale; the Protocol clearly favours the former.

140 'This Protocol does not alter the parties' rights and obligations' – paragraph 1.2.

141 Notice that the Protocol talks of what the lender 'should' do, not what it 'must' do.

142 Note also that many borrowers voluntarily surrender possession without any court intervention when they realise they cannot pay the sums due.

borrower. It can render a family homeless or require them to live apart. Consequently, much attention has been paid, judicially and academically, to assessing whether there are other grounds for keeping a mortgagee out of his right. Most of the possible 'solutions' to this 'problem'[143] are either narrow in scope or arise in very special circumstances. They are outlined below.

1   In *Quennell* v. *Maltby* (1979), Lord Denning suggested that a court of equity could restrain a mortgagee from taking possession whenever there was no justifiable reason for that possession. His view was that possession could be sought only for a *bona fide* realisation of the mortgagee's security. Obviously, this directly contradicts the mortgagee's pure right of possession springing from their status as a deemed holder of estate in the land. Consequently, it is doubtful whether the *dicta* in *Quennell* are correct and they have found little support in subsequent cases.[144]

2   Following on from *Mortgage Services Funding* v. *Palk* (1993) in the Court of Appeal, it appears that a court may suspend a mortgagee's possession application or order if it concurrently orders sale of the property at the request of the mortgagor under section 91 of the LPA 1925. This presents no difficulty if the proceeds of sale would pay off the entire sum owed – anyway, section 36 of the AJA 1970 could have been used to like effect. However, if the sale proceeds would not pay off the whole debt – as in *Palk* itself – section 36 is inapplicable and so the suspension of the mortgagee's possession in *Palk* seems to have derived from the wide discretionary power found in section 91 itself. This is a novel use of section 91, and in *Cheltenham & Gloucester BS* v. *Krausz* (1997), the Court of Appeal *appears* to have held that there is no power to suspend a mortgagee's possession unless section 36 could be used. Yet, *Krausz* does not overrule *Palk* (itself followed in *Lloyds Bank* v. *Polonski* (1999)), because *Palk* is said to be limited to its 'special facts'. In fact, the distinction drawn by the Court in *Krausz* between it and *Palk* is not convincing, and while, at present, the balance of authority favours the narrow *Krausz* view, the matter is not yet finally determined. Therefore, for the present, if the mortgagor applies for sale under section 91 of the LPA 1925, there *may* be an opportunity for the court to utilise an ancillary power to suspend a mortgagee's possession order while the sale takes place, whether or not the sale would pay off the entire debt.

3   *Albany Home Loans* v. *Massey* (1997) establishes that a mortgagee cannot be granted possession of land mortgaged by joint mortgagors where, in fact, the mortgage turns out to be binding on only one of them. In that case, the mortgage of the house had been executed by the man and woman jointly and they were in default. However, the mortgage was held void as against the woman on the grounds of undue influence. In consequence, possession of the land could not be ordered, even though the man would remain living on the land with his partner.[145]

---

143 Not everyone would agree that there is a 'problem'. After all, the existence of an effective and inexpensive means of realising the security might encourage easy and inexpensive lending by mortgagees.

144 Note, however, a similar argument found favour in *Meretz Investments* v. *ACP Ltd* (2006) in relation to a mortgagee exercising its power of sale: section 10.10.2 above.

145 Note, however, that the mortgagee may still apply for a forced sale of the land under section 14 of TOLATA 1996 which, if successful, will result in the land being sold and the innocent mortgagor receiving their equity as a first call on the proceeds of sale – see, for example, *First National Bank* v. *Achampong* (2003).

4   There are other statutory restrictions on the mortgagee's right to possession, which arise in very particular circumstances. These include attempts by the mortgagee to gain possession outside the time limit set by the Limitation Act 1980 (*National Westminster Bank v. Ashe* (2008))[146] or in contravention of the Consumer Credit Act 1974 (as amended), the Rent Act 1977 and the Housing Acts 1985–96, or contrary to the dictates of the insolvency legislation.

5   It remains to be seen whether a mortgagor can claim that the *mortgagee's* exercise of the right of possession contravenes the borrower's right to peaceful enjoyment of their property[147] or their right to family life[148] guaranteed by the European Convention on Human Rights, as implemented in the United Kingdom by the Human Rights Act 1998. Such an argument is tenable[149] and the law of human rights is dynamic and still of uncertain scope in its relationship with English land law. On the other hand, a mortgagee's claim to possession is in pursuit of their legitimate rights under the mortgage, especially if such possessory rights are a proportionate response to the mortgagor's default. At present, the tenor of decisions in related issues surrounding possession is against the success of this argument,[150] and this view has been strengthened by the decision in *Horsham Properties v. Clark*.[151]

10.10.4   Appointment of a receiver

The ability of a mortgagee to appoint a receiver to manage and administer the mortgaged property is another method by which it can recover the interest owed, and possibly sell the mortgaged property as a 'going concern'.[152] The right to appoint a receiver is often expressly included in the mortgage contract, but, in any event, such a power will be implied into every mortgage by deed (section 101 of the LPA 1925). The implied power becomes exercisable only in those circumstances in which the power of sale becomes exercisable, and it is often an alternative to that remedy (or used in conjunction with it[153]) and the duties of a receiver may generally be regarded as similar to those imposed on a selling mortgagee.[154] The great advantage of the appointment of a receiver is, however, that it avoids the dangers of the mortgagee taking possession of the property themselves. This is because the receiver is deemed to be the agent of the mortgagor, not of the mortgagee[155] with the consequence that any negligence in the administration of the property is not attributable to the mortgagee and neither is the mortgage liable to account for any income generated (or not generated) by the receiver.

---

146   The borrower remained in possession for more than 12 years after the bank's right to possession had arisen. Consequently, the mortgage was extinguished under sections 15 and 17 of the Limitation Act 1980.

147   Protocol 1, Article 1.

148   Article 8.

149   See *Barca v. Mears* (2004) in the context of a sale of family property after bankruptcy.

150   *London Borough of Harrow v. Qazi* (2008); *Kay v. Lambeth LBC* (2006); *Pye v. UK* (2008); *Doherty v. Birmingham City Council* (2008).

151   Above section 10.10.2.4.

152   See, for example, the *Billy Row* case (2000).

153   As in *Horsham Properties v. Clark* (2009).

154   *Silven Properties v. Royal Bank of Scotland* (2003). See, generally, *Medforth v. Blake* (2000).

155   *Chatsworth Properties v. Effiom* (1971); *Lloyds Bank v. Bryant* (1996).

10.10.5   Foreclosure

The remedy of foreclosure is *potentially* the most powerful remedy in the armoury of the mortgagee, although it is now used very infrequently. If successful, foreclosure will extinguish the equity of redemption and result in the transfer of the mortgaged property to the mortgagee, free of any rights of the mortgagor. In other words, the effect of a foreclosure is to vest the mortgagor's estate in the mortgagee and to extinguish the mortgage and its terms (section 88 of the LPA 1925).[156] So, if the property is freehold, the mortgagee will acquire that freehold, and similarly for a leasehold. The mortgagee's right of foreclosure arises as soon as the legal date for redemption is passed, although it is common for the mortgagee to promise not to foreclose without notice, and only in respect of specified breaches of covenant. Essentially, should the need arise, the mortgagee will begin an action in court asking for foreclosure unless the mortgagor repays the mortgage within a specified time. If repayment does not occur, the mortgagee will be given a foreclosure *nisi*, which, in effect, gives the mortgagor a further period (usually six months) in which to raise the money to pay off the loan. Failing that, the order of foreclosure will be made 'absolute', and the mortgagor's interest in the property will be extinguished. This is usually the end of the matter, save that, in exceptional circumstances, the court may open a foreclosure absolute and allow the mortgagor to redeem the mortgage at a later date. This is very unlikely if the mortgagee has already sold the property to a purchaser who has no notice of the previous mortgage (*Campbell v. Holyland* (1877)).

10.10.5.1   *Statutory control of foreclosure*

In view of the powerful nature of foreclosure, the court has power, under section 91(2) of the LPA 1925, to order sale in lieu of a foreclosure. If such a sale occurs, the proceeds will be distributed according to section 105 of the LPA 1925 (as above in the context of a mortgagee's sale), and this means that the mortgagor will receive surplus funds (if any) after the mortgage is paid off. Obviously, such a solution is desirable from the mortgagor's point of view, especially where the mortgage debt is less than the value of the property. In fact, the ability of the court to order sale in lieu of foreclosure has meant a steep decline in the number of successful foreclosure actions. After all, it is a remedy that can destroy the mortgagor's entire interest in the property and for that reason alone should be viewed with some suspicion.

10.10.5.2   *Effect of foreclosure on other mortgagees*

If a mortgagee successfully forecloses, this necessarily has consequences for any other mortgagees who have also lent money to the mortgagor. First, the rights of mortgagees under mortgages that were created *before* the mortgage that triggers the foreclosure are unaffected. In other words, whoever obtains the land after the foreclosure takes it subject to all prior mortgages. Second, the rights of mortgagees under mortgages that were created *after* the mortgage that triggers the foreclosure will be destroyed. This is because the

---

156   The mortgage is extinguished completely, and so the mortgagee may not sue the mortgagor personally for any shortfall.

foreclosure vests the mortgagor's estate in the 'foreclosing mortgagee' free of any subsequent interests. However, the subsequent mortgagees are given an opportunity to redeem any previous mortgages if foreclosure is likely. In effect, they are given the opportunity to take the place of previous mortgagees by paying them off.

10.11 The Rights of a Mortgagee under an Equitable Mortgage

The rights and remedies of a mortgagee under an equitable mortgage or charge are similar to that of the legal mortgagee, although modified, because the mortgagee cannot be treated as having a legal estate in the land. Briefly, first, the equitable mortgagee or chargee has the right to sue for the money due in the same way as the legal mortgagee. This right is founded in the contract between the parties. Second, where the equitable mortgage is made by deed, the mortgagee has the power of sale, although no power to convey the legal estate to a purchaser. This defect can be overcome by conveyancing devices in appropriate cases.[157] Where the power of sale does not exist, the equitable mortgagee may apply for sale at the court's discretion under section 91(2) of the LPA 1925. Third, an equitable mortgagee under a mortgage created by an equitable lease/sublease probably has the right to possess the property (i.e. as an equitable tenant), or may be given this expressly in the mortgage contract. An equitable chargee does not have a right of possession, as they have no estate in the land, unless possession is specifically given in the mortgage contract. Fourth, the position in respect of the appointment of a receiver is the same as with the power of sale. Finally, an equitable mortgagee has a right of foreclosure in the same way as a legal mortgagee. An equitable chargee does not, as they have no estate in the land.

10.12 Chapter Summary

10.12.1 The essential nature of a mortgage

A mortgage is a contract and the mortgagor and mortgagee are free to stipulate whatever terms they wish for repayment of the loan, the rate of interest and so forth. However, a mortgage also generates a proprietary interest in the land for both parties: both mortgagee and mortgagor have (or are treated as having) an estate in the land.

10.12.2 The classic definition of a mortgage

A mortgage is security for a loan. A mortgage of land comprises a transfer (conveyance) of a legal or equitable interest in the borrower's land to the mortgagee, with a provision that the mortgagee's interest shall lapse upon repayment of the loan plus interest and costs.

---

157 This explains why even equitable mortgages are often made by deed.

10.12.3 The creation of mortgages

For a legal mortgage, the mortgagor (having a legal estate) may grant a legal mortgage of a registered title by means of a charge by deed expressed to be by way of legal mortgage: sections 23 of the LRA 2002, and sections 85(1) and 87 of the LPA 1925. Legal mortgages of unregistered land may be created by a charge (and usually are) but also by the 'long lease' method. Equitable mortgages may exist when there is a mortgage of an equitable interest, when there is an informal mortgage of a legal interest (i.e. when writing but not a deed is used, or where registration of a deed does not take place), under the rules for equitable charges, and via the operation of proprietary estoppel.

10.12.4 The rights of the mortgagor: The equity of redemption

The mortgagor has a contractual right to redeem the mortgage on the date specified in the mortgage contract. Under the maxim 'once a mortgage always a mortgage', a court of equity would allow redemption after the legal date for redemption had passed. A mortgagor also enjoys the equity of redemption, which represents the sum total of the mortgagor's rights in the property, including his paramount title out of which the mortgage is granted. The mortgagor's rights within the equity of redemption include: the rule against irredeemability; the invalidity of a mortgagee's option to purchase the property; the insistence on unfettered redeemability and the scrutiny of collateral advantages; and the objection to unconscionable terms.

10.12.5 Undue influence

A mortgage (or a severable part of it) may be struck down if it was obtained by the undue influence of the mortgagee or a third party acting on behalf of the mortgagee. Undue influence may be 'actual' or 'presumed'. In cases of actual undue influence, it is not necessary to prove that the mortgage was to the 'manifest disadvantage' of the mortgagor. In cases of 'presumed' undue influence, this is necessary. In cases in which the mortgagor is claiming that they were unfairly induced to enter the mortgage not by the mortgagee directly, but by another person, then the mortgagee will not be able to enforce the mortgage if either:

1 the real inducer was acting as agent of the mortgagee (rare); or
2 the mortgagee had actual or constructive notice of the inducer's unfair conduct and had not taken the steps specified in *Royal Bank of Scotland v. Etridge* (No. 2) (2001) to ensure that the claimant was independently advised and thereby itself protected.

10.12.6 Unlawful credit bargains

Mortgages are subject to statutory controls designed to protect an impecunious borrower from the unfair practices of unscrupulous lenders: the Consumer Credit Act 1974, as amended and enhanced by the Consumer Credit Act 2006.

10.12.7 Restraint of trade

A mortgage that attempts to 'tie' a mortgagor to a particular company or mortgagee may fall foul of the contractual rules prohibiting contracts in restraint of trade.

10.12.8 The rights of the mortgagee under a legal mortgage: Remedies for default

1   *An action on the contract for recovery of the debt* – The mortgage is a contract and can be sued on in the normal way.
2   *The power of sale* – If the power of sale has both arisen and become exercisable, the mortgagee may sell the property and apply the proceeds of sale to meet the mortgage debt and associated liabilities according to the provisions of section 105 of the LPA 1925. It is not dependent on the mortgagee first taking possession.
3   *The right to possession* – By virtue of the way in which legal mortgages are created, the mortgagee will have the equivalent of an estate in the land and an immediate right to possession, even if the mortgagor is not in default, subject only to any provision to the contrary in the mortgage itself or in statute. The consequences of taking possession are that the mortgagee will be called to account strictly for any income generated by their possession. If a mortgagee brings an action to recover possession of land 'which consists of or includes a dwelling house', the mortgagor may plead the protection of section 36 of the AJA 1970 (as amended by section 8 of the AJA 1973). Certain other limitations on the mortgagee's right to possession may exist.
4   *Appointment of a receiver* – The right to appoint a receiver is often expressly included in the mortgage and such a power will be implied into every mortgage by deed: section 101 of the LPA 1925. The receiver is deemed to be the agent of the mortgagor, not of the mortgagee, and so the mortgagee can avoid the dangers of taking possession.
5   *Foreclosure* – If successful, foreclosure will extinguish the equity of redemption and result in the transfer of the mortgaged property, to the mortgagee, free of any rights of the mortgagor: section 88 of the LPA 1925. The court has power, under section 91(2) of the LPA, to order sale in lieu of a foreclosure and the proceeds will be distributed according to section 105 of the LPA 1925. The rights of a mortgagee under a mortgage created before the mortgage that triggers the foreclosure are unaffected, but the rights of a mortgagee under a mortgage that was created after the mortgage that triggers the foreclosure will be destroyed.

10.12.9 The rights of a mortgagee under an equitable mortgage

The rights and remedies of a mortgagee under an equitable mortgage or charge are similar to those of a legal mortgagee, although modified because the equitable mortgagee does not have a legal estate in the land. The equitable mortgagee has the right to sue for the money due on the contract; where the equitable mortgage is made by deed, the mortgagee has the power of sale, although no power to convey the legal estate to a purchaser. Where the power of sale does not exist, the equitable mortgagee may apply for sale at the court's discretion under section 91(2) of the LPA 1925. An equitable mortgagee under a mortgage created by an equitable lease/sublease probably has the right to possess the property or may be given this expressly in the mortgage contract. An equitable chargee does not have a right of possession as he has no estate in the land, unless possession is given specifically in the mortgage contract; the appointment of a receiver is as the power of sale; an equitable mortgagee has a right of foreclosure in the same way as a legal mortgagee. An equitable chargee does not, as he has no estate in the land.

Further reading

Bamforth, N, 'Lord Macnaughten's puzzle: The mortgage of real property in English law' [1996] CLP 207

Capper, D, 'Undue influence and unconscionability' (1998) 114 LQR 479

Dixon, M, 'Combating the mortgagee's right to possession: New hope for the mortgager in chains?' (1998) 18 LS 279

Dixon, M and **Harpum**, C, 'Fraud, undue influence and mortgages of registered land' [1994] Conv 421

Haley, M, 'Mortgage default: Possession, relief and judicial discretion' (1997) 16 LS 483

Horsham Properties Group Ltd v. *Clark* [2009] Conv 283

Law Commission *Land Mortgages*, Report No. 204, London: HMSO, 1991

Roplaigeach v. *Barclays Bank* [1999] 3 WLR 17; [1999] CLJ 281

Chapter 11
Adverse Possession

Introduction

The law of adverse possession is something of a peculiarity in English law. It is, in effect, a set of rules that offers an opportunity[1] to a mere trespasser actually to acquire a better title to land than the person who 'legally' owns it and to whom it was once formally conveyed with all of the solemnity of a deed or registered disposition. In fact, adverse possession is rooted in the feudal origins of English land law, for it is the most obvious modern example of the 'relativity of title' that once lay at the heart of the doctrine of estates. Given that in English law no person may own land itself – only an estate in it – it is in theory perfectly possible for someone other than the 'paper' or 'formal' owner to gain a better title without any formal transfer of 'ownership'. A person's title to land, including the paper owner's, is, as a matter of theory, only as good as the absence of a person with a better title. However, as we shall see, this justification for adverse possession is fast becoming out of date. Although it remains the case under the Land Registration Act (LRA) 2002 that a person is still registered with an estate – not with the land itself[2] – registration as proprietor under the 2002 Act is a more absolute guarantee of ownership than anything that has gone before. As we have seen in Chapter 2, there is still room for alteration of the register, and adverse possession of a registered title is not impossible – just impossibly difficult – but registration of a person as proprietor under the LRA 2002 is the closest thing in over 900 years to absolute ownership of land.[3] This has led to a radical overhaul of the law of adverse possession as it applies to registered land, and this must be remembered in the ensuing discussion. It is dealt with more fully below.

Despite the radical surgery performed by the LRA 2002, the fact that the common law should have developed a set of principles that might operate to deprive a 'paper' owner of his title to land is not as remarkable as might first appear. Historically, the common law always has been more concerned with the development of remedies for concrete situations, rather than the formulation of abstract rights, and so the apparent lack of regard for the 'rights' of the paper owner, expressed in terms of a denial of a remedy if the defendant can plead adverse possession, is not particularly surprising or unique. It is also clear that a doctrine of adverse possession can be justified on substantive grounds, even in an age of registration of title. In terms of the legal process, adverse possession is an expression of a policy that denies legal assistance to those who sleep on their rights, as well as ensuring that there is an end to disputes concerning ownership of land.[4] Similarly, land is a finite and scarce resource, and the principles of adverse possession can help to ensure its full economic and/or social utilisation, as in *Hounslow* v. *Minchinton* (1997), in which the adverse possessor brought neglected land back into use. All this said, however, it would be a mistake to accept unquestioningly the relevance of adverse possession in our modern system of land law, especially one that is moving towards electronic dealings with land.

---

1   As we shall see, the LRA 2002 has diminished substantially the chance of a successful claim to adverse possession of a registered title. Just how much of an 'opportunity' now exists remains a matter of debate.

2   Hence the Crown is authorised to grant itself an estate in order to register its own land – it cannot just 'register it'.

3   See for example, sections 23 and 58 of the LRA 2002 and see *Baxter* v. *Mannion* [2010] EWHC 573 (Ch) where the register was rectified in the context of an adverse possession claim.

4   *RB Policies* v. *Butler* (1950).

This is especially so in the context of land of registered title where entry of the 'paper owner' on the register of title – with a title guaranteed by the State – seems to preclude even the possibility that some interloper might acquire that ownership by mere possession of the land. Indeed, in so far as adverse possession had developed as a response to difficulties of proving title to land (e.g. where deeds were lost or no good 'root of title' could be shown), compulsory and widespread registration of title has removed its *raison d'etre*. Indeed, there is a point of principle here. If being registered as proprietor of an estate in the land is supposed to be a guarantee of the validity of that title to the whole world (subject only to the limited power to rectify the register under the LRA 2002), should the registered owner *ever* be susceptible to the claim of a mere trespasser? Moreover, how can we move to a system of e-conveyancing if the 'mere' fact of possession by another person might defeat the e-title of the e-vendor?

Such concerns have, of course, proved decisive, and the LRA 2002 establishes a new regime for adverse possession in respect of registered land – and we should remember that registered land now comprises over 85 per cent of all titles. Indeed, given that the relevant parts of the 2002 Act are in force, successful new claims to adverse possession of registered land[5] are likely to slow to a thin trickle – if that. However, for the present, and for so long as there remain large areas of unregistered land,[6] we need to understand the substantive law of adverse possession. Thus, in the modern law, there remains one common set of rules concerning *how* adverse possession might be established, but *two* sets of divergent rules about the effect of a claim on the paper owner's title. The rules common to both registered and unregistered land are the substantive principles developed through case law over many decades and now largely codified by the House of Lords in J A Pye Ltd v. *Graham* (2002). These rules establish when a claim of adverse possession might succeed factually and apply equally to registered and unregistered title. Beyond this, however, there is divergence, with the 'traditional principles' of limitation applying to land of unregistered title and the statutory scheme of the LRA 2002 applying to registered title. In fact, it is difficult to imagine a contrast so marked as now exists: adverse possession of unregistered land remains a real possibility, but successful[7] adverse possession of registered land is highly improbable in the vast majority of cases. Indeed, so safe is land of registered title from the claims of an adverse possessor that owners of unregistered estates – particularly local authorities and public bodies with scattered and unmonitored holdings – are applying for voluntary first registration of title primarily to bring themselves within the protective umbrella of the new legislation.

---

5 That is, claims in which the adverse possessor had not completed 12 years' adverse possession of the registered title prior to 13 October 2003 – the date of entry into force of the LRA 2002. See *Baxter* v. *Mannion*.

6 Although there are less than 15 per cent of unregistered titles, this comprises somewhere between 30 to 35 per cent of land by area. In other words, unregistered titles comprise large parcels of land, often owned by the Crown, the Church, ancient institutions and local authorities.

7 'Successful' in the sense of the adverse possessor actually acquiring title.

11.1   How is Adverse Possession Established? The Rules Common to Unregistered and Registered Land

Whether the claim for adverse possession is made in respect of unregistered land, or registered land subject to the old regime of the LRA 1925[8] or registered land subject to the new regime of the LRA 2002, the crucial question still remains: when will the possession of a trespasser be such as to establish a claim? Or, to put it another way, how is 'adverse possession' established factually? Fortunately, the rules about this are the same, irrespective of whether the land is of unregistered or registered title.[9]

The relevant principles are not found in statute, not even in the Limitation Act 1980 itself,[10] but have been developed through case law over generations. As judge-made law, these are flexible, changeable, and malleable and have not always been uniform in approach. Apparently inconsistent decisions are not difficult to find. This has the advantage that the substantive principles may respond to changing times, but the disadvantage of making it less easy to predict a court's decision. There is no doubt, for example, that some recent decisions have been 'adverse-possessor-friendly', in the sense that the courts no longer manifest an inbuilt hostility to the adverse possessor (e.g. *Port of London Authority* v. *Ashmore* (2009)[11]), although as a matter of law, adverse possession cannot operate in respect of land over which a public right of way exists.[12] On the other hand, it is now clear that the acquisition of title by adverse possession does not violate the human rights of the paper owner – see *Ofulue* v. *Bossert* (2008) and the acceptance in *Ofulue* of the authority of the ECHR decision in *Pye* v. *UK* (2008).[13]

Given the almost unlimited circumstances in which a claim of adverse possession could arise, it is a considerable advantage that the House of Lords has provided a framework within which cases can be decided. In *J A Pye Ltd* v. *Graham* (2002), the House sought to codify the principles of adverse possession in an attempt to bring some certainty and clarity to the law. Together with the earlier decision of the Court of Appeal in

---

8 Being land where the adverse possession was completed before the 13 October 2003, the date of entry into force of the LRA 2002.

9 See Schedule 6, paragraph 11 of the LRA 2002.

10 This governs the situation in unregistered land and, prior to the LRA 2002, the position in registered land also. It is considered more fully below.

11 In which the court held that it was possible to acquire title by adverse possession to that portion of river bed beneath a moored barge and on which the barge rested at low tide.

12 *Bromley LBC* v. *Morritt* (2000); *R (on the application of Smith)* v. *Land Registry (Peterborough Office)* (2009).

13 In which the Grand Chamber of the ECtHR decided that the law of adverse possession under the LRA 1925 (i.e. the law applicable to registered titles before the 2002 Act entered in to force) was human rights compliant. Therefore, so must be the law under the LRA 2002, given that it is less generous to adverse possessors. Contrast this with the High Court decision in *Beaulane Properties* v. *Palmer* (2005), which attacked the essence of the law of adverse possession on human rights grounds. *Beaulane* must now be regarded as unreliable, in the light of the decision in *Ofulue*. HM Land Registry no longer regards *Beaulane* as good law – see Land Registry Practice Guide No. 5, November 2008.

Buckinghamshire CC v. Moran (1990),[14] the judgment in *Graham* provides a definitive statement of the fundamentals of the modern law, without inhibiting its application to unique circumstances. The reasoning of the House in *Graham* forms the basis of the following discussion. In simple terms, adverse possession may be established by demonstrating the required degree of exclusive physical possession of the land, coupled with an intention to possess the land to the exclusion of all others, including the paper owner. It is, therefore, the conjunction of acts of possession with an *animus possidendi* (intention to possess) that establishes adverse possession.

11.1.1 An intention to possess

As recognised by Slade J in *Powell v. McFarlane* (1979), the requirement that the adverse possessor must 'intend' to possess the land adversely to the exclusion of all others to some extent is artificial. For example, some adverse possessors may appreciate fully that the land is not theirs and act deliberately to exclude the world; others may believe honestly that the land is theirs already, and so do not for one moment think they are excluding the 'true' owner; others still may have formulated no intention at all, but simply treat the land as their own because it is there. In other words, we are not looking here for 'intention' in the traditional legal sense of *mens rea*, either objectively or subjectively established. What is required is evidence that the adverse possessor, for whatever reason, had an intention to possess the land and put it to his own use, whether or not he also knew that some other person had a claim or right to the land.

Most importantly, as *Graham* makes clear, this means that the 'necessary intent is an intent to possess not to own and an intention to exclude the paper owner only so far as is reasonably possible'.[15] In other words, the claimant is not required to prove that he believed that the land was his, or wanted to acquire it, but, more simply, that he meant to exclude all others if he could.[16] This is crucial. It means that the focus is on the intentions of the claimant, not the landowner. Consequently, it is immaterial whether the claimant was aware that the landowner had an intention to use the land in the future that was consistent with the actual present use by the claimant – the landowner's state of mind is irrelevant. This makes clear, if it were needed, that the 'implied licence' theory (wherein the claimant is automatically deemed to have been given a licence to use the land simply because his actions were not contrary to an intended use by the landowner) is invalid and incorrect in law.[17] It is, in the language of Lord Brown-Wilkinson, 'heretical and wrong'. As much was settled by *Moran*, and although there may be occasions for the *genuine*

---

14 In turn, this decision owed much to the earlier remarkable judgment of Slade J in *Powell v. McFarlane* (1977), which was explicitly approved in *Moran* and in *Graham*. According to Lord Browne-Wilkinson in *Graham*, 'the principles set out by Slade J as subsequently approved by the Court of Appeal in *Buckinghamshire County Council v. Moran* [1990] Ch 623 cannot be improved upon'.

15 Lord Browne-Wilkinson at [46]. Or, in the words of Slade J in *Powell*, 'an intention, in one's own name and on one's own behalf, to exclude the world at large, including the owner with the paper title if he be not himself the possessor, so far as is reasonably practicable and so far as the processes of the law will allow'.

16 *Williams v. Jones* (2003).

17 See also Limitation Act 1980, Schedule 1, paragraph 8(4).

implication of such licence, Lord Bowne-Wilkinson in *Graham* also makes it clear that this will be exceptional. As he says, if the claimant:

> is aware of a special purpose for which the paper owner uses or intends to use the land and the use made by the adverse possessor does not conflict with that use, that may provide some support for a finding as a question of fact that the adverse possessor had no intention to possess the land in the ordinary sense but only an intention to occupy it until needed by the paper owner. For myself I think there will be few occasions in which such inference could be properly drawn in cases where the true owner has been physically excluded from the land. But it remains a possible, if improbable, inference in some cases.[18]

Likewise, the intention to possess[19] can still exist even if the claimant would have been prepared to accept permission to use the land had it been offered,[20] or even if he would have quitted possession if required.[21] Such willingness is not inconsistent with a current intention to possess even if any subsequent actual acceptance of permission (e.g. acceptance of a lease or licence) would destroy the intention. A later admission of the landowner's title by the claimant is not inconsistent with the claimant having an intention to possess in the meantime. This was, in fact, the situation in *Graham* itself, in which Graham had made it clear that he would have accepted a grazing licence from Pye, but as one was not offered, Graham's current intention to possess the land until a licence was offered (and accepted) was enough to secure title by adverse possession. Conversely, however, although the adverse possessor's mere knowledge of another's claim to the land is no bar to adverse possession,[22] a belief that the land is *currently* possessed with the permission of the paper owner is fatal. This was the case in *Clowes Developments* v. *Walters* (2005), in which the claimant's belief – even if mistaken – that the land was held under a licence meant that they simply could not have the relevant intention to possess. Awareness that the land belongs to another cannot prevent the existence of a current intention to possess (*Blackburn*), but an acknowledgment that the land belongs to another will do so.[23] Put simply, you cannot intend to treat the land as within *your* ultimate control if you believe that you are permitted to be there by the owner. Finally, as also demonstrated by *Graham*, if the alleged adverse possessor once occupied the land with the permission of the paper owner, any continued possession after that permission has ended (e.g. the lease or licence has ended but the claimant stays in possession) may be sufficient to support a claim of adverse possession if the *animus possidendi* is shown.

It will be appreciated immediately that this intention to possess might be difficult to prove. There are few difficulties if the alleged adverse possessor has acknowledged the true

---

18   A case that comes close is *Stadium Capital* v. *St. Marylebone Property Company plc* (2009) – adverse possession denied. However, there may have been an express licence in this case.

19   Sometimes known as the *animus possidendi*.

20   So, in *Lambeth LBC* v. *Blackburn* (2001), Blackburn was able to demonstrate an intention to possess the land – through clear acts of possession – even though he knew that the land was another's and would have accepted a permission (a lease) if one had been offered.

21   *J Alston & Sons Ltd* v. *BOCM Pauls Ltd* (2008).

22   The contrary view in *Batt* v. *Adams* (2001) cannot be good law after *Graham*.

23   *BRB (Residuary)* v. *Cully* (2001).

owner's title in some way[24] or, conversely, if the adverse possessor has placed a sign at the entrance to the land saying 'Keep Out: Private Property'. Most cases are, however, somewhere in between. *Moran* itself establishes that the actions of the adverse possessor in seeking to assert physical possession of the land also may give a strong indication as to whether the necessary intention exists. This must be correct, for it is wrong to regard the question of intention and of physical possession as being entirely separate and disconnected. They are part and parcel of the same inquiry: that is, has the claimant established adverse possession? So, enclosing land by a fence may constitute both the act of possession and demonstrate the intention to possess (*Moran*), as might changing locks to a flat (*Blackburn*) or grazing animals within an enclosed field (*Graham*), and the burden of proving the intention may be lighter in cases in which the true owner has, to the knowledge of the adverse possessor, abandoned the land (*Minchinton*). It is clear, then, that unequivocal conduct in relation to acts of possession on the land is the best evidence of an intention to possess. Such acts may need to be more forceful where the land was once occupied with permission, but it will be a question of degree in each case.

11.1.2 Physical possession of the land

As well as demonstrating an intention to possess the land, the adverse possessor must also demonstrate a physical assumption of possession. Before the decision in *Graham*, much academic and judicial ink had been spilt in trying to determine in what circumstances possession could be deemed to have been taken and when it also was 'adverse' to the paper owner. So, there was much discussion of the apparent differences between discontinuance of possession by the paper owner followed by possession by the claimant, and dispossession of the paper caused by the possession of the claimant. However, in *Graham*, Lord Browne-Wilkinson explained why too much analysis was a bad thing. In his view, 'much confusion and complication would be avoided if reference to adverse possession were to be avoided so far as possible . . . The question is simply whether the defendant squatter has dispossessed the paper owner by going into ordinary possession of the land for the requisite period without the consent of the owner'. In other words, we should not seek to overconceptualise what is 'adverse' and what is not, but ask ourselves the simple ordinary question: is the claimant in possession of the land without the permission of the landowner?

Seen in this light, factual possession means a sufficient degree of physical custody and control for one's own use. It is, in essence, a matter that must depend on the circumstances of each case, the particular nature of the land and the manner in which that land is commonly used.[25] The ultimate touchstone is, in the words of Slade J in *Powell*, whether 'the alleged possessor has been dealing with the land in question as an occupying owner might have been expected to deal with it and that no-one else has done so'. Thus, the taking of possession might reside in a series of events,[26] or some one-off activity that is maintained thereafter.[27] It is not necessary for the paper owner to be aware that they have

---

24 For example, in *Archangel v. Lambeth LBC* (2000), the alleged adverse possessor had acknowledged the landowner's title in written correspondence. See also *Rehman v. Benfield* (2006).

25 This essentially is the test put forward in *Powell* and adopted in *Graham*.

26 The last of which crystallises the moment of possession.

27 For example, enclosing the land and gating it.

lost possession,[28] or for the paper owner to be inconvenienced by the acts of possession.[29] Moreover, whereas possession will not be presumed lightly from acts that are equivocal in nature or temporary in purpose, such as growing vegetables, or clearing land to enable one's children to play,[30] even small acts of custody and control might suffice if the land has been abandoned, is inaccessible by the paper owner or is of such quality that it does not readily admit of significant possessory acts.[31] Thus, in *Purbrick v. Hackney* (2003), the successful adverse possessor had cleared a derelict shed, erected a new roof and fitted a makeshift door and fixed a chain. He could have done more to secure possession, but he had done enough in all of the circumstances. Neither does it matter that the acts of possession serve a dual purpose, so long as they give custody and control to the claimant for his own benefit. For example, in *Minchinton*, the successful adverse possessor had fenced off part of the claimant's land, apparently to prevent the escape of her dogs, which she exercised on the land. Not surprisingly, counsel for the paper owner submitted that the enclosure was not designed to exclude the world, but to confine the animals, and should not, therefore, be regarded as possession. The court, however, took the view that it was the effect of the adverse possessor's actions that was important, not the motive with which they were done.[32] So, if the effect of the fence was to keep out the world as well as keep in the dogs, it amounted to physical possession. So it is then, that in answering the question 'has the adverse possessor demonstrated physical possession of the land?', in the sense of acquiring custody and control for his own use, it is the whole of his activity on the land that is relevant. The individual activities may seem equivocal or trivial, but if taken together they paint a picture of a person in control of land, they will amount to possession.

This clear and uncompromising approach to possession, affirmed by the House of Lords, lays to rest old ghosts and places the substantive principles of adverse possession on a firm footing. In *Beaulane Properties v. Palmer* (2005), Deputy Judge Strauss QC, sitting in the Chancery Division of the High Court, had sought to reintroduce a version of the 'heresy' rejected by the House of Lords in *Graham* as a means of dealing with an *apparent* inconsistency between the principles of adverse possession and human rights obligations guaranteed by the Human Rights Act 1998.[33] It is now clear, following the decision of the Grand Chamber of the European Court of Human Rights in *Pye v. UK* (2007), that the law of adverse possession as it

---

28 *Powell v. Mcfarlane* (1979).

29 *Treloar v. Nute* (1976).

30 *Techbild v. Chamberlain* (1969). In *Central Midlands Estates v. Leicester Dyers*, (2003), the parking of an unlimited number of cars on the land was not sufficient as it did not amount to enough control of the land to establish factual possession.

31 For example, one would not expect significant acts of possession on marshland, accessible only by boat: *Red House Farms v. Catchpole* (1977). See also *Williams v. Jones* (2003), in which grazing sheep on quarry land constituted sufficient acts of possession.

32 Of course, the adverse possessor was still required to demonstrate an intention to possess, although, in *Wreatham v. Ross* (2005), the court notes that the search for factual possession is more important than the question of whether the adverse possessor intended to exclude the paper owner.

33 The issue turned on adverse possession under the old law of the LRA 1925. The judge in *Beualane* took the view that the new mechanisms of the LRA 2002 whereby the registered proprietor did not automatically lose title (in fact, he is very likely to retain it) meant that the LRA 2002 was consistent with human rights principles. This must be correct – see *Pye v. UK* (2007).

applies to claims under the LRA 1925[34] (and therefore to claims to unregistered title) is consistent with human rights law, in particular with Article 1 of Protocol 1 to the Convention. The law of adverse possession is a proportionate and legitimate response to a public interest concerning the need to limit claims in relation to land. Consequently, there is no need to 'reinterpret' principles of adverse possession in order to make them human rights compliant (because they already are), and the gloss placed on the *Graham* principle by *Beaulane* is no longer good law. In *Ofulue v. Bossert* (2008), the Court of Appeal confirmed that principles of adverse possession were, *as a matter of principle*, compliant with human rights law and thus a landowner could not seek to challenge a loss of title on human rights grounds because of his own particular circumstances. The law is, therefore, as that stated in *Pye v. Graham*, and this is now the view taken by HM Land Registry. Indeed, this is consistent with the general approach of the House of Lords to the relationship between property law and human rights: see *Harrow London Borough Council v. Qazi* and *Doherty v. Birmingham City Council* (2008).[35]

Assuming that the claimant has established both an intention to possess and factual possession of the land under the *Graham* rules, what does this mean? The answer is that it may mean much, particularly in unregistered land, or it may in the end mean very little, particularly in registered land. However, without establishing this evidential base for adverse possession there can be no claim at all, and many cases fall at this hurdle before consideration is ever given to what happens next. In fact, 'what happens next' depends on whether the adverse possession has been evidentially established against an unregistered or registered title.

11.2 The Basic Principle of Adverse Possession in Unregistered Land

The ability of an adverse possessor to acquire a better title than the paper owner to unregistered land is based on the principle of limitation of actions. In simple terms,

---

34 Being where the adverse possession was completed before the entry into force of the LRA 2002. This means, almost certainly, that the law applicable under the LRA 2002 is also human rights compliant.

35 In *Qazi*, Lord Scott decided that principles of human rights law were not engaged at all if a recognised property claim was being enforced, while Lord Millet and Lord Hope decided that the enforcement of a proprietary right could not, as a matter of principle, cause a violation of the Convention. The minority (Lord Bingham and Lord Steyn) disagreed, and felt that there might be occasions (albeit rare) on which the enforcement of a recognised property right might call for an examination of compliance with the Convention. *Qazi* attracted strong criticism because it essentially ruled out human rights issues in private property matters except in the most extreme circumstances. In *Connors v. UK* (2005), the European Court of Human Rights had decided that the enforcement of a property right by a local authority against a group of gypsies did indeed violate the Convention, and this appeared to contradict the rationale on which *Qazi* was based. However, in *Price v. Leeds City Council; Kay v. Lambeth* (2006), the House of Lords again confirmed that the enforcement of a property right valid under English law would not violate the Convention, irrespective of the personal circumstances of the 'victim', unless the law on which the enforcement was based was itself flawed. This has been confirmed again by the House of Lords in *Doherty v. Birmingham City Council* (2008), effectively disregarding the intervening ECtHR decision in *McCann v. UK* (2008) on the basis that, in *McCann*, the ECtHR fundamentally misunderstood the nature of possession proceedings in UK law. Note, however, the Supreme Court is due to revisit the question again in the summer of 2010 when *Manchester City Council v. Pinnock* will be heard by a nine-judge bench.

'limitation of actions' expresses the idea that a person must sue for an alleged wrong within a specified period of time from the moment the alleged wrong took place.[36] In the context of adverse possession of unregistered land, this means that a person (i.e. the paper owner of the land) may be 'statute-barred' from bringing a claim against the adverse possessor to recover possession of their land after the period of limitation has passed. Thus, as against the adverse possessor, the paper owner has no means of recovering the land, and so the adverse possessor has 'acquired' a better title to the land. To look at it slightly differently, if an unregistered estate owner sleeps on his rights, those rights will be extinguished in the sense that a court will not enforce them against the person actually in possession of the land. In this sense, therefore, adverse possession operates negatively: it prevents an estate owner from suing on his rights and operates to extinguish his title. Conventionally, this is taken to mean that adverse possession does not actually give a title to the adverse possessor but, by virtue of the doctrine of relativity of title, the person now in actual possession may have the best claim to the land, and may thereby become 'owner' of it to all intents and purposes. Importantly, the idea of limitation of actions has no application to land of registered title governed by the LRA 2002[37] where it has been replaced by a statutory mechanism that protects the registered proprietor in all but a limited number of situations.[38]

11.2.1 The limitation period for unregistered land

If the essence of adverse possession of unregistered land is that a paper owner will be prevented from bringing an action to recover land against the person in actual possession of it, it is crucial to know exactly when this 'bar' will come into effect. In other words, how long must an adverse possessor be in adverse possession before the paper owner is statute-barred from bringing an action? How long is the limitation period for unregistered land? It should come as no surprise to learn, first of all, that the limitation period for actions concerning land depends on the circumstances of each particular case. Fortunately, there are some general rules.

First, in the great majority of cases, the limitation period will be 12 years from the moment of adverse possession of the unregistered title by the adverse possessor (section 15 of the Limitation Act 1980). This is the normal period of limitation for actions concerning land but, of course, it has no application to land of registered title governed by the LRA 2002. Second, where the paper owner of the land is a 'sole' charitable corporation (such as a bishop), the period of limitation is 30 years from the moment of adverse possession (Schedule 1, paragraph 10 of the Limitation Act 1980). Third, where the paper owner of the land is the Crown, the period of limitation is 30 years from the moment of adverse possession (Schedule 1, paragraph 11 of the Limitation Act 1980). Fourth, if land is owned by someone for life, with remainder in fee simple to another person (for example, to A for life, remainder in fee simple to B), then the limitation period is either adverse possession of six years from the date at which the interest in remainder

---

36 See currently the Limitation Act 1980.

37 It does apply to registered land where the adverse possession was completed prior to the entry into force of the LRA 2002.

38 See section 11.4 below.

falls into possession (i.e. the death of the life tenant), if 12 years or more already have been completed against the life tenant; or adverse possession of 12 years from the time the life tenant was dispossessed, whichever is the longer (section 15 of the Limitation Act 1980). So, assuming land is held by A for life, remainder to B, adverse possession of 12 years or more against A will extinguish A's interest, and a further six years will be necessary on the death of A also to extinguish B's interest. Fifth, if the current paper owner is a tenant of the land under a lease, the period of limitation against the tenant is 12 years.[39] Expiry of the period will, therefore, extinguish the tenant's title against the adverse possessor. Importantly, however, extinguishment of the tenant's title has no immediate effect on the title of the reversioner (i.e. usually the freehold landlord), simply because, until the end of the lease, the landlord has no right to possess the land at all. Therefore, time does not begin to run against the landlord until the original term of the lease expires (or, possibly, is otherwise brought to an end: see section 11.2.2.3 below). When the original term of the lease expires, and assuming 12 years' adverse possession against the tenant, the landlord will have a further 12 years to recover the land (section 15 and Schedule 1, paragraph 4 of the Limitation Act 1980). Obviously, it is crucial for the application of these rules to know when the lease has ended. This will usually be the expiry of the stated term (or statutory extension thereof), and, for a periodic tenancy, this is treated as the end of the last period for which rent was paid. Note, however, that although the normal rule is that the land-lord's right of action against the adverse possessor arises when the original term of the lease ends, there is an exception to this. So, if the lease itself gives the tenant an option to renew the lease when it expires, the adverse possessor who has evicted that tenant also may rely on the right to renew to defeat the landlord's claim to possession.[40] The landlord (and any person claiming through the landlord, such as an alleged new tenant) must, it seems, wait until the period given under the right to renew also has expired. The rationale is that, as the landlord could not have evicted the original tenant (because of the option to renew), so the landlord cannot evict the adverse possessor who has displaced that tenant. This is logical, but it does give the lie to the idea that the adverse possessor's title is completely unconnected to that of the paper owner he dispossesses.

Whatever period of limitation is applicable, it starts to run against the relevant paper owner of the unregistered title from the first moment of adverse possession. Consequently, if the alleged adverse possessor never, in fact, has been in adverse possession, time cannot start against the owner, and he cannot lose title. For example, in Smith v. Lawson (1997), the defendant had been given an occupation licence of the disputed land for life, and so her possession was not adverse. Although this meant that the claimant had no right to recover the land during the defendant's life, it also meant that the defendant had no claim in adverse possession. However, once time has started, it is sufficient to establish that the full period has been completed at any time before the paper owner seeks to enforce his title to the land. It is not necessary to establish that the adverse possessor is in adverse possession at the moment the action for recovery is commenced, provided that the period has by then been completed.[41] For example, if S, the adverse possessor, has adversely possessed A's land for 12 years, but has left possession before A commences an action to recover the land,

---

39 Chung Ping Kwan v. Lam Island Development Co (1996).

40 Chung v. Lam (1996).

41 Hounslow v. Minchinton (1997).

A's title will be barred and he will be unable to recover the land from whomever now is in possession. A's title to the unregistered land has been extinguished, and the person in possession has the best *relative* title. Of course, if S has left the land and nobody is in possession, then A may retake possession, but will, himself, have to wait a further 12 years before being confident of defeating a returning S. Note, however, that the issue is complicated if the paper owner applies for first registration of title after the adverse possessor has completed 12 years' adverse possession, In that case, at first registration of title, the registered proprietor (against whom adverse possession has run for the limitation period) is bound only by adverse possession of which he has notice, or by the rights of an adverse possession as an overriding interest if (but only if) the adverse possessor is in actual occupation – section 11 of the LRA 2002.[42] This means that, absent notice, an adverse possessor going out of possession, even after completing the relevant period of adverse possession against an unregistered title, will have no rights against the first registered proprietor.[43]

11.2.2   Stopping the clock of limitation for unregistered land

Assuming that the land is unregistered land, if the claimant is in adverse possession of the land, this means that the paper owner has the limitation period (usually 12 years) to assert their paramount title and recover possession. It is thus important to determine what action may 'stop the clock' of limitation and so prevent the adverse possessor from completing the required period. If the clock is stopped successfully, then the paper owner's title is secure unless, of course, the adverse possessor beings to possess afresh – in which case the clock of limitation starts afresh.

1   A *successful* action for possession (or an action seeking a declaration of title) by the paper owner before expiry of the period will necessarily 'stop the clock' and any claim of adverse possession will have to begin again.[44] In this respect, a letter sent by the paper owner merely asserting title is not sufficient to stop the clock,[45] nor in most cases is the mere issuing of a claim for possession.[46]

2   Sections 29 and 30 of the Limitation Act 1980 provide that an adverse possessor cannot succeed if they have 'acknowledged' the paper owner's title before[47] the expiry of the limitation period. This may be by the payment of rent or by a written acknowledgment of title. What amounts to a written acknowledgment of tile is,

---

42 See Schedule 1, paragraph 2 of the LRA 2002 for interests that override at first registration.

43 It remains unclear whether the adverse possessor who has completed the 12-year period prior to first registration but whose interest does not override under Schedule 1 could apply successfully for rectification of the register. It seems unlikely, given the effect of section 11 of the LRA 2002, but the point is undecided. We should not forget, however, that the occasions on which the first registered proprietor does not have notice of the adverse possession *and* where the adverse possessor is not in actual occupation will be rare indeed.

44 This is so even if the proceedings are not possession proceedings, provided that the court has determined that the paper owner has title: *Higgs v. Leshel Maryas Investment Co Ltd* (2009).

45 *Moran.*

46 *Markfield Investments Ltd v. Evans* (2001).

47 Note, however, the decision in *Colchester Borough Council v. Smith* (1992): see section 11.2.3 below.

however, not always clear, and it seems that every case falls to be determined on its own facts. Obviously, a signed document will be entirely sufficient. In *Ofulue v. Bossert* (2009), the House of Lords determined that a statement in court pleadings could amount to an acknowledgment of title for the purpose of section 29 of the Limitation Act 1980, but also that any written acknowledgment usually operated only at the time it was given and did not amount to a continuing acknowledgment. Thus, if the adverse possessor continued to assert adverse possession after giving a written acknowledgment of title, time would begin to run afresh from the date of the acknowledgment and the adverse possessor would acquire title if a 'new' period of limitation was completed – as in *Ofulue* itself. Further, as also made clear in *Ofulue*, if what appears to be a written acknowledgment of title is made in correspondence between the paper owner and the adverse possessor that is formally 'without prejudice' (that is, usually when the parties negotiate without meaning to affect or compromise their strict legal position), then it does not operate as an acknowledgment in law and may be discounted.

3   It *may* be sufficient for the paper owner to retake physical possession of the land himself before the expiry of the limitation period. However, such self-help is not always successful and may attract the attention of the criminal law. As *Smith v. Waterman* (2003) illustrates, the claimant's adverse possession cannot be interrupted *merely* by the paper owner going on to the land – otherwise, a simple entry on the land at some time by the paper owner would always stop the limitation clock. Indeed, as the judge said in *Waterman*, factual possession (by the claimant) does not require continuous physical occupation, for much depends on the nature of the land itself. Consequently, recovery of possession through self-help by the landowner in order to 'stop the clock' must also be such as to demonstrate a retaking of custody and control of the land.

11.2.3   The effect of a successful claim of adverse possession in unregistered land

This section deals with the effects of a successful claim of adverse possession on land of unregistered title: that is, when the evidential base of adverse possession has been proved and the limitation period has expired. In these cases, it should come as no surprise to learn that the effects of a successful claim of adverse possession vary according to the perspective of the parties involved. In particular, the effect on tenants has attracted much interest in recent years.

11.2.3.1   *Effect on the paper owner*

It is settled law that once the limitation period has run its course in respect of unregistered land, both the paper owner's right to sue and their title are extinguished by operation of statute (section 17 of the Limitation Act 1980). After this date, the conventional wisdom is that no acknowledgment of the paper owner's title, written or otherwise, and no payment, rent or other sum can revive the title.[48] This should be uncontroversial, as it is simply the

---

48 *Nicholson v. England* (1926).

consequence of the application of the Limitation Act 1980 and an expression of its underlying policy. However, the Court of Appeal has held, in *Colchester BC v. Smith* (1992), that in
some circumstances a written acknowledgment of the paper owner's title by the adverse
possessor, given *after* the period of limitation has ended, can be enough to prevent the
adverse possessor relying on adverse possession when faced with an action for possession
by the paper owner. This interesting decision appears to be based on an application of the
estoppel doctrine, in that the adverse possessor is estopped from denying the paper
owner's title by the written acknowledgment, freely given. Surprisingly, the court offers
no convincing reason why the Limitation Act 1980 should be ignored in this fashion,
or even why the paper owner deserves to benefit from an estoppel: after all, the paper
owner has slept on his rights, and why should a court of equity now come running to his
aid? Neither does the court offer any reason why *Nicholson v. England* (1926) can be ignored
(where an acknowledgment after expiry of the period was not sufficient to prevent
adverse possession) and, in this sense, the decision in *Smith* might be regarded as *per
incuriam*. However, at present, the *Colchester* decision appears to be authority for the proposition that a *bona fide* compromise of a dispute between two persons (i.e. the paper owner
and adverse possessor), both of whom had legal advice, should be upheld on public
policy grounds, even if the 12-year period of limitation has run. This is supported by the
decision in the *Trustees in the Charity of Sir John Morden v. Mayrick* (2007), in which the claimant
was not permitted to disavow a compromise agreement relating to ownership of land (on
the ground that he had in fact completed adverse possession prior to conclusion of the
agreement), because he had entered into the agreement freely and had raised no argument
based on adverse possession at the time. In other words, a man will be bound by his
contract.[49]

11.2.3.2   *Effect on the adverse possessor: Freeholds*

The traditional doctrinal position is that a successful plea of adverse possession against
unregistered land does not transfer the paper owner's title to the adverse possessor. It operates negatively to prevent the paper owner suing the adverse possessor (or person now in
possession: for example, a purchaser from the adverse possessor) and extinguishes the paper
title (section 17 of the Limitation Act 1980). There is no conveyance of the land from paper
owner to adverse possessor. Moreover, because the adverse possessor is not a purchaser from
(or even transferee from) the paper owner, the adverse possessor takes the land subject to all
pre-existing proprietary obligations, whether these are registered as Land Charges or not. So,
for example, an adverse possessor will be bound by the burden of unprotected equitable
easements and unprotected restrictive covenants (as well as those protected as Land Charges)
because the adverse possessor can never be 'equity's darling'. Yet, it must be the case that an

---

49 In the context of adverse possession, this seemingly unobjectionable principle does not recognise that there is also a
policy consideration – recognised and effected by Act of Parliament, no less – to the effect that sleeping on one's
rights deprives a person of those rights. The judgment in *Smith* fails to explain why a contract between the parties can
override the express provisions of an Act of Parliament. Although some commentators accept that, in principle,
contracting out of the Limitation Act 1980 should be possible, it is submitted that this should not be permitted, save
in the most exceptional circumstances. The policy argument is more justifiable in the *Mayrick* case because, prior to
the compromise agreement, adverse possession had not been an issue between the parties.

adverse possessor acquires *something* as a result of a successful adverse possession because the adverse possessor may go on to deal with the land as if it were his own. He may sell it, lease it, devise it (i.e. leave it by will), give it away, grant easements over it and generally do those things that an estate owner might do. In other words, a successful adverse possessor does acquire a valuable asset. How, in practice, does this work?

As noted above, in unregistered land, the adverse possessor does not take, and is not treated as taking, a conveyance from the paper owner. Consequently, the paper owner has a bundle of worthless title documents and the adverse possessor has no proof of title at all. Yet, in practice, an adverse possessor with proof of established adverse possession usually can find a willing purchaser and will convey the land by deed to that purchaser. This new deed will be the first evidence of the adverse possessor's title and first evidence of that of the new purchaser.[50] Necessarily, of course, the adverse possessor will not be able to make out a good 'root of title',[51] but the purchaser may be happy with a statutory declaration of good title, supported perhaps by 'title insurance'.[52] In effect then, a 'new' title is generated by the conveyancing process and this title will be confirmed and guaranteed when the transferee (from the adverse possessor) successfully applies for first registration of title under the LRA 2002.

11.2.3.3   *Effect on the adverse possessor: Leaseholds*

The traditional doctrine that there is no conveyance of the paper owner's unregistered estate to the adverse possessor has some unusual consequences in the context of leaseholds. It will be remembered that a successful 12 years' adverse possession against a tenant extinguishes only the tenant's estate, and that the landlord has a further period of 12 years after the end of the original period of the lease in which to eject the adverse possessor before he also finds his title extinguished. This is perfectly proper because, as noted above, time can only run against a person when he has a right to recover land, and a landlord only has such a right when the lease expires. However, while it is true that the tenant has lost his estate by adverse possession *vis-à-vis* the adverse possessor, it is also true that the tenant remains as tenant *vis-à-vis* the landlord for the entire duration of the original lease.[53] Title is relative. So, during the currency of the lease, the landlord can bring forfeiture proceedings against the tenant (for, say, non-payment of rent), even though the adverse possessor is in possession of the land under a successful adverse possession. The effect of such forfeiture is to terminate the lease and bring forward the landlord's right to eject the adverse possessor![54] Note, however, that the converse of the rule – that the ejected tenant remains

---

50 The purchaser will then use this deed and the pre-existing claim of adverse possession to apply for first registration of title under the LRA 2002.

51 See Chapter 3.

52 This is an insurance policy, paid for by the adverse possessor and purchased from a specialist company, guaranteeing compensation if the adverse possessor's title should prove to be defective. It is very common in legal systems that do not have a State-backed guarantee of title.

53 See also *Chan Suk Yin v. Harvest Good Development Ltd* (2005), per Lord Hoffmann, giving judgment in the Hong Kong Court of Final Appeal.

54 In which proceedings the adverse possessor has no right to apply for relief, having no rights under the lease – *Tickner v. Buzzacott* (1965).

'tenant' of the landlord – is that the adverse possessor is not to be regarded as the tenant, nor an assignee of the tenant, so cannot be liable on any leasehold covenants save those enforceable as restrictive covenants under the rule in *Tulk v. Moxhay* (1848).[55]

Although apparently complicated, the picture painted above is quite simple: the adverse possessor has extinguished the tenant's title as far as he is concerned, but the tenant remains the tenant of the landlord. The difficulties arise when the ejected tenant seeks to manipulate his continuing relationship with the landlord to defeat the adverse possessor. For example, we have just noted that the landlord may forfeit the lease in an action against the dispossessed tenant, thereby bringing forward the landlord's right of action against the adverse possessor. In other words, the landlord does not have to wait until the lease term has expired because he has terminated the term in virtue of his rights as landlord. What, however, if the tenant surrenders his lease to the landlord, despite having 'lost' title *vis-à-vis* the adverse possessor? Does this also terminate the lease and bring forward the landlord's right of action? In unregistered land, the case of *Fairweather v. St Marylebone Property Co Ltd* (1963) provides a clear answer. In that case, a tenant against whom adverse possession had been completed successfully surrendered the lease to the landlord, and the House of Lords held that this was effective to terminate the lease. In other words, the lease was brought to an end by a person (the ejected tenant) who still had an estate *vis-à-vis* the landlord. Moreover, given that the lease was now terminated, the adverse possessor had no right to remain on the land in the face of an action by the landlord, because the landlord's right to possession was now active. As a matter of strict logic and theory, this is difficult to fault. However, on a common-sense view, it is difficult to see why the ejected tenant should have the power to surrender a lease that, to all intents and purposes, is an empty shell. The inequity to the adverse possessor is even more apparent if the landlord, after having evicted the adverse possessor, regrants a new lease to the ejected tenant![56] Despite powerful criticisms of this rule judicially and academically, it now seems likely that it will not be overruled. Of course, it applies only in the context of unregistered title and unregistered title is rapidly decreasing in significance.

11.2.4   The substantive nature of the adverse possessor's rights prior to completing the period of limitation in unregistered land

Pending completion of the period of limitation in respect of unregistered land, the adverse possessor is taken to have certain rights in the land, even though these can be completely

---

55 See Chapter 8.

56 Before the LRA 2002 made comparisons between registered and unregistered land pointless, the position in registered land under the LRA 1925 was different from that pertaining in unregistered land. In *Central London Commercial Estates Ltd v. Kato Kagaku Ltd* (1998), the ejected tenant surrendered its lease to the freeholder, and the registered title to that lease was closed. The freeholder sought to evict the adverse possessor before the lease had expired. However, the court held that the effect of section 75 of the LRA 1925 (which was then operative) was to ensure that the tenant's interest was held on trust for the adverse possessor, and that the tenant could not surrender after the period of limitation had run. In effect, the court held that the tenant's interest in the lease did pass to the adverse possessor, and the adverse possessor could remain on the land for the remainder of the term. Sedley J goes so far as to say that there was, in reality, a statutory conveyance of the original lease with benefits and burdens intact.

defeated by the paper owner recovering possession within the limitation period. Thus, an adverse possessor awaiting completion of the period may transfer such rights as they do have (e.g. two years' worth of possession, ten years' worth, etc.) to another person either by will or *inter vivos* (*Asher* v. *Whitlock* (1865)). The period so transferred may then be added to any period successfully completed by the legatee/assignee of the adverse possessor's rights in order to make up a total of 12 years' worth of adverse possession. The same is true if one adverse possessor dispossess another: the current adverse possessor is able to claim the combined period of adverse possession in respect of the paper owner.[57]

11.3   Adverse Possession under the Land Registration Act 1925

If the land is registered title, but is governed by the Land Registration Act 1925 (i.e. adverse possession was completed before the entry into force of the LRA 2002) the same limitation period applies as in land of unregistered title; that is, usually adverse possession of 12 years. Similarly, the same principles apply when considering whether the paper owner has managed to stop the clock of limitation. This means that a person who has *completed* 12 years' adverse possession before 12 October 2003 (the date of entry into force of the LRA 2002) is *entitled* to be registered as proprietor of the land.[58] Pending such registration, the land is held on trust by the registered proprietor for the successful adverse possessor.[59] This entitlement to be registered is enforceable against a purchaser of the land from the registered proprietor, who by definition is not in possession of title if he (the adverse possessor) is able to claim an interest that overrides by reason of his discoverable actual occupation of the land within the meaning of Schedule 3, paragraph 2 of the LRA 2002.[60] If the transferee is not a purchaser, the right to be registered is binding under the basic priority rule found in section 28 of the LRA 2002.[61]

Importantly, if the adverse possessor had not fully completed 12 years' adverse possession before the entry into force of the 2002 Act, his situation is governed in its entirety by the 2002 scheme. This is so even if the period of adverse possession was nearing completion on the day the Act entered into force. For example, if a claimant had completed 11 years' adverse possession on the day the LRA 2002 entered into force, they do not acquire a right to be registered with the title when 12 years have passed. In all such cases, the period of adverse possession (being less than 12 years on 13 October 2003) may count

---

57 In a contest between the adverse possessors, the current possessor can claim only that time which has elapsed since dispossessing the previous possessor.

58 Schedule 12, paragraph 18 of the LRA 2002.

59 Section 75 of the LRA 1925.

60 Sections 29 and 30 of the LRA 2002.

61 If an adverse possessor who is entitled to be registered (having completed 12 years' adverse possession before the entry into force of the LRA 2002) does not have priority over a purchaser (i.e. they are not in discoverable actual occupation), they lose their claim. Note, however, that it has been argued that the adverse possessor in this position may claim rectification of the register, but this would rather seem to defeat the point of the priority rules found in sections 28 and 29 of the LRA 2002.

for the relevant period under the LRA 2002, but as we shall see this is very far from giving them any right to title of the land. Consequently, the traditional rules of adverse possession will apply to registered land only in so far as the 12-year period of limitation is completed before 13 October 2003.

11.4 Adverse Possession under the Land Registration Act 2002

Most of the current case law in respect of adverse possession deals with either land of unregistered title or claims to adverse possession under the LRA 1925. However, while the law concerning *how* adverse possession is established applies just as much to registered land as it does to unregistered, the scheme for regulating the *effects* of adverse possession on land whose title is registered is now radically different, having been modified substantially by the LRA 2002.[62] This scheme, which is now fully in force, will come to govern the vast majority of claims of adverse possession in the future. It is premised on the fundamental belief that a State-guaranteed title, readily provable from a title register, should not be lost because of the 'mere' possession of a stranger, irrespective of how long that possession lasts. Similarly, it is believed that a system of e-conveyancing can be effective only if the title register can be regarded in the vast majority of cases as conclusive of ownership. Anything that detracts from this – such as title through adverse possession – is an anathema to e-conveyancing and should be severely circumscribed, if not removed altogether.

11.4.1 The basic principle

Under the LRA 2002, there is no period of limitation against a registered title and no sense in which a registered proprietor can lose title *merely* because another person has adversely possessed the land for a fixed period of time (section 96 of the LRA 2002). Consequently, even if factual possession plus an intention to possess is established, no period of possession *of itself* can deprive the registered proprietor of his title. However, the 2002 Act recognises that claims of adverse possession are a fact of life and that merely removing a period of limitation will not stop disputes between persons over title to land. Consequently, in place of a limitation principle *per se*, the 2002 Act establishes an application procedure whereby the adverse possessor may apply to the registrar to be registered as proprietor of the title and this application then triggers the statutory scheme spelt out in Schedule 6 to the Act. In this sense, the onus of making a claim to a registered title shifts squarely on to the shoulders of the adverse possessor and the registered owner need do nothing to maintain his title save take action when (and if) the adverse possessor applies for registration. A registered proprietor does not, therefore, have to remain vigilant in the vindication of his title but can rely on this new system to alert him to any adverse claim, a claim to which he can then respond to safeguard his interest.

---

62 Note, however, that even under the LRA 2002, the old limitation period applies in respect of a claim by one squatter to have ousted another squatter. This must be so as the ousted squatter has no registered title.

11.4.2   The statutory scheme

Under the 2002 Act, where a person claims to have completed at least ten years' adverse possession,[63] that person may apply to the registrar to be registered as proprietor. If the registrar takes the view that the application discloses an arguable case for registration,[64] the application will cause a notice to be sent to the current registered proprietor (and certain other persons: Schedule 6, paragraph 2 of the LRA 2002). On receipt of this notice, the registered proprietor has the choice of threes responses.[65] Option one is that he may consent to the application, in which case the adverse possessor will be registered as proprietor. No doubt, this will not be commonplace. The second option is that the registered proprietor may object to the application. If he objects, the application for registration cannot be finalised until the objection has been dealt with. In the absence of a negotiated settlement, the matter may be referred to the adjudicator for decision. The nature of the objection is likely to be that the factual basis of the claim of adverse possession is false, but even if this is the case, the registered proprietor may well be advised both to object and to serve a counternotice (see option three, considered below), because the counternotice procedure allows the registered proprietor to defeat the application *whether or not* the factual basis for the claim of adverse possession exists. Consequently, this second response, simple objection by the registered proprietor, is likely to occur only if the registered proprietor clearly can defeat the factual claim for possession or is unable to plead the benefit of the 'two-year rule' considered below.[66]

The third option open to the registered proprietor, and the most likely to be pursued, is to serve a counternotice (either with or without an objection under option 2). This counternotice requires the registrar to deal with the application under paragraph 5 of Schedule 6 to the 2002 Act. In essence, this means that, irrespective of whether the factual basis for adverse possession is made out, the adverse possessor *cannot* be entered as the new registered proprietor unless any one of three exceptional grounds is made out. Moreover, and most importantly, assuming none of these grounds to be made out (and we must await litigation for their meaning to be elucidated – see below), the registered proprietor will then have two further years following the application by the adverse possessor to recover possession of the land. Recovery of possession during this two-year period of grace

---

63 Thus there is a ten-year threshold, but it is not a period of limitation, merely the point before which an application cannot be made. The existence of adverse possession for ten years is to be assessed by reference to the traditional principles explained in *Pye v. Graham* and discussed above in the context of unregistered land – Schedule 6, paragraph 11 of the LRA 2002.

64 That is, that adverse possession under the substantive law arguably has been established. The registrar is likely to reject applications only in the most obvious cases.

65 Should the registered proprietor not respond to the notice within the prescribed time limit, the applicant (the adverse possessor) may be registered as proprietor. See the preliminary issue in *Baxter v. Mannion*. Consequently, the scheme assumes that the registered proprietor actually receives the notice from HM Land Registry. If the address for service is the registered land itself, there is a danger that the adverse possessor will destroy the notice and so the proprietor may never be warned! This is a primary reason why registered proprietors should avail themselves of the opportunity of lodging more than one address for service of notices with HM Land Registry. If possible, this should include an email address.

66 This may be because the adverse possessor can claim the benefit of one of the exceptions to the two-year rule.

is as of right – i.e. simply because he is the owner – and is available irrespective of how long the adverse possessor has actually been in possession. If the registered proprietor does not so recover within these additional two years – possible, but unlikely – then the adverse possessor may reapply at the expiry of the two-year period and he will be entered as proprietor of the title.[67]

Clearly, this new scheme will have a dramatic effect on the frequency and success of claims of adverse possession. In essence, a registered proprietor will receive notice of any application by an adverse possessor to become the new proprietor and (putting aside consent and simple objection), unless one of the three exceptional grounds is made out, will have two years from that date to recover possession by normal court action. This action for possession will be successful simply by reason of the paper owner proving his title. No further reason need be given. It will require the minimum of effort and only the most indolent or uninterested proprietors are likely to fail to recover possession during the two-year period of grace. Moreover, this process will apply whether the adverse possessor applies for registration after ten years or 110 years: there is no period of limitation. So, if the adverse possessor makes no application for registration, or does so and is evicted (assuming the exceptions do not apply), the registered proprietor is safe. This explains why landowners with large and diverse land holdings – such as local authorities – are applying for first registration of title. It offers considerable protection against the claims of adverse possessors.

11.4.3   The exceptions

Given the robust protection offered to a registered proprietor by the LRA 2002, it is anticipated that most future litigation will concern the meaning of the exceptions listed in Schedule 6 to the Act. This is likely to be the real battleground. After all, if a registered proprietor can evict an adverse possessor within two years of the adverse possessor's application for registration even if the factual basis of adverse possession exists, plainly the adverse possessor will seek to rely, if at all possible, on the exceptions. It is only if the adverse possessor is able to establish adverse possession according to the substantive law *and* is able to rely on one of these exceptions, that the adverse possessor stands any realistic chance of being registered as proprietor consequent upon his application.[68]

The exceptional cases are listed in Schedule 6, paragraph 5 of the LRA 2002. These are where: first, it would be unconscionable for the current proprietor to dispossess the adverse possessor because of an estoppel and the circumstances are such that the adverse possessor ought to be registered; second, where the adverse possessor is 'for some other reason' entitled to be registered as proprietor; or third, where there is a boundary dispute concerning adjoining land and for at least ten years the applicant reasonably believed the disputed land to be his, provided that the disputed land had been registered land for more than one year prior to the application.

---

67 In such a case, the adverse possessor takes the land subject to any interests affecting the estate, except any registered charge (unless registration is because of the exceptional situations outlined above): Schedule 6, paragraph 9 of the LRA 2002.

68 Of course, the adverse possessor will also be successful if the registered proprietor does not respond to the notice, consents to the application or fails to recover possession within two years.

11.4.3.1 *Exception 1: Estoppel, unconscionability and 'ought to be registered'*

This first condition is meant to import substantive principles of proprietary estoppel into the law of adverse possession. This is perfectly consistent with the use of estoppel as a remedy for unconscionable conduct. It suggests that as well as establishing adverse possession (factual possession and intention) for at least ten years, the applicant must also show that he has detrimentally relied on some assurance by the registered proprietor in circumstances in which it would be unconscionable for the assurance to be withdrawn. The two examples given by HM Land Registry are where the squatter has built on the registered proprietor's land in the mistaken belief that he was the owner of it and the proprietor has knowingly acquiesced in his mistake, and where neighbours have entered into an informal sale agreement for valuable consideration by which one agrees to sell the land to the other. The 'buyer' pays the price, takes possession of the land and treats it as his own, but no steps are taken to perfect his title by registration and there is no binding contract. This illustrates that it is envisaged that estoppel may be used when the 'assurance' is both express and implied by acquiescence, and where it supports a failed contract.[69] Obviously, given the flexible nature of estoppel and the reluctance of courts to 'pigeonhole' cases – see Chapter 9 – it remains to be seen whether this is a wide or narrow ground for gaining title by adverse possession. In this regard, two further points may be made. First, if a squatter can rely on estoppel *per se*, why would they wish to claim adverse possession at all? As we know, estoppel itself is a sword capable of attacking the proprietor's title and it is not immediately obvious why an adverse possessor would wait ten years and choose to tie his estoppel to a claim in adverse possession. It may be because a successful estoppel claim does not guarantee that the claimant will acquire title – see *Jennings v. Rice* (2003)[70] – whereas an adverse possession/estoppel claim within Schedule 6 could do so.[71] Nevertheless, given the overlap, there is an obvious need to reflect carefully when advising an adverse possessor who might also be able to claim estoppel. Secondly, Schedule 6, paragraph 5(2) does *not* say that an adverse possessor will be registered as proprietor if they can support the possession claim by an estoppel – in addition, the applicant must establish that they 'ought to be registered.'[72] Does this mean that the court has a discretion to refuse registration to an applicant even though he has made out ten years' adverse possession and has established an estoppel? If so, on what basis will a refusal be given, especially because by definition the paper owner must have behaved unconscionably for an estoppel to exit in the first place? Further, if there is a refusal to register the adverse possessor despite at least ten years' possession and an estoppel, can the adverse possessor then pursue an independent claim in estoppel for the same, or a different, remedy? Clearly, the exact scope of this exception will need to be clarified by judicially.

---

69 Assuming, of course, that this is not an attempt to avoid the statutory rules requiring contracts to be made in writing and that there is unconscionability.

70 Discussed in Chapter 9.

71 For example, where the estoppel is merely incidental.

72 Schedule 6, paragraph 5(2)(b).

11.4.3.2   *Exception 2: The squatter is for some other reason entitled to be registered as the proprietor*

This appears to be something of a 'catch-all' condition and its unspecific nature makes it ripe for use by adverse possessors who fear that the registered proprietor may simply take advantage of the two-year period of grace. The examples provided by HM Land Registry are where the squatter is entitled to the land under the will or intestacy of the deceased proprietor, and where the squatter contracted to buy the land and paid the purchase price, but the legal estate was never transferred to him.[73] Indeed, in both of these examples, the applicant need not rely on adverse possession at all to establish title and it raises the question why a claimant would need adverse possession where he was for some other reason 'entitled' to be registered. Perhaps the point is that, absent adverse possession, a person 'entitled' would have to make an application for rectification of the register against the proprietor under Schedule 4 of the 2002 Act, and perhaps such an application for rectification might be refused. Hence, perhaps the intention is that where adverse possession supports an entitlement, the claimant can avoid the limits on rectification[74] by using the route of adverse possession. Again, the scope of this exception is not immediately obvious.

11.4.3.3   *The boundary exception*

The third exception reflects the reality of neighbourhood living where the exact boundary line between adjoining properties may be uncertain or have been altered over time without any formal transfer or registration. It preserves the valuable role of adverse possession as a practical solution to often intractable and bitter boundary disputes. As HM Land Registry indicates:

> the condition may be useful in situations where the boundaries as they appear on the ground and as they are according to the title plan do not coincide, for example: where physical features suggest the boundary is in one place but according to the title plan it is in another; or where the dividing walls or fences on an estate were erected in the wrong place and not in accordance with the plans in the title deeds.[75]

This at least represents a common sense view of land ownership and title registration, and it has the great merit of providing a practical solution to often intractable boundary problems between warring neighbours. It may well come to be the most commonly used of the three exceptions and, of all three, it is the only one where the claimant may acquire a title simply because he has adversely possessed. There is no need to prove anything in addition, save only that the boundary exception applies.

As is apparent, the intention behind these three exceptions is to ensure that the adverse possessor is registered as owner when, in a broad sense, he 'deserves' to be and has supported this by ten years' adverse possession. As noted above, the expectation is that normally the registered proprietor will either object to the application in its entirety

---

73 The squatter-buyer is a beneficiary under a bare trust.

74 See Chapter 2.

75 Land Registry Practice Guide No. 4.

or simply utilise the two-year period of grace. The exceptions are meant to be truly exceptional. However, it is not fanciful to suppose that we may well see 'sympathetic' interpretations of these exceptions so as to permit adverse possession of registered land in a wider range of circumstances than is really intended by the 2002 Act. This remains to be seen, but it may well be that not all judges share the view that claims to adverse possession should be strangled under the regime of the LRA 2002. What is clear, however, is that this scheme as a whole means the end of one of the last operative feudal elements of English land law. Possibly, we should not lament it. On the other hand, we must also ask whether the LRA 2002 scheme will do anything to encourage negligent or inefficient landowners to make the most of their precious resource called 'land'. Prior to entry into force of the LRA 2002, a landowner had to be attentive to his estate and failure to use his land meant that others could acquire title to it and, perhaps, use it more beneficially (see *Lambeth LBC v. Ellis* (2000) and *Purbrick v. Hackney LB* (2003)). After the entry into force of the LRA 2002, a landowner with registered title can sit back and wait for the registrar to inform him that his land is subject to another's claim and then he can – usually – evict at any time within the next two years. Then he can sink back into slumber.

11.4.4   Effect of registration of the adverse possessor under the LRA 2002

If the adverse possessor is successful and is registered as proprietor, he takes the land subject to any interests affecting the estate, except any registered charge, save that if registration is the result of the application of one of the three exceptions, he takes the land also subject to any registered charge.[76] The difference arises because the registered chargee – a bank or other lender – that holds a mortgage over the land will have been served with a notice and so could have requested that the application be dealt with under the two-year rule if it wished to preserve its security. Consequently, it can hardly object to the loss of its charge if, having been served with notice, it fails to take action to evict the adverse possessor. However, if the adverse possessor is registered as a result of one of the exceptions, by definition the mortgagee will have been unable to take advantage of the two-year rule and will not be able to challenge the registration.[77] Thus it is entirely appropriate that the adverse possessor in those circumstances should take the title subject to all incumbrances including the mortgage.

11.5   Adverse Possession and Human Rights

It is clear from the preceding analysis that the rules of adverse possession – particularly in relation to unregistered land and registered land operating under the LRA 1925 – can result in the destruction of the title of a land 'owner'. On one view – indeed the view favoured in *Beaulane Properties v. Palmer* (2005) – this might be thought to contradict a person's right to peaceful enjoyment of their property as protected by Article 1, Protocol 1

---

76 Schedule 6, paragraph 9 of the LRA 2002.

77 Assuming, of course, that the substance of the adverse possession claim is made out.

of the European Convention on Human Rights, as enacted in to English law by the Human Rights Act 1998. Apart from the decision in *Beaulane*, this argument had been raised previously by counsel for Pye Developments Ltd in the Court of Appeal hearing in *Pye v. Graham* (2001). As it turned out, the discussion by their Lordships in the Court of Appeal in that case was *obiter* as the decision then handed down (subsequently overturned by the House of Lords) was that adverse possession was not made out on the facts and hence the alleged violation of the paper owner's right of property was not in issue. However, Mummery LJ in the Court of Appeal gave a robust response to the human rights argument. In his view, it was clear that rules imposing a time limit on when persons could bring claims, such as the paper owner, was not itself a contravention of any Convention right. More importantly, in his view, the rules on adverse possession prior to the introduction of the LRA 2002 were a lawful and proportionate application of limitation principles (themselves a manifestation of a public interest) and so a title defeated by adverse possession was not a title denied in violation of Article 1 of Protocol 1 of the Convention. This is powerful reasoning because the right guaranteed in Article 1 of Protocol 1 is not absolute in its own terms and must yield in the face of public policy. Consequently, much turns on the extent and manner in which the rules limiting claims in respect of title to land (and thereby denying title to the paper owner) can be seen as a proportionate application of the public interest. In the House of Lords in *Pye v. Graham*, in which, on the facts, adverse possession was established, the view was taken that the Convention was not in issue at all because all material matters arose before the Human Rights Act 1998 came into force.[78] However, there was certainly some disquiet among their Lordships in *Graham*[79] about the human rights position in respect of adverse possession under the old law had the Convention been in issue, and it is not apparent that they shared Mummery LJ's robust position.[80]

This uncertainty was seized on by the judge in *Beaulane* and then by the majority in the first instance decision of the European Court of Human Rights in *Pye v. UK*, and in both cases the application of adverse possession to registered land governed by the LRA 1925 was found to be in contravention of the Convention. However, that was not the end of the matter. The slim four–three majority at first instance in *Pye v. UK*, plus the paucity of reasoning, made an appeal by the UK inevitable. In 2007, the Grand Chamber of the European Court of Rights gave judgment in the appeal of *Pye v. UK*. This time, although again by a majority, the Grand Chamber found that the principles of adverse possession as

---

78 It was accepted that the Human Rights Act 1998 did not have retrospective effect, a view confirmed by the House of Lords in *Wilson v. First County Trust Ltd* (2003).

79 See, for example, the judgment of Lord Hope in *Pye v. Graham* at [73].

80 In *Family Housing Association v. Donellan* (2001), when considering the same issue, Park J suggested that 'adverse possession' was not contrary to Article 1 of Protocol 1 because this Article was designed to prevent State (i.e. governmental) interference with property rights. In his view, it was not meant to interfere with 'private law' issues like adverse possession, the latter being one individual 'denying' the property right of another and having nothing to do with the State. This has echoes of *Qazi*. Of course, this formulation revisits by another route the argument about whether the Human Rights Act 1998 is 'vertically' effective (applicable only where a public authority is one of the parties) or 'horizontally' effective (applicable where the parties are private litigants). The answer to that question really revolves around the meaning of the Human Rights Act 1998, particularly sections 3 and 6. It is not to be found in a restrictive interpretation of the very rights themselves.

they applied to land governed by the LRA 1925 were not in violation of the Convention.[81] Adverse possession did not deprive a landowner of their title *per se*; rather it amounted to control of land for the public good. Consequently, the absence of compensation for a title owner who lost their title through adverse possession did not signify a breach of the Convention. In essence, the Grand Chamber decided that the principles of adverse possession are a legitimate and proportionate response, within the UK's margin of appreciation, to a public interest: the interest in settling claims to land. In *Ofulue v. Bossert* (2008), the Court of Appeal[82] has made it clear that *Pye v. UK* establishes, as a matter of principle, that the law of adverse possession is Convention-compliant and that this decision of the Grand Chamber must be followed within the English legal system. This seems entirely correct and is now accepted by HM Land Registry.

11.6   Chapter Summary

11.6.1   The traditional principle of adverse possession: The limitation of actions

The ability of an adverse possessor (or 'trespasser') to acquire a better right to the land than the paper owner is based on the principle of limitation of actions. This means that a person (e.g. the paper owner of the land) may be 'statute-barred' from bringing a claim against the adverse possessor to recover possession of the land after the period of limitation has passed. In this sense, adverse possession operates negatively: it prevents an estate owner from suing on his rights and operates to extinguish his title. These principles will continue to govern cases in relation to unregistered land and registered land where the period of adverse possession is completed before 13 October 2003, the entry into force of the Land Registration Act 2002.

11.6.2   The limitation period under the 'old law': Unregistered land and registered land where adverse possession is completed before 13 October 2003

In most cases, where a limitation period is applicable at all (i.e. not in respect of registered titles under the LRA 2002), that period will be 12 years from the moment of adverse possession by the claimant (section 15 of the Limitation Act 1980). If the current paper owner is a tenant of the land under a lease, the period of limitation against the tenant is 12 years. The period for the landlord is also 12 years, but does not start to run until the original term of the tenancy has ended (Schedule 1, paragraph 4 of the Limitation Act 1980).

---

81 It follows that the principles in their application to unregistered land (where the public interest is greater) and to land governed by the LRA 2002 (where the effect of adverse possession is much less severe) are also Convention-compliant.

82 The issue was not before the House of Lords in the later appeal in *Ofulue*, the point having been settled conclusively by the Court of Appeal.

11.6.3   Adverse possession under the LRA 2002

There is no period of limitation. The adverse possessor may apply for registration of title after ten years' adverse possession and this triggers a notice to the registered proprietor. In all but three exceptional cases, the registered proprietor will have a further two years to remove the adverse possessor simply by asserting his title.

11.6.4   The substantive law: An intention to possess

The requirement that the adverse possessor must 'intend' to possess the land adversely to the exclusion of all others to some extent is artificial. For example, some adverse possessors may appreciate fully that the land is not theirs and act deliberately to exclude the world; others may believe honestly that the land is theirs already, and so do not for one moment think they are excluding the 'true' owner; others still may have formulated no intention at all, but simply treat the land as their own because it is there. In other words, we are not looking here for 'intention' in the traditional legal sense of a *mens rea*, either objectively or subjectively established. What is required is evidence that the adverse possessor, for whatever reason, had an intention to possess the land and put it to his own use, whether or not he also knew that some other person had a claim or right to the land.

11.6.5   The substantive law: Physical possession

As well as demonstrating an intention to possess the land, the adverse possessor must also demonstrate a physical assumption of possession. Before the decision in *Graham*, much academic and judicial ink had been spilt in trying to determine in what circumstances possession could be deemed to have been taken and when it also was 'adverse' to the paper owner. So, there was much discussion of the apparent differences between discontinuance of possession by the paper owner followed by possession by the claimant, and dispossession of the paper caused by the possession of the claimant. However, in *Graham*, Lord Browne-Wilkinson explained why too much analysis was a bad thing. In his view, 'much confusion and complication would be avoided if reference to adverse possession were to be avoided so far as possible . . . The question is simply whether the defendant squatter has dispossessed the paper owner by going into ordinary possession of the land for the requisite period without the consent of the owner'. In other words, we should not seek to overconceptualise what is 'adverse' and what is not, but ask ourselves the simple ordinary question: is the claimant in possession of the land without the permission of the landowner?

11.6.6   Stopping the clock of limitation in unregistered land and registered land governed by the LRA 1925

A successful action for possession will necessarily 'stop the clock', as will an acknowledgment of the paper owner's title in writing, the payment of rent (sections 29 and 30 of the Limitation Act 1980) and possibly physical repossession of the land by self-help. Once the limitation period has expired (where applicable), both the paper owner's right to sue and his title are extinguished by operation of statute (section 17 of the Limitation Act 1980). After this date, the conventional wisdom is that no acknowledgment, written or otherwise, and no payment or rent or other sum, can revive the paper owner's title: *Nicholson v. England* (1962), but see *Colchester BC v. Smith* (1992). The same principles can stop the ten-year period under the LRA 2002.

11.6.7 The effect of a successful claim of adverse possession of unregistered land and registered land governed by the LRA 1925

On the paper owner generally: successful adverse possession prevents the paper owner suing and effectively extinguishes his title (section 17 of the Limitation Act 1980). On the adverse possessor in unregistered land: conventional wisdom is that a successful adverse possession does not transfer title to the claimant. The claimant may sell or otherwise deal with the land because the absence of title deeds is dealt with by appropriate conveyancing devices (e.g. statutory declaration, title insurance).

On the adverse possessor in registered land governed by the LRA 1925: the paper owner will be the registered proprietor but is deemed to hold his estate in the land on trust for the claimant until such time as the adverse possessor can apply for rectification of the register and registration as proprietor (section 75 of the LRA 1925).

On the adverse possessor claiming against a tenant: in unregistered land, it seems the displaced tenant remains in a relationship with his landlord and can surrender his lease, so allowing the landlord to take early action against the claimant to evict. In registered land, recent authority suggests that the adverse possessor steps into the shoes of the tenant (section 75 of the LRA 1925; *Central London Commercial Estates Ltd v. Kato Kaguka Ltd* (1998)), so allowing the claimant to remain in possession for the remainder of the tenant's full term and even to enjoy rights granted to the tenant – such as the right to extend the lease.

11.6.8 Adverse possession under the Land Registration Act 2002 where the 12-year period of adverse possession was *not* completed before 13 October 2003

Under the new scheme, there will be no period of limitation and no sense in which a registered proprietor loses title merely because another person has adversely possessed the land for a fixed period of time (section 96 of the LRA 2002). The onus shifts from the true owner to the adverse possessor. Where a person claims to have completed at least ten years' adverse possession (and this is to be assessed by the traditional rules: Schedule 6, paragraph 11 of the LRA 2002), that person may apply to the registrar to be registered as proprietor. This application will trigger notice to the current registered proprietor (and certain other persons: Schedule 6, paragraph 2 of the LRA 2002) and the registered proprietor then has three options: consent, objection or ask for the application of the statutory two-year rule. If the two-year rule is requested, the adverse possessor cannot be entered as new registered proprietor unless either of three exceptional grounds is established (estoppel where the adverse possessor ought to be registered, or where the adverse possessor is 'for some other reason' entitled to be registered as proprietor, or where there is a boundary dispute). During the two-year period, absent the exceptional circumstances, the proprietor may evict the possessor simply by proving title. If the adverse possessor is not evicted during the two-year period, he may reapply for registration and must be so registered.

Further Reading

Cooke, E, 'Adverse possession, problems of title in registered land' (1994) 14 LS 1

Dixon, M, 'Adverse possession and registered land' [2009] Conv 169

Dockray, M, 'Why do we need adverse possession?' [1985] Conv 272

Fox, L and **Cobb**, N (2008) 27 *Legal Studies* Vol. 2: 236–260

Harpum, C, '*Buckinghamshire County Council v Moran*' [1990] CLJ 23

Harpum, C and **Radley-Gardner**, O, 'Adverse possession and the intention to possess: A reply' [2001] Conv 155

Tee, L, 'Adverse possession and intention to possess' [2000] Conv 113

Human rights and property law

Gray, K and **Gray**, S, in **Tee**, L (ed.), *Essays in Land Law*, Devon: Willan, 2002

Halstead, P, 'Human property rights' [2002] Conv 153

Howell, J, 'The Human Rights Act 1998' in Cooke, E (ed.) *Modern Studies in Property Law*, Vol. 1, Oxford: Hart, 2001

Index